펼쳐 보면 느껴집니다

단 한 줄도 배움의 공백이 생기지 않도록
문장 한 줄마다 20년이 넘는
해커스의 영어교육 노하우를 담았음을

덮고 나면 확신합니다

수많은 선생님의 목소리와
정확한 출제 데이터 분석으로 꽉 찬
교재 한 권이면 충분함을

해커스북 중·고등
HackersBook.com

기출로 적중

해커스 중학영문법 과 함께하면

점수가 확 오르는 이유!

기출 분석으로 완벽히 적중시키니까!

1 전국 중학교 내신
기출문제 빅데이터
철저히 분석 및 반영

2 최신 개정 교과서의
모든 문법 포인트
빠짐없이 반영

중학영문법
1학년

중학영문법
2학년

중학영문법
3학년

촘촘한 훈련으로 확실히 내 것이 되니까!

3 중간·기말·서술형
실전문제로
내신 완벽 대비

4 암기리스트·단어 암기장
+워크북으로
반복 훈련 가능

최신 개정 교과서 완벽 반영

기출로 적중
해커스
중학영문법

2학년

이 책을 검토해주신 선생님들

강상훈 경기 평촌비상에듀학원 / **김가영** 서울 송정중학교 / **김원덕** 경기 올림피아드학원 / **박유정** 서울 반포중학교 / **박윤정** 경기 이지베스트학원

박은혜 서울 송파중학교 / **박정은** 서울 대청중학교 / **양세희** 서울 양세희수능영어학원 / **이계윤** 서울 씨앤씨학원 / **이유빈** 서울 잉글리쉬&매쓰매니저학원

이혜원 서울 대청중학교 / **정혜은** 서울 용곡중학교 / **최다빈** 서울 최강영어 / **최승복** 경기 오른어학원 / **최지영** 경기 다른영어학원

목차

목차

구성 미리 보기

○ 시험에 나온, 또 나올 **기출 적중 문법 POINT 학습**

기출 적중 POINT

최신 개정 교과서와 전국 내신 기출 빅데이터에서 뽑아낸 문법 포인트를 빠짐없이 학습할 수 있습니다.

핵심 문법 사항

내신 시험 대비에 꼭 필요한 문법 사항을 명쾌한 설명과 예문을 통해 정확하게 이해할 수 있습니다.

심화 문법 TIP

어렵지만 실제 내신 시험에서 출제된 적이 있는 문법 사항을 학습하여 고난도 문제에 대비할 수 있습니다.

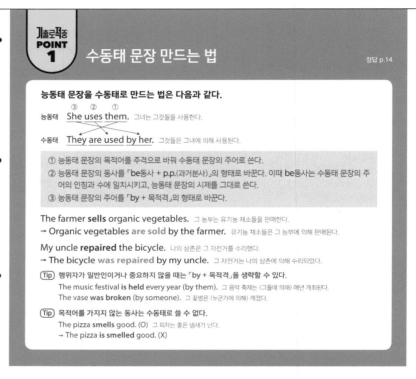

기출로적중 POINT 1 수동태 문장 만드는 법

정답 p.14

능동태 문장을 수동태로 만드는 법은 다음과 같다.

능동태 ③She ②uses ①them. 그녀는 그것들을 사용한다.

수동태 They are used by her. 그것들은 그녀에 의해 사용된다.

① 능동태 문장의 목적어를 주격으로 바꿔 수동태 문장의 주어로 쓴다.
② 능동태 문장의 동사를 「be동사 + p.p.(과거분사)」의 형태로 바꾼다. 이때 be동사는 수동태 문장의 주어의 인칭과 수에 일치시키고, 능동태 문장의 시제를 그대로 쓴다.
③ 능동태 문장의 주어를 「by + 목적격」의 형태로 바꾼다.

The farmer **sells** organic vegetables. 그 농부는 유기농 채소들을 판매한다.
→ Organic vegetables **are sold** by the farmer. 유기농 채소들은 그 농부에 의해 판매된다.

My uncle **repaired** the bicycle. 나의 삼촌은 그 자전거를 수리했다.
→ The bicycle **was repaired** by my uncle. 그 자전거는 나의 삼촌에 의해 수리되었다.

Tip 행위자가 일반인이거나 중요하지 않을 때는 「by + 목적격」을 생략할 수 있다.
The music festival **is held** every year (by them). 그 음악 축제는 (그들에 의해) 매년 개최된다.
The vase **was broken** (by someone). 그 꽃병은 (누군가에 의해) 깨졌다.

Tip 목적어를 가지지 않는 동사는 수동태로 쓸 수 없다.
The pizza **smells** good. (O) 그 피자는 좋은 냄새가 난다.
→ The pizza **is smelled** good. (X)

연습문제 A 괄호 안에서 알맞은 것을 고르시오.

1 Spanish is (speak / spoken) in Mexico.

2 This picture was (took / taken) by Sophie.

3 We (cleaned / were cleaned) the classroom.

4 *Sunflowers* was (drawing / drawn) by Vincent Van Gogh.

5 Pop-up books (love / are loved) by children.

6 Minsu was (raising / raised) by his grandparents.

7 I (returned / was returned) the library book on time.

8 North America was (discovering / discovered) by Columbus.

9 Carrots and cabbages (eat / are eaten) by rabbits.

10 That chef's steak (tastes / is tasted) wonderful.

연습문제 B 괄호 안의 동사를 알맞은 형태로 바꿔 빈칸에 쓰시오. (단, 현재형으로 쓰시오.)

1 The wooden toys _____ _____ by Mr. Tucker. (make)

2 This song _____ _____ by a popular K-pop singer. (sing)

3 You _____ _____ to my birthday party. (invite)

4 Some sentences _____ _____ on the board. (write)

5 Most coffee beans _____ _____ in Brazil. (grow)

6 The street market _____ _____ by tourists. (visit)

7 These carpets _____ _____ in India. (produce)

8 These magazines _____ _____ by lots of teenagers. (read)

9 Many movies _____ _____ at the theater. (show)

10 The newspaper _____ _____ every morning. (deliver)

연습문제 C 다음 능동태 문장을 수동태로 바꿔 쓰시오.

1 Junho moved the sofa.
→ _____

2 Gina wrote a beautiful poem.
→ _____

3 Albus collects old coins.
→ _____

4 Ms. Miller baked some apple pies.
→ _____

5 Many kinds of sea animals eat shrimps.
→ _____

6 My mother wore a wedding dress.
→ _____

기출 적중문제

다음 문장에서 어법상 어색한 부분을 찾아 쓰고 바르게 고쳐 쓰시오.

The film saw by many people around the world last year.

_____ → _____

수동태 문장의 동사는
「be동사 + p.p.(과거분사)」의
형태예요.

연습문제

다양한 유형과 많은 양의 연습 문제를 통해 문법 사항을 암기하지 않고도 자연스럽게 이해할 수 있습니다.

기출 적중문제

빈출 포인트가 적용된 실전 문제를 풀어보며 실제 내신 시험의 출제 방식을 미리 경험해볼 수 있습니다.

기출 해결 TIP

빈출 포인트가 적용된 실전 문제의 해결 TIP을 통해 실제 내신 시험에서의 정답 적중률을 높일 수 있습니다.

구성 미리 보기

○ 체계적으로 시작하는 **기초 문법**

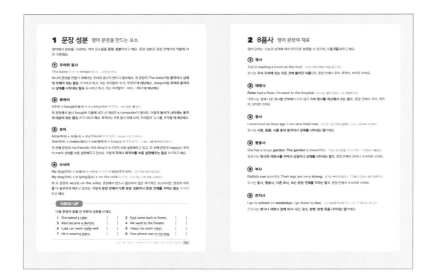

<< 중학영문법을 이해하기 위해 꼭 알아야 하는 기초 문법이 정리되어 있어 문법 실력이 부족한 학생들도 영문법을 체계적으로 학습할 수 있습니다.

○ 서술형 평가에 강해지는 **서술형 대비 문제**

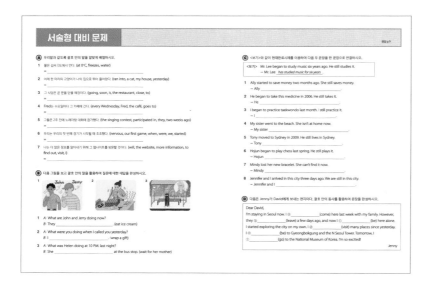

<< 다양한 유형의 서술형 대비 문제를 풀어보며 서술형을 강조하는 최근 내신 평가 트렌드에 대비할 수 있습니다.

○ 정답 적중률을 높이는 **중간·기말고사 실전 문제**

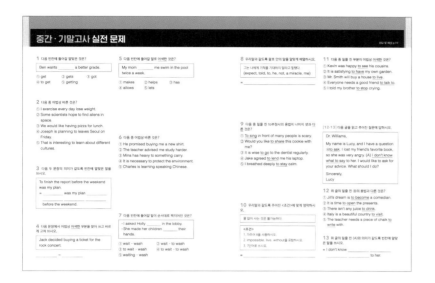

<< 전국 내신 기출문제의 빈출 유형과 문법 포인트가 반영된 객관식·주관식 문제를 풀어보며 실제 내신 시험에서의 정답 적중률을 높일 수 있습니다.

○ 학습 효과를 더욱 높이는 **워크북과 부록**

+

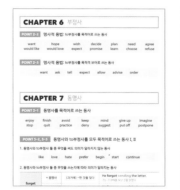

워크북

풍부한 양의 추가 문제를 풀면서 부족한 부분을 파악하고 보완할 수 있습니다.

문법 암기리스트

교재에 수록된 문법 사항 중 꼭 암기해야 할 사항을 언제 어디서나 학습할 수 있습니다.

단어 암기장

교재에서 사용된 중학 필수 단어 및 표현을 암기하며 어휘력을 향상할 수 있습니다.

기초 문법

영어 문법, 그 기초부터 알고 들어가자!

본격적인 학습 전에, 영어 문법의 기초가 되는 문장 성분, 8품사, 구와 절에 대해 배워보도록 해요!

1 문장 성분 영어 문장을 만드는 요소

영어에서 문장을 구성하는 여러 요소들을 **문장 성분**이라고 해요. 문장 성분은 문장 안에서의 역할에 따라 구분돼요.

① 주어와 동사

The baby(주어) **+ sleeps**(동사). 그 아기는 잔다.

하나의 문장을 만들기 위해서는 주어와 동사가 반드시 필요해요. 위 문장의 The baby처럼 **동작이나 상태의 주체가 되는 말**을 주어라고 하고, 이는 우리말의 '누가, 무엇이'에 해당해요. sleeps처럼 **주어의 동작이나 상태를 나타내는 말**을 동사라고 하고, 이는 우리말의 '~이다, ~하다'에 해당해요.

② 목적어

I(주어) + bought(동사) **+ a computer**(목적어). 나는 컴퓨터를 샀다.

위 문장에서 동사 bought 다음에 내가 산 대상인 a computer가 왔어요. 이렇게 **동사가 나타내는 동작의 대상이 되는 말**을 목적어라고 해요. 목적어는 주로 동사 뒤에 오며, 우리말의 '누구를, 무엇을'에 해당해요.

③ 보어

Amy(주어) + is(동사) **+ my friend**(주격 보어). Amy는 나의 친구이다.
She(주어) + makes(동사) + me(목적어) **+ happy**(목적격 보어). 그녀는 나를 행복하게 만든다.

첫 번째 문장의 my friend는 주어 Amy가 누구인지 보충 설명해주고 있고, 두 번째 문장의 happy는 목적어 me의 상태를 보충 설명해주고 있어요. 이렇게 **주어나 목적어를 보충 설명해주는 말**을 보어라고 해요.

④ 수식어

My dog(주어) + is(동사) **+ very**(수식어) + lazy(주격 보어). 나의 개는 매우 게으르다.
My dog(주어) + is lying(동사) **+ on the sofa**(수식어). 나의 개는 소파 위에 누워있다.

위 두 문장의 very와 on the sofa는 문장에서 반드시 필요하지 않은 부가적인 요소이지만, 문장의 의미를 더 풍부하게 해주고 있어요. 이렇게 **문장 안에서 다른 문장 성분이나 문장 전체를 꾸미는 말**을 수식어라고 해요.

CHECK-UP

다음 문장의 밑줄 친 부분의 성분을 쓰세요.

1 She baked <u>a cake</u>. [　　] **2** <u>Paul</u> came back to Korea. [　　]
3 Alex became <u>a dentist</u>. [　　] **4** We <u>went</u> to the theater. [　　]
5 Luke can swim <u>really</u> well. [　　] **6** I keep my room <u>clean</u>. [　　]
7 He is wearing <u>jeans</u>. [　　] **8** Your phone was <u>in my bag</u>. [　　]

정답 1 목적어 2 주어 3 보어 4 동사 5 수식어 6 보어 7 목적어 8 수식어

2 8품사 영어 문장의 재료

영어 단어는 기능과 성격에 따라 8가지로 분류할 수 있으며, 이를 **8품사**라고 해요.

① 명사

Suji is reading a **book** on the **bed.** 수지는 침대 위에서 책을 읽고 있다.

명사는 **우리 주위에 있는 모든 것에 붙여진 이름**으로, 문장 안에서 주어, 목적어, 보어로 쓰여요.

② 대명사

Peter had a fever. **He** went to the hospital. Peter는 열이 있었다. 그는 병원에 갔다.

대명사는 앞에 나온 명사를 반복해서 쓰지 않기 위해 **명사를 대신해서 쓰는 말**로, 문장 안에서 주어, 목적어, 보어로 쓰여요.

③ 동사

I **exercised** an hour ago. I **am** very tired now. 나는 한 시간 전에 운동했다. 나는 지금 매우 피곤하다.

동사는 **사람, 동물, 사물 등의 동작이나 상태를 나타내는 말**이에요.

④ 형용사

She has a **large** garden. **The** garden is **beautiful.** 그녀는 큰 정원을 가지고 있다. 그 정원은 아름답다.

형용사는 **명사와 대명사를 꾸며서 성질이나 상태를 나타내는 말**로, 문장 안에서 보어나 수식어로 쓰여요.

⑤ 부사

Rabbits **run quickly.** Their legs are **very strong.** 토끼는 빠르게 달린다. 그것들의 다리는 매우 튼튼하다.

부사는 **동사, 형용사, 다른 부사, 또는 문장 전체를 꾸미는 말**로, 문장 안에서 수식어로 쓰여요.

⑥ 전치사

I go **to school on weekdays.** I go there **by bus.** 나는 평일에 학교에 간다. 나는 거기에 버스로 간다.

전치사는 **명사나 대명사 앞에 와서 시간, 장소, 방향, 방법 등을 나타내는 말**이에요.

⑦ 접속사

I need **a notebook and a pencil.** 나는 공책과 연필이 필요하다.
Sam listens to music when he exercises. Sam은 운동할 때 노래를 듣는다.

접속사는 **단어와 단어, 구와 구, 절과 절을 연결해주는 말**이에요.

⑧ 감탄사

Wow! We won the game! 우와! 우리가 경기를 이겼어!
Oops! I spilled the milk. 아이쿠! 나는 우유를 쏟았어.

감탄사는 **기쁨, 놀람, 슬픔과 같은 다양한 감정을 표현해주는 말**이에요.

(Tip) 각 품사는 문장 안에서 쓰일 수 있는 성분이 정해져 있어요.

명사(대명사)	주어
동사	동사
형용사	목적어
부사	보어
	수식어

CHECK-UP

다음 문장의 밑줄 친 부분의 품사를 쓰세요.

1 The movie was <u>really</u> boring.   [   ]
2 <u>We</u> climbed the mountain.   [   ]
3 I'll have coffee <u>or</u> tea.   [   ]
4 <u>Oh</u>! It's snowing outside!   [   ]
5 <u>Seoul</u> is a great city.   [   ]
6 Your shoes are <u>pretty</u>.   [   ]
7 He <u>knows</u> my secret.   [   ]
8 Turn right <u>at</u> the corner.   [   ]
9 Ron can play chess <u>well</u>.   [   ]
10 Close the window <u>if</u> it's cold.   [   ]

정답 1 부사 2 대명사 3 접속사 4 감탄사 5 명사 6 형용사 7 동사 8 전치사 9 부사 10 접속사

---

3 구와 절 말 덩어리

두 개 이상의 단어가 모여 하나의 의미를 나타내는 말 덩어리를 **구**나 **절**이라고 해요. 구는 in the morning 처럼 주어와 동사를 포함하지 않고, 절은 after I brushed my teeth처럼 주어와 동사를 포함해요. 구와 절은 문장 안에서 명사, 형용사, 부사 역할을 할 수 있어요.

① 명사 역할

명사 역할을 하는 명사구와 명사절은 문장 안에서 명사처럼 주어, 목적어, 보어로 쓰여요.

명사구   **Learning a new language** is interesting. <주어> 새로운 언어를 배우는 것은 흥미롭다.

명사절   I think **that math is difficult**. <목적어> 나는 수학이 어렵다고 생각한다.

② 형용사 역할

형용사 역할을 하는 형용사구와 형용사절은 형용사처럼 명사나 대명사를 꾸며요.

형용사구   The **jacket on the chair** is mine. 의자 위에 있는 재킷은 나의 것이다.

형용사절   I ate the **pizza which she made**. 나는 그녀가 만든 피자를 먹었다.

③ 부사 역할

부사 역할을 하는 부사구와 부사절은 부사처럼 동사, 형용사, 다른 부사, 또는 문장 전체를 꾸며요.

부사구   He **drinks** a glass of milk **in the morning**. 그는 아침에 우유 한 잔을 마신다.

부사절   I **took** a shower **after I brushed my teeth**. 나는 나의 이를 닦은 후에 샤워를 했다.

CHECK-UP

다음 문장의 밑줄 친 부분이 해당하는 것을 고르세요.

1   I hope <u>to win the competition</u>.   (명사구 / 명사절)
2   The movie <u>which I watched yesterday</u> was sad.   (형용사구 / 형용사절)
3   The game was canceled <u>because it rained a lot</u>.   (명사절 / 부사절)
4   The clock <u>on the wall</u> is broken.   (형용사구 / 부사구)

정답   1 명사구   2 형용사절   3 부사절   4 형용사구

CHAPTER 1
문장의 형식

Dennis needs a new computer. Dennis는 새 컴퓨터가 필요하다.
주어 동사   목적어

위 문장은 주어 **Dennis**, 동사 **needs**, 목적어 **a new computer**로 이루어진 완전한 문장이에요. 완전한 문장에는
필수적인 문장 요소가 포함되어야 하는데, 주어와 동사는 반드시 필요하며 동사의 성격에 따라 보어나 목적어가 필요
하기도 해요. 이렇게 동사가 어떤 문장 요소를 필요로 하는지에 따라 다섯 가지로 **문장의 형식**이 나뉘어요.

기출로 적중 POINT

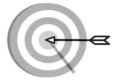

내신 100점 적중!
기출 출제율

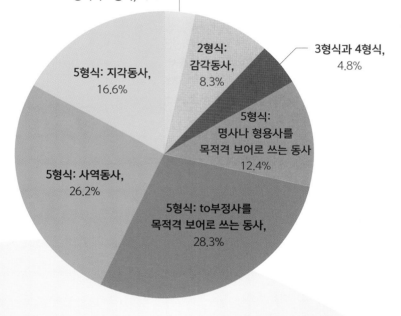

1형식과 2형식, 3.4%

2형식:
감각동사,
8.3%

3형식과 4형식,
4.8%

5형식: 지각동사,
16.6%

5형식:
명사나 형용사를
목적격 보어로 쓰는 동사
12.4%

5형식: 사역동사,
26.2%

5형식: to부정사를
목적격 보어로 쓰는 동사,
28.3%

TOP 1 **5형식: to부정사를 목적격 보어로 쓰는 동사 (28.3%)**
특정 동사의 목적격 보어 자리에 to부정사가 쓰이는 경우를 묻는 문제가 자주
출제된다.

TOP 2 **5형식: 사역동사 (26.2%)**
문장 안에서 사역동사의 쓰임을 묻는 문제가 자주 출제된다.

TOP 3 **5형식: 지각동사 (16.6%)**
문장 안에서 지각동사의 쓰임을 묻는 문제가 자주 출제된다.

1. **1형식 문장은 「주어 + 동사」의 형태로, 수식어(구)와 함께 쓰이기도 한다.**

   She **laughed**. 그녀는 웃었다.

   Birds **sing** beautifully. 새들이 아름답게 노래한다.

   The castle **stands** on the hill. 그 성은 언덕 위에 있다.

   (Tip) 「There + be동사」(~이 있다/있었다)는 1형식 문장이며, be동사 뒤에 오는 명사가 주어이다.

   There is a cup on the table. 식탁 위에 한 개의 컵이 있다.

   There were some peaches in the basket. 바구니 안에 약간의 복숭아가 있었다.

2. **2형식 문장은 「주어 + 동사 + 주격 보어」의 형태이다. 주격 보어는 주어를 보충 설명하는 말로, 주격 보어 자리에는 명사나 형용사가 온다.**

   My brother **became** a lawyer. 나의 형은 변호사가 되었다.

   The subway **is** convenient. 지하철은 편리하다.

   (Tip) · 상태(~이다, ~하다)를 나타내는 2형식 동사: be, stay, keep, remain 등

   You should **stay** calm. 너는 침착하게 있어야 한다.

   · 상태의 변화(~이 되다, ~하게 되다)를 나타내는 2형식 동사: become, get, turn, grow 등

   The weather will **get** warm soon. 날씨는 곧 따뜻해질 것이다.

연습문제 다음 문장이 1형식인지 2형식인지 고르시오.

1 The candy melted. (1형식 / 2형식)

2 My uncle is a dentist. (1형식 / 2형식)

3 The snail moves slowly. (1형식 / 2형식)

4 The sky grew dark. (1형식 / 2형식)

5 Mr. and Mrs. Jones got rich. (1형식 / 2형식)

6 James went to the art museum. (1형식 / 2형식)

7 The kids played in the snow. (1형식 / 2형식)

8 Leaves turn green in the spring. (1형식 / 2형식)

9 We must keep quiet in the hallway. (1형식 / 2형식)

10 An accident happened yesterday. (1형식 / 2형식)

11 Olivia became a ballerina. (1형식 / 2형식)

12 There are many dishes in the cupboard. (1형식 / 2형식)

13 The stars will shine brightly tonight. (1형식 / 2형식)

기출로적중 POINT 1-2 2형식: 감각동사

정답 p.2

1. **감각동사는 감각을 나타내는 2형식 동사로, 감각동사의 주격 보어 자리에는 형용사만 온다.**

   look   sound   smell   taste   feel

   You **look** lovely today. 너는 오늘 아름답게 보인다.
   His plan **sounds** exciting. 그의 계획은 신나게 들린다.
   The cat's fur **felt** soft. 그 고양이의 털은 부드럽게 느껴졌다.

2. **감각동사 뒤에 명사가 올 때는 전치사 like와 함께 「감각동사 + like + 명사」의 형태로 쓴다.**

   The soap **smelled like** a flower. 그 비누는 꽃 같은 냄새가 났다.
   This ice cream **tastes like** mango. 이 아이스크림은 망고 같은 맛이 난다.

연습문제 괄호 안에서 알맞은 것을 고르시오.

1 The man looks (strong / strongly).

2 The pasta tasted (salt / salty).

3 It (looks / looks like) a racing car.

4 The blueberry pie smells (fresh / freshly).

5 The paper (felt / felt like) silk.

6 Lena's voice sounded (amazing / amazingly).

7 This (tastes / tastes like) tomato soup.

8 We felt (nervous / nervously) on the stage.

9 These coffee beans (smell / smell like) chocolate.

10 My new neighbors look (friend / friendly).

11 Liam (feels / feels like) terrible about the mistake.

기출 적중문제

다음 문장에서 <u>틀린</u> 부분을 바르게 고쳐 완전한 문장을 쓰시오.

The story sounds a lie.
→ _____

1. **3형식 문장은 「주어 + 동사 + 목적어」의 형태이다. 목적어는 동사의 대상이 되는 말로, 목적어 자리에는 명사나 대명사 등이 온다.**

   I **studied** **history** last night. 나는 어젯밤에 역사를 공부했다.
   Mary doesn't **know** **him**. Mary는 그를 알지 못한다.

2. **4형식 문장은 「주어 + 동사 + 간접 목적어(~에게) + 직접 목적어(−을)」의 형태이다. 4형식 문장의 동사는 두 개의 목적어를 필요로 하는 수여동사로, 수여동사는 '~에게 −을 (해)주다'라는 의미를 나타낸다.**

give	send	bring	pass	show	teach	tell
write	read	lend	sell	pay	buy	cook
find	make	get	build	ask		

   Gary **gave** **her** **a hairband**. Gary는 그녀에게 머리띠를 줬다.
   The teacher **asked** **me** **some questions**. 선생님은 나에게 몇몇 질문을 하셨다.

3. **4형식 문장은 동사에 따라 전치사 to/for/of 중 하나를 사용하여 3형식으로 바꿀 수 있다.**

   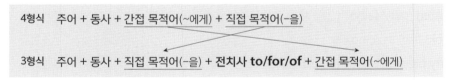

   4형식 주어 + 동사 + 간접 목적어(~에게) + 직접 목적어(−을)

   3형식 주어 + 동사 + 직접 목적어(−을) + 전치사 to/for/of + 간접 목적어(~에게)

to를 쓰는 동사	give, send, bring, pass, show, teach, tell, write, read, lend, sell, pay 등	The clerk **showed** me a nice shirt. → The clerk **showed** a nice shirt **to** me. 그 점원은 나에게 괜찮은 셔츠를 보여줬다.
for를 쓰는 동사	buy, cook, find, make, get, build 등	Dad **cooked** us a delicious meal. → Dad **cooked** a delicious meal **for** us. 아빠는 우리에게 맛있는 식사를 요리해주셨다.
of를 쓰는 동사	ask 등	Can I **ask** you a favor? → Can I **ask** a favor **of** you? 내가 너에게 부탁을 해도 되니?

연습문제 A 우리말과 같도록 괄호 안의 말을 알맞게 배열하시오.

1 Donald는 현대 미술을 좋아한다. (modern art, loves)

= Donald _____.

2 우리는 그 새들에게 집을 만들어줬다. (a house, built, the birds)

= We _____ .

3 그녀는 나에게 나의 의견을 물었다. (my opinion, asked, me)

= She _____ .

4 그들은 과학 과제를 끝냈다. (the science project, finished)

= They _____ .

5 나는 Rachel에게 약간의 한국 과자를 보내줬다. (sent, some Korean snacks, Rachel)

= I _____ .

6 Jenny는 그녀의 할머니께 신문을 읽어드렸다. (her grandmother, the newspaper, read)

= Jenny _____ .

연습문제 **B** | 다음 4형식 문장은 3형식으로, 3형식 문장은 4형식으로 바꿔 쓰시오.

1 I lent her my cell phone.

→ _____

2 Josh gave a box of cookies to me.

→ _____

3 We made Sandra a birthday card.

→ _____

4 Can you bring an umbrella to me?

→ _____

5 Jinsu sent his best friend a package.

→ _____

6 I will get you a bottle of water.

→ _____

7 The journalist asked the president some questions.

→ _____

기출 적중문제 🎯

다음 빈칸에 들어갈 말이 순서대로 짝지어진 것은?

· He will sell his car _____ his friend.
· My parents bought a new laptop _____ me.

① to - to   ② to - for   ③ for - to
④ for - of   ⑤ of - for

4형식 문장을 3형식 문장으로 바꿀 때는 동사에 따라 알맞은 전치사를 써야 해요.

5형식: 명사나 형용사를 목적격 보어로 쓰는 동사

정답 p.2

5형식 문장은 「주어 + 동사 + 목적어 + 목적격 보어」의 형태이다. 목적격 보어는 목적어를 보충 설명하는 말로, 다음 동사의 목적격 보어 자리에는 명사나 형용사가 온다.

| call | make | keep | find |

We **call** <u>our kitten</u> <u>Sunny</u>. 우리는 우리의 새끼 고양이를 Sunny라고 부른다.
This album **made** <u>him</u> <u>a superstar</u>. 이 앨범은 그를 슈퍼스타로 만들었다.
The dog **made** <u>my shoes</u> <u>dirty</u>. 그 개는 나의 신발을 지저분하게 만들었다.
Eating vegetables **keeps** <u>us</u> <u>healthy</u>. 채소를 먹는 것은 우리를 건강하게 유지한다.

연습문제 우리말과 같도록 괄호 안에서 알맞은 것을 고르시오.

1 나는 이 수프를 따뜻하게 유지하기를 원한다.
= I want to keep this soup (warm / warmly).

2 그들은 나를 주장으로 만들었다.
= They made (me the captain / the captain me).

3 민수는 수학 시험이 쉽다고 생각했다.
= Minsu found the math test (easy / easily).

4 너는 나를 거짓말쟁이라고 불렀니?
= Did you call (a liar me / me a liar)?

5 Samuel은 정원을 항상 깨끗하게 유지한다.
= Samuel always keeps (the garden clean / clean the garden).

6 그 액션 영화는 그녀를 유명 인사로 만들었다.
= The action film made (a celebrity her / her a celebrity).

7 나의 가족은 그 TV 쇼가 흥미롭다고 생각했다.
= My family found the TV show (interestingly / interesting).

기출 적중문제

우리말과 같도록 괄호 안의 말을 알맞게 배열하시오.

사람들은 이 음식을 케밥이라고 부른다. (a kebab, call, people, this food)

= _____

기출로적중 POINT 3-2 5형식: to부정사를 목적격 보어로 쓰는 동사

정답 p.2

다음 동사의 목적격 보어 자리에는 to부정사가 온다.

want   ask   tell   expect   allow   advise   order

I **want** you **to wash** the dishes.   나는 네가 설거지하기를 원한다.
Mr. Kim **told** the students **to speak** quietly.   김 선생님은 학생들에게 조용히 이야기하라고 말했다.
Please **allow** me **to buy** a tablet PC.   제가 태블릿 PC를 사는 것을 허락해주세요.

연습문제 우리말과 같도록 괄호 안의 말을 활용하여 문장을 완성하시오.

1 우리는 Adam에게 우리와 함께 점심을 먹을 것을 요청했다. (ask, have)
= We _____ lunch with us.

2 나는 그가 나의 생일 파티에 오기를 기대했다. (come, expect)
= I _____ to my birthday party.

3 나의 부모님은 내가 나의 여동생에게 사과하기를 원하신다. (apologize, want)
= My parents _____ to my sister.

4 경찰은 그들에게 문을 열라고 명령했다. (order, open)
= The police _____ the door.

5 아빠는 내가 컴퓨터 게임을 하는 것을 허락하셨다. (play, allow)
= Dad _____ computer games.

6 Joseph은 그녀에게 독서 동아리에 가입하라고 말했다. (tell, join)
= Joseph _____ the book club.

7 치과 의사는 Amy에게 더 자주 이를 닦으라고 조언했다. (brush, advise)
= The dentist _____ her teeth more often.

기출 적중문제 ◎

다음 중 어법상 어색한 것은?

① I call my friend Einstein.
② They told him to get up early.
③ Hojun usually keeps his room tidy.
④ The teacher advised her study hard.
⑤ Lisa expects me to come home early.

5형식: 사역동사

1. 사역동사는 '~가 −하게 하다'라는 의미의 동사로, 사역동사의 목적격 보어 자리에는 동사원형이 온다.

make	have	let

   This book **made** me **think** positively. 이 책은 내가 긍정적으로 생각하게 했다.
   I will **have** him **call** you back. 나는 그가 너에게 다시 전화하게 할 것이다.
   Mom doesn't **let** me **go** out late at night. 엄마는 내가 밤늦게 외출하게 허락하지 않으신다.

2. 준사역동사 help와 get

   ❶ help가 5형식 문장에 쓰일 때는 목적격 보어 자리에 동사원형과 to부정사가 둘 다 올 수 있다.
   Science **helps** us **(to) understand** the world. 과학은 우리가 세계를 이해하는 것을 돕는다.

   ❷ get이 사역동사의 의미로 쓰일 때는 목적격 보어 자리에 to부정사가 온다.
   She **got** Juwon **to keep** his promise. 그녀는 주원이가 그의 약속을 지키게 했다.

연습문제 괄호 안에서 알맞은 것을 <u>모두</u> 고르시오.

1 Don't let a child (watch / to watch) this movie.

2 Mr. Evans had them (paint / to paint) the wall.

3 She couldn't make the baby (stop / to stop) crying.

4 The doctor got me (take / to take) the medicine.

5 Can you help us (find / to find) the nearest station?

6 Let me (explain / to explain) the rules of this game.

7 I helped my little brother (put / to put) on his socks.

8 What made you (sleep / to sleep) so late yesterday?

기출 적중문제

다음 빈칸에 들어갈 말로 <u>어색한</u> 것을 <u>모두</u> 고르시오.

My mother _____ me sweep the floor.

① made ② had ③ expected
④ helped ⑤ got

기출로 적중 POINT 3-4   5형식: 지각동사

정답 p.3

지각동사는 '~가 −하는 것을 보다/듣다/냄새 맡다/느끼다'라는 의미의 동사로, 지각동사의 목적격 보어 자리에는 동사원형이나 V-ing형이 온다. 지각동사의 목적격 보어 자리에 V-ing 형이 오면 진행 중인 동작이 강조된다.

| see | watch | hear | listen to | smell | feel |

I often **see** my sister **read** books. 나는 종종 나의 누나가 책을 읽는 것을 본다.
Sophie **heard** Laura **speaking** on the phone. Sophie는 Laura가 통화하고 있는 것을 들었다.
Can you **feel** the wind **blowing**? 너는 바람이 불고 있는 것을 느낄 수 있니?

연습문제 우리말과 같도록 괄호 안의 말을 알맞게 배열하시오.

1 나는 그 개가 큰 소리로 짖는 것을 들었다. (the dog, heard, bark)
= I _____ loudly.

2 우리는 한 남자가 거리에서 춤을 추고 있는 것을 봤다. (dancing, watched, a man)
= We _____ on the street.

3 그들은 한 시간 전에 땅이 흔들리고 있는 것을 느꼈다. (felt, shaking, the ground)
= They _____ an hour ago.

4 너는 무언가가 타고 있는 것을 냄새 맡을 수 있니? (something, burning, smell)
= Can you _____ ?

5 나는 그녀가 Thomas에게 귓속말하는 것을 들었다. (whisper, her, listened to)
= I _____ to Thomas.

6 Foster씨는 그의 아들이 풍경화를 그리고 있는 것을 봤다. (drawing, saw, his son)
= Ms. Foster _____ a landscape picture.

7 Maria는 뱀이 나무를 오르는 것을 봤다. (a snake, watched, climb)
= Maria _____ up the tree.

기출 적중문제 🎯

다음 문장에서 틀린 부분을 바르게 고쳐 완전한 문장을 쓰시오.

The teacher heard someone to laugh out loud in the classroom.

→ _____
_____

지각동사의 목적격 보어 자리에는 동사원형이나 V-ing형이 와요.

A 밑줄 친 부분이 어법상 맞으면 O를 쓰고, 틀리면 바르게 고쳐 쓰시오.

1 That skirt looks too <u>shortly</u> for you. → _____

2 The cotton candy <u>tasted like</u> apples. → _____

3 This store stays <u>openly</u> all night. → _____

4 Your idea <u>sounds like</u> fantastic. → _____

5 The air smells <u>freshly</u> in the morning. → _____

6 Mr. Brown <u>looks</u> a friendly person. → _____

7 The movie became <u>famous</u> worldwide. → _____

8 Some children felt <u>sleepy</u> during the show. → _____

9 The people got <u>quietly</u> suddenly. → _____

B 우리말과 같도록 괄호 안의 말을 활용하여 주어진 지시대로 문장을 완성하시오.

1 Janet은 그 아기에게 장난감들을 만들어줬다. (made, toys)
= (3형식으로) Janet _____ .

2 너는 나에게 너의 사전을 빌려줄 수 있니? (lend, your dictionary)
= (4형식으로) Can you _____ ?

3 Davis씨는 그녀의 아들에게 동화를 읽어줬다. (read, a fairy tale)
= (3형식으로) Ms. Davis _____ .

4 그 농부는 우리에게 신선한 수박을 팔았다. (sold, fresh watermelons)
= (4형식으로) The farmer _____ .

5 나는 Kevin에게 도시락을 가져다줄 것이다. (get, a lunch box)
= (3형식으로) I will _____ .

6 그녀는 그들에게 중요한 교훈을 가르쳐줬다. (taught, an important lesson)
= (4형식으로) She _____ .

7 Emily는 그녀의 선생님께 몇몇 질문을 했다. (asked, some questions)
= (3형식으로) Emily _____ .

8 우리는 그녀에게 진짜 이유를 말해줄 수 없었다. (tell, the real reason)
= (4형식으로) We couldn't _____ .

C 다음은 Nick의 가족들이 Nick에게 하는 말이다. <보기>와 같이 가족들의 말에 나온 표현을 활용하여 문장을 완성하시오.

| <보기> | Study hard. | Nick's father told him _to study hard_ . |

1 Eat some fruit.   Nick's mother made him _____.

2 Can you open the window?   Nick's uncle asked him _____.

3 Don't skip breakfast.   Nick's sister didn't let him _____.

4 Pick up the laundry.   Nick's brother wanted him _____.

D <보기>와 같이 다음 두 문장을 한 문장으로 연결하시오.

> <보기> I went to bed early. My mom wanted me to do that.
> → My mom wanted _me to go to bed early_ .
>
> I watched my grandmother. She was cooking dinner.
> → I watched _my grandmother cooking[cook] dinner_ .

1 Claire finished her homework. I told her to do that.
→ I told _____.

2 I saw Yumi. She was playing the violin.
→ I saw _____.

3 John found his smartphone. Ann helped him do that.
→ Ann helped _____.

4 Julie watched Alex. He was sending a text message.
→ Julie watched _____.

5 I sang a song in front of my classmates. My teacher made me do that.
→ My teacher made _____.

6 Benjamin saw his friends. They were taking a walk.
→ Benjamin saw _____.

중간 · 기말고사 실전 문제

1 다음 중 어법상 어색한 것은?

① My puppy got sick.
② Let's keep silent.
③ The milk became sourly.
④ Yura's face turned red.
⑤ The doctors were very tired.

2 다음 빈칸에 들어갈 말로 어색한 것을 <u>모두</u> 고르시오.

> A: How did Diana look yesterday?
> B: She looked _____.

① lonely   ② nicely   ③ healthy
④ sadly   ⑤ lovely

3 다음 빈칸에 들어갈 말이 순서대로 짝지어진 것은?

> · Mr. Park will teach chemistry _____ us next semester.
> · May I ask a favor _____ you?

① to – of   ② to – to   ③ for – of
④ for – to   ⑤ of – of

4 다음 중 어법상 <u>어색한</u> 것은?

① The waffle smells delicious.
② Your sister looks like a ballerina.
③ This plan sounds perfect to me.
④ The popcorn tasted like cheese.
⑤ I felt like confident about the contest.

5 다음 빈칸에 들어갈 알맞은 것은?

> We expected the Korean player _____ the gold medal.

① win   ② won
③ winning   ④ to win
⑤ is winning

6 우리말과 같도록 괄호 안의 말을 알맞게 배열하시오.

> 강한 바람은 나뭇잎이 떨어지게 했다. (made, fall, the leaves)

= The strong wind _____.

7 다음 중 어법상 바른 것을 <u>모두</u> 고르시오.

① Do you want me make some lemonade?
② Someone asked us to talk quietly.
③ Mr. Rogers advised me studying law.
④ The police made the man to tell the truth.
⑤ Suho told Jennifer to arrive on time.

8 우리말과 같도록 괄호 안의 말을 알맞게 배열하시오.

> 지우는 매일 아침 그 고양이들에게 약간의 음식을 준다. (some food, Jiwoo, the cats, gives)

= _____ every morning.

[9-10] 다음 빈칸에 들어갈 말로 어색한 것을 고르시오.

9

> They _____ Mr. Wood making a speech.

① watched ② saw ③ heard
④ made ⑤ listened to

10

> Our teacher will _____ us do our history project.

① make ② help ③ get
④ let ⑤ have

11 괄호 안의 말을 알맞게 배열하시오.

> Brian is very good at music, so _____ _____. (Mozart, call, we, him)

12 다음 우리말을 영작할 때 빈칸에 들어갈 알맞은 것은?

> 엄마는 내가 초콜릿을 먹는 것을 허락하지 않으신다.
> = Mom doesn't _____ chocolate.

① allow eat me ② allow to eat me
③ allow me eat ④ allow me eating
⑤ allow me to eat

13 다음 우리말을 알맞게 영작한 것은?

> Luna의 부모님은 그녀가 애완동물을 기르게 허락하지 않으신다.

① Luna's parents don't let her having a pet.
② Luna's parents don't let her to have a pet.
③ Luna's parents don't let her have a pet.
④ Luna's parents let her not have a pet.
⑤ Luna's parents let her not to have a pet.

14 다음 중 밑줄 친 부분이 어법상 어색한 것은?

① Monica is really <u>friendly</u>.
② The carrots taste <u>sweet</u>.
③ It's getting <u>cold</u> outside.
④ They looked very <u>busily</u>.
⑤ Everyone became <u>excited</u>.

15 다음 중 주어진 문장과 문장의 형식이 같은 것은?

> This novel made him popular.

① She got me some water.
② The students look bored.
③ I didn't start the fight.
④ Natalie calls her dog Coco.
⑤ The new year will come quickly.

16 다음 빈칸에 들어갈 말로 어색한 것은?

> I _____ him to come home before nine o'clock.

① ordered ② told ③ expected
④ had ⑤ asked

17 다음 중 밑줄 친 부분이 어법상 어색한 것은?

① Edward got me to write a postcard.
② The guide made us stand in line.
③ Clara told her daughter make the bed.
④ My father wants me to take swim lessons.
⑤ She always helps me look on the bright side.

18 다음 빈칸에 들어갈 말이 순서대로 짝지어진 것은?

> · He doesn't allow us _____ our cell phone during class.
> · I heard my sister _____ the stars.

① use – count　　　② using – to count
③ using – counting　　④ to use – to count
⑤ to use – counting

19 다음 빈칸에 공통으로 들어갈 알맞은 것은?

> · Don't show my photos _____ anyone.
> · I advised her _____ think carefully.

① of　　　② for　　　③ to
④ with　　⑤ about

20 다음 중 어법상 바른 것끼리 묶인 것은?

> ⓐ I didn't see Jacob to smile at me.
> ⓑ Let's listen to the musicians play a song.
> ⓒ Did you hear someone cried?
> ⓓ Have you watched dolphins swimming in the sea?
> ⓔ I felt someone to touch my shoulder.

① ⓐ, ⓑ　　② ⓐ, ⓒ　　③ ⓑ, ⓒ
④ ⓑ, ⓓ　　⑤ ⓓ, ⓔ

21 다음 중 밑줄 친 kept의 쓰임이 나머지 넷과 다른 것은?

① The blanket kept us warm.
② Sam kept his desk clean.
③ A cup of coffee kept her awake.
④ I kept my passport in the drawer.
⑤ The security guard kept the bank safe.

[22-23] 다음 두 문장을 한 문장으로 연결하시오.

22

> Mark threw out some garbage outside.
> Cameron made him do that.
> → Cameron made _____
> _____ outside.

23

> I saw Ruby yesterday. She was getting on the bus.
> → I saw _____
> yesterday.

24 다음 빈칸에 공통으로 들어갈 알맞은 것은?

> · She _____ me forgive Lucy.
> · I _____ my friend a muffler.
> · Serena _____ delicious cream pasta.

① helped　　② gave　　③ wanted
④ let　　　⑤ made

25 다음 중 4형식 문장은 3형식으로, 3형식 문장은 4형식으로 바르게 바꾼 것은?

① Jake passed Martin the ball.
→ Jake passed the ball for Martin.
② Please tell the truth to me.
→ Please tell the truth me.
③ Could you teach me the rules of chess?
→ Could you teach the rules of chess to me?
④ I'm going to cook breakfast for you.
→ I'm going to cook you for breakfast.
⑤ Jen's parents asked her some questions.
→ Jen's parents asked some questions for her.

26 다음 중 문장의 형식이 같은 것끼리 묶인 것은?

ⓐ There is a box under the desk.
ⓑ She helped me study math for the test.
ⓒ His mother wrote him a short message.
ⓓ Did you show your ticket to the man at the door?
ⓔ I listened to the rain falling last night.
ⓕ Joanna looks great today.

① ⓐ, ⓕ   ② ⓑ, ⓔ   ③ ⓒ, ⓓ
④ ⓐ, ⓑ, ⓓ   ⑤ ⓑ, ⓒ, ⓕ

27 <보기>와 같이 괄호 안의 말을 활용하여 문장을 완성하시오.

<보기> I told Robert _to wear his coat_ .
(wear his coat)

(1) I asked Sophia _____.
(water the plants)

(2) I had Dave _____.
(walk the dog)

(3) I helped Mina _____.
(move a closet)

28 다음 글의 밑줄 친 ⓐ~ⓔ 중 어법상 어색한 것을 찾아 기호를 쓰고 바르게 고쳐 쓰시오.

Today was my sister's birthday. My parents and I ⓐbaked a birthday cake this morning. It ⓑtasted deliciously, and she loved it. Later, her friends ⓒcame to our house. They ⓓbrought her some gifts. The gifts ⓔmade her to feel happy.

(1) _____ → _____
(2) _____ → _____

CHAPTER 2
다양한
문장의 종류

It is a very good idea. 그것은 매우 좋은 생각이다.
What a good idea it is! 그것은 정말 좋은 생각이구나!

첫 번째 문장은 그것이 매우 좋은 생각이라는 사실을 전달하는 평서문이에요. 하지만 문장 맨 앞에 **What**을 쓰고 어순을 바꾼 뒤 문장 맨 뒤에 느낌표를 붙이면 그것이 정말 좋은 생각이라고 말하며 놀라움을 나타내는 **감탄문**이 돼요. 이렇게 특정한 의도를 나타내기 위해 감탄문, 의문문 등 다양한 종류의 문장을 사용할 수 있어요.

기출로 적중 POINT

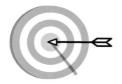

내신 100점 적중!
기출 출제율

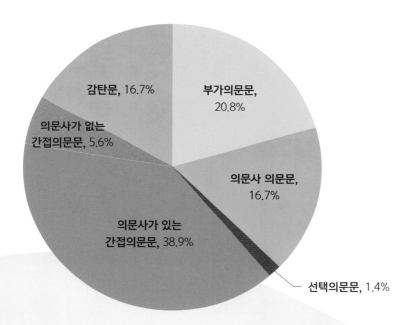

감탄문, 16.7%

의문사가 없는
간접의문문, 5.6%

부가의문문,
20.8%

의문사 의문문,
16.7%

의문사가 있는
간접의문문, 38.9%

선택의문문, 1.4%

TOP 1 **의문사가 있는 간접의문문 (38.9%)**
의문사가 있는 간접의문문의 형태를 묻는 문제가 자주 출제된다.

TOP 2 **부가의문문 (20.8%)**
문장에 따라 알맞은 부가의문문을 쓰는 문제가 자주 출제된다.

TOP 3 **감탄문 (16.7%)**
의문사 의문문 (16.7%)
감탄문의 의미와 형태를 묻는 문제가 자주 출제된다. 의문사 의문문의 형태를 묻
는 문제가 자주 출제된다.

감탄문은 '정말 ~이구나/하구나!'의 의미로, 기쁨이나 놀라움 등의 감정을 나타내는 문장이다.
문장 맨 뒤의 「주어 + 동사」는 생략할 수도 있다.

❶ What 감탄문은 명사를 강조한다.

| What | + | (a/an) | + | 형용사 | + | 명사 | + | (주어 + 동사) | ! |

That is a very tall building. 저것은 매우 높은 건물이다.
→ **What a tall building** (that is)! (저것은) 정말 높은 건물이구나!

(Tip) What 감탄문이 복수명사나 셀 수 없는 명사를 강조할 때는 a/an을 쓰지 않는다.
What pretty eyes (he has)! (그는) 정말 예쁜 눈을 가지고 있구나!
What useful information (it was)! (그것은) 정말 유용한 정보였구나!

❷ How 감탄문은 형용사나 부사를 강조한다. How 감탄문이 부사를 강조할 때는 문장 맨 뒤의 「주어 + 동사」를 생략할 수 없다.

| How | + | 형용사 | + | (주어 + 동사) | ! |

The movie was really boring. 그 영화는 아주 지루했다.
→ **How boring** (the movie was)! (그 영화는) 정말 지루했구나!

| How | + | 부사 | + | 주어 + 동사 | ! |

He swims very well. 그는 수영을 매우 잘한다.
→ **How well** he swims! 그는 수영을 정말 잘하는구나!

연습문제 A 괄호 안에서 알맞은 것을 고르시오.

1 (What / How) a cute baby!

2 (What / How) friendly Emily is!

3 (What / How) small your feet are!

4 (What / How) pretty skirts!

5 (What / How) fun the trip was!

6 (What / How) an excellent speech!

7 (What / How) heavily it rained!

8 (What / How) long hair she has!

9 (What / How) sweet oranges they are!

10 (What / How) fast the airplane moves!

연습문제 B 다음 문장을 감탄문으로 바꿔 쓰시오.

1 Your kittens are really lovely.

→ _____

2 The chair is very comfortable.

→ _____

3 Jinho has a very low voice.

→ _____

4 They are very delicious strawberries.

→ _____

5 I was really lucky.

→ _____

6 We had a really wonderful time.

→ _____

7 She drove very carefully.

→ _____

8 It is really beautiful weather.

→ _____

9 Turtles live very long.

→ _____

10 The bread smells really nice.

→ _____

11 This is very helpful advice.

→ _____

12 That was a very exciting game.

→ _____

기출 적중문제

다음 빈칸에 들어갈 말이 나머지 넷과 <u>다른</u> 것은?

① _____ clear the water looks!
② _____ difficult the test was!
③ _____ surprising news it was!
④ _____ strangely he acts!
⑤ _____ brave the soldiers are!

> What 감탄문은 명사를 강조하고, How 감탄문은 형용사나 부사를 강조해요.

의문사 의문문은 구체적인 정보를 묻는 의문사로 시작하는 의문문이며, 의문사 의문문에는 Yes나 No가 아닌 각 의문사가 묻는 정보로 대답한다.

❶ be동사가 있는 의문사 의문문: 「의문사 + be동사 + 주어 ~?」

Who is this girl in the picture? 사진에 있는 이 소녀는 누구니?
- My sister, Mina. 나의 여동생인 미나야.

What were you reading? 너는 무엇을 읽고 있었니?
- I was reading a comic book. 나는 만화책을 읽고 있었어.

❷ 일반동사가 있는 의문사 의문문: 「의문사 + do/does/did + 주어 + 동사원형 ~?」

When do you usually **exercise**? 너는 보통 언제 운동하니?
- I usually exercise after dinner. 나는 보통 저녁 식사 후에 운동해.

Why did Leo quit the basketball club? Leo는 왜 농구 동아리를 그만뒀니?
- Because he broke his arm. 그의 팔이 부러졌기 때문이야.

❸ 조동사가 있는 의문사 의문문: 「의문사 + 조동사 + 주어 + 동사원형 ~?」

Where will you go for your vacation? 너는 너의 휴가로 어디에 갈 거니?
- To France and Italy. 프랑스와 이탈리아에.

How can I turn on this machine? 내가 이 기계를 어떻게 켤 수 있니?
- Press the green button. 초록색 버튼을 눌러.

(Tip) How come은 '어째서, 왜'라는 의미이며, 「How come + 주어 + 동사 ~?」의 형태로 쓴다.
How come (~~did you arrive~~, **you arrived**) late? 너는 어째서 늦게 도착했니?

(Tip) 의문문의 주어가 의문사인 경우 「의문사 + 동사 ~?」의 형태이며, 의문사는 3인칭 단수 취급한다.
What makes you happy? 무엇이 너를 행복하게 만드니?
Who called you this morning? 누가 오늘 아침에 너에게 전화했니?

연습문제 A 우리말과 같도록 괄호 안의 말을 알맞게 배열하시오.

1 이 버스는 언제 떠나니? (this bus, does, leave, when)

= _____

2 어젯밤에 무슨 일이 일어났니? (happened, what, last night)

= _____

3 우리의 담임 선생님은 누가 되실까? (our homeroom teacher, be, will, who)

= _____

4 학교에서의 너의 첫날은 어땠니? (was, your first day, how, at school)

= _____

5 Brandon은 지금 어디에 가고 있니? (is, going, where, Brandon, now)

= _____

6 너는 점심 식사로 무엇을 원하니? (for lunch, want, do, you, what)

= _____

7 그는 어째서 그의 가방을 잃어버렸니? (his bag, lost, how come, he)

= _____

8 누가 그녀를 울게 했니? (who, cry, her, made)

= _____

9 우리는 어디에서 화장실을 찾을 수 있니? (find, we, where, can, the toilet)

= _____

10 Johnson씨는 어떻게 그 정보를 얻었니? (the information, how, Mr. Johnson, did, get)

= _____

11 나는 왜 Linda에게 사과해야 하니? (should, why, to Linda, apologize, I)

= _____

12 너는 언제 부산으로 이사했니? (you, when, move, did, to Busan)

= _____

연습문제 **B** | 자연스러운 대화가 되도록 질문과 대답을 연결하시오.

1 Who is your favorite artist? ·   · ⓐ We can get to the airport by bus.

2 How can we get to the airport? ·   · ⓑ Because this show is very funny.

3 When do you go to bed on weekends? ·   · ⓒ The cold weather.

4 Why are you laughing? ·   · ⓓ Van Gogh.

5 Where were you yesterday? ·   · ⓔ I was at home.

6 What made your brother sick? ·   · ⓕ Around 11:30 P.M.

기출 적중문제 ◎→

괄호 안의 말을 알맞게 배열하시오.

A: Josie, _____?

(about Korean culture, you, like, do, what)

B: I like traditional Korean food.

선택의문문은 or를 사용하여 상대방의 선택을 묻는 의문문이며, 선택의문문에는 제시된 것 중 하나를 선택하여 대답한다.

Is this **your phone or Minji's phone**? 이것은 너의 전화기니, 아니면 민지의 전화기니?
- It's mine. 그것은 나의 것이야.

Did he **go home or play soccer** after school? 그는 방과 후에 집에 갔니, 아니면 축구를 했니?
- He played soccer. 그는 축구를 했어.

Who wrote this letter, **Henry or Paul**? Henry와 Paul 중 누가 이 편지를 썼니?
- Paul wrote it. Paul이 그것을 썼어.

Which do you like better, **juice or tea**? 너는 주스와 차 중 어느 것을 더 좋아하니?
- Juice. 주스.

연습문제 A 우리말과 같도록 빈칸에 알맞은 말을 쓰시오.

1 너는 중학생이니, 아니면 고등학생이니?

= _____ you a middle school student _____ a high school student?

2 너는 초록색과 노란색 중 어느 것을 선호하니?

= _____ do you prefer, green _____ yellow?

3 나는 오전과 오후 중 언제 너에게 전화해야 하니?

= _____ should I call you, in the morning _____ in the afternoon?

4 너는 학교에 버스를 타고 가니, 아니면 지하철을 타고 가니?

= _____ you go to school by bus _____ by subway?

연습문제 B 자연스러운 대화가 되도록 질문과 대답을 연결하시오.

1 Do you like classical music or hip-hop music? ·   · ⓐ My uncle.

2 Is the woman Chinese or Japanese? ·   · ⓑ Yejin.

3 Who is he, your father or your uncle? ·   · ⓒ I read a book.

4 Was the story true or false? ·   · ⓓ Classical music.

5 Who broke the window, Minsu or Yejin? ·   · ⓔ A tablet PC.

6 Did you watch a movie or read a book last night? ·   · ⓕ It was true.

7 Which do you need, a laptop or a tablet PC? ·   · ⓖ She's Japanese.

POINT 4-1 의문사가 있는 간접의문문

정답 p.5

1. 다른 문장의 일부로 쓰여 질문의 내용을 간접적으로 묻는 의문문을 간접의문문이라 한다.
   의문사가 있는 간접의문문은 「의문사 + 주어 + 동사」의 형태이다.

   I'm not sure. + What is his name?
   → I'm not sure **what** **his name is**. 나는 그의 이름이 무엇인지 확실히 알지 못한다.

   Can you tell me? + Where did you buy this shirt?
   → Can you tell me **where** **you bought** this shirt?
   네가 어디에서 이 셔츠를 샀는지 나에게 말해줄 수 있니?

   Do you know? + When will Susan visit Korea?
   → Do you know **when** **Susan will visit** Korea? 너는 Susan이 언제 한국을 방문할지 알고 있니?

   (Tip) 간접의문문의 주어가 의문사인 경우 「의문사 + 동사」의 형태이다.
   I wonder. + Who made this cake?
   → I wonder **who** **made** this cake. 나는 누가 이 케이크를 만들었는지 궁금하다.

2. 간접의문문을 포함하는 문장의 동사가 생각이나 추측을 나타내는 think, believe, guess, imagine 등인 경우 간접의문문의 의문사를 문장 맨 앞에 쓴다.

   Do you **think**? + **What** is the answer?
   → **What** do you **think** the answer is? 너는 답이 무엇이라고 생각하니?

   Do you **believe**? + **Who** sent these flowers?
   → **Who** do you **believe** sent these flowers? 너는 누가 이 꽃을 보냈다고 생각하니?

연습문제 A | <보기>와 같이 다음 의문문을 간접의문문으로 바꿔 쓰시오.

<보기> How did the fire start?
   → Do you know _how the fire started_ ?

1 Who is she?
   → Can you tell me _____ ?

2 When does the bank open?
   → Please tell me _____ .

3 When will the next train arrive?
   → I'm not sure _____ .

4 Where can I find the library?
   → I want to know _____ .

5 Who took my bike?

→ I don't know _____ .

6 When did the dinosaurs disappear?

→ Do you know _____ ?

7 Why is Jason so upset?

→ I wonder _____ .

8 How does the movie end?

→ I don't remember _____ .

연습문제 **B** 다음 두 문장을 한 문장으로 연결하시오.

1 Do you think? + What is the dog eating?

→ _____

2 Do you believe? + When can we take a break?

→ _____

3 Do you guess? + What will the next song be?

→ _____

4 Do you think? + Who is telling a lie?

→ _____

5 Do you believe? + Where did you lose your bag?

→ _____

6 Do you imagine? + Why did he act rudely?

→ _____

기출 적중문제

우리말과 같도록 괄호 안의 말을 알맞게 배열하시오.

(1) 나는 그 콘서트가 언제 시작하는지 모른다. (starts, I, the concert, know, when, don't)

= _____

(2) 너는 그녀가 어떻게 높은 점수를 받았다고 생각하니? (got, think, a high score, she, how, you, do)

= _____

기출로적중 POINT 4-2 의문사가 없는 간접의문문

정답 p.5

의문사가 없는 간접의문문은 「if[whether](~인지 아닌지) + 주어 + 동사」의 형태이다.

I'm not sure. + Is this the right answer?

→ I'm not sure **if[whether] this is** the right answer. 나는 이것이 정답인지 아닌지 확실히 알지 못한다.

Do you remember? + Did you lock the door?

→ Do you remember **if[whether] you locked** the door? 너는 네가 문을 잠갔는지 아닌지 기억하니?

Do you know? + Will he like my gift?

→ Do you know **if[whether] he will like** my gift? 너는 그가 나의 선물을 좋아할지 아닌지 아니?

연습문제 다음 두 문장을 한 문장으로 연결하시오.

1 Please tell me. + Can Anna ride a bike?

→ Please tell me _____.

2 I wonder. + Do you have a pet?

→ I wonder _____.

3 I don't know. + Will Kenny buy a new wallet?

→ I don't know _____.

4 Can you tell me? + Is Alex at home?

→ Can you tell me _____?

5 Do you know? + Are they playing outside?

→ Do you know _____?

6 I'm not sure. + Will it rain tomorrow?

→ I'm not sure _____.

7 Do you remember? + Did James come to school last Friday?

→ Do you remember _____?

기출 적중문제 🎯

우리말과 같도록 괄호 안의 말을 활용하여 문장을 완성하시오.

> 나는 그녀가 매운 음식을 먹을 수 있는지 아닌지 궁금하다. (eat)

= I wonder _____ spicy food.

POINT 5 부가의문문

1. 부가의문문은 상대방에게 확인이나 동의를 구하기 위해 문장 뒤에 덧붙이는 의문문이다.

①, ②
Tom is diligent, **isn't he?** Tom은 성실해, 그렇지 않니?
③

– **Yes, he is. / No, he isn't.** 응, 그는 성실해. / 아니, 그는 성실하지 않아.
④ ④

① 긍정문 뒤에는 부정의 부가의문문을, 부정문 뒤에는 긍정의 부가의문문을 덧붙인다. (단, 부정형은 축약형으로 쓴다.)
② 앞 문장의 동사가 be동사면 be동사를, 일반동사면 do/does/did를, 조동사면 조동사를 사용한다.
③ 부가의문문의 주어는 앞 문장의 주어와 맞는 인칭대명사를 사용한다.
④ 부가의문문에 대답할 때는 질문의 형태와 상관없이 대답의 내용이 긍정이면 Yes, 부정이면 No로 답한다.

Cindy studied with you, **didn't she?** Cindy는 너와 함께 공부했어, 그렇지 않니?
 – **Yes, she did.** 응, 그녀는 나와 함께 공부했어. / **No, she didn't.** 아니, 그녀는 나와 함께 공부하지 않았어.

You can't play the piano, **can you?** 너는 피아노를 칠 수 없어, 그렇지?
 – **Yes, I can.** 아니, 나는 피아노를 칠 수 있어. / **No, I can't.** 응, 나는 피아노를 칠 수 없어.

(Tip) ① I'm으로 시작하는 문장의 부가의문문으로는 「aren't I?」를 쓴다.
  I'm your best friend, (~~amn't~~, **aren't**) **I?** 나는 너의 가장 친한 친구야, 그렇지 않니?

② 앞 문장의 주어가 지시대명사 this/that이거나 this/that이 포함되어 있을 때는 부가의문문의 주어로 it을 쓰고, these/those이거나 these/those가 포함되어 있을 때는 they를 쓴다.
  This isn't your book, is (~~this~~, **it**)? 이것은 너의 책이 아니야, 그렇지?
  Those pictures look old, don't (~~those~~, **they**)? 저 사진들은 오래되어 보여, 그렇지 않니?

③ 「There + be동사」 구문의 부가의문문의 주어로는 there를 쓴다.
  There were many people on the bus, weren't **there?** 버스에 많은 사람들이 있었어, 그렇지 않니?

2. 명령문과 청유문의 부가의문문

명령문, will you?	Stay in your seat, **will you?** 너의 자리에 그대로 있어라, 알겠니? Don't lie to me, **will you?** 나에게 거짓말하지 마라, 알겠니?
청유문, shall we?	Let's play a game, **shall we?** 게임을 하자, 어떠니? Let's not go outside, **shall we?** 밖으로 나가지 말자, 어떠니?

연습문제 **A** 다음 빈칸에 알맞은 부가의문문을 쓰시오.

1 The movie wasn't very funny, _____?

2 Your friends can speak Chinese well, _____ ?

3 Minho has a new camera, _____ ?

4 I'm quite clever, _____ ?

5 That is Patrick's coat, _____ ?

6 You went to Spain last summer, _____ ?

7 Don't be mean to your little brother, _____ ?

8 There aren't any cookies in the box, _____ ?

9 These leaves will turn red soon, _____ ?

10 Let's ask Mr. Lee for advice, _____ ?

연습문제 B   <보기>와 같이 질문에 대한 대답이 괄호 안의 내용과 일치하도록 빈칸에 쓰시오.

> **<보기>**   *A*: It isn't snowing, is it?
> *B*: _No_ , _it_ _isn't_ . (It isn't snowing.)

1 *A*: You didn't burn the cake, did you?
   B: _____ , _____ _____ . (I didn't burn the cake.)

2 *A*: Penguins can swim quickly, can't they?
   B: _____ , _____ _____ . (They can swim quickly.)

3 *A*: Nick doesn't like rock music, does he?
   B: _____ , _____ _____ . (He doesn't like rock music.)

4 *A*: Those are your earrings, aren't they?
   B: _____ , _____ _____ . (They aren't my earrings.)

5 *A*: The weather will be nice tomorrow, won't it?
   B: _____ , _____ _____ . (It will be nice tomorrow.)

기출 적중문제

다음 대화의 빈칸에 들어갈 알맞은 부가의문문은?

> *A*: Lily called you last night, _____ ?
> *B*: No, she forgot to call me.

① did she   ② didn't she   ③ didn't Lily
④ was she   ⑤ wasn't she

A 밑줄 친 부분이 어법상 맞으면 O를 쓰고, 틀리면 바르게 고쳐 쓰시오.

1 <u>How</u> a busy day it was! → _____

2 She will go on a trip next week, <u>won't she</u>? → _____

3 <u>What</u> lovely tulips! → _____

4 I'm taller than you, <u>am not I</u>? → _____

5 How brightly <u>shine the stars</u>! → _____

6 Thomas has two cats, <u>hasn't he</u>? → _____

7 <u>How</u> funny his joke is! → _____

8 Which do you prefer, pork <u>and</u> beef? → _____

9 What <u>beautiful a smile</u> you have! → _____

10 That red hat is yours, <u>isn't that</u>? → _____

B <보기>와 같이 알맞은 의문사를 활용하여 대화를 완성하시오.

<보기>   A: <u>*When does the bookstore close?*</u>
B: The bookstore closes at 9 P.M.

1 A: _____
　 B: Angela's smartphone was under the pillow.

2 A: _____
　 B: My favorite subject is biology.

3 A: _____
　 B: Jane Austen wrote this novel.

4 A: _____
　 B: The plane will land in an hour.

5 A: _____
　 B: You can make chocolate brownies with this recipe.

6 A: _____
　 B: Jacob looked sad because his friend moved to a different city.

C 다음 두 문장을 한 문장으로 연결하시오.

1 Can you tell me? + What are you doing?

→ _____

2 Do you know? + Who broke the mirror?

→ _____

3 Do you think? + When will we meet Yuna again?

→ _____

4 I want to know. + Where did he put the knife?

→ _____

5 I wonder. + Does Jenny like this restaurant?

→ _____

6 Do you believe? + Why were they so shocked?

→ _____

7 Please tell me. + How can I get to the bus station?

→ _____

8 I don't remember. + Did I turn off the light?

→ _____

D 다음 그림을 보고 빈칸에 알맞은 말을 넣어 대화를 완성하시오.

1  **2**  **3**

1 *A* : Sumin always keeps her room clean, _____ _____?

B : _____, _____ _____.

2 *A* : These are your clothes, _____ _____?

B : _____, _____ _____.

3 *A* : Jim can reach the top shelf, _____ _____?

B : _____, _____ _____.

중간·기말고사 실전 문제

1 다음 문장을 감탄문으로 바르게 바꾼 것은?

It was a really terrible storm.

① How a terrible storm it was!
② How terrible it was a storm!
③ What a terrible storm it was!
④ What a terrible storm was it!
⑤ What a storm terrible it was!

2 다음 중 어법상 어색한 것은?

① When does the game begin?
② How your trip to Busan was?
③ Where should I put my jacket?
④ Why did you join the book club?
⑤ Who came to your birthday party?

3 우리말과 같도록 빈칸에 알맞은 말을 쓰시오.

너는 여름과 겨울 중 어느 것을 더 좋아하니?

= _____ do you like better, summer or winter?

4 다음 빈칸에 들어갈 알맞은 것은?

You have some problems, _____?

① haven't you   ② have you
③ don't you   ④ do you
⑤ didn't you

5 다음 빈칸에 공통으로 들어갈 알맞은 의문사는?

· _____ does he want to get married?
· _____ is the Children's Day?

① Who   ② What   ③ Why
④ Where   ⑤ When

6 다음 빈칸에 들어갈 알맞은 것은?

Do you remember _____ the thief was wearing a mask?

① what   ② who   ③ which
④ where   ⑤ whether

7 다음 두 문장을 한 문장으로 바르게 연결한 것은?

Do you know? Why do zebras have stripes?

① Do you know why do zebras have stripes?
② Do you know why zebras have stripes?
③ Do you know if zebras have stripes?
④ Why do you know do zebras have stripes?
⑤ Why do you know zebras have stripes?

[8-9] 다음 대화의 빈칸에 들어갈 알맞은 것을 고르시오.

8

A: _____ bright the moon is!
B: Yes, it is very shiny.

① What   ② Where
③ How   ④ Which
⑤ Why

9

A: Let's take a picture together, _____?
B: Sure. I want to remember this moment.

① will you   ② won't you
③ will we   ④ shall we
⑤ don't we

10 다음 중 어법상 어색한 것은?

① Who arrived at school first today?
② What do you see in the hole?
③ Can you tell me where is Ms. Park?
④ I wonder who will be the president of our class.
⑤ I want to know why we celebrate Thanksgiving.

[11-12] 다음 문장을 감탄문으로 바꿔 쓰시오.

11

She is a really excellent dancer.

→ _____

12

This orange juice tastes very sweet.

→ _____

13 다음 빈칸에 공통으로 들어갈 알맞은 것은?

· Stop jumping on the bed, _____?
· Don't use a cell phone when you cross the street, _____?

① won't you   ② will you
③ don't you   ④ do you
⑤ shall we

14 다음 중 밑줄 친 what의 쓰임이 나머지 넷과 다른 것은?

① What made her so angry?
② What is your answer to the question?
③ Do you know what he did last weekend?
④ What wonderful songs these are!
⑤ I'm not sure what our parents want for dinner.

15 다음 빈칸에 들어갈 말이 나머지 넷과 다른 것은?

① _____ lucky Jeff was!
② _____ slow the snail moves!
③ _____ hard he studies!
④ _____ nice jeans you have!
⑤ _____ strong the firefighters were!

16 괄호 안의 말을 알맞게 배열하시오.

A: I don't know _____ .
   (is, when, your birthday)
B: It's November 25.

17 다음 (A)~(C)에 들어갈 말이 바르게 짝지어진 것은?

· I'm talking too loudly, ___(A)___ ?
· He won't forgive me, ___(B)___ ?
· There were many flowers in your
  garden, ___(C)___ ?

	(A)	(B)	(C)
①	am I	won't he	were there
②	am I	will he	weren't it
③	aren't I	will he	weren't it
④	amn't I	won't he	weren't there
⑤	aren't I	will he	weren't there

18 다음 질문에 대한 대답으로 가장 알맞은 것은?

A: How will we get to our aunt's house?
B: _____

① We are going to visit her.
② This Saturday.
③ Because she needs our help.
④ We will take a bus.
⑤ She is planting some tomatoes now.

19 우리말과 같도록 주어진 <조건>에 맞게 영작하시오.

그 콘서트 홀은 정말 크구나!

<조건>
1. 감탄문으로 쓰시오.
2. 6단어로 쓰시오.
3. the concert hall, big을 활용하시오.

= _____

20 다음 대화의 밑줄 친 우리말을 알맞게 영작한 것은?

A: Jane doesn't know the truth, does
   she?
B: 아니, 그녀는 그 사실을 알아.

① Yes, she doesn't.　② No, she doesn't.
③ Yes, she is.　④ No, she does.
⑤ Yes, she does.

21 다음 대답에 대한 질문으로 가장 알맞은 것은?

> A: _____
> B: I shopped online.

① Are you shopping now?
② Did you shop at a mall or online?
③ How do you shop online?
④ Can you shop online?
⑤ Why do you shop at a mall?

22 다음 중 밑줄 친 부분이 어법상 바른 것은?

① That wasn't your fault, <u>was that</u>?
② Be quiet here, <u>shall we</u>?
③ Donald isn't British, <u>isn't he</u>?
④ These pens are hers, <u>aren't these</u>?
⑤ She brought her passport, <u>didn't she</u>?

23 다음 빈칸에 들어갈 말이 순서대로 짝지어진 것은?

> · Do you remember _____ you fed your dog?
> · Can you tell me _____ sent this package?

① what – who
② what – why
③ if – how
④ if – who
⑤ if – why

24 다음 중 어법상 바른 것을 <u>모두</u> 고르시오.

① What huge a balloon it is!
② What they are sharp scissors!
③ What a handsome horse!
④ How deep the river is!
⑤ How sweet tastes this cookie!

25 다음 빈칸에 공통으로 들어갈 알맞은 것은?

> · _____ shocking news!
> · _____ is the most important thing in your life?

① Who
② How
③ Which
④ What
⑤ When

26 다음 대답에 대한 질문으로 알맞은 것은?

> A: _____
> B: Last week.

① Who made you change your mind?
② Where did you change your mind?
③ How did you change your mind?
④ Why did you change your mind?
⑤ When did you change your mind?

[27-28] 다음 두 문장을 한 문장으로 연결하시오.

27

Please tell me. How did you become a
soccer player?

→ _____

_____

28

I'm not sure. Will it be sunny tomorrow?

→ _____

_____

[30-31] 우리말과 같도록 괄호 안의 말을 알맞게 배열하시오.

30

나는 준수가 어디에 그의 자전거를 주차했는지 궁금하다. (where, parked, I, Junsu, wonder)

= _____

his bicycle.

31

너는 우리가 언제 집에 가야 한다고 생각하니?
(should, believe, do, we, when, you, go)

= _____

home?

29 다음 대화의 빈칸에 들어갈 말이 순서대로 짝지어진 것은?

A: Do you have any plans for this
    weekend?
B: I'm going to meet my friends.
A: _____ will you and your friends
    go?
B: We will go to the National Gallery for
    an exhibition.
A: That sounds interesting. _____ is
    the theme of the exhibition?
B: It's about the ancient art of Egypt.

① Why – How   ② Where – What
③ Who – How   ④ Who – What
⑤ Where – How

32 다음 중 어법상 바른 것끼리 묶인 것은?

ⓐ What cheap a shirt it is!
ⓑ Do you know where is my phone?
ⓒ How fast the motorcycle moves!
ⓓ When you visited your grandparents
    with your family?
ⓔ What will you order, pasta or salad?

① ⓐ, ⓑ   ② ⓐ, ⓒ   ③ ⓑ, ⓓ
④ ⓒ, ⓓ   ⑤ ⓒ, ⓔ

33 우리말과 같도록 주어진 <조건>에 맞게 영작하시오.

> 너는 누가 경주에서 우승할 것이라고 생각하니?

> **<조건>**
> 1. 간접의문문을 사용하시오.
> 2. 8단어로 쓰시오.
> 3. think, win, the race를 활용하시오.

= _____

34 다음 글의 빈칸에 들어갈 알맞은 것은?

> _____ It's because Queen Victoria wore a white dress on her wedding day. People thought it was very pretty, so it became a tradition to wear a white dress to a wedding.

① When do you know are wedding dresses white?
② Why do you know wedding dresses are white?
③ Do you know why wedding dresses are white?
④ Do you know why are wedding dresses white?
⑤ Do you know when wedding dresses are white?

35 다음 대화의 빈칸에 들어갈 알맞은 것은?

> *A*: I asked you to return some books to the library. However, _____, did you?
> *B*: I'm sorry. I'll return them tomorrow.

① you won't return the books
② you will return the books
③ you returned the books
④ you don't return the books
⑤ you didn't return the books

36 다음 글의 밑줄 친 ⓐ~ⓔ 중 어법상 어색한 것을 찾아 기호를 쓰고 바르게 고쳐 쓰시오.

> ⓐWhat your plan is for this summer? Many people recommend visiting Busan. Do you know ⓑwhy do they like Busan? First, there are amazing beaches in the city. How beautiful ⓒthe beaches are! ⓓWhat do you think Busan is also famous for? Its food. Busan has many well-known seafood restaurants. You want to visit Busan, ⓔdo you?

(1) _____ → _____
(2) _____ → _____
(3) _____ → _____

CHAPTER 3
시제

Suji **lived** in Jejudo a year ago. 수지는 1년 전에 제주도에 살았다.
Suji **has lived** in Jejudo for a year. 수지는 1년 동안 제주도에 살아왔다.

동사 live(살다)의 형태를 **lived**(살았다), **has lived**(살아왔다)로 바꿔 수지가 제주도에 산 시점을 나타냈어요. 이렇게 동사의 형태를 바꿔 행동이나 사건이 발생한 시간을 표현하는 것을 **시제**라고 해요.

기출로 적중 POINT

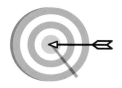

내신 100점 적중!
기출 출제율

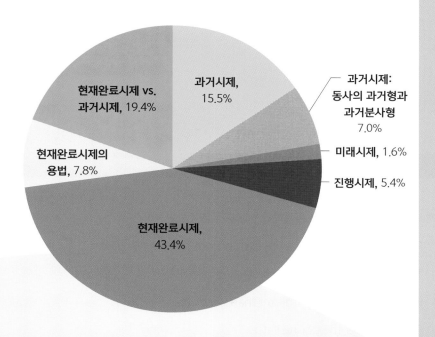

현재완료시제 vs. 과거시제, 19.4%

과거시제, 15.5%

과거시제: 동사의 과거형과 과거분사형 7.0%

미래시제, 1.6%

진행시제, 5.4%

현재완료시제의 용법, 7.8%

현재완료시제, 43.4%

TOP 1 **현재완료시제 (43.4%)**
현재완료시제의 의미와 형태를 묻는 문제가 자주 출제된다.

TOP 2 **현재완료시제 vs. 과거시제 (19.4%)**
현재완료시제와 과거시제를 구별하는 문제가 자주 출제된다.

TOP 3 **과거시제 (15.5%)**
문장 안에서 과거시제가 쓰이는 경우를 묻는 문제가 자주 출제된다.

POINT 1 현재시제

정답 p.7

현재시제는 다음과 같을 때 쓴다.

현재의 상태를 나타낼 때	I **live** in Suwon with my parents. 나는 나의 부모님과 함께 수원에 산다.
현재의 습관이나 반복되는 일을 나타낼 때	Jim **drinks** two cups of milk every day. Jim은 매일 우유 두 컵을 마신다. They **go** hiking on weekends. 그들은 주말마다 하이킹하러 간다. (Tip) 습관이나 반복을 나타내는 부사(구): every day, every Saturday, on weekends, always, sometimes, once a month, twice a week 등
일반적·과학적 사실이나 속담·격언을 말할 때	Water **boils** at 100℃. 물은 섭씨 100도에서 끓는다. Actions **speak** louder than words. 행동이 말보다 더 중요하다.

(Tip) ① go, come, start, leave, arrive 등의 왕래발착 동사는 현재형이나 현재진행형으로 미래의 일을 나타낼 수 있으며, 이때 미래를 나타내는 부사(구)와 주로 함께 쓰인다.
The train for Chicago **leaves** soon. 시카고행 기차는 곧 떠날 것이다.

② 시간이나 조건을 나타내는 부사절에서는 미래시제 대신 현재시제를 쓴다.
I'll finish my homework **before** the class (~~will start~~, **starts**).
나는 수업이 시작하기 전에 나의 숙제를 끝낼 것이다.
I'll stay home **if** it (~~will rain~~, **rains**) tomorrow. 만약 내일 비가 온다면 나는 집에 머무를 것이다.

연습문제 괄호 안의 동사를 활용하여 현재시제 문장을 완성하시오.

1 Robin _____ at the gym on weekends. (exercise)

2 The sun _____ early in summer. (rise)

3 Blood _____ thicker than water. (be)

4 Please answer the phone if it _____. (ring)

5 The plane _____ at 11:30 A.M. tomorrow. (leave)

6 Mars _____ lower gravity than the Earth. (have)

7 This teddy bear _____ to my sister. (belong)

8 The early bird _____ the worm. (catch)

9 Colin always _____ songs when he takes a shower. (sing)

10 Mr. and Mrs. Evans _____ for the same company. (work)

11 I will start my birthday party when my father _____. (arrive)

12 Sojin and her brother _____ bikes to school every morning. (ride)

POINT 2-1 과거시제

정답 p.7

과거시제는 다음과 같을 때 쓴다.

과거의 동작이나 상태를 나타낼 때	My grandfather **built** this house ten years ago. 나의 할아버지는 10년 전에 이 집을 지으셨다. Mr. Brown was my English teacher last year. Brown 선생님은 작년에 나의 영어 선생님이셨다.
역사적 사실을 말할 때	The Korean War **ended** in 1953. 한국 전쟁은 1953년에 끝났다.

(Tip) 과거시제와 주로 함께 쓰이는 부사(구): yesterday, last month, two weeks ago, in 1990 등

연습문제 괄호 안에서 알맞은 것을 고르시오.

1 (Is / Was) the weather sunny yesterday?

2 Edward (sends / sent) me a letter three days ago.

3 She (finds / found) her old diary last Monday.

4 The First World War (breaks / broke) out in 1914.

5 No news (is / was) good news.

6 Lily (reads / read) sci-fi novels every night.

7 Korea (holds / held) the World Cup in 2002.

8 Ketchup (is / was) a medicine in the 1830s.

9 I'll say goodbye to everyone before I (go / went) home.

10 Jessica (meets / met) Mike when she went to the mall.

11 It's cold today because it (rains / rained) heavily last night.

12 The students (go / went) on a field trip last month.

13 Surin (is / was) an elementary school student two years ago.

기출 적중문제

다음 중 밑줄 친 부분이 어법상 어색한 것은?

① The museum <u>was</u> empty last weekend.

② He <u>fixed</u> my old computer yesterday.

③ She will be sad if she <u>hears</u> the news.

④ Rachel <u>eats</u> breakfast three hours ago.

⑤ The city <u>has</u> a flower festival every year.

과거시제: 동사의 과거형과 과거분사형

정답 p.7

1. 동사의 과거형은 대부분 동사원형에 -(e)d를 붙여 만들며, 과거형이 규칙적으로 변하는 동사의 과거형과 과거분사형(p.p.)은 형태가 같다.

대부분의 동사	동사원형 + -ed	want – want**ed**	watch – watch**ed**
-**e**로 끝나는 동사	동사원형 + -d	like – like**d**	invite – invite**d**
「자음 + **y**」로 끝나는 동사	y를 i로 바꾸고 + -ed	cry – cr**ied** hurry – hurr**ied** Tip 「모음 + y」로 끝나는 동사: stay – stay**ed**	
「단모음 + 단자음」으로 끝나는 동사	마지막 자음을 한 번 더 쓰고 + -ed	plan – plan**ned** prefer – prefer**red** Tip 강세가 앞에 오는 2음절 동사: visit – visit**ed** enter – enter**ed**	

2. 일부 동사의 과거형과 과거분사형(p.p.)은 불규칙하게 변한다.

❶ **A-A-A형**: 원형-과거형-과거분사형이 모두 같다.

원형	과거형	과거분사형	원형	과거형	과거분사형
cost 비용이 들다	cost	cost	hurt 다치게 하다	hurt	hurt
let ~하게 하다	let	let	read [riːd] 읽다	read [red]	read [red]
shut 닫다	shut	shut	spread 펼치다	spread	spread

❷ **A-B-A형**: 원형-과거분사형이 같다.

원형	과거형	과거분사형	원형	과거형	과거분사형
become ~이 되다	became	become	come 오다	came	come
overcome 극복하다	overcame	overcome	run 달리다	ran	run

❸ **A-B-B형**: 과거형-과거분사형이 같다.

원형	과거형	과거분사형	원형	과거형	과거분사형
bring 가져오다	brought	brought	build 짓다, 만들다	built	built
feed 먹이를 주다	fed	fed	feel 느끼다	felt	felt
find 찾다	found	found	get 얻다	got	got(ten)
have 가지다	had	had	hear 듣다	heard	heard
keep 유지하다	kept	kept	lay 놓다, 낳다	laid	laid

원형	과거형	과거분사형	원형	과거형	과거분사형
lead 이끌다	led	led	leave 떠나다	left	left
lose 잃다, 지다	lost	lost	make 만들다	made	made
meet 만나다	met	met	send 보내다	sent	sent
sleep 자다	slept	slept	spend 쓰다	spent	spent
think 생각하다	thought	thought	understand 이해하다	understood	understood

❹ A-B-C형: 원형-과거형-과거분사형이 모두 다르다.

원형	과거형	과거분사형	원형	과거형	과거분사형
be ~이다, ~하다	was/were	been	begin 시작하다	began	begun
break 깨다	broke	broken	choose 선택하다	chose	chosen
do 하다	did	done	drive 운전하다	drove	driven
eat 먹다	ate	eaten	fall 떨어지다, 넘어지다	fell	fallen
fly 날다	flew	flown	forget 잊다	forgot	forgotten
give 주다	gave	given	go 가다	went	gone
grow 자라다	grew	grown	know 알다	knew	known
mistake 실수하다	mistook	mistaken	ride 타다	rode	ridden
ring 울리다	rang	rung	rise 오르다	rose	risen
see 보다	saw	seen	sing 노래하다	sang	sung
steal 훔치다	stole	stolen	swim 수영하다	swam	swum
take 가지고 가다	took	taken	throw 던지다	threw	thrown
wear 입고 있다	wore	worn	write 쓰다	wrote	written

연습문제 A | 다음 동사의 과거형을 쓰시오.

1 start　　　－ ＿＿＿＿＿＿＿　　　**2** improve　　　－ ＿＿＿＿＿＿＿

3 stop　　　－ ＿＿＿＿＿＿＿　　　**4** try　　　－ ＿＿＿＿＿＿＿

5 listen　　　－ ＿＿＿＿＿＿＿　　　**6** play　　　－ ＿＿＿＿＿＿＿

7 believe　　　－ ＿＿＿＿＿＿＿　　　**8** chat　　　－ ＿＿＿＿＿＿＿

9	enjoy	– _____	10	remember	– _____
11	carry	– _____	12	shop	– _____
13	invent	– _____	14	agree	– _____
15	enter	– _____	16	study	– _____

연습문제 B 다음 동사의 과거형과 과거분사형을 쓰시오.

1	grow	– _____ – _____	2	hear	– _____ – _____
3	throw	– _____ – _____	4	make	– _____ – _____
5	run	– _____ – _____	6	become	– _____ – _____
7	spend	– _____ – _____	8	lay	– _____ – _____
9	eat	– _____ – _____	10	sleep	– _____ – _____
11	cost	– _____ – _____	12	have	– _____ – _____
13	be	– _____ – _____	14	read	– _____ – _____
15	leave	– _____ – _____	16	build	– _____ – _____
17	let	– _____ – _____	18	shut	– _____ – _____
19	write	– _____ – _____	20	keep	– _____ – _____
21	break	– _____ – _____	22	rise	– _____ – _____
23	take	– _____ – _____	24	think	– _____ – _____
25	do	– _____ – _____	26	spread	– _____ – _____
27	see	– _____ – _____	28	feed	– _____ – _____
29	know	– _____ – _____	30	find	– _____ – _____
31	bring	– _____ – _____	32	hurt	– _____ – _____
33	forget	– _____ – _____	34	drive	– _____ – _____

기출 적중문제

다음 중 동사의 과거형과 과거분사형이 잘못된 것은?

① wear – wore – worn
② lead – led – led
③ swim – swam – swam
④ delay – delayed – delayed
⑤ steal – stole – stolen

1. **미래시제는 미래의 일을 예측할 때 쓰며, 「will + 동사원형」이나 「be going to + 동사원형」의 형태이다.**

   Sophia **will be** 16 years old next year.   Sophia는 내년에 16살이 될 것이다.
   = Sophia **is going to be** 16 years old next year.

   It **won't snow** tomorrow.   내일 눈이 오지 않을 것이다.
   = It **isn't going to snow** tomorrow.

   (Tip) 미래시제와 주로 함께 쓰이는 부사(구): tomorrow, next Monday, next week, soon 등

2. **단, 주어의 의지나 말하는 시점에 결정된 미래의 일을 나타낼 때는 「will + 동사원형」을 쓰고, 예정된 미래의 일을 나타낼 때는 「be going to + 동사원형」을 쓴다.**

   I**'ll wait** here until you come.   나는 네가 올 때까지 여기에서 기다리겠다. (기다리겠다는 주어의 의지)
   This dress is pretty. I**'ll buy** it.   이 드레스는 예쁘다. 나는 그것을 살 것이다. (말하는 시점에 사기로 결정됨)
   I**'m going to leave** tomorrow.   나는 내일 떠날 예정이다. (떠나기로 예정됨)

연습문제 다음 문장을 괄호 안의 말을 활용하여 미래시제로 바꿔 쓰시오.

1 They watch a baseball game together. (will)

→ _____ tomorrow night.

2 The sky is clear. (be going to)

→ _____ this afternoon.

3 Peter bakes a cake for Sally's birthday. (will)

→ _____ next Wednesday.

4 A strong typhoon hits the city. (be going to)

→ _____ next week.

5 Luke does not invite me to his house. (will)

→ _____ this weekend.

6 Do you and your brother call your grandparents? (will)

→ _____ tomorrow?

7 The restaurant moves to a new location. (be going to)

→ _____ soon.

8 What does Mr. Jenkins cook for breakfast? (be going to)

→ _____ on Sunday morning?

1. **진행시제는 특정 시점에 진행되고 있는 동작을 나타낼 때 쓰며, 「be + V-ing」의 형태이다.**

현재진행시제	Junsu **is using** the computer now. 준수는 지금 그 컴퓨터를 쓰고 있다. **Are** they **listening** to K-pop music? 그들은 케이팝 음악을 듣고 있니? (Tip) 현재진행시제는 미래를 나타내는 부사(구)와 주로 함께 쓰여 예정된 가까운 미래의 일을 나타낼 수 있다. She **is coming** to New York **next month**. 그녀는 다음 달에 뉴욕에 올 예정이다. What **are** you **doing tomorrow**? 너는 내일 무엇을 할 예정이니?
과거진행시제	I **was walking** my dog an hour ago. 나는 한 시간 전에 나의 개를 산책시키고 있었다. We **weren't playing** soccer at that time. 우리는 그때 축구를 하고 있지 않았다.

2. **소유(have 등), 인식(think, know 등), 감정(love, hate 등), 감각(smell, taste 등) 등의 상태를 나타내는 동사는 진행형으로 쓸 수 없다.**

The man (~~is having~~, **has**) a small boat. 그 남자는 작은 배를 가지고 있다.

Those cupcakes (~~are smelling~~, **smell**) good. 저 컵케이크들은 좋은 냄새가 난다.

(Tip) have, think, smell, taste 등의 동사가 상태가 아닌 동작을 나타낼 때는 진행형으로 쓸 수 있다.

Dennis and I **are having** dinner. Dennis와 나는 저녁을 먹고 있다.

Mr. Shaw **is tasting** the wine. Shaw씨는 그 와인을 맛보고 있다.

연습문제 **A** 우리말과 같도록 괄호 안의 동사를 활용하여 빈칸에 쓰시오.

1 Mona는 그때 공원에서 조깅하고 있었다. (jog)

= Mona ＿＿＿＿＿＿ ＿＿＿＿＿＿ in the park at that time.

2 너는 Josie와 무엇을 공부하고 있니? (study)

= What ＿＿＿＿＿ you ＿＿＿＿＿ with Josie?

3 나는 그때 Sarah와 말다툼하고 있지 않았다. (argue)

= I ＿＿＿＿＿ ＿＿＿＿＿ with Sarah then.

4 유빈이는 이번 금요일에 브라질로 떠날 예정이다. (leave)

= Yubin ＿＿＿＿＿ ＿＿＿＿＿ for Brazil this Friday.

5 네가 초인종을 눌렀을 때 나는 샤워를 하고 있었다. (take)

= I ＿＿＿＿＿ ＿＿＿＿＿ a shower when you rang the doorbell.

6 군인들은 그들의 지휘관의 명령을 기다리고 있다. (wait)

= Soldiers ＿＿＿＿＿ ＿＿＿＿＿ for their captain's order.

7 Penny와 Annie은 소풍을 위해 김밥을 만들고 있다. (make)

= Penny and Annie _____ _____ gimbap for the picnic.

8 그는 내일 언제 집에 도착할 예정이니? (arrive)

= When _____ he _____ home tomorrow?

9 그들은 어젯밤에 Gina를 위한 깜짝 파티를 계획하고 있었다. (plan)

= They _____ _____ a surprise party for Gina last night.

10 많은 학생들은 요즘 중국어를 배우고 있다. (learn)

= Many students _____ _____ Chinese these days.

11 윤호의 부모님은 다음 주에 그의 학교를 방문하실 예정이다. (visit)

= Yunho's parents _____ _____ his school next week.

12 나는 그 고양이가 나타났을 때 식물에 물을 주고 있었다. (water)

= I _____ _____ plants when the cat appeared.

연습문제 B 밑줄 친 부분이 어법상 맞으면 O를 쓰고, 틀리면 바르게 고쳐 쓰시오.

1 I am knowing your girlfriend. → _____

2 Ms. Jones hates rainy days. → _____

3 Jenny is having brown hair and blue eyes. → _____

4 We were having lunch two hours ago. → _____

5 The flowers in the garden are smelling amazing. → _____

6 Molly is loving her younger sister. → _____

7 Mr. Clark has the biggest house in the town. → _____

8 This ice cream tastes like mint chocolate. → _____

9 They have a good time in France right now. → _____

10 Hyeri is tasting a free sample of bread. → _____

기출 적중문제

다음 중 어법상 바른 것은?

① Katie cleaning her room yesterday.

② Elena is having an expensive ring.

③ Where were they going now?

④ He is writing in his diary when I called him.

⑤ The baby wasn't sleeping at that time.

현재완료시제

1. **현재완료시제는 과거에 발생한 일이 현재까지 영향을 미칠 때 쓰며, 「have/has + p.p.」의 형태이다.**

과거 ────────────────→ 현재

I **have lived** in China since last year. 나는 작년 이후로 중국에서 살아왔다.

(= I started to live in China last year. I still live there.)
나는 작년에 중국에서 살기 시작했다. 나는 여전히 거기에 산다.

Minho **has broken** his left arm. 민호는 왼팔이 부러졌다.

(= Minho broke his left arm. It is still broken.) 민호는 왼팔이 부러졌다. 그것은 아직도 부러져있다.

2. **현재완료시제의 부정문:「have/has + not + p.p.」**

I **have not[haven't] seen** Jake for two months. 나는 두 달 동안 Jake를 보지 못해왔다.

She **has not[hasn't] finished** her homework yet. 그녀는 아직 그녀의 숙제를 끝내지 못했다.

3. **현재완료시제의 의문문과 대답**

의문문	긍정의 대답	부정의 대답
Have/Has + 주어 + p.p. ~?	Yes, 주어 + have/has.	No, 주어 + have/has + not.

Have you ever **been** to Africa? 너는 아프리카에 가본 적이 있니?

– **Yes, I have.** 응, 가본 적이 있어. / **No, I haven't.** 아니, 가본 적이 없어.

(Tip) 의문사가 있는 현재완료시제의 의문문:「의문사 + have/has + 주어 + p.p. ~?」
Why have you been late for school recently? 너는 최근에 왜 학교에 늦었니?

연습문제 A 괄호 안의 동사를 활용하여 현재완료시제 문장을 완성하시오. (단, 긍정문으로 쓰시오.)

1 He _____ about his promise. (forget)

2 Joseph _____ to Seoul once. (be)

3 I _____ a bad cold since Monday. (have)

4 Gloria _____ the piano for three hours. (play)

5 The hockey team _____ a lot of games recently. (lose)

6 The temperature _____ to 35℃. (rise)

7 They _____ at this company since 2008. (work)

연습문제 B | 다음 문장을 괄호 안의 지시대로 바꿔 쓰시오.

1 We have been to Dokdo before. (부정문으로)

→ _____

2 They have lost their bags and passports. (의문문으로)

→ _____

3 Joshua has seen a rainbow. (부정문으로)

→ _____

4 You have told your parents about the problem. (의문문으로)

→ _____

5 I have tried the recipe for onion soup. (부정문으로)

→ _____

6 Tina has run a marathon recently. (의문문으로)

→ _____

연습문제 C | 우리말과 같도록 괄호 안의 말을 알맞게 배열하시오.

1 어젯밤 이후로 비가 많이 오고 있다. (a lot, rained, it, has)

= _____ since last night.

2 우리는 5년 동안 서로를 알아왔다. (each other, we, known, have)

= _____ for five years.

3 Collins씨는 전에 조종사로 일해본 적이 있니? (worked, has, as a pilot, Mr. Collins)

= _____ before?

4 나는 최근에 새 영화를 보지 않았다. (new movies, watched, not, I, have)

= _____ lately.

5 그 학생들은 무엇을 깨뜨렸니? (broken, what, the students, have)

= _____ ?

6 우민이는 1년 동안 치과에 가지 않아 왔다. (to the dentist, been, not, Woomin, has)

= _____ for a year.

기출 적중문제

우리말과 같도록 괄호 안의 말을 활용하여 영작하시오.

> 너는 그의 소설을 읽어본 적이 있니? (read, novel)

= _____

현재완료시제의 용법

정답 p.8

현재완료시제의 용법과 의미는 다음과 같다.

용법	의미	예문
완료	~했다	과거에 발생한 일이 현재에 완료되었음을 나타내며, just, already, yet, lately, recently 등의 표현과 주로 함께 쓴다. The musical **has just ended**. 그 뮤지컬은 방금 끝났다. The train **hasn't arrived yet**. 그 기차는 아직 도착하지 않았다.
경험	~해본 적이 있다	과거부터 현재까지의 경험을 나타내며, once, ~ times, ever, never, before 등의 표현과 주로 함께 쓴다. I**'ve eaten** at this restaurant **twice**. 나는 이 식당에서 두 번 식사해본 적이 있다. **Have** you **ever seen** a camel? 너는 낙타를 본 적이 있니?
계속	~해왔다, ~했다	과거부터 현재까지 계속되는 일을 나타내며, for, since, how long 등의 표현과 주로 함께 쓴다. People **have had** rice **for** thousands of years. 사람들은 수천 년 동안 쌀을 먹어왔다. I **have been** sick **since** last night. 나는 어젯밤부터 아팠다. (Tip) for(~ 동안)는 일이 지속된 기간과 함께 쓰이고, since(~ 이후로)는 일이 시작된 시점과 함께 쓰인다. Cam has kept his rabbit **for four years**. Cam은 그의 토끼를 4년 동안 길러왔다. Cam has kept his rabbit **since 2010**. Cam은 2010년 이후로 그의 토끼를 길러왔다.
결과	~했다 (지금은 ~이다)	과거에 발생한 일의 결과가 현재까지 영향을 미치고 있음을 나타낸다. She **has lost** her bag. 그녀는 그녀의 가방을 잃어버렸다. (지금은 가방이 없다.) Jamie **has left** for Brazil. Jamie는 브라질로 떠났다. (지금은 여기에 없다.)

(Tip) have/has been to는 경험을 나타내고, have/has gone to는 결과를 나타낸다.
Jinsu **has been to** Canada. 진수는 캐나다에 가본 적이 있다.
Jinsu **has gone to** Canada. 진수는 캐나다에 갔다. (지금은 여기에 없다.)

연습문제 A 우리말과 같도록 괄호 안의 동사를 활용하여 빈칸에 쓰시오.

1 너는 얼음 위에서 넘어져본 적이 있니? (fall)

= _____ you ever _____ down on the ice?

2 Marcus의 삼촌은 일하기 위해 이라크에 가셨다. (go)

= Marcus's uncle _____ _____ to Iraq to work.

3 나는 그 미술관에 한 번 방문해본 적이 있다. (visit)

= I _____ _____ the art museum once.

4 지희는 이미 그녀의 역사 숙제를 했다. (do)

= Jihee _____ already _____ her history homework.

5 그는 실수로 그 꽃병을 깨트렸다. (break)

= He _____ _____ the vase by mistake.

6 보스턴행 버스는 아직 떠나지 않았다. (leave)

= The bus to Boston _____ _____ yet.

7 Luna와 Martha는 얼마나 오래 가장 친한 친구였니? (be)

= How long _____ Luna and Martha _____ best friends?

8 플라스틱은 수년 동안 많은 문제를 초래해왔다. (cause)

= Plastics _____ _____ lots of problems for many years.

연습문제 B 밑줄 친 부분의 용법을 <보기>에서 골라 그 기호를 쓰시오.

<보기> ⓐ 완료 ⓑ 경험 ⓒ 계속 ⓓ 결과

1 Ms. Johnson has worked as a teacher since 1997.　　[　　　]

2 Isaac and his friends have just arrived at the library.　　[　　　]

3 My aunt has gone to France with her kids.　　[　　　]

4 He has seen the movie three times.　　[　　　]

5 We haven't eaten lunch yet.　　[　　　]

6 Ella has grown tulips for a month.　　[　　　]

7 Have you ever been to San Francisco?　　[　　　]

8 Jonathan has sold his bicycle, so he doesn't have it now.　　[　　　]

9 I haven't heard the rumor before.　　[　　　]

10 She has already finished writing the science report.　　[　　　]

기출 적중문제 🎯

다음 중 밑줄 친 부분의 용법이 나머지 넷과 다른 것은?

① Max has never seen a raccoon.

② I have known Benny for a long time.

③ Have you ever watched this TV show?

④ Have you been to London before?

⑤ We have taken the yoga class five times.

1. 현재완료시제는 과거에 발생하여 현재까지 영향을 미치는 일을 나타낼 때 쓰고, 과거시제는 과거에 발생하고 완료된 일을 나타낼 때 쓴다.

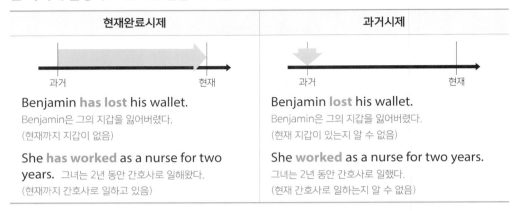

현재완료시제	과거시제
Benjamin **has lost** his wallet.	Benjamin **lost** his wallet.
Benjamin은 그의 지갑을 잃어버렸다.	Benjamin은 그의 지갑을 잃어버렸다.
(현재까지 지갑이 없음)	(현재 지갑이 있는지 알 수 없음)
She **has worked** as a nurse for two years. 그녀는 2년 동안 간호사로 일해왔다.	She **worked** as a nurse for two years. 그녀는 2년 동안 간호사로 일했다.
(현재까지 간호사로 일하고 있음)	(현재 간호사로 일하는지 알 수 없음)

2. 현재완료시제는 yesterday, last ~, ~ ago, 「in + 연도」, when 등의 특정한 과거 시점을 나타내는 표현과 함께 쓸 수 없다.

He (~~has stayed~~, **stayed**) at my home **last month**. 그는 지난달에 나의 집에 머물렀다.
I (~~have learned~~, **learned**) to play the cello **when** I was young.
나는 어렸을 때 첼로를 연주하는 것을 배웠다.

연습문제 A 괄호 안에서 알맞은 것을 고르시오.

1 Anna (studied / has studied) Italian for five weeks.

2 It (snowed / has snowed) a lot last winter.

3 The plane (left / has left) ten minutes ago.

4 Suho (bought / has bought) a new laptop yesterday.

5 I (didn't read / haven't read) any books since last month.

6 When (did you clean / have you cleaned) the kitchen?

7 I (had / have had) a glass of orange juice this morning.

8 The family (lived / has lived) near Hangang park since last year.

9 (Did you know / Have you known) Sara for a long time?

10 Kate (cooked / has cooked) some soup for me when I was sick.

11 Daniel (went / has gone) to Seoul a year ago, and I (didn't see / haven't seen) him since then.

연습문제 B 괄호 안의 동사를 활용하여 빈칸에 쓰시오. (단, 부정문에서는 줄임말로 쓰시오.)

1 She _____ in her hometown two days ago. (arrive)

2 _____ the bookstore _____ open since last year? (be)

3 We _____ just _____ some flowers in the garden. (plant)

4 Thomas _____ _____ to Paris yet. (not, be)

5 Minsu's family _____ to Jeonju last month. (move)

6 He _____ _____ the same computer since 2007. (use)

7 I _____ the amusement park when I was 13 years old. (visit)

8 My brothers had a fight yesterday, and they _____ _____ since then. (not, talk)

연습문제 C 밑줄 친 부분이 어법상 맞으면 O를 쓰고, 틀리면 바르게 고쳐 쓰시오.

1 I haven't had breakfast yet. → _____

2 James practiced dancing since April. → _____

3 The first McDonald's has opened in 1955. → _____

4 Charles has already watched the documentary film. → _____

5 She hasn't gone to Italy last summer. → _____

6 Our soccer team has won the game yesterday. → _____

7 I have tried vegan food before. → _____

8 Mario has written short stories three years ago. → _____

9 When have you taken the photo? → _____

10 How long have you waited outside? → _____

11 My sister has graduated from middle school last year. → _____

12 We have seen the sunset together yesterday evening. → _____

기출 적중문제

현재완료시제는 특정한 과거 시점을 나타내는 표현과 함께 쓸 수 없어요.

다음 빈칸에 들어갈 말로 어색한 것을 모두 고르시오.

We have visited their new house _____.

① in 2008　　② before　　③ twice
④ recently　　⑤ a week ago

(A) 우리말과 같도록 괄호 안의 말을 알맞게 배열하시오.

1 물은 섭씨 0도에서 언다. (at 0°C, freezes, water)

= _____

2 어제 한 마리의 고양이가 나의 집으로 뛰어 들어왔다. (ran into, a cat, my house, yesterday)

= _____

3 그 식당은 곧 문을 닫을 예정이다. (going, soon, is, the restaurant, close, to)

= _____

4 Fred는 수요일마다 그 카페에 간다. (every Wednesday, Fred, the café, goes to)

= _____

5 그들은 2주 전에 노래자랑 대회에 참가했다. (the singing contest, participated in, they, two weeks ago)

= _____

6 우리는 우리의 첫 번째 경기가 시작될 때 초조했다. (nervous, our first game, when, were, we, started)

= _____

7 나는 더 많은 정보를 알아내기 위해 그 웹사이트를 방문할 것이다. (will, the website, more information, to find out, visit, I)

= _____

(B) 다음 그림을 보고 괄호 안의 말을 활용하여 질문에 대한 대답을 완성하시오.

1 *A*: What are John and Jerry doing now?

B: They _____. (eat ice cream)

2 *A*: What were you doing when I called you yesterday?

B: I _____. (wrap a gift)

3 *A*: What was Helen doing at 10 P.M. last night?

B: She _____ at the bus stop. (wait for her mother)

C <보기>와 같이 현재완료시제를 이용하여 다음 두 문장을 한 문장으로 연결하시오.

> <보기> Mr. Lee began to study music six years ago. He still studies it.
>   → Mr. Lee *has studied music for six years* .

1 Ally started to save money two months ago. She still saves money.
→ Ally _____ .

2 He began to take this medicine in 2006. He still takes it.
→ He _____ .

3 I began to practice taekwondo last month. I still practice it.
→ I _____ .

4 My sister went to the beach. She isn't at home now.
→ My sister _____ .

5 Tony moved to Sydney in 2009. He still lives in Sydney.
→ Tony _____ .

6 Hojun began to play chess last spring. He still plays it.
→ Hojun _____ .

7 Mindy lost her new bracelet. She can't find it now.
→ Mindy _____ .

8 Jennifer and I arrived in this city three days ago. We are still in this city.
→ Jennifer and I _____ .

D 다음은 Jenny가 David에게 보내는 편지이다. 괄호 안의 동사를 활용하여 문장을 완성하시오.

> Dear David,
> I'm staying in Seoul now. I ⓐ_____(come) here last week with my family. However,
> they ⓑ_____(leave) a few days ago, and now I ⓒ_____(be) here alone.
> I started exploring the city on my own. I ⓓ_____(visit) many places since yesterday.
> I ⓔ_____(be) to Gyeongbokgung and the N Seoul Tower. Tomorrow, I
> ⓕ_____(go) to the National Museum of Korea. I'm so excited!
>
> Jenny

중간·기말고사 실전 문제

[1-2] 다음 중 동사의 과거형과 과거분사형이 <u>잘못된</u> 것을 고르시오.

1

① feed – fed – fed
② invite – invited – invited
③ sing – sang – sung
④ cost – cost – cost
⑤ teach – teached – teached

2

① lay – laid – laid
② throw – threw – thrown
③ mistake – mistook – mistook
④ stay – stayed – stayed
⑤ spread – spread – spread

3 다음 중 밑줄 친 부분이 어법상 바른 것은?

① I <u>heared</u> someone scream last night.
② He <u>broken</u> the window yesterday.
③ Chinese people <u>invented</u> silk.
④ My sisters <u>have drinked</u> all the milk.
⑤ Mr. Hall <u>has drove</u> a sports car once.

4 다음 빈칸에 들어갈 말로 어색한 것은?

> Ms. Nelson has _____ many books lately.

① borrowed   ② read
③ bought   ④ wrote
⑤ published

5 우리말과 같도록 괄호 안의 동사를 활용하여 빈칸에 쓰시오.

> 그 버스는 이미 출발했다. (depart)

= The bus _____ already _____.

6 다음 중 어법상 <u>어색한</u> 것은?

① Emily has long brown hair.
② The snow festival starts soon.
③ Jonathan Swift writes *Gulliver's Travels* in 1726.
④ Water covers 71 percent of the earth's surface.
⑤ Jackson watched the musical *Aladdin* yesterday.

[7-8] 다음 빈칸에 들어갈 알맞은 것을 고르시오.

7

> Carrie _____ her mom to plant cucumbers last weekend.

① helps   ② helped
③ will help   ④ is helping
⑤ has helped

8

> It _____ six years since you and I graduated from high school.

① be   ② is
③ was   ④ is going to be
⑤ has been

9 괄호 안의 동사를 활용하여 질문에 대한 대답을 완성하시오.

A: What did your parents do three days ago?
B: They _____ hiking with their friends. (go)

12 다음 빈칸에 들어갈 말이 순서대로 짝지어진 것은?

· I _____ when you sent me a text message.
· Neil Armstrong _____ on the moon in 1969.

① was sleeping – will land
② am sleeping – has landed
③ was sleeping – has landed
④ am sleeping – landed
⑤ was sleeping – landed

10 다음 중 밑줄 친 부분이 어법상 바른 것을 모두 고르시오.

① I will study hard for the test last week.
② Erica was listening to music now.
③ Is Mark angry at me yesterday?
④ The sun will rise at 5:30 A.M. tomorrow morning.
⑤ Jake goes to the museum twice a year.

13 다음 중 밑줄 친 부분이 어법상 어색한 것은?

① I haven't washed my hair for two days.
② Have you ever been to Egypt?
③ The tree fell down yesterday.
④ Ms. Watson drank three cups of coffee since 9 A.M.
⑤ Someone knocked on the door a few minutes ago.

11 다음 두 문장의 의미가 같도록 빈칸에 알맞은 말을 쓰시오.

A famous scientist will visit Korea next week.
= A famous scientist _____
_____ _____ _____
Korea next week.

14 다음 중 밑줄 친 부분이 어법상 어색한 것은?

A: Has your family ①planned anything for the holiday?
B: Yes, we ②have. We ③are going to go on a picnic if it ④will be sunny tomorrow. It ⑤will be very fun.

15 다음 빈칸에 들어갈 알맞은 것을 <u>모두</u> 고르시오.

> The orchestra is performing at the concert hall _____.

① tomorrow   ② an hour ago
③ last month   ④ before
⑤ next Saturday

16 다음 우리말을 알맞게 영작한 것은?

> 예린이는 지난달에 매우 흥미로운 책을 읽었다.

① Yerin reads a very interesting book last month.
② Yerin read a very interesting book last month.
③ Yerin was reading a very interesting book last month.
④ Yerin has read a very interesting book last month.
⑤ Yerin will read a very interesting book last month.

17 다음 중 어법상 <u>어색한</u> 것은?

① We were solving the puzzle yesterday.
② Cam is having a short beard now.
③ I'm preparing dinner with my brother.
④ My aunt was driving a car an hour ago.
⑤ Eunji is tasting an orange at the market.

18 다음 문장에서 <u>틀린</u> 부분을 바르게 고쳐 완전한 문장을 쓰시오.

> Columbus has landed in North America in 1492.
> → _____
> _____

19 다음 중 밑줄 친 부분의 의미가 나머지 넷과 <u>다른</u> 것은?

① It <u>is going to</u> rain on Sunday.
② Susan <u>is going to</u> be late again.
③ Ronald <u>is going to</u> city hall.
④ He <u>is going to</u> wake up early tomorrow.
⑤ My sister <u>is going to</u> buy a new camera.

20 다음 글의 빈칸에 들어갈 말이 순서대로 짝지어진 것은?

> Jiwon _____ the school band last May. He has been a member of the band _____ three months.

① joins – for
② joined – since
③ joined – for
④ has joined – since
⑤ has joined – for

21 다음 대화의 밑줄 친 우리말과 같도록 괄호 안의 말을 활용하여 문장을 완성하시오.

> A: 너는 전에 이 노래를 들어본 적이 있니? (hear, this song)
> B: Yes, it is my favorite song.

= _____ before?

[22-23] 주어진 문장의 밑줄 친 부분과 용법이 같은 것을 고르시오.

22

> Emma has taught us English since last month.

① Nate has been to Hong Kong three times.
② Have you already gotten a birthday gift for Jane?
③ I have stopped swimming for six months.
④ Has your brother gone to England?
⑤ Lisa hasn't bought the concert tickets yet.

23

> He has never written me a letter.

① It has been cloudy since last night.
② Susie has just left the hospital.
③ Victor has lost his hat on the bus.
④ My sister has gone to New York for her job.
⑤ Katherine has met the actor once.

24 다음 문장을 주어진 지시대로 바꿔 쓰시오.

> Anne and Diana have been friends since 2015.

(1) 부정문으로
→ _____
_____

(2) 의문문으로
→ _____
_____

25 다음 (A)~(C)에 들어갈 말이 바르게 짝지어진 것은?

> Something scary happened yesterday.
> I ___(A)___ TV when I heard a noise.
> The noise ___(B)___ from upstairs.
> But nobody ___(C)___ there since last month. My hands started to shake with fear.

	(A)	(B)	(C)
①	was watching	comes	has lived
②	was watching	came	has lived
③	am watching	comes	has lived
④	was watching	came	lived
⑤	am watching	came	lived

26 다음 빈칸에 들어갈 말이 나머지 넷과 다른 것은?

① Tom has lived in Brazil _____ 2001.
② He has stayed at the hotel _____ November.
③ I have studied German _____ I was nine years old.
④ Monica's father has worked as a teacher _____ 20 years.
⑤ My brother has been sick _____ last night.

27 다음 빈칸에 들어갈 알맞은 것을 모두 고르시오.

> I have waited for the Christmas party
> _____.

① three days ago   ② since last week
③ yesterday   ④ for a month
⑤ last evening

28 다음 중 밑줄 친 부분의 쓰임이 나머지 넷과 다른 것은?

① Is it snowing heavily there?
② Are you listening to the news?
③ Ronald is going to the post office.
④ I am flying to Busan tomorrow afternoon.
⑤ The students are doing a science project now.

29 다음은 Alex와 Iris가 경험해본 것을 나타낸 표이다. 표를 보고 현재완료시제 문장을 완성하시오.

	Alex	Iris
ride a horse	O	X
visit Vietnam	O	O

> Alex has ridden a horse, but Iris
> _____. Alex
> and Iris _____.

[30-31] 다음 대화를 읽고 주어진 질문에 답하시오.

> *Don*: Have you ever had a dog?
> *Joe* : _____ But I (A) have had an iguana before.

30 위 질문에 대한 대답으로 알맞은 것은?

① No, I didn't.   ② Yes, I did.
③ No, I haven't.   ④ Yes, I haven't.
⑤ No, I don't.

31 위 대화의 밑줄 친 (A)의 용법과 같은 것은?

① Ms. Clark has lost her luggage.
② I haven't eaten anything yet.
③ My uncle has worked at the bank for twelve years.
④ The train has just arrived at the station.
⑤ Have you ever tried skydiving?

32 다음 중 어법상 바른 것은?

① I knew him since 2004.
② When have they built this castle?
③ Amy has visited her old teachers a week ago.
④ Eric has played the online game for six hours.
⑤ The children have found the treasure yesterday.

33 괄호 안의 말을 활용하여 질문에 대한 대답을 완성하시오.

A: What were your father and brother doing when you got home?

B: _____ _____ _____
_____ . (play, baduk)

[34-36] 현재완료시제를 이용하여 다음 두 문장을 한 문장으로 연결하시오.

34

Jane and Jim moved to London in 2012. They still live in London.
→ Jane and Jim _____
_____ .

35

Martin started to work at the restaurant five years ago. He still works there.
→ Martin _____
_____ .

36

Yumi went to Russia. She isn't here now.
→ Yumi _____ .

37 다음 글의 밑줄 친 ⓐ~ⓔ 중 어법상 어색한 것을 찾아 기호를 쓰고 바르게 고쳐 쓰시오.

Dr. Anderson is a scientist. He ⓐhas done medical experiments for ten years. A few years ago, he ⓑhas decided to do research on cancer cells. He ⓒspent most of his time working on it since then. He has worked hard ⓓfor many years. Finally, he ⓔis going to release a cure next week.

*cancer cell 암세포

(1) _____ → _____
(2) _____ → _____

38 다음 그림을 보고 괄호 안의 말을 활용하여 빈칸에 쓰시오.

20 years ago	Now

Mr. Smith _____ _____
_____ _____ _____
_____ . (grow, corn)

39 괄호 안의 동사를 활용하여 문장을 완성하시오.

Lucy and her friends ⓐ_____
(volunteer) at a children's center since
last September. They ⓑ_____
(bake) chocolate chip cookies for the
children last weekend. And the children
ⓒ_____(write) letters to them.
They were so moved by the letters.

40 다음 중 자연스럽지 <u>않은</u> 대화는?

① A: Where have you been?
   B: I have been in the classroom since
      8:30.
② A: Did he go for a walk last night?
   B: Yes, he did. He walked with me.
③ A: How long has Jacob been in Jeonju?
   B: He has been there for a week.
④ A: Have you ever watched any French
      movies?
   B: No, I don't. I want to see one someday.
⑤ A: What did you eat for breakfast today?
   B: I ate a bowl of chicken salad.

41 다음 중 어법상 <u>어색한</u> 것의 개수는?

ⓐ Natalie has lived in Hawaii for a long
   time.
ⓑ I have read *Little Women* two years
   ago.
ⓒ My mother lost a pair of earrings
   yesterday.
ⓓ Josh has played tennis since two
   years.
ⓔ When have you met each other last
   time?

① 1개   ② 2개   ③ 3개
④ 4개   ⑤ 5개

42 우리말과 같도록 괄호 안의 말을 활용하여 영작하
시오.

많은 학생들이 그 수수께끼를 풀지 못해왔다.
(solve, many, the riddle)

= _____

_____

43 다음 중 밑줄 친 부분이 어법상 바른 것은?

Have you ever heard of Seoullo 7017?
It is a pedestrian bridge above a road
near Seoul Station. It ①is a railroad in
the past. However, it ②will have some
safety issues in the 1990s. So, the
government ③turned it into a public
space for citizens and tourists. Now, it
④had many trees and benches. Many
visitors ⑤visited Seoullo 7017 since it
opened.

*pedestrian 보행자용의

44 다음 글의 밑줄 친 ⓐ~ⓔ 중 어법상 어색한 것을 찾아 기호를 쓰고 바르게 고쳐 쓰시오.

Emperor penguins ⓐhave live in the Antarctic for a long time. They ⓑare bigger than all the other penguins. They look like they ⓒare wearing tuxedos, so they ⓓis having a nickname. People often ⓔcall them the gentlemen of the Antarctic.

*emperor penguin 황제 펭귄

(1) _____ → _____
(2) _____ → _____

45 다음 중 밑줄 친 부분이 어법상 어색한 것을 모두 고르시오.

I ①haven't been to Australia before. But I ②am going there to meet my friend, Alice, soon. I ③met her last year when she visited my home in Canada. We ④will have a lot of fun at that time. I ⑤wanted to visit her home since then. I finally got that chance!

46 다음은 Julie의 일정표이다. 표에 나온 표현을 활용하여 대화를 완성하시오.

Julie's Schedule	
Mon	read newspaper
Tues	go to soccer practice
Wed	clean my room
Thu	go shopping
Fri	study English

Paul: What are you doing now?
Julie: I'm cleaning my room. I clean my room every Wednesday.
Paul: What about soccer practice?
Julie: I (A) _____ _____ _____ _____ yesterday.
Paul: I see. Are you busy tomorrow?
Julie: A little bit. I (B) _____ _____ _____ tomorrow.
Paul: Why don't you watch a movie with me instead?
Julie: Sure. I can go shopping another time.

CHAPTER 4
조동사

Lena keeps her promises. Lena는 그녀의 약속을 지킨다.
Lena **should** keep her promises. Lena는 그녀의 약속을 지켜야 한다.

'Lena는 그녀의 약속을 지킨다.'라는 문장에 조동사 **should** (~해야 한다)가 포함되어 'Lena는 그녀의 약속을 지켜야 한다.'라는 문장이 됐어요. 이렇게 다른 동사와 함께 쓰여 여러 가지 의미를 더하는 동사를 **조동사**라고 해요.

기출로 적중 POINT

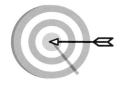

내신 100점 적중!
기출 출제율

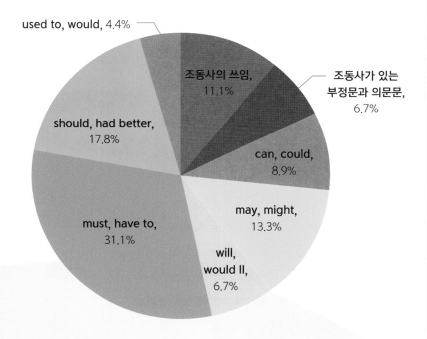

used to, would, 4.4%

조동사의 쓰임,
11.1%

조동사가 있는
부정문과 의문문,
6.7%

should, had better,
17.8%

can, could,
8.9%

must, have to,
31.1%

may, might,
13.3%

will,
would II,
6.7%

TOP 1 **must, have to (31.1%)**
조동사 must, have to의 의미와 쓰임을 묻는 문제가 자주 출제된다.

TOP 2 **should, had better (17.8%)**
조동사 should, had better의 의미와 쓰임을 묻는 문제가 자주 출제된다.

TOP 3 **may, might (13.3%)**
조동사 may, might의 의미와 쓰임을 묻는 문제가 자주 출제된다.

1. **조동사는 「조동사 + 동사원형」의 형태로 쓴다.**

   I **can play** the guitar well. 나는 기타를 잘 연주할 수 있다.
   You **must be** quiet in the museum. 너는 박물관에서 조용히 해야 한다.

2. **조동사는 주어의 인칭이나 수에 따라 형태가 변하지 않는다.**

   Jack (~~shoulds~~, **should**) **go** to the hospital. Jack은 병원에 가야 한다.

3. **조동사는 한 번에 하나만 쓴다.**

   We (~~will can~~, **will be able to**) **meet** them soon. 우리는 곧 그들을 만날 수 있을 것이다.
   Cindy (~~may must~~, **may have to**) **cancel** the reservation.
   Cindy는 그 예약을 취소해야 할지도 모른다.

연습문제 | 괄호 안에서 알맞은 것을 고르시오.

1 We should (recycle / recycled) the cans.

2 Miso's sister (mays / may) be at the playground.

3 You must (wearing / wear) your seat belt on the bus.

4 Emma (can / cans) speak four languages fluently.

5 People (will be able to / will can) travel in space someday.

6 This medicine may (make / makes) you feel sleepy.

7 Richard must (return / returned) the books to the library.

8 We (may must / may have to) wait long.

9 You should (are / be) proud of yourself.

10 Their son (wills / will) be a university student next year.

기출 적중문제

다음 중 어법상 바른 것은?

① This book will is very boring.
② Ben will can make lunch for us.
③ We should be polite to others.
④ She musts get up early tomorrow.
⑤ The team may needed more practice.

조동사가 있는 부정문과 의문문

1. 조동사가 있는 부정문: 「조동사 + not + 동사원형」

I **cannot[can't] find** my wallet. 나는 나의 지갑을 찾을 수 없다.
Jamie **may not like** spicy food. Jamie는 매운 음식을 좋아하지 않을지도 모른다.
It **will not[won't] be** sunny tomorrow. 내일은 화창하지 않을 것이다.
You **should not[shouldn't] drink** this old milk. 너는 이 오래된 우유를 마시면 안 된다.

2. 조동사가 있는 의문문: 「조동사 + 주어 + 동사원형 ~?」

Can your puppy **swim**? 너의 강아지는 수영할 수 있니?
Will Sam **join** the basketball team? Sam은 농구팀에 가입할 거니?

연습문제 다음 문장을 괄호 안의 지시대로 바꿔 쓰시오.

1 Mr. Davis can drive a truck. (부정문으로)
→ _____ a truck.

2 I should wear warmer clothes. (의문문으로)
→ _____ warmer clothes?

3 We may have time to eat snacks. (부정문으로)
→ _____ time to eat snacks.

4 Jimin can run 100 meters in 15 seconds. (의문문으로)
→ _____ 100 meters in 15 seconds?

5 She will be at home this Sunday. (부정문으로)
→ _____ at home this Sunday.

6 Gary and Mindy will get married next year. (의문문으로)
→ _____ married next year?

7 You should use a pencil on the test. (부정문으로)
→ _____ a pencil on the test.

기출 적중문제

다음 문장에서 <u>틀린</u> 부분을 바르게 고쳐 완전한 문장을 쓰시오.

This math problem may be not easy.
→ _____

기출로 적중 POINT 2 can, could

정답 p.11

can/could는 능력·가능, 허가, 요청, 추측의 의미를 나타낸다.

능력·가능 (~할 수 있다)	능력·가능을 나타내는 can의 과거형은 could이며, 이때 can/could는 be able to로 바꿔 쓸 수 있다. A camel **can** survive long without water. 낙타는 물 없이 오래 살아남을 수 있다. = A camel **is able to** survive long without water. Paul **couldn't** solve the problem. Paul은 그 문제를 해결할 수 없었다. = Paul **wasn't able to** solve the problem. **Can** Minji run faster than her sister? 민지는 그녀의 언니보다 더 빠르게 뛸 수 있니? = **Is** Minji **able to** run faster than her sister?
허가 (~해도 된다)	You **can** try on these shoes. 너는 이 신발을 신어봐도 된다. They **cannot** talk loudly here. 그들은 여기에서 큰 소리로 말하면 안 된다. **Can** I ask you something? 내가 너에게 무언가를 물어봐도 되니? **Could** I use your pen? 제가 당신의 펜을 써도 되나요? └→ 허가의 의미로 질문할 때 could를 쓰면 더 정중한 표현이 된다.
요청 (~해주겠니?)	**Can** you carry the boxes for me? 나를 위해 그 상자들을 날라주겠니? **Could** you please pass me the salt? 저에게 소금을 건네주시겠어요? └→ 요청의 의미로 질문할 때 could를 쓰면 더 정중한 표현이 된다.
추측	~일 리가 없다 The rumor **can't** be true. 그 소문은 사실일 리가 없다. ~일 수도 있다 This bag **could** be Lily's. 이 가방은 Lily의 것일 수도 있다. └→ could는 can보다 약한 추측을 나타낸다.

연습문제 A   <보기>와 같이 두 문장의 의미가 같도록 문장을 완성하시오.

> <보기>   Miranda can write her name in Korean.
>   = *Miranda is able to write*   her name in Korean.

1   Tony can bake blueberry muffins.

= _____ blueberry muffins.

2   Amy couldn't find her favorite socks.

= _____ her favorite socks.

3   Can you hear my voice?

= _____ my voice?

4 Mr. Clark can't see well without glasses.

= _____ well without glasses.

5 They couldn't sleep because of the noise.

= _____ because of the noise.

6 Can she tell us the whole story?

= _____ us the whole story?

7 My little brother can read Chinese characters.

= _____ Chinese characters.

8 We can't meet each other this weekend.

= _____ each other this weekend.

연습문제 **B** │ 밑줄 친 부분의 의미를 <보기>에서 골라 그 기호를 쓰시오.

<보기> ⓐ 능력·가능   ⓑ 허가   ⓒ 요청   ⓓ 추측

1 Monkeys <u>can</u> climb trees very well.　　　　　[　　　　　]

2 <u>Can</u> you do me a favor?　　　　　[　　　　　]

3 <u>Can</u> I sit next to you during the lecture?　　　　　[　　　　　]

4 They <u>can</u> get to the subway station on time.　　　　　[　　　　　]

5 Alex <u>can't</u> be sleepy. He slept for over ten hours.　　　　　[　　　　　]

6 <u>Could</u> you open the window?　　　　　[　　　　　]

7 You <u>can</u> keep healthy by exercising regularly.　　　　　[　　　　　]

8 <u>Could</u> I bring my dog into the store?　　　　　[　　　　　]

9 Your answer <u>could</u> be right, but I don't agree with you.　　　　　[　　　　　]

10 <u>Can</u> you wait for me for a while?　　　　　[　　　　　]

11 You <u>cannot</u> touch anything in the museum.　　　　　[　　　　　]

12 The girl in this picture <u>can't</u> be Gloria. I know her face.　　　　　[　　　　　]

기출 적중문제 ◎

다음 중 밑줄 친 <u>can</u>의 의미가 나머지 넷과 <u>다른</u> 것은?

① <u>Can</u> I please have a drink?

② <u>Can</u> I go to the toilet now?

③ <u>Can</u> I turn on the air conditioner?

④ <u>Can</u> you send me the package?

⑤ You <u>can</u> use my eraser if you don't have one.

POINT 3 may, might

정답 p.11

may/might는 약한 추측이나 허가의 의미를 나타낸다.

약한 추측 (~일지도 모른다)	The guests **may** arrive soon. 손님들이 곧 도착할지도 모른다. I **may not** get there by eight. 나는 8시까지 거기에 도착하지 않을지도 모른다. He **might** be interested in music. 그는 음악에 흥미가 있을지도 모른다. └→ might는 may보다 불확실한 추측을 나타낸다.
허가 (~해도 된다)	You **may** take a break now. 너는 지금 휴식을 취해도 된다. Visitors **may not** enter this room. 방문객들은 이 방에 들어가면 안 된다. **May** I use this printer? 내가 이 프린터를 사용해도 되니?

연습문제 밑줄 친 부분의 의미와 같은 것을 <보기>에서 골라 그 기호를 쓰시오.

<보기>   ⓐ My sister <u>may</u> be upset.   ⓑ You <u>may</u> go to your room now.

1 She <u>may</u> like Vietnamese food.   [   ]   **2** You <u>may</u> take a picture here.   [   ]

3 May I look at this album?   [   ]   **4** Luke <u>may</u> be from Canada.   [   ]

5 My brother <u>may</u> catch a cold.   [   ]   **6** This <u>may</u> be a bad idea.   [   ]

7 You <u>may</u> borrow my book.   [   ]   **8** May I see your passport?   [   ]

<보기>   ⓐ The story <u>may not</u> be true.   ⓑ You <u>may not</u> turn off the lights.

9 You <u>may not</u> open the present yet. [   ]   **10** James <u>may not</u> be busy now.   [   ]

11 We <u>may not</u> run in the hallway.   [   ]   **12** We <u>may not</u> eat food here.   [   ]

13 They <u>may not</u> believe the news.   [   ]   **14** The answer <u>may not</u> be correct.   [   ]

15 You <u>may not</u> skip a meal.   [   ]   **16** This purse <u>may not</u> be Kate's.   [   ]

기출 적중문제

다음 중 밑줄 친 may의 의미가 나머지 넷과 다른 것은?

① He <u>may</u> be allergic to peanuts.

② It <u>may</u> snow on Christmas Day.

③ You <u>may</u> leave when you finish the exam.

④ My cats <u>may</u> like these new toys.

⑤ I <u>may</u> cry at my graduation ceremony.

will, would I

will/would는 미래, 의지, 요청의 의미를 나타낸다.

미래 (~할 것이다)	미래를 나타내는 will은 be going to로 바꿔 쓸 수 있다. It **will** rain tomorrow morning. 내일 아침에 비가 올 것이다. = It **is going to** rain tomorrow morning. We **won't** be here two months later. 우리는 두 달 뒤에 여기에 있지 않을 것이다. = We **aren't going to** be here two months later.
의지 (~하겠다)	I **will** buy these earrings. 나는 이 귀걸이를 사겠다. We**'ll pass** the exam. 우리는 그 시험을 통과하겠다.
요청 (~해주겠니?)	**Will** you close the door? 문을 닫아주겠니? **Would** you speak more slowly? 더 천천히 말씀해주시겠어요? ↳ 요청의 의미로 질문할 때 would를 쓰면 더 정중한 표현이 된다.

연습문제 A 다음 두 문장의 의미가 같도록 be going to를 활용하여 문장을 완성하시오.

1 They will travel to France. = _____ to France.

2 My father won't buy a new car. = _____ a new car.

3 Will Kevin visit your house soon? = _____ your house soon?

4 The survey will take about five minutes. = _____ about five minutes.

5 Will your brothers wash the dishes? = _____ the dishes?

연습문제 B 우리말과 같도록 괄호 안의 동사를 활용하여 빈칸에 쓰시오.

1 우리는 이번 주말에 토마토를 심을 것이다. (plant)

= _____ _____ _____ tomatoes this weekend.

2 그들은 내가 그 영화를 보는 것을 허락하지 않을 것이다. (allow)

= _____ _____ _____ me to see the movie.

3 이 열쇠를 나의 책상 위에 놓아주겠니? (put)

= _____ _____ _____ this key on my desk?

4 나는 올해 10권 이상의 책을 읽겠다. (read)

= _____ _____ _____ more than ten books this year.

5 한 시간 후에 저에게 전화해주시겠어요? (call)

= _____ _____ _____ me in an hour?

will, would Ⅱ

정답 p.11

1. 「would like + 명사」는 '~을 원하다'라는 의미이며, 「want + 명사」로 바꿔 쓸 수 있다.

   I **would like** a cup of **green tea**. 나는 녹차 한 잔을 원한다.
   = I **want** a cup of **green tea**.

   Would you **like** some more **rice**? 너는 약간의 밥을 더 원하니?
   = Do you **want** some more **rice**?

2. 「would like to + 동사원형」은 '~하기를 원하다'라는 의미이며, 「want to + 동사원형」으로 바꿔 쓸 수 있다.

   I'd like to move to New York. 나는 뉴욕으로 이사하기를 원한다.
   = I **want to move** to New York.

   Would you **like to listen** to the song again? 너는 그 노래를 다시 듣기를 원하니?
   = Do you **want to listen** to the song again?

연습문제 | 괄호 안의 주어와 would like (to)를 활용하여 문장을 완성하시오.

1 _____ some advice? (you)

2 _____ buy a ticket to Busan. (I)

3 _____ watch the action movie? (you)

4 _____ a piece of cake? (you)

5 _____ come with us? (you)

6 _____ more information? (you)

7 _____ reserve a room. (I)

8 _____ some coffee, please. (I)

9 _____ help other people. (I)

기출 적중문제 ◎

다음 문장에서 <u>틀린</u> 부분을 바르게 고쳐 완전한 문장을 쓰시오.

> Would you like go to the concert together?
> → _____

must, have to

1. must는 의무나 강한 추측의 의미를 나타낸다.

의무 (~해야 한다)	의무를 나타내는 must는 have/has to로 바꿔 쓸 수 있다. You **must** finish your homework by 5 P.M. 너는 오후 5시까지 너의 숙제를 끝내야 한다. = You **have to** finish your homework by 5 P.M. Everyone **must** wear a seat belt. 모든 사람은 안전벨트를 매야 한다. = Everyone **has to** wear a seat belt. (Tip) 의무를 나타내는 must의 과거형은 had to를 쓰고, 미래형은 will have to를 쓴다. I **had to** clean the classroom after school. 나는 방과 후에 교실을 청소해야 했다. I **will have to** clean the classroom after school. 나는 방과 후에 교실을 청소해야 할 것이다.
강한 추측 (~임에 틀림없다)	Sumin didn't come to school today. She **must** be ill. 수민이는 오늘 학교에 오지 않았다. 그녀는 아픈 것임에 틀림없다. (Tip) 강한 추측을 나타내는 must의 부정은 can't(~일 리가 없다)를 쓴다. Our dog **can't** be hungry now. 우리의 개는 지금 배고플 리가 없다.

2. must not은 '~하면 안 된다(강한 금지)'라는 의미이며, don't have to는 '~할 필요가 없다(불필요)'라는 의미이다.

You **must not** lie to your parents. 너는 너의 부모님께 거짓말하면 안 된다.
Eric **doesn't have to** hurry. Eric은 서두를 필요가 없다.

(Tip) don't have to는 don't need to나 need not으로 바꿔 쓸 수 있다.
We **don't have to** wear suits. 우리는 정장을 입을 필요가 없다.
= We **don't need to** wear suits.
= We **need not** wear suits.

연습문제 A | 다음 빈칸에 must, can't, must not 중 알맞은 것을 쓰시오.

1 We're talking too loudly. We _____ be quiet here.

2 Sally didn't sleep at all yesterday. She _____ be very tired now.

3 You _____ water the cactuses too often. Cactus doesn't need much water.

4 That girl _____ be Linda. She left for the U.S. last week.

5 We _____ avoid using plastics. They're not good for the environment.

6 Students _____ smoke. Smoking is harmful.

7 Your cat looks so hungry. You _____ feed him now.

8 Jonathan _____ be very happy. He can finally spend time with his family.

연습문제 B 우리말과 같도록 must 또는 have to와 괄호 안의 동사를 활용하여 문장을 완성하시오.

1 우리는 다른 문화를 존중해야 한다. (respect)

= We _____ other cultures.

2 너희들은 산에 너희들의 쓰레기를 두고 가면 안 된다. (leave)

= You _____ your trash on the mountain.

3 Max는 지난주에 그의 개를 수의사에게 데리고 가야 했다. (take)

= Max _____ his dog to the vet last week.

4 너는 나가기 전에 너의 옷을 갈아입어야 할 것이다. (change)

= You _____ your clothes before you go out.

5 그들은 그녀에 대해 걱정할 필요가 없다. (worry)

= They _____ about her.

6 Mina는 그녀의 행동을 책임져야 한다. (take)

= Mina _____ responsibility for her actions.

7 나는 어제 나의 할머니가 저녁 식사를 준비하시는 것을 도와야 했다. (help)

= I _____ my grandmother make dinner yesterday.

8 Bell씨는 주차 요금을 낼 필요가 없다. (pay)

= Mr. Bell _____ a parking fee.

9 너는 내일 적극적으로 토론에 참여해야 할 것이다. (participate)

= You _____ in the discussion actively tomorrow.

기출 적중문제

다음 대화의 빈칸에 들어갈 알맞은 것을 <u>모두</u> 고르시오.

> *A*: Oh, no! It's raining outside. We may have to cancel tomorrow's picnic.
> *B*: The news says that the rain will stop tonight. We _____ cancel it.

① must   ② will   ③ don't have to
④ need not   ⑤ have to

기출로적중 POINT 6 should, had better

정답 p.12

---

1. should는 '~해야 한다(충고·의무)'라는 의미이다.

We **should** eat healthy food. 우리는 건강에 좋은 음식을 먹어야 한다.

You **shouldn't** play the piano at night. 너는 밤에 피아노를 치면 안 된다.

Should I wear a helmet when I ride a bike? 나는 자전거를 탈 때 헬멧을 써야 하니?

2. had better는 '~하는 것이 낫다(강한 충고)'라는 의미이며, 주로 축약형인 'd better의 형태로 쓰인다. 부정형은 had better not이다.

We**'d better** call him. 우리는 그에게 전화하는 것이 낫겠다.

You**'d better not** be rude to your parents. 너는 너의 부모님에게 무례하게 대하지 않는 것이 낫다.

연습문제 우리말과 같도록 should 또는 had better와 괄호 안의 동사를 활용하여 빈칸에 쓰시오.

1 우리는 물을 절약해야 한다. (save)

= _____ _____ _____ water.

2 너는 수업 중에 잠들면 안 된다. (fall)

= _____ _____ _____ asleep during class.

3 그는 우산을 가지고 가는 것이 낫겠다. (take)

= _____ _____ _____ an umbrella.

4 나는 Brenda를 나의 생일 파티에 초대해야 하니? (invite)

= _____ _____ _____ Brenda to my birthday party?

5 우리는 누군가에게 길을 묻는 것이 낫겠다. (ask)

= _____ _____ _____ someone for directions.

6 너는 그의 이야기를 믿지 않는 것이 낫다. (believe)

= _____ _____ _____ _____ his story.

기출 적중문제

우리말과 같도록 괄호 안의 말을 알맞게 배열하시오.

너는 여기에 너의 가방을 두지 않는 것이 낫다. (put, you, better, had, your bag, here, not)

= _____

had better의 부정형은 had better not이에요.

1. **used to는 과거의 반복적인 습관(~하곤 했다)이나 과거의 상태(전에는 ~이었다)를 나타낸다.**

   Yura **used to** get up early on weekdays. 유라는 평일에 일찍 일어나곤 했다.

   My dog **used to** be very small. 나의 개는 전에는 매우 작았다.

   There **used to** be a pharmacy in this building. 전에는 이 건물 안에 약국이 있었다.

   (Tip) 「be used to + V-ing」는 '~하는 데 익숙하다'라는 의미이다.
   I **am used to speaking** in English. 나는 영어로 말하는 데 익숙하다.

2. **would는 과거의 반복적인 습관(~하곤 했다)을 나타낸다.**

   I **would** go to the movies every month. 나는 매달 영화를 보러 가곤 했다.

   They **would** have lunch together on Fridays. 그들은 금요일마다 함께 점심을 먹곤 했다.

   (Tip) would는 과거의 상태를 나타낼 수 없다.
   He (~~would~~, **used to**) be a famous model. 그는 전에는 유명한 모델이었다.

연습문제 | 우리말과 같도록 used to 또는 would와 괄호 안의 동사를 활용하여 빈칸에 쓰시오.

1 그녀는 전에는 짧은 머리를 가지고 있었다. (have)

= She _____ _____ _____ short hair.

2 Thomas는 주말마다 배드민턴을 치곤 했다. (play)

= Thomas _____ _____ badminton on weekends.

3 전에는 나의 집 옆에 빵집이 있었다. (be)

= There _____ _____ _____ a bakery next to my house.

4 나는 사람들이 붐비는 도시에서 사는 데 익숙하다. (live)

= I _____ _____ _____ _____ in a crowded city.

5 나의 아빠는 출장에서 돌아오실 때 선물을 가지고 오시곤 했다. (bring)

= My dad _____ _____ a present when he came back from a business trip.

기출 적중문제 🎯

우리말과 같도록 괄호 안의 말을 활용하여 문장을 완성하시오.

> Becky는 매일 요가를 하곤 했다. (do yoga)

= _____ every day.

기출로적중 POINT 8 do

정답 p.12

1. do는 일반동사의 부정문과 의문문에 쓴다.

Jay **does** not give up easily. Jay는 쉽게 포기하지 않는다.
Do you know his phone number? 너는 그의 전화번호를 아니?

2. do는 동사 앞에서 동사를 강조할 때 쓴다.

This dress **looks** beautiful. 이 드레스는 아름답게 보인다.
→ This dress **does** **look** beautiful. 이 드레스는 정말 아름답게 보인다.

I **saw** my favorite singer yesterday. 나는 어제 내가 가장 좋아하는 가수를 봤다.
→ I **did** **see** my favorite singer yesterday. 나는 어제 내가 가장 좋아하는 가수를 정말 봤다.

3. do는 대동사로서 동사(구)의 반복을 피할 때 쓴다.

I **run** faster than my sister **does**(= **runs**). 나는 나의 언니가 달리는 것보다 더 빠르게 달린다.
Did you **sleep well**? – Yes, I **did**(= **slept well**). 너는 잘 잤니? – 응. 나는 잘 잤어.

연습문제 밑줄 친 부분의 쓰임과 같은 것을 <보기>에서 골라 그 기호를 쓰시오.

<보기> ⓐ Don't you know how to swim?
　　　　ⓑ These grapes do taste good.
　　　　ⓒ I know him better than you do.

1　I do like cycling along the river.　　　　　　[　　　]
2　Did you do the laundry last night?　　　　　[　　　]
3　Do you write in your diary every day? – Yes, I do.　[　　　]
4　Elizabeth loves bulgogi more than I do.　　　[　　　]
5　I did win the lottery a month ago.　　　　　[　　　]
6　The café doesn't open on Mondays.　　　　[　　　]

기출 적중문제 ◎

우리말과 같도록 괄호 안의 말을 배열할 때 세 번째에 오는 것을 쓰시오.

Jessica는 노래를 매우 잘한다. (very, sing, Jessica, well, does)

→ _____

do가 동사를 강조할 때 쓰이면 동사 앞에 와요.

서술형 대비 문제

A 밑줄 친 부분이 어법상 맞으면 O를 쓰고, 틀리면 바르게 고쳐 쓰시오.

1 My belief could <u>is</u> wrong. → _____

2 <u>Can peel you</u> the potatoes? → _____

3 You <u>must not take</u> the medicine before bedtime. → _____

4 Jenny can <u>hold</u> her breath for a minute. → _____

5 A new Italian restaurant <u>mights</u> open in my town. → _____

6 My parents <u>will be not</u> at home tomorrow. → _____

7 We may <u>must</u> change our plans because of the snow. → _____

8 John <u>would like travel</u> to Greece someday. → _____

9 Visitors <u>had better not</u> touch animals at the zoo. → _____

10 I used to <u>eating</u> meat before, but I'm a vegetarian now. → _____

B 우리말과 같도록 <보기>의 조동사와 괄호 안의 동사를 활용하여 문장을 완성하시오.

> <보기> can   will   should   used to

1 우리는 우리의 호텔에서 바다를 볼 수 있다. (see)
= _____ the sea from our hotel.

2 나의 삼촌은 전에는 변호사셨다. (be)
= _____ a lawyer.

3 나는 이번 여름까지 살을 빼겠다. (lose)
= _____ weight until this summer.

4 내가 피자 한 조각을 먹어도 되니? (have)
= _____ a slice of pizza?

5 Mia는 그녀의 방을 일주일에 두 번 청소해야 한다. (clean)
= _____ her room twice a week.

6 그 학생들은 학예회에서 공연할 것이다. (perform)
= _____ at the school arts festival.

7 너는 너의 친구들에게 부드럽게 말해야 한다. (speak)
= _____ gently to your friends.

C <보기>의 말과 괄호 안의 동사를 활용하여 문장을 완성하시오.

> <보기>   could   would like to   had better

1 The sky is getting cloudy. It _____ soon. (rain)

2 You _____ a warm coat. It's very cold outside. (wear)

3 I saw a picture of a beautiful temple in Korea. I _____ it. (visit)

> <보기>   may not   must   used to

4 Luna studied all day for the exam. She _____ exhausted now. (be)

5 I _____ Jeff every day. But I haven't seen him for a month. (meet)

6 You _____ five books. Students can borrow only two books at a time. (borrow)

D 우리말과 같도록 괄호 안의 말을 알맞게 배열하시오.

1 너는 노크할 필요가 없다. (you, have, knock, to, don't)

= _____

2 저 차는 비싼 것임에 틀림없다. (be, car, expensive, that, must)

= _____

3 너는 나의 도움을 원하니? (help, you, like, my, would)

= _____

4 이 레모네이드는 정말 신맛이 난다. (taste, lemonade, does, sour, this)

= _____

5 그들은 그들의 기차를 놓칠지도 모른다. (their, they, miss, train, may)

= _____

6 그 영화는 실화일 리가 없다. (be, story, can't, a, the, movie, true)

= _____

7 우리의 도시는 그 행사를 가을에 개최할 것이다. (is, hold, to, the, event, our, city, the, fall, going, in)

= _____

8 Noah는 어제 학교에 갈 수 없었다. (not, to, go, able, school, was, to, yesterday, Noah)

= _____

1 다음 빈칸에 들어갈 알맞은 것은?

> Headaches may _____ a sign of stress.

① is   ② was   ③ are
④ been   ⑤ be

2 다음 중 어법상 <u>어색한</u> 것은?

① Can we talk privately?
② We had better call the police.
③ You should be careful with that knife.
④ I may have to leave soon.
⑤ This song wills make you feel calm.

3 다음 문장에서 <u>틀린</u> 부분을 바르게 고쳐 완전한 문장을 쓰시오.

> The plane will takes off in a minute.
> → _____

4 다음 중 not이 들어갈 위치는?

> You ① had ② better ③ go ④ outside ⑤ because of the yellow dust.

5 다음 빈칸에 들어갈 가장 알맞은 것은?

> I'm not sure where she is from, but she _____ be from Finland.

① must   ② has to   ③ would
④ might   ⑤ should

6 다음 대화의 밑줄 친 부분과 의미가 같은 것은?

> A: <u>Can</u> I see your ID, please?
> B: Sure. Here it is.

① May   ② Will   ③ Do
④ Must   ⑤ Should

[7-8] 다음 글의 빈칸에 들어갈 알맞은 것을 고르시오.

7

> You _____ jump on the floor at night. Your downstairs neighbors will get angry.

① must   ② should
③ might   ④ should not
⑤ don't have to

8

> I _____ play baduk well when I was young. However, I can't remember how to play baduk now.

① can   ② can't
③ am able to   ④ could
⑤ couldn't

[9-10] 다음 우리말을 영작할 때 빈칸에 들어갈 알맞은 것을 고르시오.

9

> 우리를 위해 노래를 불러주겠니?
> = _____ you sing a song for us?

① Should   ② Will   ③ May
④ Must   ⑤ Do

10

> 장시간 동안 TV를 보는 것은 좋지 않은 시력을 초래할지도 모른다.
> = Watching TV for many hours _____ cause poor eyesight.

① may   ② would   ③ must
④ has to   ⑤ had better

11 다음 중 어법상 바른 것은?

① Claire used to biting her nails.
② You don't may stay at the gym after 10 P.M.
③ Will you take me to the hospital?
④ You won't must stand in line to buy the ticket.
⑤ I have to go to the grocery store yesterday.

12 다음 밑줄 친 부분과 바꿔 쓸 수 있는 것은?

> You <u>don't have to</u> make a decision right now.

① should not   ② must not
③ will not   ④ need not
⑤ cannot

13 다음 글의 빈칸에 들어갈 가장 알맞은 것은?

> This place _____ be an empty field ten years ago. However, there are many buildings here now.

① had to   ② should   ③ used to
④ will   ⑤ had better

14 우리말과 같도록 괄호 안의 말을 활용하여 빈칸에 쓰시오.

> James는 안경을 써야 한다. (wear)

= James _____ _____ _____ glasses.

15 다음 대화의 빈칸에 들어갈 가장 알맞은 것은?

> A: Can you lend me your math textbook for my next class?
> B: Yes, I can. But you _____ give it back to me right after your class. I also have math class today.

① can   ② may   ③ will
④ must   ⑤ would

16 주어진 문장의 밑줄 친 부분과 쓰임이 같은 것은?

My brother and I <u>do</u> like the movie series, *Harry Potter*.

① <u>Do</u> you want me to help you?
② Water <u>doesn't</u> mix with oil.
③ I will <u>do</u> some exercise tonight.
④ Jane studies harder than I <u>do</u>.
⑤ You <u>did</u> look gorgeous yesterday.

17 우리말과 같도록 괄호 안의 말을 활용하여 영작하시오.

이 나무는 오래된 것임에 틀림없다. (be, old)

= _____

18 다음 대화의 빈칸에 들어갈 알맞은 것은?

A: I'm sorry, but _____ your beverage into the shop.
B: OK. Then, I'll just drink it all now.

① you should bring
② you can bring
③ you won't bring
④ you can't bring
⑤ you don't have to bring

19 다음 빈칸에 들어갈 말이 순서대로 짝지어진 것은?

· I _____ introduce Marcus to you.
· You _____ talk on the phone during the movie.

① would like – should
② would like – should not
③ would like to – should
④ would like to – should not
⑤ would like to – need not

20 주어진 문장과 의미가 같은 것은?

My dad was a baseball player, but he is a coach now.

① My dad can't be a baseball player.
② My dad must be a baseball player.
③ My dad used to be a baseball player.
④ My dad was able to be a baseball player.
⑤ My dad may be a baseball player.

21 다음 두 문장의 의미가 같도록 빈칸에 알맞은 말을 쓰시오.

Send me an e-mail if you want more information.
= Send me an e-mail if you _____ _____ more information.

22 다음 밑줄 친 부분과 바꿔 쓸 수 있는 것은?

> I couldn't finish reading the book
> because I didn't have much time last
> week.

① am not able to ② wasn't able to
③ may not ④ shouldn't
⑤ didn't have to

23 다음 대화의 밑줄 친 우리말과 같도록 괄호 안의 말을 활용하여 영작하시오.

> A: I feel so cold. What should I do?
> B: 너는 뜨거운 차를 마시는 것이 낫겠다. (drink, hot tea)

= _____

24 다음 중 밑줄 친 may의 의미가 나머지 넷과 다른 것은?

① May I change the television channel?
② You may ride the bus for free.
③ May I drink this juice on the table?
④ She may want to get some sleep.
⑤ You may play a computer game after you wash the dishes.

25 다음 빈칸에 공통으로 들어갈 알맞은 것은?

> · Passengers _____ fasten their seat belt right now.
> · Ava didn't talk to me all day, so she _____ be angry at me.

① used to ② would ③ might
④ has to ⑤ must

26 다음 대화의 빈칸에 들어갈 말로 어색한 것은?

> A: Excuse me, sir. You _____ take this elevator.
> B: Why?
> A: It is only for doctors and nurses at this hospital. The elevators for patients and visitors are over there.
> B: All right. I see.

① cannot ② must not
③ should not ④ don't have to
⑤ may not

27 다음 중 밑줄 친 부분의 의미가 나머지 넷과 다른 것은?

① She used to ride a bike on weekends.
② Jeremy used to walk to school.
③ Most Koreans are used to recycling.
④ My family used to eat out every Saturday night.
⑤ He used to play tennis with his friend.

28 우리말과 같도록 괄호 안의 말을 알맞게 배열하시오.

> 그 아기가 잠이 들어서, 우리는 시끄럽게 하지 않는 것이 낫겠다. (had, noisy, be, not, we, better)

= The baby is asleep, so _____

_____.

29 다음은 Hailey와 Luke가 해야 하는 것을 나타낸 표이다. 표를 바르게 설명한 것은?

Hailey	Luke
· water the plants · wash the clothes · throw out the garbage	· clean the bathroom · walk the dog · make dinner

① Hailey must walk the dog.
② Luke must not clean the bathroom.
③ Luke doesn't have to wash the clothes.
④ Hailey and Luke have to make dinner.
⑤ Hailey doesn't need to throw out the garbage.

30 주어진 문장의 밑줄 친 must와 의미가 다른 것은?

> I must go home by 9 o'clock.

① You must take this medicine twice a day.
② We must do our best for the test.
③ She must keep the money safe.
④ Tom must be tired after his long trip.
⑤ You must write your name on this paper.

31 다음 대화의 밑줄 친 부분과 의미가 같은 것은?

> A: Olivia is the most popular girl in our class.
> B: Right. She is very funny and kind.
> A: I agree. Don't you think that she has a beautiful smile?
> B: Yes, she does.

① is very funny
② is kind
③ has a beautiful smile
④ isn't very funny
⑤ doesn't have a beautiful smile

32 다음 (A)~(C)에 들어갈 말이 바르게 짝지어진 것은?

> When you first see koalas, you ___(A)___ think they are the cutest animals in the world. However, you ___(B)___ be careful when you meet them in the wild. They have sharp teeth and claws, so you ___(C)___ touch them.

	(A)	(B)	(C)
①	might	have to	don't have to
②	should	have to	must not
③	may	could	don't have to
④	should	could	don't need to
⑤	may	have to	must not

33 다음 표지판을 보고 괄호 안의 말을 활용하여 문장을 완성하시오.

You _____ in the museum. (must, take a picture)

34 다음 문장을 부정문으로 바꿔 쓰시오.

There must be a problem with my phone.

→ _____

_____

35 우리말과 같도록 괄호 안의 말을 활용하여 빈칸에 쓰시오.

나의 여동생은 매일 저녁 플루트를 연주하곤 했다. (play the flute)

= My sister _____ _____

_____ _____ every evening.

36 다음은 시우와 지안이가 초등학생 때 할 수 있었던 것과 할 수 없었던 것을 나타낸 표이다. 표를 보고 빈칸에 알맞은 말을 쓰시오.

	Siwoo	Jian
ride a bike	O	X
speak Chinese	X	X

When Siwoo was an elementary school student, she _____ _____

_____ ride a bike. Siwoo and Jian

_____ _____

_____ speak Chinese at that time.

37 다음 대화의 밑줄 친 우리말과 같도록 대화에 나온 표현을 활용하여 영작하시오.

 I'm too nervous. I do want to win the first prize in the singing contest.

Don't worry. 너는 그 노래 자랑 대회에서 1등 상을 탈 수 있을 거야. You've practiced a lot.

= _____

_____

CHAPTER 5
수동태

Sumi **opened** the door. 수미는 그 문을 열었다.
The door **was opened** by Sumi. 그 문은 수미에 의해 열렸다.

'수미는 그 문을 열었다.'라는 문장에서 주어인 수미가 문을 여는 행위를 하고 있는데, 이렇게 주어가 행위의 주체가 되는 것을 **능동태**라고 해요. 반면에 '그 문은 수미에 의해 열렸다.'라는 문장에서는 그 문이 주어가 되어 수미에 의해 열리는 행위를 당하고 있어요. 이렇게 주어가 행위의 대상이 되는 것을 **수동태**라고 해요.

기출로 적중 POINT

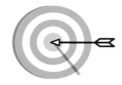

내신 100점 적중!
기출 출제율

5형식 문장의 수동태, 3.7%

수동태 관용 표현, 2.4%

4형식 문장의 수동태, 1.2%

조동사가 있는 수동태, 2.4%

수동태의 부정문과
의문문, 4.9%

수동태의 시제,
8.5%

수동태 문장 만드는 법,
76.8%

TOP 1 **수동태 문장 만드는 법 (76.8%)**
수동태의 쓰임과 수동태 문장을 만드는 방법을 묻는 문제가 자주 출제된다.

TOP 2 **수동태의 시제 (8.5%)**
다양한 시제에 따른 수동태의 형태를 묻는 문제가 자주 출제된다.

TOP 3 **수동태의 부정문과 의문문 (4.9%)**
수동태의 부정문과 의문문의 형태를 묻는 문제가 자주 출제된다.

수동태 문장 만드는 법

능동태 문장을 수동태로 만드는 법은 다음과 같다.

능동태   ③ ② ①
She uses them.   그녀는 그것들을 사용한다.

수동태   They are used by her.   그것들은 그녀에 의해 사용된다.

① 능동태 문장의 목적어를 주격으로 바꿔 수동태 문장의 주어로 쓴다.
② 능동태 문장의 동사를 「be동사 + p.p.(과거분사)」의 형태로 바꾼다. 이때 be동사는 수동태 문장의 주어의 인칭과 수에 일치시키고, 능동태 문장의 시제를 그대로 쓴다.
③ 능동태 문장의 주어를 「by + 목적격」의 형태로 바꾼다.

The farmer **sells** organic vegetables.   그 농부는 유기농 채소들을 판매한다.
→ Organic vegetables **are sold** by the farmer.   유기농 채소들은 그 농부에 의해 판매된다.

My uncle **repaired** the bicycle.   나의 삼촌은 그 자전거를 수리했다.
→ The bicycle **was repaired** by my uncle.   그 자전거는 나의 삼촌에 의해 수리되었다.

(Tip) 행위자가 일반인이거나 중요하지 않을 때는 「by + 목적격」을 생략할 수 있다.
The music festival **is held** every year (by them).   그 음악 축제는 (그들에 의해) 매년 개최된다.
The vase **was broken** (by someone).   그 꽃병은 (누군가에 의해) 깨졌다.

(Tip) 목적어를 가지지 않는 동사는 수동태로 쓸 수 없다.
The pizza **smells** good. (O)   그 피자는 좋은 냄새가 난다.
→ The pizza **is smelled** good. (X)

연습문제 A   괄호 안에서 알맞은 것을 고르시오.

1 Spanish is (speak / spoken) in Mexico.

2 This picture was (took / taken) by Sophie.

3 We (cleaned / were cleaned) the classroom.

4 *Sunflowers* was (drawing / drawn) by Vincent Van Gogh.

5 Pop-up books (love / are loved) by children.

6 Minsu was (raising / raised) by his grandparents.

7 I (returned / was returned) the library book on time.

8 North America was (discovering / discovered) by Columbus.

9 Carrots and cabbages (eat / are eaten) by rabbits.

10 That chef's steak (tastes / is tasted) wonderful.

연습문제 B 괄호 안의 동사를 알맞은 형태로 바꿔 빈칸에 쓰시오. (단, 현재형으로 쓰시오.)

1 The wooden toys _____ _____ by Mr. Tucker. (make)

2 This song _____ _____ by a popular K-pop singer. (sing)

3 You _____ _____ to my birthday party. (invite)

4 Some sentences _____ _____ on the board. (write)

5 Most coffee beans _____ _____ in Brazil. (grow)

6 The street market _____ _____ by tourists. (visit)

7 These carpets _____ _____ in India. (produce)

8 These magazines _____ _____ by lots of teenagers. (read)

9 Many movies _____ _____ at the theater. (show)

10 The newspaper _____ _____ every morning. (deliver)

연습문제 C 다음 능동태 문장을 수동태로 바꿔 쓰시오.

1 Junho moved the sofa.

→ _____

2 Gina wrote a beautiful poem.

→ _____

3 Albus collects old coins.

→ _____

4 Ms. Miller baked some apple pies.

→ _____

5 Many kinds of sea animals eat shrimps.

→ _____

6 My mother wore a wedding dress.

→ _____

기출 적중문제

다음 문장에서 어법상 <u>어색한</u> 부분을 찾아 쓰고 바르게 고쳐 쓰시오.

> The film saw by many people around the world last year.

_____ → _____

> 수동태 문장의 동사는
> 「be동사 + p.p.(과거분사)」의
> 형태예요.

기출로적중 POINT 2 수동태의 시제

정답 p.14

수동태의 시제는 be동사로 나타내며, 능동태의 시제를 그대로 쓴다.

현재시제	「am/is/are + p.p.」	Kids **visit** this website. 아이들은 이 웹사이트를 방문한다. → This website **is visited** by kids. 이 웹사이트는 아이들에 의해 방문된다.
과거시제	「was/were + p.p.」	Thomas Edison **invented** the light bulb. 토마스 에디슨은 전구를 발명했다. → The light bulb **was invented** by Thomas Edison. 전구는 토마스 에디슨에 의해 발명되었다.
미래시제	「will be + p.p.」	He **will explain** the reason. 그가 그 이유를 설명할 것이다. → The reason **will be explained** by him. 그 이유는 그에 의해 설명될 것이다.
현재완료시제	「have/has been + p.p.」	A thief **has stolen** my wallet. 도둑이 나의 지갑을 훔쳤다. → My wallet **has been stolen** by a thief. 나의 지갑은 도둑에 의해 훔쳐졌다.

연습문제 A 다음 능동태 문장은 수동태로, 수동태 문장은 능동태로 바꿔 쓰시오.

1 Students pick the class president.
→ _____ by students.

2 The watch was lost by Howard.
→ _____ .

3 My family will plant some trees.
→ _____ by my family.

4 This essay was written by my friend.
→ _____ .

5 The history museum will be visited by Maria.
→ _____ .

6 We recycle plastic bottles on Fridays.
→ _____ on Fridays by us.

7 My father has prepared a delicious meal.

→ _____ by my father.

8 King Sejong is respected by many Koreans.

→ _____ .

9 Jacob will paint the fence.

→ _____ by Jacob.

10 Amy put the plates on the table.

→ _____ on the table by Amy.

11 They have built the house for three years.

→ _____ for three years by them.

12 The chair has been broken by Cindy and her brothers.

→ _____ .

연습문제 B 괄호 안의 동사를 알맞은 형태로 바꿔 문장을 완성하시오.

1 His right leg _____ last week. (break)

2 A brand new laptop _____ next month. (release)

3 The science experiment _____ tomorrow. (finish)

4 The pasta _____ an hour ago by Tony. (cook)

5 Cars _____ since 1885. (make)

6 The room _____ yesterday by Joey. (decorate)

기출 적중문제

다음 중 문장의 태를 바르게 바꾼 것은?

① The toast was burned by her.

→ She burns the toast.

② The workers have fixed the elevator.

→ The elevator has been fix by the workers.

③ Steve will buy some pears today.

→ Some pears will be bought today by Steve.

④ The guitar is practiced every day by Lucy.

→ Lucy practiced the guitar every day.

⑤ The team will finish the work.

→ The work will be finishing by the team.

수동태의 부정문과 의문문

정답 p.14

1. **수동태의 부정문: 「be동사 + not + p.p.」**

   I **didn't write** this letter. 나는 이 편지를 쓰지 않았다.

   → This letter **wasn't written** by me. 이 편지는 나에 의해 쓰이지 않았다.

2. **수동태의 의문문: 「(의문사 +) be동사 + 주어 + p.p. ~?」**

   Do you **clean** the floor regularly? 너는 정기적으로 바닥을 청소하니?

   → **Is** the floor **cleaned** regularly? 바닥은 정기적으로 청소되니?

   Where did they **build** the library? 그들은 어디에 그 도서관을 지었니?

   → **Where was** the library **built**? 그 도서관은 어디에 지어졌니?

   (Tip) 능동태 문장의 주어가 의문사 who인 경우 수동태의 의문문: 「By whom + be동사 + 주어 + p.p. ~?」
   Who drew this painting? 누가 이 그림을 그렸니?
   → **By whom was** this painting **drawn**? 이 그림은 누구에 의해 그려졌니?

연습문제 다음 능동태 문장을 수동태로 바꿀 때 빈칸에 알맞은 말을 쓰시오.

1 The snake didn't bite my dog.
   → My dog _____ _____ by the snake.

2 Does Kevin understand the questions?
   → _____ the questions _____ by Kevin?

3 Emily doesn't read fantasy novels.
   → Fantasy novels _____ _____ by Emily.

4 How did you make this bracelet?
   → _____ _____ this bracelet _____?

5 Who invented the telephone?
   → _____ _____ _____ the telephone _____?

기출 적중문제

다음 문장을 수동태로 바꿔 쓰시오.

> Did Noah lock the door?
> → _____ by Noah?

POINT 4 조동사가 있는 수동태

정답 p.14

조동사가 있는 수동태: 「조동사 + be + p.p.」

Sam **can speak** French. Sam은 프랑스어를 말할 수 있다.

→ French **can be spoken** by Sam. 프랑스어는 Sam에 의해 말해질 수 있다.

People **must not touch** the sculpture. 사람들은 그 조각상에 손대면 안 된다.

→ The sculpture **must not be touched**. 그 조각상은 손대지면 안 된다.

Should we **recycle** these cans? 우리는 이 깡통들을 재활용해야 하니?

→ **Should** these cans **be recycled**? 이 깡통들은 재활용되어야 하니?

연습문제 우리말과 같도록 괄호 안의 말을 활용하여 빈칸에 쓰시오.

1 그 병은 쉽게 열릴 수 있다. (can, open)

= The bottle _____ _____ _____ easily.

2 그 소포는 다음 주에 보내져도 된다. (may, send)

= The package _____ _____ _____ next week.

3 여분의 종이는 이 상자에 넣어져야 한다. (should, put)

= Extra paper _____ _____ _____ in this box.

4 그 자동차는 곧 고쳐지지 않을 것이다. (will, fix)

= The car _____ _____ _____ _____ soon.

5 바나나는 냉장고에 보관되어야 하니? (should, keep)

= _____ bananas _____ _____ in the refrigerator?

6 미래는 예측될 수 있니? (can, predict)

= _____ the future _____ _____ ?

7 야생에 있는 동물들은 사냥되면 안 된다. (must, hunt)

= The animals in the wild _____ _____ _____ .

기출 적중문제

우리말과 같도록 괄호 안의 말을 알맞게 배열하시오.

> 그 스웨터는 차가운 물에 세탁되어야 한다. (must, washed, the sweater, be)

= _____ in cold water.

기출로적중 POINT 5 · 4형식 문장의 수동태

1. 4형식 문장은 목적어가 두 개이므로 각 목적어를 주어로 하는 두 개의 수동태 문장을 만들 수 있다. 이때 직접 목적어가 주어인 수동태 문장은 간접 목적어 앞에 to/for/of 중 하나를 쓴다.

Dan **gave** <u>Brandon</u> <u>a nice gift</u>. Dan은 Brandon에게 좋은 선물을 줬다.
　　　　　　간접 목적어　　직접 목적어

간접 목적어가 주어 → **Brandon was given** a nice gift by Dan.
　　　　　　　　　　Brandon은 Dan에 의해 좋은 선물을 받았다.

직접 목적어가 주어 → **A nice gift was given to Brandon** by Dan.
　　　　　　　　　　좋은 선물이 Dan에 의해 Brandon에게 주어졌다.

2. 직접 목적어가 주어인 수동태 문장에서 쓰는 전치사는 동사에 따라 다르다.

to를 쓰는 동사	give, send, bring, show, teach, tell, write, lend 등	Jake **told** her the rumor. Jake는 그녀에게 그 소문을 말해줬다. → The rumor **was told to** her by Jake. 그 소문은 Jake에 의해 그녀에게 말해졌다.
for를 쓰는 동사	buy, cook, make, get, build 등	Mom **made** me these muffins. 엄마는 나에게 이 머핀들을 만들어주셨다. → These muffins **were made for** me by Mom. 이 머핀들은 엄마에 의해 나에게 만들어졌다.
of를 쓰는 동사	ask 등	He **asked** the teacher some questions. 그는 선생님께 몇몇 문제를 물었다. → Some questions **were asked of** the teacher **by him.** 몇몇 문제가 그에 의해 선생님께 물어졌다.

(Tip) bring, write, buy, cook, make 등의 동사가 쓰인 4형식 문장은 주로 직접 목적어를 수동태 문장의 주어로 쓴다.

I cooked him **pasta**. 나는 그에게 파스타를 요리해줬다.
→ **Pasta** was cooked for him by me. (O) 파스타가 나에 의해 그에게 요리되었다.
→ He was cooked pasta by me. (X)

연습문제 A | 다음 빈칸에 to, for, of 중 알맞은 것을 쓰시오.

1 This letter was written _____ Susan by Josh.

2 A newspaper was brought _____ him by his dog.

3 A pair of shoes was bought _____ her by Billy.

4 Those photo albums were made _____ me by my sister.

5 The postcards were sent _____ Liam by Chris.

6 The soup was cooked _____ Tina by me.

7 A question was asked _____ the mayor by the reporter.

8 The award was given _____ the best student by the teacher.

연습문제 **B** 다음 능동태 문장을 수동태로 바꿔 쓰시오.

1 Jenny showed Matt the pictures of cats.

→ Matt _____.

→ The pictures of cats _____.

2 Emma made me chocolate cupcakes.

→ Chocolate cupcakes _____.

3 Jonathan gives people helpful advice.

→ People _____.

→ Helpful advice _____.

4 She bought Joseph a new video game.

→ A new video game _____.

5 My friend sent me a text message.

→ I _____.

→ A text message _____.

6 The old man asked him a favor.

→ He _____.

→ A favor _____.

7 Sophia teaches children English.

→ Children _____.

→ English _____.

기출 적중문제

다음 문장을 수동태로 바르게 바꾼 것은?

They built the hero a statue.

① The hero was built for a statue by them.

② The hero was built to a statue by them.

③ A statue was built hero by them.

④ A statue was built for the hero by them.

⑤ A statue was built to the hero by them.

직접 목적어가 주어인 수동태 문장에서는 동사에 따라 간접 목적어 앞에 알맞은 전치사를 써야 해요.

5형식 문장의 수동태

정답 p.15

1. **목적격 보어가 명사, 형용사, to부정사인 5형식 문장을 수동태로 바꿀 때는 목적격 보어를 「be동사 + p.p.」 뒤에 그대로 쓴다.**

   People **call** this food **bulgogi**. 사람들은 이 음식을 불고기라고 부른다.
   → This food **is called** bulgogi. 이 음식은 불고기라고 불린다.

   Dad **asked** me **to help** my brother. 아빠는 나에게 나의 형을 도와줄 것을 요청하셨다.
   → I **was asked** to help my brother by Dad. 나는 아빠에 의해 나의 형을 도와줄 것을 요청받았다.

2. **사역동사나 지각동사가 쓰인 5형식 문장을 수동태로 바꿀 때는 목적격 보어로 쓰인 동사원형을 to부정사로 바꾼다.**

   사역동사　The movie **made** us **cry**. 그 영화는 우리가 울게 했다.
   　　　　　→ We **were made** to cry by the movie. 우리는 그 영화에 의해 울게 되었다.

   지각동사　Minji **saw** him **play** the drum. 민지는 그가 드럼을 치는 것을 봤다.
   　　　　　→ He **was seen** to play the drum by Minji. 그는 민지에 의해 드럼을 치는 것이 보였다.

   (Tip) 지각동사의 목적격 보어가 V-ing형일 때는 to부정사로 바꾸지 않고 그대로 쓴다.
   　　　Marcus **heard** the dog **barking**. Marcus는 그 개가 짖고 있는 것을 들었다.
   　　　→ The dog **was heard** barking by Marcus. 그 개는 Marcus에 의해 짖고 있는 것이 들어졌다.

연습문제 ｜ 다음 능동태 문장을 수동태로 바꿔 쓰시오.

1 Mr. Smith keeps the building clean.

→ _____

2 His friends call him Teddy.

→ _____

3 My parents expect me to come home early.

→ _____

4 Nina heard some children laugh.

→ _____

5 The members elected her the leader.

→ _____

6 She made Suho stay at home.

→ _____

7 My teacher advised me to study harder.

→ _____

POINT 7 수동태 관용 표현

정답 p.15

다음은 수동태를 사용한 관용 표현이다.

be made of	~으로 만들어지다 (재료 성질이 변하지 않음)	be known to	~에게 알려져 있다
be made from	~으로 만들어지다 (재료 성질이 변함)	be known for	~으로 유명하다
be filled with	~으로 가득 차 있다	be known as	~으로서 알려져 있다
be covered with	~으로 덮여 있다	be interested in	~에 흥미가 있다
be satisfied with	~에 만족하다	be surprised at	~에 놀라다
be pleased with	~에 기뻐하다	be disappointed at[by]	~에 실망하다

This toy **is made of** plastic.   이 장난감은 플라스틱으로 만들어진다.
Paper **is made from** wood.   종이는 나무로 만들어진다.
The cabinet **is filled with** snacks.   그 수납장은 간식으로 가득 차 있다.

연습문제 다음 빈칸에 알맞은 전치사를 쓰시오.

1 Cheese is made _____ milk.

2 The shoes are covered _____ mud.

3 Ronald is interested _____ physics.

4 These bowls are made _____ clay.

5 Jane is satisfied _____ the new dress.

6 This bakery is known _____ its pumpkin pie.

7 Jejudo is known _____ a lot of foreign travelers.

8 David was surprised _____ the size of the computer screen.

기출 적중문제

우리말과 같도록 괄호 안의 말을 활용하여 문장을 완성하시오.

그 차의 트렁크는 도구들로 가득 차 있었다. (fill, tools)

= The trunk of the car _____.

Ⓐ 밑줄 친 부분이 어법상 맞으면 O를 쓰고, 틀리면 바르게 고쳐 쓰시오.

1 The television was repaired by <u>he</u>. → _____

2 The dishes aren't <u>washed</u> by Ginny. → _____

3 The new robot will be <u>present</u> by the scientists. → _____

4 My flight was <u>cancels</u> because of the storm. → _____

5 My arm was <u>broke</u> while I was playing basketball. → _____

6 Each country's traditions must <u>be respected</u>. → _____

7 A hanbok can <u>rented</u> at many shops in Seoul. → _____

8 Olive oil has <u>be used</u> to cook for a long time. → _____

9 Was the first *Harry Potter* book <u>published</u> in 1997? → _____

10 The Winter Olympics was <u>holding</u> in Pyeongchang in 2018. → _____

Ⓑ 다음 문장을 괄호 안의 지시대로 바꿔 쓰시오.

1 You should water the plant. (수동태로)

→ _____

2 He sliced the onions. (수동태 의문문으로)

→ _____

3 The journalist provided the information. (수동태 부정문으로)

→ _____

4 James will copy those documents. (수동태로)

→ _____

5 The children damaged the bicycle. (수동태 부정문으로)

→ _____

6 Beth found the earrings under the bed. (수동태 의문문으로)

→ _____

7 The flu patients must take this medicine. (수동태로)

→ _____

C 다음 능동태 문장은 수동태로, 수동태 문장은 능동태로 바꿔 쓰시오.

1 Jiho heard someone sneeze.

→ _____

2 A guitar was bought for me by my father.

→ _____

3 Luke was made to shop for groceries by her.

→ _____

4 The police officer asked us some questions.

→ _____

5 She is called Sunny by her fans.

→ _____

6 Benjamin lent me a digital camera.

→ _____

D 다음은 민지의 일기이다. 괄호 안의 동사를 활용하여 빈칸에 알맞은 말을 쓰시오.

1

March 8, Sunday

It was my little brother's birthday yesterday. For his birthday gift, I gave him a box. He was
ⓐ_____ _____(disappoint) the box at first. However, he found that the
box was ⓑ_____ _____(fill) presents. Among them, his favorite gift was
the toy trains. They were ©_____ _____(make) wood. He was so
ⓓ_____ _____(please) the gifts that he was smiling all day.

2

March 22, Friday

I'm very ⓐ_____ _____(interest) cooking. I like to cook delicious food
and share it with other people. Last week, I baked a cake for my friends. It was
ⓑ_____ _____(cover) cream and strawberries. They were
©_____ _____(surprise) my cooking skills. Now, I'm ⓓ_____
_____(know) my friends as Chef Park. I want to be a real chef in the future.

중간·기말고사 실전 문제

1 괄호 안의 동사를 활용하여 빈칸에 알맞은 말을 쓰시오.

> The fly was _____ by the spider.
> (catch)

2 다음 중 어법상 어색한 것은?

① Ms. Jones is respect by her students.
② The ring was found on the floor.
③ This magazine is read by many travelers.
④ The seals were followed by a killer whale.
⑤ A lot of nice cars are made in Germany.

3 다음 빈칸에 들어갈 알맞은 것은?

> A soccer ball _____ really hard by Oliver.

① kick ② kicks
③ kicked ④ was kicked
⑤ were kicked

4 다음 문장에서 틀린 부분을 바르게 고쳐 완전한 문장을 쓰시오.

> This singer loves by many teenagers.
> → _____

5 다음 문장을 수동태로 바르게 바꾼 것은?

> Lewis Carroll wrote *Alice in Wonderland* in 1865.

① *Alice in Wonderland* written in 1865 by Lewis Carroll.
② *Alice in Wonderland* is wrote in 1865 by Lewis Carroll.
③ *Alice in Wonderland* was write in 1865 by Lewis Carroll.
④ *Alice in Wonderland* is written in 1865 by Lewis Carroll.
⑤ *Alice in Wonderland* was written in 1865 by Lewis Carroll.

6 우리말과 같도록 괄호 안의 동사를 활용하여 빈칸에 쓰시오.

> 여름에, 비치 타월은 많은 고객들에 의해 구매된다.
> (purchase)

= In the summer, beach towels _____ _____ _____ many customers.

7 다음 밑줄 친 부분을 바르게 고친 것은?

> The guests greet at the door by the hotel manager.

① greets ② greeted
③ was greeted ④ were greeted
⑤ were greet

8 다음 문장을 수동태로 바꿔 쓰시오.

> I brush my teeth three times a day.
> → _____ three times a day by me.

9 다음 중 밑줄 친 부분이 어법상 <u>어색한</u> 것은?

① The kite <u>was flown</u> at the park.
② Lunch <u>will be provided</u> at noon.
③ The mountain <u>was hidden</u> by the clouds.
④ Short stories <u>have written</u> since 2015 by Julie.
⑤ The letters <u>are delivered</u> by the mail carrier.

10 다음 중 어법상 바른 것끼리 묶인 것은?

> ⓐ That sandcastle was built by he.
> ⓑ Delicious pasta is sold at that restaurant.
> ⓒ These books were published two years ago.
> ⓓ Costumes are wearing on Halloween.
> ⓔ The vacuum cleaner uses by my father every day.

① ⓐ, ⓑ   ② ⓐ, ⓓ   ③ ⓑ, ⓒ
④ ⓑ, ⓓ   ⑤ ⓒ, ⓔ

11 다음 문장을 주어진 지시대로 바꿔 쓰시오.

> Jason washed the shirt last night.

(1) 수동태 부정문으로

   → _____
      _____

(2) 수동태 의문문으로

   → _____
      _____

12 다음 중 자연스러운 대화를 <u>모두</u> 고르시오.

① A: Where is the restroom in this building?
  B: It located on the second floor.
② A: Was that cartoon drawn by Patrick?
  B: No, it wasn't. It was drawn by Eric.
③ A: When were these sandwiches made?
  B: They were make in the morning.
④ A: What happened to your leg?
  B: I bite by the dog.
⑤ A: Which sport was created by Americans?
  B: Baseball was created by Americans.

13 다음 문장을 수동태로 바꿀 때 빈칸에 들어갈 알맞은 것은?

> Ellen cooked me a great meal.
> → A great meal was cooked _____ me by Ellen.

① by   ② for   ③ of
④ to   ⑤ from

14 다음 중 수동태 문장으로 바꿀 수 <u>없는</u> 것을 <u>모두</u> 고르시오.

① Hyemi went to London for shopping.
② Ben put the pizza in the oven.
③ That plan sounds terrible to me.
④ My best friends and I attend the festival every spring.
⑤ The parrot opened the cage door.

15 우리말과 같도록 괄호 안의 말을 활용하여 빈칸에 쓰시오.

> 그 TV 프로그램은 모든 연령의 사람들에 의해 보아질 수 있다. (can, watch)

= The TV program _____ _____
_____ by people of all ages.

16 다음 중 문장의 태를 <u>잘못</u> 바꾼 것은?

① Steven will wipe the dust.
  → The dust will be wiped by Steven.
② The cook chopped the lettuce.
  → The lettuce is chopped by the cook.
③ Money was stolen from the bank by the thieves.
  → The thieves stole money from the bank.
④ Susie has raised three cats for many years.
  → Three cats have been raised for many years by Susie.
⑤ Our roof will be painted next week by a few workers.
  → A few workers will paint our roof next week.

17 우리말과 같도록 괄호 안의 말을 배열할 때 네 번째에 오는 것을 쓰시오.

> 중국어는 Mark에 의해 배워질 것이다. (by, be, will, Mark, Chinese, learned)

→ _____

[18-19] 다음 우리말을 수동태 문장으로 알맞게 영작한 것을 고르시오.

18

> Mary는 오늘 오후에 쿠키를 구울 것이다.

① The cookies bake this afternoon by Mary.
② The cookies were baked this afternoon by Mary.
③ The cookies will bake this afternoon by Mary.
④ The cookies have been baked this afternoon by Mary.
⑤ The cookies will be baked this afternoon by Mary.

19

> 김 선생님은 우리에게 미술을 가르치신다.

① We taught art by Ms. Kim.
② We are taught for art by Ms. Kim.
③ Art is taught to us by Ms. Kim.
④ Art is taught for us by Ms. Kim.
⑤ Art teaches to us by Ms. Kim.

20 다음 문장에서 어법상 <u>어색한</u> 부분을 찾아 쓰고 바르게 고쳐 쓰시오.

> The field is covered of snow.

_____ → _____

[21-22] 괄호 안의 말을 활용하여 빈칸에 알맞은 말을 쓰시오.

21

The N Seoul Tower _____ _____ in 1969. (build)

22

Presidential elections _____ _____ every five years now in Korea. (hold)

23 다음 문장을 수동태로 바르게 바꾼 것을 <u>모두</u> 고르시오.

He gave Lisa a free ticket.

① Lisa was given to a free ticket by him.
② Lisa was given a free ticket by him.
③ A free ticket was given Lisa by him.
④ A free ticket was given to Lisa by him.
⑤ A free ticket was given of Lisa by him.

24 다음 표지판을 바르게 표현한 것은?

① The birds must fed.
② The birds must be fed.
③ The birds not must fed.
④ The birds must not be fed.
⑤ The birds not must be fed.

25 괄호 안의 동사를 활용하여 빈칸에 알맞은 말을 쓰시오.

The family album _____ _____ _____ Martha last weekend by her grandma. (show)

26 다음 중 밑줄 친 부분이 어법상 <u>어색한</u> 것은?

① That used lamp <u>can be bought</u> for eight dollars.
② Cars <u>shouldn't be parked</u> here.
③ Fire <u>must be treated</u> carefully.
④ A child <u>may not be leave</u> alone at home.
⑤ The store <u>might be closed</u> tomorrow.

27 다음 빈칸에 들어갈 알맞은 것은?

Lake Baikal is known _____ its clear water and unique wildlife.

① for　　② to　　③ as
④ at　　⑤ with

28 다음 중 문장의 태를 바르게 바꾼 것은?

① Nick enjoyed the fireworks.
　→ The fireworks be enjoyed by Nick.
② We must protect the forests.
　→ The forests must be protected.
③ Lola will send the package tonight.
　→ The package will sent tonight by Lola.
④ I didn't break the plates.
　→ The plates weren't broken by I.
⑤ People can't bring knives on the plane.
　→ Knives can't be bring on the plane.

29 우리말과 같도록 괄호 안의 동사를 활용하여 빈칸에 쓰시오.

> Nicole은 공상 과학 영화에 흥미가 있다. (interest)

= Nicole _____ _____ _____
science fiction movies.

30 다음 빈칸에 들어갈 말이 나머지 넷과 <u>다른</u> 것은?

① The doughnut is filled _____ strawberry jam.
② My hands are covered _____ ink.
③ The hockey fans weren't satisfied _____ the match.
④ Nora is pleased _____ her new haircut.
⑤ Kim Yuna's talent is known _____ everyone in the world.

31 다음 중 어법상 <u>어색한</u> 것은?

① Jimmy was disappointed by the dish.
② My bedroom is kept to neat all the time.
③ The first machine was invented in 1939.
④ We were asked to turn off our phone.
⑤ A blueberry pie was made for me by Surin.

32 우리말과 같도록 괄호 안의 말을 알맞게 배열하시오.

> 그녀는 2008년에 부사장으로 선출되었다. (vice president, she, elected, was)

= _____ in 2008.

33 다음 빈칸에 들어갈 말이 순서대로 짝지어진 것은?

> · Some books were lent _____ him by Cathy.
> · Questions were asked _____ the soccer player by the reporters.

① to – for   ② to – of   ③ of – to
④ for – to   ⑤ for – of

34 다음 빈칸에 to가 들어갈 수 <u>없는</u> 것은?

① The baby was heard _____ cry by his mother.
② The sun was seen _____ set by us.
③ We were made _____ speak only English during class.
④ Minho was told _____ finish his bowl of vegetables.
⑤ Sandra's new doll was named _____ Annabelle.

35 다음 빈칸에 for가 들어갈 수 <u>없는</u> 것을 <u>모두</u> 고르시오.

① A new school was built _____ the students in our town.
② The bouquet was given _____ the bride's friend.
③ This bracelet was made _____ me by Samantha.
④ Flowers are bought _____ my mom every month by my dad.
⑤ Funny jokes were told _____ the audience by the comedian.

36 괄호 안의 동사를 활용하여 다음 대화의 빈칸에 알맞은 말을 쓰시오.

> A: _____ this window _____ by Paul? (break)
> B: I think so. He was playing with a baseball an hour ago.

37 다음 대화의 밑줄 친 ⓐ~ⓔ 중 어법상 어색한 것을 찾아 기호를 쓰고 바르게 고쳐 쓰시오.

> A: When was Tutankhamen's tomb ⓐdiscover?
> B: In 1922.
> A: Could you tell me more about it?
> B: While other tombs ⓑrobbed by treasure hunters and thieves, this boy pharaoh's tomb ⓒwas kept safe. It ⓓis known for being undamaged.
> A: Do you know why?
> B: Its entrance was hidden well ⓔby the builders.
>
> *tomb 무덤
> *pharaoh 파라오(고대 이집트의 왕)

(1) _____ → _____
(2) _____ → _____

38 다음 빈칸에 들어갈 말이 순서대로 짝지어진 것은?

> · We were surprised _____ the size of the diamond.
> · This wine is made _____ excellent grapes.

① with – by   ② with – from
③ at – from   ④ for – of
⑤ at – of

39 다음 중 밑줄 친 부분을 생략할 수 있는 것은?

① Were these tomatoes grown <u>by your grandpa</u>?
② Peter was told to clean his desk <u>by the teacher</u>.
③ This dog is called Buddy <u>by Serena</u>.
④ Portuguese is spoken in Brazil <u>by people</u>.
⑤ This video wasn't filmed <u>by George</u>.

40 다음 문장을 수동태로 바꿔 쓰시오.

> British people call a bathroom a loo.
> → _____
> _____

41 다음 중 어법상 바른 것의 개수는?

> ⓐ Was the green tea ordered by Henry?
> ⓑ Where did your lost key found yesterday?
> ⓒ Was how the puzzle solved by her?
> ⓓ This mobile phone wasn't made at our factory.
> ⓔ These events not are held in the winter.

① 1개   ② 2개   ③ 3개
④ 4개   ⑤ 5개

CHAPTER 6
부정사

My dream is **to become** a soccer player. 나의 꿈은 축구 선수가 되는 것이다.

'~이 되다'라는 의미의 동사 become 앞에 to를 붙여 '~이 되는 것'이라는 의미를 나타냈어요. 이렇게 동사 앞에 to를 붙인 「to + 동사원형」의 형태를 **to부정사**라고 하며, to부정사는 문장 안에서 명사·형용사·부사 역할을 할 수 있어요.

기출로 적중 POINT

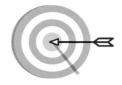

내신 100점 적중!
기출 출제율

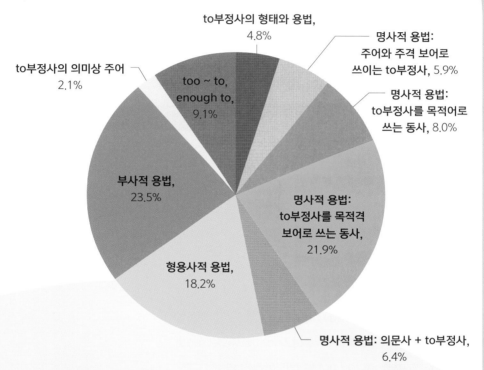

to부정사의 형태와 용법,
4.8%

명사적 용법:
주어와 주격 보어로
쓰이는 to부정사, 5.9%

명사적 용법:
to부정사를 목적어로
쓰는 동사, 8.0%

to부정사의 의미상 주어
2.1%

too ~ to,
enough to,
9.1%

부사적 용법,
23.5%

명사적 용법:
to부정사를 목적격
보어로 쓰는 동사,
21.9%

형용사적 용법,
18.2%

명사적 용법: 의문사 + to부정사,
6.4%

TOP 1 **부사적 용법 (23.5%)**
to부정사의 부사적 용법의 다양한 의미를 묻는 문제가 자주 출제된다.

TOP 2 **명사적 용법: to부정사를 목적격 보어로 쓰는 동사 (21.9%)**
특정 동사의 목적격 보어 자리에 to부정사가 쓰이는 경우를 묻는 문제가 자주
출제된다.

TOP 3 **형용사적 용법 (18.2%)**
형용사적 용법으로 쓰인 to부정사의 역할과 문장 안에서의 위치를 묻는 문제
가 자주 출제된다.

to부정사의 형태와 용법

정답 p.17

1. to부정사는 「to + 동사원형」의 형태로, 문장 안에서 명사·형용사·부사 역할을 한다.

명사적 용법	주어·보어·목적어로 쓰임	I want **to have** some water. 나는 약간의 물을 마시기를 원한다.
형용사적 용법	명사·대명사 수식	Ella didn't have a chance **to talk**. Ella는 말할 기회가 없었다.
부사적 용법	동사·형용사·부사· 문장 전체 수식	He jogs regularly **to lose** weight. 그는 살을 빼기 위해 규칙적으로 조깅한다.

2. to부정사의 부정형: 「not to + 동사원형」

I decided **not to go** out today. 나는 오늘 외출하지 않기로 결심했다.
He told me **not to be** late again. 그는 나에게 또 늦지 말라고 말했다.

연습문제 괄호 안에서 알맞은 것을 고르시오.

1 Her plan is (learn / to learn) French this year.

2 I went to the library (to study / studied).

3 Jeonju is an exciting city to (visited / visit).

4 Do you have anything (drank / to drink)?

5 He decided (not to sleep / to sleep not) late.

6 Miso is saving money to (buy / buying) a ring.

7 My mom asked me (to don't waste / not to waste) food.

8 She promised (tell not to / not to tell) my secret.

9 (To get / Get) enough sleep is important for our health.

기출 적중문제

다음 중 밑줄 친 부분이 어법상 바른 것은?

① She ran fast <u>catch</u> the bus.
② I want <u>to going</u> to the festival.
③ His plan is <u>to write</u> a good novel.
④ We chose <u>stay not to</u> at a hotel.
⑤ I expected him <u>to called</u> me tonight.

POINT 2-1 명사적 용법: 주어와 주격 보어로 쓰이는 to부정사 정답 p.17

1. to부정사는 주어로 쓰이며, 이때 주로 주어 자리에 가주어 it을 쓰고 원래 주어인 진주어 to부정사(구)를 뒤로 보낸다.

   To read comic books is fun. 만화책을 읽는 것은 재미있다.
   = **It** is fun **to read** comic books.

   To achieve my goal wasn't easy. 나의 목표를 달성하는 것은 쉽지 않았다.
   = **It** wasn't easy **to achieve** my goal.

   (Tip) 주어로 쓰인 to부정사(구)는 항상 단수 취급한다.
   To keep your promises **is** important. 너의 약속을 지키는 것은 중요하다.

2. to부정사는 주어를 보충 설명하는 주격 보어로 쓰인다.

   Her job is **to manage** a hotel. 그녀의 직업은 호텔을 운영하는 것이다.
   Bob's plan is **to build** a huge house. Bob의 계획은 거대한 집을 짓는 것이다.

연습문제 **A** 다음 문장을 가주어 it을 사용한 문장으로 바꿔 쓰시오.

1 To study history is important.

→ _____

2 To travel to the moon is hard.

→ _____

3 To swim in this river isn't safe.

→ _____

4 To use that machine was confusing.

→ _____

5 To brush your teeth is necessary.

→ _____

6 To play online games is exciting.

→ _____

7 To climb this mountain wasn't difficult.

→ _____

8 To spend the summer in Europe is my dream.

→ _____

9 To collect stamps is Junsu's hobby.

→ _____

10 To predict our future is impossible.

→ _____

연습문제 B 우리말과 같도록 괄호 안의 말을 활용하여 빈칸에 쓰시오.

1 Katie의 소망은 세계를 여행하는 것이다. (Katie's wish, travel)

= _____ _____ _____ the world.

2 그의 꿈은 화가가 되는 것이었다. (his dream, become)

= _____ _____ _____ _____ an artist.

3 야구 경기를 보는 것은 재미있다. (fun, watch)

= _____ _____ _____ _____ baseball games.

4 그 요리사의 목표는 새로운 식당을 여는 것이다. (the chef's goal, open)

= _____ _____ _____ _____ a new restaurant.

5 그녀의 취미는 피아노를 치는 것이었다. (her hobby, play)

= _____ _____ _____ _____ the piano.

6 그의 직업은 시민들을 보호하는 것이다. (his job, protect)

= _____ _____ _____ _____ the citizens.

7 과일과 채소를 먹는 것은 좋다. (good, eat)

= _____ _____ _____ _____ fruits and vegetables.

8 나의 엄마의 조언은 많은 물을 마시는 것이었다. (my mom's advice, drink)

= _____ _____ _____ lots of water.

9 자기 자신을 믿는 것은 중요하다. (important, believe)

= _____ _____ _____ _____ in yourself.

10 나의 계획은 올해 더 열심히 공부하는 것이다. (my plan, study)

= _____ _____ _____ _____ harder this year.

기출 적중문제

다음 중 밑줄 친 to부정사의 쓰임이 나머지 넷과 다른 것은?

① It is hard to become a lawyer.
② Cam's wish is to see a rainbow.
③ To wear a hat during class is rude.
④ It isn't easy to take care of a pet.
⑤ To learn foreign languages is interesting.

기출로적중 POINT 2-2 명사적 용법: to부정사를 목적어로 쓰는 동사

정답 p.17

다음 동사들은 to부정사를 목적어로 쓴다.

| want | hope | wish | decide | plan | need | agree |
| would like | would love | expect | promise | learn | choose | refuse |

We **are planning to watch** a movie tonight. 우리는 오늘 밤에 영화를 보기로 계획하고 있다.

I**'d like to join** the book club. 나는 독서 동아리에 가입하기를 원한다.

Jinho **promised not to lie** anymore. 진호는 더는 거짓말하지 않기로 약속했다.

연습문제 우리말과 같도록 괄호 안의 말을 활용하여 문장을 완성하시오.

1 Jane은 그녀의 오랜 친구를 찾기를 바란다. (find, wish)

= Jane _____ her old friend.

2 Daniel은 나에게 그의 필기를 빌려주기로 동의했다. (lend, agree)

= Daniel _____ me his notes.

3 Parker씨는 새 차를 구매하지 않기로 정했다. (purchase, choose)

= Mr. Parker _____ a new car.

4 나는 산책하러 가기를 원한다. (would love, go)

= I _____ for a walk.

5 대부분의 사람들은 8시간 동안 잘 필요가 있다. (need, sleep)

= Most people _____ for eight hours.

6 우리는 세상을 더 좋은 곳으로 만들기를 바란다. (make, hope)

= We _____ the world a better place.

7 기린은 매우 어린 나이에 걷는 것을 배운다. (walk, learn)

= Giraffes _____ at a very young age.

8 Steve는 혼잡 시간대에 택시를 타지 않기로 결심했다. (decide, take)

= Steve _____ a taxi during rush hour.

기출 적중문제 🎯

다음 문장에서 어법상 어색한 부분을 찾아 쓰고 바르게 고쳐 쓰시오.

Liam refused answering the questions.

_____ → _____

명사적 용법: to부정사를 목적격 보어로 쓰는 동사 정답 p.17

다음 동사들은 to부정사를 목적격 보어로 쓴다.

want	ask	tell	expect	allow	advise	order

My mom **wants** me **to clean** the floor. 나의 엄마는 내가 바닥을 청소하기를 원하신다.
The doctor **advised** her **not to eat** fast food. 그 의사는 그녀에게 패스트푸드를 먹지 말라고 조언했다.

연습문제 Nina와 Sam의 대화를 보고 대화에 나온 표현을 활용하여 문장을 완성하시오.

1 Could you turn down the volume?　　All right.

→ Nina asks Sam _____.

2 You can use my cell phone.　　Thank you.

→ Sam allowed Nina _____.

3 Will you close the window?　　Sure.

→ Sam wants Nina _____.

4 You'll study with me today, won't you?　　Of course.

→ Nina expects Sam _____.

5 You shouldn't play the piano at night.　　Sorry, I won't.

→ Sam advised Nina _____.

기출 적중문제

우리말과 같도록 괄호 안의 말을 활용하여 문장을 완성하시오.

나의 부모님은 항상 나에게 조심하라고 말씀하신다. (tell, be careful)

= My parents always _____.

POINT 2-4 명사적 용법: 의문사 + to부정사

정답 p.17

「의문사 + to부정사」는 문장 안에서 명사처럼 쓰이며, 의문사에 따라 의미가 달라진다.

what + to부정사 무엇을 ~할지   when + to부정사 언제 ~할지
where + to부정사 어디에(서)/어디로 ~할지   how + to부정사 어떻게 ~할지

Anna couldn't decide **what to eat** for lunch. Anna는 점심으로 무엇을 먹을지 결정할 수 없었다.
Please tell me **where to buy** a nice watch. 저에게 좋은 시계를 어디에서 살지 말해주세요.

(Tip) 「의문사 + to부정사」는 「의문사 + 주어 + should + 동사원형」으로 바꿔 쓸 수 있다.
I'm not sure **when to leave**. 나는 언제 떠날지 확실히 알지 못한다.
= I'm not sure **when I should leave**.
He showed me **how to use** the Internet. 그는 나에게 인터넷을 어떻게 사용하는지 보여줬다.
= He showed me **how I should use** the Internet.

연습문제 우리말과 같도록 괄호 안의 동사를 활용하여 빈칸에 쓰시오.

1 그녀는 우리에게 다음에 무엇을 할지 말해줬니? (do)
= Did she tell us _____ _____ _____ next?

2 나는 나의 여행 가방을 어디에 놓을지 모른다. (put)
= I don't know _____ _____ _____ my suitcase.

3 그는 학생들에게 그 문제를 어떻게 해결할지 가르쳐줬다. (solve)
= He taught the students _____ _____ _____ the problem.

4 그 도시는 그 행사를 언제 개최할지 결정할 수 없다. (hold)
= The city can't decide _____ _____ _____ the event.

5 Jamie는 나에게 지도에서 어디에 방문할지 보여줬다. (visit)
= Jamie showed me _____ _____ _____ on the map.

기출 적중문제

다음 빈칸에 알맞은 말을 넣어 대화를 완성하시오.

A: Can you tell me _____ _____ _____
_____ _____ _____ ?
B: You can get to city hall by taking bus number 11.

형용사적 용법

정답 p.17

1. to부정사는 형용사 역할을 할 때 명사나 대명사를 뒤에서 수식할 수 있으며, 이때 '~할, ~하는'의 의미이다.

   The monkey needs **bananas to eat**. 그 원숭이는 먹을 바나나가 필요하다.

   I don't have **anything to tell** you. 나는 너에게 말해줄 어떤 것도 없다.

2. -thing, -body, -one으로 끝나는 대명사가 형용사와 to부정사의 수식을 동시에 받을 때는 「-thing/-body/-one + 형용사 + to부정사」의 형태로 쓴다.

   Jiho wants **something warm to wear**. 지호는 입을 따뜻한 무언가를 원한다.

3. to부정사가 수식하는 명사나 대명사가 전치사의 목적어인 경우 to부정사 뒤에 반드시 전치사를 쓴다.

   Please lend me **a pencil to write with**. (← write with a pencil) 저에게 쓸 연필을 빌려주세요.

   I hope to buy **a house to live in**. (← live in a house) 나는 살 집을 사기를 바란다.

   He found **someone to play with**. (← play with someone) 그는 함께 놀 누군가를 찾았다.

연습문제 A 우리말과 같도록 괄호 안의 말을 알맞게 배열하시오.

1 John은 마실 커피 한 잔을 가져왔다. (to, a cup of coffee, drink, brought)

= John _____.

2 우리는 쉴 약간의 시간이 필요하다. (rest, to, need, some time)

= We _____.

3 너는 먹을 무언가를 가지고 있니? (eat, have, anything, to)

= Do you _____?

4 나는 나의 방에서 사용할 새 컴퓨터를 원한다. (to, want, use, a new computer)

= I _____ in my room.

5 도서관은 읽을 많은 책들을 가지고 있다. (have, to, read, many books)

= Libraries _____.

6 그는 이 문제를 해결할 똑똑한 누군가를 찾고 있다. (to, is looking for, smart, someone, solve)

= He _____ this problem.

7 민하는 그 정원에 심을 세 송이의 꽃을 찾았다. (three flowers, plant, found, to)

= Minha _____ in the garden.

8 여름은 수영할 가장 좋은 계절이다. (swim, is, the best season, to)

= Summer _____ .

9 너는 평일에 할 많은 숙제가 있니? (a lot of homework, do, have, to)

= Do you _____ on weekdays?

10 Susie는 입을 좋은 무언가를 샀다. (something, to, nice, bought, wear)

= Susie _____ .

11 한수는 서울에서 방문할 많은 관광지를 안다. (knows, to, many tourist sites, visit)

= Hansu _____ in Seoul.

연습문제 B <보기>와 같이 to부정사를 이용하여 다음 두 문장을 한 문장으로 연결하시오.

> **<보기>** We have some topics. We will talk about the topics.
> → We *have some topics to talk about* .

1 Mr. and Mrs. Brown bought a house. They will live in the house.

→ Mr. and Mrs. Brown _____ .

2 Penny met new friends. She will talk to the new friends.

→ Penny _____ .

3 Billy recommended a song. I will listen to the song.

→ Billy _____ .

4 Give me a piece of paper. I need to write on the piece of paper.

→ Give me _____ .

5 There isn't any chair. I can sit on a chair.

→ There _____ .

기출 적중문제

다음 중 어법상 <u>어색한</u> 것은?

① This is the best way to get to school.

② I want something cold to drink.

③ The festival has fun activities to do.

④ Jaemin needs a spoon to eat with.

⑤ Do you have any pens to write?

> to부정사가 수식하는 명사가 전치사의 목적어인 경우 to부정사 뒤에 반드시 전치사를 써야 해요.

부사적 용법

정답 p.18

to부정사는 부사 역할을 할 때 동사·형용사·부사·문장 전체를 수식할 수 있으며, 다양한 의미를 나타낸다.

목적	~하기 위해	목적을 나타낼 때 to 대신 in order to나 so as to를 쓸 수 있다. I went outside **to take** a walk. 나는 산책하기 위해 밖으로 나갔다. = I went outside **in order to[so as to] take** a walk. He ran **not to miss** the bus. 그는 버스를 놓치지 않기 위해 뛰었다. = He ran **in order not to[so as not to] miss** the bus.
형용사 수식	~하기에	This book isn't **easy to understand**. 이 책은 이해하기에 쉽지 않다.
감정의 원인	~해서, ~하니	주로 감정을 나타내는 형용사(glad, sad, surprised 등) 뒤에 쓰인다. Narae was **glad to win** the contest. 나래는 그 대회에서 우승해서 기뻤다.
판단의 근거	~하다니	주로 추측을 나타내는 조동사(must, can't 등)와 함께 쓰인다. Charlie **must** be smart **to solve** this puzzle. 이 퍼즐을 풀다니 Charlie는 똑똑함에 틀림없다.
결과	(…해서 결국) ~하다	주로 grow up, live 등과 함께 쓰인다. She **grew up to be** a famous singer. 그녀는 자라서 유명한 가수가 되었다.

연습문제 A 우리말과 같도록 괄호 안의 말을 활용하여 빈칸에 쓰시오.

1 우리는 식료품을 사기 위해 시장에 갔다. (buy, groceries)

= We went to the market _____ _____ _____.

2 그 물은 마시기에 안전하지 않다. (safe, drink)

= The water is _____ _____ _____ _____.

3 그 아이는 자라서 소방관이 되었다. (grow up, be)

= The child _____ _____ _____ _____ a firefighter.

4 이 바지는 집에서 입기에 편하다. (comfortable, wear)

= These pants are _____ _____ _____ at home.

5 Dave의 글씨는 읽기에 매우 어렵다. (difficult, read)

= Dave's writing is very _____ _____ _____.

6 Luke는 나에게 무언가를 물어보기 위해 전화했다. (ask, something)

= Luke called _____ _____ _____ _____.

연습문제 B <보기>와 같이 to부정사를 이용하여 다음 두 문장을 한 문장으로 연결하시오.

> <보기>   I met you. I was glad.
> → I _was glad to meet you_ .

1   Terry heard the bad news. He was sad.
→ Terry _____.

2   She repairs computers. She must be clever.
→ She _____.

3   We won the first prize. We were excited.
→ We _____.

4   He tells many lies. He can't be honest.
→ He _____.

5   Julie saw me in the market. She was surprised.
→ Julie _____.

연습문제 C 밑줄 친 to부정사의 쓰임을 <보기>에서 골라 그 기호를 쓰시오.

> <보기>   ⓐ 목적   ⓑ 형용사 수식   ⓒ 감정의 원인   ⓓ 판단의 근거   ⓔ 결과

1   Sarah went to the bakery to buy some bread.   [   ]
2   I was disappointed to lose the game.   [   ]
3   Volleyball is impossible to play alone.   [   ]
4   My grandma lived to be 101 years old.   [   ]
5   Emma must be foolish to trust Adam.   [   ]
6   You need your ID to open a bank account.   [   ]

기출 적중문제

주어진 문장의 밑줄 친 to부정사와 쓰임이 같은 것은?

> Violet is going to the theater to watch a play.

① He must be very angry to scream like that.
② The boy grew up to be a pilot.
③ I was shocked to see a rat in the house.
④ Jina visited Busan to see her cousins.
⑤ This math question is difficult to solve.

to부정사의 의미상 주어

정답 p.18

1. **to부정사의 의미상 주어는 to부정사가 나타내는 동작의 주체이며, 문장의 주어와 다를 때 「for + 목적격」의 형태로 to부정사 앞에 쓴다.**

   It is easy **for me to speak** Russian. 내가 러시아어로 말하는 것은 쉽다.
   It is impossible **for him to wake** up early. 그가 일찍 일어나는 것은 불가능하다.

2. **to부정사의 의미상 주어가 사람의 성격을 나타내는 형용사 뒤에 쓰일 때는 「of + 목적격」 의 형태로 쓴다.**

kind	nice	brave	polite	rude	selfish	foolish	careless

   It is **kind of her to help** us. 그녀가 우리를 도와주다니 친절하다.
   It was **foolish of me to make** that mistake. 내가 그 실수를 하다니 어리석었다.

연습문제 A 괄호 안에서 for나 of 중 알맞은 것을 고르시오.

1 It is fun (for / of) me to play the guitar.

2 It was nice (for / of) you to carry Mary's bags.

3 It was foolish (for / of) them to skip breakfast.

4 It was selfish (for / of) Brian to eat the pizza by himself.

5 It is necessary (for / of) some animals to sleep in the winter.

연습문제 B 우리말과 같도록 괄호 안의 말을 활용하여 빈칸에 쓰시오.

1 내가 문법을 이해하는 것은 어렵다. (understand)
   = It is difficult _____ _____ _____ _____ grammar.

2 그녀가 그 질문을 하다니 무례했다. (ask)
   = It was rude _____ _____ _____ _____ the question.

3 우리가 규칙을 따르는 것은 중요하다. (follow)
   = It is important _____ _____ _____ the rules.

4 그가 그의 지갑을 잃어버리다니 부주의했다. (lose)
   = It was careless _____ _____ _____ _____ his wallet.

5 고양이들이 높은 곳에서 뛰어내리는 것은 가능하다. (jump)
   = It is possible _____ _____ _____ _____ off from high places.

기출로적중 POINT 6 too ~ to, enough to

정답 p.18

1. 「too + 형용사/부사 + to부정사」는 '…하기에 너무 ~한'이라는 의미로, 「so + 형용사/부사 + that + 주어 + can't + 동사원형」으로 바꿔 쓸 수 있다.

We are **too busy to take** a break. 우리는 휴식을 취하기에 너무 바쁘다.
= We are **so busy that we can't take** a break. 우리는 너무 바빠서 휴식을 취할 수 없다.

2. 「형용사/부사 + enough + to부정사」는 '…할 만큼 충분히 ~한'이라는 의미로, 「so + 형용사/부사 + that + 주어 + can + 동사원형」으로 바꿔 쓸 수 있다.

He is **tall enough to reach** the ceiling. 그는 천장에 닿을 만큼 충분히 키가 크다.
= He is **so tall that he can reach** the ceiling. 그는 매우 키가 커서 천장에 닿을 수 있다.

(Tip) 문장의 주어가 to부정사의 목적어인 경우 that절에 반드시 목적어를 쓴다.
The movie was too scary **for me to watch**. 그 영화는 내가 보기에 너무 무서웠다.
= **The movie** was so scary that **I couldn't watch it**. 그 영화는 너무 무서워서 나는 그것을 볼 수 없었다.
The boxes are light enough **for Amy to lift**. 그 상자들은 Amy가 들어 올릴 만큼 충분히 가볍다.
= **The boxes** are so light that **Amy can lift them**.
그 상자들은 매우 가벼워서 Amy는 그것들을 들어 올릴 수 있다.

연습문제 A 우리말과 같도록 괄호 안의 말을 활용하여 빈칸에 쓰시오.

1 오늘은 밖에서 놀기에 너무 덥다. (hot, play)
= It is _____ _____ _____ _____ outside today.

2 민수는 그 침대를 옮길 만큼 충분히 힘이 세다. (strong, move)
= Minsu is _____ _____ _____ _____ the bed.

3 나는 집중하기에 너무 배가 고팠다. (hungry, concentrate)
= I was _____ _____ _____ _____.

4 Brad는 나를 도울 만큼 충분히 친절했다. (kind, help)
= Brad was _____ _____ _____ _____ me.

5 나는 시험을 통과할 만큼 충분히 열심히 공부했다. (hard, pass)
= I studied _____ _____ _____ _____ the test.

6 저 말은 경주에서 우승하기에 너무 느리다. (slow, win)
= That horse is _____ _____ _____ _____ the race.

7 그 카레는 내가 먹기에 너무 매웠다. (spicy, eat)
= The curry was _____ _____ _____ _____ _____ _____.

CHAPTER 6 부정사 기출로 적중 해카스 중학영문법 2학년

8 그는 거미를 잡을 만큼 충분히 용감했다. (brave, catch)

= He was _____ _____ _____ _____ the spider.

9 Samantha는 학교에 가기에 너무 아프다. (ill, go)

= Samantha is _____ _____ _____ _____ to school.

10 그 방은 우리가 파티를 열 만큼 충분히 컸다. (large, throw)

= The room was _____ _____ _____ _____ _____ a party.

연습문제 B | 다음 두 문장의 의미가 같도록 문장을 완성하시오.

1 Noah is smart enough to be a doctor.

= Noah _____ .

2 Ashley is so sleepy that she can't read the book.

= Ashley _____ .

3 The laptop is so small that it can fit in my bag.

= The laptop _____ .

4 That lemonade was too sour for me to drink.

= That lemonade _____ .

5 Suho was so tired that he couldn't walk home.

= Suho _____ .

6 She is funny enough to make me laugh.

= She _____ .

7 This knife is so sharp that it can cut everything.

= This knife _____ .

8 The skirt is too long for her to wear.

= The skirt _____ .

기출 적중문제 🎯

다음 두 문장의 의미가 같도록 괄호 안의 말을 배열할 때 다섯 번째에 오는 것은?

> The movie was too boring for children to watch.
> = The movie was _____ .
> (watch, boring, children, it, so, that, couldn't)

① that   ② it   ③ couldn't

④ watch   ⑤ children

POINT 7 원형부정사

정답 p.18

원형부정사는 to부정사에서 to가 없는 동사원형의 형태이며, 사역동사나 지각동사의 목적격 보어로 쓰인다.

사역동사 (make, have, let)	My dad **made** me **set** the table. 나의 아빠는 내가 식탁을 차리게 하셨다. (Tip) 준사역동사 help의 목적격 보어 자리에는 to부정사와 원형부정사가 모두 올 수 있다. I'll **help** Gina **(to) find** her wallet. 나는 Gina가 그녀의 지갑을 찾는 것을 도울 것이다.
지각동사 (see, watch, hear, listen to, smell, feel)	I **saw** him **sing** on the stage. 나는 그가 무대 위에서 노래하는 것을 봤다. (Tip) 지각동사의 목적격 보어 자리에 V-ing형이 오면 진행 중인 동작이 강조된다. Minji **heard** someone **knocking** on the door. 민지는 누군가가 문을 두드리고 있는 것을 들었다.

연습문제 괄호 안에서 알맞은 것을 모두 고르시오.

1 I watched Dan (play / to play / playing) basketball.

2 The letter made me (feel / to feel / feeling) sad.

3 Jonathan heard me (sing / to sing / singing) in the shower.

4 Susan saw her sister (break / to break / breaking) the vase.

5 I will help you (wash / to wash / washing) the dishes.

6 The police had the driver (get / to get / getting) out of the car.

7 Hannah let her friend (borrow / to borrow / borrowing) her umbrella.

8 The chef smelled something (burn / to burn / burning) in the oven.

9 Our teacher made us (write / to write / writing) a very long report.

10 We felt the ground (shake / to shake / shaking) because of the earthquake.

기출 적중문제 🎯

다음 빈칸에 들어갈 알맞은 것은?

This song makes me _____ asleep easily.

① fall   ② falls   ③ to fall
④ fell   ⑤ falling

서술형 대비 문제

Ⓐ 밑줄 친 부분이 어법상 맞으면 O를 쓰고, 틀리면 바르게 고쳐 쓰시오.

1 Jackson's job is <u>to take</u> photographs. → _____

2 What did you choose <u>wearing</u>? → _____

3 Hyeri taught me <u>what to bake</u> a cake. → _____

4 Can you bring me something warm <u>drink</u>? → _____

5 It isn't easy <u>of</u> me to speak in public. → _____

6 Ms. Hall told her son <u>not to play</u> with fire. → _____

7 To protect wild animals <u>are</u> important. → _____

8 It was rude <u>of</u> him to shout at you. → _____

9 <u>That</u> is fun to hang out with my friends. → _____

10 There weren't any benches <u>to sit</u> in this park. → _____

Ⓑ 다음 문장을 가주어 it을 사용한 문장으로 바꿔 쓰시오.

1 To plan a trip is exciting.

  → _____

2 To listen to his songs is wonderful.

  → _____

3 To shop online is convenient.

  → _____

4 To become an astronaut is my dream.

  → _____

5 To ride a bike without a helmet is dangerous.

  → _____

6 To find an empty seat on the subway was impossible.

  → _____

7 To spend too much time on computer games is not wise.

  → _____

(C) 우리말과 같도록 괄호 안의 말을 알맞게 배열하시오.

1 이 버섯은 먹기에 안전하지 않다. (eat, safe, not, to, is)

= This mushroom _____.

2 Elena는 그 문제에 대해 이야기하는 것을 거부했다. (about the problem, talk, to, refused)

= Elena _____.

3 보라는 쓸 공책이 필요하다. (in, needs, write, a notebook, to)

= Bora _____.

4 그 거북은 200살까지 살았다. (be, lived, to, 200 years old)

= The turtle _____.

5 James는 잘 시간이 없다. (time, not, sleep, to, does, have)

= James _____.

6 우리는 별똥별을 봐서 놀랐다. (to, the shooting star, were, see, surprised)

= We _____.

7 저에게 읽을 재미있는 무언가를 건네주시겠어요? (read, pass, something, to, fun, me)

= Could you _____?

8 코끼리는 의사소통을 하기 위해 그들의 코를 사용한다. (communicate, to, use, their trunks)

= Elephants _____.

(D) 다음 두 문장의 의미가 같도록 문장을 완성하시오.

1 She is so young that she can't drive a car.

= She _____.

2 Peter was generous enough to forgive me.

= Peter _____.

3 The camera was too expensive for me to buy.

= The camera _____.

4 The baseball player is so good that he can play in the major leagues.

= The baseball player _____.

5 That cookie is too hard for me to chew.

= That cookie _____.

중간 · 기말고사 실전 문제

1 다음 빈칸에 들어갈 알맞은 것은?

> Ben wants _____ a better grade.

① get ② gets ③ got
④ to get ⑤ getting

2 다음 중 어법상 바른 것은?

① I exercise every day lose weight.
② Some scientists hope to find aliens in space.
③ We would like having pizza for lunch.
④ Joseph is planning to leaves Seoul on Friday.
⑤ That is interesting to learn about different cultures.

3 다음 두 문장의 의미가 같도록 빈칸에 알맞은 말을 쓰시오.

> To finish the report before the weekend was my plan.
> = _____ was my plan _____
> _____ _____ _____
> before the weekend.

4 다음 문장에서 어법상 어색한 부분을 찾아 쓰고 바르게 고쳐 쓰시오.

> Jack decided buying a ticket for the rock concert.

_____ → _____

5 다음 빈칸에 들어갈 말로 어색한 것은?

> My mom _____ me swim in the pool twice a week.

① makes ② helps ③ has
④ allows ⑤ lets

6 다음 중 어법상 바른 것은?

① He promised buying me a new shirt.
② The teacher advised me study harder.
③ Mina has heavy to something carry.
④ It is necessary to protect the environment.
⑤ Charles is learning speaking Chinese.

7 다음 빈칸에 들어갈 말이 순서대로 짝지어진 것은?

> · I asked Holly _____ in the lobby.
> · She made her children _____ their hands.

① wait – wash ② wait – to wash
③ to wait – wash ④ to wait – to wash
⑤ waiting – wash

8 우리말과 같도록 괄호 안의 말을 알맞게 배열하시오.

그는 나에게 기적을 기대하지 말라고 말했다.
(expect, told, to, he, not, a miracle, me)

= _____

9 다음 중 밑줄 친 to부정사의 용법이 나머지 넷과 다른 것은?

① To sing in front of many people is scary.
② Would you like to share this cookie with me?
③ It is wise to go to the dentist regularly.
④ Jake agreed to lend me his laptop.
⑤ I breathed deeply to stay calm.

10 우리말과 같도록 주어진 <조건>에 맞게 영작하시오.

물 없이 사는 것은 불가능하다.

<조건>
1. 가주어 it을 사용하시오.
2. impossible, live, without을 포함하시오.
3. 7단어로 쓰시오.

= _____

11 다음 중 밑줄 친 부분이 어법상 어색한 것은?

① Kevin was happy to see his cousins.
② It is satisfying to have my own garden.
③ Mr. Smith will buy a house to live.
④ Everyone needs a good friend to talk to.
⑤ I told my brother to stop crying.

[12-13] 다음 글을 읽고 주어진 질문에 답하시오.

Dr. Williams,

My name is Lucy, and I have a question ⓐto ask. I lost my friend's favorite book, so she was very angry. (A) I don't know what to say to her. I would like to ask for your advice. What should I do?

Sincerely,
Lucy

12 위 글의 밑줄 친 ⓐ의 용법과 다른 것은?

① Jill's dream is to become a comedian.
② It is time to open the presents.
③ There isn't any juice to drink.
④ Italy is a beautiful country to visit.
⑤ The teacher needs a piece of chalk to write with.

13 위 글의 밑줄 친 (A)와 의미가 같도록 빈칸에 알맞은 말을 쓰시오.

= I don't know _____ _____
_____ _____ to her.

[14-15] 우리말과 같도록 괄호 안의 말을 알맞게 배열하시오.

14

> 태양으로부터 너의 눈을 보호할 약간의 방법들이 있다. (eyes, some, to, ways, your, protect)

= There are _____

_____ from the sun.

15

> 나는 오랜 친구로부터 편지를 받아서 놀랐다. (letter, receive, a, surprised, to)

= I was _____

from an old friend.

16 다음 중 어법상 어색한 것은?

① Mr. Jones had his son pick up the trash.
② We heard someone ask for help.
③ My sister let me wear her dress yesterday.
④ Did you see Eric painting the fence?
⑤ That TV show always makes me laughing.

17 다음 빈칸에 들어갈 말이 순서대로 짝지어진 것은?

> · Birds build nests to live _____.
> · I need a fork to eat _____.

① in – to   ② in – with   ③ at – to
④ on – to   ⑤ on – with

[18-19] 다음 글을 읽고 주어진 질문에 답하시오.

> Tigers are excellent hunters. They use their senses ⓐto find other animals in the jungle. When a tiger finds its prey, it gets close enough and then attacks. (A) 그것은 그 동물을 붙잡을 날카로운 이빨을 가지고 있다. (sharp teeth, the animal, grab) Nothing can escape from those teeth.
>
> *prey 먹이, 사냥감

18 위 글의 밑줄 친 ⓐ의 쓰임과 같은 것을 모두 고르시오.

① She called the police to report the accident.
② The students were sad to graduate from middle school.
③ This river is dangerous to swim in.
④ Dustin must be foolish to believe the jokes.
⑤ He turned on the computer to shop online.

19 위 글의 밑줄 친 우리말 (A)와 같도록 괄호 안의 말을 활용하여 문장을 완성하시오.

= It _____.

20 다음 빈칸에 공통으로 들어갈 알맞은 것은?

> · My cat is _____ heavy to jump on the table.
> · Luna was _____ upset to speak with anyone.

① so   ② too   ③ enough
④ such   ⑤ that

21 다음 대화에 나온 표현을 활용하여 빈칸에 알맞은 말을 쓰시오.

> *Linda*: I couldn't understand what you said. Could you speak more slowly?
> *Brian* : Oh, sorry. I'll try.

→ Linda asked Brian _____ _____
_____ _____.

22 주어진 문장의 밑줄 친 to부정사와 용법이 같은 것은?

> There are some apples <u>to eat</u> on the table.

① I'm going to London <u>to visit</u> Buckingham Palace.
② Nate went to the hospital <u>to see</u> a doctor.
③ I decided not <u>to spend</u> too much money.
④ Lisa has a lot of nice shoes <u>to wear</u>.
⑤ Our team expects <u>to win</u> the final game.

23 to부정사를 이용하여 다음 두 문장을 한 문장으로 연결하시오.

> · Harin bought a new doll.
> · She will play with it.

→ Harin bought _____.

[24-25] 다음 두 문장의 의미가 같도록 문장을 완성하시오.

24

> Some snakes are so poisonous that they can kill people.
> = Some snakes are _____
> _____.

25

> The room was so dark that I couldn't read the magazine.
> = The room was _____
> _____.

26 다음 밑줄 친 to부정사의 용법이 같은 것끼리 묶인 것은?

> ⓐ Regina didn't have time <u>to eat</u> lunch.
> ⓑ It is dangerous <u>to touch</u> some jellyfish.
> ⓒ Evan didn't bring a book <u>to read</u> on the plane.
> ⓓ This is a great apartment <u>to live</u> in.
> ⓔ I stayed up late <u>to study</u> for the final exam.

① ⓐ, ⓑ, ⓒ   ② ⓐ, ⓒ, ⓓ   ③ ⓑ, ⓒ, ⓓ
④ ⓑ, ⓓ, ⓔ   ⑤ ⓒ, ⓓ, ⓔ

27 우리말과 같도록 괄호 안의 말을 활용하여 빈칸에 쓰시오.

> Jerry는 제시간에 그의 숙제를 끝내서 기뻤다.
> (finish, homework)

= Jerry was glad _____ _____

_____ _____ on time.

30 다음 중 밑줄 친 부분이 어법상 어색한 것은?

① Isn't it easy <u>for</u> you to make new friends?

② It was polite <u>of</u> them to listen to my speech patiently.

③ It was nice <u>for</u> you to send me the flowers.

④ This game is too difficult <u>for</u> him to play.

⑤ It is very selfish <u>of</u> her to act like that.

[28-29] 다음 대화를 읽고 주어진 질문에 답하시오.

> *Beth*: (A) 민호는 영어를 어떻게 말하는지 배우기 위해 미국에 갈 예정이야. (speak)
> *Jisu* : Which city is he going to stay in?
> *Beth*: He is planning to stay in New York for three months.
> *Jisu* : Really? I'm so jealous ⓐto hear that!
> *Beth*: I hope Minho learns a lot.

28 위 대화의 밑줄 친 우리말 (A)와 같도록 괄호 안의 동사를 활용하여 빈칸에 쓰시오.

= Minho is going to America to learn

_____ _____ _____

_____.

[31-32] 우리말과 같도록 괄호 안의 말을 배열할 때 다섯 번째에 오는 것을 쓰시오.

31

> 우리가 다른 사람들을 존중하는 것은 중요하다. (to, important, others, is, respect, for, it, us)

→ _____

32

> 그는 먹을 맛있는 무언가를 요리할 것이다. (cook, delicious, will, something, eat, he, to)

→ _____

29 위 대화의 밑줄 친 ⓐ의 쓰임과 같은 것은?

① Jim called me <u>to invite</u> me to his birthday party.

② Kate was depressed <u>to lose</u> her favorite necklace.

③ Lola must be a genius <u>to come</u> up with that idea.

④ We went to the library <u>to borrow</u> some books.

⑤ She grew up <u>to be</u> the first female pilot.

33 다음 빈칸에 들어갈 말이 나머지 넷과 <u>다른</u> 것은?

① It is impossible _____ her to keep the secret.

② It is hard _____ me to write a diary every day.

③ It is important _____ children to read good books.

④ It was kind _____ him to help us find the way.

⑤ It was easy _____ me to solve math problems.

34 다음 문장과 의미가 같은 것은?

> Robert sings well enough to become a singer.

① Robert sings too well to become a singer.
② Robert sings so well that he can become a singer.
③ Robert sings so well that he can't become a singer.
④ Robert doesn't sing so well that he can become a singer.
⑤ Robert doesn't sing too well to become a singer.

[35-36] 다음 빈칸에 알맞은 말을 넣어 대화를 완성하시오.

35

> A: It was foolish _____ _____
>   to tell Fred everything.
> B: I know. I feel really stupid.

36

> A: Did you decide _____ _____
>   _____?
> B: I decided to move on March 9.

37 다음 빈칸에 들어갈 말이 나머지 넷과 다른 것은?

① She is small _____ to hide in the closet.
② The wind is strong _____ to fly a kite.
③ Jason is tall _____ to join the basketball club.
④ Marie is _____ scared to open her eyes.
⑤ The curtain is not long _____ to cover this window.

38 다음 밑줄 친 to부정사의 용법이 같은 것끼리 묶인 것은?

> ⓐ We should avoid fast foods <u>to stay</u> healthy.
> ⓑ Alex was satisfied <u>to pass</u> the test.
> ⓒ My goal is <u>to win</u> the competition.
> ⓓ It is difficult <u>to see</u> snow in Africa.
> ⓔ There are many rules <u>to follow</u> in baseball.
> ⓕ My sister saved $1,000 <u>to buy</u> a violin.

① ⓐ, ⓑ, ⓕ ② ⓐ, ⓒ, ⓔ ③ ⓑ, ⓒ, ⓓ
④ ⓑ, ⓓ, ⓕ ⑤ ⓒ, ⓔ, ⓕ

CHAPTER 7
동명사

I enjoy **playing** the guitar. 나는 기타를 연주하는 것을 즐긴다.

'연주하다'라는 의미의 동사 play를 V-ing형으로 바꿔 '연주하는 것'이라는 의미를 나타냈어요. 이렇게 동사가 V-ing형으로 쓰여 문장 안에서 명사 역할을 하는 것을 **동명사**라고 해요.

기출로 적중 POINT

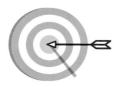

내신 100점 적중!
기출 출제율

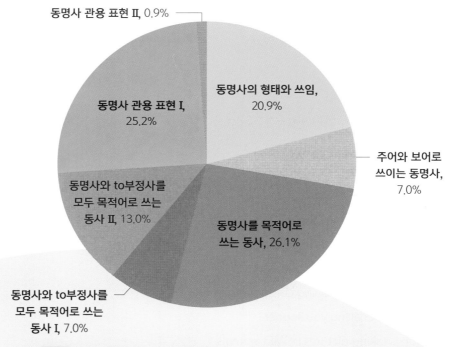

동명사 관용 표현 II, 0.9%

동명사의 형태와 쓰임, 20.9%

동명사 관용 표현 I, 25.2%

주어와 보어로 쓰이는 동명사, 7.0%

동명사와 to부정사를 모두 목적어로 쓰는 동사 II, 13.0%

동명사를 목적어로 쓰는 동사, 26.1%

동명사와 to부정사를 모두 목적어로 쓰는 동사 I, 7.0%

TOP 1 **동명사를 목적어로 쓰는 동사 (26.1%)**
특정 동사 뒤에 동명사가 목적어로 쓰이는 경우를 묻는 문제가 자주 출제된다.

TOP 2 **동명사 관용 표현 I (25.2%)**
전치사의 목적어로 동명사를 쓰는 관용 표현을 묻는 문제가 자주 출제된다.

TOP 3 **동명사의 형태와 쓰임 (20.9%)**
동명사의 형태와 쓰임을 묻는 문제가 자주 출제된다.

동명사의 형태와 쓰임

정답 p.20

1. **동명사는 V-ing의 형태로 문장 안에서 명사처럼 주어·보어·목적어로 쓰이며, '~하는 것, ~하기'의 의미이다.**

주어	**Writing** an excellent poem is difficult. 훌륭한 시를 쓰는 것은 어렵다.
보어	My hobby is **watching** soccer games. 나의 취미는 축구 경기를 보는 것이다.
동사의 목적어	Cam **enjoys** **jogging** in the morning. Cam은 아침에 조깅하는 것을 즐긴다.
전치사의 목적어	Sujin is good **at** **cooking** Italian food. 수진이는 이탈리아 음식을 요리하는 것을 잘한다.

2. **동명사의 부정형은 동명사 앞에 not을 붙여 만든다.**

Not sleeping enough makes us tired. 충분히 자지 않는 것은 우리를 피곤하게 만든다.

I regret **not apologizing** to my friend. 나는 나의 친구에게 사과하지 않은 것을 후회한다.

연습문제 밑줄 친 동명사의 쓰임을 <보기>에서 골라 그 기호를 쓰시오.

<보기>   ⓐ 주어   ⓑ 보어   ⓒ 동사의 목적어   ⓓ 전치사의 목적어

1 My dog started <u>digging</u> a hole.　　　　　[　　　]

2 <u>Drinking</u> enough water is necessary.　　　[　　　]

3 I kept <u>waiting</u> for her at the bus stop.　　　[　　　]

4 My favorite activity is <u>playing</u> computer games.　　[　　　]

5 I'm sorry for not <u>calling</u> you sooner.　　　[　　　]

6 Mark's job is <u>taking</u> pictures of wild animals.　　[　　　]

7 <u>Knitting</u> a sweater takes a lot of time.　　　[　　　]

8 I'm interested in <u>learning</u> new instruments.　　[　　　]

기출 적중문제

다음 문장에서 어법상 어색한 부분을 찾아 쓰고 바르게 고쳐 쓰시오.

> Go to bed before midnight is good for your skin.

_____ → _____

기출로적중 POINT 2 주어와 보어로 쓰이는 동명사

정답 p.20

1. **동명사는 주어로 쓰이며, 이때 항상 단수 취급한다. 주어로 쓰인 동명사는 to부정사로 바꿔 쓸 수 있다.**

   Studying foreign languages **is** not easy. 외국어를 공부하는 것은 쉽지 않다.
   = **To study** foreign languages **is** not easy.
   = **It** is not easy **to study** foreign languages.

2. **동명사는 보어로 쓰이며, 이때 to부정사로 바꿔 쓸 수 있다.**

   My plan is **visiting** grandpa on Friday. 나의 계획은 금요일에 할아버지를 방문하는 것이다.
   = My plan is **to visit** grandpa on Friday.

연습문제 다음 두 문장의 의미가 같도록 동명사를 이용하여 문장을 완성하시오.

1 It is exciting to watch a magic show.
   = _____ exciting.

2 Jacob's hobby is to collect movie posters.
   = Jacob's hobby is _____ .

3 It is good to exercise regularly.
   = _____ good.

4 It is difficult to break old habits.
   = _____ difficult.

5 My dream is to meet my favorite actor.
   = My dream is _____ .

6 It is really interesting to explore a new city.
   = _____ really interesting.

7 Jenna's goal is to read more books this year.
   = Jenna's goal is _____ .

기출 적중문제 ◎

> 주어로 쓰인 동명사는 항상 단수 취급해요.

우리말과 같도록 괄호 안의 말을 활용하여 영작하시오. (단, 5단어로 쓰시오.)

좋은 친구들이 있는 것은 중요하다. (have, good, be)

= _____

다음 동사는 동명사를 목적어로 쓴다.

enjoy	finish	avoid	keep	mind	give up	imagine
stop	quit	practice	deny	suggest	put off	postpone

Eunji **finished** baking the cupcakes. 은지는 컵케이크를 굽는 것을 끝냈다.

The thief **denied** stealing the money. 그 도둑은 돈을 훔친 것을 부인했다.

We had to **put off** going on a field trip. 우리는 현장 학습을 가는 것을 미뤄야 했다.

연습문제 A 우리말과 같도록 괄호 안의 말을 활용하여 문장을 완성하시오.

1 나는 재즈 음악을 듣는 것을 즐긴다. (enjoy, listen)

= I _____ to jazz music.

2 나의 남동생은 나의 안경을 숨긴 것을 부인했다. (hide, deny)

= My brother _____ my glasses.

3 그들은 왜 부산으로 이사하기로 결심했니? (decide, move)

= Why did they _____ to Busan?

4 나는 혼잡 시간대에 버스를 타는 것을 피한다. (avoid, take)

= I _____ the bus during rush hour.

5 치과에 가는 것을 미루지 마라. (go, put off)

= Don't _____ to the dentist.

6 한수는 마침내 그의 보고서를 쓰는 것을 끝냈다. (write, finish)

= Hansu finally _____ his report.

7 나의 책상 위에 있는 그 시계는 작동하는 것을 멈췄다. (work, stop)

= The clock on my desk _____.

8 너는 어느 나라를 가장 방문하기를 원하니? (visit, want)

= Which country do you _____ most?

9 Erica는 그 아름다운 풍경에 대해 생각하는 것을 계속했다. (keep, think)

= Erica _____ about the beautiful scenery.

10 아이들은 그들의 친구들과 함께 밖에서 놀 필요가 있다. (need, play)

= Children _____ outside with their friends.

11 나는 때때로 해변 옆에서 사는 것을 상상한다. (imagine, live)

= I sometimes ＿＿＿＿＿＿＿＿＿＿＿＿＿ by the beach.

12 주말마다 운동하는 것을 포기하지 말자. (give up, exercise)

= Let's not ＿＿＿＿＿＿＿＿＿＿＿＿＿ on the weekends.

13 너는 너의 시간을 낭비하는 것을 그만둬야 한다. (waste, quit)

= You should ＿＿＿＿＿＿＿＿＿＿＿＿＿ your time.

14 너는 얼마나 오래 여기에 머무르기를 예상하니? (stay, expect)

= How long do you ＿＿＿＿＿＿＿＿＿＿＿＿＿ here?

15 그 의사는 건강한 음식을 먹는 것을 제안했다. (eat, suggest)

= The doctor ＿＿＿＿＿＿＿＿＿＿＿＿＿ healthy foods.

16 James는 항상 저녁 식사 이후에 플루트를 연주하는 것을 연습한다. (practice, play)

= James always ＿＿＿＿＿＿＿＿＿＿＿＿＿ the flute after dinner.

연습문제 B 밑줄 친 부분이 어법상 맞으면 O를 쓰고, 틀리면 바르게 고쳐 쓰시오.

1 I put off <u>to do</u> my homework. → ＿＿＿＿＿＿＿

2 We would like <u>tasting</u> the new dish. → ＿＿＿＿＿＿＿

3 Do you mind <u>closing</u> the window? → ＿＿＿＿＿＿＿

4 Ginny promises <u>keeping</u> my secret. → ＿＿＿＿＿＿＿

5 Does she enjoy <u>to ride</u> the roller coaster? → ＿＿＿＿＿＿＿

6 We postponed <u>to go</u> on a summer vacation. → ＿＿＿＿＿＿＿

7 The farmer is planning <u>to sell</u> the peaches. → ＿＿＿＿＿＿＿

8 The kids denied <u>eating</u> the ice cream. → ＿＿＿＿＿＿＿

9 William's dad gave up <u>to smoke</u> for his children. → ＿＿＿＿＿＿＿

10 Jessica imagined <u>to win</u> the lottery. → ＿＿＿＿＿＿＿

기출 적중문제 🎯

다음 중 어법상 <u>어색한</u> 것은?

① I'll avoid making the same mistake again.

② Nick doesn't enjoy watching TV.

③ The students wish going home early.

④ Do you mind turning off the heater?

⑤ He suggested going to the theater.

동명사와 to부정사를 모두 목적어로 쓰는 동사 Ⅰ

정답 p.21

다음 동사는 동명사와 to부정사를 모두 목적어로 쓰며, 둘 중 무엇을 써도 의미가 달라지지 않는다.

| like | love | hate | prefer | begin | start | continue |

George **likes shopping** online. George는 온라인으로 쇼핑하는 것을 좋아한다.
= George **likes to shop** online.

It **began snowing** heavily today. 오늘 눈이 많이 오기 시작했다.
= It **began to snow** heavily today.

연습문제 괄호 안에서 알맞은 것을 <u>모두</u> 고르시오.

1 Mr. Brown doesn't like (waiting / to wait) in line.

2 Why don't we give up (using / to use) plastic cups?

3 I've always wanted (seeing / to see) an aurora.

4 The baby started (crying / to cry) at 2 A.M.

5 What are you planning (doing / to do) this weekend?

6 We'll begin (doing / to do) the history project soon.

7 Jason hates (waking / to wake) up early in the morning.

8 I practiced (speaking / to speak) Chinese with my friend.

9 My puppies love (spending / to spend) time in the park.

10 Noah enjoys (meeting / to meet) new people.

11 I prefer (studying / to study) alone in my room.

12 The scientists will continue (working / to work) with each other.

기출 적중문제

다음 대화의 빈칸에 공통으로 들어갈 알맞은 것은?

> *A*: Why do you like _____ leather bags? It
>   would be cheaper to buy them.
> *B*: Actually, I enjoy _____ them. It's really fun.

① make　　② made　　③ making
④ to make　　⑤ to making

동명사와 to부정사를 모두 목적어로 쓰는 동사 Ⅱ

정답 p.21

다음 동사는 동명사와 to부정사를 모두 목적어로 쓰며, 둘 중 무엇을 쓰는지에 따라 의미가 달라진다.

forget	+ 동명사	(과거에) ~한 것을 잊다	He **forget sending** the letter. 그는 그 편지를 보낸 것을 잊었다.
	+ to부정사	(미래에) ~할 것을 잊다	He **forgot to send** the letter. 그는 그 편지를 보낼 것을 잊었다.
remember	+ 동명사	(과거에) ~한 것을 기억하다	Do you **remember calling** him? 너는 그에게 전화한 것을 기억하니?
	+ to부정사	(미래에) ~할 것을 기억하다	Do you **remember to call** him? 너는 그에게 전화할 것을 기억하니?
regret	+ 동명사	~한 것을 후회하다	I **regret telling** you my secret. 나는 너에게 나의 비밀을 말해준 것을 후회한다.
	+ to부정사	~하게 되어 유감이다	I **regret to tell** you the news. 나는 너에게 그 소식을 말하게 되어 유감이다.
try	+ 동명사	(시험 삼아) ~해보다	Sally **tried writing** a fantasy novel. Sally는 판타지 소설을 써봤다.
	+ to부정사	~하려고 노력하다	Sally **tried to write** a fantasy novel. Sally는 판타지 소설을 쓰려고 노력했다.

(Tip) 「stop + 동명사」(~하는 것을 멈추다)에서 동명사는 stop의 목적어이며, 「stop + to부정사」(~하기 위해 멈추다)에서 to부정사는 부사적 용법으로 쓰여 목적을 나타낸다.

Luke **stopped asking** questions. Luke는 질문하는 것을 멈췄다.
Luke **stopped to ask** questions. Luke는 질문하기 위해 멈췄다.

연습문제 A 우리말과 같도록 괄호 안의 말을 활용하여 문장을 완성하시오.

1 나는 불을 끈 것을 기억한다. (remember, turn)
= I _____ off the lights.

2 정문을 잠그는 것을 잊지 마라. (forget, lock)
= Don't _____ the front door.

3 새 피자집에서 주문해보자. (try, order)
= Let's _____ from a new pizza place.

4 민우는 그의 남동생과 싸운 것을 후회했다. (regret, fight)
= Minwoo _____ with his brother.

5 Matthew는 금요일까지 그의 숙제를 끝내려고 노력했다. (try, finish)

= Matthew _____ his homework by Friday.

6 내일 약간의 식료품을 살 것을 기억해라. (remember, buy)

= _____ some groceries tomorrow.

7 우리는 너에게 그 사고에 대해 말하게 되어 유감이다. (regret, tell)

= We _____ you about the accident.

8 나는 내가 가장 좋아하는 가수를 본 것을 결코 잊지 않을 것이다. (forget, see)

= I'll never _____ my favorite singer.

연습문제 B 괄호 안의 동사를 알맞은 형태로 바꿔 문장을 완성하시오.

1 I don't mind _____ my snacks with you. (share)

2 You should avoid _____ alone at night. (walk)

3 Gina forgot _____ off the oven and burned the bread. (turn)

4 Jeff forgot _____ me before, so he asked my name again. (meet)

5 Did you finish _____ the picture? (draw)

6 Claire tried _____ her dog down, but she couldn't. (calm)

7 Kelly regrets _____ so much money last month. (spend)

8 Do you remember _____ France when you were young? (visit)

9 I tried _____ soap to remove the stain, and it worked. (use)

10 Remember _____ your teeth before you go to bed. (brush)

기출 적중문제

다음 우리말을 영작한 것 중 <u>어색한</u> 것은?

① 나는 그 결정을 한 것을 후회한다.

= I regret making that decision.

② 나의 여동생은 탄산음료를 마시는 것을 멈췄다.

= My sister stopped drinking soda.

③ 그 소년은 처음으로 자전거를 타봤다.

= The boy tried riding a bicycle for the first time.

④ 나는 나의 전화기를 침대 위에 둔 것을 잊었다.

= I forgot putting my phone on the bed.

⑤ Joseph은 선물을 숨긴 것을 기억했다.

= Joseph remembered to hide the present.

POINT 4-1 동명사 관용 표현 I

다음은 전치사의 목적어로 동명사를 쓰는 관용 표현이다.

be good at + V-ing ~하는 것을 잘하다
succeed in + V-ing ~하는 데 성공하다
think of + V-ing ~하는 것을 생각하다
be afraid of + V-ing ~하는 것을 무서워하다
thank … for + V-ing ~에 대해 …에게 감사하다
be used to + V-ing ~하는 데 익숙하다
look forward to + V-ing ~하는 것을 기대하다
on + V-ing ~하자마자

be bad at + V-ing ~하는 것을 못하다
be interested in + V-ing ~하는 것에 흥미가 있다
be tired of + V-ing ~하는 것에 싫증이 나다
feel like + V-ing ~하고 싶다
be sorry for[about] + V-ing ~에 대해 미안해하다
get used to + V-ing ~하는 데 익숙해지다
keep[prevent] … from + V-ing …가 ~하지 못하게 하다
by + V-ing ~함으로써

I **thanked** Ben **for inviting** me to the party. 나는 나를 파티에 초대한 것에 대해 Ben에게 감사했다.
She's **looking forward to meeting** her friends. 그녀는 그녀의 친구들을 만나는 것을 기대하고 있다.
On arriving at the airport, I called my parents. 공항에 도착하자마자, 나는 나의 부모님께 전화했다.

연습문제 A 우리말과 같도록 괄호 안의 동사를 활용하여 문장을 완성하시오.

1 나는 너를 보는 것을 기대한다. (see)
= I _____ you.

2 대부분의 사람들은 실패하는 것을 무서워한다. (fail)
= Most people _____ .

3 Benny는 이름을 기억하는 것을 못한다. (remember)
= Benny _____ names.

4 너는 규칙적으로 운동함으로써 체중을 줄일 수 있다. (exercise)
= You can lose weight _____ regularly.

5 나는 어제 나의 개를 돌본 것에 대해 Sam에게 감사했다. (take)
= I _____ care of my dog yesterday.

6 곰은 나무를 오르는 것을 잘한다. (climb)
= Bears _____ trees.

7 Thomas는 나의 생일을 잊은 것에 대해 미안해했다. (forget)
= Thomas _____ my birthday.

8 하나는 달콤한 무언가를 먹고 싶었다. (eat)
= Hana _____ something sweet.

9 우리는 우리의 농장에서 사과를 키우는 것을 생각했다. (grow)

= We _____ apples on our farm.

10 그녀의 부모님을 보자마자, 그 아기는 행복하게 웃었다. (see)

= _____ her parents, the baby smiled happily.

11 그는 작은 마을에 사는 것에 싫증이 난다. (live)

= He _____ in a small town.

12 그 소음은 내가 시험에 집중하지 못하게 했다. (focus)

= The noise _____ on the test.

13 Alex는 다른 문화에 대해 배우는 것에 흥미가 있다. (learn)

= Alex _____ about other cultures.

14 라이트 형제는 비행기를 발명하는 데 성공했다. (invent)

= The Wright brothers _____ the airplane.

연습문제 B 다음 빈칸에 알맞은 말을 <보기>에서 한 번씩만 골라 알맞은 형태로 바꿔 쓰시오.

<보기> carry solve do use swim study arrive talk

1 I'm afraid of _____ in the sea.

2 Thank you for _____ the heavy boxes for me.

3 We can see Mars by _____ a telescope.

4 Jenny doesn't feel like _____ her homework.

5 Sorry for _____ so late for the class.

6 Mason is interested in _____ Korean history.

7 Sherlock Holmes is good at _____ mysteries.

8 Colin can't get used to _____ in front of a lot of people.

기출 적중문제

우리말과 같도록 괄호 안의 말을 활용하여 빈칸에 쓰시오.

우리는 플라스틱 병을 재활용함으로써 지구를 보호할 수 있다.
(recycle, plastic bottles)

= We can protect the earth _____ _____

_____ _____ .

기출로적중 POINT 4-2 동명사 관용 표현 II

정답 p.21

다음은 동명사를 쓰는 관용 표현이다.

go + V-ing ~하러 가다
It's no use + V-ing ~해도 소용없다
spend + 시간/돈 + V-ing ~하는 데 시간/돈을 쓰다
cannot help + V-ing ~하지 않을 수 없다
(= cannot but + 동사원형)

be busy + V-ing ~하느라 바쁘다
be worth + V-ing ~할 가치가 있다
have trouble + V-ing ~하는 데 어려움을 겪다
How[What] about + V-ing ~? ~하는 게 어때?
(= What do you say to + V-ing ~?)

He is **having trouble** finding a perfect house. 그는 완벽한 집을 찾는 데 어려움을 겪고 있다.
How[What] about watching a movie tonight? 오늘 밤에 영화를 보는 게 어때?

연습문제 우리말과 같도록 괄호 안의 말을 활용하여 문장을 완성하시오.

1 Lily는 어젯밤에 빨래를 하느라 바빴다. (do)
= Lily _____ the laundry last night.

2 나는 크루아상을 위한 요리법을 따르는 데 어려움을 겪었다. (follow)
= I _____ the recipe for croissants.

3 나는 그 과학 보고서를 쓰는 데 세 시간을 썼다. (three hours, write)
= I _____ the science report.

4 저 오래된 텔레비전을 수리해도 소용없다. (repair)
= _____ that old television.

5 좋은 매트리스는 살 가치가 있다. (buy)
= A good mattress _____ .

6 Adam은 그 호수로 주말마다 낚시하러 간다. (fish)
= Adam _____ every weekend to the lake.

7 나는 그녀의 용기를 존경하지 않을 수 없다. (respect)
= I _____ her courage.

기출 적중문제 🎯

다음 문장에서 어법상 어색한 부분을 찾아 쓰고 바르게 고쳐 쓰시오.

How about wear a cat costume on Halloween?

_____ → _____

Ⓐ 다음 그림을 보고 <보기>의 말을 활용하여 문장을 완성하시오.

<보기>	play badminton	touch a spider	eat chocolate cake
	take a nap	become a violinist	plant flowers

1

2

3

4

5

6

1 _____ is scary for Linda.

2 Elena's dream is _____ .

3 Jinho enjoys _____ with his sister.

4 My cat likes _____ on the sofa.

5 Molly is planning _____ in her garden.

6 _____ makes me happy.

Ⓑ 밑줄 친 부분이 어법상 맞으면 O를 쓰고, 틀리면 바르게 고쳐 쓰시오.

1 Catching thieves <u>are</u> Mr. Holt's job.　→ _____

2 I'm sorry for <u>not answering</u> the phone.　→ _____

3 Jack prefers <u>get</u> up early in the morning.　→ _____

4 Reading books <u>is</u> a great way to relax.　→ _____

5 We can't imagine <u>having not</u> electricity.　→ _____

6 <u>Plays</u> fair is the most important thing in sports.　→ _____

C 괄호 안의 동사를 알맞은 형태로 바꿔 문장을 완성하시오.

1 Carl enjoys _____ great musicals. (watch)

2 Never give up _____ your dreams. (follow)

3 Susan wants _____ Paris with her family someday. (visit)

4 You'd better avoid _____ that old milk. (drink)

5 The city had to put off _____ the festival. (hold)

6 Minsu tried _____ awake during the biology class. (stay)

7 Let's practice _____ for our contest next week. (dance)

8 I would like _____ chicken salad and soup. (order)

9 Ronald stopped _____ in order to ask directions. (walk)

10 My parents promised _____ me a new computer. (buy)

11 I forgot _____ the library book and missed the due date. (borrow)

D 우리말과 같도록 괄호 안의 말을 활용하여 문장을 완성하시오.

1 Gloria는 항상 차에서 자는 데 어려움을 겪는다. (sleep)
= Gloria always _____ in a car.

2 너는 해외로 여행하는 것을 기대하고 있니? (travel)
= Are you _____ abroad?

3 Chris는 프랑스어를 배우는 것에 흥미가 있다. (learn)
= Chris _____ French.

4 나는 같은 노래를 반복해서 듣는 것에 싫증이 난다. (listen)
= I _____ to the same song over and over again.

5 회사들은 새 기술을 개발하는 데 많은 돈을 쓴다. (lots of money, develop)
= Companies _____ new technologies.

6 북극곰은 추운 날씨에서 사는 데 익숙하다. (live)
= Polar bears _____ in cold weather.

7 우리는 우리를 위해 저녁 식사를 준비한 것에 대해 Jamie에게 감사했다. (prepare)
= We _____ dinner for us.

중간·기말고사 실전 문제

[1-3] 다음 빈칸에 들어갈 알맞은 것을 고르시오.

1

_____ the mountain is great exercise.

① Climb ② Climbed
③ Climbs ④ To climbing
⑤ Climbing

2

The man's job is _____ mystery novels.

① write ② writes
③ to wrote ④ writing
⑤ written

3

Mary enjoys _____ cold coffee even in winter.

① drink ② drinking
③ drank ④ to drink
⑤ to drinking

4 우리말과 같도록 괄호 안의 동사를 활용하여 빈칸에 쓰시오.

안전벨트를 매지 않는 것은 매우 위험하다. (wear)

= _____ _____ a seat belt is very dangerous.

5 다음 중 어법상 어색한 것은?

① Do you hate riding a bicycle?
② Beth avoided answering the question.
③ I want to apologize for my behavior.
④ Do you mind holding the door for me?
⑤ They finished to clean their classroom.

6 다음 글의 빈칸에 들어갈 말이 순서대로 짝지어진 것은?

Michael likes daydreaming. Today, he imagined _____ in the sky like a bird. He thought of _____ wings on his back, and it seemed wonderful.

① flying – to have ② to fly – having
③ flying – having ④ to fly – have
⑤ flying – have

7 다음 빈칸에 들어갈 수 있는 것을 <u>모두</u> 고르시오.

Yejin continued _____ the Internet until she found useful information.

① search ② searched
③ searching ④ to search
⑤ to searching

8 다음 대화의 빈칸에 들어갈 알맞은 것은?

> A: I regret _____ my little brother that Santa Claus doesn't exist.
> B: Oh, was he disappointed?
> A: Yes. He even cried!

① tell ② told ③ to tell
④ telling ⑤ to telling

9 다음 중 어법상 어색한 것은?

① Monica keeps losing her earrings.
② He began to sing with his friend.
③ I suggest not to take the subway now.
④ How about going to the mall tonight?
⑤ The fence prevents people from entering the garden.

10 주어진 문장의 밑줄 친 부분과 쓰임이 다른 것은?

> You should stop biting your nails.

① I will quit eating too much junk food.
② My dream is drawing cartoons for children.
③ Ben's team is winning the soccer game.
④ Snowboarding is a fun winter activity.
⑤ Sora records her feelings by writing a diary.

11 다음 빈칸에 들어갈 말로 어색한 것은?

> Sandra _____ swimming in the pool.

① loves ② plans ③ imagined
④ stopped ⑤ enjoys

12 다음 대화의 빈칸에 들어갈 말이 순서대로 짝지어진 것은?

> A: Don't forget _____ your umbrella when you go out. It's going to rain in the afternoon.
> B: OK. Thank you for _____ me.

① to take – reminded
② taking – reminding
③ to take – reminding
④ taking – to remind
⑤ to take – to remind

13 다음 중 어법상 어색한 것은?

① Don't be afraid of trying new things.
② The child is not used to using chopsticks.
③ I couldn't but cry after watching the movie.
④ Joe was busy preparing for the exam all weekend.
⑤ Amy felt like to join the school band.

14 <보기>와 같이 다음 두 문장을 한 문장으로 연결하시오.

<보기>   I met Cindy at the library. I remember it.
→ *I remember meeting Cindy at the library.*

Emily saw the Queen of England. Emily will never forget it.

→ _____

_____

15 다음 중 밑줄 친 부분의 쓰임이 나머지 넷과 다른 것은?

① Our goal is reducing food waste.
② Janice's plan for the holiday is visiting her friend in Seoul.
③ Ms. White's job is editing magazine articles.
④ My mom is baking a pie for our family.
⑤ The key to success is believing in yourself.

16 우리말과 같도록 괄호 안의 말을 활용하여 빈칸에 쓰시오.

새 언어를 배우는 것은 많은 시간이 걸린다. (a new language, take)

= _____ _____ _____

_____ a lot of time.

17 다음 빈칸에 들어갈 말이 순서대로 짝지어진 것은?

· You shouldn't wear your sister's clothes without _____ her first.
· Luna finally succeeded in _____ the difficult math problem.

① to ask - to solve   ② asking - to solve
③ to ask - solving   ④ asking - solving
⑤ ask - solve

18 다음은 미나에 대한 정보를 나타낸 표이다. 표에 나온 표현을 활용하여 문장을 완성하시오.

What her dream is	be a fashion designer
What she likes	design new clothes
What she is good at	draw pictures, knit sweaters

(1) Mina's dream is _____

_____.

(2) Mina likes _____.

(3) Mina is good at _____

and _____.

19 우리말과 같도록 괄호 안의 말을 알맞게 배열하시오.

그 문제에 대해 언쟁해도 소용없다. (no, the, about, arguing, use, problem, it's)

= _____

20 다음 빈칸에 들어갈 말이 순서대로 짝지어진 것은?

> · I'm tired _____ to Lisa's complaints.
> · Why did you postpone _____ to Canada?

① listening – to move
② to listening – to move
③ of listening – moving
④ of listening – to move
⑤ to listening – moving

21 다음 중 어법상 바른 것의 개수는?

> ⓐ The man denied to steal the wallet.
> ⓑ Emma tried not to eat anything after 9 P.M.
> ⓒ I started take art lessons last month.
> ⓓ My uncle quit smoking for his health.
> ⓔ Most chefs prefer to use sharp knives.

① 1개   ② 2개   ③ 3개
④ 4개   ⑤ 5개

22 다음 글에 나온 표현을 활용하여 빈칸에 공통으로 들어갈 알맞은 말을 쓰시오.

> Lucas loves _____ the piano. He has played it since he was very little, so he is very good at _____ the piano.

[23-24] 다음 문장에서 어법상 어색한 부분을 찾아 쓰고 바르게 고쳐 쓰시오.

23

> What about to have a pajama party on Saturday?

_____ → _____

24

> I couldn't help feel excited about the news.

_____ → _____

25 다음 (A)~(C)에 들어갈 말이 바르게 짝지어진 것은?

> Yujin: I'm planning ___(A)___ a new phone.
> Lucy: Really? Why?
> Yujin: I'm having trouble ___(B)___ other people with this phone. Also, I can't check any new text messages.
> Lucy: That sounds inconvenient. I suggest ___(C)___ the newest model. It will work fine.

	(A)	(B)	(C)
①	to get	calling	buying
②	getting	to call	to buy
③	to get	calling	to buy
④	getting	calling	to buy
⑤	to get	to call	buying

26 다음 밑줄 친 ⓐ~ⓔ 중 어법상 어색한 것을 찾아 기호를 쓰고 바르게 고쳐 쓰시오.

- Her job is ⓐteaching music to children.
- Can you imagine ⓑlive on Mars?
- Reading these books ⓒhelp you understand world history.
- We are looking forward to ⓓvisit the aquarium.
- Dad had to put off ⓔwashing the car because it was raining.

(1) _____ → _____
(2) _____ → _____
(3) _____ → _____

27 다음 대화의 빈칸에 들어갈 말이 순서대로 짝지어진 것은?

A: Do you feel like _____ that roller coaster again?
B: Of course. It was very thrilling. On _____ at the end, I wanted to ride it again.

① ride – to arrive
② to ride – arriving
③ to ride – arrive
④ riding – arriving
⑤ riding – to arrive

28 다음 두 문장의 의미가 같도록 빈칸에 알맞은 말을 쓰시오.

It is important to wash your hands before eating.
= _____ _____ _____ before eating _____ important.

29 다음 중 짝지어진 두 문장의 의미가 다른 것은?

① Liam doesn't like to eat broccoli.
= Liam doesn't like eating broccoli.
② The angry man started shouting at me.
= The angry man started to shout at me.
③ Jisu prefers walking to school.
= Jisu prefers to walk to school.
④ I hate going outside when it's hot.
= I hate to go outside when it's hot.
⑤ Tim stopped to buy lemonade from the café.
= Tim stopped buying lemonade from the café.

30 다음 우리말을 영작할 때 빈칸에 들어갈 알맞은 것은?

나는 안경 없이 보는 데 어려움을 겪는다.
= I have trouble _____ without glasses.

① see
② seeing
③ saw
④ to see
⑤ seen

31 다음 밑줄 친 부분의 쓰임이 같은 것끼리 묶인 것은?

ⓐ The baby is afraid of sleeping alone.
ⓑ His goal is inventing something useful.
ⓒ Finishing this puzzle is impossible.
ⓓ My hobby is running along the river.
ⓔ My parents kept worrying about me.

① ⓐ, ⓑ
② ⓐ, ⓒ
③ ⓑ, ⓓ
④ ⓒ, ⓓ
⑤ ⓓ, ⓔ

32 우리말과 같도록 괄호 안의 말을 활용하여 문장을 완성하시오.

> 소방관들이 불을 끄려고 노력하고 있다. (try, put out)

= The firefighters are _____ a fire.

33 다음 우리말을 알맞게 영작한 것은?

> 나는 어젯밤에 너에게 전화한 것을 기억할 수 없다.

① I can't remember call you last night.
② I can't remember called you last night.
③ I can't remember to call you last night.
④ I can't remember calling you last night.
⑤ I can't remember to calling you last night.

34 다음 대화의 빈칸에 들어갈 알맞은 것은?

> *A*: I'm planning to go hiking tomorrow.
> *B*: Really? I heard that it's going to be cold. _____
> *A*: All right. Thanks!

① Forget to take your jacket.
② Don't forget taking your jacket.
③ Don't remember to take your jacket.
④ Remember taking your jacket.
⑤ Don't forget to take your jacket.

[35-36] 다음 두 문장의 의미가 같도록 빈칸에 알맞은 말을 쓰시오.

35

> How about taking a walk with me?
> = _____ _____ _____
> _____ _____ _____
> a walk with me?

36

> I cannot but wonder about my future.
> = I _____ _____ _____
> about my future.

37 다음 중 어법상 어색한 것끼리 묶인 것은?

> ⓐ Not skipping meals is important for your health.
> ⓑ Tina's goal is saving enough money to buy a new watch.
> ⓒ Do you prefer not putting ketchup on your burger?
> ⓓ Nicholas denied to break the vase on the table.
> ⓔ Taking care of animals require a lot of responsibility.

① ⓐ, ⓑ
② ⓐ, ⓔ
③ ⓑ, ⓒ
④ ⓒ, ⓓ
⑤ ⓓ, ⓔ

CHAPTER 8
분사

There is a sleeping puppy. 자고 있는 강아지가 있다.

'자다'라는 의미의 동사 sleep을 V-ing형으로 바꿔 '자고 있는'이라는 의미를 나타냈어요. 이렇게 동사가 V-ing형이나 p.p.형으로 쓰여 형용사 역할을 하는 것을 **분사**라고 해요.

기출로 적중 POINT

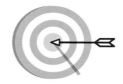

내신 100점 적중!
기출 출제율

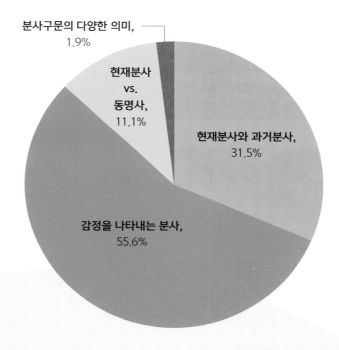

분사구문의 다양한 의미, 1.9%

현재분사 vs. 동명사, 11.1%

현재분사와 과거분사, 31.5%

감정을 나타내는 분사, 55.6%

TOP 1 **감정을 나타내는 분사 (55.6%)**
감정을 나타내는 분사의 의미에 따라 알맞은 형태를 쓰는 문제가 자주 출제된다.

TOP 2 **현재분사와 과거분사 (31.5%)**
현재분사와 과거분사를 구별하는 문제가 자주 출제된다.

TOP 3 **현재분사 vs. 동명사 (11.1%)**
문장 안의 V-ing형이 현재분사인지 동명사인지 구별하는 문제가 자주 출제된다.

분사는 V-ing(현재분사)나 p.p.(과거분사)의 형태로, 형용사처럼 명사를 수식하거나 문장 안에서 보어로 쓰인다.

❶ 분사가 단독으로 쓰이면 명사 앞에서 명사를 수식하고, 구를 이루어 쓰이면 명사 뒤에서 명사를 수식한다.

Look at that **dancing boy**. 춤을 추고 있는 저 소년을 봐라.

This is the **house built by my grandfather**. 이것은 나의 할아버지에 의해 지어진 집이다.

❷ 분사는 주어나 목적어를 보충 설명하는 보어로 쓰인다.

The play sounded **boring**. 그 연극은 지루하게 들렸다.
The audience got **bored**. 그 관중은 지루해졌다.

She heard **someone calling** her name. 그녀는 누군가가 그녀의 이름을 부르고 있는 것을 들었다.
She heard **her name called**. 그녀는 그녀의 이름이 불린 것을 들었다.

연습문제 밑줄 친 부분의 쓰임과 같은 것을 <보기>에서 골라 그 기호를 쓰시오.

<보기>   ⓐ Who is the shouting man?
          ⓑ Your dress looks amazing.

1 The boiling soup smells very nice.   [   ]
2 They sounded excited because of the snow.   [   ]
3 Can you see the shining stars in the sky?   [   ]
4 The girl wearing a pink hat looks like Jenny.   [   ]
5 I bought a used bicycle from my friend.   [   ]
6 David tried to open the locked door.   [   ]
7 Mary looked worried because she had an exam.   [   ]
8 We heard an interesting fact about the human brain. [   ]
9 The actor became known to many teenagers.   [   ]
10 Jinho saw his dog hiding under the sofa.   [   ]
11 I enjoyed reading the book written by Steve Jobs.   [   ]
12 Did you have the television fixed?   [   ]
13 All the soccer players felt tired after the game.   [   ]

기출로적중 POINT 2 · 현재분사와 과거분사

정답 p.23

1. 현재분사는 능동·진행의 의미를 나타내고, 과거분사는 수동·완료의 의미를 나타낸다.

현재분사(V-ing)	과거분사(p.p.)
능동(~하는)	수동(~된, 당한)
명사와 분사의 관계가 능동이면 현재분사를 쓴다.	명사와 분사의 관계가 수동이면 과거분사를 쓴다.
I heard the **surprising** news. 나는 그 놀라운 소식을 들었다. **The news** was **surprising**. 그 소식은 놀라웠다.	A **surprised** kid started to cry. 놀란 아이는 울기 시작했다. **The kid** was very **surprised**. 그 아이는 매우 놀랐다.
진행(~하고 있는)	완료(~된)
You should watch out for the **boiling** water. 너는 끓고 있는 물을 조심해야 한다.	He drank two cups of **boiled** water. 그는 끓여진 물 두 잔을 마셨다.

2. 현재분사는 진행시제를 만들기도 하고, 과거분사는 완료시제와 수동태를 만들기도 한다.

Brandon **is eating** lunch now. Brandon은 지금 점심을 먹고 있다.
I **have** just **finished** my homework. 나는 나의 숙제를 방금 끝냈다.
This artwork **was created** by Elizabeth. 이 예술작품은 Elizabeth에 의해 만들어졌다.

연습문제 A | 다음 그림을 보고 괄호 안의 말을 활용하여 문장을 완성하시오.

1 The _____ feels so sad. (cry, baby)

2 There is a _____ on the floor. (break, toy)

3 Junsu is fishing on the _____. (freeze, lake)

4 He can see some _____. (swim, in the lake, fish)

5 The _____ looks peaceful.
(sleep, boy)

6 The _____ can't wake him up.
(ring, alarm)

7 There is a _____. (sing, bird)

8 Susie is making a _____.
(cover with strawberry cream, cake)

연습문제 B 괄호 안의 동사를 알맞은 형태로 바꿔 빈칸에 쓰시오.

1 Have you tried the dish _____ bulgogi? (call)

2 Who is that girl _____ on the bench? (sit)

3 The birds are _____ south for the winter. (fly)

4 Susan bought a purse _____ in Italy. (make)

5 Justin has just _____ in the classroom. (arrive)

6 We woke up before 5 A.M. to see the _____ sun. (rise)

7 The Eiffel Tower was _____ in 1887. (build)

8 Let's keep the lights _____ on until midnight. (turn)

9 Would you like a doughnut _____ with chocolate? (fill)

10 You can see zebras _____ across the road in Africa. (walk)

11 The woman _____ a red scarf is my aunt. (wear)

12 Look at that building _____ by the earthquake. (damage)

기출 적중문제

다음 문장에서 어법상 어색한 부분을 찾아 쓰고 바르게 고쳐 쓰시오.

> Peter is living in the house painting yellow.

_____ → _____

현재분사는 능동의 의미를
나타내고, 과거분사는
수동의 의미를 나타내요.

감정을 나타내는 분사

현재분사와 과거분사로 감정을 나타낼 수 있다.

현재분사(~한 감정을 일으키는)		과거분사(~한 감정을 느끼는)	
surprising	놀라게 하는	surprised	놀란
amazing	놀라게 하는	amazed	놀란
worrying	걱정하게 하는	worried	걱정하는
interesting	흥미롭게 하는	interested	흥미로워하는
boring	지루하게 하는	bored	지루해하는
exciting	신이 나게 하는	excited	신이 난
pleasing	기쁘게 하는	pleased	기뻐하는
depressing	우울하게 하는	depressed	우울해하는
tiring	피곤하게 하는	tired	피곤해하는
moving	감동하게 하는	moved	감동한
touching	감동하게 하는	touched	감동한
shocking	충격을 주는	shocked	충격을 받은
confusing	혼란스럽게 하는	confused	혼란스러워하는
satisfying	만족스럽게 하는	satisfied	만족스러워하는
disappointing	실망스럽게 하는	disappointed	실망스러워하는
embarrassing	당황스럽게 하는	embarrassed	당황해하는
fascinating	황홀하게 하는	fascinated	황홀해하는

Lisa is taking an **interesting** class.
Lisa는 흥미로운 수업을 듣고 있다. (수업이 Lisa에게 흥미로운 감정을 일으킴)
Lisa is **interested** in the class. Lisa는 그 수업에 흥미로워한다. (Lisa가 수업에 흥미로운 감정을 느낌)

The play was **disappointing**. 그 연극은 실망스러웠다. (연극이 실망스러운 감정을 일으킴)
We were **disappointed** by the play. 우리는 그 연극에 실망했다. (우리가 연극에 실망스러운 감정을 느낌)

연습문제 A 괄호 안에서 알맞은 것을 고르시오.

1 The music festival was (exciting / excited).

2 He felt (depressing / depressed) about losing his watch.

3 Your painting looks really (amazing / amazed).

4 I find science experiments (interesting / interested).

5 My mother was (disappointing / disappointed) by my grades.

6 The history of Rome is (fascinating / fascinated).

7 Abby's letter was very (touching / touched).

8 Mr. Smith was (shocking / shocked) by the price of the car.

연습문제 B 괄호 안의 동사를 알맞은 형태로 바꿔 빈칸에 쓰시오.

1 (move)
① The principal's speech was _____.
② The students were _____ by his speech.

2 (tire)
① I was _____ because of the long journey.
② The long journey was _____.

3 (shock)
① The news was _____ to everyone.
② Everyone was _____ by the news.

4 (embarrass)
① Her mistake was _____.
② She felt _____ by her mistake.

5 (bore)
① Mark was _____ of playing board games.
② Playing board games was _____ for him.

6 (disappoint)
① The ending of the movie made us _____.
② The ending of the movie was very _____.

7 (satisfy)
① Sujin was _____ with the sandwich for lunch.
② The sandwich was _____.

8 (surprise)
① The magic performance was _____.
② The kids were _____ by the magic performance.

9 (confuse)
① The recipe for the macaron was _____.
② Melissa was _____ by the recipe.

기출 적중문제 ◎

다음 중 밑줄 친 부분이 어법상 어색한 것은?

① Having nice friends is pleasing.
② Today's soccer practice was tired.
③ Samantha feels depressed when it rains.
④ The tourist is confused about the directions.
⑤ The meal at the restaurant was disappointing.

> 감정을 일으키면 현재분사를 쓰고, 감정을 느끼면 과거분사를 써요.

현재분사 vs. 동명사

현재분사는 형용사 역할을 하고, 동명사는 명사 역할을 한다.

현재분사	동명사
능동·진행(~하는, ~하고 있는)의 의미로 명사를 수식한다. Don't wake the **sleeping** lion. 자고 있는 사자를 깨우지 마라.	명사의 용도·목적(~하기 위한)을 나타낸다. Did you bring your **sleeping** bag? 너는 너의 침낭을 가져왔니? (sleeping bag ≠ 자고 있는 가방)
보어로 쓰인다. **The book** sounds **interesting**. 그 책은 흥미롭게 들린다. We saw **a helicopter** **flying** above us. 우리는 헬리콥터가 우리 위에서 날고 있는 것을 봤다.	주어, 보어, 동사나 전치사의 목적어로 쓰인다. **Studying** Russian is difficult. 러시아어를 공부하는 것은 어렵다. His job is **teaching** science. 그의 직업은 과학을 가르치는 것이다. Lauren **enjoys** **jogging** in the park. Lauren은 공원에서 조깅하는 것을 즐긴다.
be동사와 함께 진행시제를 만든다. The architect **is** **designing** a building. 그 건축가는 건물을 설계하고 있다.	He is good **at** **surfing** in the ocean. 그는 바다에서 서핑하는 것을 잘한다.

연습문제 A 밑줄 친 부분의 쓰임과 같은 것을 <보기>에서 골라 그 기호를 쓰시오.

<보기> ⓐ The laughing child made me smile.
ⓑ Please stay in the waiting room for a minute.

1 Biting your nails is a bad habit. [ ]

2 They got out of the burning house. [ ]

3 It was raining heavily last night. [ ]

4 I can hear someone knocking on the door. [ ]

5 Where can I find a shopping cart? [ ]

6 Did you finish watering the plants in the garden? [ ]

7 There is my friend waiting in the lobby. [ ]

8 Yuna's hobby is watching e-sports games. [ ]

9 I'm looking forward to meeting your family. [ ]

10 Ms. Park is writing something on the board. [ ]

11 The crossword puzzle looked confusing to me. [ ]

12 That washing machine isn't working anymore. [ ]

우리말과 같도록 괄호 안의 말을 알맞게 배열하시오.

1 노래를 부르는 저 소녀는 나의 반 친구이다. (my, is, singing, classmate, that, girl)

= _____

2 너의 운동화는 어디에 있니? (where, shoes, your, are, running)

= _____

3 그녀의 취미는 만화를 그리는 것이다. (drawing, her, cartoons, hobby, is)

= _____

4 나는 약간의 식수가 필요하다. (need, water, some, I, drinking)

= _____

5 그 벌은 꽃 위에서 쉬고 있다. (is, on, resting, a, flower, bee, the)

= _____

6 그 요리사는 스테이크를 요리하고 있다. (steak, cooking, the, chef, a, is)

= _____

7 우리는 계속 앞으로 걸어야 한다. (keep, to, we, walking, have, forward)

= _____

8 나는 그가 누군가에게 소리치고 있는 것을 들었다. (someone, heard, I, at, yelling, him)

= _____

9 너는 날고 있는 나비를 잡을 수 있니? (butterfly, you, a, can, catch, flying)

= _____

10 Ken은 수영장 안으로 뛰어들었다. (into, Ken, swimming, the, dove, pool)

= _____

11 그 짖는 개는 사람들을 무서워하게 만들었다. (people, the, scared, barking, made, dog)

= _____

12 새로운 언어를 배우는 것은 재미있다. (is, learning, languages, fun, new)

= _____

기출 적중문제

다음 중 밑줄 친 부분의 쓰임이 나머지 넷과 다른 것은?

① My dream is becoming a writer.
② Do you have your own hiding place?
③ That child helping the old lady is kind.
④ Nick is afraid of being alone in the dark.
⑤ You shouldn't put off going to the dentist.

POINT 5-1 분사구문 만드는 법

정답 p.24

분사구문은 분사를 이용하여 「접속사 + 주어 + 동사」 형태의 부사절을 부사구로 바꾼 것이다.

<u>When</u> <u>he</u> <u>saw</u> me, he waved his hand. 그는 나를 봤을 때, 그의 손을 흔들었다.
　①　②　③
　　　　↓
　　　Seeing me, he waved his hand.

① 부사절의 접속사를 생략한다. 단, 분사구문의 의미를 분명하게 하기 위해 접속사를 생략하지 않기도 한다.
② 주절과 부사절의 주어가 같을 때는 부사절의 주어를 생략한다.
③ 부사절의 동사를 V-ing형으로 바꾼다.

While he played basketball, he got hurt. 그는 농구를 하면서, 다쳤다.
= **Playing** basketball, he got hurt.

(Tip) 분사구문의 부정형은 분사 앞에 not을 붙여 만든다.
　　As she **didn't wake** up early, she missed the train. 그녀는 일찍 일어나지 않았기 때문에, 기차를 놓쳤다.
　　= **Not waking** up early, she missed the train.

연습문제 다음 두 문장의 의미가 같도록 분사구문을 이용하여 문장을 완성하시오. (단, 접속사를 생략하시오.)

1 When she looked out the window, she saw the clear sky.
= _____, she saw the clear sky.

2 Because I felt sick, I went to the hospital.
= _____, I went to the hospital.

3 While I ate breakfast, I watched TV.
= _____, I watched TV.

4 As she is too short, she can't ride this roller coaster.
= _____, she can't ride this roller coaster.

5 Since I didn't have much time, I had to run really fast.
= _____, I had to run really fast.

6 After he talked to his friend, he felt much better.
= _____, he felt much better.

7 While we waited in line, we told each other some jokes.
= _____, we told each other some jokes.

8 Because she didn't know what to do, she called her mom.
= _____, she called her mom.

분사구문의 다양한 의미

정답 p.24

분사구문은 접속사에 따라 다양한 의미를 나타낸다.

의미	접속사	예문	
시간	when ~할 때 while ~하는 동안 before ~하기 전에 after ~한 후에	**When she opened** the box, she found a ring. = **Opening** the box, she found a ring. 그녀는 그 상자를 열었을 때, 반지를 찾았다.	
이유	because/since/as ~이기 때문에	**Because he was** late, he couldn't see the play. = **Being** late, he couldn't see the play. 그는 늦었기 때문에, 그 연극을 볼 수 없었다.	
동시동작	while/as ~하면서	**While I take a bath**, I listen to music. = **Taking** a bath, I listen to music. 나는 목욕을 하면서, 음악을 듣는다.	
연속동작	and ~하고 나서	She slipped on the ice, **and she broke** her leg. = She slipped on the ice, **breaking** her leg. 그녀가 얼음 위에서 미끄러지고 나서, 그녀의 다리가 부러졌다.	
양보	although/though 비록 ~이지만	양보를 나타내는 분사구문은 의미를 분명하게 하기 위해 주로 접속사를 생략하지 않는다. **Although I am** tired, I can finish this report. = **Although being** tired, I can finish this report. 비록 나는 피곤하지만, 이 보고서를 끝낼 수 있다.	

(Tip) 「with + 명사 + 분사」는 '…가 ~한 채로'라는 의미로, 동시에 일어나는 상황을 나타낸다. 이때 명사와 분사의 관계가 능동이면 현재분사를 쓰고, 수동이면 과거분사를 쓴다.
I was sleeping **with the music playing** loudly. 나는 음악이 크게 울리는 채로 자고 있었다.
She is sitting on the sofa **with her legs crossed**. 그녀는 그녀의 다리를 꼰 채로 소파에 앉아있다.

연습문제 A 우리말과 같도록 괄호 안의 말을 활용하여 분사구문을 완성하시오.

1 나는 계단을 뛰어 올라간 후에, 땀을 많이 흘렸다. (run, up the stairs)
= _____, I sweated a lot.

2 그는 너무 우울했기 때문에, 우는 것을 멈출 수 없었다. (be, so depressed)
= _____, he couldn't stop crying.

3 나는 은행에 도착했을 때, 그곳이 문을 닫은 것을 발견했다. (reach, the bank)
= _____, I found it closed.

4 그는 산을 오르는 동안, 그의 발목을 다쳤다. (climb, the mountain)

= _____, he hurt his ankle.

5 나는 충분한 돈을 가지고 있지 않기 때문에, 새 휴대폰을 살 수 없었다. (have, enough money)

= _____, I couldn't buy a new cell phone.

6 우리는 해변에 앉아서, 저녁노을을 봤다. (sit, on the beach)

= _____, we watched the sunset.

7 그녀는 책을 읽는 동안, 잠이 들었다. (read, a book)

= _____, she fell asleep.

8 그는 열심히 공부했기 때문에, 시험에서 높은 점수를 받았다. (study, hard)

= _____, he got a high score on the test.

9 나는 집 밖으로 나와서, 문을 잠갔다. (lock, the door)

= I came out of the house, _____.

10 그는 언덕에 서 있으면서, 별들을 관찰했다. (stand, on the hill)

= _____, he observed the stars.

연습문제 B | <보기>에서 가장 알맞은 접속사를 한 번씩만 골라 다음 두 문장의 의미가 같도록 문장을 완성하시오.

<보기> when   after   because   and

1 Feeling sleepy, I took a nap.

= _____, I took a nap.

2 Taking a walk , she found a four-leaf clover.

= _____, she found a four-leaf clover.

3 Graduating from university, he became a famous architect.

= _____, he became a famous architect.

4 We departed at 8:45, arriving in Hong Kong at noon.

= We departed at 8:45, _____.

기출 적중문제 ◎

다음 밑줄 친 부분과 바꿔 쓸 수 있는 것은?

As he waited for his friend, he had a sandwich.

① Wait   ② Waits   ③ Waited
④ Waiting   ⑤ Been waiting

서술형 대비 문제

A 밑줄 친 부분이 어법상 맞으면 O를 쓰고, 틀리면 바르게 고쳐 완전한 문장을 쓰시오.

1 He had his shirt <u>washing</u>. → _____

2 Sehun's new pink hair looks <u>shocked</u>. → _____

3 It's hard to read a book <u>written</u> in English. → _____

4 Gina was <u>pleasing</u> with her final grades. → _____

5 Who is that man <u>taken</u> pictures? → _____

6 I need to fix my <u>break</u> computer. → _____

7 Terry sleeps with the window <u>closing</u>. → _____

8 Luke got me cheese <u>making</u> in France. → _____

9 I saw Jason <u>giving</u> a girl some flowers. → _____

10 I want to raise a <u>talked</u> parrot. → _____

B 다음은 Sophia와 Charles가 뮤지컬 '알라딘'을 본 소감이다. 괄호 안의 말을 활용하여 빈칸에 알맞은 말을 쓰시오.

1

Sophia

The musical *Aladdin* was very ⓐ_____ (excite). First, I was ⓑ_____ (amaze) by the beautiful costumes. I especially liked Princess Jasmine's clothes. Also, all of the songs in the musical were very ⓒ_____ (touch), and the melodies were beautiful. I was ⓓ_____ (fascinate) by the wonderful singers. I would love to watch it again.

2

I thought the musical wasn't ⓐ_____ (interest). I was a little ⓑ_____ (disappoint). I think the movie version was better, because it had great special effects. I also thought the songs in the musical were a little ⓒ_____ (bore). They weren't as good as the ones in the film. Lastly, the musical was really long. I was a little ⓓ_____ (tire) by the end.

Charles

C <보기>와 같이 우리말과 같도록 괄호 안의 말을 활용하여 문장을 완성하시오.

> <보기> 나는 늦게 일어났기 때문에, 뛰어야 했다. (wake up late)
> = Because _I woke up late_, I had to run.
> = _Waking up late_, I had to run.

1 우리는 영화를 보면서, 팝콘을 먹었다. (watch a movie)

= While _____, we ate popcorn.

= _____, we ate popcorn.

2 나는 펜을 가지고 있지 않았기 때문에, 양식에 서명할 수 없었다. (have a pen)

= Since _____, I couldn't sign the form.

= _____, I couldn't sign the form.

3 나는 거미를 봤을 때, 비명을 질렀다. (see a spider)

= When _____, I screamed.

= _____, I screamed.

4 그녀는 두통이 있었기 때문에, 약을 먹었다. (have a headache)

= Because _____, she took medicine.

= _____, she took medicine.

5 그들은 함께 조깅하는 동안, 서로에게 이야기했다. (jog together)

= While _____, they talked to each other.

= _____, they talked to each other.

6 Sara는 새장을 열고 나서, 그 새를 풀어줬다. (let the bird out)

= Sara opened the cage, and _____.

= Sara opened the cage, _____.

7 그는 키가 컸기 때문에, 선반 꼭대기에서 접시를 꺼낼 수 있었다. (be tall)

= As _____, he could take out the plate from the top shelf.

= _____, he could take out the plate from the top shelf.

8 나는 나의 방을 청소할 때, 나의 잃어버린 목걸이를 발견했다. (clean my room)

= When _____, I found my lost necklace.

= _____, I found my lost necklace.

9 그는 줄을 서서, 표를 사기 위해 기다렸다.(wait to buy a ticket)

= He stood in line, and _____.

= He stood in line, _____.

중간·기말고사 실전 문제

[1-3] 다음 빈칸에 들어갈 알맞은 것을 고르시오.

1

> Do you know that girl _____ the red raincoat?

① wear ② wearing
③ to wear ④ wore
⑤ worn

2

> When Thomas arrived home, he found the window _____.

① break ② broke
③ breaking ④ broken
⑤ breaks

3

> The price of the new smartphone was _____.

① shock ② shocks
③ shocked ④ shocking
⑤ to shocking

4 다음 중 밑줄 친 부분이 어법상 바른 것은?

① Paul likes the sound of fallen rain.
② Please keep the radio turning on.
③ I bought a chair making of wood.
④ Amy saw her brother reading her diary.
⑤ Camping in the woods was a satisfied experience.

5 다음 (A)~(C)에 들어갈 말이 바르게 짝지어진 것은?

> *Lucy*: Did you see the woman __(A)__ the piano in the lobby?
>
> *Jack*: Yes. I was very __(B)__ by her music.
>
> *Lucy*: Me, too. Her performance was __(C)__. She is a talented pianist.

	(A)	(B)	(C)
①	playing	moved	fascinated
②	played	moved	fascinating
③	playing	moving	fascinated
④	playing	moved	fascinating
⑤	played	moving	fascinating

6 우리말과 같도록 괄호 안의 동사를 활용하여 빈칸에 쓰시오.

> Jill은 길에서 콘서트가 열린 것을 봤다. (hold)

= Jill watched a concert _____ on the street.

7 다음 빈칸에 들어갈 말로 어색한 것을 모두 고르시오.

> The students looked _____ after the math test.

① tired ② worried
③ pleasing ④ confused
⑤ disappointing

8 다음 중 자연스러운 대화는?

① A: You look very tiring today.
　 B: I had to stay up all night.
② A: How are your new boots?
　 B: They are actually disappointed.
③ A: Did you enjoy your trip to Seoul?
　 B: Yes, I was touching by kind people.
④ A: I don't know how to play baseball.
　 B: Me, either. The rules are confused.
⑤ A: Why did you stop baking?
　 B: I got bored. I need a new hobby.

[9-10] 분사를 이용하여 다음 두 문장을 한 문장으로 연결하시오.

9

The shoes were under the sofa. They were hidden by my dog.
→ The shoes _____ were under the sofa.

10

The man is a police officer. He is checking our IDs.
→ The man _____ is a police officer.

11 다음 중 어법상 어색한 것은?

① I finally found the stolen laptop.
② Do you know the person waving at you?
③ The sculpture made by da Vinci is in Italy.
④ That machine made a strange noise is out of order.
⑤ Yeri loves to eat boiled potatoes.

12 우리말과 같도록 괄호 안의 말을 활용하여 빈칸에 쓰시오.

나의 가족과 나는 이 식당의 서비스에 실망했다.
(disappoint)

= My family and I were _____ by the service at this restaurant.

13 다음 빈칸에 들어갈 말이 순서대로 짝지어진 것은?

· There are some dolphins _____ in the river.
· Henry had his bike _____ yesterday.

① living – repair　　② living – repairing
③ lived – repairing　④ lived – repaired
⑤ living – repaired

14 다음 (A)~(C)에 들어갈 말이 바르게 짝지어진 것은?

> · The hotel has an ____(A)____ view of the ocean.
> · The after-school program offers many ____(B)____ activities.
> · Are you ____(C)____ in collecting rare coins?

	(A)	(B)	(C)
①	amazed	exciting	interested
②	amazing	exciting	interested
③	amazing	excited	interested
④	amazing	exciting	interesting
⑤	amazed	excited	interesting

[15-16] 우리말과 같도록 괄호 안의 말을 활용하여 빈칸에 쓰시오.

15

> 그녀는 답을 알지 못했기 때문에, 계속 조용하게 있었다. (know, the answer)

= _____ _____ _____
_____, she kept quiet.

16

> 화가 난 아이는 문이 잠긴 채로 그의 방에 그대로 있었다. (the door, lock)

= The angry kid stayed in his room
_____ _____ _____
_____.

17 주어진 문장의 밑줄 친 부분과 쓰임이 같은 것은?

> Suho is bringing the package into the house.

① Recycling plastic helps the environment.
② Did you start preparing for the contest?
③ Her job is treating sick animals in the wild.
④ The number of crimes is decreasing.
⑤ I enjoy eating vanilla ice cream for dessert.

18 다음 빈칸에 들어갈 말이 순서대로 짝지어진 것은?

> · This library is full of _____ students.
> · Look at all the people _____ in line to enter the concert hall.

① studied – waiting
② studying – waiting
③ studying – waited
④ studied – waited
⑤ study – waiting

19 다음 중 밑줄 친 부분이 어법상 어색한 것은?

① The sunflowers are facing the sun.
② The kitchen floor is cleaned every day.
③ Ben has traveled to Africa three times.
④ I had my tooth pulling out by my father.
⑤ I can't hear you talking since it's too loud here.

20 다음 문장의 밑줄 친 부분을 분사구문으로 바꿔 쓰시오.

Because she didn't have her wallet, she walked home.

= _____, she walked home.

21 다음 중 밑줄 친 부분의 쓰임이 나머지 넷과 <u>다른</u> 것은?

① I had to throw out my old <u>swimming</u> suit.
② You should bring your own <u>sleeping</u> bag.
③ Our grandpa is looking for his <u>walking</u> stick.
④ I see a few children <u>playing</u> outside.
⑤ Is there anyone in the <u>dressing</u> room?

22 다음 대화의 빈칸에 들어갈 말이 순서대로 짝지어진 것은?

A: What are you going to do this summer?
B: Our family is going on a trip to Europe. We've never been there, so it will be very _____.
A: Wow. You must be really _____.
B: Yes, I'm looking forward to it.

① amaze – exciting
② amazing – excited
③ amazed – excite
④ amazing – exciting
⑤ amazed – excited

23 다음 문장을 분사구문을 이용하여 바꿔 쓰시오.

When I had some free time, I went outside to play.

= _____, I went outside to play.

24 다음 밑줄 친 부분의 쓰임이 같은 것끼리 묶인 것은?

ⓐ Don't get too close to a <u>burning</u> candle.
ⓑ Hyeri is <u>standing</u> at the bus stop.
ⓒ My goal is <u>winning</u> a Nobel Prize.
ⓓ Don't give up <u>following</u> your dream.
ⓔ There is a child <u>running</u> in the field.

① ⓐ, ⓑ, ⓒ   ② ⓐ, ⓑ, ⓔ   ③ ⓐ, ⓒ, ⓓ
④ ⓑ, ⓒ, ⓔ   ⑤ ⓒ, ⓓ, ⓔ

25 다음 문장을 분사구문을 이용하여 바꿔 쓸 때 빈칸에 들어갈 알맞은 것은?

While I watched TV, I texted my friend.

= _____, I texted my friend.

① Watch TV   ② Watches TV
③ Watched TV   ④ Watching TV
⑤ I watched TV

26 다음 두 문장을 한 문장으로 연결할 때 빈칸에 들어갈 알맞은 것은?

I heard Ryan and Emily. They were arguing outside.
→ I heard Ryan and Emily _____ outside.

① argues   ② to argue
③ arguing   ④ argued
⑤ be argued

27 다음 중 어법상 어색한 것은?

① He was embarrassed because he fell down the stairs.
② The depressed weather made me feel sad.
③ The breakfast cooked by my dad was amazing.
④ Sarah looked tired after she took care of her nephew.
⑤ I was worried about turning in my homework late.

28 주어진 문장의 밑줄 친 부분과 쓰임이 같은 것은?

Alice was scared of the barking dog.

① Using your time wisely is important.
② Stop thinking about your past mistakes.
③ Let's help the old man carrying the heavy boxes.
④ Exercising is necessary to stay healthy.
⑤ Camels can survive in the desert without drinking water.

29 다음 빈칸에 들어갈 말이 순서대로 짝지어진 것은?

· _____ for a train, I read a comic book.
· Is that _____ car your father's?

① Waited - parked   ② Waiting - parked
③ Waited - parking   ④ Waiting - parking
⑤ Wait - parked

30 다음 밑줄 친 부분과 바꿔 쓸 수 있는 것은?

Being thirsty, I drank three cups of cold water.

① As I was thirsty
② And I was thirsty
③ When I am thirsty
④ Before I was thirsty
⑤ Although I am thirsty

31 다음 대화의 밑줄 친 부분의 쓰임이 나머지 넷과 다른 것은?

A: I want to try ①cooking pancakes by myself. I'm ②planning to do it this weekend.
B: ③Making pancakes for the first time is going to be difficult.
A: I know, but it will be worth ④trying.
B: All right. I look forward to ⑤eating your pancakes.

32 다음 중 어법상 <u>어색한</u> 것의 개수는?

ⓐ I was touched by Leo's story.
ⓑ That roller coaster doesn't look excited.
ⓒ We saw lots of amazed paintings at the gallery.
ⓓ There were some confusing questions on the exam.
ⓔ You will be satisfying when you complete the puzzle.

① 1개　　　　② 2개　　　　③ 3개
④ 4개　　　　⑤ 5개

33 우리말과 같도록 괄호 안의 말을 활용하여 빈칸에 쓰시오.

그녀는 방에 들어온 후에, 코트를 벗었다. (enter the room)

= ＿＿＿＿＿ ＿＿＿＿＿ ＿＿＿＿＿
＿＿＿＿＿ ＿＿＿＿＿, she took off her coat.

= ＿＿＿＿＿ ＿＿＿＿＿ ＿＿＿＿＿,
she took off her coat.

34 다음 밑줄 친 부분과 바꿔 쓸 수 있는 것은?

<u>Because he has many friends</u>, he is always busy.

① Have many friends
② Has many friends
③ Having many friends
④ Had many friends
⑤ To have many friends

35 다음 문장에서 어법상 <u>어색한</u> 부분을 찾아 쓰고 바르게 고쳐 쓰시오.

Go into my room, I turned on the lights.

＿＿＿＿＿＿ → ＿＿＿＿＿＿

36 다음 중 어법상 <u>어색한</u> 것끼리 묶인 것은?

ⓐ Mr. Harold's history class is so confused.
ⓑ Listening to classical music, Minho felt relaxed.
ⓒ I wore a muffler knitting by my mother.
ⓓ The wind blew hard, making the tree fall down.
ⓔ Jane is sitting with her arms folded.

① ⓐ, ⓑ　　　② ⓐ, ⓒ　　　③ ⓑ, ⓒ
④ ⓒ, ⓓ　　　⑤ ⓓ, ⓔ

37 다음 글의 밑줄 친 ⓐ~ⓔ 중 어법상 <u>어색한</u> 것을 찾아 기호를 쓰고 바르게 고쳐 쓰시오.

Last night, Tony was home alone. He was really ⓐ<u>boring</u>. But around 8 o'clock, he heard someone ⓑ<u>breaking</u> into his house. He was scared, so he listened very carefully. He realized that the noise sounded like a ⓒ<u>crying</u> animal. ⓓ<u>Followed</u> the noise, he found an ⓔ<u>injuring</u> bird.

(1) ＿＿＿ → ＿＿＿＿＿
(2) ＿＿＿ → ＿＿＿＿＿
(3) ＿＿＿ → ＿＿＿＿＿

CHAPTER 9
명사와 관사

Tommy and his **brother** are drinking **soda** at the **park**.
Tommy와 그의 형은 공원에서 탄산음료를 마시고 있다.

Tommy, **brother**, **soda**, **park** 와 같이 사람, 사물, 장소 등의 이름을 나타내는 말을 **명사**라고 해요. 명사는 brother나 park와 같이 셀 수 있는 명사와 Tommy나 soda와 같이 셀 수 없는 명사로 구분할 수 있어요.

기출로 적중 POINT

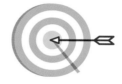

내신 100점 적중!
기출 출제율

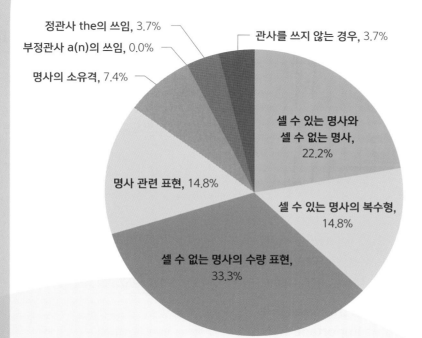

정관사 the의 쓰임, 3.7%

부정관사 a(n)의 쓰임, 0.0%

명사의 소유격, 7.4%

관사를 쓰지 않는 경우, 3.7%

셀 수 있는 명사와 셀 수 없는 명사, 22.2%

명사 관련 표현, 14.8%

셀 수 있는 명사의 복수형, 14.8%

셀 수 없는 명사의 수량 표현, 33.3%

TOP 1 **셀 수 없는 명사의 수량 표현 (33.3%)**
셀 수 없는 명사의 수량을 나타내는 단위의 종류와 쓰임을 묻는 문제가 자주 출제된다.

TOP 2 **셀 수 있는 명사와 셀 수 없는 명사 (22.2%)**
셀 수 있는 명사와 셀 수 없는 명사를 구별하는 문제와 명사의 다양한 종류를 묻는 문제가 자주 출제된다.

TOP 3 **셀 수 있는 명사의 복수형 (14.8%)**
        명사 관련 표현 (14.8%)
셀 수 있는 명사의 복수형을 묻는 문제가 자주 출제된다. 다양한 명사 관련 표현을 묻는 문제가 자주 출제된다.

셀 수 있는 명사와 셀 수 없는 명사

정답 p.26

1. **셀 수 있는 명사가 단수일 때는 명사 앞에 a(n)을 붙이고, 복수일 때는 복수형으로 쓴다. 셀 수 있는 명사에는 보통명사와 집합명사가 있다.**

보통명사	일반적인 사람·동물·사물을 나타내는 명사 baby, teacher, monkey, building, desk, violin, pineapple 등
집합명사	사람·동물·사물이 모인 집합을 나타내는 명사 class, family, team, group, band, club, audience 등

A **boy** and two **cats** are on the **roof**. 한 명의 소년과 두 마리의 고양이가 지붕 위에 있다.
My **family** consists of four **members**. 나의 가족은 네 명의 구성원으로 이루어진다.

(Tip) 셀 수 있는 명사의 복수형은 many, a lot of[lots of], (a) few, some, any 등의 수를 나타내는 형용사와 함께 쓸 수 있다.
I planted **many flowers** in the garden. 나는 정원에 많은 꽃들을 심었다.
Some families were invited to the wedding. 몇몇 가족들은 그 결혼식에 초대되었다.

2. **셀 수 없는 명사는 명사 앞에 a(n)을 붙일 수 없고, 복수형으로도 쓸 수 없다. 셀 수 없는 명사에는 고유명사, 추상명사, 물질명사가 있다.**

고유명사	사람, 장소, 요일, 월 등의 고유한 이름을 나타내는 명사 Lisa, Minho, Korea, Vancouver, Hallasan, Monday, September 등
추상명사	눈에 보이지 않는 추상적인 개념을 나타내는 명사 peace, love, kindness, news, advice, information, luck 등
물질명사	일정한 형태가 없는 물질을 나타내는 명사 water, bread, rice, sugar, paper, money, trash, oxygen 등

Harry will visit **Seoul** this weekend. Harry는 이번 주말에 서울을 방문할 것이다.
Happiness is more important than **money**. 행복은 돈보다 더 중요하다.

(Tip) 셀 수 없는 명사는 much, a lot of[lots of], (a) little, some, any 등의 양을 나타내는 형용사와 함께 쓸 수 있다.
Mr. Andrews gave me **a little advice**. Andrews씨는 나에게 약간의 조언을 주셨다.
There wasn't **any salt** in the jar. 병 안에 약간의 소금도 있지 않았다.

연습문제 A 다음 명사가 셀 수 있는 명사이면 O, 셀 수 <u>없는</u> 명사이면 X를 쓰시오.

1 city → _____ **2** milk → _____ **3** club → _____

4 truth → _____ **5** sand → _____ **6** uncle → _____

7 group → _____ **8** New York → _____ **9** homework → _____

10	oxygen	→ _____	11	dictionary	→ _____	12	luck	→ _____
13	April	→ _____	14	money	→ _____	15	tiger	→ _____
16	information	→ _____	17	student	→ _____	18	Ms. Kim	→ _____

연습문제 B 다음 문장의 밑줄 친 명사와 종류가 <u>다른</u> 것을 고르시오.

1 Spread <u>jam</u> on a piece of bread.　　　① class　② rice　③ cheese

2 My <u>advice</u> is to practice harder.　　　① peace　② trust　③ country

3 There is no <u>water</u> in the bottle.　　　① paper　② oil　③ school

4 My <u>family</u> loves camping.　　　① food　② audience　③ team

5 You should turn off your <u>phone</u>.　　　① truck　② honesty　③ cup

6 <u>Tim Burton</u> is known for his fantasy movies.　　① Taiwan　② rain　③ David

연습문제 C 괄호 안에서 알맞은 것을 고르시오.

1 How many (chair / chairs) will we need?

2 I have (a question / question) about the new rule.

3 Would you like to drink (orange juice / orange juices)?

4 Could you lend me some (money / moneys)?

5 Have you climbed (a Hallasan / Hallasan) before?

6 Jonathan's (family / families) is large.

7 Did you put (a sugar / sugar) in the cookie dough?

8 We can get more (information / informations) from the website.

9 (An elephant / Elephant) has a very long nose.

10 There are four basketball (team / teams) in the playground.

11 (A December / December) is the twelfth month of the year.

기출 적중문제

다음 중 밑줄 친 부분이 어법상 <u>어색한</u> 것은?

① I won't forget your <u>kindness</u>.
② Is this pie made with <u>apples</u>?
③ The plastic bag is full of <u>trashes</u>.
④ Many <u>families</u> live in this neighborhood.
⑤ You should take my <u>advice</u>.

셀 수 없는 명사는 복수형으로 쓸 수 없어요.

POINT 2 셀 수 있는 명사의 복수형

셀 수 있는 명사의 복수형은 대부분 명사에 -(e)s를 붙여 만들며, 일부는 불규칙하게 변한다.

대부분의 명사	명사 + -s	shirt – shirt**s**	game – game**s**
-s, -x, -ch, -sh로 끝나는 명사	명사 + -es	address – address**es** peach – peach**es**	fox – fox**es** dish – dish**es**
「자음 + o」로 끝나는 명사	명사 + -es	tomato – tomato**es** (Tip) · 예외: piano – pianos photo – photos · 「모음 + o」로 끝나는 명사: radio – radios	hero – hero**es**
「자음 + y」로 끝나는 명사	y를 i로 바꾸고 + -es	party – part**ies** (Tip) 「모음 + y」로 끝나는 명사: day – days	baby – bab**ies**
-f, -fe로 끝나는 명사	f, fe를 v로 바꾸고 + -es	wolf – wol**ves** (Tip) 예외: roof – roofs cliff – cliffs	knife – kni**ves**
불규칙 변화		man – m**e**n woman – w**o**men child – child**ren** mouse – mi**ce** ox – ox**en** goose – g**ee**se foot – f**ee**t tooth – t**ee**th sheep – **sheep** deer – **deer** fish – **fish** salmon – **salmon**	

Foxes are normally smaller than **wolves**. 여우들은 보통 늑대들보다 더 작다.
Some **children** are playing hide-and-seek. 몇몇 아이들은 숨바꼭질을 하고 있다.

연습문제 A 다음 명사의 복수형을 쓰시오.

1 bottle – _____ **2** city – _____

3 watch – _____ **4** mouse – _____

5 potato – _____ **6** friend – _____

7 ox – _____ **8** goose – _____

9 deer – _____ **10** brush – _____

11 tomato – _____ **12** woman – _____

13 dish – _____ **14** bicycle – _____

15 roof – _____ **16** key – _____

17 photo – _____ **18** zoo – _____

19 knife   – _____   **20** dolphin   – _____

21 sheep   – _____   **22** activity   – _____

23 camera   – _____   **24** life   – _____

25 baby   – _____   **26** radio   – _____

27 foot   – _____   **28** memory   – _____

29 bus   – _____   **30** neighbor   – _____

31 shelf   – _____   **32** cliff   – _____

연습문제 B   괄호 안의 명사를 알맞은 형태로 바꿔 빈칸에 쓰시오.

1 Four _____ are singing on the stage. (man)

2 Rick was teaching some _____ how to swim. (child)

3 There are a few _____ at the gym. (girl)

4 The _____ are on sale now. (piano)

5 The movie is about a team of three _____ . (hero)

6 This _____ doesn't have a public library. (town)

7 Ronald visited a _____ in Korea last year. (temple)

8 The monster's _____ are yellow and dirty. (tooth)

9 _____ fall on the street during autumn. (leaf)

10 He bought me a _____ for my birthday present. (ring)

11 We can watch many _____ for free on the Internet. (video)

12 The _____ are running away from the police. (thief)

13 Some _____ don't allow students to park on campus. (university)

14 The bank will require an _____ to open an account. (address)

15 Lots of _____ were damaged because of the storm. (roof)

기출 적중문제

다음 중 명사의 복수형이 <u>잘못된</u> 것은?

① wife – wives   ② factory – factories

③ deer – deers   ④ fish – fish

⑤ vegetable – vegetables

셀 수 없는 명사의 수량 표현

정답 p.27

셀 수 없는 명사는 그것을 담는 그릇이나 단위를 나타내는 명사를 활용하여 수량을 나타내고,
복수형은 그릇이나 단위를 나타내는 단위명사에 -(e)s를 붙여 만든다.

수량 표현	함께 쓰이는 명사	수량 표현	함께 쓰이는 명사
a glass of	water, milk, juice	**a cup of**	water, tea, coffee
a bottle of	water, milk, juice, ink	**a can of**	coke, soda, paint
a bowl of	soup, rice, salad, cereal	**a spoonful of**	salt, sugar, rice
a slice of	pizza, ham, cheese, bread, cake, toast	**a loaf of**	bread
a bar of	chocolate, soap, gold	**a sheet of**	paper, newspaper
a piece of	pizza, cheese, bread, cake, paper, furniture, news, advice, information		

Can I have **a bowl of** cereal? 내가 시리얼 한 그릇을 먹어도 되니?
Give them **eight loaves of** bread. 그들에게 빵 여덟 덩어리를 줘라.
I bought **four pieces of** pizza and **two cans of** coke. 나는 피자 네 조각과 콜라 두 캔을 샀다.

연습문제 **A** | 다음 그림을 보고 괄호 안의 말을 활용하여 질문에 대한 대답을 완성하시오. (단, 숫자는 영어로 쓰시오.)

1

A: How much water do you drink a day?
B: I drink _____ a day. (glass, water)

2

A: What do you want to eat?
B: I'd like _____. (slice, cake)

3

A: How much salt do I have to put in the pot?

B: You have to put _____.
   (spoonful, salt)

4

A: Do you have a problem, sir?

B: Yes. We didn't order _____.
   (bowl, salad)

연습문제 B 괄호 안에서 알맞은 것을 고르시오.

1 Here is a (cup / loaf) of green tea for you.

2 Could you pass me five (slice / slices) of ham?

3 A bar of (gold / golds) weighs about 27 pounds.

4 Please add four (spoonfuls / sheets) of sugar.

5 Can I order two bowls of (rice / rices)?

6 There are three (loaf of breads / loaves of bread) on the plate.

7 A (glass / glasses) of chocolate milk always makes me happy.

8 The man ate twenty (slice / slices) of pizza at a time.

9 I heard a (sheet / piece) of information about the new student.

10 You cannot use more than ten (sheets of paper / sheet of papers).

11 We need two (pieces of furniture / piece of furnitures).

12 Janice used four (cans / pieces) of paint to finish this painting.

13 Could you buy three (bottle of milks / bottles of milk) on the way home?

14 My father always drinks a (cup / cups) of coffee after work.

기출 적중문제 🎯

우리말과 같도록 괄호 안의 말을 활용하여 문장을 완성하시오. (단, 숫자는 영어로 쓰시오.)

> 나는 빵 두 덩어리와 수프 한 그릇을 먹기를 원한다. (bread, soup)

= I would like to have _____ and

_____.

명사 관련 표현

1. 한 쌍이 짝을 이루는 다음 명사는 항상 복수형으로 쓰고, a pair of를 활용하여 수량을 나타낸다. 단, 한 쌍 중 하나만 나타낼 때는 단수형으로 쓴다.

| glasses | sunglasses | gloves | shoes | sneakers |
| socks | pants | jeans | shorts | scissors |

Brian gave me **a pair of pants**. Brian은 나에게 바지 한 벌을 줬다.
We need **three pairs of gloves** to play baseball.
우리는 야구를 하기 위해 장갑 세 켤레가 필요하다.
The dog is playing with **a shoe**. 그 개는 신발 한 짝을 가지고 놀고 있다.

2. 「숫자 + 단위명사」는 하이픈(-)으로 연결되어 형용사처럼 명사 앞에서 명사를 수식할 수 있다. 이때 단위명사는 항상 단수형으로 쓴다.

The **ten-hour flight** was very tiring. 10시간의 비행은 매우 피곤했다.
The ten-hours flight was very tiring. (X)

Thomas is a **thirteen-year-old boy**. Thomas는 13살짜리 소년이다.
Thomas is a thirteen-years-old boy. (X)

3. 명사나 대명사 뒤에 콤마(,)나 that을 써서 부연 설명을 덧붙일 수 있으며, 이를 동격이라고 한다.

Have you met **my sister, Diana**? 너는 나의 여동생인 Diana를 만나본 적이 있니?

He knows **the fact that I lied to him**. 그는 내가 그에게 거짓말했다는 사실을 알고 있다.

연습문제 A 우리말과 같도록 괄호 안의 말을 활용하여 문장을 완성하시오. (단, 숫자는 영어로 쓰시오.)

1 Edward는 선글라스 한 쌍이 필요하다. (sunglass)

= Edward needs _____.

2 유라의 가족은 작년에 3개월의 휴가를 갔다. (month, vacation)

= Yura's family took a _____ ` _____ last year.

3 빨간 양말 다섯 켤레가 벽난로에 걸려있었다. (red sock)

= _____ were hanging on the fireplace.

4 나의 삼촌은 문이 두 개인 차를 가지고 계신다. (door, car)

= My uncle has a _____.

5 그 가수는 새 운동화 10켤레를 기부할 것이다. (new sneaker)

= The singer will donate _____.

6 그들은 방 세 개짜리 집을 사기를 원한다. (room, house)

= They want to buy a _____.

7 나의 친구는 공원에서 장갑 한 짝을 잃어버렸다. (glove)

= My friend lost _____ in the park.

8 그녀의 5살짜리 남동생은 정말 영리하다. (year, old, brother)

= Her _____ is really clever.

9 Allen씨는 그의 아이들을 위해 반바지 네 벌을 샀다. (short)

= Mr. Allen bought _____ for his kids.

10 Lucy는 어제 길에서 20달러짜리 지폐를 발견했다. (dollar, bill)

= Lucy found a _____ on the street yesterday.

11 맨 위 서랍 안에 가위 한 자루가 있다. (scissor)

= There is _____ in the top drawer.

연습문제 B 다음 문장의 밑줄 친 부분과 동격인 부분에 밑줄을 치시오.

1 This is my cat, Nabi.

2 His wife, Teresa, is a nurse.

3 The rumor that Paul likes Karen is not true.

4 I love Heungmin Son, the best soccer player.

5 Mom's advice that I should read more books was very helpful.

6 The fact that the climate is changing makes me scared.

7 That is the *Mona Lisa*, one of the world's most famous paintings.

8 Did you hear the announcement that the flight has been canceled?

기출 적중문제

다음 중 밑줄 친 부분이 어법상 어색한 것은?

① A seven-story building will be built here.

② I'll pack three pairs of shoes for the journey.

③ This eleven-months-old baby is my nephew, Ken.

④ My grandmother has a pair of glasses.

⑤ Sumin is reading a four hundred-page book.

기출로 적중 POINT 5 — 명사의 소유격

1. 사람이나 동물을 나타내는 명사의 소유격은 명사에 -'(s)를 붙여 만든다.

단수명사	명사 + 's	the **girl's** phone 그 소녀의 전화기 my **friend's** bag 나의 친구의 가방	**Betty's** jeans Betty의 청바지 the **dog's** tail 그 개의 꼬리
-s로 끝나지 않는 복수명사		**men's** shoes 남자들의 신발 old **people's** home 양로원	**Children's** Day 어린이날 **women's** clothing 여성복
-s로 끝나는 복수명사	명사 + '	**students'** names 학생들의 이름 **teachers'** room 교무실	**boys'** school 남학교 **cats'** toys 고양이들의 장난감

(Tip) 소유격 뒤의 명사가 앞에 나온 명사와 같거나 집·상점 등을 나타내면 생략할 수 있다.
These **clothes** are the **kid's** (clothes). 이 옷은 그 아이의 옷이다.
Where did he stay last weekend? – He stayed at **Mr. Jackson's** (house).
그는 지난 주말에 어디에 머물렀니? – 그는 Jackson씨네 집에 머물렀어.

2. 무생물을 나타내는 명사의 소유격은 주로 「of + 명사」로 나타낸다.

the door **of the car** 그 차의 문   legs **of the chair** 그 의자의 다리들

(Tip) 시간·거리·가격·무게를 나타내는 명사의 소유격은 명사에 -'(s)를 붙여 만든다.
today's weather 오늘의 날씨   three **miles'** distance 3마일의 거리
a **dollar's** worth 1달러의 가치   two **tons'** weight 2톤의 무게

연습문제 우리말과 같도록 괄호 안의 말을 활용하여 영작하시오.

1 Sally의 인형들 = _____ (Sally, dolls)

2 여자 화장실 = _____ (women, restroom)

3 그 깃발의 색깔 = _____ (the flag, the color)

4 어버이날 = _____ (Parents, Day)

5 그 산의 꼭대기 = _____ (the mountain, the top)

6 어제의 신문 = _____ (yesterday, newspaper)

7 그 군인의 군복 = _____ (the soldier, uniform)

8 동물들의 행동 = _____ (animals, behavior)

9 이 영화의 제목 = _____ (this movie, the title)

10 5파운드의 무게 = _____ (five pounds, weight)

기출로작중 POINT 6-1 부정관사 a(n)의 쓰임

정답 p.27

1. **부정관사 a(n)은 정해지지 않은 막연한 것을 가리킬 때 쓰며, 셀 수 있는 명사의 단수형 앞에만 쓴다.**

   Ms. Adams is **a lawyer**.   Adams씨는 변호사이다.
   Maria needs **an umbrella**.   Maria는 우산이 필요하다.

2. **부정관사 a(n)은 다음과 같은 경우에도 쓴다.**

'하나의(one)'를 나타낼 때	Grace lent me **a pencil**. Grace는 나에게 한 자루의 연필을 빌려줬다.
'~마다(per)'를 나타낼 때	My brother usually goes to the movies once **a week**. 나의 오빠는 보통 일주일마다 한 번 영화를 보러 간다.
종족 전체를 대표할 때	**A sloth** is a very slow animal. 나무늘보는 매우 느린 동물이다.

   (Tip) a와 an은 뒤따라오는 단어의 첫소리에 따라 구별해서 쓴다.
   ① 첫소리가 자음으로 발음되는 단어 앞에는 a를 쓴다.
   　a frog, **a** brown egg, **a** university, **a** European, **a** year
   ② 첫소리가 모음으로 발음되는 단어 앞에는 an을 쓴다.
   　an eraser, **an** onion, **an** old car, **an** hour, **an** honest man

---

연습문제 | 밑줄 친 a(n)의 의미와 같은 것을 <보기>에서 골라 그 기호를 쓰시오.

<보기>　ⓐ He didn't say a word today.
　　　　ⓑ Suji visits her grandfather three times a year.
　　　　ⓒ A cat can see well in the dark.

1 Anna has a younger brother. 　　　　　　[　　　　]
2 An owl is active at night. 　　　　　　[　　　　]
3 Marco's family eats out twice a month. 　　　　　　[　　　　]
4 Rome was not built in a day. 　　　　　　[　　　　]
5 You should take this medicine once a week. 　　　　　　[　　　　]
6 A shark is a very dangerous creature. 　　　　　　[　　　　]
7 I drink eight glasses of water a day. 　　　　　　[　　　　]
8 She hopes to buy an expensive car. 　　　　　　[　　　　]
9 An elephant uses its trunk to eat food. 　　　　　　[　　　　]
10 There is a hole in your sweater. 　　　　　　[　　　　]

정관사 the의 쓰임

정답 p.27

정관사 the는 정해진 특정한 것을 가리킬 때 쓰며, 셀 수 있는 명사와 셀 수 없는 명사 앞에 모두 쓸 수 있다.

앞에서 언급된 명사가 반복될 때	I read an **article**. **The article** was about the Antarctic. 나는 하나의 기사를 읽었다. 그 기사는 남극에 관한 것이었다.
서로 알고 있는 것을 말할 때	Can you turn off **the light**? 그 불을 꺼주겠니?
구나 절의 수식을 받는 명사 앞에	**The pasta in the photo** looks delicious. 그 사진 속의 파스타는 맛있게 보인다.
유일한 것을 말할 때	**The Sun** is much bigger than our planet. 태양은 우리의 행성보다 훨씬 더 크다.
종족 전체를 대표할 때	**The koala** is one of Australia's best-known animals. 코알라는 호주의 가장 잘 알려진 동물들 중 하나이다.
악기 이름 앞에	Yunho is good at playing **the cello**. 윤호는 첼로를 연주하는 것을 잘한다.
서수, 최상급, **only**, **same** 앞에	He is **the only** person in the waiting room. 그는 대기실에 있는 유일한 사람이다.

연습문제 다음 빈칸에 a(n)이나 the 중 알맞은 것을 쓰시오.

1 _____ bread on the dish wasn't soft.

2 It's too cold here. Please turn on _____ heater.

3 You'd better exercise four times _____ week.

4 Let's look at _____ moon with this telescope.

5 Minjun and Jia go to _____ same middle school.

6 Do you have _____ problem with your friends?

7 I think that *The Dark Knight* is _____ greatest movie.

8 Have you ever learned how to play _____ guitar?

9 It is snowing for _____ first time this winter.

10 Eating _____ apple every morning is good for your health.

11 I bought a beautiful skirt online. _____ skirt will arrive tomorrow.

기출로적중 POINT 6-3 관사를 쓰지 않는 경우

정답 p.27

다음과 같은 경우에는 명사 앞에 관사를 쓰지 않는다.

운동, 식사, 과목 이름 앞에	How about playing **basketball** with us? 우리와 함께 농구를 하는 게 어때? I always eat **dinner** at 7:30 P.M. 나는 항상 오후 7시 30분에 저녁을 먹는다. Minseo is really good at **math**. 민서는 수학을 정말 잘한다.
「by + 교통·통신수단」	Dave went to the theater **by taxi**. Dave는 택시로 극장에 갔다. I sent you the pictures **by e-mail**. 나는 너에게 이메일로 그 사진들을 보냈다.
장소나 건물이 본래의 목적으로 쓰일 때	Students don't go to **school** on weekends. 학생들은 주말에 학교에 가지 않는다. (Tip) 장소나 건물이 본래의 목적으로 쓰이지 않을 때는 관사를 써야 한다. My parents came to **the** school to pick me up. 나의 부모님은 나를 태우기 위해 학교에 오셨다.

연습문제 다음 빈칸에 a(n)이나 the 중 알맞은 것을 쓰고, 필요하지 않으면 X를 쓰시오.

1 Tom's favorite subject is _____ history.

2 My father goes fishing once _____ month.

3 I want to know every secret of _____ universe.

4 Miranda went to _____ bed early last night.

5 He was _____ only man in the yoga class.

6 You're not _____ child anymore.

7 _____ fish in the pond are so huge.

8 Do your parents go to work by _____ bus?

9 Stella likes to listen to the sound of _____ trumpet.

10 We are going to play _____ soccer tomorrow.

11 She bought the concert ticket by _____ phone yesterday.

12 They went to _____ hospital to see their sick friend.

13 What are you going to have for _____ lunch?

14 Does anyone in your family go to _____ church on Sundays?

서술형 대비 문제

A 밑줄 친 부분이 어법상 맞으면 O를 쓰고, 틀리면 바르게 고쳐 쓰시오.

1 Where did you get these fresh <u>tomatos</u>? → _____

2 Two hundred <u>sheeps</u> live on this farm. → _____

3 We need <u>advice</u> about the issue. → _____

4 The <u>leafes</u> will turn red and yellow soon. → _____

5 *Lord of the Rings* is a <u>three-volumes</u> book. → _____

6 I took many <u>picture</u> during the trip. → _____

7 A few <u>gooses</u> are flying in the sky. → _____

8 Emily went to an amusement park on <u>Children' Day</u>. → _____

9 I think this necklace brought a lot of <u>lucks</u> to me. → _____

10 Please tell me <u>the rules of the game</u> one more time. → _____

11 This park has an <u>eight-mile-long</u> trail. → _____

12 She should buy lots of <u>furnitures</u> for her apartment. → _____

13 Do you know where <u>Mina's classroom</u> is? → _____

14 I won't forget our <u>two-weeks</u> trip to Mexico. → _____

B 다음 글의 빈칸에 a(n)이나 the 중 알맞은 것을 쓰고, 필요하지 않으면 X를 쓰시오.

1

There is ⓐ_____ new French restaurant in my town. ⓑ_____ week ago, my family and I went to ⓒ_____ restaurant to have ⓓ_____ lunch. My younger brother was very hungry because he ate only ⓔ_____ egg that morning. So, we went there by ⓕ_____ taxi. The food was wonderful.

2

Last night, Eunho went to ⓐ_____ bed after midnight because he did a group project about the shape of ⓑ_____ moon with his classmates. They had to find lots of information on the Internet for ⓒ_____ project and write ⓓ_____ report. After finishing it, they sent the report to their teacher by ⓔ_____ e-mail. It was one of ⓕ_____ most tiring days of his life, but he felt proud.

C 다음 그림을 보고 괄호 안의 명사를 활용하여 대화를 완성하시오.

1

Jiyun : Hello.

Mom : Jiyun, it's Mom. Did you buy everything on the list?

Jiyun : Yes, I bought ⓐ_____(orange juice) and ⓑ_____
_____(pizza) for dinner.

Mom : Did you buy ⓒ_____(bread) too?

Jiyun : I did. Also, I bought ⓓ_____(sunglasses) for next week's trip.

Mom : That's nice. You got ⓔ_____(coke) as well, didn't you?

Jiyun : Of course. I got them too.

2

Jane : Wow, you prepared lots of things for our pajama party!

Cindy : Sure, I was looking forward to this. There are ⓐ_____
(milk), ⓑ_____(cake), and ⓒ_____
(chocolate).

Jane : I brought ⓓ_____(paper). We can write letters to each other
later.

Cindy : That's a good idea. Here is ⓔ_____(shorts), so you can
change your clothes.

Jane : Thank you. After I change my clothes, let's watch a movie together.

중간 · 기말고사 실전 문제

1 다음 중 명사의 복수형이 바른 것은?

① knife – knifes ② brush – brushes
③ foot – foots   ④ baby – babys
⑤ mouse – mise

2 다음 중 명사의 종류가 서로 다른 것끼리 짝지어진 것은?

① team, class, audience
② Alex, Italy, Seoul
③ cup, apple, cello
④ tree, peace, juice
⑤ hope, information, honesty

3 다음 빈칸에 들어갈 말로 어색한 것을 모두 고르시오.

> There is _____ in the refrigerator.

① water   ② bread   ③ pear
④ butter   ⑤ egg

4 다음 우리말을 알맞게 영작한 것은?

① 햄 열 조각 = ten slice of ham
② 비누 한 개 = a bar of soaps
③ 가구 한 점 = a sheet of furniture
④ 커피 두 잔 = two cup of coffees
⑤ 쌀 다섯 그릇 = five bowls of rice

5 다음 글의 빈칸에 들어갈 알맞은 것은?

> Look over there. There are many
> _____.

① bus   ② leaf   ③ deer
④ tomato   ⑤ goose

6 다음 중 밑줄 친 부분이 어법상 어색한 것은?

① One of the radios is not working.
② How many oxes are there in the field?
③ They have to move hundreds of boxes.
④ Five men walked into the room.
⑤ The teacher told us some stories about Hangeul.

7 다음 빈칸에 공통으로 들어갈 알맞은 것은?

> · Would you like _____ cake?
> · Please give me _____ paper.

① a slice of   ② a piece of
③ a sheet of   ④ a loaf of
⑤ a glass of

8 다음 중 어법상 어색한 것은?

① She goes to the library twice a month.
② Look at the painting on the wall.
③ Jina has played a flute for three years.
④ The Moon goes around the Earth.
⑤ Humans are the only animals that can speak.

9 다음 <보기> 중 빈칸에 들어갈 수 있는 것의 개수는?

<보기>	cheese	hat	books
	wine	flour	pencil case

Susan is going to buy a _____ at the shopping mall tomorrow.

① 1개 ② 2개 ③ 3개
④ 4개 ⑤ 5개

13 다음 빈칸에 들어갈 말이 순서대로 짝지어진 것은?

· My brother ate three _____ of chocolate right after dinner.
· Sojin ordered a _____ of soup at the restaurant.

① loaves - glass ② loaf - glasses
③ bar - bowl ④ bars - bowl
⑤ bars - glass

[10-11] 우리말과 같도록 괄호 안의 명사를 활용하여 문장을 완성하시오. (단, 숫자는 영어로 쓰시오.)

10

나는 어제 양말 한 켤레를 샀다. (sock)

= I bought _____ yesterday.

11

너는 Maria에게 빵 두 덩어리를 줄 수 있니? (bread)

= Can you give Maria _____?

14 다음 중 밑줄 친 부분이 어법상 어색한 것끼리 묶인 것은?

ⓐ I'll get you a glass of water.
ⓑ We have five cans of sodas.
ⓒ Could you lend me a pair of scissor?
ⓓ Let's put two spoonfuls of salt into the pot.
ⓔ Yuna gave him three bananas.

① ⓐ, ⓒ ② ⓐ, ⓔ ③ ⓑ, ⓒ
④ ⓑ, ⓓ ⑤ ⓒ, ⓔ

12 다음 중 밑줄 친 부분이 어법상 바른 것은?

① A knowledge is power.
② Add a little sugar to your tea.
③ We can't live without an air.
④ I drank some milks in the morning.
⑤ The woman told us too much informations.

15 주어진 문장의 밑줄 친 부분과 의미가 같은 것은?

I take a shower once a day.

① There is a man waiting for a taxi.
② The police have found a clue.
③ A whale is one of the biggest animals.
④ They're going to stay here for a week.
⑤ How many times do you eat out a month?

[16-17] 다음 문장에서 <u>틀린</u> 부분을 바르게 고쳐 완전한 문장을 쓰시오.

16

> Daniel is a 15-years-old boy.
>
> → _____

17

> They asked for seven glass of orange juices.
>
> → _____

[18-19] 우리말과 같도록 괄호 안의 말을 활용하여 문장을 완성하시오.

18

> 이것은 나의 조부모님의 집이다. (my grandparents, house)

= This is _____ .

19

> 그 우산의 모양은 꽤 특이하게 보인다. (the umbrella, the shape)

= _____ looks quite unusual.

20 다음 중 밑줄 친 부분의 쓰임이 나머지 넷과 <u>다른</u> 것은?

① Have you tried bulgogi, a Korean food?
② We, human beings, cannot live alone.
③ If you hurry, you can catch the train.
④ He is reading *Damien*, his favorite novel.
⑤ Minju, our class president, is very smart.

21 다음 (A)~(C)에 들어갈 말이 바르게 짝지어진 것은?

> · Hayun is a five-___(A)___-old baby.
> · There are many ___(B)___ in my neighborhood.
> · All the furniture is covered with ___(C)___ .

	(A)	(B)	(C)
①	month	bookstore	dust
②	months	bookstore	dust
③	month	bookstores	dust
④	months	bookstores	dusts
⑤	month	bookstores	dusts

22 다음 빈칸에 the가 들어갈 수 있는 것은?

① People normally go to _____ church on Sundays.
② A lot of tourists visit _____ capital city of France every year.
③ Do you often listen to music when you study _____ math?
④ You'd better go to the airport by _____ subway.
⑤ Let's go for a walk after eating _____ dinner.

[23-24] 다음 그림을 보고 괄호 안의 말을 활용하여 질문에 대한 대답을 완성하시오. (단, 숫자는 영어로 쓰시오.)

23

A: What did you have for breakfast?
B: I had _____ and _____. (cereal, bread)

24

A: How much ink and paint did you buy?
B: I bought _____ and _____. (ink, paint)

25 다음 글의 밑줄 친 @~@를 바르게 고치지 <u>못한</u> 것은?

Jeff was waiting for a bus at a bus station yesterday evening. He was very hungry because he didn't have @<u>the lunch</u>. So, he went to the supermarket near the bus station to buy ⓑ<u>two bars of chocolates</u> and ©<u>a can of sodas</u>. When he left ⓓ<u>a supermarket</u>, he saw the bus passing the bus station. He had to wait more than 40 minutes for the next bus, so he just went home by ⓔ<u>the taxi</u>.

① @ the lunch → lunch
② ⓑ two bars of chocolates → two bars of chocolate
③ © a can of sodas → a can of soda
④ ⓓ a supermarket → the supermarket
⑤ ⓔ the taxi → a taxi

26 다음 글의 밑줄 친 @~ⓔ 중 어법상 <u>어색한</u> 것을 찾아 기호를 쓰고 바르게 고쳐 쓰시오.

I'm going to take care of three @<u>child</u> this afternoon. They are my cousin, Jenny, and her friends. I've prepared special things for them. First, I'll show them a movie about two ⓑ<u>fish</u> living in a pond together. ©<u>Jenny's</u> friends will like it a lot. Also, I'll make them a few ⓓ<u>sandwich</u> and give them each ⓔ<u>a bottle of</u> apple juice. I hope they have a great time with me.

(1) _____ → _____
(2) _____ → _____

CHAPTER 10
대명사

My brother = He
a book = it

My brother bought **a book** yesterday. **He** is reading **it** now.
나의 오빠는 어제 한 권의 책을 샀다. 그는 지금 그것을 읽고 있다.

두 번째 문장에서 첫 번째 문장의 **My brother** 대신에 **He**를 쓰고, **a book** 대신에 **it**을 썼어요. 이렇게 앞에서 언급된 특정한 명사를 반복하지 않기 위해 대신해서 쓰는 말을 **대명사**라고 해요.

기출로 적중 POINT

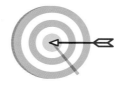

내신 100점 적중!
기출 출제율

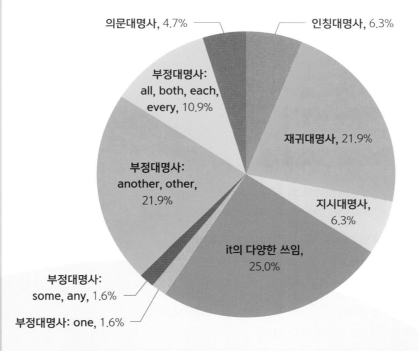

의문대명사, 4.7%

인칭대명사, 6.3%

부정대명사:
all, both, each,
every, 10.9%

재귀대명사, 21.9%

부정대명사:
another, other,
21.9%

지시대명사,
6.3%

it의 다양한 쓰임,
25.0%

부정대명사:
some, any, 1.6%

부정대명사: one, 1.6%

TOP 1 **it의 다양한 쓰임 (25%)**
it의 다양한 쓰임을 묻는 문제와 이를 구별하는 문제가 자주 출제된다.

TOP 2 **재귀대명사 (21.9%)**
부정대명사: another, other (21.9%)
재귀대명사의 쓰임과 재귀대명사를 이용한 관용 표현을 묻는 문제가 자주 출제된다. 부정대명사 another, other를 이용한 다양한 표현을 묻는 문제가 자주 출제된다.

TOP 3 **부정대명사: all, both, each, every (10.9%)**
부정대명사 all, both, each, every의 의미와 쓰임을 묻는 문제가 자주 출제된다.

인칭대명사

정답 p.29

인칭대명사는 사람이나 사물의 이름을 대신하는 말로, 인칭·수·격에 따라 형태가 다르다.

인칭·수	격	주격	소유격	목적격	소유대명사
1인칭	단수	I	my	me	mine
	복수	we	our	us	ours
2인칭	단수·복수	you	your	you	yours
3인칭	단수	he	his	him	his
		she	her	her	hers
		it	its	it	–
	복수	they	their	them	theirs

❶ 주격은 '~은, ~이'의 의미로, 문장의 주어 역할을 한다.
  She is a very smart student. 그녀는 매우 똑똑한 학생이다.
  We enjoy playing badminton together. 우리는 함께 배드민턴을 치는 것을 즐긴다.

❷ 소유격은 '~의'의 의미로, 명사 앞에서 명사와의 소유 관계를 나타낸다.
  I lost **my wallet** on the subway. 나는 지하철에서 나의 지갑을 잃어버렸다.
  Their house has a huge swimming pool. 그들의 집에는 큰 수영장이 있다.

❸ 목적격은 '~을, ~에게'의 의미로, 동사나 전치사의 목적어 역할을 한다.
  I can't **stand it** anymore. 나는 그것을 더는 참을 수 없다.
  Emily is waiting **for him** outside. Emily는 밖에서 그를 기다리고 있다.

❹ 소유대명사는 '~의 것'의 의미로, 「소유격 + 명사」를 대신한다.
  Is this jacket **yours**(= **your jacket**)? 이 재킷은 너의 것이니?
  My hair is longer than **hers**(= **her hair**). 나의 머리는 그녀의 것보다 더 길다.

연습문제 A 괄호 안에서 알맞은 것을 고르시오.

1 (You / Your) have to follow the rules.

2 (My / Me) grades were good last semester.

3 Benny will bake a cake for (our / us) soon.

4 Mr. and Mrs. Smith washed (their / them) car yesterday.

5 Please show the picture to (my / me).

6 Why don't you speak to (she / her)?

7 I often bite (my / me) nails when I'm nervous.

8 Jennifer gave (my / me) a box of chocolate cookies.

9 I've been to Norway. (It / Its) scenery was amazing.

10 Could you tell me (you / your) phone number?

11 Look at that girl. Do you know (she / her) name?

12 Do you see the police officer over there? (He / His) is my uncle.

13 Irene has a parrot. (It / Its) can say some words.

14 My family and I will miss our flight if (we / us) don't leave now.

15 Have you seen my glasses? I can't find (they / them) anywhere.

16 Mr. Kim teaches students science at school. They like (he / him) very much.

연습문제 B 우리말과 같도록 괄호 안의 인칭대명사를 알맞은 형태로 바꿔 빈칸에 쓰시오.

1 (I) ① 나의 노트북은 책상 위에 있다. = _____ laptop is on the desk.

② 책상 위에 있는 그 노트북은 나의 것이다. = The laptop on the desk is _____.

2 (you) ① 이것들은 너의 양말이니? = Are these _____ socks?

② 너의 것은 매우 깨끗하다. = _____ are very clean.

3 (he) ① 나는 그의 휴대폰을 빌렸다. = I borrowed _____ cell phone.

② 그 은색의 것은 그의 것이다. = The silver one is _____.

4 (she) ① 그녀는 그녀의 목걸이에 50달러를 지불했다. = She paid $50 for _____ necklace.

② 그녀의 것은 매우 예쁘고 반짝거린다. = _____ is very pretty and shiny.

5 (we) ① 저 아름다운 마을은 우리의 것이다. = That beautiful town is _____.

② 우리는 우리의 마을을 깨끗하게 유지해야 한다. = We should keep _____ town clean.

6 (they) ① 그 큰 차는 그들의 것이다. = The large car is _____.

② 그들의 차는 그 건물 앞에 있다. = _____ car is in front of the building.

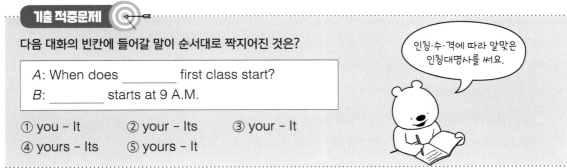

기출 적중문제

다음 대화의 빈칸에 들어갈 말이 순서대로 짝지어진 것은?

A: When does _____ first class start?
B: _____ starts at 9 A.M.

인칭·수·격에 따라 알맞은 인칭대명사를 써요.

① you - It   ② your - Its   ③ your - It
④ yours - Its   ⑤ yours - It

1. 재귀대명사는 '~ 자신, ~ 자체'의 의미로, 인칭대명사의 소유격이나 목적격에 -self(단수)/ -selves(복수)를 붙인 형태이다.

인칭 ＼ 수	단수	복수
1인칭	I - **my**self	we - **our**selves
2인칭	you - **your**self	you - **your**selves
3인칭	he - **him**self / she - **her**self / it - **it**self	they - **them**selves

2. 재귀대명사는 재귀 용법이나 강조 용법으로 쓰인다.

재귀 용법	동사나 전치사의 목적어가 주어와 같은 대상일 때 목적어로 재귀대명사를 쓴다. 이때 재귀대명사는 생략할 수 없다. Can **you** introduce **yourself**? 너 자신을 소개해주겠니? **I** don't like talking about **myself**. 나는 나 자신에 대해 이야기하는 것을 좋아하지 않는다.
강조 용법	문장의 주어·보어·목적어를 강조하기 위해 강조하는 말 바로 뒤나 문장 맨 뒤에 재귀대명사를 쓴다. 이때 재귀대명사는 생략할 수 있다. **He (himself)** made it. = **He** made it **(himself)**. 그는 그것을 직접 만들었다. I interviewed **the musician (herself)**. 나는 그 음악가 본인을 인터뷰했다.

3. 다음은 재귀대명사를 쓰는 관용 표현이다.

> by oneself 혼자서, 홀로
> in itself 그 자체가, 본질적으로
> talk to oneself 혼잣말을 하다
> help oneself to ~을 마음껏 먹다
>
> for oneself 혼자 힘으로, 스스로
> enjoy oneself 즐거운 시간을 보내다
> think to oneself 혼자 생각하다
> make oneself at home (집에서처럼) 편히 쉬다

Katie always does everything **for herself**. Katie는 항상 혼자 힘으로 모든 것을 한다.
Help yourself to the pizza. 그 피자를 마음껏 먹어라.

연습문제 A 괄호 안에서 알맞은 것을 고르시오.

1 My dog opened the door (him / himself).

2 They bought (her / herself) a teddy bear.

3 Jessica was angry at (herself / itself) for losing the race.

4 Could you bring (me / myself) a bottle of water, please?

5 Your friends must be proud of (ourselves / themselves).

6 I (me / myself) saw the accident yesterday.

7 My aunt cooked a pork cutlet for (us / ourselves).

8 We have to keep (us / ourselves) safe from the flu.

연습문제 **B** 밑줄 친 부분을 생략할 수 있으면 O를 쓰고, 생략할 수 없으면 X를 쓰시오.

1 Let me introduce <u>myself</u>. → _____

2 Jane made this bookshelf <u>herself</u>. → _____

3 You should take care of <u>yourself</u>. → _____

4 She doesn't like the clothes <u>themselves</u>. → _____

5 Minho <u>himself</u> painted this landscape painting. → _____

6 The chimpanzee looked at <u>itself</u> in the mirror. → _____

7 We thought of <u>ourselves</u> as great dancers. → _____

연습문제 **C** 우리말과 같도록 문장을 완성하시오.

1 Jake는 종종 혼잣말을 한다.
= Jake often _____.

2 그 아이들은 쿠키를 마음껏 먹었다.
= The children _____ the cookies.

3 Becky는 혼자서 영화를 보러 갔다.
= Becky went to the movies _____.

4 너희들은 그 콘서트에서 즐거운 시간을 보냈니?
= Did you _____ at the concert?

5 우리는 앉아서 편히 쉬었다.
= We sat down and _____.

6 나는 "Amy가 왜 화가 났지?"라고 혼자 생각했다.
= I _____, "Why is Amy angry?"

7 그 이야기는 그 자체가 인상적이었다.
= The story _____ was impressive.

8 그는 혼자 힘으로 사업을 시작했다.
= He started a business _____.

기출 적중문제

다음 중 밑줄 친 부분을 생략할 수 있는 것을 모두 고르시오.

① They enjoyed the festival <u>itself</u>.
② I made a promise to <u>myself</u>.
③ We were surprised to see <u>ourselves</u> on TV.
④ Owen cut <u>himself</u> with a pair of scissors.
⑤ My mom <u>herself</u> planted the tomatoes.

재귀대명사가 재귀 용법으로 쓰이면 생략할 수 없고, 강조 용법으로 쓰이면 생략할 수 있어요.

POINT 3 지시대명사

1. 지시대명사 this/these/that/those는 특정한 사람이나 사물을 가리킬 때 쓴다.

가까이 있는 사람·사물	단수	this 이 사람, 이것	**This** is my best friend. 이 사람은 나의 가장 친한 친구이다.
	복수	these 이 사람들, 이것들	**These** are Bob's shoes. 이것들은 Bob의 신발이다.
멀리 있는 사람·사물	단수	that 저 사람, 저것	**That** is my father's car. 저것은 나의 아버지의 차이다.
	복수	those 저 사람들, 저것들	**Those** are not Lisa's earrings. 저것들은 Lisa의 귀걸이가 아니다.

(Tip) that/those는 비교 표현에서 앞에 나온 명사의 반복을 피하기 위해서도 쓴다.

The price of gold is higher than **that**(= the price) of silver. 금의 가격은 은의 그것보다 더 높다.
The effects of smoking are as harmful as **those**(= the effects) of drinking.
흡연의 영향들은 음주의 그것들만큼 해롭다.

2. this/these/that/those는 '이 ~, 저 ~ '라는 의미의 지시형용사로 쓰여 명사 앞에서 명사를 수식할 수 있다.

This pancake smells delicious. 이 팬케이크는 맛있는 냄새가 난다.
Those students are studying hard. 저 학생들은 열심히 공부하고 있다.

연습문제 A 다음 그림을 보고 빈칸에 this, these, that, those 중 알맞은 것을 쓰시오.

1

2

3

4

1 Look at _____ men wearing sunglasses.

2 Is _____ your homeroom teacher?

3 _____ orange is for you.

4 Do you know who sent _____ letters?

연습문제 **B** 밑줄 친 부분의 쓰임과 같은 것을 <보기>에서 골라 그 기호를 쓰시오.

> <보기> ⓐ This is my little sister.
> ⓑ I like this wooden chair.

1 Those are my friends from school.   [   ]

2 These snakes are not poisonous.   [   ]

3 That building is over 100 years old.   [   ]

4 Please do not touch this.   [   ]

5 Natalie broke those eggs.   [   ]

6 Are these made in Italy?   [   ]

7 That is the largest tree in the world.   [   ]

8 This article was written by Ms. Johnson.   [   ]

연습문제 **C** 다음 빈칸에 that이나 those 중 알맞은 것을 쓰시오.

1 My bag is heavier than _____ of my brother.

2 Jenny's paintings are as great as _____ of professional artists.

3 Roy's birthday is earlier than _____ of Kelly.

4 The lives of dogs are shorter than _____ of humans.

5 The colors of the flowers were as beautiful as _____ of rainbows.

기출 적중문제

다음 중 밑줄 친 that의 쓰임이 나머지 넷과 다른 것은?

① Where did you get that camera?

② I'd like to eat that sandwich.

③ Do you know that boy over there?

④ That is a wonderful idea.

⑤ That house is really expensive.

it은 대명사, 비인칭 주어, 가주어로 쓰일 수 있다.

❶ 대명사 it은 특정한 대상을 가리킬 때 쓰며, '그것'이라고 해석한다.

Do you see **the bike** over there? **It** is my brother's.
너는 저기에 있는 자전거가 보이니? 그것은 나의 형의 것이야.

❷ 비인칭 주어 it은 날씨·계절·시간·요일·날짜·명암·거리를 나타낼 때 쓰며, '그것'이라고 해석하지 않는다.

날씨	**It** is raining now.	지금 비가 오고 있다.
계절	**It** is still winter here.	여기는 아직 겨울이다.
시간	**It** is five o'clock.	5시다.
요일	**It** is Friday today.	오늘은 금요일이다.
날짜	**It** is August 14.	8월 14일이다.
명암	**It** is too dark there.	저기는 너무 어둡다.
거리	**It** is only one kilometer to my school.	나의 학교까지 단지 1킬로미터이다.

❸ to부정사(구)나 명사절 등이 문장의 주어로 쓰였을 때는 주로 주어 자리에 가주어 it을 쓰고 원래 주어인 진주어를 뒤로 보낸다.

It is difficult **to learn Vietnamese**. 베트남어를 배우는 것은 어렵다.
가주어 it 　진주어(to부정사구)

It is certain **that Tim will visit Korea soon**. Tim이 곧 한국을 방문할 것은 확실하다.
가주어 it 　진주어(명사절)

연습문제 **A**   우리말과 같도록 괄호 안의 말을 알맞게 배열하시오.

1 눈사람을 만드는 것은 어렵지 않다. (a snowman, to, hard, isn't, make)
= It _____.

2 너의 약속을 지키는 것은 중요하다. (keep, is, to, important, your promises)
= It _____.

3 우리의 여행이 내일 끝난다는 것은 슬프다. (ends, our journey, sad, is, tomorrow, that)
= It _____.

4 약간의 과학적 사실들을 아는 것은 유용하다. (useful, some scientific facts, know, is, to)
= It _____.

5 미래를 예언하는 것은 불가능하다. (impossible, the future, is, predict, to)
= It _____.

6 네가 나의 주소를 기억한다는 것은 놀랍다. (is, that, my address, remember, you, surprising)

= It _____ .

7 매일 한 개의 사과를 먹는 것은 건강에 좋다. (healthy, to, every day, an apple, is, eat)

= It _____ .

8 아기 물개들이 수영할 수 없다는 것은 흥미롭다. (interesting, swim, baby seals, can't, is, that)

= It _____ .

| 연습문제 B | 밑줄 친 it의 쓰임과 같은 것을 <보기>에서 골라 그 기호를 쓰시오. |

> <보기> ⓐ It was an interesting show.
> ⓑ It will snow in a few hours.
> ⓒ It is helpful to exercise regularly.

1 Is it Monday tomorrow?　　　　　　　　　　　　　　　　[　　　　　]

2 The song was popular in 2007. I loved it.　　　　　　[　　　　　]

3 It is November 26.　　　　　　　　　　　　　　　　　　[　　　　　]

4 It is nice to ride a bike along the riverside.　　　　　[　　　　　]

5 It is a great place to go for a vacation.　　　　　　　[　　　　　]

6 It is certain that she will win the gold medal.　　　　[　　　　　]

7 It isn't easy to wake up early in the morning.　　　　[　　　　　]

8 Let's go to bed. It's already 11 P.M.　　　　　　　　　[　　　　　]

9 Have you ever smelled a durian? It smells quite bad.　[　　　　　]

10 It is surprising that Josh can play the flute.　　　　　[　　　　　]

11 It is about 400 meters from here to the supermarket.　[　　　　　]

12 My grandmother told me an old story. It was really funny.　[　　　　　]

기출 적중문제 🎯

주어진 문장의 밑줄 친 It과 쓰임이 같은 것은?

> It is hard to focus on studying at home.

① It was too hot yesterday.

② It was on the sofa.

③ It is getting bright outside.

④ It was good to see you again.

⑤ It isn't Katherine's fault.

부정대명사: one

정답 p.30

1. **one**은 앞에서 언급된 명사와 같은 종류의 불특정한 사람이나 사물을 가리킬 때 쓰며, 복수형은 **ones**이다.

   Jack's **phone** was stolen. He will buy a new **one**.
   Jack의 전화기가 도난당했다. 그는 새것을 살 것이다.

   I don't like these **shoes**. Can I try those **ones** on?
   저는 이 신발이 마음에 들지 않아요. 제가 저것들을 신어봐도 되나요?

   (Tip) 앞에서 언급된 특정한 대상을 가리킬 때는 **it**이나 **they/them**을 쓴다.

   Jack's **phone** was stolen. Somebody took **it** yesterday.
   Jack의 전화기가 도난당했다. 누군가가 어제 그것을 가져갔다.

   I don't like **these shoes**. I don't want to try **them** on.
   저는 이 신발이 마음에 들지 않아요. 저는 그것들을 신어보기를 원하지 않아요.

2. **one**은 일반적인 사람을 나타낼 때도 쓴다.

   One should obey the law. 사람은 법을 지켜야 한다.

연습문제 | 다음 빈칸에 알맞은 말을 <보기>에서 골라 쓰시오.

<보기> one   ones   it   them

1 Mr. Brown plans to buy a car. He will buy a cheap _____ .

2 There are some cupcakes on the table. I baked _____ myself.

3 These are not my cups. The _____ in the cupboard are mine.

4 There is a big hole in my blue shirt. I can't wear _____ anymore.

5 I need large paper clips, but the store only sells small _____ .

6 Would you like a sandwich? – No, I already had _____ .

7 He has a red tomato and three green _____ .

8 Molly sent you some text messages. Did you read _____ ?

9 Is the bag on the desk Ben's? – No, his is the _____ on the chair.

10 Where did you buy this sofa? – I bought _____ on the Internet.

11 Sumi lost her wallet, so she is using her old _____ now.

12 _____ should not judge others by their appearance.

13 When did you borrow those books? – I borrowed _____ last week.

부정대명사: some, any

정답 p.30

some/any는 '약간(의), 조금(의), 몇몇(의)'라는 의미이며, 대명사나 형용사로 쓰인다.

some	주로 긍정문과 권유·요청을 나타내는 의문문에 쓴다. I'm making **some** soup. Would you like to have **some**? 나는 약간의 수프를 만들고 있어. 너는 조금 먹기를 원하니? Can you bring me **some** tea? 나에게 약간의 차를 가져다주겠니?
any	주로 부정문과 의문문에 쓴다. I don't have **any** pens. Do you have **any**? 나는 약간의 펜도 가지고 있지 않아. 너는 조금 가지고 있니?

(Tip) some/any에 -thing이 붙으면 불특정한 사물을 나타내고, -body/-one이 붙으면 불특정한 사람을 나타낸다.

I saw **something** in the garden. 나는 정원에서 무언가를 봤다.
Do you have **anything** cold to drink? 너는 마실 차가운 무언가를 가지고 있니?
Mark needs **somebody** to help him. Mark는 그를 도와줄 누군가가 필요하다.
There isn't **anyone** in this room. 이 방에는 아무도 없다.

연습문제 | 괄호 안에서 알맞은 것을 고르시오.

1 Let's buy (some /any) onions and cucumbers.

2 Can I have (some / any) milk, please?

3 There isn't (some / any) pasta left.

4 I can do it by myself, so I don't need (some / any) help.

5 She is looking for (some / any) paper to write on.

6 Would you buy (some / any) flour on the way home?

7 I don't have (some / any) time to talk.

8 If you need more tissues, take (some / any).

9 Mary has a lot of homework, but I don't have (some / any).

10 There is fried chicken in the refrigerator. Do you want (some / any)?

11 Will you show me (something / anything) fun?

12 Is (somebody / anybody) feeling cold?

13 (Someone / Anyone) knocked on the door a minute ago.

14 We should do (something / anything) to fix the house.

15 Please don't say (something / anything).

16 (Someone / Anyone) is looking through the window.

부정대명사: another, other

정답 p.30

1. another는 '하나 더, 또 다른 하나'라는 의미이다.

This muffin is delicious. I will have **another**. 이 머핀은 맛있다. 나는 하나 더 먹겠다.

(Tip) 「another + 단수명사」는 '또 다른 ~'이라는 의미이다.

Let's look at **another example**. 또 다른 사례를 보자.

2. other는 '(불특정한) 다른 사람들/것들'이라는 의미이며, 주로 복수형인 others로 쓰인다. 「the + other(s)」는 '나머지'라는 의미이다.

Helping **others** feels great. 다른 사람들을 돕는 것은 정말 좋은 기분이 든다.

One of the four strawberries was sweet, but **the others** were sour.
네 개의 딸기들 중 하나는 달았지만, 나머지 전부는 시큼했다.

(Tip) 「other + 복수명사」는 '다른 ~'이라는 의미이다.

We have to think of **other plans**. 우리는 다른 계획들을 생각해내야 한다.

3. one, another, other(s), some을 써서 여럿 중 일부를 나타낼 수 있다.

one ~, the other –	**one ~, another –, the other ⋯**
(둘 중) 하나는 ~, 나머지 하나는 –	(셋 중) 하나는 ~, 다른 하나는 –, 나머지 하나는 ⋯
There are two flowers. **One** is a rose, and **the other** is a tulip. 두 송이의 꽃이 있다. 하나는 장미이고, 나머지 하나는 튤립이다.	There are three flowers. **One** is a rose, **another** is a tulip, and **the other** is a lily. 세 송이의 꽃이 있다. 하나는 장미이고, 다른 하나는 튤립이고, 나머지 하나는 백합이다.
some ~, others –	**some ~, the others –**
(여럿 중) 몇몇은 ~, 다른 사람들/것들은 –	(여럿 중) 몇몇은 ~, 나머지 전부는 –
There are lots of flowers. **Some** are roses, and **others** are tulips. 많은 꽃들이 있다. 몇몇은 장미이고, 다른 것들은 튤립이다.	There are ten flowers. **Some** are roses, and **the others** are tulips. 열 송이의 꽃이 있다. 몇몇은 장미이고, 나머지 전부는 튤립이다.

연습문제 A 괄호 안에서 알맞은 것을 고르시오.

1 He always makes (another / others) laugh.

2 Would you like to have (another / other) glass of juice?

3 I like carrots, but I don't like (another / other) vegetables.

4 If you buy two snacks, you can get (another / other) for free.

연습문제 B 다음 그림을 보고 빈칸에 알맞은 말을 <보기>에서 골라 쓰시오.

<보기>　one　another　others　the other　the others　some

1 Two boys are sitting on the bench. ＿＿＿＿＿＿ is reading a book, and ＿＿＿＿＿＿ is listening to music.

2 Five people are watching a movie in the theater. ＿＿＿＿＿＿ are eating popcorn, and ＿＿＿＿＿＿ are drinking soda.

3 I met three new friends at the international culture festival. ＿＿＿＿＿＿ is from Indonesia, ＿＿＿＿＿＿ is from Italy, and ＿＿＿＿＿＿ is from Kenya.

4 There are lots of puppies in the garden. ＿＿＿＿＿＿ are brown, and ＿＿＿＿＿＿ are white.

 기출 적중문제

다음 글의 밑줄 친 우리말과 같도록 문장을 완성하시오.

> Sojin bought two ingredients for the soup. 하나는 소고기이고, 나머지 하나는 브로콜리이다.

= ＿＿＿＿＿＿ is beef, and ＿＿＿＿＿＿ is broccoli.

부정대명사: all, both, each, every

정답 p.30

부정대명사 all, both, each, every의 쓰임은 다음과 같다.

	쓰임		예문
all 모든	복수 취급	all (of) + 복수명사	**All (of) the questions were** easy to solve. 모든 문제들은 풀기에 쉬웠다.
	단수 취급	all (of) + 셀 수 없는 명사	**All (of) my homework is** finished. 나의 모든 숙제는 끝났다.
both 둘 다	복수 취급	both (of) + 복수명사	**Both (of) my sisters enjoy** reading poetry. 나의 여동생들 둘 다 시를 읽는 것을 즐긴다.
each 각각(의)	단수 취급	each + 단수명사	**Each person has** a different personality. 각각의 사람은 서로 다른 성격을 가지고 있다.
		each of + 복수명사	**Each of the students has** to turn in an essay. 학생들 각각은 과제물을 제출해야 한다.
every 모든	단수 취급	every + 단수명사	**Every room is** reserved until August. 모든 방은 8월까지 예약되었다.
		everything / everybody / everyone	**Everything is** going smoothly. 모든 것은 순조롭게 진행되고 있다.

(Tip) each other는 '(둘 사이에) 서로', one another는 '(셋 이상 사이에) 서로'라는 의미의 대명사이다.
Peter and I know **each other** well. Peter와 나는 서로를 잘 안다.
Friends shouldn't lie to **one another**. 친구들은 서로에게 거짓말하면 안 된다.

(Tip) all, both, every가 not 등의 부정어와 함께 쓰이면 일부를 부정하는 부분 부정을 나타낸다.
Not all people like soccer. 모든 사람이 축구를 좋아하는 것은 아니다.
They are not both middle school students. 그들 둘 다 중학생인 것은 아니다.
Not every fruit tastes sweet. 모든 과일이 단맛이 나는 것은 아니다.

연습문제 A | 우리말과 같도록 괄호 안의 말을 알맞게 배열하시오.

1 모든 학생들은 교복을 입어야 한다. (the students, wear, have to, all, a uniform)
= _____

2 그 차 둘 다 독일에서 만들어졌다. (made, the cars, both, in Germany, are)
= _____

3 그 소녀들 각각은 서로 다른 취미를 가지고 있다. (has, each of, the girls, a different hobby)
= _____

4 모든 돈은 그 도둑에 의해 훔쳐졌다. (the money, was, all of, stolen, by the thief)

= _____

5 동물들은 서로 의사소통할 수 있다. (can, one, communicate with, another, animals)

= _____

6 모든 한국인이 매운 음식을 좋아하는 것은 아니다. (Korean, spicy food, likes, every, not)

= _____

7 각각의 하키팀은 최종 경기를 준비하고 있다. (preparing for, is, hockey team, the final match, each)

= _____

8 지구와 달은 서로를 끌어당긴다. (each, pull, the Earth and the Moon, other)

= _____

9 모든 사람은 보드 게임을 하고 있었다. (a board game, was, everybody, playing)

= _____

10 모든 지방이 너의 건강에 나쁜 것은 아니다. (all, is, bad for, your health, fat, not)

= _____

연습문제 B | 괄호 안에서 알맞은 것을 고르시오.

1 Both cities (is / are) popular among tourists.

2 All of the milk (was / were) spilt on the floor.

3 Everyone (knows / know) that wine is made from grapes.

4 All guests (needs / need) to show their invitation card.

5 Both of his daughters (is / are) studying law.

6 Each of the farmers (grows / grow) different crops.

7 Everything (looks / look) great on you.

8 Each of the bottles (was / were) marked with a yellow sticker.

9 Every book on this shelf (is / are) interesting.

10 Each country (sends / send) their best athletes to the Olympic Games.

기출 적중문제 🎯

다음 중 어법상 어색한 것은?

① Every child needs attention.

② Both my laptops were broken.

③ Each of the doughnuts cost two dollars.

④ I've already watched both of the movies.

⑤ All of the food has been eaten by my brother.

who, what, which는 각각 '누구, 무엇, 어느 것'이라는 구체적인 정보를 묻는 의문대명사이다.

who	who는 사람에 대해 물을 때 쓰며, 격에 따라 whose나 whom으로 형태가 변한다. 주격　**Who** ate the last piece? – Daeho did. 　　　누가 그 마지막 조각을 먹었니? – 대호가 먹었어. 소유격　**Whose hat** is this? – It's mine.　이것은 누구의 모자니? – 그것은 나의 것이야. 　　　= **Whose** is this hat?　이 모자는 누구의 것이니? 　　　└→ whose는 '누구의 것'이라는 의미로 명사 없이 단독으로 쓰이기도 한다. 목적격　**Who[Whom]** did you have lunch with? – Carla. 　　　너는 누구와 함께 점심을 먹었니? – Carla. 　　　= With **whom** did you have lunch? 　　　└→ 전치사를 의문대명사 앞에 쓰면 who가 아닌 whom을 써야 한다.
what	what은 동물이나 사물, 또는 사람의 직업이나 성격에 대해 물을 때 쓴다. **What** will you order? – A hamburger.　너는 무엇을 주문할 거니? – 햄버거. **What** does Amy do? – She is a doctor.　Amy는 무슨 일을 하니? – 그녀는 의사야. (Tip) what은 '무슨, 어떤'이라는 의미의 의문형용사로 쓰여 명사 앞에서 명사를 수식할 수 있다. 　　　**What genre** is the movie? – It's a horror movie. 　　　그 영화는 무슨 장르니? – 그것은 공포 영화야.
which	which는 정해진 범위 안에서의 선택을 물을 때 쓴다. **Which** do you want, juice or coffee? – I want juice. 너는 주스와 커피 중 어느 것을 원하니? – 나는 주스를 원해. (Tip) which는 '어느, 어떤'이라는 의미의 의문형용사로 쓰여 명사 앞에서 명사를 수식할 수 있다. 　　　**Which color** do you like among these? – Pink. 　　　너는 이것들 중 어느 색을 좋아하니? – 분홍색.

(Tip) what은 정해지지 않은 범위에서 질문할 때 쓰고, which는 정해진 범위 안에서의 선택을 물을 때 쓴다.
　　What flavor do you like best?　너는 무슨 맛을 가장 좋아하니?
　　Which flavor of these three do you like best?　너는 이 셋 중 어느 맛을 가장 좋아하니?

연습문제 A　괄호 안에서 알맞은 것을 고르시오.

1　(Who / Whom) wrote the play *Romeo and Juliet*?

2　(What / Which) fruit do you prefer, watermelon or peach?

3　(Whose / Whom) name is written on the paper?

4　(What / Which) does the building look like?

5　To (who / whom) is James talking?

연습문제 B 다음 빈칸에 알맞은 의문대명사를 넣어 대화를 완성하시오.

1 A: _____ did Beth make for breakfast? B: She made some toast.

2 A: _____ music do you prefer, R&B or hip hop? B: R&B.

3 A: _____ cat is it? B: I think it is Sam's cat.

4 A: _____ did you meet last Sunday? B: I met Jihye.

5 A: _____ called you five minutes ago? B: Mike did.

6 A: By _____ was the window broken? B: My little brother.

7 A: _____ is taller, a giraffe or an elephant? B: A giraffe is taller.

8 A: _____ do you want to be in the future? B: I want to be a lawyer.

연습문제 C 우리말과 같도록 괄호 안의 말을 알맞게 배열하시오.

1 너는 어느 식당을 추천하니? (recommend, do, restaurant, you, which)

= _____

2 너의 가족은 어느 호텔을 예약할 거니? (which, your family, will, hotel, book)

= _____

3 세미는 무슨 과목을 공부하는 것을 좋아하니? (to study, does, like, what, subject, Semi)

= _____

4 Eric은 Samantha에게 무슨 꽃을 줬니? (did, flower, give, what, Eric, to Samantha)

= _____

5 너는 그 영화에서 어느 영웅을 좋아하니? (like, hero, in the movie, you, which, do)

= _____

기출 적중문제

다음 대화의 빈칸에 알맞은 말을 <보기>에서 한 번씩만 골라 쓰시오.

<보기> who   what   which

(1) A: _____ shirt of these two will you wear?
   B: The white one.

(2) A: _____ taught you how to ride a bike?
   B: My dad did.

(3) A: _____ are you going to do after dinner?
   B: I'm going to jog in the park.

Ⓐ 다음 빈칸에 알맞은 재귀대명사를 쓰시오.

1 Ronald hurt _____ playing hockey.

2 We need to believe in _____ .

3 She _____ told me the truth.

4 The plan _____ was not so bad.

5 People can express _____ by writing in a diary.

6 Minji talks to _____ when she washes the dishes.

7 I went to John's apartment and made _____ at home.

8 The selfish man always thinks about _____ only.

9 Did you make the gimbap for the picnic _____ ?

Ⓑ 우리말과 같도록 괄호 안의 말을 알맞게 배열하시오.

1 내일은 추울 것이다. (cold, be, it, will)
= _____ tomorrow.

2 그것은 전혀 나의 생각이 아니었다. (my idea, wasn't, it)
= _____ at all.

3 극장 안은 매우 어두웠다. (dark, it, very, was)
= _____ in the theater.

4 매일 아침을 먹는 것은 중요하다. (is, eat, it, to, breakfast, important)
= _____ every day.

5 애완동물이 아이들에게 좋은 친구라는 것은 사실이다. (true, are, good friends, pets, is, it, that)
= _____ to children.

6 네가 자고 있는 동안 감기에 걸리는 것은 쉽다. (catch, is, it, to, a cold, easy)
= _____ while you are sleeping.

7 오늘은 9월 12일이고, 나의 생일이다. (is, it, September 12)
= _____ today, and it is my birthday.

8 나의 팀이 어제 그 경기를 진 것은 실망스러웠다. (was, that, my team, the game, disappointing, it, lost)
= _____ yesterday.

C 우리말과 같도록 괄호 안의 말을 활용하여 문장을 완성하시오.

1 두 개의 가방이 있다. 하나는 핸드백이고, 나머지 하나는 배낭이다. (a handbag, a backpack)

= There are two bags. _____ , and _____ .

2 나는 일곱 개의 상자를 찾았다. 몇몇은 갈색이고, 나머지 전부는 회색이다. (brown, gray)

= I found seven boxes. _____ , and _____ .

3 세 벌의 옷이 있다. 하나는 재킷이고, 다른 하나는 코트이고, 나머지 하나는 치마이다. (a jacket, a coat, a skirt)

= There are three pieces of clothes. _____ , _____ ,

and _____ .

4 Luke는 많은 과일을 샀다. 몇몇은 배이고, 다른 것들은 멜론이다. (pears, melons)

= Luke bought many fruits. _____ , and _____ .

5 지붕 위에 두 마리의 고양이가 있다. 하나는 자고 있고, 나머지 하나는 앉아 있다. (sleeping, sitting)

= Two cats are on the roof. _____ , and _____ .

6 바구니 안에 아홉 개의 공이 있다. 몇몇은 야구공이고, 나머지 전부는 농구공이다. (baseballs, basketballs)

= Nine balls are in the basket. _____ , and _____ .

7 삶에 세 가지 중요한 것이 있다. 하나는 행복이고, 다른 하나는 사랑이고, 나머지 하나는 건강이다. (happiness, love, health)

= There are three important things in life. _____ , _____ ,

and _____ .

D 밑줄 친 부분이 어법상 맞으면 O를 쓰고, 틀리면 바르게 고쳐 쓰시오.

1 Both child love eating ice cream. → _____

2 Everybody has their own opinion. → _____

3 All of the buses was crowded an hour ago. → _____

4 Every passengers has to wear a seat belt. → _____

5 Each of the stones has a different shape. → _____

6 All of the information were totally wrong. → _____

7 Each classes takes 45 minutes. → _____

8 Each of this postcard costs one dollar. → _____

9 Both of my hand got dirty while gardening. → _____

중간·기말고사 실전 문제

1 다음 대화의 빈칸에 들어갈 말이 순서대로 짝지어진 것은?

> A: Can I borrow _____ phone for a second?
> B: Sure. What happened to _____ ?
> A: Its battery died.

① you – your
② your – yours
③ your – your
④ yours – yours
⑤ yours – your

2 다음 중 밑줄 친 it의 쓰임이 나머지 넷과 다른 것은?

① It's 10:30 A.M. now.
② How much is it?
③ It's too bright in this hall.
④ It will be cloudy tomorrow.
⑤ How far is it from here to the café?

3 다음 중 밑줄 친 부분이 어법상 바른 것은?

① Where did you get that gloves?
② These is Bella's pencil case.
③ The black suit in the closet is him.
④ Soyoung lent her bicycle to me.
⑤ The grammar of English is easier than those of Korean.

4 다음 중 밑줄 친 부분을 생략할 수 있는 것을 모두 고르시오.

① I'm growing all of the plants myself.
② Minjae always believes in himself.
③ Ms. Green herself painted the room.
④ You don't have to blame yourself.
⑤ They forgave themselves for the mistake.

5 우리말과 같도록 빈칸에 알맞은 말을 쓰시오.

> 그 칼을 조심해라. 너는 너 자신을 벨지도 모른다.

= Be careful with the knife. You might cut
_____.

6 다음 글의 빈칸에 들어갈 말이 순서대로 짝지어진 것은?

> Canada has two official languages. _____ is English, and _____ is French.

① One – others
② Some – others
③ One – the other
④ Some – the other
⑤ Another – the others

7 다음 대화의 빈칸에 들어갈 알맞은 것은?

> A: Where do those birds spend the winter?
> B: Some fly to Mexico, and _____ travel to South America.

① one ② another ③ other
④ others ⑤ the other

8 다음 빈칸에 들어갈 알맞은 것은?

> Some people feel uncomfortable to talk about _____ in front of many people.

① our ② they
③ ourselves ④ themselves
⑤ their

9 다음 중 어법상 바른 것은?

① Why don't you love you?
② He bought me the new computer.
③ Do you know why cats wash myself so much?
④ I'm going to draw a picture of me.
⑤ A chameleon hides themselves by changing color.

10 다음 빈칸에 들어갈 말이 순서대로 짝지어진 것은?

> · _____ of the potatoes is a different size.
> · _____ the stores were closed on Lunar New Year.

① Each – Every ② All – Every
③ Both – Each ④ Both – All
⑤ Each – All

11 우리말과 같도록 빈칸에 알맞은 말을 쓰시오.

> 너는 당근 케이크와 레몬 케이크 중 어느 케이크를 더 좋아하니?

= _____ cake do you like more, carrot cake or lemon cake?

12 다음 빈칸에 들어갈 알맞은 것은?

> The clown gave me a small balloon, but I wanted a big _____.

① it ② them ③ that
④ one ⑤ ones

13 다음 빈칸에 들어갈 말이 순서대로 짝지어진 것은?

> · All the articles _____ written in English.
>
> · Each bus _____ different numbers on it.

① was – have   ② was – has
③ were – have   ④ were – has
⑤ be – have

14 주어진 문장의 밑줄 친 it과 쓰임이 같은 것을 모두 고르시오.

> It is interesting to learn a new language.

① Is it Thursday tomorrow?
② I've been to the restaurant. It is on the second floor.
③ It is the most beautiful place on earth.
④ It is amazing that Minsu got the highest score in his class.
⑤ It is important to follow the law.

15 다음 글에서 어법상 어색한 부분을 찾아 쓰고 바르게 고쳐 쓰시오.

> I have two pieces of news for you. One is good news, and other is bad news. Which one would you like to hear first?

_____ → _____

16 우리말과 같도록 재귀대명사를 이용하여 빈칸에 알맞은 말을 쓰시오.

> 나의 친구들과 나는 학교 축제에서 즐거운 시간을 보냈다.

= My friends and I _____ _____ at the school festival.

17 다음 중 밑줄 친 it의 쓰임이 같은 것끼리 묶인 것은?

> ⓐ Is it summer in New Zealand now?
> ⓑ It is an old song by the Beatles.
> ⓒ It is too expensive for us.
> ⓓ It is certain that I turned off the stove.
> ⓔ It was a very difficult question to answer.

① ⓐ, ⓑ   ② ⓐ, ⓓ   ③ ⓑ, ⓓ
④ ⓑ, ⓒ, ⓔ   ⑤ ⓒ, ⓓ, ⓔ

18 다음 빈칸에 들어갈 말이 순서대로 짝지어진 것은?

> · He wrote a letter and sent _____ to his grandparents.
>
> · These gloves are too expensive. Do you have cheaper _____?

① it – them   ② one – them
③ it – ones   ④ one – one
⑤ one – ones

19 다음 빈칸에 another가 들어갈 수 없는 것은?

① There is _____ coin in my pocket.
② This chair is too hard. Do you have _____?
③ My mother doesn't have a car. She needs _____.
④ We should find _____ way to solve the problem.
⑤ Can I have _____ slice of pizza?

20 다음 중 어법상 어색한 것은?

① Each room is beautifully decorated.
② Both of the author are from England.
③ Every customer should use paper bags.
④ All the information will be kept safe.
⑤ Each of you has to introduce yourselves for three minutes.

21 다음 대화의 빈칸에 들어갈 말이 순서대로 짝지어진 것은?

A: Help _____ to the fried chicken.
B: Thanks. Would you pass me _____ sauce?
A: Here you go.

① you – any   ② you – some
③ your – any   ④ yourself – any
⑤ yourself – some

22 다음 빈칸에 공통으로 들어갈 알맞은 것은?

· _____ like watching action movies, but others don't like watching them.
· I have _____ questions to ask the math teacher.

① One[one]   ② Ones[ones]
③ Some[some]   ④ Any[any]
⑤ The other[the other]

23 주어진 문장의 밑줄 친 부분과 쓰임이 같은 것을 모두 고르시오.

We must do our homework ourselves.

① I myself made the kimchi.
② Be careful not to hurt yourself.
③ The woman thought to herself, "Let it go."
④ The artist created the new design himself.
⑤ Those cats are looking at themselves in the mirror.

24 다음 (A)~(C)에 들어갈 말이 바르게 짝지어진 것은?

Some countries use three colors in their flags. For example, Germany's flag has three colors. _____(A)_____ is black, _____(B)_____ is red, and _____(C)_____ is yellow.

	(A)	(B)	(C)
①	One	another	the other
②	One	other	the other
③	One	another	the others
④	Ones	other	the others
⑤	Ones	another	others

25 다음 빈칸에 who가 들어갈 수 <u>없는</u> 것은?

① _____ is the tallest student in your class?
② Do you know _____ that boy is?
③ _____ can fix this computer?
④ With _____ did you go to the theater?
⑤ _____ drew the picture on the wall?

26 다음 중 어법상 바른 것은?

① Both her parents likes sweet desserts.
② Every password have to be different.
③ Not all monkeys eats bananas.
④ All the cabbages was destroyed by the heavy rain.
⑤ Each of the players has special skills.

27 다음 대화의 밑줄 친 those와 쓰임이 같은 것을 <u>모두</u> 고르시오.

A: Why did <u>those</u> trees fall?
B: Because of the storm last night.

① <u>Those</u> are my father's diaries.
② Michael is a fan of <u>those</u> sports teams.
③ Are <u>those</u> real flowers?
④ What kinds of meats are <u>those</u>?
⑤ You can find <u>those</u> places on the map.

28 우리말과 같도록 괄호 안의 말을 활용하여 문장을 완성하시오.

환경을 보호하기 위해 플라스틱을 재활용하는 것은 중요하다. (important, recycle plastics)

= It _____ in order to protect the environment.

29 다음 글의 빈칸에 들어갈 말이 순서대로 짝지어진 것은?

I have two little brothers. One is eleven years old, and _____ is nine years old. They fight with _____ about everything, so I always have to stop them.

① the other – one another
② other – one another
③ the other – each other
④ another – each other
⑤ another – one another

30 다음 중 밑줄 친 부분이 어법상 <u>어색한</u> 것끼리 묶인 것은?

ⓐ I burned <u>myself</u> while cooking yesterday.
ⓑ Did you make the pie for <u>them</u>?
ⓒ Is Jonathan talking to <u>yourself</u> now?
ⓓ Maria was very disappointed in <u>herself</u>.
ⓔ I've seen the famous actor <u>him</u> on the street.

① ⓐ, ⓑ   ② ⓐ, ⓒ   ③ ⓑ, ⓓ
④ ⓒ, ⓔ   ⑤ ⓓ, ⓔ

31 다음 빈칸에 알맞은 말을 <보기>에서 한 번씩만 골라 쓰시오.

<보기> this   that   these

(1) Here is a phone. Is _____ yours?

(2) The population of China is larger than _____ of India.

(3) _____ laptops are new models. Those are old ones.

32 다음 대화의 빈칸에 들어갈 알맞은 것은?

A: To _____ are you going to send the package?

B: To my cousin, Fred. I bought a watch for his birthday present.

① who   ② whom   ③ whose
④ which   ⑤ what

33 다음 중 밑줄 친 부분이 어법상 어색한 것은?

① Diana met many new people at the party. Some were nice, and <u>others</u> were not.

② Jason chose a red hat, and I chose a black <u>one</u>.

③ There are ten horses on the farm. Some are brown, and <u>the others</u> are white.

④ Mr. Lee has two sons. One is a dentist, and <u>another</u> is a teacher.

⑤ I have many necklaces, but I want to buy new <u>ones</u>.

34 다음 글의 밑줄 친 it과 쓰임이 <u>다른</u> 것을 모두 고르시오.

Petroleum is the main energy source in lots of countries. However, <u>it</u> causes some environmental problems. So, we need to find another energy source to protect the earth.

*petroleum 석유

① Have you ever heard of <u>it</u>?

② <u>It</u> was so cold last winter.

③ You can find <u>it</u> in the box under the bed.

④ <u>It</u> is a good habit to drink a liter of water every day.

⑤ There was a big dog in front of the building. Did you see <u>it</u>?

35 다음 그림을 보고 주어진 <조건>에 맞게 문장을 완성하시오.

<조건>
1. play, the violin을 활용하시오.
2. 진행시제로 쓰시오.

There are five musicians on the stage.
_____, and
_____ the cello.

CHAPTER 11
형용사

I have a **soft** pillow. 나는 부드러운 베개를 가지고 있다.

My pillow is **soft**. 나의 베개는 부드럽다.

그냥 '베개'라고 말하는 것보다 '부드러운 베개' 또는 '베개는 부드럽다.'라고 말하면 어떤 베개인지 더 자세하게 알 수 있어요. 이렇게 사람이나 사물의 모양, 상태 등을 설명해주는 것을 **형용사**라고 해요. 형용사는 크기, 색깔, 모양, 감정, 상태, 날씨, 숫자 등을 나타낼 수 있어요.

기출로 적중 POINT

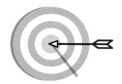

내신 100점 적중!
기출 출제율

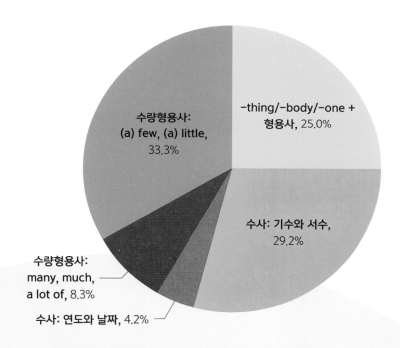

-thing/-body/-one + 형용사, 25.0%

수량형용사: (a) few, (a) little, 33.3%

수사: 기수와 서수, 29.2%

수량형용사: many, much, a lot of, 8.3%

수사: 연도와 날짜, 4.2%

TOP 1 **수량형용사: (a) few, (a) little (33.3%)**
수량형용사 (a) few와 (a) little의 쓰임을 묻는 문제가 자주 출제된다.

TOP 2 **수사: 기수와 서수 (29.2%)**
기수와 서수를 영어로 나타내는 문제가 자주 출제된다.

TOP 3 **-thing/-body/-one + 형용사 (25%)**
-thing/-body/-one으로 끝나는 대명사를 수식하는 형용사의 위치를 묻는 문제가 자주 출제된다.

형용사의 용법

정답 p.33

---

1. 한정적 용법: 주로 명사 앞에서 명사를 수식한다.

Marie is a **small dog**. Marie는 작은 개이다.

I picked up a **wooden toy**. 나는 나무로 된 장난감을 주웠다.

2. 서술적 용법: 보어로 쓰여 주어나 목적어를 보충 설명한다.

주격 보어 **This watch** is very **expensive**. 이 시계는 매우 비싸다.

목적격 보어 Bobby made **me angry**. Bobby는 나를 화나게 만들었다.

(Tip) 다음 형용사는 서술적 용법으로만 쓰인다.

asleep 잠든	awake 깨어있는	alive 살아있는	alone 혼자의
alike 비슷한	afraid 무서워하는	glad 반가운	pleased 기쁜

The frog is **alive**. (O) 그 개구리는 살아있다.
It is an alive frog. (X)

연습문제 A <보기>와 같이 다음 문장을 바꿔 쓰시오.

<보기> The tree is tall. → It _is a tall tree_ .

1 The stone is round. → It _____ .

2 The musical was amazing. → It _____ .

3 This diamond is shiny. → This _____ .

4 That car is old and broken. → That _____ .

5 The boy is clever. → He _____ .

6 The singer was rich and famous. → She _____ .

연습문제 B 괄호 안에서 알맞은 것을 고르시오.

1 The twins are very (like / alike).

2 Look at that (live / alive) octopus.

3 The (scared / afraid) girl screamed loudly.

4 My great-grandmother is still (live / alive).

5 The (sleeping / asleep) baby is John's younger sister.

기출로적중 POINT 2

-thing/-body/-one + 형용사

정답 p.33

-thing, -body, -one으로 끝나는 대명사를 수식할 때는 형용사가 대명사 뒤에 온다.

I want **something** delicious. 나는 맛있는 무언가를 원한다.
Is there **anything** wrong with your food? 너의 음식에 잘못된 무언가가 있니?
There was **nobody** familiar to me. 나에게 친숙한 사람이 아무도 없었다.
Someone smart solved the problem. 똑똑한 누군가가 그 문제를 해결했다.

(Tip) 명사 thing(것, 물건)을 수식할 때는 형용사가 명사 앞에 온다.
　　Many **useful** things are on this shelf. 많은 유용한 것들이 이 선반 위에 있다.

연습문제 │ 괄호 안의 형용사를 알맞은 곳에 넣어 완전한 문장을 쓰시오.

1 Would you like to have something? (sweet)

→ _____

2 Have you ever met anyone? (famous)

→ _____

3 Nothing happened last night. (special)

→ _____

4 My mother met somebody at the post office. (kind)

→ _____

5 He couldn't find anything with his computer. (wrong)

→ _____

6 We can learn things when we travel abroad. (new)

→ _____

7 There was somebody at Mina's birthday party. (funny)

→ _____

기출 적중문제

다음 글에서 어법상 어색한 부분을 찾아 쓰고 바르게 고쳐 쓰시오.

> There was sticky something on the kitchen
> table. The sticky thing was melted ice cream.

_____ → _____

-thing으로 끝나는
대명사는 형용사가 뒤에서
수식해요.

기출로적중 POINT 3 the + 형용사

「the + 형용사」는 '~한 사람들'이라는 의미로, 복수 취급한다.

The young(= **Young people**) should respect **the old**(= **old people**).
젊은 사람들은 나이 든 사람들을 공경해야 한다.

The rich(= **Rich people**) pay higher taxes than **the poor**(= **poor people**).
부유한 사람들은 가난한 사람들보다 더 높은 세금을 낸다.

Rick donated some money for **the blind**(= **blind people**).
Rick은 눈이 먼 사람들을 위해 약간의 돈을 기부했다.

연습문제 A | <보기>와 같이 다음 문장을 바꿔 쓰시오.

<보기>   The doctor is helping sick people in Africa.
   → *The doctor is helping the sick in Africa.*

1 Young people should listen to their parents.

→ _____

2 We did some volunteer work for poor people.

→ _____

3 Many charities offer free meals to homeless people.

→ _____

4 The school trains guide dogs for blind people.

→ _____

5 They took care of injured people at the hospital.

→ _____

연습문제 B | 괄호 안에서 알맞은 것을 고르시오.

1 (A / The) weak should be protected.

2 The truth is that the rich (is / are) not always happy.

3 The deaf usually (use / uses) their hands to communicate.

4 (Does / Do) the disabled get government support?

5 The young (have / has) to learn how to save money.

6 Her dream is to build a special school for (the blind / the blinds).

POINT 4-1 수사: 기수와 서수

정답 p.33

1. 기수는 개수를 말할 때 쓰고, 서수는 순서를 말할 때 쓴다.

기수		서수		기수		서수	
1	one	1st	first	12	twelve	12th	twelfth
2	two	2nd	second	20	twenty	20th	twentieth
3	three	3rd	third	40	forty	40th	fortieth
4	four	4th	fourth	60	sixty	60th	sixtieth
5	five	5th	fifth	61	sixty-one	61st	sixty-first
6	six	6th	sixth	62	sixty-two	62nd	sixty-second
7	seven	7th	seventh	63	sixty-three	63rd	sixty-third
8	eight	8th	eighth	90	ninety	90th	ninetieth
9	nine	9th	ninth	100	a[one] hundred	100th	one hundredth
10	ten	10th	tenth	1,000	a[one] thousand	1,000th	one thousandth

Jonathan's older sister is **twenty** years old. Jonathan의 누나는 스무 살이다.
Her **twentieth** birthday was yesterday. 그녀의 스무 번째 생일은 어제였다.

2. 「hundreds/thousands/millions + of + 복수명사」는 막연하게 큰 숫자를 나타낸다.

Hundreds of volunteers cleaned the beach. 수백 명의 자원봉사자들이 그 해변을 청소했다.
There are **millions of** books in that library. 저 도서관에는 수백만 권의 책이 있다.

(Tip) 정해진 큰 숫자를 나타낼 때는 hundred/thousand/million에 -s를 붙이지 않는다.
I have **eight** thousand won in my pocket. 나는 나의 주머니에 8,000원을 가지고 있다.

연습문제 A 다음 기수는 서수로, 서수는 기수로 바꿔 쓰시오. (단, 영어로 쓰시오.)

1 nine   → _____   **2** four   → _____

3 tenth   → _____   **4** thirty-one   → _____

5 twenty-two   → _____   **6** seventy   → _____

7 eighty   → _____   **8** thirty-third   → _____

9 one hundredth   → _____   **10** sixty-second   → _____

11 eleven   → _____   **12** eighteenth   → _____

13 seventy-five → _____   **14** a thousand → _____

15 fifty-ninth → _____   **16** fortieth → _____

연습문제 **B** 우리말과 같도록 괄호 안의 말을 활용하여 문장을 완성하시오. (단, 숫자는 영어로 쓰시오.)

1 리어왕은 세 명의 딸이 있었다. 세 번째 딸은 매우 현명했다. (daughter)

= King Lear had _____ . The _____ was very wise.

2 그들은 오십 명의 손님을 초대했다. 오십 번째 손님은 늦게 도착했다. (guest)

= They invited _____ . The _____ arrived late.

3 우리는 식당에서 여섯 개의 요리를 주문했다. 여섯 번째 요리는 스테이크였다. (dish)

= We ordered _____ at the restaurant. The _____ was steak.

4 나의 아파트에는 스물 다섯 개의 층이 있다. 나는 스물 다섯 번째 층에 산다. (floor)

= There are _____ in my apartment. I live on the _____ .

5 Josie는 열두 개의 색연필을 가지고 있다. 열두 번째 색연필은 보라색이다. (colored pencil)

= Josie has _____ . The _____ is violet.

연습문제 **C** 우리말과 같도록 괄호 안의 말을 활용하여 문장을 완성하시오. (단, 숫자는 영어로 쓰시오.)

1 수백만 달러가 지난주에 그 은행에서 도난당했다. (dollar)

= _____ were stolen from the bank last week.

2 그 끔찍한 사고 이후로 4,000일이 지났다. (day)

= _____ have passed since the terrible accident.

3 그들은 그들의 여동생의 결혼식을 위해 수백 송이의 꽃을 샀다. (flower)

= They bought _____ for their sister's wedding.

4 고대의 그리스 신전들은 수천 년 전에 지어졌다. (year)

= The ancient Greek temples were built _____ ago.

5 그 환경 보호 단체는 백만 그루의 나무를 심었다. (tree)

= The environmental group planted _____ .

기출 적중문제

다음 문장에서 <u>틀린</u> 부분을 바르게 고쳐 완전한 문장을 쓰시오.

Thousand of koalas live in Australia.

→ _____

기출로적중 POINT 4-2 수사: 분수, 배수, 횟수

정답 p.33

1. 분수는 분자를 먼저 기수로 읽고, 다음으로 분모를 서수로 읽는다. 단, 분자가 2 이상일 때는 분모에 -s를 붙인다.

$\frac{1}{3}$ → one-third[a third]　　$\frac{4}{7}$ → four-sevenths　　$\frac{3}{8}$ → three-eighths

$\frac{1}{2}$ → one-half[a half]　　$\frac{1}{4}$ → one-quarter[a quarter] 또는 one-fourth[a fourth]

$2\frac{3}{5}$ → two and three-fifths　　　　$5\frac{11}{13}$ → five and eleven-thirteenths

2. 배수와 횟수는 once(한 번), twice(두 배, 두 번), 그 이후부터는 「기수 + times」(~ 배, ~ 번)로 나타낸다.

Judy's smartphone is **twice** as expensive as mine.
Judy의 스마트폰은 나의 것보다 두 배 더 비싸다.

Mr. Jones takes his medicine **three times** a day.　Jones씨는 하루에 세 번 그의 약을 먹는다.

연습문제 우리말과 같도록 문장을 완성하시오. (단, 숫자는 영어로 쓰시오.)

1 나는 저녁으로 피자의 4분의 1을 먹었다.
= I ate _____ of the pizza for dinner.

2 Carol은 한 달에 한 번 그녀의 조부모님을 방문한다.
= Carol visits her grandparents _____ a month.

3 나의 사전은 윤호의 것보다 두 배 더 무겁다.
= My dictionary is _____ as heavy as Yunho's.

4 우리는 버터의 6분의 5를 사용해야 한다.
= We have to use _____ of the butter.

5 그릇에 3과 3분의 2컵의 밀가루를 넣어라.
= Put _____ cups of flour in the bowl.

6 Jane의 할머니는 Jane보다 다섯 배 더 나이가 많으시다.
= Jane's grandmother is _____ older than Jane.

7 나의 여동생과 나는 1년에 네 번 그 영화를 함께 본다.
= My sister and I watch the movie together _____ a year.

8 학생들의 9분의 2가 오늘의 수업에 오지 않았다.
= _____ of the students didn't come to today's class.

기출로적중 POINT 4-3 수사: 연도와 날짜

1. **연도는 주로 두 자리씩 끊어 읽는다. 단, 2000년 이상은 끊어 읽지 않기도 한다.**

   1542년 → fifteen forty-two

   2009년 → two thousand (and) nine

   2031년 → two thousand (and) thirty-one 또는 twenty thirty-one

   (Tip) 연대는 연도에 -(e)s를 붙여 읽는다.

   1700년대 → the seventeen hundreds 또는 1700s

   1940년대 → the nineteen forties 또는 1940s

2. **날짜는 서수로 읽는다.**

   5월 24일 → May (the) twenty-fourth 또는 the twenty-fourth of May

   8월 9일 → August (the) ninth 또는 the ninth of August

연습문제 다음 연도와 날짜를 영어로 쓰시오.

1 1958년 → _____

2 7월 15일 → _____

3 11월 31일 → _____

4 1265년 → _____

5 1990년대 → _____

6 2007년 → _____

7 1월 1일 → _____

8 1400년대 → _____

9 9월 4일 → _____

기출 적중문제 ◎⊶

다음 그림을 보고 질문에 대한 대답을 완성하시오. (단, 숫자는 영어로 쓰시오.)

JUNE
23

A: What's the date today?

B: It's _____.

정답 p.34

기출로적중 POINT 5-1 수량형용사: many, much, a lot of

many/much/a lot of는 모두 '많은'이라는 의미이다. many는 셀 수 있는 명사와 함께 쓰고, much는 셀 수 없는 명사와 함께 쓴다. a lot of는 셀 수 있는 명사, 셀 수 없는 명사 모두와 함께 쓸 수 있다.

many = a number of (수가) 많은	+ 셀 수 있는 명사의 복수형	Yuna has **many friends** from various countries. 유나는 다양한 나라에서 온 많은 친구들이 있다. There are **a number of cafés** on this street. 이 길 위에는 많은 카페가 있다.
much (양이) 많은	+ 셀 수 없는 명사	Do you have **much time** to read books? 너는 책을 읽을 많은 시간이 있니?
a lot of = lots of = plenty of (수·양이) 많은	+ 셀 수 있는 명사의 복수형/ 셀 수 없는 명사	Jiho bought **a lot of shirts** yesterday. 지호는 어제 많은 셔츠를 샀다. We can save **lots of water** with this plan. 우리는 이 계획으로 많은 물을 절약할 수 있다. Did he take **plenty of food** to the picnic? 그는 소풍에 많은 음식을 가지고 갔니?

연습문제 A 다음 빈칸에 many나 much 중 알맞은 것을 쓰시오.

1 The firefighters save _____ lives.

2 You shouldn't drink so _____ soda.

3 You can see _____ stars in the countryside.

4 Sophia spent too _____ money buying a tablet PC.

5 How _____ fish did your father catch?

6 _____ students in my class wear glasses.

7 We didn't add _____ sugar to the cookie dough.

8 Ronald hasn't seen Max for _____ months.

9 There wasn't _____ information in the guidebook.

10 It won't take _____ time to wash the dishes.

11 How _____ milk should we buy?

12 She couldn't answer _____ questions on the math test.

13 Ms. Park gave us too _____ homework.

14 The school will buy _____ new computers for the students.

15 It requires _____ patience to finish the marathon.

연습문제 B 다음 문장의 밑줄 친 부분을 many나 much로 바꿔 완전한 문장을 쓰시오.

1 My neighbor has a lot of flowers in her garden.

→ _____

2 Is there plenty of water in the bottle?

→ _____

3 You should eat lots of vegetables.

→ _____

4 We don't have plenty of time to get ready.

→ _____

5 Do you save lots of money every month?

→ _____

6 A number of soldiers fought for peace.

→ _____

7 She made a lot of friends on her trip to Europe.

→ _____

8 Alex's mentor didn't give him lots of advice.

→ _____

9 Did you have a lot of fun at the summer camp?

→ _____

10 There were a number of problems with the new machine.

→ _____

기출 적중문제

다음 대화에서 어법상 어색한 부분을 찾아 쓰고 바르게 고쳐 쓰시오.

> *A*: Did you eat many bread for lunch?
> *B*: I only ate two pieces of bread.

_____ → _____

수량형용사: (a) few, (a) little

정답 p.34

1. **a few/a little은 '약간의, 조금 있는'이라는 의미이다. a few는 셀 수 있는 명사와 함께 쓰고, a little은 셀 수 없는 명사와 함께 쓴다.**

a few + 셀 수 있는 명사의 복수형	**a little** + 셀 수 없는 명사

There are **a few tomatoes** in the bowl. 그릇에 약간의 토마토들이 있다.	There is **a little juice** in the cup. 컵에 약간의 주스가 있다.

2. **few/little은 '거의 없는'이라는 의미이다. few는 셀 수 있는 명사와 함께 쓰고, little은 셀 수 없는 명사와 함께 쓴다.**

few + 셀 수 있는 명사의 복수형	**little** + 셀 수 없는 명사

There are **few tomatoes** in the bowl. 그릇에 토마토들이 거의 없다.	There is **little juice** in the cup. 컵에 주스가 거의 없다.

연습문제 A 괄호 안에서 알맞은 것을 고르시오.

1 (Few / Little) plants can live in a desert.

2 Jennifer has (few / little) time to change her clothes.

3 There is (a few / a little) ice on the road.

4 I'm going to buy (a few / a little) books at the bookstore.

5 Betty always puts (a few / a little) honey in her tea.

6 My mother threw away (a few / a little) shirts yesterday.

7 I bought (a few / a little) postcards to give to my friends.

8 Robert knows (few / little) Korean words.

9 Spread (a few / a little) oil in the pan before you heat it.

10 (A few / A little) hours ago, the spaceship successfully landed on Mars.

연습문제 B 우리말과 같도록 <보기>의 말과 괄호 안의 명사를 활용하여 문장을 완성하시오.

<보기> a few   a little   few   little

1 약간의 새들이 지붕 위에 앉아있다. (bird)

= _____ are sitting on the roof.

2 나의 돼지 저금통에 동전이 거의 없었다. (coin)

= There were _____ in my piggy bank.

3 민수는 요즘 아침으로 쌀을 거의 먹지 않는다. (rice)

= Minsu eats _____ for breakfast these days.

4 우리는 수프를 더 진하게 만들기 위해 약간의 밀가루를 사용했다. (flour)

= We used _____ to make the soup thicker.

5 나는 나의 집 가까이에 있는 연못에서 개구리들을 거의 보지 못했다. (frog)

= I saw _____ in the pond near my house.

6 너는 너의 핫도그 위에 약간의 케첩을 원하니? (ketchup)

= Would you like _____ on your hot dog?

7 과거에는 관광객들이 한국을 거의 방문하지 않았다. (tourist)

= _____ visited Korea in the past.

8 Patrick은 그의 겨울 코트에서 약간의 달러를 발견했다. (dollar)

= Patrick found _____ in his winter coat.

9 선호는 그의 숙제를 하기 위해 도움이 거의 필요하지 않다. (help)

= Sunho needs _____ to do his homework.

기출 적중문제

다음 중 밑줄 친 부분이 어법상 바른 것을 모두 고르시오.

① Do you need <u>a few</u> salt?

② Please show me <u>a little</u> examples.

③ <u>Few</u> bananas are left on the table.

④ There is <u>a few</u> sand in my shoe.

⑤ Have some cookies with <u>a little</u> apple juice.

수량형용사: some, any

some/any는 '약간의, 조금의'라는 의미로, 셀 수 있는 명사, 셀 수 없는 명사 모두와 함께 쓸 수 있지만 쓰임이 다르다.

	쓰임	예문
some	긍정문	I need to buy **some** clothes. 나는 약간의 옷을 살 필요가 있다.
	권유나 요청을 나타내는 의문문	Would you like to have **some** biscuits? 너는 약간의 비스킷을 먹기를 원하니? Could you please give me **some** coffee? 저에게 약간의 커피를 주시겠어요?
	긍정의 대답을 예상하는 의문문	You look very happy. Did you succeed in booking **some** tickets? 너는 매우 행복하게 보여. 너는 약간의 티켓을 예약하는 데 성공했니?
any	부정문	My dog didn't eat **any** food today. 나의 개는 오늘 약간의 먹이도 먹지 않았다.
	의문문	Do you have **any** medicine? 너는 약간의 약을 가지고 있니?
	조건을 나타내는 if절	Please send me an e-mail if you have **any** questions. 만약 당신이 약간의 질문이 있다면 저에게 이메일을 보내주세요.
	'어떤 ~이라도'를 의미하는 긍정문	You can borrow **any** book in the library. 너는 도서관에 있는 어떤 책이라도 빌릴 수 있다.

연습문제 괄호 안에서 알맞은 것을 고르시오.

1 (Some / Any) cats were chasing the mouse.

2 Did the men find (some / any) gold in the mine?

3 If you need (some / any) advice, you can call me.

4 Would you like (some / any) cold water to drink?

5 Can you get (some / any) snacks from the store for me?

6 There isn't (some / any) cake left in the refrigerator.

7 Seojin needs (some / any) balloons for the party tomorrow.

8 If you want to go to city hall, take (some / any) bus here.

9 Let's take (some / any) time to think about the matter.

10 You can use this credit card at (some / any) store.

11 If you have (some / any) food in your bag, please take it out.

A 밑줄 친 부분이 어법상 맞으면 O를 쓰고, 틀리면 바르게 고쳐 쓰시오.

1 My sister was still <u>awake</u> after midnight.　　　→ _____

2 Turkey has <u>hundred of beautiful beaches</u>.　　　→ _____

3 <u>The twenty-five</u> of December is my favorite day of a year.　→ _____

4 Will you please bring me <u>some</u> dry towels?　　　→ _____

5 The telephone was invented in <u>the nineteen-twentieths</u>.　→ _____

6 The deaf <u>need</u> subtitles when they watch TV.　　　→ _____

7 Matt took <u>any</u> pictures during his trip to Italy.　　　→ _____

8 I'll call you if <u>some</u> customers cancel a reservation.　　　→ _____

9 Vaccines have saved <u>millions of life</u>.　　　→ _____

10 Asia covers <u>one-thirds</u> of the earth.　　　→ _____

B 우리말과 같도록 <보기>의 말과 괄호 안의 형용사를 활용하여 문장을 완성하시오.

| <보기>　anything　anybody　someone　thing |

1 너는 그 지저분한 것을 닦기 위해 알코올을 사용해야 한다. (dirty)
= You should use alcohol to clean the _____.

2 너는 이 근처에서 이상한 누군가를 본 적이 있니? (strange)
= Have you seen _____ around here?

3 나는 나의 복통 때문에 매운 어떤 것도 먹을 수 없다. (spicy)
= I can't eat _____ because of my stomachache.

4 요즘에는 바둑에 흥미가 있는 누군가를 찾는 것이 어렵다. (interested)
= It is hard to find _____ in Baduk these days.

| <보기>　something　nothing　somebody　nobody |

5 그 영화에는 유명한 사람이 아무도 없었다. (famous)
= There was _____ in the movie.

6 소미는 그녀의 삶을 재미있게 만들기 위해 새로운 무언가를 배울 것이다. (new)

= Somi will learn _____ to make her life fun.

7 Jake는 낚시에 유용한 어떤 것도 가져오지 않았다. (useful)

= Jake brought _____ for fishing.

8 나의 팀은 과학 과제를 위해 창의적인 누군가를 찾고 있다. (creative)

= My team is looking for _____ for the science project.

C 우리말과 같도록 <보기>의 말과 괄호 안의 명사를 활용하여 문장을 완성하시오.

<보기>	many	much	a few	a little	few	little

1 숲은 많은 면에서 우리에게 중요하다. (way)

= Forests are important to us in _____.

2 너는 너의 목표를 달성하기 위해 약간의 용기가 필요하다. (courage)

= You need _____ to achieve your goal.

3 다행히도, 그 지진은 많은 피해를 초래하지 않았다. (damage)

= Fortunately, the earthquake didn't cause _____.

4 약간의 아이들이 놀이터에서 놀고 있었다. (child)

= _____ were playing in the playground.

5 나는 외국인들과 의사소통할 기회가 거의 없었다. (chance)

= I had _____ to communicate with foreigners.

6 너무 많은 곤충은 농작물에 해롭다. (insect)

= Too _____ are harmful to the crops.

7 도훈이는 낮 동안 약간의 잠을 잤다. (sleep)

= Dohun got _____ during the day.

8 그 호수는 많은 쓰레기로 오염되었다. (trash)

= The lake was polluted with _____.

9 한국에서는 이번 여름에 비가 거의 오지 않았다. (rain)

= There was _____ this summer in Korea.

10 그 축구 선수들은 어제 경기에서 약간의 실수를 했다. (mistake)

= The soccer players made _____ in the game yesterday.

1 다음 중 밑줄 친 형용사의 용법이 나머지 넷과 다른 것은?

① The boy found the golden ticket.
② Korean food is usually very healthy.
③ This poem always makes me sad.
④ Tom and I built a huge sandcastle.
⑤ There were useful tips on the website.

2 다음 중 어법상 어색한 것은?

① Do you have any small bags?
② I was so sad to hear the story.
③ The box was full of old toys.
④ Yunji and her sister don't look alike.
⑤ The tree has been live for hundreds of years.

3 다음 대화에서 어법상 어색한 부분을 찾아 쓰고 바르게 고쳐 쓰시오.

> A: Do you notice different anything about me?
> B: Sure. You've changed your hair color.

_____ → _____

4 다음 글의 빈칸에 들어갈 알맞은 것은?

> It was so cold in the morning. However, I felt warm after I drank _____ tea.

① a few   ② many   ③ a little
④ little   ⑤ few

5 다음 밑줄 친 부분과 바꿔 쓸 수 있는 것을 모두 고르시오.

> Jinsu and his father caught a lot of fish last Friday.

① many   ② much
③ little   ④ a few
⑤ a number of

6 다음 두 문장의 의미가 같도록 문장을 완성하시오.

> We should keep some parking spaces empty for disabled people.
> = We should keep some parking spaces empty for _____.

7 다음 글의 빈칸에 들어갈 말이 순서대로 짝지어진 것은?

> _____ people were worried about Matthew when he was injured in a car accident. And _____ friends visited him in the hospital.

① Many – a little   ② Much – few
③ Many – little   ④ Much – a few
⑤ Many – a few

8 우리말과 같도록 괄호 안의 말을 배열할 때 다섯 번째에 오는 것을 쓰시오.

> 너는 전에 유명한 누군가를 만나본 적이 있니? (have, met, famous, you, anyone, before)

→ _____

9 다음 중 어법상 바른 것은?

① Jellyfish don't have some bones.
② Would you like to have any more rice?
③ Does Joseph have some brothers?
④ She added some ingredients to the bread.
⑤ If you have some problems, please call me right away.

10 다음 빈칸에 들어갈 말이 순서대로 짝지어진 것은?

· I have _____ to tell you.
· Don't you need _____ salt in your soup?

① nothing important – a few
② nothing important – a little
③ important nothing – a few
④ important nothing – a little
⑤ nothing important – few

11 다음 중 어법상 어색한 것은?

① Can you recommend anything interesting to read?
② There is new someone in my class.
③ The injured should be treated immediately.
④ Let's find somebody clever to solve this problem.
⑤ The young change their phones more often than the old do.

12 다음 중 영어로 바르게 읽은 것끼리 묶인 것은?

ⓐ 82 → eighty-second
ⓑ $6\frac{3}{5}$ → six and three-fifths
ⓒ 1951년 → nineteen fifty-ones
ⓓ 11월 12일 → the twelve of November
ⓔ $\frac{1}{4}$ → one-fourths
ⓕ 1300년대 → thirteen hundreds

① ⓐ, ⓑ   ② ⓐ, ⓔ   ③ ⓑ, ⓕ
④ ⓑ, ⓒ, ⓔ   ⑤ ⓒ, ⓓ, ⓕ

13 다음 빈칸에 들어갈 말로 어색한 것은?

Were there _____ children in the library?

① a lot of   ② a few   ③ plenty of
④ a little   ⑤ lots of

14 다음 빈칸에 a few가 들어갈 수 없는 것은?

① Do you have _____ questions to ask of me?
② There were _____ kites flying in the sky.
③ Please put _____ cream on my drink.
④ Could you wait outside for _____ minutes?
⑤ The hens lay _____ eggs every morning.

[15-16] 다음 대화의 밑줄 친 우리말과 같도록 문장을
완성하시오. (단, 숫자는 영어로 쓰시오.)

15

> A: How often do you go to the dentist?
> B: 나는 치과에 1년에 네 번 가.

= I go to the dentist _____
a year.

16

> A: When does your summer vacation
> start?
> B: 7월 25일에.

= On _____.

17 다음 (A)~(C)에 들어갈 말이 바르게 짝지어진 것
은?

> Alice: I'm so tired today. What do you
> think I should do to feel better?
> Mark: Eating ___(A)___ will help you.
> Would you like ___(B)___
> chocolate? I got ___(C)___ bars of
> it in my bag.
> Alice: Thanks. That will be nice.

	(A)	(B)	(C)
①	something sweet	some	two
②	sweet something	any	two
③	something sweet	any	second
④	sweet something	some	two
⑤	something sweet	some	second

18 다음 중 어법상 <u>어색한</u> 것은?

① Hundreds of turtles live in the lake.
② Paul called me twice last night.
③ You need to brush your teeth three times
a day.
④ We've prepared special something for
you.
⑤ The most important thing is making good
friends.

19 다음 중 밑줄 친 부분이 어법상 바른 것은?

① Don't drink too <u>many</u> soda before the
movie starts.
② Susie has <u>few</u> interest in cooking.
③ It took <u>little</u> hours to finish painting the
picture.
④ <u>A few</u> women gathered around the table.
⑤ I learned that most fish have <u>a few</u> fat.

20 다음 중 어법상 바른 것은?

① He invested million of dollars in AI
technology.
② The dinner course costs forty-five
thousands won.
③ A plastic bottle takes thousands of years
to decay.
④ The eight planet in our solar system is
Neptune.
⑤ Hundreds of customer visited this
museum today.

21 다음 중 어법상 <u>어색한</u> 것의 개수는?

ⓐ I found a few socks in my dog's house.
ⓑ The thief stole a lot of money from the bank.
ⓒ All of the guests arrived a little minutes ago.
ⓓ Carrie spent many time swimming in the ocean.
ⓔ The Arctic is so cold that few plants can grow.

① 1개   ② 2개   ③ 3개
④ 4개   ⑤ 5개

22 다음 글의 밑줄 친 우리말과 같도록 문장을 완성하시오.

The pond was full of water when I was ten years old. <u>그러나, 이제 연못에 물이 거의 없다.</u>

= However, there is _____ in the pond now.

23 다음 밑줄 친 부분과 공통으로 바꿔 쓸 수 있는 것은?

· The students have to write <u>a few</u> essays.
· Can you please give me <u>a little</u> advice?

① many   ② a number of
③ any   ④ some
⑤ much

24 다음 (A)~(C)에 들어갈 말이 바르게 짝지어진 것은?

· Junsu got ___(A)___ sleep last night because it was too noisy upstairs.
· Joe has lived in several countries, so he can speak ___(B)___ languages.
· We need ___(C)___ tomatoes to make tomato sauce.

	(A)	(B)	(C)
①	little	many	a little
②	a little	much	a few
③	a little	a few	few
④	little	many	a few
⑤	few	any	few

25 다음 글의 밑줄 친 부분 중 어법상 바른 것을 <u>모두</u> 고르시오.

This is a story about a girl who couldn't use both of her hands. The girl wanted to be an artist and give hope to ①<u>the disabled</u>. Even though she had to hold a brush with her mouth, she didn't give up her dream. She painted ②<u>lots of</u> paintings, and they became very ③<u>famously</u>. People could get ④<u>any</u> positive energy from her works. We can learn ⑤<u>meaningful something</u> from her touching story. We can do anything we want, so start to act and try hard.

CHAPTER 12
부사

Minsu is eating his breakfast **quickly**.   민수는 서둘러서 그의 아침을 먹고 있다.

그냥 '먹고 있다'라고 말하는 것보다 '서둘러서 먹고 있다'라고 말하면 어떻게 먹고 있는지 더 자세하게 알 수 있어요.
이렇게 다른 품사를 수식하여 의미를 강조하거나 풍부하게 하는 것을 **부사**라고 해요.

기출로 적중 POINT

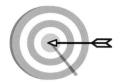

내신 100점 적중!
기출 출제율

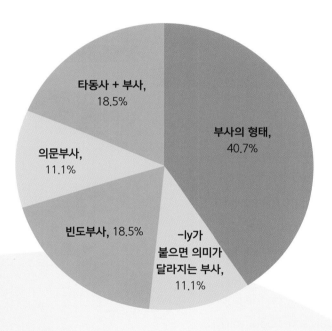

부사의 형태,
40.7%

타동사 + 부사,
18.5%

의문부사,
11.1%

빈도부사, 18.5%

-ly가
붙으면 의미가
달라지는 부사,
11.1%

TOP 1 **부사의 형태 (40.7%)**
부사의 형태를 묻는 문제가 자주 출제된다.

TOP 2 **빈도부사 (18.5%)**
타동사 + 부사 (18.5%)
빈도부사의 종류와 위치를 묻는 문제가 자주 출제된다. 「타동사 + 부사」의 목적
어의 위치를 묻는 문제가 자주 출제된다.

TOP 3 **-ly가 붙으면 의미가 달라지는 부사 (11.1%)**
의문부사 (11.1%)
-ly가 붙어서 의미가 달라지는 부사의 의미를 구별하는 문제가 자주 출제된다.
의문부사의 의미와 쓰임을 묻는 문제가 자주 출제된다.

부사는 동사·형용사·다른 부사·문장 전체를 수식한다.

동사 수식	Snails **move slowly**. 달팽이는 느리게 움직인다. Fred **speaks** Korean **fluently**. Fred는 한국어를 유창하게 말한다.
형용사 수식	The roses were **really beautiful**. 그 장미들은 아주 아름다웠다.
다른 부사 수식	Sarah can cook **very well**. Sarah는 요리를 매우 잘 할 수 있다.
문장 전체 수식	**Unfortunately, my computer is broken**. 불행하게도, 나의 컴퓨터가 고장 났다.

연습문제 다음 문장의 밑줄 친 부사가 수식하는 부분에 밑줄을 치시오.

1 My family arrived at the hotel <u>safely</u>.

2 She made her room <u>perfectly</u> clean.

3 Bees flew <u>busily</u> around the flowers.

4 <u>Luckily</u>, the bus came on time.

5 The runners ran <u>extremely</u> fast.

6 The boy told his story <u>clearly</u>.

7 A woman talked <u>loudly</u> on the phone.

8 Are you <u>absolutely</u> sure about this?

9 Mr. Scott spends his money <u>wisely</u>.

10 Henry finished his homework <u>so</u> quickly.

11 We answered all of the questions <u>easily</u>.

12 Don't make the decision <u>too</u> hastily.

13 <u>Finally</u>, the soccer team won the championship.

14 My uncle drove his new sports car very <u>carefully</u>.

15 The weather forecast was <u>completely</u> wrong.

기출로적중 POINT 2-1 부사의 형태

정답 p.36

부사는 대부분 형용사에 -ly를 붙여 만든다.

대부분의 형용사	형용사 + -ly	loud – loud**ly** main – main**ly**	rude – rude**ly** careful – careful**ly**
「자음 + y」로 끝나는 형용사	y를 i로 바꾸고 + -ly	happy – happ**ily**	noisy – nois**ily**
-le로 끝나는 형용사	e를 없애고 + -y	terrible – terrib**ly**	gentle – gent**ly**
-ll로 끝나는 형용사	형용사 + -y	full – full**y**	dull – dull**y**
-ue로 끝나는 형용사	e를 없애고 + -ly	true – tru**ly**	
-ic로 끝나는 형용사	형용사 + -ally	basic – basic**ally** energetic – energetic**ally**	
불규칙 변화	good – **well**		

Everyone clapped **happily** after the play. 그 연극 후에 모든 사람이 행복하게 박수를 쳤다.
Jacob's brother plays the violin **well**. Jacob의 형은 바이올린을 잘 연주한다.

(Tip) 다음 단어는 -ly로 끝나지만 부사가 아닌 형용사이다.

friendly 친절한 **lovely** 사랑스러운 **lonely** 외로운 **weekly** 주간의 **costly** 값비싼 **likely** 그럴듯한

연습문제 A 다음 형용사를 부사로 바꿔 쓰시오.

1 nice → _____ **2** final → _____

3 careful → _____ **4** easy → _____

5 gentle → _____ **6** wise → _____

7 strange → _____ **8** lucky → _____

9 sad → _____ **10** clear → _____

11 lazy → _____ **12** different → _____

13 perfect → _____ **14** good → _____

15 full → _____ **16** real → _____

17 busy → _____ **18** polite → _____

19 heavy → _____ **20** comfortable → _____

21 safe → _____ **22** certain → _____

23 noisy	→ _____	24 serious	→ _____
25 true	→ _____	26 angry	→ _____
27 sudden	→ _____	28 simple	→ _____
29 responsible	→ _____	30 quiet	→ _____
31 energetic	→ _____	32 horrible	→ _____
33 brave	→ _____	34 sincere	→ _____
35 proper	→ _____	36 fantastic	→ _____
37 dull	→ _____	38 special	→ _____
39 nervous	→ _____	40 possible	→ _____

연습문제 B 괄호 안의 말을 알맞은 형태로 바꿔 빈칸에 쓰시오.

1 (heavy) ① We have to carry the _____ boxes.
　　　　　 ② It snowed _____ last weekend.

2 (gentle) ① Ben's voice was nice and _____.
　　　　　 ② My mother always kisses me _____ on the cheek.

3 (basic) ① _____, children have to read as many books as they can.
　　　　　② Napa cabbage is a _____ ingredient for kimchi.

4 (good) ① Mongolians are known to have _____ eyesight.
　　　　　② Although the printer is old, it still works _____.

5 (true) ① The news can't be _____.
　　　　　② I'm _____ sorry for forgetting your birthday.

6 (full) ① I'm _____ ready for the final exams.
　　　　　② The basket was _____ of rainwater.

7 (real) ① Mitch threw the ball _____ hard.
　　　　　② Do you know what the _____ problem is?

기출 적중문제

우리말과 같도록 괄호 안의 말을 활용하여 문장을 완성하시오.

Roberts씨는 그 자동차를 쉽게 고칠 수 있다. (fix, easy)

= Mr. Roberts can _____.

POINT 2-2 형용사와 형태가 같은 부사

정답 p.36

CHAPTER 12 부사 기출로 적중 해카스 중학영문법 2학년

다음 단어는 형용사와 부사의 형태가 같다.

late	형 늦은	부 늦게	high	형 높은	부 높이
early	형 이른	부 일찍	long	형 긴	부 길게, 오래
fast	형 빠른	부 빠르게	enough	형 충분한	부 충분히
hard	형 어려운, 단단한	부 열심히	pretty	형 예쁜	부 꽤

Tim solved a really **hard** math problem. Tim은 아주 어려운 수학 문제를 풀었다.
Tim studied **hard** for the math exam. Tim은 수학 시험을 위해 열심히 공부했다.

> (Tip) enough가 명사를 수식하는 형용사로 쓰일 때는 명사 앞에 오고, 형용사나 부사를 수식하는 부사로 쓰일 때는 형용사나 부사 뒤에 온다.
> I don't have **enough** money to buy the bag. 나는 그 가방을 사기에 충분한 돈을 가지고 있지 않다.
> His sister is **old enough** to drive now. 그의 누나는 이제 운전할 만큼 충분히 나이가 많다.

연습문제 다음 중 밑줄 친 부분이 부사인 것을 고르시오.

1 ① He is speaking too <u>fast</u>.
　　② Look at that <u>fast</u> racing car.

2 ① The street is quiet in the <u>early</u> morning.
　　② Jaemin left <u>early</u> to catch the bus.

3 ① The eagles are flying <u>high</u>.
　　② The kid couldn't reach the <u>high</u> shelf.

4 ① It was very <u>hard</u> to focus on the music.
　　② Hyeri is practicing the dance <u>hard</u>.

5 ① Jill wore a <u>long</u> dress to the party.
　　② Do I have to wait <u>long</u>?

6 ① The rainy season came <u>late</u> this year.
　　② Oliver was <u>late</u> for school again.

7 ① This pond is large <u>enough</u> for the geese.
　　② Do you have <u>enough</u> time to talk with me?

8 ① I will buy something <u>pretty</u> for my mom.
　　② The house looks <u>pretty</u> old.

기출 적중문제

우리말과 같도록 괄호 안의 말을 알맞게 배열하시오.

> 그 소파는 충분히 편안하니? (comfortable, the sofa, enough)

= Is _____ ?

enough가 형용사를 수식하는 부사로 쓰일 때는 형용사 뒤에 와요.

Chapter 12 부사 **255**

-ly가 붙으면 의미가 달라지는 부사

정답 p.36

다음 부사에 -ly가 붙으면 의미가 다른 부사가 된다.

late 늦게 – lately 최근에	John came home **late** yesterday. John은 어제 집에 늦게 왔다. I haven't drunk coffee **lately**. 나는 최근에 커피를 먹지 않았다.
high 높이 – highly 매우, 대단히	We don't have to climb **high**. 우리는 높이 오를 필요가 없다. She is a **highly** successful lawyer. 그녀는 매우 성공한 변호사이다.
hard 열심히 – hardly 거의 ~않다	My parents always work **hard**. 나의 부모님은 항상 열심히 일하신다. We **hardly** know each other. 우리는 서로를 거의 알지 못한다.
close 가까이 – closely 면밀히	The puppy sat **close** to me. 그 강아지는 나에게 가까이 앉았다. He observed the frogs **closely**. 그는 개구리들을 면밀히 관찰했다.
near 가까이 – nearly 거의	Paul lives **near** to my house. Paul은 나의 집에 가까이 산다. The milk bottle is **nearly** empty. 그 우유병은 거의 비어있다.

연습문제 괄호 안에서 알맞은 것을 고르시오.

1 The weather has been too cold (late / lately).

2 Jason hit the baseball (high / highly) into the air.

3 I could (hard / hardly) move because of my headache.

4 New Year's Day is coming (near / nearly).

5 The students listened to the lecture (close / closely).

6 The pizza was delivered (late / lately), so it wasn't hot.

7 Riding a bike without a helmet is (high / highly) dangerous.

8 Ms. Johnson's new sculpture is (near / nearly) finished.

9 Mr. Choi parked his car (close / closely) to ours.

10 Study (hard / hardly), or you won't pass the test.

기출 적중문제

다음 중 밑줄 친 부분이 어법상 어색한 것은?

> I ①hardly ②exercise these days. I have to
> ③work out ④hardly in order to stay ⑤fit.

POINT 3 빈도부사

정답 p.36

1. **빈도부사는 어떤 일이 얼마나 자주 발생하는지를 나타내는 부사이다.**

100%					0%
always	usually	often	sometimes	seldom/rarely/hardly	never
항상	보통, 대개	종종, 자주	때때로, 가끔	거의 ~않다	결코 ~않다

Mary **always** eats breakfast at 8 A.M. Mary는 항상 오전 8시에 아침을 먹는다.
I **seldom** wake up early on Sundays. 나는 일요일에 거의 일찍 일어나지 않는다.

2. **빈도부사는 be동사나 조동사 뒤 또는 일반동사 앞에 온다.**

be동사나 조동사 뒤	It **is** **hardly** cold in May. 5월에는 거의 춥지 않다. You **can** **usually** see tulips in spring. 너는 보통 봄에 튤립을 볼 수 있다. I **have** **never** told a lie to you. 나는 너에게 결코 거짓말을 한 적이 없다.
일반동사 앞	My dog **often** **barks** at cats. 나의 개는 종종 고양이들에게 짖는다. Do you and your sister **sometimes** **fight** with each other? 너와 너의 언니는 때때로 서로 싸우니?

연습문제 A 우리말과 같도록 빈칸에 알맞은 빈도부사를 쓰시오.

1 공포 영화는 때때로 보기에 너무 무섭다.

= Horror movies are _____ too scary to watch.

2 너는 종종 공부하기 위해 도서관에 가니?

= Do you _____ go to the library to study?

3 아이들은 결코 낯선 사람을 따라가면 안 된다.

= Children should _____ follow strangers.

4 우리는 항상 그를 훌륭한 배우로 기억할 것이다.

= We will _____ remember him as a great actor.

5 그 체육관은 토요일 아침에 보통 사람들로 가득하다.

= The gym is _____ full of people on Saturday morning.

6 Emily는 바쁘기 때문에 거의 집에 머무르지 않는다.

= Emily _____ stays at home because she is busy.

7 나는 전에 결코 이집트로 여행해본 적이 없다.

= I have _____ traveled to Egypt before.

8 별은 보통 도시 밖에서 더 밝게 빛난다.

= Stars _____ shine brighter outside of the city.

9 사하라 사막에는 거의 비가 오지 않는다.

= It _____ rains in the Sahara Desert.

연습문제 B | 괄호 안의 빈도부사를 알맞은 곳에 넣어 완전한 문장을 쓰시오.

1 I drink soda. (seldom)

→ _____

2 The restaurant is busy on Friday night. (always)

→ _____

3 What do you buy online? (usually)

→ _____

4 You can see rainbows after heavy rain. (often)

→ _____

5 It is possible to swim across the river. (hardly)

→ _____

6 The café will be open during the holiday. (always)

→ _____

7 This word is used in modern English. (rarely)

→ _____

8 I have been to the movie theater alone. (never)

→ _____

9 I hear the birds singing in the morning. (sometimes)

→ _____

10 Lightning hits in the same place twice. (hardly)

→ _____

기출 적중문제

괄호 안의 말을 알맞게 배열하시오.

> A: What does your brother do on weekends?
>
> B: _____
>
> on weekends. (plays, he, usually, computer games)

> 빈도부사는 be동사나
> 조동사의 뒤,
> 일반동사의 앞에 와요.

기출로적중 POINT 4-1 다양한 부사: already, still, yet

정답 p.37

already/still/yet은 긍정문, 부정문, 의문문에서 쓰일 때 각각 다른 의미를 나타낸다.

	쓰임	의미	예문
already	긍정문	이미	I have **already** seen the movie three times. 나는 이미 그 영화를 세 번 봤다.
	의문문	벌써	already가 의문문에서 쓰이면 놀라움을 나타낸다. Have you **already** finished your homework? 너는 벌써 너의 숙제를 끝냈니?
still	긍정문/ 부정문/ 의문문	아직, 여전히	still은 긍정문, 부정문, 의문문에서 모두 쓰이고, 부정문에서 쓰일 때는 부정어 앞에 온다. Bob is **still** waiting for you outside. Bob은 아직 밖에서 너를 기다리고 있다. I **still don't** understand why she was upset. 나는 아직 그녀가 왜 속상했는지 이해하지 못한다. Do you **still** exercise every evening? 너는 아직 저녁마다 운동하니?
yet	부정문	아직	yet은 주로 부정문이나 의문문 맨 뒤에 온다. The building hasn't been completed **yet**. 그 건물은 아직 완성되지 않았다.
	의문문	이미, 벌써	Have you heard the rumor **yet**? 너는 이미 그 소문을 들었니?

연습문제 괄호 안에서 알맞은 것을 고르시오.

1 It's (still / yet) snowing here.

2 Has the package arrived (still / yet)?

3 Is it (already / yet) 6 o'clock?

4 Ms. Evans has (already / still) booked a flight to Brazil.

5 I haven't started painting my room (still / yet).

6 Did you (already / still) tell her the news?

7 We haven't decided what to eat for lunch (still / yet).

8 Do you (still / yet) have his phone number?

9 Luke (already / still) doesn't know his faults.

다양한 부사: too, either

정답 p.37

too/either는 '또한, 역시'라는 의미이다. too는 긍정문에 대한 동의를 나타내고, either는 부정문에 대한 동의를 나타낸다.

too	Kenny **likes** reading books. I **like** reading books, **too**. Kenny는 책을 읽는 것을 좋아한다. 나 또한 책을 읽는 것을 좋아한다. Diana **will leave** soon. David **will leave** soon, **too**. Diana는 곧 떠날 것이다. David 또한 곧 떠날 것이다.
either	I **don't drink** milk. My sister **doesn't drink** milk, **either**. 나는 우유를 마시지 않는다. 나의 여동생 또한 우유를 마시지 않는다. He **can't play** the flute. I **can't play** the flute, **either**. 그는 플루트를 연주할 수 없다. 나 또한 플루트를 연주할 수 없다.

(Tip) too가 '너무, 매우'라는 의미인 경우 형용사나 부사 앞에 온다.
This desk is **too** heavy to carry. 이 책상은 나르기에 너무 무겁다.
Don't eat **too** much before you sleep. 자기 전에 너무 많이 먹지 마라.

연습문제 다음 빈칸에 too나 either를 넣어 대화를 완성하시오.

1 A: I can swim. B: I can swim, _____.

2 A: I'm not feeling hungry. B: I'm not feeling hungry, _____.

3 A: I have heard the song. B: I have heard the song, _____.

4 A: I don't like cucumbers. B: I don't like cucumbers, _____.

5 A: I was in Busan last weekend. B: Norah was in Busan last weekend, _____.

6 A: I am afraid of insects. B: I am afraid of insects, _____.

7 A: Alice won't change her mind. B: Dennis won't change his mind, _____.

8 A: She went to the library yesterday. B: I went to the library yesterday, _____.

9 A: I didn't break the window. B: I didn't break the window, _____.

10 A: I haven't been to Canada. B: I haven't been to Canada, _____.

11 A: Sujin might know the truth. B: Junsu might know the truth, _____.

12 A: I voted for Linda as our group leader. B: I voted for her, _____.

13 A: My father can't eat raw fish. B: My father can't eat raw fish, _____.

14 A: He can ride a bicycle. B: She can ride a bicycle, _____.

기출로적중 POINT 4-3 다양한 부사: so, neither

정답 p.37

so/neither는 '~도 그렇다'라는 의미이며, 「So/Neither + 동사 + 주어」의 형태로 앞 문장에 대한 동의를 나타낼 때 쓴다. so는 긍정문에 대한 동의를 나타내고 neither는 부정문에 대한 동의를 나타내며, 이때 동사는 앞 문장에 쓰인 동사에 따라 달라진다.

❶ 앞 문장에 be동사가 쓰인 경우: 「So/Neither + be동사 + 주어」
   I **am** so tired. – **So am** I. 나는 너무 피곤해. – 나도 그래.
   He **wasn't** angry. – **Neither was** she. 그는 화나지 않았었어. – 그녀도 그랬어.

❷ 앞 문장에 일반동사가 쓰인 경우: 「So/Neither + do/does/did + 주어」
   I **lived** in here. – **So did** Minho. 나는 여기에 살았어. – 민호도 그랬어.
   Irene **doesn't like** science. – **Neither do** I. Irene은 과학을 좋아하지 않아. – 나도 그래.

❸ 앞 문장에 조동사가 쓰인 경우: 「So/Neither + 조동사 + 주어」
   Peter **will** join the club. – **So will** Jimin. Peter는 그 동아리에 가입할 거야. – 지민이도 그럴 거야.
   I **can't** understand the riddle. – **Neither can** I. 나는 그 수수께끼를 이해할 수 없어. – 나도 그래.

연습문제 so 또는 neither와 괄호 안의 말을 활용하여 대화를 완성하시오.

1 A: She is ten years old.   B: _____ (Michael)

2 A: I don't have a cat.   B: _____ (he)

3 A: He can drive a car.   B: _____ (she)

4 A: I'm allergic to peanuts.   B: _____ (I)

5 A: I can't speak Italian.   B: _____ (I)

6 A: Suho will come to the party.   B: _____ (Rachel)

7 A: I often have toast for breakfast.   B: _____ (she)

8 A: I wasn't prepared for the test.   B: _____ (I)

9 A: Alex will help you.   B: _____ (Luke)

10 A: I'm not interested in baking.   B: _____ (he)

11 A: Dojin enjoys riding roller coasters.   B: _____ (Yeri)

12 A: I won't go out tonight.   B: _____ (I)

13 A: I didn't see the newspaper yesterday.   B: _____ (I)

14 A: I wasn't good at English in high school.   B: _____ (he)

정답 p.37

1. 다음은 목적어를 가질 수 있는 「타동사 + 부사」이다.

turn on ~을 켜다	turn off ~을 끄다	put on ~을 입다/쓰다
take off ~을 벗다	try on ~을 입어보다/신어보다	pick up ~을 줍다/들어 올리다
wake up ~를 깨우다	give up ~을 포기하다/그만두다	write down ~을 적다
throw away ~을 버리다	put off ~을 미루다	hand[turn] in ~을 제출하다
find out ~을 알아내다	look up ~을 찾아보다	give back ~을 돌려주다

Can I **turn off** the air conditioner? 내가 에어컨을 꺼도 되니?
You should **write down** your name here. 너는 여기에 너의 이름을 적어야 한다.
Jiho **looked up** the word in a dictionary. 지호는 사전에서 그 단어를 찾아봤다.

2. 「타동사 + 부사」는 목적어가 명사인지 대명사인지에 따라 어순이 달라진다.

목적어	어순	예문
명사	「타동사 + 부사 + 목적어」/ 「타동사 + 목적어 + 부사」	George **put on** a coat. George는 코트를 입었다. = George **put** a coat **on**. **Hand in** the report now. 지금 그 보고서를 제출해라. = **Hand** the report **in** now.
대명사	「타동사 + 목적어 + 부사」	Don't **wake** me **up** until nine. 9시까지 나를 깨우지 마라. I had to **give** it **up**. 나는 그것을 포기해야 했다.

(Tip) 「자동사 + 전치사」는 「자동사 + 전치사 + 목적어」의 어순으로만 쓴다.
Are you **looking at** his phone? Don't **look at** it. 너는 그의 전화기를 보고 있니? 그것을 보지 마라.

연습문제 A 우리말과 같도록 빈칸에 알맞은 말을 쓰시오.

1 나는 한 시간 후에 나의 누나를 깨울 것이다.

= I am going to _____ _____ my sister in an hour.

2 수업 후에 너희들의 숙제를 제출해라.

= _____ _____ your homework after class.

3 수민이는 그녀의 꿈을 포기하지 않기로 결심했다.

= Sumin decided not to _____ _____ her dream.

4 당신의 주소를 적어주시겠어요?

= Could you _____ _____ your address?

5 James는 또렷하게 보기 위해 그의 안경을 써야 한다.

= James must ＿＿＿＿＿＿ ＿＿＿＿＿＿ his glasses to see clearly.

6 너는 어제 길 위에서 100달러를 주웠니?

= Did you ＿＿＿＿＿＿ ＿＿＿＿＿＿ a hundred dollars on the street yesterday?

7 더 많은 정보를 알아내기 위해 그 웹사이트를 방문하세요.

= Please visit the website to ＿＿＿＿＿＿ ＿＿＿＿＿＿ more information.

8 너는 안으로 들어올 때 너의 신발을 벗어야 한다.

= You must ＿＿＿＿＿＿ ＿＿＿＿＿＿ your shoes when you come inside.

9 네가 떠나기 전에 불을 끌 것을 잊지 마라.

= Don't forget to ＿＿＿＿＿＿ ＿＿＿＿＿＿ the lights before you leave.

10 우리는 폭우 때문에 그 경기를 미뤄야 했다.

= We had to ＿＿＿＿＿＿ ＿＿＿＿＿＿ the game because of the heavy rain.

연습문제 B 괄호 안에서 알맞은 것을 <u>모두</u> 고르시오.

1 Don't (give it up / give up it).

2 Can I (try on them / try on these sunglasses)?

3 Let's (find it out / find the truth out) together.

4 Did you (give them back / give back them) to her?

5 Could you (wake up me / wake me up) at 7 A.M.?

6 I always (turn off the heater / turned off it) when I go to sleep.

7 (Look at me / Look me at) while I'm talking to you.

8 We need to (take off them / take off our caps) in class.

9 You can (look up the words / look them up) on the Internet.

10 I wanted to listen to the radio, so I (turned on it / turned it on).

11 You should (hand in the document / hand in it) before tomorrow.

12 Don't (throw away my clothes / throw them away) without asking me.

기출 적중문제

다음 중 어법상 <u>어색한</u> 것은?

① Someone has turned the TV on.
② Samantha had to put the plan off.
③ He picked up the trash from the floor.
④ Please give back it by next week.
⑤ Let's look them up in the textbook.

「타동사 + 부사」의 목적어가 대명사인 경우 「타동사 + 대명사 + 부사」의 어순으로 써요.

1. where, when, why, how는 각각 장소, 시간·날짜, 이유, 방법·상태의 구체적인 정보를 묻는 의문부사이다.

where	장소	**Where** are my socks? – They're in the drawer. 나의 양말은 어디에 있니? – 그것들은 서랍 안에 있어.
when	시간, 날짜	**When** do you arrive? – Soon. 너는 언제 도착하니? – 곧.
why	이유	**Why** didn't you like the soup? – Because it was salty. 너는 왜 그 수프를 좋아하지 않았니? – 그것이 짰기 때문이야.
how	방법, 상태	**How** did you come here? – I walked. 너는 어떻게 여기에 왔니? – 나는 걸어왔어.

2. 「How + 형용사/부사 ~?」는 '얼마나 ~하니?'라는 의미로, 높이, 크기, 시간, 거리 등의 구체적인 정보를 물을 때 쓴다.

How tall ~?	높이, 키	**How tall** are you? – I'm 162 centimeters. 너는 얼마나 키가 크니? – 나는 162센티미터야.
How big ~?	크기	**How big** is your new room? – It's not that large. 너의 새 방은 얼마나 크니? – 그것은 그렇게 크지 않아.
How long ~?	시간, 길이	**How long** will you stay there? – A month. 너는 거기에 얼마나 오래 머무를 거니? – 한 달.
How far ~?	거리	**How far** is it from here to the bank? – It's a block away. 여기에서 은행까지 얼마나 머니? – 그것은 한 블록 떨어져 있어.
How old ~?	나이	**How old** is your dog? – He's seven. 너의 개는 몇 살이니? – 그는 일곱 살이야.
How often ~?	빈도	**How often** does the subway come? – Every five minutes. 지하철은 얼마나 자주 오니? – 5분마다.
How many ~?	개수	**How many** cousins do you have? – Six. 너는 얼마나 많은 사촌들이 있니? – 여섯 명.
How much ~?	양, 가격	**How much** is the ticket? – It's 40 dollars. 그 표는 얼마니? – 그것은 40달러야.

연습문제 A | 다음 빈칸에 Where, When, Why, How 중 알맞은 것을 넣어 대화를 완성하시오.

1 *A*: _____ are your parents going now?   *B*: To the supermarket.

2 A: _____ did you meet each other?   B: We went to the same elementary school.

3 A: _____ is Emma's birthday?   B: It's December 13.

4 A: _____ should I apologize to Martin? B: Because you were rude to him.

5 A: _____ can I find the carrots?   B: They're in the vegetable section.

6 A: _____ didn't you do the dishes?   B: Because I was cleaning my room.

7 A: _____ are you doing?   B: I'm doing well.

8 A: _____ does your plane leave?   B: In an hour.

연습문제 B 다음 빈칸에 알맞은 말을 넣어 대화를 완성하시오.

1   A: How _____ do you take a shower?   B: Every day.

2   A: How _____ is the Sun?   B: It's much bigger than the Earth.

3   A: How _____ are those kiwis?   B: One dollar each.

4   A: How _____ is your brother?   B: He is two years older than me.

5   A: How _____ is the Statue of Liberty?   B: It's 93 meters tall.

6   A: How _____ do you get your hair cut?   B: Once a month.

7   A: How _____ people were at the concert?   B: There were hundreds of people.

8   A: How _____ is this ring?   B: It's 30 dollars.

9   A: How _____ does it take to go home?   B: Almost an hour.

10 A: How _____ is it from here to the bus station? B: It's about 50 meters.

11 A: How _____ books did you read last week?   B: Only one.

기출 적중문제

다음 대화의 빈칸에 들어갈 말이 순서대로 짝지어진 것은?

> A: _____ do you exercise?
> B: About five times a week.
> A: Wow! _____ do you usually exercise?
> B: Right after I wake up.
> A: You are very diligent.

① How many – Where   ② How many – When
③ How often – Why   ④ How often – Where
⑤ How often – When

서술형 대비 문제

(A) 괄호 안의 말을 알맞은 형태로 바꿔 빈칸에 쓰시오.

1 Seonmi is moving the vase very _____. (careful)

2 Don't come home too _____ at night. (late)

3 I can _____ believe her words. (hard)

4 I feel _____ when I'm with my family. (comfortable)

5 The scenery in Hawaii is _____ beautiful. (true)

6 The water is warm _____ for the baby. (enough)

7 EU citizens can travel _____ between EU countries. (free)

8 _____, Ms. Brown is hiding something important. (clear)

9 It was the most _____ experience in my life. (terrible)

10 Bill Gates is _____ respected for his charity work. (high)

11 They are talking _____ so as not to wake up the baby. (quiet)

(B) 우리말과 같도록 괄호 안의 말을 알맞게 배열하시오.

1 비타민 C는 종종 감기를 예방하는 데 도움이 된다. (a cold, vitamin C, to prevent, helpful, often, is)
= _____

2 아프리카에 있는 나일강은 얼마나 기니? (long, the Nile in Africa, how, is)
= _____

3 여자들은 보통 남자들보다 더 오래 사니? (do, live, women, longer than men, usually)
= _____

4 너의 여동생은 얼마나 자주 그녀의 방을 청소하니? (clean, your sister, her room, does, often, how)
= _____

5 Brian은 전에 결코 그리스 음식을 먹어본 적이 없다. (eaten, has, before, Greek food, never, Brian)
= _____

6 우리는 가끔 우리의 점심시간 동안 축구를 한다. (during our lunch hour, sometimes, soccer, we, play)
= _____

7 우주를 여행하는 것은 항상 나의 꿈이었다. (always, my dream, has, traveling in space, been)
= _____

C 다음 빈칸에 알맞은 말을 <보기>에서 한 번씩만 골라 쓰시오.

> <보기> already   still   yet

1 I have _____ ordered fried chicken for dinner.

2 Do you _____ keep in touch with your old teacher?

3 Minji hasn't sent a text message to Hojun _____ .

> <보기> too   so   either   neither

4 He takes an art class. – _____ do I.

5 I don't like swimming. – I don't like swimming, _____ .

6 William isn't selfish. – _____ is Sandra.

7 Kate can speak sign language. – I can speak sign language, _____ .

D 다음 문장의 밑줄 친 부분을 괄호 안의 대명사로 바꿔 완전한 문장을 쓰시오.

1 Let's put off our meeting until next week. (it)
→ _____

2 Can I try on these clothes in the fitting room? (them)
→ _____

3 The journalists found the facts out finally. (them)
→ _____

4 My mother gave up drinking coffee last year. (it)
→ _____

5 I always wake my brother up in the morning. (him)
→ _____

6 You don't have to turn the air conditioner off now. (it)
→ _____

7 Daniel felt chilly, so he put on a sweater. (it)
→ _____

중간·기말고사 실전 문제

1 다음 중 짝지어진 관계가 나머지 넷과 다른 것은?

① dull – dully
② simple – simply
③ final – finally
④ busy – busily
⑤ week – weekly

2 다음 중 어법상 어색한 것을 모두 고르시오.

① The moon and stars shine brightly.
② Serious crimes have increased in the city.
③ You should speak your opinion clear.
④ Hopefully, we'll get there on time.
⑤ Did you sleep good last night?

3 다음 빈칸에 공통으로 들어갈 알맞은 것은?

> · Could you turn the music _____?
> · If you like the dress, you can try it
>   _____.

① off   ② out   ③ up
④ on   ⑤ in

4 다음 빈칸에 공통으로 들어갈 알맞은 의문부사를 쓰시오.

> · _____ can I get to the bank?
> · _____ are your parents doing
>   these days?

5 다음 (A)~(C)에 들어갈 말이 바르게 짝지어진 것은?

> · You are ___(A)___ for your own
>   mistakes.
> · Nami ___(B)___ didn't recognize her old
>   friend on the street.
> · Please don't sit so ___(C)___ to me. It's
>   too hot today.

	(A)	(B)	(C)
①	responsible	nearly	close
②	responsibly	nearly	close
③	responsible	nearly	closely
④	responsibly	near	closely
⑤	responsible	near	close

6 다음 중 밑줄 친 hard의 쓰임이 나머지 넷과 다른 것은?

① This wooden chair feels hard.
② The judge must make a hard decision.
③ My friends studied hard to win the math
   competition.
④ Jennifer found the crossword hard.
⑤ Hard cookies made my teeth hurt.

7 다음 중 어법상 바른 것을 모두 고르시오.

① Why did you arrive at school so lately?
② We hardly ate anything for lunch.
③ Children should talk polite to their
   parents.
④ It was raining so heavily last night.
⑤ This medicine is high effective for
   headaches.

8 다음 빈칸에 too가 들어갈 수 <u>없는</u> 것은?

① I can speak Spanish, _____.
② Monica is a very good singer, _____.
③ My uncle stopped smoking, _____.
④ I didn't eat the ice cream, _____.
⑤ He will go to the museum with me,
   _____.

9 다음 중 어법상 바른 것은?

① The dog always is friendly to strangers.
② You can see rarely people at night here.
③ Snow on the top of Mount Everest never melts.
④ We see sometimes the man playing the guitar in his yard.
⑤ My family usually has been to Jejudo every summer.

[10-11] 다음 대화의 빈칸에 알맞은 의문부사를 쓰시오.

10

> A: _____ did you go for your three-week vacation?
> B: I went to Bali with my best friend.

11

> A: Do you remember _____ you got this pretty necklace?
> B: I bought it a month ago.

12 다음 빈칸에 들어갈 말이 순서대로 짝지어진 것은?

> · Every person should be treated _____.
> · The dentist came _____ to him to check his teeth.

① equal – nearly
② equal – near
③ equally – nearly
④ equally – near
⑤ equality – nearly

13 다음 대화의 빈칸에 들어갈 알맞은 것은?

> Mom: Did either of you spill the milk on the kitchen floor?
> Amy : I didn't spill it.
> Sam : _____ Maybe our cat spilled the milk.

① Neither I did.
② So I did.
③ Neither did I.
④ So did I.
⑤ Neither didn't I.

14 다음 중 밑줄 친 <u>enough</u>의 쓰임이 나머지 넷과 다른 것은?

① Is your apple juice cold <u>enough</u>?
② The runner didn't run fast <u>enough</u> to win the race.
③ He isn't old <u>enough</u> to apply for an ID card.
④ Juwon is trying to save <u>enough</u> money to buy a laptop.
⑤ This ladder isn't long <u>enough</u> for us to reach the roof.

15 다음 중 어법상 <u>어색한</u> 것끼리 묶인 것은?

ⓐ Don't throw away any trash on the floor.
ⓑ Jane tried writing a novel, but she gave it up quickly.
ⓒ The necktie was so uncomfortable, so Bill took off it.
ⓓ Dami asked me to wake up her two hours later.
ⓔ My mother wrote a recipe for corn soup down for me.

① ⓐ, ⓑ   ② ⓐ, ⓒ   ③ ⓑ, ⓔ
④ ⓒ, ⓓ   ⑤ ⓓ, ⓔ

16 다음 글의 빈칸에 들어갈 말이 순서대로 짝지어진 것은?

_____ books do you read for a year? Nowadays, lots of students find watching videos more interesting than reading books. Then, _____ should we read books? Because, through reading, we can experience what we've never done before. For example, you can explore an ancient city or even meet a king.

① How often – when
② How often – why
③ How many – why
④ How many – where
⑤ How much – where

17 다음 빈칸에 알맞은 말을 <보기>에서 한 번씩만 골라 쓰시오.

<보기>   already   still   yet

(1) Have you received my letters _____?

(2) Did you _____ finish doing the laundry?

(3) My brother _____ doesn't know the capital of Canada.

18 다음 (A)~(C)에 들어갈 말이 바르게 짝지어진 것은?

· I felt so ___(A)___ because someone helped me to find my missing phone.
· Listen ___(B)___ to this strange sound.
· You must not play music ___(C)___ at night.

	(A)	(B)	(C)
①	lucky	closely	loudly
②	lucky	close	loudly
③	lucky	closely	loud
④	luckily	close	loud
⑤	luckily	closely	loud

19 다음 중 어법상 <u>어색한</u> 것끼리 묶인 것은?

> ⓐ The Titanic was enormously hugely.
> ⓑ Andy is pretty sure that his answer is correct.
> ⓒ Semi woke up enough early to make breakfast for her family.
> ⓓ The dance was international popular in the 2000s.
> ⓔ The flu spreads among people very quickly.

① ⓐ, ⓔ   ② ⓑ, ⓓ   ③ ⓒ, ⓔ
④ ⓐ, ⓒ, ⓓ   ⑤ ⓑ, ⓓ, ⓔ

20 다음 표를 보고 <보기>의 빈도부사를 활용하여 문장을 완성하시오.

How often do you go jogging?					
	Mon	Tue	Wed	Thu	Fri
Chanho	O	O	O	O	O
Jihee	O	X	X	O	X
Yerim	X	X	X	X	O

<보기>	seldom	sometimes	always

(1) Chanho _____ on weekdays.

(2) Jihee _____ on weekdays.

(3) Yerim _____ on weekdays.

21 다음 중 어법상 바른 것의 개수는?

> ⓐ I want to find it out for myself.
> ⓑ When you finish using the pen, please give back it to me.
> ⓒ Will you never tell a lie again?
> ⓓ Do often you go to a theater alone?
> ⓔ Why don't you look at yourself in the mirror?

① 1개   ② 2개   ③ 3개
④ 4개   ⑤ 5개

22 다음 중 밑줄 친 부분이 어법상 <u>어색한</u> 것을 <u>모두</u> 고르시오.

> A: I've been interested in skateboarding ①<u>lately</u>.
> B: Really? I didn't know that you liked it. ②<u>How often</u> do you ride a skateboard?
> A: Almost every day. I ③<u>ride always</u> it after dinner. It feels like I become a ④<u>complete</u> different person when I ride it.
> B: You seem to love skateboarding so much. But make sure to ⑤<u>put on a helmet</u> so as not to get hurt.
> A: I will. Thanks.

CHAPTER 13
비교구문

A car is **as fast as** a bus. 자동차는 버스만큼 빠르다.
A car is **faster than** a bicycle. 자동차는 자전거보다 더 빠르다.
A plane is **the fastest** of the four. 비행기는 넷 중에서 가장 빠르다.

위 문장에서 여러 교통수단의 속도를 비교하고 있는데, 이렇게 두 가지 이상의 대상을 서로 견주어 비교하는 문장을 **비교구문**이라고 해요. 비교하는 두 대상의 정도가 비슷하거나 같음을 나타낼 때는 **원급**, 두 대상 간 정도의 차이를 나타낼 때는 **비교급**, 셋 이상의 비교 대상 중 하나의 정도가 가장 높음을 나타낼 때는 **최상급**을 써요.

기출로 적중 POINT

1-1 • 규칙 변화

1-2 • 불규칙 변화

2-1 • 원급 비교: as + 원급 + as

2-2 • 원급 비교: as + 원급 + as + 주어 + can[could]

2-3 • 원급 비교: 배수사 + as + 원급 + as

3-1 • 비교급 비교: 비교급 + than

3-2 • 비교급 비교: the + 비교급, the + 비교급

3-3 • 비교급 비교: 비교급 + and + 비교급

4-1 • 최상급 비교: the + 최상급

4-2 • 최상급 비교: one of the + 최상급 + 복수명사

4-3 • 최상급 비교: 원급과 비교급을 이용한 최상급 표현

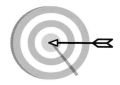

내신 100점 적중!
기출 출제율

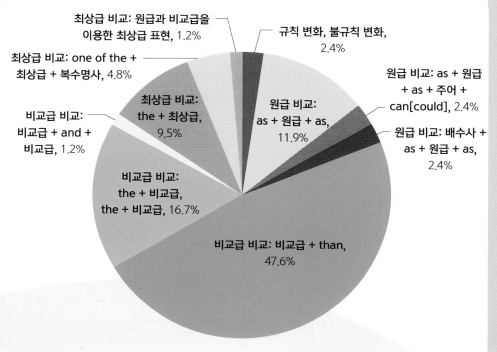

최상급 비교: 원급과 비교급을
이용한 최상급 표현, 1.2%

규칙 변화, 불규칙 변화,
2.4%

최상급 비교: one of the +
최상급 + 복수명사, 4.8%

원급 비교: as + 원급
+ as + 주어 +
can[could], 2.4%

비교급 비교:
비교급 + and +
비교급, 1.2%

최상급 비교:
the + 최상급,
9.5%

원급 비교:
as + 원급 + as,
11.9%

원급 비교: 배수사 +
as + 원급 + as,
2.4%

비교급 비교:
the + 비교급,
the + 비교급, 16.7%

비교급 비교: 비교급 + than,
47.6%

TOP 1 **비교급 비교: 비교급 + than (47.6%)**
비교급 비교의 형태와 쓰임 및 비교급을 강조하는 법을 묻는 문제가 자주 출제
된다.

TOP 2 **비교급 비교: the + 비교급, the + 비교급 (16.7%)**
「the + 비교급, the + 비교급」의 의미와 형태를 묻는 문제가 자주 출제된다.

TOP 3 **원급 비교: as + 원급 + as (11.9%)**
원급 비교의 형태와 쓰임을 묻는 문제가 자주 출제된다.

1. 원급은 형용사나 부사의 원래 형태이며, 비교급은 대부분 원급에 -(e)r을, 최상급은 대부분 원급에 -(e)st를 붙여 만든다.

비교급/최상급 만드는 법		원급	비교급	최상급
대부분의 형용사·부사	+ -er/-est	small	smaller	smallest
-e로 끝나는 형용사·부사	+ -r/-st	close	closer	closest
「자음 + y」로 끝나는 형용사·부사	y를 i로 바꾸고 + -er/-est	lazy	lazier	laziest
「단모음 + 단자음」으로 끝나는 형용사·부사	마지막 자음을 한 번 더 쓰고 + -er/-est	thin	thinner	thinnest

2. 다음 형용사나 부사의 비교급은 원급 앞에 more를, 최상급은 원급 앞에 most를 붙여 만든다.

비교급/최상급 만드는 법		원급	비교급	최상급
대부분의 2음절 이상인 형용사·부사 (-y로 끝나는 형용사 제외)	more/most + 원급	useful	more useful	most useful
분사 형태의 형용사		tired	more tired	most tired
「형용사 + ly」 형태의 부사		gladly	more gladly	most gladly

연습문제 | 다음 형용사나 부사의 비교급과 최상급을 쓰시오.

1 smart – _____ – _____

2 hot – _____ – _____

3 big – _____ – _____

4 loud – _____ – _____

5 beautiful – _____ – _____

6 nice – _____ – _____

7 easily – _____ – _____

8 great — _____ — _____

9 strange — _____ — _____

10 healthy — _____ — _____

11 helpful — _____ — _____

12 dark — _____ — _____

13 young — _____ — _____

14 thin — _____ — _____

15 serious — _____ — _____

16 hungry — _____ — _____

17 cheap — _____ — _____

18 long — _____ — _____

19 expensive — _____ — _____

20 quickly — _____ — _____

21 warm — _____ — _____

22 few — _____ — _____

23 interesting — _____ — _____

24 strong — _____ — _____

25 scary — _____ — _____

26 sweet — _____ — _____

27 important — _____ — _____

28 wide — _____ — _____

29 tired — _____ — _____

30 lonely — _____ — _____

31 useless — _____ — _____

32 wet — _____ — _____

33 boring — _____ — _____

34 tasty — _____ — _____

35 close — _____ — _____

36 gladly — _____ — _____

POINT 1-2 불규칙 변화

일부 형용사나 부사의 비교급과 최상급은 불규칙하게 변한다.

원급		비교급	최상급	원급		비교급	최상급
good	좋은	better	best	many	(수가) 많은	more	most
well	건강한, 잘			much	(양이) 많은		
bad	나쁜	worse	worst	little	(양이) 적은	less	least
badly	나쁘게			late	(시간이) 늦은	later	latest
ill	아픈, 병든				(순서가) 늦은	latter	last
old	나이 든, 오래된	older	oldest	far	(거리가) 먼	farther	farthest
	연상의	elder	eldest		(정도가) 더욱	further	furthest

연습문제 다음 형용사나 부사의 비교급과 최상급을 쓰시오.

1 much – _____ – _____

2 bad – _____ – _____

3 old – _____ – eldest

4 little – _____ – _____

5 well – _____ – _____

6 many – _____ – _____

7 far – _____ – farthest

8 badly – _____ – _____

9 good – _____ – _____

10 late – latter – _____

11 old – older – _____

12 ill – _____ – _____

13 late – _____ – latest

14 far – further – _____

기출 적중문제

다음 중 원급–비교급–최상급 형태가 잘못된 것을 모두 고르시오.

① ill – worse – worst

② far – further – furthest

③ safely – safelier – safeliest

④ bored – more bored – most bored

⑤ good – more – most

기출로적중 POINT 2-1 원급 비교: as + 원급 + as

정답 p.39

1. 「as + 원급 + as」는 '…만큼 ~한/하게'라는 의미로, 비교하는 두 대상의 정도가 비슷하거나 같음을 나타낸다.

   Minho is **as tall as** his father. 민호는 그의 아버지만큼 키가 크다.

   Jenny walked **as slowly as** I did. Jenny는 나만큼 느리게 걸었다.
   = Jenny walked **as slowly as** me.
   └→ as 뒤의 「주어 + 동사」는 목적격으로 바꿔 쓸 수 있다.

2. 「not + as[so] + 원급 + as」는 '…만큼 ~하지 않은/않게'라는 의미이다.

   This pillow is **not as[so] comfortable as** that one. 이 베개는 저것만큼 편안하지 않다.
   I can**not** cook **as[so] well as** Paul. 나는 Paul만큼 요리를 잘하지 못한다.

   (Tip) 「not + as[so] + 원급 + as」는 주어에 따라 「비교급 + than」이나 「less + 원급 + than」으로 바꿔 쓸 수 있다.

   Victory is**n't as[so] important as** fair play. 승리는 페어플레이만큼 중요하지 않다.
   = Fair play is **more important than** victory. 페어플레이는 승리보다 더 중요하다.
   = Victory is **less important than** fair play. 승리는 페어플레이보다 덜 중요하다.

연습문제 A 우리말과 같도록 괄호 안의 말을 활용하여 문장을 완성하시오.

1 너의 손은 얼음만큼 차갑다. (cold)

= Your hands are _____ ice.

2 Jamie는 운동선수만큼 자주 운동한다. (often)

= Jamie exercises _____ an athlete.

3 이 수건은 저것만큼 마르지 않았다. (dry)

= This towel is _____ that one.

4 그 코트는 깃털만큼 가볍게 느껴진다. (light)

= The coat feels _____ a feather.

5 저 딸기들은 설탕만큼 달다. (sweet)

= Those strawberries are _____ sugar.

6 그 시험은 지난 것만큼 어렵지 않았다. (difficult)

= The exam was _____ the last one.

7 Tim은 Carol만큼 학교에 늦게 도착했다. (late)

= Tim arrived at school _____ Carol did.

8 이 컵들은 싱크대 안에 있는 그것들만큼 더럽지 않다. (dirty)

= These cups are _____ the ones in the sink.

9 Danny는 그의 형만큼 예의 바르지 않다. (polite)

= Danny is _____ his brother.

10 민재는 그의 부모님만큼 일찍 일어난다. (early)

= Minjae wakes up _____ his parents do.

11 곰은 말만큼 빠르게 달릴 수 있다. (quickly)

= Bears can run _____ horses.

12 밴쿠버의 기온은 토론토의 것만큼 낮지 않다. (low)

= Vancouver's temperature is _____ that of Toronto.

연습문제 B <보기>와 같이 다음 세 문장의 의미가 같도록 문장을 완성하시오.

> <보기> Turtles don't move as fast as rabbits.
>
> = Rabbits move _faster than_ turtles.
>
> = Turtles move _less fast than_ rabbits.

1 Fall is not as hot as summer.

= Summer is _____ fall.

= Fall is _____ summer.

2 My suitcase is not as heavy as your suitcase.

= Your suitcase is _____ my suitcase.

= My suitcase is _____ your suitcase.

3 Ralph can't jump as high as Steven.

= Steven can jump _____ Ralph.

= Ralph can jump _____ Steven.

4 Vegetables are not as delicious as junk food.

= Junk food is _____ vegetables.

= Vegetables are _____ junk food.

기출 적중문제

다음 밑줄 친 ⓐ~ⓔ 중 어법상 <u>어색한</u> 것을 찾아 기호를 쓰고 바르게 고쳐 쓰시오.

> <u>Her</u> eyes <u>are</u> <u>as</u> <u>brighter</u> as <u>stars</u>.
> ⓐ   ⓑ   ⓒ   ⓓ   ⓔ

_____ → _____

POINT 2-2
원급 비교: as + 원급 + as + 주어 + can[could]

정답 p.39

「as + 원급 + as + 주어 + can[could]」는 '…가 할 수 있는 한 ~한/하게'라는 의미이며, 「as + 원급 + as + possible」로 바꿔 쓸 수 있다.

I drink water **as often as I can.** 나는 내가 할 수 있는 한 자주 물을 마신다.
= I drink water **as often as possible.** 나는 가능한 한 자주 물을 마신다.

He kicked the ball **as hard as he could.** 그는 그가 할 수 있는 한 세게 공을 찼다.
= He kicked the ball **as hard as possible.** 그는 가능한 한 세게 공을 찼다.

연습문제 다음 두 문장의 의미가 같도록 문장을 완성하시오.

1 We should walk as much as we can.
= We should walk _____.

2 Kate folded her clothes as neatly as possible.
= Kate folded her clothes _____.

3 He tried to drive as safely as possible.
= He tried to drive _____.

4 You need to complete this project as quickly as you can.
= You need to complete this project _____.

5 The visitors looked at the painting as closely as they could.
= The visitors looked at the painting _____.

6 Please call me back as soon as possible.
= Please call me back _____.

7 The children are singing as loudly as possible.
= The children are singing _____.

8 Tony answered the questions as honestly as he could.
= Tony answered the questions _____.

기출 적중문제 ◎

우리말과 같도록 괄호 안의 말을 활용하여 빈칸에 쓰시오.

나는 내가 할 수 있는 한 빨리 돌아와야 했다. (soon)

= I had to return _____ _____ _____ _____ _____.

원급 비교: 배수사 + as + 원급 + as

정답 p.40

> 「배수사 + as + 원급 + as」는 '…보다 −배 더 ~한/하게'라는 의미이며, 「배수사 + 비교급 + than」으로 바꿔 쓸 수 있다.
>
> This doll is **six times as expensive as** that one. 이 인형은 저것보다 6배 더 비싸다.
> = This doll is **six times more expensive than** that one.
>
> Russia is **26 times as big as** France. 러시아는 프랑스보다 26배 더 크다.
> = Russia is **26 times bigger than** France.

연습문제 다음 두 문장의 의미가 같도록 문장을 완성하시오.

1 Humans live seven times longer than dogs.
= Humans live _____ dogs.

2 This bag is ten times as light as that one.
= This bag is _____ that one.

3 An elephant is about 1,500 times heavier than a rabbit.
= An elephant is about _____ a rabbit.

4 My grandmother is eight times as old as me.
= My grandmother is _____ me.

5 Gilbert's room is three times larger than that of Suho.
= Gilbert's room is _____ that of Suho.

6 Fleas can jump 200 times as high as their height.
= Fleas can jump _____ their height.

7 Jupiter is five times farther than the Earth from the Sun.
= Jupiter is _____ the Earth from the Sun.

기출 적중문제 🎯

우리말과 같도록 괄호 안의 말을 알맞게 배열하시오.

> 이 책은 저것보다 두 배 더 두껍다. (as, thick, that one, twice, as, is, this book)

= _____

POINT 3-1 비교급 비교: 비교급 + than

기출로적중

정답 p.40

1. 「비교급 + than」은 '…보다 더 ~한/하게'라는 의미로, 비교하는 두 대상 간 정도의 차이를 나타낸다.

   Light travels **faster than** sound. 빛은 소리보다 더 빠르게 이동한다.
   His car is **newer than** mine. 그의 차는 나의 것보다 더 새 것이다.

   I am **more popular than** he is. 나는 그보다 더 인기 있다.
   = I am **more popular than** him.
   └→ than 뒤의 「주어 + 동사」는 목적격으로 바꿔 쓸 수 있다.

2. 비교급 앞에 much, even, still, far, a lot을 써서 '훨씬'이라는 의미로 비교급을 강조할 수 있다.

   Grapes are **much** sweeter than lemons. 포도는 레몬보다 훨씬 더 달다.
   The castle is **even** **more beautiful** than I thought.
   그 성은 내가 생각했던 것보다 훨씬 더 아름답다.

   (Tip) very는 비교급이 아닌 원급을 강조한다.
   Mr. Johnson lives in a **very** (**nice**, ~~nicer~~) house. Johnson씨는 매우 좋은 집에서 산다.

연습문제 A 괄호 안의 말을 비교급 형태로 바꿔 문장을 완성하시오.

1 The Sun is _____ the moon. (bright)

2 That magazine is _____ this one. (interesting)

3 An earthworm moves _____ a snail. (slow)

4 Jinho arrived _____ Bora. (soon)

5 Today is _____ yesterday was. (cold)

6 Your sandwich looks _____ mine. (tasty)

7 Children's bones are _____ those of adults. (soft)

8 My parents were _____ I was. (nervous)

9 The movie was _____ I expected. (sad)

10 Playing soccer is _____ watching it. (exciting)

11 Nate is normally _____ me on weekdays. (busy)

12 The final exam is _____ the midterm exam. (important)

<보기>   expensive   tall   many   old   heavy   fast   young

1   Yuri is nine years old. Hana is twelve years old.

→ Yuri is _____ Hana.

2   Dan is 185 cm. Liam is 178 cm.

→ Dan is _____ Liam.

3   My dog is 8 kg. His dog is 5 kg.

→ My dog is _____ his.

4   This house was built in 1995. That house was built in 2008.

→ This house is _____ that house.

5   Lisa runs 50 meters in seven seconds. Jasmine runs 50 meters in ten seconds.

→ Lisa runs _____ Jasmine.

6   The banana muffin is 3,500 won. The chocolate muffin is 2,000 won.

→ The banana muffin is _____ the chocolate muffin.

7   Jake has eight shirts. Ben has five shirts.

→ Jake has _____ shirts _____ Ben does.

연습문제 **C**   괄호 안에서 알맞은 것을 고르시오.

1   Beth has a (very / much) big family.

2   Kelly's grades were (high / higher) than mine.

3   These pants are (very / even) tighter than I thought.

4   Seoul is (much / more) crowded than Jeonju.

5   Carl's plan sounds (very / a lot) better than Sam's.

6   People say airplanes are (safe / safer) than cars.

기출 적중문제 🎯

다음 중 어법상 바른 것은?

① I'm more stronger than him.

② My sister's food tastes better as mine.

③ A horse is far bigger than an ant.

④ The noise was even loud than thunder.

⑤ A golf ball is very lighter than a basketball.

비교급 비교: the + 비교급, the + 비교급

정답 p.40

POINT 3-2

「the + 비교급, the + 비교급」은 '~하면 할수록 더 …하다'라는 의미이다.

The older she grew, **the wiser** she became.　그녀는 나이가 들면 들수록 더 현명해졌다.
The more pizza I had, **the fuller** I got.　나는 더 많은 피자를 먹으면 먹을수록 더 배불러졌다.
The faster we walk, **the earlier** we'll arrive.　우리는 빠르게 걸으면 걸을수록 더 일찍 도착할 것이다.
The longer the speaker spoke, **the more bored** the audience felt.
발표자가 길게 말하면 말할수록 청중은 더 지루하게 느꼈다.

연습문제 A　우리말과 같도록 괄호 안의 말을 활용하여 문장을 완성하시오.

1　바다는 깊으면 깊을수록 더 어둡다. (deep, dark)

= ＿＿＿＿＿＿＿＿＿＿ the ocean is, ＿＿＿＿＿＿＿＿＿＿ it is.

2　네가 열심히 공부하면 할수록 너의 성적은 더 좋아질 것이다. (good, hard)

= ＿＿＿＿＿＿＿＿＿＿ you study, ＿＿＿＿＿＿＿＿＿＿ your grade will be.

3　비가 심하게 내리면 내릴수록 나의 신발은 더 축축해졌다. (heavily, wet)

= ＿＿＿＿＿＿＿＿＿＿ it rained, ＿＿＿＿＿＿＿＿＿＿ my shoes got.

4　너는 브로콜리를 자주 먹으면 먹을수록 더 건강해질 것이다. (healthy, often)

= ＿＿＿＿＿＿＿＿＿＿ you eat broccoli, ＿＿＿＿＿＿＿＿＿＿ you will be.

5　추우면 추울수록 나는 더 우울해진다. (cold, depressed)

= ＿＿＿＿＿＿＿＿＿＿ it is, ＿＿＿＿＿＿＿＿＿＿ I become.

6　그 카페가 인기 있어지면 질수록 더 많은 사람들이 방문했다. (popular, many)

= ＿＿＿＿＿＿＿＿＿＿ the café got, ＿＿＿＿＿＿＿＿＿＿ people visited.

7　음악이 커지면 커질수록 나의 귀는 더 아팠다. (loud, much)

= ＿＿＿＿＿＿＿＿＿＿ the music grew, ＿＿＿＿＿＿＿＿＿＿ my ears hurt.

8　손님들은 오래 기다리면 기다릴수록 더 화가 났다. (angry, long)

= ＿＿＿＿＿＿＿＿＿＿ the customers waited, ＿＿＿＿＿＿＿＿＿＿ they got.

9　날씨가 따뜻해지면 질수록 그 정원은 더 아름다워졌다. (warm, beautiful)

= ＿＿＿＿＿＿＿＿＿＿ the weather got, ＿＿＿＿＿＿＿＿＿＿ the garden became.

10　우리는 산을 높이 올라가면 갈수록 더 멀리 볼 수 있다. (far, high)

= ＿＿＿＿＿＿＿＿＿＿ we go up the mountain, ＿＿＿＿＿＿＿＿＿＿ we can see.

11　네가 더 많은 문제에 답하면 답할수록 더 많은 점수를 받을 것이다. (many)

= ＿＿＿＿＿＿＿＿＿＿ questions you answer, ＿＿＿＿＿＿＿＿＿＿ points you will
receive.

<보기>와 같이 다음 문장을 「the + 비교급, the + 비교급」을 이용하여 바꿔 쓰시오.

> <보기> If you read more books, you will become smarter.
> → *The more books you read, the smarter you will become.*

1 If Emma goes to bed earlier, she can sleep longer.

→ _____

2 As the box got emptier, it became lighter.

→ _____

3 When it got cloudier, John felt more disappointed.

→ _____

4 As I thought about the test more, I got more nervous.

→ _____

5 When I have more free time, I feel more relaxed.

→ _____

6 When the restaurant is more crowded, it becomes noisier.

→ _____

7 As the actor became more famous, he got busier.

→ _____

8 If you invite more friends to the party, it will be more exciting.

→ _____

9 If you exercise more often, you will become stronger.

→ _____

10 If the item has less packaging, it is cheaper.

→ _____

기출 적중문제

다음 글의 밑줄 친 (A)를 「the + 비교급, the + 비교급」을 이용하여 바꿔 쓰시오.

> When I first started to learn the cello, I wasn't good at playing it. So, I practiced really hard. (A) As I practiced more, I played the cello better.

→ _____

비교급 비교: 비교급 + and + 비교급

정답 p.40

「비교급 + and + 비교급」은 '점점 더 ~한/하게'라는 의미이다.

The child is growing **taller and taller**. 그 아이는 점점 더 키가 커지고 있다.

The weather became **warmer and warmer**. 날씨가 점점 더 따뜻해졌다.

The drama is getting **more and more interesting**. 그 드라마는 점점 더 흥미로워지고 있다.

↳ 비교급이 「more + 원급」의 형태인 경우 「more and more + 원급」으로 쓴다.

연습문제 우리말과 같도록 괄호 안의 말을 활용하여 문장을 완성하시오.

1 하늘이 점점 더 밝아지고 있다. (bright)

= The sky is getting _____.

2 낮은 겨울에 점점 더 짧아진다. (short)

= The days become _____ in winter.

3 빗방울이 점점 더 커졌다. (big)

= The raindrops grew _____.

4 그 배구 경기는 점점 더 흥미진진해졌다. (exciting)

= The volleyball game became _____.

5 그녀는 점점 더 빠르게 말하기 시작했다. (fast)

= She began to talk _____.

6 인공지능은 점점 더 똑똑해지고 있다. (smart)

= Artificial intelligence is getting _____.

7 Jenna의 얼굴은 점점 더 빨개지고 있다. (red)

= Jenna's face is turning _____.

8 그 안전벨트는 점점 더 조여졌다. (tight)

= The seat belt got _____.

9 유기농 채소는 점점 더 인기 있어지고 있다. (popular)

= Organic vegetables are becoming _____.

10 주호의 영어는 점점 더 좋아지고 있다. (good)

= Juho's English is becoming _____.

11 바람이 불 수록, 나의 연은 점점 더 높이 날았다. (high)

= As the wind blew, my kite flew _____.

POINT 4-1 최상급 비교: the + 최상급

1. 「the + 최상급」은 '가장 ~한/하게'라는 의미로, 셋 이상의 비교 대상 중 하나의 정도가 가장 높음을 나타낸다. 부사의 최상급은 the를 생략하기도 한다.

   This is **the oldest** tree in my yard. 이것은 나의 마당에서 가장 오래된 나무이다.

   Hansu practices **(the) hardest** of the players. 한수는 그 선수들 중에서 가장 열심히 연습한다.

2. 최상급은 보통 in이나 of를 사용하여 비교 범위를 나타낸다.

   in + 장소/집단   Irene is **the kindest** girl **in her class.**   Irene은 그녀의 반에서 가장 친절한 소녀이다.

   of + 비교 대상   Tom is **the tallest** **of my friends.**   Tom은 나의 친구들 중에서 가장 키가 크다.

   (Tip) 최상급 뒤에 「(that) + 주어 + have/has + (ever) + p.p.」의 형태도 종종 쓰이며, '…한 것 중에서 가장 ~한'이라는 의미이다.

   It is **the scariest** story **(that) I've (ever) heard.** 그것은 내가 들어본 것 중에서 가장 무서운 이야기이다.

연습문제 A   다음 그림을 보고 <보기>의 말을 활용하여 빈칸에 쓰시오.

<보기> heavy   large   expensive   long   short   fast

1

2

3

4

5

6

1   Matt is _____ _____ of all the students.

2   The orange cat is _____ _____ of all the cats.

3   Jessica runs _____ _____ of the three.

4   I want to buy _____ _____ _____ sneakers in the store.

5   This dress is _____ _____ in the closet.

6 The pineapple is _____ _____ fruit in the basket.

우리말과 같도록 괄호 안의 말을 활용하여 문장을 완성하시오.

1 러시아는 아시아에서 가장 큰 나라이다. (big country, Asia)
= Russia is _____ .

2 아나콘다는 정글에서 가장 위험한 동물이다. (dangerous animal, the jungle)
= The anaconda is _____ .

3 이것은 우리 집에서 가장 푹신한 의자이다. (soft chair, our house)
= This is _____ .

4 Gino's는 이 마을에서 가장 맛있는 피자를 판다. (delicious pizza, this town)
= Gino's sells _____ .

5 가족은 나의 삶에서 가장 중요한 것이다. (important thing, my life)
= Family is _____ .

6 Jason은 나의 모든 친구들 중에서 가장 노래를 잘 하는 사람이다. (good singer, all my friends)
= Jason is _____ .

7 제주도는 한국에서 가장 아름다운 해변을 가지고 있다. (beautiful beach, Korea)
= Jejudo has _____ .

8 봄은 넷 중에서 가장 알록달록한 계절이다. (colorful season, the four)
= Spring is _____ .

9 저 그림은 미술관에서 가장 훌륭한 예술 작품이다. (excellent artwork, the gallery)
= That painting is _____ .

기출 적중문제

다음 빈칸에 들어갈 말이 순서대로 짝지어진 것은?

> A hummingbird is _____ bird _____ the world.

① a small – in　　② a smaller – of
③ a smaller – in　　④ the smallest – of
⑤ the smallest – in

최상급 비교: one of the + 최상급 + 복수명사 정답 p.41

「one of the + 최상급 + 복수명사」는 '가장 ~한 것들 중 하나'라는 의미이다.

That pyramid is **one of the oldest structures** on earth.
저 피라미드는 지구에서 가장 오래된 구조물들 중 하나이다.

The Great Gatsby was **one of the most popular novels**.
'위대한 개츠비'는 가장 인기 있는 소설들 중 하나였다.

One of the biggest museums is in France. 가장 큰 박물관들 중 하나는 프랑스에 있다.

연습문제 | 우리말과 같도록 괄호 안의 말을 활용하여 문장을 완성하시오.

1 나일강은 아프리카에서 가장 긴 강들 중 하나이다. (long, river)

= The Nile is _____ in Africa.

2 시드니는 살기에 가장 좋은 도시들 중 하나이다. (good, city)

= Sydney is _____ to live in.

3 Smith는 미국에서 가장 흔한 성들 중 하나이다. (common, last name)

= Smith is _____ in the United States.

4 '노트북'은 내가 본 것 중에서 가장 슬픈 영화들 중 하나였다. (sad, movie)

= *The Notebook* was _____ I've ever watched.

5 레오나르도 다 빈치는 역사에서 가장 위대한 예술가들 중 한 명이었다. (great, artist)

= Leonardo da Vinci was _____ in history.

6 한글은 가장 과학적인 문자 체계들 중 하나이다. (scientific, writing system)

= Hangeul is _____.

7 지구 온난화는 세계에서 가장 심각한 문제들 중 하나이다. (serious, problem)

= Global warming is _____ in the world.

기출 적중문제

다음 중 어법상 <u>어색한</u> 것을 <u>모두</u> 고르시오.

① He is one of the most famous writers in England.

② The chef cooks one of the tastiest steaks in the town.

③ Jackson is one of funnier kids in his class.

④ She is one of the best violinists in the orchestra.

⑤ Today was one of the hottest day in August.

POINT 4-3 최상급 비교: 원급과 비교급을 이용한 최상급 표현

정답 p.41

원급이나 비교급을 이용하여 최상급의 의미를 나타낼 수 있다.

the + 최상급 가장 ~한/하게
= No (other) + 단수명사 ~ as[so] + 원급 + as (다른) 어떤 …도 -만큼 ~하지 않은
= No (other) + 단수명사 ~ 비교급 + than (다른) 어떤 …도 -보다 더 ~하지 않은
= 비교급 + than any other + 단수명사 다른 어떤 …보다 더 ~한
= 비교급 + than all the other + 복수명사 다른 모든 …보다 더 ~한

Amy is **the smartest student** in my school. Amy는 나의 학교에서 가장 똑똑한 학생이다.
= **No (other) student** is **as[so] smart as** Amy in my school.
나의 학교에서 (다른) 어떤 학생도 Amy만큼 똑똑하지 않다.
= **No (other) student** is **smarter than** Amy in my school.
나의 학교에서 (다른) 어떤 학생도 Amy보다 더 똑똑하지 않다.
= Amy is **smarter than any other student** in my school.
Amy는 나의 학교에서 다른 어떤 학생보다 더 똑똑하다.
= Amy is **smarter than all the other students** in my school.
Amy는 나의 학교에서 다른 모든 학생들보다 더 똑똑하다.

연습문제 다음 문장들의 의미가 같도록 문장을 완성하시오.

1 Incheon Grand Bridge is the longest bridge in Korea.
= _____ is _____ Incheon Grand Bridge in Korea.
= _____ is _____ Incheon Grand Bridge in Korea.
= Incheon Grand Bridge is _____ in Korea.
= Incheon Grand Bridge is _____ in Korea.

2 Venus is the brightest planet in our solar system.
= _____ is _____ Venus in our solar system.
= _____ is _____ Venus in our solar system.
= Venus is _____ in our solar system.
= Venus is _____ in our solar system.

3 The Bermuda Triangle is the most mysterious place in the world.
= _____ is _____ the Bermuda Triangle in the world.
= _____ is _____ the Bermuda Triangle in the world.
= The Bermuda Triangle is _____ in the world.
= The Bermuda Triangle is _____ in the world.

Ⓐ 밑줄 친 부분이 어법상 맞으면 O를 쓰고, 틀리면 바르게 고쳐 쓰시오.

1 Today was the <u>goodest</u> day in my life.　　　　→ _____

2 The TV is <u>lighter than</u> the refrigerator.　　　　→ _____

3 This winter isn't <u>as cold so</u> the last one.　　　　→ _____

4 The movie *Deep Blue Sea* was <u>as shocking as</u> *Jaws*.　→ _____

5 The triathlon is <u>toughest</u> race in the Olympics.　→ _____

6 Luke sings <u>very</u> nicer than all the other boys.　→ _____

7 Usain Bolt is the fastest man <u>of</u> the world.　　→ _____

8 My mother thinks that I am as <u>smarter</u> as Einstein.　→ _____

Ⓑ 다음 그림을 보고 괄호 안의 말을 활용하여 문장을 완성하시오.

[1-4]

1 Ricky is _____ of the four. (short)

2 Peter is _____ Katie. (tall)

3 Katie is _____ David. (young)

4 Peter is _____ any other kid in the room. (old)

[5-8]

5 The notebook is _____ of the three. (cheap)

6 The textbook is _____ the notebook. (four times, expensive)

7 The dictionary is _____ the textbook. (thick)

8 The notebook is _____ all the other books on the shelf. (thin)

C 다음은 여러 도시의 특징을 비교하는 표이다. 괄호 안의 말을 활용하여 빈칸에 알맞은 말을 쓰시오.

도시	Seoul	London	Manila	Moscow
크기	605 km²	1,572 km²	43 km²	2,511 km²
인구	9,963,000	9,046,000	1,780,148	12,410,000
기온	15℃	3℃	27℃	8℃

1 Seoul is _____ _____ London. (small)

2 Moscow is _____ _____ of the four. (large)

3 Manila's population is not _____ _____ _____ Seoul's. (big)

4 London is _____ _____ of all the cities. (cold)

5 Manila is _____ _____ Moscow. (hot)

D 우리말과 같도록 괄호 안의 말을 활용하여 빈칸에 쓰시오.

1 그 환자는 점점 더 나아졌다. (good)

= The patient got _____ _____ _____.

2 시금치는 가장 건강에 좋은 채소들 중 하나이다. (healthy, vegetable)

= Spinach is _____ _____ _____ _____ _____.

3 더워지면 질수록 우리는 더 많은 물을 마실 필요가 있다. (hot, much)

= _____ _____ it gets, _____ _____ water we need to drink.

4 스마트폰은 점점 더 유용해지고 있다. (useful)

= Smartphones are becoming _____ _____ _____ _____.

5 시험이 어려우면 어려울수록 학생들은 더 혼란스럽게 느낀다. (hard, confused)

= _____ _____ the test is, _____ _____ _____ the students feel.

6 우리는 비행기를 타기 위해 가능한 한 일찍 일어났다. (early)

= We got up _____ _____ _____ _____ to catch the flight.

7 Jay는 뉴욕에서 가장 좋은 집들 중 하나에 산다. (fine, house)

= Jay lives in _____ _____ _____ _____ _____ in New York.

8 너는 네가 할 수 있는 한 자주 어항을 청소해야 한다. (often)

= You must clean the fishbowl _____ _____ _____ _____ _____.

중간·기말고사 실전 문제

[1-2] 다음 중 원급-비교급-최상급 형태가 <u>잘못된</u> 것을 고르시오.

1

① hot – hotter – hottest
② wide – wider – widest
③ bored – more bored – most bored
④ strange – more strange – most strange
⑤ creative – more creative – most creative

2

① little – less – least
② old – elder – eldest
③ late – latter – latest
④ bad – worse – worst
⑤ far – farther – farthest

3 다음 중 밑줄 친 부분이 어법상 <u>어색한</u> 것은?

Chocolate cream cake <u>is</u> <u>one</u> of
           ① ②

<u>most popular</u> <u>items</u> in this bakery.
   ③   ④ ⑤

4 다음 빈칸에 들어갈 말이 순서대로 짝지어진 것은?

· Gwangju is not _____ crowded as Seoul.
· A melon is bigger _____ a cherry.

① as – as
② so – as
③ as – so
④ so – than
⑤ than – than

[5-7] 다음 빈칸에 들어갈 알맞은 것을 고르시오.

5

These boxes are as _____ as rocks.

① heavy
② heavier
③ more heavy
④ heaviest
⑤ most heavy

6

Whales are able to dive _____ than dolphins.

① deep
② deeper
③ more deep
④ the deepest
⑤ the most deep

7

Who is _____ actor in your country?

① famouser
② more famous
③ the famousest
④ most famous
⑤ the most famous

8 다음 밑줄 친 ⓐ~ⓔ 중 어법상 <u>어색한</u> 것을 찾아 기호를 쓰고 바르게 고쳐 쓰시오.

I am not a bad dancer, but Luna dances
         ⓐ   ⓑ

<u>much</u> <u>well</u> than <u>me</u>.
  ⓒ   ⓓ   ⓔ

_____ → _____

9 다음은 여러 동물의 무게를 비교하는 표이다. 다음 표를 **잘못** 설명한 것은?

Cat	Dog	Panda	Lion
6kg	6kg	80kg	130kg

① A cat is lighter than a lion.
② A dog is heavier than a panda.
③ A cat is as light as a dog.
④ A lion is the heaviest of the four.
⑤ A panda is not as heavy as a lion.

[10-11] 우리말과 같도록 괄호 안의 말을 알맞게 배열하시오.

10

보라는 그녀가 할 수 있는 한 빠르게 그녀의 숙제를 끝냈다. (finished, she, her, as, Bora, quickly, as, homework, could)

= _____

_____

11

Judy의 머리카락은 나의 것보다 세 배 더 길다. (three, hair, times, than, Judy's, mine, is, longer)

= _____

_____

12 다음 중 어법상 어색한 것을 **모두** 고르시오.

① The chair is cheaper as the sofa.
② I can speak English as fluently as him.
③ This laptop is the best in the store.
④ Cameron is as young as Benjamin.
⑤ Your dress is beautiful than hers.

13 다음 빈칸에 들어갈 말이 순서대로 짝지어진 것은?

Minjun is a _____ good basketball player, but Jinsu is a _____ better player than Minjun.

① much – far
② much – still
③ very – very
④ very – far
⑤ even – very

14 괄호 안의 말을 활용하여 다음 두 문장을 한 문장으로 바꿔 쓰시오.

· The gloves are twenty dollars.
· The scarf is twenty dollars.

→ The gloves are _____ the scarf. (cheap)

15 다음 글의 밑줄 친 (A)를 비교급 문장으로 바꿔 쓰시오.

Bicycles are a fast and eco-friendly means of transportation in cities.
(A) Bicycles are not as fast as cars.
However, they can be faster than cars in traffic jams. Moreover, bicycles don't produce any gas, so they don't cause air pollution.

*means 수단, 방법

→ Cars _____.

18 다음 문장에서 어법상 <u>어색한</u> 부분을 찾아 쓰고 바르게 고쳐 쓰시오.

Math is the more difficult subject of all.

_____ → _____

19 다음 빈칸에 들어갈 말이 순서대로 짝지어진 것은?

As we talked louder, our teacher got angrier.
= _____ we talked, _____ our teacher got.

① Louder – angrier
② Louder – the angrier
③ The louder – angrier
④ The louder – more angry
⑤ The louder – the angrier

[16-17] 다음 두 문장의 의미가 같도록 빈칸에 알맞은 말을 쓰시오.

16

Eric is more diligent than any other student in our class.
= Eric is _____ _____ _____ _____ in our class.

17

Monkeys are smarter than dogs.
= Dogs are not _____ _____ _____ monkeys.

20 다음은 세 종류의 컴퓨터를 비교하는 표이다. 다음 표를 바르게 설명한 것을 <u>모두</u> 고르시오.

컴퓨터	A	B	C
출시 연도	2015	2018	2020
가격	$700	$2,300	$1,500
인기도	★★	★★★★	★★★★

① Computer A is the most expensive computer.
② Computer B is older than computer A.
③ Computer B is not as cheap as computer C.
④ Computer C is the oldest computer of all.
⑤ Computer C is as popular as computer B.

21 다음 중 어법상 어색한 것은?

① This is the best documentary I've ever watched.
② An octopus is one of the smartest animals in the ocean.
③ The many friends you have, the happy you are.
④ It is becoming darker and darker.
⑤ Please reply to the message as soon as possible.

22 주어진 문장의 밑줄 친 much와 의미가 같은 것은?

> I love pepperoni pizza <u>much</u> more than cheese pizza.

① There isn't <u>much</u> water in the bottle.
② Daniel is <u>much</u> stronger than I am.
③ I don't have <u>much</u> time to watch TV.
④ How <u>much</u> money did you spend on your hair?
⑤ Don't put too <u>much</u> salt in the soup.

23 우리말과 같도록 괄호 안의 말을 활용하여 문장을 완성하시오.

> 우리는 밖에 오래 머무르면 머무를수록 더 추워졌다. (long, cold)

= _____ we stayed outside, _____ we became.

24 다음 중 문장의 의미가 나머지 넷과 다른 것은?

① Jogging is the easiest way to become healthy.
② No other way is easier than jogging to become healthy.
③ Jogging is easier than all the other ways to become healthy.
④ Jogging is one of the easiest ways to become healthy.
⑤ No other way is so easy as jogging to become healthy.

25 다음 두 문장의 의미가 같도록 문장을 완성하시오.

> If a house is larger, cleaning it is harder.
> = _____ a house is, _____ cleaning it is.

26 다음은 세 명의 학생을 비교하는 표이다. 괄호 안의 말을 활용하여 문장을 완성하시오.

	Brad	Charlie	Diana
나이	15	16	18
키	170 cm	178 cm	165 cm

(1) Charlie is _____ _____ of the three. (tall)

(2) Brad is not _____ _____ _____ Diana. (short)

(3) Brad is _____ _____ all the other students. (young)

(4) No other student is _____ _____ _____ Diana. (old)

27 다음 빈칸에 들어갈 말이 순서대로 짝지어진 것은?

> · This is one of _____ hotels in the city.
> · He is _____ than any other comedian in Korea.

① finest – funny
② finest – funniest
③ the most fine – funnier
④ the finest – funnier
⑤ the finest – the funniest

28 다음 두 문장의 의미가 같도록 비교급을 이용하여 문장을 완성하시오.

> Ken's house is the most luxurious house in my neighborhood.
> = No other _____
>   Ken's house in my neighborhood.

29 다음 중 어법상 바른 것의 개수는?

> ⓐ This is the smallest shirt in the store.
> ⓑ Kim Gu is one of the most important people in Korean history.
> ⓒ The more you travel, the more things you can see.
> ⓓ Silk is a lot softer than cotton.
> ⓔ When it gets warmer, fruits turn more and more sweet.

① 1개   ② 2개   ③ 3개
④ 4개   ⑤ 5개

30 다음 두 문장의 의미가 같도록 빈칸에 알맞은 말을 쓰시오.

> Write down your name as clearly as possible.
> = Write down your name _____
>   _____ _____ _____
>   _____.

31 우리말과 같도록 괄호 안의 말을 활용하여 문장을 완성하시오.

> 그 곰은 우리에게 점점 더 가까이 왔다. (close)

= The bear came _____
  to us.

32 다음 우리말을 영작할 때 빈칸에 들어갈 알맞은 것은?

> 이것은 그 영화에서 가장 흥미로운 장면이다.
> = This is _____.

① interesting scene in the movie
② interestinger scene in the movie
③ more interesting scene in the movie
④ the interestingest scene in the movie
⑤ the most interesting scene in the movie

33 다음 중 어법상 바른 것은?

① My mom's pie is the most tasty of all.
② Samantha is the kindest in the four.
③ Today was the gloomier day in her life.
④ Please try to laugh as more as you can.
⑤ Hamburgers are the most popular food in America.

34 우리말과 같도록 괄호 안의 말을 알맞게 배열하시오.

인터넷은 20세기의 가장 위대한 발명품들 중 하나이다. (greatest, one, the Internet, of, inventions, is, the)

= _____

of the 20th century.

35 다음 빈칸에 들어갈 말이 순서대로 짝지어진 것은?

_____ we recycle, _____ we damage the environment.

① More – less
② The more – the less
③ The more – the least
④ The most – the least
⑤ The most – the less

36 다음 대화에서 어법상 어색한 부분을 찾아 쓰고 바르게 고쳐 쓰시오.

A: *Pride and Prejudice* is one of the most impressive novel in the 1800s.
B: Really? I should read it.

_____ ➔ _____

37 다음 빈칸에 들어갈 말로 어색한 것은?

Riding a bike without a helmet is _____ more dangerous than you think.

① very   ② a lot   ③ even
④ much   ⑤ far

38 다음 문장과 의미가 같은 것은?

These new shoes aren't as comfortable as those old shoes.

① These new shoes are more comfortable than those old shoes.
② Those old shoes aren't more comfortable than these new shoes.
③ Those old shoes are more comfortable than these new shoes.
④ Those old shoes aren't as comfortable as these new shoes.
⑤ These new shoes are more comfortable than all the other shoes.

39 다음 중 어법상 바른 것을 모두 고르시오.

① The children danced as best as they could.
② James tries to eat as slowly as me.
③ Elephants live as longer as humans.
④ The Eiffel Tower is the most famous tourist site in Paris.
⑤ Ronald is even strong than his older brother.

CHAPTER 14
전치사

The cats are on the sofa. 고양이들은 소파 위에 있다.

명사 the sofa 앞에 **on**이 와서 '소파 위에'라는 의미를 나타냈어요. 이렇게 명사나 대명사 앞에 와서 시간, 장소, 위치, 방향 등을 나타내는 것을 **전치사**라고 해요.

기출로 적중 POINT

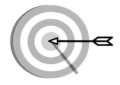

내신 100점 적중!
기출 출제율

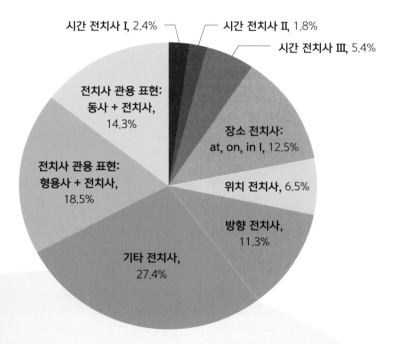

시간 전치사 I, 2.4%

시간 전치사 II, 1.8%

시간 전치사 III, 5.4%

전치사 관용 표현:
동사 + 전치사,
14.3%

장소 전치사:
at, on, in I, 12.5%

전치사 관용 표현:
형용사 + 전치사,
18.5%

위치 전치사, 6.5%

방향 전치사,
11.3%

기타 전치사,
27.4%

TOP 1 **기타 전치사 (27.4%)**
다양한 의미를 나타내는 전치사의 의미와 쓰임을 묻는 문제가 자주 출제된다.

TOP 2 **전치사 관용 표현: 형용사 + 전치사 (18.5%)**
형용사와 함께 쓰이는 전치사 관용 표현을 묻는 문제가 자주 출제된다.

TOP 3 **전치사 관용 표현: 동사 + 전치사 (14.3%)**
동사와 함께 쓰이는 전치사 관용 표현을 묻는 문제가 자주 출제된다.

시간 전치사 Ⅰ

정답 p.43

at, on, in은 '~에'라는 의미로 시간을 나타낸다.

at	시각	**at** 2 o'clock 2시에　　**at** 6:10 6시 10분에
	시점	**at** dawn 새벽에　　**at** noon 정오에　　**at** night 밤에 **at** the beginning of the year 연초에
on	요일	**on** Thursday 목요일에　　**on** Sunday 일요일에 (Tip) 「on + 요일s」: (요일)마다　　**on** Monday**s** 월요일마다
	날짜, 기념일	**on** November 25, 1971 1971년 11월 25일에 **on** Thanksgiving Day 추수감사절에　　**on** my birthday 나의 생일에
in	월, 계절	**in** July 7월에　　**in** summer 여름에
	연도, 세기	**in** 2002 2002년에　　**in** the 21st century 21세기에
	아침·오후·저녁	**in** the morning/afternoon/evening 아침/오후/저녁에 (Tip) 특정한 날의 아침·오후·저녁을 나타낼 때는 on을 쓴다. 　　**on** Friday morning 금요일 아침에 　　**on** Halloween evening 핼러윈 저녁에
	기타	**in** the past 과거에　　**in** the future 미래에 (Tip) 예외: **at** present 현재에

(Tip) every, last, next 등의 시간을 나타내는 부사구와 전치사 at, on, in은 함께 쓰지 않는다.
　　We threw a huge party **last night**. 우리는 어젯밤에 성대한 파티를 열었다.
　　We threw a huge party at last night. (X)

연습문제 괄호 안에서 at, on, in 중 알맞은 것을 고르시오.

1 John was born (at / on / in) 1998.

2 I'll start preparing dinner (at / on / in) 5 P.M.

3 Hyeri is going to France (at / on / in) April 2.

4 We like to go skiing (at / on / in) winter.

5 My dream is to be a lawyer (at / on / in) the future.

6 I got lots of chocolate (at / on /in) Valentine's Day.

7 Ben always takes a short walk (at / on / in) noon.

8 The festival will be held (at / on / in) Saturday afternoon.

9 My brother plays soccer with his friends (at / on /in) Sundays.

기출로작중 POINT 1-2 시간 전치사 II

다음 전치사는 시간을 나타낸다.

before	~ 전에	I do yoga **before** breakfast. 나는 아침 식사 전에 요가를 한다. Turn the light off **before** leaving the house. 집을 떠나기 전에 불을 꺼라.
after	~ 후에	**After** school, I play computer games. 방과 후에, 나는 컴퓨터 게임을 한다. Frank washed his hands **after** returning home. Frank는 집으로 돌아온 후에 그의 손을 씻었다. **(Tip)** '(기간) 후에'라는 의미를 나타내기 위해 「in + 기간을 나타내는 표현」을 쓸 수 있다. The science exhibition will end **in** a week. 그 과학 전시회는 1주일 후에 끝날 것이다.
from	~부터	The library is open **from** 9 A.M. 그 도서관은 오전 9시부터 문을 연다. **(Tip)** 「from ~ to …」는 '~부터 …까지'라는 의미로, 기간을 나타낸다. You can buy the tickets **from** March 29 **to** April 4. 너는 3월 29일부터 4월 4일까지 표를 살 수 있다.
since	~ 이후로	since는 주로 완료시제와 함께 쓰여 특정 시점부터 어떤 행동이나 상황이 계속되는 것을 나타낸다. I **have lived** in Seoul **since** 2009. 나는 2009년 이후로 서울에 계속 살아왔다.
by	~까지 (완료)	by는 정해진 시점까지 어떤 행동이나 상황이 완료되는 것을 나타낸다. Students must arrive at school **by** 8:30. 학생들은 8시 30분까지 학교에 도착해야 한다. I need to finish my homework **by** Monday. 나는 월요일까지 나의 숙제를 끝내야 한다.
until	~까지 (계속)	until은 특정 시점까지 어떤 행동이나 상황이 계속되는 것을 나타낸다. I will wait for the invitation **until** this Friday. 나는 이번 주 금요일까지 초대장을 기다릴 것이다. Let's stay awake **until** midnight. 자정까지 자지 않고 깨어 있자.

연습문제 A 다음 빈칸에 before나 after 중 알맞은 것을 쓰시오.

1 I'll have dinner and then walk my dog.

　① I'll walk my dog _____ having dinner.

　② _____ walking my dog, I'll have dinner.

2 I look both ways and then cross the street.

　① I look both ways _____ crossing the street.

　② I cross the street _____ looking both ways.

3 Sara took a deep breath and then started her speech.

① _____ starting her speech, Sara took a deep breath.

② _____ taking a deep breath, Sara started her speech.

4 Bake the pie for 50 minutes and then take it out of the oven.

① _____ baking the pie for 50 minutes, take it out of the oven.

② Bake the pie for 50 minutes _____ taking it out of the oven.

연습문제 **B** 괄호 안에서 알맞은 전치사를 고르시오.

1 I'll stay at my friend's house (by / until) tomorrow.

2 Mary has lived in this town (from / since) 2005.

3 Turn in your science report (by / until) next week.

4 (From / Since) October, the bookstore will be closed.

5 The art exhibition will continue (by / until) the first of May.

6 Abraham Lincoln was the president of the US (from / since) 1861 to 1865.

7 This apartment has been empty (from / since) last month.

8 Please come to the airport (by / until) 7 o'clock to pick me up.

9 Jimin watched the movie (by / until) midnight.

10 It has rained heavily (from / since) yesterday.

11 The amusement park gives discounts to students (from / since) Monday to Friday.

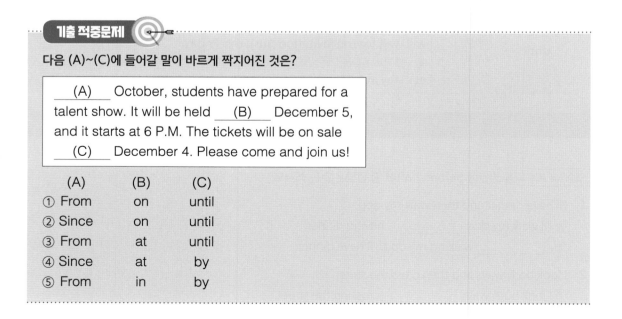

기출 적중문제

다음 (A)~(C)에 들어갈 말이 바르게 짝지어진 것은?

_____(A)_____ October, students have prepared for a talent show. It will be held _____(B)_____ December 5, and it starts at 6 P.M. The tickets will be on sale _____(C)_____ December 4. Please come and join us!

	(A)	(B)	(C)
①	From	on	until
②	Since	on	until
③	From	at	until
④	Since	at	by
⑤	From	in	by

기출로적중 POINT 1-3 시간 전치사 Ⅲ

정답 p.43

for와 during은 둘 다 '~ 동안'이라는 의미이지만, for 뒤에는 숫자를 포함한 기간 표현이 오고 during 뒤에는 특정 기간을 나타내는 명사가 온다.

for	+ 숫자를 포함한 기간 표현	Suji has studied English **for ten years.** 수지는 10년 동안 영어를 공부해왔다. We talked about our favorite actor **for two hours.** 우리는 두 시간 동안 우리가 가장 좋아하는 배우에 대해 이야기했다. (Tip) 예외: **for a while** 잠시 동안
during	+ 특정 기간을 나타내는 명사	We cleaned the house **during the day.** 우리는 낮 동안 집을 청소했다. Sam visited Italy **during the summer vacation.** Sam은 여름 방학 동안 이탈리아를 방문했다.

연습문제 A 다음 빈칸에 for나 during 중 알맞은 것을 쓰시오.

1 Boil the eggs _____ seven minutes.

2 You shouldn't use your phone _____ the class.

3 The man kept sneezing _____ the movie.

4 Many people lost their families _____ the war.

5 If you have a headache, lie down _____ a while.

6 I will do my homework _____ the evening.

7 I have practiced jazz dance _____ five months.

8 My parents have been married _____ over 20 years.

9 Jeremy stayed at the hotel _____ a week.

10 Bears sleep in their caves _____ the winter.

연습문제 B 우리말과 같도록 알맞은 전치사와 괄호 안의 말을 활용하여 문장을 완성하시오.

1 제 컴퓨터를 수요일까지 고쳐주시겠어요? (Wednesday)
= Could you fix my computer _____ ?

2 6월 12일부터 6월 15일까지 기말고사가 있을 것이다. (June 12, June 15)
= There will be a final exam _____ .

3 어젯밤 이후로 매우 추웠다. (last night)

= It has been very cold _____.

4 우리는 스테이크를 넣기 전에 오븐을 데워야 한다. (putting)

= We have to heat up the oven _____ the steak in it.

5 그 가게는 이번 주 금요일까지 문을 닫을 것이다. (this Friday)

= The store will be closed _____.

6 전자 기타는 20세기에 발명되었다. (the 20th century)

= The electronic guitar was invented _____.

7 너는 공연 동안 약간의 사진도 찍으면 안 된다. (the performance)

= You shouldn't take any pictures _____.

8 지진 후에 많은 건물들이 파괴되었다. (the earthquake)

= Many buildings were destroyed _____.

9 나는 연말에 남아메리카에 있을 것이다. (the end of the year)

= I'll be in South America _____.

10 나는 3일 동안 Ally와 이야기하지 않았다. (three days)

= I haven't talked to Ally _____.

11 소희와 그녀의 남동생들은 10시 전에 집으로 돌아갈 것이다. (10 o'clock)

= Sohee and her brothers will come back home _____.

12 불행하게도, 눈은 내일까지 계속 내릴 것이다. (tomorrow)

= Unfortunately, the snow will continue to fall _____.

13 그들은 잠시 동안 낮잠을 잘 수 있었다. (a while)

= They could take a nap _____.

14 그 영화를 본 후에 극장 안에 있는 모두가 울었다. (watching)

= Everyone in the theater cried _____ the movie.

기출 적중문제 ◎

다음 글의 빈칸에 들어갈 말이 순서대로 짝지어진 것은?

> Mr. Davis will make a speech about air pollution
> _____ an hour. Please keep quiet _____
> the speech.

① for – during   ② during – for

③ for – from   ④ during – since

⑤ from – during

POINT 2-1 장소 전치사: at, on, in I

at, on, in은 장소를 나타낸다.

at ~에, ~에서	비교적 좁은 장소나 하나의 지점	**at** the bus stop 버스 정류장에 **at** the corner 모퉁이에
on ~에, ~ 위에	표면에 접촉한 상태	**on** the table 탁자 위에 **on** the grass 잔디 위에 **on** the wall 벽에 **on** the roof 지붕 위에
in ~에, ~ 안에	비교적 넓은 장소나 공간의 내부	**in** London 런던에 **in** Korea 한국에 **in** the room 방 안에 **in** the building 건물 안에

연습문제 다음 그림을 보고 빈칸에 at, on, in 중 알맞은 것을 쓰시오.

[1-4]

[5-8]

1 A girl is standing _____ the window.

2 A grocery bag is _____ the floor.

3 Some apples are _____ the grocery bag.

4 There are many magnets _____ the refrigerator.

5 A big map is _____ the wall.

6 A woman is standing _____ the corner.

7 A pigeon is _____ the bench.

8 A man has two books _____ his backpack.

기출 적중문제

다음 그림을 보고 빈칸에 알맞은 전치사를 쓰시오.

A woman is waiting _____ the bus stop.
She is sitting _____ a bench, and there
are some flowers _____ her basket.

at, on, in은 다양한 상황을 나타내기도 한다.

at	일상적으로 다니는 장소	**at** home 집에서 **at** school 학교에서 **at** work 직장에서 **at** the airport 공항에서 **at** the library 도서관에서
	행사, 모임	**at** a concert 콘서트에서 **at** a meeting 회의에서 **at** a party 파티에서 **at** a contest 대회에서
	기타	**at** the top/bottom of ~의 상단/하단에 (Tip) 예외: **in** the middle of ~의 가운데에
on	길, 층	**on** the street 길 위에 **on** the third floor 3층에
	교통수단	**on** a bus 버스에 **on** a subway 지하철에 **on** a train 기차에 **on** a plane 비행기에 (Tip) 예외: **in** a car 차에 **in** a taxi 택시에
	통신수단	**on** the Internet 인터넷에서 **on** the phone 전화로
	기타	**on** the[one's] way home 집으로 가는 길에 **on** the[one's] way to the station 역으로 가는 길에 **on** the[one's] left/right 왼쪽에/오른쪽에
in	자연환경	**in** the sky 하늘에 **in** the ocean 바다에 **in** the world 세상에 **in** space 우주에
	인쇄물	**in** a book 책에 **in** a dictionary 사전에 **in** a newspaper 신문에 **in** a picture 그림/사진에
	(특정 장소에서) ~하는 중인	**in** bed 취침 중인 **in** prison 수감 중인 **in** the hospital 입원 중인
	기타	**in** red shoes 빨간 신발을 신은 **in** half 반으로 **in** danger 위험에 빠진 **in** a hurry 서두르는 **in** a line 한 줄로 **in** French 프랑스어로

연습문제 | 괄호 안에서 at, on, in 중 알맞은 것을 고르시오.

1 I'm (at / on / in) the bus, so I'll call you later.

2 My dad is (at / on / in) work right now.

3 Can you read that sign written (at / on / in) Chinese?

4 Jonathan is planning to stay (at / on / in) home today.

5 Not all dolphins live (at / on / in) the ocean.

6 Russia has the deepest lake (at / on / in) the world.

7 The tower is (at / on / in) the middle of the city.

8 Don't talk (at / on / in) the phone while you're driving.

9 Minji was (at / on / in) bed all morning.

10 Please buy some milk (at / on / in) the way home.

11 Let's cut the bread (at / on / in) half and share it.

12 I looked up the word (at / on / in) the dictionary.

13 There is no gravity (at / on / in) space.

14 Junho is (at / on / in) a train to Daegu.

15 The woman (at / on / in) a blue dress is my English teacher.

16 Could you check the weather report (at / on / in) the Internet?

17 Serena and her friend had a great time (at / on / in) the party.

18 The new shopping mall is (at / on / in) Main Street.

19 He told the students to stand (at / on / in) a line.

20 I read an interesting article (at / on / in) the newspaper.

21 Our classroom is (at / on / in) the second floor.

22 Lizards sometimes lose their tails when they're (at / on / in) danger.

23 Walk two blocks, and you'll see the bank (at / on / in) your right.

24 We can borrow books (at / on / in) the library.

25 I always listen to the radio (at / on / in) the way to school.

26 Did you lose your wallet when you were (at / on / in) the taxi?

27 The criminal has been (at / on / in) prison for ten years.

기출 적중문제

다음 빈칸에 공통으로 들어갈 알맞은 것은?

· Let's go swimming _____ the river.

· The baby _____ the picture looks so cute.

· Where is the bathroom _____ this building?

① from   ② on   ③ at

④ in   ⑤ along

위치 전치사

정답 p.44

다음 전치사는 위치를 나타낸다.

in front of	~ 앞에	The boy is standing **in front of** the bike. 그 소년은 자전거 앞에 서 있다.
behind	~ 뒤에	The bike is parked **behind** the boy. 그 자전거는 소년 뒤에 세워져 있다.
over	(덮여 있듯이 바로) ~ 위에	There is an old bridge **over** the river. 강 위에 오래된 다리가 있다.
under	(덮여 있듯이 바로) ~ 아래에	My puppy is hiding **under** the sofa. 나의 강아지는 소파 아래에 숨어 있다.
above	~(보다) 위에	The plane is **above** the clouds. 비행기는 구름보다 위에 있다.
below	~(보다) 아래에	The clouds are **below** the plane. 구름은 비행기보다 아래에 있다.
next to, by, beside	~ 옆에	Mina is sitting **next to[by/beside]** Yunho. 미나는 윤호 옆에 앉아 있다.
near	~ 가까이에	Samantha is sitting **near** Jason. Samantha는 Jason 가까이에 앉아 있다.
between	(둘) 사이에	The mouse is **between** two cats. 그 쥐는 두 마리의 고양이 사이에 있다.
among	(셋 이상) 사이에	The cat is **among** the mice. 그 고양이는 쥐들 사이에 있다.

연습문제 다음 그림을 보고 괄호 안에서 가장 알맞은 전치사를 고르시오.

1

2

3

1 A kid is lying (over / under) the tree.

2 The sun is shining (over / under) the rainbow.

3 The picture of my family is (in front of / next to) the lamp.

4 Ducks are swimming (over / near) the swans.

5 There is a stove (behind / beside) the refrigerator.

6 Two pairs of shoes are (above / below) the mirror.

7 The hat was hanging (above / among) my other clothes.

8 Ms. Hall parked her car (in front of / behind) the house.

9 The bank is (between / among) the school and the police station.

10 The man is fishing (below / by) the river.

11 The teacher drew a circle (above / below) a triangle on the board.

12 Charlie is standing (in front of / behind) Amy.

기출 적중문제

다음 빈칸에 들어갈 알맞은 것은?

> My dog always tries to sleep _____ my mom and me.

① to   ② among   ③ from
④ above   ⑤ between

방향 전치사

정답 p.44

다음 전치사는 방향을 나타낸다.

up	~ 위로	Jiho is going **up** the hill. 지호는 언덕 위로 올라가고 있다.
down	~ 아래로	Jiho is going **down** the hill. 지호는 언덕 아래로 내려가고 있다.
into	~ 안으로	Diane went **into** the room. Diane은 방 안으로 들어갔다.
out of	~ 밖으로	Diane came **out of** the room. Diane은 방 밖으로 나왔다.
across	~을 가로질러	They are running **across** the field. 그들은 들판을 가로질러 뛰고 있다.
along	~을 따라서	We walked **along** the lake. 우리는 호수를 따라서 걸었다.
around	~ 주위에	Four children are dancing **around** the campfire. 네 명의 아이는 모닥불 주위에서 춤을 추고 있다.
through	~을 통해서	The cars went **through** the tunnel. 차들은 터널을 통해서 갔다.
over	~을 넘어서	The cat jumped **over** the table. 그 고양이는 식탁을 뛰어 넘었다.
from	~으로부터	The students are going home **from** school. 학생들은 학교로부터 집에 가고 있다.
to	~으로, ~에	to는 주로 동사 go, come, get, return과 함께 쓰여 도착 지점을 나타낸다. Kenny **went to** New York. Kenny는 뉴욕으로 갔다.
for	~으로, ~을 향해	for는 주로 동사 leave, start, depart, head와 함께 쓰여 가고자 하는 방향을 나타낸다. Kenny **left for** New York. Kenny는 뉴욕으로 떠났다.

연습문제 다음 그림을 보고 괄호 안에서 가장 알맞은 전치사를 고르시오.

1

2

3

1 Larry is walking (up / down) the stairs.

2 The golf ball fell (into / out of) the hole.

3 The thief is climbing (around / over) the wall.

4 Cassie is walking (across / along) the street.

5 The train departs (from / for) Busan at 8 o'clock.

6 The magician took the dove (into / out of) his hat.

7 Peter is going (from / to) the science museum.

8 Ms. Jones wrapped the scarf (around / over) her neck.

9 I can hear the birds singing (along / through) the window.

10 The monkey ran (up / down) the tree.

11 Beth is coming back (from / to) the library.

12 Many flowers are planted (across / along) the river.

기출 적중문제

우리말과 같도록 빈칸에 알맞은 전치사를 쓰시오.

> 나의 형은 새벽에 체육관으로 떠났다.

= My brother left _____ the gym at dawn.

POINT 5 기타 전치사

정답 p.44

다음 전치사는 다양한 의미를 나타낸다.

with	~과 함께	How about watching the movie **with** me? 나와 함께 그 영화를 보는 게 어때?
	~을 가진	That man **with** a long beard is my uncle. 긴 수염을 가진 저 남자는 나의 삼촌이다.
	~을 이용해서 (도구)	You can even cut glass **with** this knife. 너는 이 칼을 이용해서 유리도 자를 수 있다.
without	~ 없이	I went to the store **without** any cash. 나는 약간의 현금도 없이 가게에 갔다.
by	~을 타고 (교통수단)	We're going to travel the world **by** train. 우리는 기차를 타고 세계를 여행할 예정이다. (Tip) 예외: **on** foot 걸어서
	~으로 (수단)	Can I pay **by** credit card? 제가 신용카드로 지불해도 되나요?
	~에 의해	This painting was painted **by** Picasso. 이 그림은 피카소에 의해 그려졌다.
about	~에 대해	Dave is reading a book **about** American history. Dave는 미국 역사에 대한 책을 읽고 있다.
like	~처럼	Sam swam **like** a mermaid. Sam은 인어처럼 수영했다.
	~ 같은	We should eat vegetables **like** carrots and spinach. 우리는 당근과 시금치 같은 채소를 먹어야 한다. (Tip) '~ 같은'을 의미하는 like는 such as로 바꿔 쓸 수 있다. I love bright colors **like**(= such as) red and yellow. 나는 빨간색과 노란색 같은 밝은 색을 좋아한다.
as	~으로서	Let's use that bottle **as** a vase. 저 병을 꽃병으로서 사용하자.
for	~을 위해	I donated money **for** homeless people. 나는 집이 없는 사람들을 위해 돈을 기부했다.
	~에 찬성하여	The teacher was **for** the students' idea. 그 선생님은 학생들의 의견에 찬성했다.
against	~에 반대하여/맞서	Our team will play basketball **against** your team. 우리 팀은 너의 팀에 맞서 농구를 할 것이다.

연습문제 A 우리말과 같도록 빈칸에 알맞은 전치사를 <보기>에서 골라 쓰시오.

<보기> without   about   as   by   with

1 나는 나의 반 친구에게 우리의 숙제에 대해 물었다.

= I asked my classmate _____ our homework.

2 풀을 이용해서 두 개의 조각을 하나로 붙여라.

= Stick the two pieces together _____ glue.

3 너는 컴퓨터 없이 살 수 있니?

= Are you able to live _____ computers?

4 Mark는 9년 동안 바리스타로서 일해왔다.

= Mark has worked _____ a barista for nine years.

5 사람들은 그들의 애완동물들과 함께 이 공원에 들어갈 수 있다.

= People can enter this park _____ their pets.

6 저에게 그 정보를 이메일로 보내주세요.

= Please send me the information _____ e-mail.

연습문제 B 괄호 안에서 알맞은 것을 고르시오.

1 There is a package (with / for) you at the door.

2 What are you planning to do (with / like) Sumin tonight?

3 People voted (as / against) the plan to move city hall.

4 Susan is wearing a hat (with / about) a yellow ribbon.

5 I usually go to school (by / for) bus in the morning.

6 Isabella sings (by / like) an angel.

7 These cupcakes were baked (by / as) my mother.

8 It takes ten minutes to get to the supermarket (by / on) foot.

기출 적중문제 🎯

다음 빈칸에 공통으로 들어갈 알맞은 것은?

· Brenda had lunch _____ her friends yesterday.

· You can start a fire _____ a glass lens.

· The man _____ a huge suitcase looks tired.

① against   ② like   ③ for

④ by   ⑤ with

다음은 형용사와 함께 쓰이는 전치사 관용 표현이다.

be good at ~을 잘하다	be bad at ~을 못하다
be afraid of ~을 무서워하다	be proud of ~을 자랑스러워하다
be full of ~으로 가득 차 있다	be late for ~에 늦다
be good for ~에 좋다	be bad for ~에 나쁘다
be famous for ~으로 유명하다	be ready for ~에 준비가 되다
be sorry for[about] ~에 대해 미안해하다	be curious about ~에 대해 호기심이 있다
be similar to ~과 비슷하다	be different from ~과 다르다

Are you **afraid of** spiders? 너는 거미를 무서워하니?
Charles **was late for** the math class. Charles는 수학 수업에 늦었다.

연습문제 │ 다음 빈칸에 알맞은 전치사를 쓰시오.

1 Italy is famous _____ its tourist sites.

2 Cameron is good _____ snowboarding.

3 I'm sorry _____ the loud noise.

4 Junsu wasn't ready _____ the final exam.

5 Eating instant foods is bad _____ our health.

6 Mr. White is proud _____ his three daughters.

7 Linda's eyes are similar _____ her mom's.

8 Santa's bag is full _____ presents for children.

9 I'm curious _____ the ending of the movie.

기출 적중문제

다음 빈칸에 들어갈 알맞은 것은?

> Is American English different _____ British English?

① to   ② for   ③ of
④ at   ⑤ from

기출로적중 POINT 6-2 전치사 관용 표현: 동사 + 전치사

다음은 동사와 함께 쓰이는 전치사 관용 표현이다.

look at ~을 보다
wait for ~을 기다리다
laugh at ~을 보고/듣고 웃다, 비웃다
belong to ~에 속하다
run[bump] into ~을(과) 우연히 만나다

look for ~을 찾다
thank … for ~에 대해 …에게 감사해하다
listen to ~을 듣다
spend 시간/돈 on ~에 시간/돈을 쓰다
take care of ~을 돌보다, ~을 신경 쓰다

Jim **laughed at** my silly joke. Jim은 나의 유치한 농담을 듣고 웃었다.
Can you **take care of** my hamster? 나의 햄스터를 돌봐주겠니?

연습문제 다음 빈칸에 알맞은 전치사를 쓰시오.

1 I ran _____ my old friend on the street.

2 The students are listening _____ their teacher.

3 Does this jacket belong _____ Laura?

4 I'm waiting _____ you in front of your house.

5 They laughed _____ my new haircut.

6 Yumi spent four days _____ this painting.

7 Would you help me look _____ my phone?

8 Whom should I thank _____ this gift?

9 We took care _____ the injured bird.

10 The detective closely looked _____ the evidence.

기출 적중문제

다음 빈칸에 공통으로 들어갈 알맞은 것은?

· What are you laughing _____ ?
· The visitors looked _____ the artwork in
  silence.

① of   ② to   ③ at
④ for   ⑤ into

서술형 대비 문제

A 다음 빈칸에 알맞은 말을 <보기>에서 한 번씩만 골라 쓰시오.

<보기>　in　on　at　for　since　by

1 It has been rainy _____ three days.

2 The Pyeongchang Olympics was held _____ 2018.

3 Your report must be done _____ tomorrow.

4 The football team has a big match _____ Saturday afternoon.

5 Anton has studied Korean _____ last month.

6 We always throw a party _____ the end of a year.

<보기>　by　with　during　about　as　against

7 My father uses his phone _____ a watch.

8 Where are you planning to visit _____ the holidays?

9 Jamie complains _____ a lot of things.

10 It took four hours to go to Busan _____ bus.

11 Paul decided to go to the concert _____ Benny.

12 Fighting with friends is _____ our class rules.

B 다음 문장의 밑줄 친 부분을 바르게 고쳐 쓰시오.

1 Young children are curious <u>for</u> everything.　→ _____

2 Jake was sorry <u>with</u> breaking the window.　→ _____

3 The red jacket on the chair belongs <u>from</u> Hailey.　→ _____

4 Tim is looking <u>with</u> something tasty to eat.　→ _____

5 Maria bumped <u>out of</u> a friend at the shopping mall.　→ _____

6 The park was full <u>by</u> people enjoying the weather.　→ _____

7 Yena took care <u>with</u> her younger brothers last weekend.　→ _____

ⓒ 다음은 Fairview 마을의 도난 사건에 대한 목격자들의 진술이다. 빈칸에 알맞은 전치사를 <보기>에서 한 번씩만 골라 쓰시오.

<보기> on   for   out of   next to

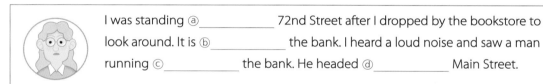

I was standing ⓐ_____ 72nd Street after I dropped by the bookstore to look around. It is ⓑ_____ the bank. I heard a loud noise and saw a man running ⓒ_____ the bank. He headed ⓓ_____ Main Street.

<보기> in   across   between   at

I was waiting for a bus ⓔ_____ the bus stop. Just before the bus arrived, a man ⓕ_____ a hurry walked ⓖ_____ Main Street. He ran onto Second Street ⓗ_____ the post office and the pharmacy.

<보기> up   above   into   in front of   with

I was talking on the phone ⓘ_____ the supermarket. A man ⓙ_____ a large bag suddenly appeared, and he walked ⓚ_____ the stairs and went ⓛ_____ the apartment on the 2nd floor ⓜ_____ the supermarket.

1 다음 빈칸에 들어갈 알맞은 것은?

> We celebrate Teacher's Day _____ May 15.

① in   ② to   ③ for
④ at   ⑤ on

2 다음 우리말을 영작할 때 빈칸에 들어갈 알맞은 전치사는?

> 박쥐들은 보통 낮 동안 잔다.
> = Bats usually sleep _____ the day.

① at   ② during   ③ from
④ since   ⑤ on

3 우리말과 같도록 빈칸에 알맞은 말을 쓰시오.

> 머핀을 위한 요리법을 인터넷에서 찾아주겠니?

= Will you search for a recipe for muffins
_____ _____ _____ ?

4 우리말과 같도록 빈칸에 알맞은 전치사를 쓰시오.

> 나의 목표는 한강을 가로질러 수영하는 것이다.

= My goal is to swim _____ the Hangang.

[5-6] 다음 빈칸에 공통으로 들어갈 알맞은 것을 고르시오.

5

> · You should return the library books _____ next Monday.
> · People can visit Dokdo _____ ship.

① in   ② at   ③ by
④ until   ⑤ from

6

> · Cam found his keys _____ the desk.
> · We need to buy some groceries _____ the way home.

① in   ② on   ③ over
④ next to   ⑤ at

7 다음 빈칸에 들어갈 말이 순서대로 짝지어진 것은?

> · Korea gained independence _____ 1945.
> · The bridge _____ the two islands was built last month.

① in – between   ② on – between
③ at – between   ④ in – among
⑤ on – among

8 다음 빈칸에 들어갈 알맞은 것은?

> Julie takes cooking classes _____ noon to 2:30.

① at   ② for   ③ from
④ on   ⑤ in

9 다음 중 밑줄 친 부분이 어법상 어색한 것은?

① Oliver cried alone <u>in</u> his room.
② I spilled some water <u>at</u> the floor.
③ Turn left <u>at</u> the next corner.
④ This building has a pool <u>on</u> its roof.
⑤ My brother has lived <u>in</u> China for a year.

10 다음 빈칸에 들어갈 말이 순서대로 짝지어진 것은?

> · Alex is looking _____ a part-time job.
> · I always eat hot dogs _____ ketchup.

① for – for   ② for – with
③ by – for   ④ by – with
⑤ with – by

11 다음 빈칸에 들어갈 전치사가 같은 것끼리 묶인 것은?

> · Walnuts are good ⓐ_____ our brain.
> · Don't be late ⓑ_____ school again.
> · Alice is old enough to take care ⓒ_____ herself.
> · Josh bumped ⓓ_____ his homeroom teacher at the park.
> · I'm curious ⓔ_____ the people living next door.

① ⓐ, ⓑ   ② ⓐ, ⓓ   ③ ⓑ, ⓒ
④ ⓒ, ⓔ   ⑤ ⓓ, ⓔ

12 다음 중 밑줄 친 부분이 어법상 어색한 것은?

① There are many beautiful houses <u>along</u> the beach.
② She learned English <u>by</u> listening to pop songs.
③ The boat sailed quietly <u>across</u> the lake.
④ You can bake a cake <u>without</u> butter.
⑤ Tom walked <u>above</u> the stairs for exercise.

13 다음 빈칸에 들어갈 전치사가 나머지 넷과 <u>다른</u> 것은?

① David is standing _____ line to buy a new phone.
② This user's manual is written _____ German.
③ Are we able to grow food _____ space?
④ He is going to wear a gray suit _____ his wedding.
⑤ My wish is to visit the Tomato Festival _____ Spain.

14 다음 그림을 <u>잘못</u> 표현한 것은?

① Doves are eating bread on the ground.
② A girl is standing between the two swings.
③ There is a stone path passing through the park.
④ Doves are in front of the ice cream truck.
⑤ There aren't any benches to sit on.

15 다음 대화의 빈칸에 들어갈 말이 순서대로 짝지어진 것은?

> A: Have you seen my favorite teddy bear?
> B: I thought I saw it _____ the other dolls in your toy box. You have so many toys in there.
> A: Hmm... It's not in the box.
> B: Did you check _____ your bed? Maybe it fell while you were sleeping.
> A: I found it!

① between – under ② among – under
③ between – above ④ among – above
⑤ among – between

16 다음 우리말을 영작할 때 빈칸에 들어갈 알맞은 전치사는?

> Nate는 핼러윈에 마법사처럼 변장했다.
> = Nate dressed up _____ a wizard on Halloween.

① about ② by ③ for
④ like ⑤ without

17 주어진 문장의 밑줄 친 <u>for</u>와 의미가 같은 것은?

> What can I do <u>for</u> you?

① Are you <u>for</u> the new traffic law?
② Please hold my bag <u>for</u> a while.
③ I'm leaving <u>for</u> Paris to study fashion.
④ I exercise <u>for</u> 30 minutes every day.
⑤ Please leave this message <u>for</u> Lucy.

18 다음 빈칸에 들어갈 말로 어색한 것은?

> I am meeting James at _____.

① 8:25
② noon
③ the morning
④ home
⑤ the station

19 다음 빈칸에 들어갈 말이 순서대로 짝지어진 것은?

> · Could you tell me how to get _____ Seoul Station?
> · He left _____ London to join the soccer team.

① to – to
② from – for
③ to – for
④ for – for
⑤ for – to

20 다음 그림을 보고 빈칸에 알맞은 전치사를 <보기>에서 골라 쓰시오.

> <보기> beside   into   in

(1) Some letters are _____ the mailbox.

(2) A bicycle is parked _____ the mailbox.

(3) A child is going _____ the garden.

21 우리말과 같도록 빈칸에 알맞은 전치사를 쓰시오.

> 사람은 태양과 물 없이 살 수 없다.

= People cannot live _____ sun and water.

22 다음 빈칸에 들어갈 전치사가 나머지 넷과 다른 것은?

① I will send you the e-mail _____ Friday morning.
② Do you like traveling _____ train?
③ Don't leave children alone _____ a car.
④ The forest was burnt _____ the terrible fire.
⑤ Will you pay _____ cash or credit card?

23 다음 빈칸에 공통으로 들어갈 알맞은 것은?

> · Nina saw a man _____ blue hair.
> · Stir the soup _____ a spoon before you eat it.

① about
② for
③ like
④ with
⑤ from

24 다음 (A)~(C)에 들어갈 말이 바르게 짝지어진 것은?

· George will stay in Seoul ___(A)___ Tuesday.
· We are very proud ___(B)___ our country.
· Jenny doesn't want to play ___(C)___ anyone now.

	(A)	(B)	(C)
①	until	of	with
②	until	with	about
③	until	of	about
④	by	of	with
⑤	by	with	with

25 다음 대화의 ⓐ~ⓔ에 알맞은 말을 <보기>에서 한 번씩만 골라 쓰시오.

<보기> for by without as against

A: I'm going to visit my aunt in Jejudo ⓐ_____ my parents for the first time.
B: Really? Weren't they ⓑ_____ it?
A: No. They even bought the ticket for me.
B: Are you going there ⓒ_____ plane?
A: I'm actually taking the ferry. I can get a discount ⓓ_____ a student.
B: I didn't know they offered discounts ⓔ_____ students.
A: I didn't know, either. My aunt told me.

*ferry 여객선, 페리

26 다음 밑줄 친 ⓐ~ⓔ 중 어법상 어색한 것을 찾아 기호를 쓰고 바르게 고쳐 쓰시오.

· Danny is good ⓐin singing and dancing.
· Robert thinks that the girl ⓑin the pink dress is pretty.
· The bakery is famous ⓒof its pies.
· That computer is very different ⓓby the other ones.
· There is a scarecrow ⓔin the middle of the corn field.

(1) _____ → _____
(2) _____ → _____
(3) _____ → _____

27 우리말과 같도록 빈칸에 알맞은 전치사를 쓰시오.

나는 나의 앵무새가 어떻게 새장 밖으로 나왔는지 모른다.

= I don't know how my parrot got _____ the cage.

28 다음 중 밑줄 친 like의 쓰임이 나머지 넷과 다른 것은?

① This place feels like home.
② The candy tastes like cherries.
③ Lisa bought a coat like mine.
④ My friends and I like playing outside.
⑤ Her younger sister doesn't look like her.

29 다음 ⓐ~ⓔ에 들어갈 전치사가 같은 것끼리 묶인 것은?

<How to Make Blueberry Muffins>

1. Mix flour, sugar, and baking powder ⓐ_____ a large bowl.
2. Add egg, milk, and blueberries. Stir until everything is mixed well.
3. Put the mix ⓑ_____ the muffin tray. Place a couple of blueberries ⓒ_____ top of each muffin.
4. Bake the muffins ⓓ_____ 20 minutes at 200°C.
5. Remove the muffins ⓔ_____ the oven, and let them cool for ten minutes.

---

① ⓐ, ⓑ　　② ⓐ, ⓒ　　③ ⓑ, ⓒ
④ ⓑ, ⓓ　　⑤ ⓓ, ⓔ

30 다음 그림을 보고 두 문장의 의미가 같도록 빈칸에 알맞은 전치사를 쓰시오.

Hannah was sitting _____ Adam at the concert.

= Adam was sitting _____ Hannah at the concert.

---

31 다음 (A)~(C)에 들어갈 말이 바르게 짝지어진 것은?

· I lost my phone ___(A)___ my way to the supermarket.
· The burning building was full ___(B)___ smoke.
· Don't play the instruments ___(C)___ night.

	(A)	(B)	(C)
①	on	of	at
②	at	for	in
③	on	for	at
④	at	of	in
⑤	on	of	on

32 다음 중 밑줄 친 부분이 어법상 어색한 것은?

① I haven't seen my cousins <u>since</u> last year.
② The store is closed from 1 P.M. <u>to</u> 2 P.M.
③ You should go <u>from</u> the dentist soon.
④ Try not to eat junk food <u>like</u> pizza and hamburgers.
⑤ Derek told me a story <u>about</u> his family.

33 다음 빈칸에 들어갈 알맞은 것은?

Kids are laughing _____ the funny clown at the birthday party.

---

① in　　　② on　　　③ at
④ for　　　⑤ without

34 다음 글의 밑줄 친 ⓐ~ⓔ 중 어법상 어색한 것을 찾아 기호를 쓰고 바르게 고쳐 쓰시오.

Last weekend, my family went to Cedar Point ⓐin a car. This amusement park is similar ⓑfrom Disneyworld. However, it is known ⓒfor scary roller coasters. My little sister was afraid ⓓwith them at first, but she decided to try. ⓔAs her brother, I held her hand when she felt scared.

(1) _____ → _____
(2) _____ → _____

35 다음 글의 빈칸에 들어갈 말이 순서대로 짝지어진 것은?

The city of Pompeii was buried _____ volcanic ash for a long time. Italy spent a lot of money _____ excavating the city. Thanks to Italy, it became a popular tourist destination attracting many people.

*volcanic ash 화산재
*excavate 발굴하다

① over – on
② over – with
③ under – on
④ under – with
⑤ over – in

36 다음 빈칸에 들어갈 알맞은 것은?

Too much sunlight comes _____ my room in the morning.

① out of
② down
③ into
④ under
⑤ next to

37 다음 대화의 빈칸에 들어갈 말이 순서대로 짝지어진 것은?

A: Justin, what are you planning to do _____ Mom's birthday?
B: Oh, no. I didn't know her birthday was coming up.
A: That's all right. I already made a reservation at a nice restaurant in town _____ her. Why don't you think of a present to give her?
B: Ok. I will.

① on – to
② in – to
③ on – for
④ in – for
⑤ at – for

38 다음 중 어느 빈칸에도 들어갈 수 없는 것은?

· I ran _____ Joey at the grocery store.
· Surin will take care _____ my cat while I'm gone.
· Lucas is ready _____ his audition.
· Busan and Pohang are famous _____ seafood.
· Mike is bad _____ speaking in public.

① for
② as
③ into
④ at
⑤ of

39 다음 글의 빈칸에 들어갈 말이 순서대로 짝지어진 것은?

The English Channel separates England from France. It made traveling _____ the two countries difficult in the past. Now, there is an underwater tunnel _____ the English Channel. People can easily get from one country to the other.

*English Channel 영국 해협

① between – beside ② between – below
③ among – above ④ among – below
⑤ among – beside

40 다음 빈칸에 공통으로 들어갈 알맞은 것은?

· Tigers belong _____ the cat family.
· Susie was listening _____ music when the doorbell rang.

① for ② to ③ with
④ of ⑤ at

41 다음 중 어법상 어색한 것은?

① Thank you to the letter and the flowers.
② You should go to bed before midnight.
③ Look at these posters on the wall.
④ The plane is going to land in five minutes.
⑤ I couldn't find my friend among the crowd.

42 다음 글의 빈칸에 들어갈 말이 순서대로 짝지어진 것은?

Many Canadians enjoy visiting Mexico _____ the winter because of its warm weather. Instead of having snow, they can lie on the beach. They can also visit the US _____ Canada and Mexico on their way home.

① for – among ② for – between
③ during – among ④ during – between
⑤ for – among

43 우리말과 같도록 괄호 안의 말을 알맞게 배열하시오.

그 개는 그것의 주인이 돌아오기를 기다리고 있다.
(for, is, its, dog, waiting, the, owner)

= _____ to come back.

44 다음 중 밑줄 친 부분이 어법상 어색한 것은?

A: Will your soccer practice end ①until dinner?
B: No, it will probably finish ②at nine. Why?
A: I bought a pizza ③at the mall, and I want to share it with you.
B: Oh, that sounds delicious. Will you put some ④in the refrigerator for me?
A: Hmm... It's full ⑤of food, so I'll just leave it on the table.

CHAPTER 15
접속사

My dog is old **but** healthy.　나의 개는 나이가 많지만 건강하다.
단어　접속사　단어

위 문장에서 두 단어 **old**와 **healthy**가 **but**이라는 말로 연결되어 있어요. 이렇게 단어와 단어, 구와 구, 절과 절을 연결하는 것을 **접속사**라고 해요.

기출로 적중 POINT

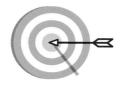

내신 100점 적중!
기출 출제율

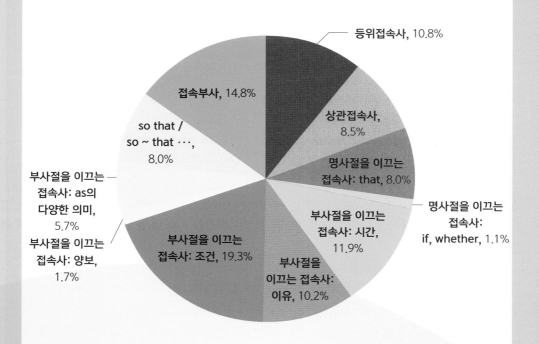

등위접속사, 10.8%

접속부사, 14.8%

상관접속사, 8.5%

so that /
so ~ that ···,
8.0%

명사절을 이끄는
접속사: that, 8.0%

부사절을 이끄는
접속사: as의
다양한 의미,
5.7%

부사절을 이끄는
접속사: 시간,
11.9%

명사절을 이끄는
접속사:
if, whether, 1.1%

부사절을 이끄는
접속사: 양보,
1.7%

부사절을 이끄는
접속사: 조건, 19.3%

부사절을
이끄는 접속사:
이유, 10.2%

TOP 1 **부사절을 이끄는 접속사: 조건 (19.3%)**
조건을 나타내는 접속사의 의미와 쓰임을 묻는 문제가 자주 출제된다.

TOP 2 **접속부사 (14.8%)**
접속부사를 지문의 문맥에 맞게 쓰는 문제가 자주 출제된다.

TOP 3 **부사절을 이끄는 접속사: 시간 (11.9%)**
시간을 나타내는 접속사의 의미와 쓰임을 묻는 문제가 자주 출제된다.

1. 등위접속사는 문법적으로 대등한 단어와 단어, 구와 구, 절과 절을 연결한다.

and	~과, 그리고, ~하고 나서	I enjoy **swimming and surfing**. 나는 수영하는 것과 서핑하는 것을 즐긴다. I need to buy **sweaters, boots, and a hat**. 나는 스웨터, 부츠, 그리고 모자를 살 필요가 있다. **Miranda arrived home, and (she) took a nap.** Miranda는 집에 도착하고 나서 낮잠을 잤다. → 등위접속사 앞뒤 절의 주어가 같을 때, 뒤 절의 주어는 생략할 수 있다.
but	하지만, 그러나	The laptop is **light but too expensive**. 그 노트북은 가볍지만 너무 비싸다. **The sky is cloudy, but it isn't raining.** 하늘이 흐리지만, 비는 오고 있지 않다.
or	또는, ~이거나	He exercises **three or four** times a week. 그는 일주일에 세 번 또는 네 번 운동한다. Should I **ride the subway or take a taxi** to get there? 나는 그곳에 가기 위해 지하철을 타거나 택시를 타야 하니?
so	그래서, 따라서	**The sun was too bright, so I put on my sunglasses.** 해가 너무 밝아서, 나는 나의 선글라스를 썼다.

2. 「명령문 + and ~」는 '…해라, 그러면 ~'이라는 의미이고, 「명령문 + or ~」는 '…해라, 그렇지 않으면 ~'이라는 의미이다. 이때 명령문은 조건을 나타내는 접속사 if를 이용하여 바꿔 쓸 수 있다.

Drink this tea, and you'll get warm. 이 차를 마셔라, 그러면 너는 따뜻해질 것이다.

(= **If you drink this tea, you'll get warm.**) 만약 네가 이 차를 마신다면, 너는 따뜻해질 것이다.

Get up now, or you'll be late. 지금 일어나라, 그렇지 않으면 너는 늦을 것이다.

(= **If you don't get up now, you'll be late.**) 만약 네가 지금 일어나지 않는다면, 너는 늦을 것이다.

연습문제 A 괄호 안에서 가장 알맞은 것을 고르시오.

1 John (and / but) Kelly live on the same street.

2 Would you like hot coffee (or / so) iced coffee?

3 Mason studied hard (but / or) his friend didn't.

4 My neighbors were very noisy, (but / so) I couldn't sleep.

5 Yura called her friend, (and / but) they talked for an hour.

6 Justin ate a lot, (but / or) he is still hungry.

7 Let's eat at a restaurant or (order / ordered) some food.

8 The birds are sitting (and / so) singing outside my window.

9 That movie is popular, (but / or) I haven't watched it yet.

10 Ants are small but very (strong / strongly).

11 Are you planning to leave today (and / or) tomorrow?

12 He finished cleaning the floor and (do / doing) the dishes.

연습문제 **B** 다음 두 문장의 의미가 같도록 문장을 완성하시오.

1 If you get some rest, you'll feel better.

= Get some rest, _____ .

2 If you study hard, you can get a good grade.

= Study hard, _____ .

3 If you don't hurry up, you'll miss the train.

= Hurry up, _____ .

4 If you exercise regularly, you'll get healthier.

= Exercise regularly, _____ .

5 If you aren't quiet, the baby will wake up.

= Be quiet, _____ .

6 If you don't wear a coat, you'll catch a cold.

= Wear a coat, _____ .

7 If you don't watch out, you'll fall down the stairs.

= Watch out, _____ .

8 If you apologize to Fred, he'll forgive you.

= Apologize to Fred, _____ .

9 If you don't leave now, you'll be late for school.

= Leave now, _____ .

우리말과 같도록 괄호 안의 말을 활용하여 문장을 완성하시오.

나는 선물로 시계를 받았지만, 나의 여동생이 그것을 고장 냈다.
(broke)

= I got a watch as a present, _____ .

상관접속사는 두 개 이상의 단어가 짝을 이뤄 문법적으로 대등한 단어와 단어, 구와 구, 절과 절을 연결하는 말이다.

both A and B	A와 B 둘 다	Amy likes **both** reading books **and** writing stories. Amy는 책을 읽는 것과 이야기를 쓰는 것을 둘 다 좋아한다.
not only A but (also) B = B as well as A	A뿐만 아니라 B도	Mark is **not only** clever **but (also)** diligent. = Mark is **diligent as well as** clever. Mark는 똑똑할 뿐만 아니라 성실하기도 하다.
either A or B	A나 B 둘 중 하나	I would like to have **either** lemonade **or** peach tea. 나는 레모네이드나 복숭아 차 둘 중 하나를 마시기를 원한다.
neither A nor B	A도 B도 아닌	My brother can **neither** swim **nor** ride a bike. 나의 남동생은 수영을 하지도 자전거를 타지도 못한다.

Tip both A and B 뒤에는 항상 복수동사를 쓰고, 나머지 상관접속사 뒤에 오는 동사는 B에 수일치시킨다.
Both Mike **and** Jenny (enjoys, **enjoy**) skiing. Mike와 Jenny는 둘 다 스키 타는 것을 즐긴다.
Not only Susan **but also** her sister (wake, **wakes**) up early in the morning.
Susan뿐만 아니라 그녀의 언니도 아침에 일찍 일어난다.

연습문제 A 다음 빈칸에 알맞은 말을 넣어 문장을 완성하시오.

1 Please bring either a black _____ blue pen.

2 Samantha is both funny _____ kind.

3 The sculptor used not only wood _____ stone.

4 Neither the children _____ their parents enjoyed the play.

5 _____ sugarcane and coffee are grown in Brazil.

6 This mattress is _____ comfortable nor cheap.

7 _____ you or I have to take care of our pet.

8 Frogs can live _____ in water but also on land.

9 _____ Janet or Mindy is going to sit next to me.

10 Both Timothy _____ Junsu walk to school.

11 She is _____ an actor but also a great singer.

12 Neither the bank _____ the bookstore is open today.

연습문제 B 우리말과 같도록 빈칸에 알맞은 말을 쓰시오.

1 나는 나의 배낭과 나의 지갑을 둘 다 잃어버렸다.

= I lost _____ my backpack _____ my wallet.

2 Peter뿐만 아니라 나도 야구를 잘한다.

= _____ _____ Peter _____ _____ I play baseball well.

3 민지도 지호도 오늘 수업에 오지 않았다.

= _____ Minji _____ Jiho came to class today.

4 그는 이탈리아어뿐만 아니라 프랑스어로도 말할 수 있다.

= He is able to speak in French _____ _____ _____ Italian.

5 너는 버스나 지하철 둘 중 하나로 그 쇼핑몰에 갈 수 있다.

= You can get to the shopping mall _____ by bus _____ by subway.

6 나는 붓뿐만 아니라 페인트 한 캔도 필요하다.

= I need _____ _____ a brush _____ _____ a can of paint.

7 Gina는 베를린과 런던 둘 다에 가본 적이 있다.

= Gina has been to _____ Berlin _____ London.

8 우리는 그 대회를 위해 노래하는 것뿐만 아니라 춤추는 것도 연습했다.

= We practiced dancing _____ _____ _____ singing for the contest.

연습문제 C 다음 빈칸에 알맞은 형태의 be동사를 쓰시오. (단, 현재형으로 쓰시오.)

1 Either Nancy or Julie _____ his friend.

2 Bacon as well as eggs _____ great for breakfast.

3 Not only Irene but also her cousins _____ tall.

4 Neither this hat nor these gloves _____ mine.

5 Both Brandon and Tiffany _____ coming to Seoul.

6 Not only the students but also the teacher _____ for the new class rule.

기출 적중문제 🎯

다음 두 문장의 의미가 같도록 as well as를 이용하여 문장을 완성하시오.

I have not only a sore throat but also a headache.

= I have _____.

> not only A but also B는 B as well as A로 바꿔 쓸 수 있어요.

명사절을 이끄는 접속사: that

that은 문장 안에서 주어·보어·목적어로 쓰이는 명사절을 이끄는 접속사이며, '~이라는 것'이라는 의미이다.

주어	**That the earth is round** is true. 지구가 둥글다는 것은 사실이다. = **It** is true **that the earth is round**. 　└→ that절이 문장 안에서 주어로 쓰였을 때는 주로 주어 자리에 가주어 it을 쓰고 진주어 that절을 뒤로 　　보낸다.
보어	The problem is **that I don't know her**. 문제는 내가 그녀를 알지 못한다는 것이다.
목적어	that절이 문장 안에서 목적어로 쓰였을 때는 that을 생략할 수 있다. I think **(that) Mr. Park is the best teacher**. 나는 박 선생님이 최고의 선생님이라고 생각한다.

(Tip) that은 지시대명사나 지시형용사로도 쓰인다.

지시대명사　He told me **that** was a lie. 그는 나에게 그것이 거짓말이었다고 말했다.

지시형용사　I saw **that** movie last weekend. 나는 지난 주말에 그 영화를 봤다.

연습문제 **A**　밑줄 친 that절의 역할을 <보기>에서 골라 그 기호를 쓰시오.

<보기>　ⓐ 주어　ⓑ 보어　ⓒ 목적어

1　I believe that I can win first prize.　　　　　　[　　　　]
2　It is exciting that we are going on a field trip.　　[　　　　]
3　The fact is that Melody is afraid of clowns.　　　[　　　　]
4　I hope that we can solve the puzzle together.　　[　　　　]
5　Some people think that whales are fish.　　　　[　　　　]
6　The truth is that I don't know how to play chess.　[　　　　]
7　It is a pity that you lost your favorite necklace.　　[　　　　]
8　Jane told me that I looked pretty in my red dress.　[　　　　]

연습문제 **B**　<보기>와 같이 다음 문장을 괄호 안의 말과 접속사 that을 활용하여 바꿔 쓰시오.

<보기>　It is time to go home.
　　→ *I think that it is time to go home.*　(I think)

1　This scarf is yours.

　→ _____ (I guess)

2 I can finish the report on time.

→ _____ (I hope)

3 I want to be an astronaut.

→ _____ (He knows)

4 Science is the easiest subject.

→ _____ (I think)

5 Patrick is a genius.

→ _____ (Everyone says)

6 You had dinner with your friends.

→ _____ (I thought)

7 Jessie called me last night.

→ _____ (I didn't know)

8 Laughing is good for our health.

→ _____ (I believe)

연습문제 C | 밑줄 친 that의 쓰임과 같은 것을 <보기>에서 골라 그 기호를 쓰시오.

> **<보기>** ⓐ I believe <u>that</u> he is a great director.
> ⓑ Is <u>that</u> your luggage over there?
> ⓒ I know <u>that</u> girl with red hair.

1 Greg likes <u>that</u> shirt more than this one.   [   ]

2 <u>That</u> is not an important issue to me.   [   ]

3 I think <u>that</u> the music is too loud.   [   ]

4 Have you visited <u>that</u> café before?   [   ]

5 <u>That</u> is Kate's smartphone on the desk.   [   ]

6 Sheldon said <u>that</u> he forgot to bring his umbrella.   [   ]

기출 적중문제

다음 중 밑줄 친 that의 쓰임이 나머지 넷과 다른 것은?

① Do you believe <u>that</u> trash is useless?

② Josh said <u>that</u> he was truly sorry.

③ Alice told me <u>that</u> I could borrow her pen.

④ Where did you buy <u>that</u> pretty purse?

⑤ I think <u>that</u> I need to go to the hospital.

명사절을 이끄는 접속사: if, whether

정답 p.47

if/whether는 명사절을 이끄는 접속사로, '~인지 아닌지'라는 의미이다. if가 이끄는 명사절은 주로 문장 안에서 동사의 목적어로 쓰인다.

Whether you are rich (or not) is not important.   네가 부자인지 아닌지는 중요하지 않다.

I don't know **if[whether] he is coming (or not)**.   나는 그가 오는지 아닌지 모른다.

I'm not sure **if[whether] the rumor is true (or not)**.

나는 그 소문이 사실인지 아닌지 확실히 알지 못한다.

연습문제 <보기>와 같이 다음 문장을 괄호 안의 접속사를 활용하여 바꿔 쓰시오.

<보기> Is he a middle school student?

→ Do you know *if he is a middle school student (or not)* ? (if)

1 Should I wait in line?

→ I asked _____. (whether)

2 Did you turn the lights off?

→ Do you remember _____? (if)

3 Will Nate join our soccer team?

→ I'm not sure _____. (whether)

4 Are monkeys smarter than parrots?

→ I wonder _____. (if)

5 Can you speak Korean?

→ Tell me _____. (whether)

6 Does Emily like red roses?

→ He wants to know _____. (if)

7 Have we met each other before?

→ I don't remember _____. (whether)

기출 적중문제

우리말과 같도록 괄호 안의 말을 활용하여 빈칸에 쓰시오.

나는 내일 비가 올지 아닌지 모른다. (it, rain)

= I don't know _____ _____ _____ _____.

POINT 4-1 부사절을 이끄는 접속사: 시간

정답 p.47

1. 부사절 접속사는 주절과 부사절을 연결하며, 부사절은 시간, 이유, 조건 등을 나타낸다. 다음 접속사는 시간을 나타내는 부사절을 이끈다.

when	~할 때	**When** I was ten, I lived in Suwon. 나는 10살이었을 때 수원에 살았다.
before	~하기 전에	Let's close all the windows **before** we go out. 우리가 나가기 전에 모든 창문들을 닫자.
after	~한 후에	**After** Anne had dinner, she washed the dishes. Anne은 저녁을 먹은 후에 설거지를 했다.
as	~하고 있을 때, ~하면서	Carl listened to music **as** he jogged. Carl은 조깅하면서 음악을 들었다.
while	~하는 동안	Your friend called you **while** you were sleeping. 네가 자고 있는 동안 너의 친구가 너에게 전화했다. (Tip) '~ 동안'이라는 의미의 전치사 during 뒤에는 명사(구)가 온다. I was so sleepy **during** the history class. 나는 역사 수업 시간 동안 너무 졸렸다.
until	~할 때까지	Be seated **until** the bell rings. 종이 울릴 때까지 앉아 있어라.
as soon as	~하자마자	**As soon as** I got home, I turned the heater on. 나는 집에 도착하자마자 히터를 켰다.
since	~한 이후로	주로 주절에는 완료시제가 쓰이고, since가 이끄는 절에는 과거시제가 쓰인다. This house **has been** empty **since** the owner **moved** out last month. 그 주인이 지난달에 이사 간 이후로 이 집은 비어져 왔다.

2. 시간을 나타내는 부사절에서는 미래시제 대신 현재시제를 쓴다.

I'll brush my teeth **after** I **eat** dessert. 나는 디저트를 먹은 후에 이를 닦을 것이다.
Until Sam **arrives**, we'll wait here. Sam이 도착할 때까지, 우리는 여기에서 기다릴 것이다.
Sunho will go hiking **as soon as** he **gets** up. 선호는 일어나자마자 등산하러 갈 것이다.

연습문제 A 괄호 안에서 가장 알맞은 접속사를 고르시오.

1 We have to do our best (when / after) we play sports.

2 Bomi has known Sumin (when / since) she was four.

3 (While / Until) I was taking a shower, someone knocked on the door.

4 My dad told me stories (as / as soon as) we were walking home.

5 (Until / As soon as) I opened the door, my cat entered the room.

연습문제 B   우리말과 같도록 <보기>의 접속사와 괄호 안의 말을 활용하여 문장을 완성하시오.

<보기>   when   after   until   while

1 나는 도움이 되는 정보를 찾을 때까지 계속 검색할 것이다. (find helpful information)

= I'll keep searching _____ .

2 그녀는 저녁을 먹는 동안 그녀의 전화기를 보지 않는다. (eat dinner)

= She doesn't look at her phone _____ .

3 너는 이 약을 먹은 후에 나아질 것이다. (take this medicine)

= You'll feel better _____ .

4 그는 준비가 될 때 연설할 것이다. (be ready)

= He'll make a speech _____ .

<보기>   before   as   as soon as   since

5 Joseph은 잠들기 전에 그 소설을 읽는 것을 끝냈다. (fall asleep)

= Joseph finished reading the novel _____ .

6 나는 모자를 사자마자 가게를 떠날 것이다. (buy a hat)

= I'm going to leave the store _____ .

7 나의 삼촌은 수술을 받으신 이후로 병원에 머물러오셨다. (have surgery)

= My uncle has stayed in the hospital _____ .

8 나는 도서관에 가면서 나의 친구를 봤다. (be going to the library)

= I saw my friend _____ .

기출 적중문제

다음 빈칸에 들어갈 말이 순서대로 짝지어진 것은?

· It was very dark _____ I turned on the lights.
· I'll make a wish when I _____ out the candles.

① after – will blow   ② after – blow
③ before – will blow   ④ before – blow
⑤ as soon as – blow

POINT 4-2 부사절을 이끄는 접속사: 이유

다음 접속사는 이유를 나타내는 부사절을 이끈다.

because	~하기 때문에	She was hungry **because** she skipped lunch. 그녀는 점심 식사를 걸렀기 때문에 배가 고팠다. (= She skipped lunch, **so** she was hungry.) 그녀는 점심 식사를 걸러서 배가 고팠다. **Because** it was snowing outside, we were excited. 밖에 눈이 오고 있었기 때문에, 우리는 신이 났다. (= It was snowing outside, **so** we were excited.) 밖에 눈이 오고 있어서, 우리는 신이 났다. (Tip) '~ 때문에'라는 의미의 because of 뒤에는 명사(구)가 온다. I can't sleep **because of** a mosquito. 나는 모기 때문에 잘 수 없다.
since		**Since** today is Sunday, the bank is closed. 오늘은 일요일이기 때문에, 은행이 문을 닫았다.
as		**As** Sarah lost her phone, she was upset. Sarah는 그녀의 전화기를 잃어버렸기 때문에 속상했다.

연습문제 A <보기>와 같이 다음 문장을 because를 이용하여 바꿔 쓰시오.

<보기>	She loves children, so she became a kindergarten teacher. → *She became a kindergarten teacher because she loves children.*

1 He missed the bus, so he arrived late.

→ _____

2 I was thirsty, so I drank two bottles of water.

→ _____

3 The wind is too weak, so the boat isn't moving.

→ _____

4 She wasn't tall enough, so she couldn't ride the roller coaster.

→ _____

5 The roads were icy, so there were many car accidents.

→ _____

6 He didn't want to cook, so he ordered pizza.

→ _____

| <보기> | since the movie was great | as you are sleepy | since it's too expensive |
| | because she is kind to others | as you lied to me | because I'm too busy |

1 I can't buy this car _____.

2 _____, you should take a nap.

3 She is very popular _____.

4 _____, I am angry at you.

5 _____, Paul watched it twice.

6 I can't help you right now _____.

연습문제 **C** 다음 빈칸에 because나 because of 중 알맞은 것을 쓰시오.

1 I was surprised _____ the loud noise.

2 Everyone had to leave the building _____ the fire.

3 Ginseng is expensive _____ it grows very slowly.

4 The soccer game was canceled _____ the storm.

5 Jason is depressed _____ his friend is moving away.

6 Glaciers are melting _____ global warming.

7 People like this song _____ its melody is beautiful.

8 The author became famous _____ his latest book.

9 I took my umbrella _____ it rained today.

10 Violet bought the fancy plates _____ they were on sale.

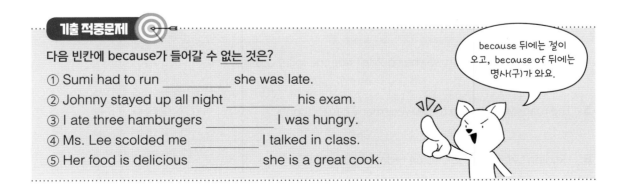

기출 적중문제

다음 빈칸에 because가 들어갈 수 <u>없는</u> 것은?

① Sumi had to run _____ she was late.

② Johnny stayed up all night _____ his exam.

③ I ate three hamburgers _____ I was hungry.

④ Ms. Lee scolded me _____ I talked in class.

⑤ Her food is delicious _____ she is a great cook.

> because 뒤에는 절이 오고, because of 뒤에는 명사(구)가 와요.

부사절을 이끄는 접속사: 조건

1. 다음 접속사는 조건을 나타내는 부사절을 이끈다.

if	만약 ~한다면	**If** you need help, go to the information desk. 만약 네가 도움이 필요하다면, 안내소로 가라. People can't enter this building **if** they don't have an ID. 만약 사람들이 신분증을 가지고 있지 않다면 그들은 이 건물에 들어갈 수 없다. (Tip) if는 '~인지 아닌지'라는 의미의 명사절 접속사로도 쓰인다. I'm not sure **if I can park here.** 나는 여기에 주차해도 되는지 아닌지 확실히 알지 못한다.
unless (= if ~ not)	만약 ~하지 않는다면	**Unless** it rains, I'll dry the clothes outside. = **If** it does **not** rain, I'll dry the clothes outside. 만약 비가 오지 않는다면, 나는 밖에서 옷을 말릴 것이다. We can't watch the musical **unless** we make a reservation. = We can't watch the musical **if** we don't make a reservation. 만약 우리가 예약하지 않는다면 우리는 그 뮤지컬을 볼 수 없다.

2. 조건을 나타내는 부사절에서는 미래시제 대신 현재시제를 쓴다.

If you **drink** old milk, you'll get a stomachache.
만약 네가 오래된 우유를 마신다면 너는 배가 아플 것이다.

This vacuum cleaner won't work **unless** you **charge** it.
만약 네가 그것을 충전하지 않는다면 이 진공청소기는 작동하지 않을 것이다.

연습문제 A │ 다음 두 문장의 의미가 같도록 문장을 완성하시오.

1 You'll feel sorry if you don't apologize to your friend.

= You'll feel sorry _____.

2 Unless you wear a sweater, you'll catch a cold.

= _____, you'll catch a cold.

3 If you don't take notes now, you'll regret it later.

= _____, you'll regret it later.

4 Unless the store is too far away, we can just walk.

= _____, we can just walk.

5 Those birds will disappear if we don't protect their habitat.

= Those birds will disappear _____.

6 Unless you have a visa, you can't travel to China.

= _____, you can't travel to China.

7 If you don't exercise regularly, you'll gain weight.

= _____, you'll gain weight.

8 If you don't try your best, you won't win the race.

= _____, you won't win the race.

9 If you aren't over 20, you can't drive in Korea.

= _____, you can't drive in Korea.

10 Unless I go to the library, I can't concentrate on studying.

= _____, I can't concentrate on studying.

연습문제 **B** 밑줄 친 부분이 어법상 맞으면 O를 쓰고, 틀리면 바르게 고쳐 쓰시오.

1 <u>If</u> you have a ticket, you can't enter the theater. → _____

2 My grandfather can't hear us <u>unless</u> we speak loudly. → _____

3 Turn the computer off <u>unless</u> you're not using it. → _____

4 We can't give you a refund <u>if</u> you bring a receipt. → _____

5 The earth will get cleaner if we <u>recycle</u> more. → _____

6 You will get ill unless you <u>will stop</u> eating junk food. → _____

7 Benny will arrive tonight unless her flight <u>will be</u> canceled. → _____

8 If I <u>see</u> my favorite actor, I will ask for his autograph. → _____

9 If you <u>will mix</u> red and blue paint, you will have purple paint. → _____

기출 적중문제 🎯

다음 우리말을 알맞게 영작한 것을 <u>모두</u> 고르시오.

만약 내일 비가 오지 않는다면, 그 축제는 열릴 것이다.

① If it rains tomorrow, the festival will be held.
② If it won't rain tomorrow, the festival will be held.
③ If it doesn't rain tomorrow, the festival will be held.
④ Unless it will rain tomorrow, the festival will be held.
⑤ Unless it rains tomorrow, the festival will be held.

unless는 if ~ not
으로 바꿔 쓸 수
있어요.

기출로적중 POINT 4-4 부사절을 이끄는 접속사: 양보

다음 접속사는 양보를 나타내는 부사절을 이끈다.

although	비록 ~이지만	**Although[Though]** Yuri doesn't sing well, she wants to be a singer. 비록 유리는 노래를 잘 못하지만 가수가 되기를 원한다.
though		
even though	비록 ~일지라도	I'll take a walk **even though** it's snowing outside. 비록 밖에 눈이 올지라도 나는 산책할 것이다.

(Tip) '~에도 불구하고'라는 의미의 despite와 in spite of 뒤에는 명사(구)가 온다.
I'll take a walk **despite[in spite of]** the snow. 눈에도 불구하고 나는 산책할 것이다.

연습문제 우리말과 같도록 괄호 안의 말을 알맞게 배열하시오.

1 비록 그 시계가 비쌀지라도, 나는 그것을 사기를 원한다. (even though, is, expensive, the watch)
= _____, I want to buy it.

2 비록 Evan은 많은 시간이 없었지만 돕겠다고 제안했다. (he, much time, though, didn't have)
= Evan offered to help _____.

3 비록 내가 큰 실수를 했지만, 나의 부모님은 화나지 않으셨다. (I, a big mistake, made, though)
= _____, my parents weren't angry.

4 비록 유나와 유진이는 쌍둥이지만 닮지 않았다. (are, although, Yuna and Yujin, twins)
= _____, they don't look alike.

5 비록 그는 하키를 잘하지만 팀에 선발되지 않았다. (plays, he, though, hockey, well)
= _____, he wasn't chosen for the team.

6 비록 음식이 맛있을지라도 나는 많이 먹지 못한다. (the food, delicious, even though, is)
= I can't eat much _____.

7 비록 우리는 최선을 다했지만 그 과학 프로젝트를 끝낼 수 없었다. (our best, did, although, we)
= _____, we couldn't finish the science project.

기출 적중문제

우리말과 같도록 괄호 안의 말을 활용하여 빈칸에 알맞은 말을 쓰시오.

> 비록 나는 우산이 있었지만 젖었다. (have)

= _____ _____ _____ _____ _____, I got wet.

부사절을 이끄는 접속사: as의 다양한 의미

정답 p.48

부사절 접속사 as는 다양한 의미를 나타낸다.

~하고 있을 때, ~하면서	I saw Mary **as** I was going to school. 나는 학교에 가면서 Mary를 봤다.
~하기 때문에	**As** it was cold outside, Harry put on a coat. 밖이 추웠기 때문에, Harry는 코트를 입었다.
~하는 대로, ~하는 듯이	Install the program **as** I say. 내가 말하는 대로 그 프로그램을 설치해라.
~할수록	**As** she grew older, she became wiser. 그녀는 나이가 들수록 더 현명해졌다.

(Tip) as는 '~으로서, ~처럼'이라는 의미의 전치사로도 쓰이며, 이때 뒤에 명사(구)가 온다.

Jim received a new hat **as a gift**. Jim은 선물로 새 모자를 받았다.

연습문제 밑줄 친 as의 의미를 <보기>에서 골라 그 기호를 쓰시오.

<보기>   ⓐ ~하고 있을 때   ⓑ ~하기 때문에   ⓒ ~하는 대로   ⓓ ~할수록   ⓔ ~으로서

1 I broke the plate as I was putting it in the sink. [   ]

2 As Jisu lives near me, I can often see her. [   ]

3 They planted the flowers as I asked. [   ]

4 As you were not home, I left the package at the door. [   ]

5 Alex is working as a fashion designer. [   ]

6 As time passed, he grew more impatient. [   ]

7 I followed the rules as I was told by my teacher. [   ]

8 This box can be used as a table. [   ]

9 James sang as he played the guitar. [   ]

10 As we climbed the mountain, the air got colder. [   ]

기출 적중문제

다음 중 밑줄 친 As의 의미가 나머지 넷과 다른 것은?

① As Julian became taller, he got stronger.

② As I forgot the password, I couldn't log in.

③ As she grew up, she got more interested in art.

④ As it gets warmer, animals become more active.

⑤ As the week passed, his cough got worse.

so that / so ~ that …

정답 p.48

1. **so that**은 '~하기 위해, ~할 수 있도록'이라는 의미로, 목적을 나타내는 부사절을 이끈다.

   I'm saving money **so that** I can buy a house. 나는 집을 사기 위해 돈을 모으고 있다.
   (= I'm saving money **(in order[so as]) to** buy a house.)

   She hurried **so that** she could catch the bus. 그녀는 버스를 잡기 위해 서둘렀다.
   (= She hurried **(in order[so as]) to** catch the bus.)

2. 「**so** + 형용사/부사 + **that** …」은 '너무 ~해서 …한'이라는 의미로, 결과를 나타낸다.

   The play was **so touching that** I cried. 그 연극은 너무 감동적이어서 나는 울었다.
   Hansu talks **so loudly that** my ears hurt. 한수는 너무 큰 소리로 말해서 나의 귀가 아프다.

   (Tip) 「so 형용사/부사 that 주어 can't」는 「too ~ to」로 바꿔 쓸 수 있다.
   This ring is **so expensive that** I **can't** buy it. 이 반지는 너무 비싸서 나는 그것을 살 수 없다.
   = This ring is **too** expensive for me **to** buy. 이 반지는 내가 사기에 너무 비싸다.

   (Tip) 「such + a(n) + 형용사 + 명사 + that …」으로도 결과를 나타낼 수 있다.
   It is **such an expensive ring that** I can't buy it. 그것은 너무 비싼 반지라서 나는 그것을 살 수 없다.

연습문제 A   <보기>와 같이 다음 두 문장의 의미가 같도록 문장을 완성하시오.

> <보기>   I jog every morning to stay fit.
>   = I jog every morning _so that I can stay fit_ .

1   I ate hot soup to keep warm.
    = I ate hot soup _____ .

2   My brother exercises a lot to get healthy.
    = My brother exercises a lot _____ .

3   Jina practiced hard to do well in her school play.
    = Jina practiced hard _____ .

4   I use a lot of honey to make the tea sweeter.
    = I use a lot of honey _____ .

5   Review your notes every day to get a good grade.
    = Review your notes every day _____ .

6   We regularly plant trees to save the environment.
    = We regularly plant trees _____ .

7 I looked at my phone to check for new messages.

= I looked at my phone _____ .

8 Jeffrey set his alarm to wake up early.

= Jeffrey set his alarm _____ .

연습문제 B <보기>와 같이 다음 두 문장을 한 문장으로 연결하시오.

> **<보기>** These shoes are uncomfortable. I'll return them.
> → These shoes are _so uncomfortable that I'll return them_ .

1 The box is heavy. I can't lift it.

→ The box is _____ .

2 Daeho was hungry. He ate the whole pie.

→ Daeho was _____ .

3 The sun is bright. People shouldn't look at it directly.

→ The sun is _____ .

4 The movie was boring. Everyone fell asleep.

→ The movie was _____ .

5 It rained heavily. We had to cancel our picnic.

→ It rained _____ .

6 This book is difficult. Many people can't understand it.

→ This book is _____ .

7 The cat ran away quickly. I couldn't catch it.

→ The cat ran away _____ .

8 My grandfather is wise. We respect him very much.

→ My grandfather is _____ .

기출 적중문제 ◎

다음 빈칸에 들어갈 알맞은 것은?

> The book became _____ it was made into a movie.

① so popular that   ② such popular that
③ so popularly that   ④ so popular what
⑤ such popularly what

기출로적중 POINT 6 접속부사

정답 p.49

접속부사는 앞 문장과 뒤 문장을 이어주는 접속사 역할을 하는 부사이다.

however	그러나, 하지만	I have a lot of things to do on weekdays. **However**, I'm free on weekends. 나는 평일에 할 것들이 많다. 그러나, 나는 주말에 한가하다.
on the other hand	반면에, 다른 한편으로는	Earth has one moon. **On the other hand**, Jupiter has 79 moons. 지구는 하나의 위성을 가지고 있다. 반면에, 목성은 79개의 위성을 가지고 있다.
for example	예를 들어	Crows are smart birds. **For example**, they use branches as tools. 까마귀는 똑똑한 새이다. 예를 들어, 그들은 나뭇가지를 도구로서 사용한다.
in addition, besides	게다가	This restaurant's food is delicious. **Besides**, the waiters are kind. 이 식당의 음식은 맛있다. 게다가, 종업원들이 친절하다.
therefore	그러므로	I had a bad toothache. **Therefore**, I had to go to the dentist. 나는 심한 치통이 있었다. 그러므로, 나는 치과에 가야 했다.

CHAPTER 15 접속사 기출로 적중 해카스 중학영문법 2학년

연습문제 괄호 안에서 가장 알맞은 접속부사를 고르시오.

1 Ants have six legs. (On the other hand / For example), spiders have eight legs.

2 Dad bought me a bicycle last year. (However / In addition), I seldom ride it.

3 The paint on the wall isn't dry yet. (On the other hand / Therefore), you shouldn't touch it.

4 The shop sells different kinds of fruits. (However / For example), it sells limes and mangoes.

5 I don't really want to go swimming. (On the other hand / Besides), it's too late.

6 I use my smartphone to watch videos. (In addition / Therefore), I read online news on it.

기출 적중문제

다음 글의 빈칸에 들어갈 가장 알맞은 것은?

> We respect our baseball coach because he gives us great advice. He said, "Winning the game is important. _____, playing fair is much more important."

① Because   ② However   ③ Therefore
④ That   ⑤ For example

Chapter 15 접속사 345

서술형 대비 문제

Ⓐ 우리말과 같도록 괄호 안의 말을 알맞게 배열하시오.

1 나는 나의 열쇠를 잃어버렸다고 생각한다. (lost, key, I, my, that)

= I think _____.

2 나는 Sally가 아픈지 아닌지 확실히 알지 못한다. (sick, if, is, Sally)

= I'm not sure _____.

3 Paul이 그 축제에 갈 수 없다는 것은 실망스럽다. (can't, Paul, the, that, go, to, festival)

= It is disappointing _____.

4 나에게 네가 한국을 다시 방문할지 아닌지 말해주겠니? (Korea, visit, whether, again, will, you)

= Can you tell me _____?

5 나는 돼지가 똑똑한 동물이라고 믿는다. (are, smart, pigs, that, animals)

= I believe _____.

6 문제는 내가 나의 숙제를 가져오지 않았다는 것이다. (that, my, bring, homework, didn't, I)

= The problem is _____.

7 그는 여기에서 머무르는 것을 즐겼다고 말했다. (that, staying, enjoyed, here, he)

= He said _____.

8 소라는 오타와가 캐나다의 수도인지 아닌지 모른다. (capital, Canada, Ottawa, the, if, of, is)

= Sora doesn't know _____.

Ⓑ 밑줄 친 부분이 어법상 맞으면 O를 쓰고, 틀리면 바르게 고쳐 쓰시오.

1 Dad may be in the living room <u>and</u> the kitchen.　　→ _____

2 Both Linda and Marcus <u>has</u> fish as pets.　　→ _____

3 Doves are symbols of love <u>as well as</u> peace.　　→ _____

4 I'll lend you my umbrella if it <u>will rain</u>.　　→ _____

5 This café has not only great coffee <u>also</u> a nice view.　　→ _____

6 Ron is good at both singing and <u>dance</u>.　　→ _____

7 Mr. Brown is not only smart but also <u>generous</u>.　　→ _____

8 A jacket as well as some pants <u>are</u> lying on the sofa.　　→ _____

9 You can play computer games or <u>watched</u> TV.　　→ _____

Ⓒ 다음 빈칸에 가장 알맞은 말을 <보기>에서 골라 쓰시오.

<보기>
though it is very expensive	if you like modern art
while he was playing football	when I called her
as soon as I came home	before you eat your sandwich
as he studied the wrong chapter	so that they can hear better
since I was very young	until they are red

1 Wash your hands _____ .

2 Don't pick the apples _____ .

3 Jamie broke his leg _____ .

4 I haven't seen a rainbow _____ .

5 I unpacked my luggage _____ .

6 Liam wants to buy the laptop _____ .

7 Rabbits have long ears _____ .

8 Jake might fail the history test _____ .

9 Elizabeth didn't answer the phone _____ .

10 You should go to that exhibition _____ .

Ⓓ 다음 그림을 보고 「so ~ that …」 구문과 괄호 안의 말을 활용하여 문장을 완성하시오.

1

2

3

1 The shirt is _____ . (can't wear it)

2 It is snowing _____ . (can't go outside)

3 The soup is _____ . (can't eat it)

중간·기말고사 실전 문제

1 다음 대화의 빈칸에 들어갈 가장 알맞은 것은?

> *A*: What did you do last weekend?
> *B*: I went to the ice rink with my friend, _____ we skated together.

① or   ② so   ③ but
④ and   ⑤ that

2 우리말과 같도록 괄호 안의 말을 활용하여 빈칸에 쓰시오.

> 이 소파는 매우 좋아 보이지만 불편하다. (it, uncomfortable)

= This sofa looks very nice, _____
_____ _____ _____ .

3 다음 글의 빈칸에 들어갈 말이 순서대로 짝지어진 것은?

> My grandmother's birthday is coming up soon, _____ I'm planning to visit her. I can go to her town by bus _____ by train. Either way, it will take about four hours.

① so – or   ② so – but   ③ or – so
④ or – but   ⑤ but – or

4 다음 중 어법상 어색한 것은?

① Not only Lucy but also her friends like the new TV show.
② Both Leonard and Jenna enjoy listening to K-pop.
③ Either Jimin or I have to finish cleaning the classroom.
④ Tom's parents as well as Tom is reading a book.
⑤ Neither Anton nor his brothers play online games.

5 다음 빈칸에 들어갈 알맞은 것을 모두 고르시오.

> _____ the price of the ticket was high, the musical was excellent.

① Although   ② Whether
③ As soon as   ④ Though
⑤ Until

6 다음 두 문장의 의미가 같도록 문장을 완성하시오. (단, as를 포함하시오.)

> Not only blue but also green looks good on you.
> = _____ looks good on you.

7 다음 밑줄 친 부분을 바르게 고친 것끼리 묶인 것은?

ⓐ Both Suho and I is wearing new running shoes. (→ am)

ⓑ Kelly enjoys neither taking walks nor plays outdoors. (→ playing)

ⓒ We can either stay home or going to the movies. (→ to go)

ⓓ A notebook as well as pencils are needed for this class. (→ is)

① ⓐ, ⓑ   ② ⓐ, ⓒ   ③ ⓑ, ⓒ
④ ⓑ, ⓓ   ⑤ ⓒ, ⓓ

8 다음 중 밑줄 친 that을 생략할 수 있는 것을 모두 고르시오.

① Nina hasn't heard about that.
② I think that Luke will arrive soon.
③ We have to cross that long bridge.
④ The earthquake destroyed that building.
⑤ Jessica didn't know that her wallet was gone.

9 다음 두 문장의 의미가 같도록 빈칸에 알맞은 접속사를 쓰시오.

I don't know if my answer is correct or not.
= I don't know _____ my answer is correct or not.

[10-11] 다음 빈칸에 들어갈 가장 알맞은 것을 고르시오.

10

It is a pity _____ you spilled the ink on your favorite shirt.

① or   ② so   ③ but
④ whether   ⑤ that

11

_____ you aren't using the computer, you should turn it off.

① Unless   ② If   ③ Before
④ So that   ⑤ Whether

12 다음 중 밑줄 친 that의 쓰임이 나머지 넷과 다른 것은?

① That elephants can't jump is interesting.
② Tony said that the concert was boring.
③ The truth is that he doesn't like his new haircut.
④ That closet is full of expensive dresses.
⑤ Judy hopes that she'll be elected class president.

13 괄호 안의 말을 알맞게 배열하여 문장을 완성하시오.

Jacob thinks _____.
(him, lied, I, that, to)

14 다음 빈칸에 들어갈 접속사가 나머지 넷과 다른 것은?

① Stay calm, _____ everything will be fine.
② Start your homework now, _____ you'll finish it by dinner.
③ Get some sleep, _____ you'll be sleepy during the exam.
④ Always try your best, _____ you won't regret the result.
⑤ Order the items before noon, _____ you'll get them tomorrow.

15 다음 그림을 보고 주어진 <조건>에 맞게 문장을 완성하시오.

<조건> if를 사용하지 마시오.

→ I'm wondering _____
_____ or not.

16 알맞은 접속사를 이용하여 다음 두 문장을 한 문장으로 연결하시오.

He was 15. He could already speak three languages then.
→ _____ he was 15, he could already speak three languages.

17 다음 우리말을 알맞게 영작한 것은?

그녀는 알람이 울리자마자 일어났다.

① She woke up before the alarm rang.
② She woke up while the alarm rang.
③ She woke up as soon as the alarm rang.
④ She woke up because the alarm rang.
⑤ She woke up if the alarm rang.

[18-19] 다음 두 문장의 의미가 같도록 빈칸에 알맞은 접속사를 쓰시오.

18

We aren't old enough, so we can't vote.
= We can't vote _____ we aren't old enough.

19

If you don't raise your hand, you can't ask questions.
= _____ you raise your hand, you can't ask questions.

20 다음 문장에서 어법상 어색한 부분을 찾아 쓰고 바르게 고쳐 쓰시오.

Mom will get very angry if she will see this mess.

_____ → _____

21 다음 중 밑줄 친 since의 의미가 나머지 넷과 다른 것은?

① I made pasta for lunch <u>since</u> it's easy to cook.
② Bob is able to help you <u>since</u> he isn't busy right now.
③ Wear comfortable shoes <u>since</u> we are going hiking.
④ Molly's father has grown corn <u>since</u> he started farming.
⑤ I left a little early <u>since</u> I wanted to stop by the store.

22 다음 빈칸에 들어갈 말이 순서대로 짝지어진 것은?

> · The teacher was worried about Ken _____ he didn't come to school today.
> · People think Yunju is rich _____ her fancy jeweiry.

① because – because of
② because – because
③ since – because
④ because of – because of
⑤ because of – because

23 다음 두 문장의 의미가 같도록 문장을 완성하시오.

> If you don't take a taxi, you'll be late.
> = Take a taxi, _____.

24 다음은 Tim의 저녁 일정표이다. <보기>와 같이 알맞은 접속사를 이용하여 질문에 대한 대답을 쓰시오.

7:00	Do my homework
7:45	Help my mom prepare dinner
8:15	Eat dinner
9:00	Brush my teeth

> **<보기>**
> Q : What does Tim do at 7:45?
> A1: *He helps his mom prepare dinner after he does his homework.*
> A2: *He helps his mom prepare dinner before he eats dinner.*

Q : What does Tim do at 8:15?
A1: _____

_____

A2: _____

25 다음 중 어법상 어색한 것의 개수는?

> ⓐ I'll call you when I'll arrive at the airport.
> ⓑ You'll feel better after you talk about your feelings.
> ⓒ Minju won't go into the pool if the water is too cold.
> ⓓ Unless you'll really want the necklace, you shouldn't buy it.
> ⓔ He can stay up late if he will drink a cup of coffee.

① 없음　　② 1개　　③ 2개
④ 3개　　⑤ 4개

26 다음 빈칸에 공통으로 들어갈 알맞은 것은?

> · _____ I go to Thailand, I'll try eating durian.
> · Do you remember _____ you locked the front door?

① That[that]　　　② Unless[unless]
③ If[if]　　　　　④ While[while]
⑤ After[after]

27 우리말과 같도록 주어진 <조건>에 맞게 영작하시오.

> 더울 뿐만 아니라 습하기도 하다.

> <조건>
> 1. it, not, also, hot, humid를 활용하시오.
> 2. 8단어로 쓰시오.

= _____

28 주어진 문장의 빈칸에 들어갈 접속사와 다음 빈칸에 들어갈 접속사가 같은 것은?

> Stores are not open today _____ it is a national holiday.

① _____ I was younger, my family used to go to museums on Sundays.
② Columbus kept sailing _____ he reached land.
③ Tell me the truth, _____ I'll forgive you.
④ Sunmi didn't know _____ her friend was furious at her yesterday.
⑤ The floor is wet _____ Olivia broke a glass filled with milk.

29 다음 밑줄 친 as와 의미가 같은 것은?

> She lost a lot of weight <u>as</u> she exercised every day.

① until　　　② that　　　③ because
④ after　　　⑤ or

30 다음 중 밑줄 친 as의 쓰임이 나머지 넷과 다른 것은?

① Ms. Bell works <u>as</u> a nurse at the hospital.
② You must be careful <u>as</u> that knife is sharp.
③ We like him <u>as</u> he has good manners.
④ I couldn't go to school <u>as</u> I had the flu.
⑤ Venus is very hot <u>as</u> it's close to the Sun.

31 다음 글의 밑줄 친 우리말과 같도록 괄호 안의 말을 활용하여 빈칸에 쓰시오.

> My friend Minho is very diligent.
> He is never late when he hands his assignments in. One day, I observed him closely as he was doing his homework. <u>그는 그가 일찍 끝낼 수 있도록 아주 열심히 집중했다.</u> (that, could, early)

= He concentrated really hard _____

_____ _____ _____

_____ _____ .

32 우리말과 같도록 괄호 안의 말을 활용하여 문장을 완성하시오.

> 너의 부모님께 솔직하게 말해라, 그러면 그들은 이해할 것이다. (understand)

= Be honest with your parents, _____

_____ .

33 다음 밑줄 친 since와 의미가 같은 것은?

Nathan sent me a card yesterday <u>since</u> it was my birthday.

① when   ② because   ③ before
④ while   ⑤ until

34 주어진 문장의 밑줄 친 as와 의미가 같은 것은?

Jack was disappointed <u>as</u> his favorite basketball team lost the game.

① I ran into Paul <u>as</u> I was going to the market.
② You don't have to prepare dinner <u>as</u> we're eating out.
③ The dog greeted Matt <u>as</u> he entered the room.
④ Children grow taller <u>as</u> they get older.
⑤ My brother received a bicycle <u>as</u> a Christmas gift.

35 우리말과 같도록 괄호 안의 말을 알맞게 배열하시오.

비록 그녀는 많은 쿠키들을 가지고 있을지라도 그것들을 나눠주기를 원하지 않는다. (she, cookies, even, many, has, though)

= _____,
she doesn't want to share them.

36 대화에 나온 표현을 활용하여 빈칸에 알맞은 말을 쓰시오.

A: The music is _____ _____
_____ _____ _____
_____ you.
B: Oh, sorry. I guess it's too loud. I'll turn down the volume.
A: Thanks! Now I can hear you.

[37-38] 다음 글을 읽고 주어진 질문에 답하시오.

Things made of metal expand in hot weather. ⓐ_____, bridges and railway lines expand during the summer. Even the Eiffel Tower becomes a little taller. We can apply this knowledge in our daily lives. ⓑ_____, try putting it in hot water. The metal lid will expand, and you will be able to open the jar more easily!

37 위 글의 빈칸 ⓐ에 들어갈 알맞은 것을 고르시오.

① For example   ② But
③ However   ④ Finally
⑤ On the other hand

38 위 글의 빈칸 ⓑ에 들어갈 가장 알맞은 것은?

① If a jar opens
② If a jar will open
③ If a jar doesn't open
④ Unless a jar won't open
⑤ Unless a jar doesn't open

39 다음 빈칸에 들어갈 말이 순서대로 짝지어진 것은?

> The bus was _____ crowded _____
> Jinho couldn't get on.

① too - to
② so - to
③ too - for
④ so - that
⑤ very - that

40 다음 (A)~(C)에 들어갈 말이 바르게 짝지어진 것은?

> Last weekend, my friends and I wanted
> to play soccer on the field. __(A)__,
> rain started to pour down. We didn't
> want to get wet. __(B)__, we played
> basketball in the gym instead. We
> promised to play soccer this weekend
> __(C)__ it doesn't rain.

	(A)	(B)	(C)
①	In addition	Besides	when
②	In addition	Therefore	if
③	However	Therefore	unless
④	However	Therefore	if
⑤	However	Besides	unless

41 다음 밑줄 친 부분과 바꿔 쓸 수 있는 것은?

> I need a calculator to add the numbers.

① so that I can add the numbers
② so that I can't add the numbers
③ to that I can add the numbers
④ so I can that add the numbers
⑤ so I can't that add the numbers

42 다음 글의 빈칸에 들어갈 말이 순서대로 짝지어진 것은?

> The west and east sides of Korea are
> different from each other. There are
> hundreds of islands in the West Sea.
> _____, there aren't many islands in
> the East Sea. _____, the west coast
> has muddy beaches, but the east coast
> has sandy ones.

① On the other hand - For example
② On the other hand - In addition
③ Therefore - In addition
④ Therefore - However
⑤ However - For example

43 「so ~ that …」 구문을 이용하여 다음 두 문장을 한 문장으로 연결하시오.

> The room was hot. I turned the air
> conditioner on.
>
> → _____
>   _____

44 다음 중 밑줄 친 when의 쓰임이 나머지 넷과 다른 것은?

① He felt terrible when he saw the accident.
② I don't know when the movie starts.
③ Jihye lived in Italy when she was seven.
④ I was washing the dishes when you
   called me.
⑤ Carol was surprised when she walked
   into the room.

45 다음 그림을 보고 괄호 안의 말을 활용하여 문장을 완성하시오.

Minsu is _____ _____. (so, excited, fall asleep)

46 다음 빈칸에 들어갈 알맞은 것을 <u>모두</u> 고르시오.

Nick was _____ on writing the report.

① too tired to focus
② too tired that he could focus
③ such tired that he couldn't focus
④ so tired to he could focus
⑤ so tired that he couldn't focus

47 주어진 문장의 밑줄 친 <u>if</u>와 쓰임이 같은 것은?

You'll get in trouble <u>if</u> you run in the hallway.

① I wonder <u>if</u> you want to join our club.
② I can't remember <u>if</u> I fed my goldfish.
③ I don't know <u>if</u> I should ask Mr. Jones for advice.
④ I'll get lonely <u>if</u> my best friend moves away.
⑤ I'm not sure <u>if</u> we're going in the right direction.

48 <보기 1>과 <보기 2>의 말을 하나씩 골라 한 문장으로 연결하시오.

<보기 1> · You'll save much energy
· Please don't play the piano
· I haven't talked to Mina

<보기 2> · since we fought last month
· if you unplug unused devices
· because it is after 10 o'clock

(1) _____

(2) _____

(3) _____

49 다음 두 문장의 의미가 같도록 문장을 완성하시오.

She writes in her diary before she goes to bed.
= _____, she goes to bed.

50 다음 밑줄 친 부분과 의미가 같은 것은?

<u>If you don't pay attention</u>, you won't be able to understand the lesson.

① Unless you don't pay attention
② Unless you pay attention
③ Though you don't pay attention
④ Though you pay attention
⑤ As soon as you pay attention

CHAPTER 16
관계사

선행사　　　관계절
The boy who is dancing is Jack.　춤을 추고 있는 그 소년은 Jack이다.

위 문장에서 who가 이끄는 절인 **who is dancing**이 명사 **The boy**를 꾸며서 '춤을 추고 있는 그 소년'이라는 의미가 됐어요. 이렇게 명사를 꾸미는 절을 관계절이라고 하고, 관계절이 꾸미는 명사를 선행사라고 해요. who처럼 두 절을 연결하는 접속사 역할을 하는 것을 **관계사**라고 하며, 관계사에는 관계대명사와 관계부사가 있어요.

기출로 적중 POINT

1 • 관계대명사의 역할과 종류

2-1 • 주격 관계대명사

2-2 • 목적격 관계대명사

2-3 • 소유격 관계대명사

3 • 관계대명사 that

4 • 관계대명사 what

5 • 관계대명사의 생략

6 • 전치사 + 관계대명사

7 • 관계부사

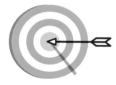

내신 100점 적중!
기출 출제율

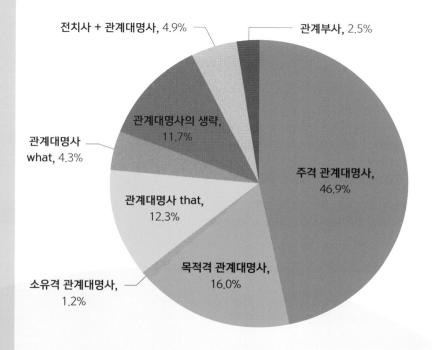

전치사 + 관계대명사, 4.9%

관계부사, 2.5%

관계대명사의 생략, 11.7%

관계대명사 what, 4.3%

관계대명사 that, 12.3%

소유격 관계대명사, 1.2%

목적격 관계대명사, 16.0%

주격 관계대명사, 46.9%

TOP 1 **주격 관계대명사 (46.9%)**
주격 관계대명사의 역할과 선행사에 따른 주격 관계대명사의 종류를 묻는 문제가 자주 출제된다.

TOP 2 **목적격 관계대명사 (16%)**
목적격 관계대명사의 역할과 선행사에 따른 목적격 관계대명사의 종류를 묻는 문제가 자주 출제된다.

TOP 3 **관계대명사 that (12.3%)**
관계대명사 that의 역할과 that을 주로 써야 하는 경우를 묻는 문제가 자주 출제된다.

1. **관계대명사는 관계대명사절을 이끄는 접속사 역할과 대명사 역할을 한다.**

   I have **a friend**. **He** is very kind. 나는 친구가 있다. 그는 매우 친절하다.
   → I have **a friend** <u>and he</u> is very kind. 나는 친구가 있고 그는 매우 친절하다.
   　　　　　　　　　접속사 + 대명사
   → I have **a friend** <u>who</u> is very kind. 나는 매우 친절한 친구가 있다.
   　　　　　　　　선행사　관계대명사

2. **관계대명사는 선행사의 종류와 관계대명사절 안에서의 선행사의 역할에 따라 다음과 같이 쓴다.**

선행사 \ 격	주격	목적격	소유격
사람	who	who(m)	whose
사물, 동물	which	which	whose
사람, 사물, 동물	that	that	–

   I'm reading **a book**. I bought **it** last week. 나는 책을 읽고 있다. 나는 그것을 지난주에 샀다.
   　　　　　　선행사(사물)　　　　목적어
   → I'm reading **a book** <u>which</u> I bought last week. 나는 내가 지난주에 산 책을 읽고 있다.

연습문제 다음 문장의 선행사에는 동그라미를 치고, 관계대명사에는 밑줄을 치시오.

1 I saw a woman who was jogging in the park.

2 You should try the bread which I baked.

3 I received a postcard which Mason sent.

4 I closed the door whose handle is metal.

5 She knows the man who used to be a doctor.

6 Sam bought some tomatoes which were fresh.

7 We met a singer whose songs are popular.

8 Jessica is the girl whom Annie introduced to me.

9 Chris destroyed the snowman that I built.

10 We're on a train which goes to Busan Station.

11 That is the bench which they painted an hour ago.

12 Miso is wearing the same jacket that she wore yesterday.

정답 p.51

POINT 2-1 주격 관계대명사

주격 관계대명사는 관계대명사절 안에서 주어 역할을 하며, 선행사의 종류에 따라 who나 which를 쓴다.

❶ 선행사가 사람인 경우: who

I have **a sister**. **She** is ten years old. 나는 여동생이 있다. 그녀는 10살이다.

→ I have **a sister who** is ten years old. 나는 10살인 여동생이 있다.

└→ 주격 관계대명사절의 동사는 선행사에 수일치시킨다.

(Tip) who는 '누구'라는 의미의 의문사로도 쓰인다.

I don't know **who** broke this window. 나는 누가 이 창문을 깼는지 모른다.

❷ 선행사가 사물이나 동물인 경우: which

The cat looks cute. **It** is taking a nap. 그 고양이는 귀엽게 보인다. 그것은 낮잠을 자고 있다.

→ **The cat which** is taking a nap looks cute. 낮잠을 자고 있는 그 고양이는 귀엽게 보인다.

연습문제 A 관계대명사를 이용하여 다음 두 문장을 한 문장으로 연결하시오.

1 My dad got me a doll. It has blue eyes.

→ _____

2 I know the man. He delivers milk every morning.

→ _____

3 I have a watch. It was made in Switzerland.

→ _____

4 The lamp is not working. It is on the table.

→ _____

5 Jimmy drank the orange juice. It was in the fridge.

→ _____

6 Ms. Lee scolded the boys. They talked during class.

→ _____

7 We bought a new sofa. It fits in our living room.

→ _____

8 A trophy was given to the woman. She won the contest.

→ _____

연습문제 B 괄호 안에서 알맞은 것을 고르시오.

1 Mr. Smith is the teacher (who / which) teaches English.

2 We're going to take the bus which (leaves / leave) at 7:30.

3 There's a cloud (who / which) looks like a sheep.

4 Jenny is the girl who (has / have) a twin brother.

5 I want a bottle (who / which) keeps the tea warm.

6 Owls are birds which (hunts / hunt) at night.

7 Look at the stars (who / which) are shining in the sky.

8 This market sells pears which (is / are) very sweet.

9 Paul smelled the flowers (who / which) were in his garden.

10 The actor (who / which) was in my favorite movie retired last month.

연습문제 C 밑줄 친 who의 쓰임과 같은 것을 <보기>에서 골라 그 기호를 쓰시오.

<보기>	ⓐ The guy who stole my wallet ran away.
	ⓑ Do you know who spilled the water on the floor?

1 I know someone who can help us.   [   ]

2 I can't remember who took that picture.   [   ]

3 People who exercise regularly live longer.   [   ]

4 Rebecca took care of the baby who was crying.   [   ]

5 They aren't sure who caused the car accident.   [   ]

6 Who is that man reading the newspaper?   [   ]

7 I wonder who sent this letter to me.   [   ]

8 Minha is my cousin who has really long hair.   [   ]

9 Mr. Collins is the architect who designed this tower.   [   ]

기출 적중문제

다음 중 어법상 바른 것은?

① I bought the camera who was cheap.

② She is a comedian which is popular.

③ A whale is a mammal who lives in the sea.

④ I ate a sandwich which was very delicious.

⑤ Listen to the boy which is playing the violin.

선행사의 종류에 따라 알맞은 관계대명사를 써야 해요.

기출로 작중 POINT 2-2 목적격 관계대명사

정답 p.52

목적격 관계대명사는 관계대명사절 안에서 목적어 역할을 하며, 선행사의 종류에 따라 who(m)이나 which를 쓴다.

❶ 선행사가 사람인 경우: who(m)

She is **the poet**. I like **her** very much. 그녀는 시인이다. 나는 그녀를 매우 좋아한다.

→ She is **the poet who[whom]** I like very much. 그녀는 내가 매우 좋아하는 시인이다.

❷ 선행사가 사물이나 동물인 경우: which

This painting is excellent. Jake drew **it**. 이 그림은 훌륭하다. Jake는 그것을 그렸다.

→ **This painting which** Jake drew is excellent. Jake가 그린 이 그림은 훌륭하다.

연습문제 A 관계대명사를 이용하여 다음 두 문장을 한 문장으로 연결하시오.

1 Yumi is my friend. I trust her.

→ Yumi is my friend _____ .

2 This bakery has a beautiful cake. I want to try it.

→ This bakery has a beautiful cake _____ .

3 I can smell the soup. My father is making it.

→ I can smell the soup _____ .

4 Stella is my classmate. I know her well.

→ Stella is my classmate _____ .

5 Einstein is the scientist. I respect him very much.

→ Einstein is the scientist _____ .

6 The computer is in the other room. We can use it.

→ The computer _____ is in the other room.

7 James threw out the plastic cups. They were already used.

→ James threw out the plastic cups _____ .

8 Ms. Lopez is a famous artist. We saw her at the gallery.

→ Ms. Lopez is a famous artist _____ .

9 I still remember the tree. We planted it five years ago.

→ I still remember the tree _____ .

10 The man called me last night. I met him at the gym.

→ The man _____ called me last night.

1 Luke는 내가 좋아하는 소년이다. (the boy, like)

= Luke is _____ .

2 나는 Clara가 보낸 이메일을 받았다. (an e-mail, sent)

= I received _____ .

3 Jacob은 나에게 그가 읽은 책을 줬다. (the book, read)

= Jacob gave me _____ .

4 내가 사용하는 그 프린터는 잉크가 다 떨어졌다. (the printer, use)

= _____ is out of ink.

5 우리가 본 그 학생들은 캐나다인이었다. (the students, saw)

= _____ were Canadians.

6 Jane은 그녀가 고등학교에서 만난 남자와 결혼했다. (the man, met)

= Jane married _____ in high school.

7 페니실린은 Alexander Fleming이 발견한 약이다. (the medicine, discovered)

= Penicillin is _____ .

8 나는 그가 길에서 파는 핫도그를 먹고 있다. (the hotdog, sells)

= I'm eating _____ on the street.

9 다람쥐는 그들이 겨울 동안 먹을 음식을 모은다. (food, will eat)

= Squirrels collect _____ during the winter.

10 우리가 뉴스에서 본 그 소방관은 힘이 셌다. (the firefighter, saw)

= _____ on the news was strong.

11 그녀가 책상 밑에서 발견한 그 연필은 나의 것이다. (the pencil, found)

= _____ under the desk was mine.

12 Nathan은 그가 지하철에 두고 온 그의 배낭을 결코 찾지 못했다. (his backpack, left)

= Nathan never found _____ on the subway.

기출 적중문제 ◎

관계대명사를 이용하여 다음 두 문장을 한 문장으로 연결하시오.

> The festival offered a lot of activities. We
> enjoyed them.

→ The festival offered _____ .

기출로적중 POINT 2-3 소유격 관계대명사

소유격 관계대명사는 관계대명사절 안에서 소유격의 역할을 하며, 선행사와 상관없이 **whose**를 쓴다. 소유격 관계대명사 뒤에는 소유의 대상이 되는 명사가 온다.

This is **my cousin**. **Her name** is Ella. 이 사람은 나의 사촌이다. 그녀의 이름은 Ella이다.

→ This is **my cousin whose name** is Ella. 이 사람은 이름이 Ella인 나의 사촌이다.

He lives in **a house**. **Its** swimming pool is large. 그는 집에 산다. 그것의 수영장은 크다.

→ He lives in **a house whose swimming pool** is large. 그는 수영장이 큰 집에 산다.

연습문제 관계대명사를 이용하여 다음 두 문장을 한 문장으로 연결하시오.

1 Coco is the rabbit. Its hair is white.

→ Coco is the rabbit _____.

2 She is the woman. Her son is a lawyer.

→ She is the woman _____.

3 I like the singer. His voice sounds amazing.

→ I like the singer _____.

4 The boy looks depressed. His phone is missing.

→ The boy _____ looks depressed.

5 Ms. Hall is the writer. Her books are popular among teens.

→ Ms. Hall is the writer _____.

6 My brother has a bicycle. Its brake is broken.

→ My brother has a bicycle _____.

7 Let's rest under the tree. Its leaves are very large.

→ Let's rest under the tree _____.

8 Timothy is my neighbor. His house has five rooms.

→ Timothy is my neighbor _____.

9 These are the students. Their test scores are over 90.

→ These are the students _____.

10 I watched the movie. Its director won three awards.

→ I watched the movie _____.

11 They are the couple. Their baby cries too much at night.

→ They are the couple _____.

관계대명사 that

정답 p.52

1. **관계대명사 that은 선행사와 상관없이 주격이나 목적격 관계대명사로 쓰인다.**

   Surin has **a brother that[who]** plays the piano well.
   수린이는 피아노를 잘 연주하는 오빠가 있다.

   Would you like to have **the muffins that[which]** I made?
   너는 내가 만든 머핀을 먹기를 원하니?

   (Tip) that은 명사절 접속사로도 쓰인다.
   　　I think **that** Josh is very polite. 나는 Josh가 매우 공손하다고 생각한다.

2. **선행사에 다음이 포함될 때 주로 관계대명사 that을 사용한다.**

사람 + 사물/동물	Look at **the man and the tiger that** are in this picture. 이 그림에 있는 남자와 호랑이를 봐.
최상급, 서수	Ken is **the tallest person that** I've ever seen. Ken은 내가 본 사람들 중에서 가장 키가 큰 사람이다.
the only, the same, the very	Susie has **the same purse that** I have. Susie는 내가 가지고 있는 같은 지갑을 가지고 있다.
-thing/-body로 끝나는 대명사	He's looking for **somebody that** can speak Chinese. 그는 중국어를 말할 수 있는 누군가를 찾고 있다.
all, no, little, much 등	These stories are **all that** I can tell you. 이 이야기들이 내가 너에게 말해줄 수 있는 전부이다.

연습문제 A 밑줄 친 that과 바꿔 쓸 수 있는 말을 모두 쓰시오.

1 She wants a robot <u>that</u> helps her clean the house.　　→ _____

2 Change the battery in the clock <u>that</u> is on the wall.　　→ _____

3 Lincoln is a president <u>that</u> many Americans admire.　　→ _____

4 Thomas is my friend <u>that</u> runs with me once a week.　　→ _____

5 Are you the person <u>that</u> ordered pizza?　　→ _____

6 The flowers <u>that</u> he bought for her were pretty.　　→ _____

7 Minho is my neighbor <u>that</u> I see every morning.　　→ _____

8 The politician <u>that</u> is making a speech on TV is my grandfather.　　→ _____

연습문제 B 관계대명사 that을 이용하여 다음 두 문장을 한 문장으로 연결하시오.

1 Elena wants something. She can eat it quickly.

→ _____

2 The beaver is the only animal. It builds dams.

→ _____

3 Is this the last bus? It goes to Gangnam.

→ _____

4 Kelly bought the same watch. I purchased it online.

→ _____

5 Cameron sat on the first chair. He saw it.

→ _____

6 There is somebody. He is knocking on the door.

→ _____

7 There are some cows and a farmer. They are resting under the tree.

→ _____

연습문제 C 밑줄 친 that의 쓰임과 같은 것을 <보기>에서 골라 그 기호를 쓰시오.

> **<보기>** ⓐ Ollie has a new bed that is soft.
> ⓑ I think that I need a vacation.

1 Jess sent the letter that she finished writing. [   ]
2 Jinho said that he can surf in the ocean. [   ]
3 I believe that Hannah should stop blaming others. [   ]
4 This is the medicine that will keep you from coughing. [   ]
5 Lisa and I wrapped the present that we'll give Julie. [   ]
6 It is true that the Internet has made our lives more convenient. [   ]

기출 적중문제

다음 중 밑줄 친 that의 쓰임이 나머지 넷과 다른 것은?

① Matt is the boy that is wearing a blue cap.
② I don't believe anything that Jeremy says.
③ I think that we should eat more vegetables.
④ This is the only shop that sells shoes for babies.
⑤ The first book that Mr. Jones wrote was excellent.

> 관계대명사 that은 불완전한 절을 이끌고, 명사절 접속사 that은 완전한 절을 이끌어요.

관계대명사 what

정답 p.52

관계대명사 what은 선행사를 포함하고 있으며, '~한 것'이라는 의미이다. 관계대명사 what
은 the thing which[that]으로 바꿔 쓸 수 있다.

What I want most is a new smartphone. 내가 가장 원하는 것은 새 스마트폰이다.
= **The thing which[that]** I want most is a new smartphone.

Alice showed me **what** she drew. Alice는 나에게 그녀가 그린 것을 보여줬다.
= Alice showed me **the thing which[that]** she drew.

(Tip) what은 '무엇, 무슨'이라는 의미의 의문사로도 쓰인다.
Can you tell me **what** the problem is? 나에게 무엇이 문제인지 말해주겠니?

연습문제 | 괄호 안에서 what이나 which 중 알맞은 것을 고르시오.

1 I can't believe (what / which) I just heard.

2 The flowers (what / which) I planted were roses.

3 Carl gave me a box (what / which) was full of chocolate.

4 Tina asked (what / which) I had for dinner.

5 (What / Which) made me angry was his rude behavior.

6 (What / Which) Mary wants for her birthday is a pet turtle.

7 Fruit (what / which) grows in hot weather is often sweet.

8 This is the new backpack (what / which) Jisu bought.

9 There are some cars (what / which) are parked along the road.

10 Jim couldn't remember (what / which) he dreamed last night.

11 I carefully thought about (what / which) you said yesterday.

12 (What / Which) my grandmother told me really moved me.

13 The doctor didn't know (what / which) made the patient so sick.

기출 적중문제

우리말과 같도록 괄호 안의 말을 활용하여 문장을 완성하시오. (단, 3단어로 쓰시오.)

Leonard가 필요한 것은 약간의 수면이다. (needs)

= _____ is some sleep.

POINT 5 관계대명사의 생략

정답 p.53

> **1. 목적격 관계대명사 who(m), which, that은 생략할 수 있다.**
>
> He is a boy **(whom)** I met at the concert. 그는 내가 콘서트에서 만난 소년이다.
> I recommend the movie **(which)** I saw last week. 나는 내가 지난주에 본 그 영화를 추천한다.
> Ben is the only person **(that)** we can trust. Ben은 우리가 믿을 수 있는 유일한 사람이다.
>
> **2. 「주격 관계대명사 + be동사」는 생략할 수 있다.**
>
> I know that man **(who is)** waving at us. 나는 우리에게 손을 흔들고 있는 저 남자를 안다.
> Vegetables **(which are)** sold in this market are fresh. 이 시장에서 판매되는 채소들은 신선하다.
> The last piece of cake **(that is)** on the plate is Jiho's.
> 접시 위에 있는 마지막 케이크 조각은 지호의 것이다.

연습문제 A 다음 문장에서 생략할 수 있는 부분에 밑줄을 치시오.

1 She is the girl whom I used to like.

2 Joey is my friend who is scared of the dark.

3 I'm reading the book which is written in English.

4 Katie ate the pasta that she cooked by herself.

5 The radio DJ played the song that I requested.

6 Howard answered the quiz that was in the magazine.

7 The butter which I bought yesterday was organic.

8 There is a large statue which is standing in the park.

9 Bomin is the smartest student that I know.

10 Mr. Johnson is an American soldier who is living in Korea.

연습문제 B 밑줄 친 부분을 생략할 수 있으면 O를 쓰고, 생략할 수 없으면 X를 쓰시오.

1 That girl <u>who is</u> acting on the stage is my older sister. → _____

2 Evan is eating the cheese <u>which</u> he brought from France. → _____

3 I have some friends <u>who</u> play the guitar very well. → _____

4 Sally talked to her neighbor <u>who was</u> walking the dog. → _____

5 Marcus collects stamps <u>that</u> are from other countries. → _____

6 I like the pie <u>which is</u> made by my grandmother. → _____

7 Is he the same person that we saw in the TV show? → _____

8 I found the vase which was buried in the garden. → _____

9 Mark forgot to hand in the report which he wrote last night. → _____

연습문제 C 우리말과 같도록 괄호 안의 말을 알맞게 배열하시오.

1 Charlie가 산 집은 해변 가까이에 있다. (Charlie, bought, the house)

= _____ is near the beach.

2 나에게 네가 너의 여행에서 찍은 사진들을 보여줘라. (the pictures, took, you)

= Show me _____ on your trip.

3 나는 내가 테니스 수업에서 만난 그 소녀와 함께 점심을 먹었다. (I, the girl, met)

= I had lunch with _____ at the tennis lesson.

4 Brown 씨에 의해 쓰인 소설들은 어디에 있니? (by Mr. Brown, written, the novels)

= Where are _____ ?

5 민수는 나에게 그가 어제 너에게 말해줬던 같은 농담을 말해줬다. (the same joke, told, he)

= Minsu told me _____ you yesterday.

6 내가 숲속에서 찾은 버섯은 독이 있었다. (found, the mushroom, I)

= _____ in the forest was poisonous.

7 내가 어제 인터뷰한 그 유명 인사는 아주 친절했다. (interviewed, I, the celebrity)

= _____ yesterday was really nice.

8 도서관에서 햄버거를 먹고 있는 저 학생은 누구니? (a hamburger, that student, eating)

= Who is _____ in the library?

9 지도를 보고 있는 그 남자는 관광객처럼 보인다. (at the map, looking, the man)

= _____ looks like a tourist.

10 소방관들은 불타는 집 안에 있는 그 사람들을 구했다. (the people, in the burning house)

= The firefighters saved _____ .

기출 적중문제

다음 중 밑줄 친 부분을 생략할 수 있는 것을 모두 고르시오.

① He wants to be a model whom everyone knows.

② I enjoy watching movies that have happy endings.

③ Holly is looking for the book whose cover is yellow.

④ The girl who is sitting beside me is very noisy.

⑤ Tony returned the pants which were too small for him.

> 목적격 관계대명사와 「주격 관계대명사 + be동사」는 생략할 수 있어요.

POINT 6 전치사 + 관계대명사

정답 p.53

관계대명사가 전치사의 목적어인 경우 전치사는 관계대명사절의 맨 뒤나 관계대명사 바로 앞에 온다. 전치사가 관계대명사 바로 앞에 올 때는 목적격 관계대명사를 생략할 수 없다.

Gina is **the girl**. I talked **about her**. Gina는 그 소녀이다. 나는 그녀에 대해 말했다.

→ Gina is **the girl** (who/whom/that) I talked **about**. Gina는 내가 말했던 그 소녀이다.

→ Gina is **the girl** about <u>whom</u> I talked.

└→ 전치사 바로 뒤에는 관계대명사 who나 that을 쓸 수 없다.

I need **a pen**. I can write **with it**. 나는 펜이 필요하다. 나는 그것으로 쓸 수 있다.

→ I need **a pen** (which/that) I can write **with**. 나는 내가 쓸 수 있는 펜이 필요하다.

→ I need **a pen** with which I can write.

연습문제 <보기>와 같이 관계대명사를 이용하여 다음 두 문장을 한 문장으로 연결하시오. (단, 관계대명사는 생략하지 마시오.)

<보기> Tom is my friend. I can depend on him.

  → *Tom is my friend who[whom/that] I can depend on.*

  → *Tom is my friend on whom I can depend.*

1 This is the toy mouse. My cat plays with it.

→ _____

→ _____

2 I know the man. You were speaking to him.

→ _____

→ _____

3 I visited the Opera House. Sydney is famous for it.

→ _____

→ _____

기출 적중문제

다음 밑줄 친 ⓐ~ⓔ 중 어법상 어색한 것을 찾아 기호를 쓰고 바르게 고쳐 쓰시오.

The <u>house</u> in <u>that</u> Fred <u>lives</u> <u>has</u> <u>many</u> windows.
     ⓐ   ⓑ   ⓒ   ⓓ   ⓔ

전치사 바로 뒤에는 that이 올 수 없어요.

_____ → _____

관계부사는 관계부사절을 이끄는 접속사 역할과 부사 역할을 하며, 장소, 시간, 이유, 방법을 나타낸다. 관계부사는 「전치사 + 관계대명사」로 바꿔 쓸 수 있다.

	선행사	관계부사	「전치사 + 관계대명사」
장소	the place, the city, the house 등	where	in/on/at/to + which
시간	the time, the year, the day 등	when	in/on/at + which
이유	the reason	why	for + which
방법	the way	how	in + which

Paris is **the city**. The Eiffel Tower is **in that city**. 파리는 도시이다. 에펠탑은 그 도시에 있다.
→ Paris is **the city** where[in which] the Eiffel Tower is. 파리는 에펠탑이 있는 도시이다.

7 o'clock is **the time**. Susan wakes up **at that time**. 7시는 시간이다. Susan은 그 시간에 일어난다.
→ 7 o'clock is **the time** when[at which] Susan wakes up. 7시는 Susan이 일어나는 시간이다.

I know **the reason**. He is upset **for that reason**. 나는 이유를 안다. 그는 그 이유로 화가 났다.
→ I know **the reason** why[for which] he is upset. 나는 그가 화가 난 이유를 안다.

Show me **the way**. You made it **in that way**. 나에게 방법을 보여줘라. 너는 그 방법으로 그것을 만들었다.
→ Show me **how** you made it. 나에게 네가 그것을 만든 방법을 보여줘라.
 └→ the way와 how는 둘 중 하나만 쓸 수 있다.
→ Show me **the way** (in which) you made it.

(Tip) 선행사가 the place나 the time과 같은 일반적인 명사인 경우 선행사나 관계부사 둘 중 하나를 생략할 수 있다.
Do you remember (**the place**) **where** we first met? 너는 우리가 처음 만난 장소를 기억하니?
= Do you remember **the place** (**where**) we first met?

연습문제 A 다음 빈칸에 알맞은 관계부사를 쓰시오.

1 May was the month _____ George moved to Korea.

2 He explained the reason _____ he didn't like cats.

3 Tomorrow is the day _____ we're going on a field trip.

4 School is the place _____ students spend most of their time.

5 Could you tell me _____ I can get a better grade in science?

6 The hospital _____ I was born turned into a shopping center.

연습문제 B 관계부사를 이용하여 다음 두 문장을 한 문장으로 연결하시오.

1 I'm going to visit the house. Monet lived in that house.
→ I'm going to visit the house _____.

2 Let me show you the way. You can solve the problem in this way.
→ Let me show you _____.

3 Beth told us the reason. She quit drinking soda for this reason.
→ Beth told us the reason _____.

4 April 5 is the day. We plant trees on that day.
→ April 5 is the day _____.

5 Do you know the way? He built the robot in that way.
→ Do you know _____?

6 There are a few regions. Coffee beans grow in those regions.
→ There are a few regions _____.

7 John remembers the day. He graduated from middle school on that day.
→ John remembers the day _____.

8 Global warming is the reason. Glaciers are melting for that reason.
→ Global warming is the reason _____.

9 This is the restaurant. I eat lunch every day at this restaurant.
→ This is the restaurant _____.

10 1953 is the year. The Korean War ended in that year.
→ 1953 is the year _____.

11 I hope to learn the way. My grandma cooked the soup in that way.
→ I hope to learn _____.

12 Is there any reason? You were late for school for this reason.
→ Is there any reason _____?

기출 적중문제

우리말과 같도록 괄호 안의 말과 관계부사를 활용하여 문장을 완성하시오.

이곳은 그들이 주말마다 야구를 하는 공원이다. (the park, play)

= This is _____
every weekend.

서술형 대비 문제

Ⓐ 빈칸에 알맞은 말을 <보기>에서 골라 관계대명사를 이용하여 쓰시오. (단, that은 쓰지 마시오.)

<보기>
color is orange	tail is long and black
everyone can trust	was drawn by Picasso
filmed popular movies	I played yesterday

1 Mr. Nolan is the director _____.

2 A carrot is a vegetable _____.

3 The painting _____ is in London.

4 The online game _____ wasn't fun.

5 We are looking for a cat _____.

6 Colin is a responsible student _____.

Ⓑ 우리말과 같도록 괄호 안의 말을 알맞게 배열하시오.

1 나는 내가 전에 잃어버린 지갑을 찾았다. (I, the wallet, lost, that)
= I found _____ before.

2 너는 너의 부모님이 말씀하시는 것을 들어야 한다. (your parents, what, say)
= You should listen to _____.

3 이것은 나의 집에서 학교로 가는 유일한 버스이다. (goes, that, the only bus)
= This is _____ to school from my house.

4 네가 필요한 것은 좋은 친구이다. (need, what, you)
= _____ is a good friend.

5 유빈이는 나에게 나의 목을 따뜻하게 유지할 목도리를 줬다. (a muffler, will keep, that)
= Yubin gave me _____ my neck warm.

6 태준이는 그가 표지판에서 읽은 것을 무시했다. (what, read, he)
= Taejun ignored _____ on the sign.

7 Eric이 그린 공룡은 티라노사우루스였다. (that, Eric, drew, the dinosaur)
= _____ was a Tyrannosaurs.

8 나를 놀라게 한 것은 줄을 서 있는 사람들의 수였다. (me, surprised, what)
= _____ was the number of people in the line.

C 다음 문장에서 생략된 부분을 넣어 완전한 문장을 쓰시오.

1 The horse I rode yesterday was gentle.

→ _____

2 I tried to catch the ball rolling down the stairs.

→ _____

3 Frank read a book written in 1999.

→ _____

4 I want to be a class president everyone likes.

→ _____

5 I miss my friend I met at summer camp last year.

→ _____

6 The Korean alphabet King Sejong invented is called Hangeul.

→ _____

7 The passenger sitting behind me keeps kicking my seat.

→ _____

D 다음 글의 빈칸에 알맞은 관계대명사나 관계부사를 쓰시오.

1

The Southwest Music Festival is the place ⓐ_____ my friends and I go every year. The festival is held in spring ⓑ_____ the weather becomes warm. During the festival, many bands play live music ⓒ_____ everyone can enjoy. Therefore, I'm sure that people ⓓ_____ enjoy music will have fun at the festival. Why don't you join us next time?

2

Do you want to try some amazing pizza? At Say Cheese Pizzeria, our pizzas are made by a skillful chef ⓐ_____ studied traditional pizza-making in Italy. We use dough ⓑ_____ is soft and fresh. We also allow you to choose your own toppings from our various ingredients. This is ⓒ_____ we make our incredible pizzas. The great taste of our pizza is the reason ⓓ_____ our customers are always satisfied. If you want a slice, visit Say Cheese Pizzeria today!

1 다음 빈칸에 들어갈 알맞은 것은?

> I'm eating the pancake _____ my dad made.

① who   ② whom   ③ whose
④ which   ⑤ what

2 다음 빈칸에 들어갈 말이 순서대로 짝지어진 것은?

> · She threw away the can _____ was empty.
> · Aaron called the man _____ dropped the wallet on the street.

① who – who   ② who – that
③ which – which   ④ which – who
⑤ that – which

3 다음 두 문장을 한 문장으로 바르게 연결한 것은?

> We tried the new Mexican dish. It was very spicy.

① We tried the new Mexican dish was very spicy.
② We tried the new Mexican dish who was very spicy.
③ We tried the new Mexican dish what was very spicy.
④ We tried the new Mexican dish which was very spicy.
⑤ The new Mexican dish was very spicy we tried.

4 다음 중 어법상 바른 것은?

① Daniel likes the girl which is in his class.
② Emily hopes to be a doctor what saves people.
③ I don't know the boy and his dog that are standing at the front door.
④ There is a bee who is gathering honey from flowers.
⑤ She is sitting on a chair whose is made of wood.

5 다음 빈칸에 공통으로 들어갈 알맞은 것은?

> · Narae takes yoga lessons _____ her older sister teaches.
> · We believe _____ a new class rule is needed.
> · An architect is a person _____ designs buildings.

① which   ② who   ③ whom
④ whose   ⑤ that

6 다음 문장에서 어법상 어색한 부분을 찾아 쓰고 바르게 고쳐 쓰시오.

> Ronald knows the man whom plays the cello in the orchestra.

_____ → _____

7 다음 중 밑줄 친 that의 쓰임이 나머지 넷과 다른 것은?

① The toys that Mr. Miller makes are all safe.
② The article that I read was about traveling.
③ The children that live next door are twins.
④ Michael is the boy that I met at the theater.
⑤ Noah repaired the laptop that I broke.

8 다음 빈칸에 들어갈 알맞은 것을 모두 고르시오.

> My parents sold _____ that were kept in our garage.

① the car
② the lamps
③ the bicycle
④ the blanket
⑤ the old books

9 주어진 문장의 밑줄 친 that과 쓰임이 같은 것은?

> The story that Harry told me wasn't true.

① Can you carry that box for me?
② I thought that his advice was useless.
③ Sumin won that in the dance contest.
④ We heard that the elevator isn't working.
⑤ Look at the ducks that are swimming in the pond.

10 우리말과 같도록 괄호 안의 말을 활용하여 빈칸에 쓰시오.

> Luna는 나를 많이 도와주는 나의 친구이다.
> (friend, help)

= Luna is _____ _____ _____ _____ me a lot.

11 다음 대화의 빈칸에 들어갈 알맞은 것은?

> A: Do you remember the time _____ the movie starts?
> B: Of course. It starts at 5:30.

① where
② when
③ how
④ why
⑤ what

12 다음 두 문장의 의미가 같도록 빈칸에 알맞은 관계부사를 쓰시오.

> A heavy thunderstorm was the reason for which the game was canceled.
> = A heavy thunderstorm was the reason _____ the game was canceled.

13 다음 중 밑줄 친 부분이 어법상 어색한 것은?

The basketball player who score the
①　　　　　②　　③
most points on the team is injured.
　　　　　　　　　　④　　⑤

14 다음 빈칸에 that이 들어갈 수 없는 것은?

① Tell me everything _____ you know about the rumor.
② The castle _____ is on the hill was built in the 17th century.
③ Humans are not the only animals _____ can use tools.
④ Liam lives in the house _____ roof is red.
⑤ I respect people _____ are polite and generous.

15 다음 두 문장을 한 문장으로 바르게 연결한 것을 모두 고르시오.

Jerry is the boy. He is playing badminton with Amy.

① Jerry is the boy who is playing badminton with Amy.
② Jerry is the boy who playing badminton with Amy.
③ Jerry is the boy what is playing badminton with Amy.
④ Jerry is the boy playing badminton with Amy.
⑤ Jerry is the boy is playing badminton with Amy.

16 다음 중 밑줄 친 that의 쓰임이 나머지 넷과 다른 것은?

① Linda's dad knows that she lied to him.
② It is exciting that I won the marathon.
③ Did you think that I was going to be late?
④ I believe that health is more important than money.
⑤ Any student that has a fever should go to the nurse's office.

17 다음 중 어느 빈칸에도 들어갈 수 없는 것은?

· Helen made the soup with potatoes _____ she grew.
· We have a new student _____ name is Emma.
· The store is looking for a new worker _____ is responsible.

① which　　② that　　③ what
④ whose　　⑤ who

18 다음 영화 평가표를 보고 관계대명사를 이용하여 문장을 완성하시오.

<Movie Review: *The Jungle Book*>

Reviewer	Review
Mac06	All family members can watch the movie together.
Joan_s	The movie's special effects are amazing.

(1) *The Jungle Book* is a movie _____

_____.

(2) *The Jungle Book* is a movie _____

_____.

19 다음 중 밑줄 친 what의 쓰임이 나머지 넷과 다른 것은?

① These shoes aren't <u>what</u> Sora decided to buy.
② <u>What</u> he ordered was tastier than mine.
③ Gary showed me <u>what</u> he was drawing.
④ Italian is <u>what</u> I plan to learn this summer.
⑤ Nobody in the room knows <u>what</u> my name is.

[20-21] 알맞은 관계대명사를 이용하여 다음 두 문장을 한 문장으로 연결하시오.

20

I borrowed a pen. Its color was blue.

→ _____

_____

21

We should help the child. She lost her cat.

→ _____

_____

22 다음 중 밑줄 친 부분을 생략할 수 <u>없는</u> 것은?

① The nurse called the patient <u>whom</u> the doctor asked for.
② We liked the salad <u>which</u> Erica made.
③ Ann is my cousin <u>who</u> I live with.
④ The avocado is a fruit <u>that</u> grows on a tree.
⑤ The vase <u>that</u> she broke was more than 100 years old.

23 우리말과 같도록 괄호 안의 말을 알맞게 배열하시오.

내가 필요한 것은 매일 운동하는 것이다. (I, to, every, exercise, need, what, day, is)

= _____

24 다음 우리말을 알맞게 영작한 것은?

진수가 들고 있던 그 사전은 무거웠다.

① Jinsu was holding the dictionary what was heavy.
② Jinsu which the dictionary was holding was heavy.
③ Jinsu which was was holding by the dictionary was heavy.
④ The dictionary which was holding Jinsu was heavy.
⑤ The dictionary which Jinsu was holding was heavy.

25 다음 중 어법상 <u>어색한</u> 것끼리 묶인 것은?

ⓐ There are some flowers that blooms at night.
ⓑ He is a ballerino which performs as the swan prince.
ⓒ I'm planning to visit the house in which Hemingway was born.
ⓓ I'm eating a snack what is called poutine.
ⓔ Robin broke the wooden toy that he was playing with.

① ⓐ, ⓑ, ⓒ   ② ⓐ, ⓑ, ⓓ   ③ ⓐ, ⓒ, ⓓ
④ ⓑ, ⓒ, ⓔ   ⑤ ⓒ, ⓓ, ⓔ

26 주어진 문장의 밑줄 친 who와 쓰임이 같은 것은?

> My aunt is the woman who has green eyes.

① Who are you eating lunch with this afternoon?
② Did the police find out who broke into the bank?
③ Vivaldi is the composer who wrote *The Four Seasons*.
④ I'm not sure who you are talking about.
⑤ We didn't know who was invited to Oliver's party.

27 다음 중 밑줄 친 부분을 생략할 수 있는 것은?

① Ms. Davis is the teacher whom I like most.
② I bought a necklace which was quite expensive.
③ Monica watched a video which made her cry.
④ Jihoon has two younger brothers that are cute.
⑤ The man who is resting on the sofa is my grandpa.

28 다음 빈칸에 공통으로 들어갈 알맞은 말을 쓰시오.

> · She was the greatest author _____ wrote more than ten best sellers.
> · The girl and the unicorn _____ are shown in the film look mysterious.
> · The only thing _____ I remember from the musical is the costumes.

29 다음 중 어법상 어색한 것을 모두 고르시오.

① Do you know the reason why Dan was late for school?
② The Internet has changed the way how people shop.
③ Mr. Adams is the chef who cook the most delicious steak in town.
④ I saw an alien whose eyes were red and scary in the movie.
⑤ A parrot is one of the animals that can talk.

30 다음 그림을 보고 괄호 안의 말을 알맞게 배열하시오.

> Paris _____
> someday. (visit, I, the, to, city, is, want, which)

31 다음 문장에서 틀린 부분을 바르게 고쳐 완전한 문장을 쓰시오.

> Jason is the astronaut about who I told you.
>
> → _____
> _____

32 다음 중 밑줄 친 부분을 생략할 수 있는 것의 개수는?

ⓐ Lots of money was in the bag which Carol found on the street.
ⓑ Marie Curie is the only woman that has won two Nobel Prizes.
ⓒ I went to the gallery which has many great sculptures.
ⓓ There is a person who is screaming loudly outside.
ⓔ Let's go to the Chinese restaurant which is located on Main Street.

① 1개　　② 2개　　③ 3개
④ 4개　　⑤ 5개

33 다음 (A)~(C)에 들어갈 말이 바르게 짝지어진 것은?

Angela is my best friend, and we are like sisters. We have many things in common. We both like the teacher ___(A)___ teaches science. Also, she is my classmate who ___(B)___ the same homework with me every day. Moreover, we love to eat the chocolate croissants ___(C)___ are sold at Greta's Bakery after school.

	(A)	(B)	(C)
①	who	do	which
②	which	does	whose
③	who	do	whose
④	which	does	that
⑤	who	does	which

34 주어진 <조건>에 맞게 다음 두 문장을 한 문장으로 연결하시오.

This park is the place. I usually take a walk in this place.

<조건>
1. 관계부사를 이용하시오.
2. the place를 활용하시오.

→ _____
_____

35 다음은 형사 Holmes가 조사한 내용이다. <보기>와 같이 관계대명사를 이용하여 문장을 완성하시오.

Holmes's memo

Name	What they did at 8 o'clock
Jamie	He answered the phone.
Chloe	She was talking to Jamie on the phone.
Martha	She went to see Minjun.
Bill	He was cooking dinner.

<보기>　Jamie is the boy _who[that] answered the phone_ .

(1) Chloe is the girl _____
_____ .

(2) Minjun is the boy _____
_____ .

(3) Bill is the boy _____
_____ .

CHAPTER 17
가정법

If I **were** tall enough, I **could ride** the roller coaster.
만약 내가 충분히 키가 크다면, 롤러코스터를 탈 수 있을 텐데.

위 문장은 내가 현재 충분히 키가 크지 않아서 롤러코스터를 못 타지만, 만약 충분히 키가 크다면 롤러코스터를 탈 수 있을 것이라고 가정하여 말하고 있어요. 이렇게 사실과 반대되거나 실현 가능성이 매우 작은 일을 가정하여 말하는 것을 **가정법**이라고 해요.

기출로 적중 POINT

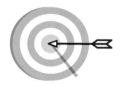

내신 100점 적중!
기출 출제율

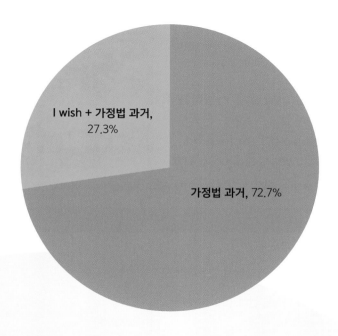

I wish + 가정법 과거, 27.3%

가정법 과거, 72.7%

TOP 1 **가정법 과거 (72.7%)**
가정법 과거의 형태와 쓰임을 묻는 문제와 가정법 문장을 직설법 문장으로 바꾸는 문제가 자주 출제된다.

TOP 2 **I wish + 가정법 과거 (27.3%)**
「I wish + 가정법 과거」의 의미와 형태를 묻는 문제가 자주 출제된다.

POINT 1-1 가정법 과거

1. **가정법 과거는 '만약 ~한다면 …할 텐데'의 의미로 현재의 사실과 반대되거나 실현 가능성이 매우 작은 일을 가정할 때 쓴다.**

If	+	주어	+	동사의 과거형 (be동사는 were)	~	주어	+	would, could should, might	+	동사원형	…

└─────────────────── if절 ───────────────────┘ └─────────────── 주절 ───────────────┘

If I **lived** here, I **could see** you more often. 만약 내가 여기에 산다면, 너를 더 자주 볼 수 있을 텐데.

If I **didn't have** homework, I **would play** outside. 만약 내가 숙제가 없다면, 밖에서 놀 텐데.

If I **were** you, I **wouldn't trust** him. 만약 내가 너라면, 그를 믿지 않을 텐데.

(Tip) 가정법은 실현 가능성이 매우 작은 일을 가정할 때 쓰고, 조건문은 현재나 미래에 일어날 수 있는 상황을 나타낼 때 쓴다. 조건문에서는 미래를 나타내더라도 현재시제를 쓴다.

가정법 If I **were** free, I **would** help you. 만약 내가 한가하다면, 너를 도울 텐데. (내가 한가할 가능성이 매우 작음)

조건문 If I **am** free, I **will** help you. 만약 내가 한가하다면, 너를 도울 것이다. (내가 한가할 가능성이 있음)

2. **가정법 과거 문장은 as나 so를 사용하는 직설법 문장으로 바꿔 쓸 수 있으며, 이때 현재시제를 쓴다.**

If I **were** 20 years old, I **could drive**. 만약 내가 스무 살이라면, 운전할 수 있을 텐데.

→ **As** I **am not** 20 years old, I **can't drive**. 나는 스무 살이 아니기 때문에, 운전할 수 없다.

→ I **am not** 20 years old, **so** I **can't drive**. 나는 스무 살이 아니라서, 운전할 수 없다.

연습문제 A 우리말과 같도록 괄호 안의 말을 활용하여 문장을 완성하시오.

1 만약 내가 부자라면, 세계를 여행할 텐데. (be, travel)

= If I _____ rich, I _____ the world.

2 만약 내가 정답을 안다면, 너에게 말해줄 텐데. (know, tell)

= If I _____ the answer, I _____ you.

3 만약 내가 너라면, Emily에게 사과할 텐데. (be, apologize)

= If I _____ you, I _____ to Emily.

4 만약 이 반지가 비싸지 않다면, 그녀는 그것을 살 수 있을 텐데. (be, buy)

= If this ring _____ expensive, she _____ it.

5 만약 그가 복권에 당첨된다면, 그의 부모님께 집을 사드릴 텐데. (win, buy)

= If he _____ the lottery, he _____ his parents a house.

6 만약 Rachel이 자전거를 가지고 있다면, 학교에 걸어가지 않을 텐데. (have, walk)

= If Rachel _____ a bike, she _____ to school.

7 만약 Josh가 그의 집에 나를 초대한다면, 나는 그를 방문할 텐데. (invite, visit)

= If Josh _____ me to his house, I _____ him.

8 만약 날씨가 화창하다면, 우리는 해변에 갈 수 있을 텐데. (be, go)

= If it _____ sunny, we _____ to the beach.

9 만약 그가 한국어를 말한다면, 나는 그와 이야기할 수 있을 텐데. (speak, have)

= If he _____ Korean, I _____ a conversation with him.

연습문제 B 다음 문장을 가정법 문장으로 바꿔 쓰시오.

1 As I'm sick, I can't go to school today.

→ _____

2 Lisa is shy, so she won't talk to strangers.

→ _____

3 As I don't have a brother or a sister, I am lonely.

→ _____

4 The suitcase is heavy, so he can't carry it.

→ _____

5 As the wind blows, I feel chilly.

→ _____

6 As you don't know how to ski, we can't ski together.

→ _____

7 As the air conditioner doesn't work, this room is hot.

→ _____

8 The concert tickets are sold out, so I am disappointed.

→ _____

기출 적중문제

다음 문장을 직설법 문장으로 바꿔 쓰시오.

If I weren't tired, I could play soccer with you.

→ As I _____

_____ .

가정법 과거완료

정답 p.55

1. 가정법 과거완료는 '만약 ~했더라면 …했을 텐데'의 의미로 과거의 사실과 반대되는 일을 가정할 때 쓴다.

If	+	주어	+	had + p.p.	~,	주어	+	would, could should, might	+	have + p.p.	…

　　　　　　　if절　　　　　　　　　　　　　주절

If she **had studied** harder, she **could have gotten** a better grade.
만약 그녀가 더 열심히 공부했더라면, 더 좋은 점수를 받을 수 있었을 텐데.

If I **had brought** my umbrella, I **wouldn't have bought** a new one.
만약 내가 나의 우산을 가져왔더라면, 새 것을 사지 않았을 텐데.

2. 가정법 과거완료 문장을 as나 so를 사용하는 직설법 문장으로 바꿔 쓸 때는 과거시제를 쓴다.

If the water **had not been** cold, I **could have swum** in the river.
만약 물이 차갑지 않았더라면, 나는 강에서 수영할 수 있었을 텐데.
→ **As** the water **was** cold, I **couldn't swim** in the river.
　물이 차가웠기 때문에, 나는 강에서 수영할 수 없었다.
→ The water **was** cold, **so** I **couldn't swim** in the river.
　물이 차가워서, 나는 강에서 수영할 수 없었다.

연습문제　괄호 안의 말을 활용하여 가정법 과거완료 문장을 완성하시오.

1 If I _____ your number, I would have called you. (know)

2 If I had been more careful, I _____ my phone. (will, not, drop)

3 If I had not woken up early, I _____ the beautiful sunrise. (will, miss)

4 If the bus _____ late, I would have missed the class. (arrive)

5 If the question _____ easier, Liam could have answered it. (be)

6 If the floor had not been slippery, my sister _____ down. (will, not, fall)

7 If he _____ to the concert, he would have enjoyed himself. (come)

8 If the book had been more interesting, Mina _____ reading it. (will, finish)

9 If the oven _____ so hot, the cake wouldn't have burned. (not, be)

10 If it had not rained so much, we _____ camping. (can, go)

11 If I _____ to water the plant, it could have lived. (not, forget)

정답 p.56

I wish + 가정법 과거

「I wish + 가정법 과거」는 '~하면 좋을 텐데'라는 의미로 현재 이룰 수 없거나 실현 가능성이 매우 작은 일을 소망할 때 쓴다.

| I wish | + | 주어 | + | 동사의 과거형 (be동사는 were) |

I wish I **were** in London right now.   내가 지금 당장 런던에 있다면 좋을 텐데.
→ I'm sorry that I**'m not** in London right now.   내가 지금 당장 런던에 있지 않아서 유감이다.

I wish you **would clean** your room.   네가 너의 방을 청소하면 좋을 텐데.
→ I'm sorry that you **won't clean** your room.   네가 너의 방을 청소하지 않을 것이라서 유감이다.

연습문제 괄호 안의 말을 활용하여 가정법 과거 문장을 완성하시오.

1 I wish I _____ a millionaire. (be)

2 I wish I _____ the contest. (can, win)

3 I wish the café _____ so early. (not, close)

4 I wish I _____ how to play chess. (know)

5 I wish I _____ a rainbow. (can, see)

6 I wish you _____ so depressed. (not, feel)

7 I wish food _____ from the sky. (will, fall)

8 I wish I _____ on a trip to Canada. (can, go)

9 I wish the store _____ nicer shoes. (sell)

10 I wish I _____ enough time to finish the report. (have)

11 I wish the author _____ more novels. (will, write)

12 I wish my brother _____ more time with me. (spend)

기출 적중문제 ◎

우리말과 같도록 can을 활용하여 빈칸에 쓰시오.

내가 그 장미 축제에 갈 수 있다면 좋을 텐데.

= I wish I _____ _____ to the rose festival.

POIN
2-2

「I wish + 가정법 과거완료」는 '~했더라면 좋았을 텐데'라는 의미로 과거에 이루지 못한 일을 소망할 때 쓴다.

| I wish | + | 주어 | + | had + p.p. |

I wish I **had eaten** salad for lunch. 내가 점심으로 샐러드를 먹었더라면 좋았을 텐데.
→ I'm sorry that I **didn't eat** salad for lunch. 내가 점심으로 샐러드를 먹지 않아서 유감이다.

I wish she **had not seen** me fall down. 내가 넘어지는 것을 그녀가 보지 않았더라면 좋았을 텐데.
→ I'm sorry that she **saw** me fall down. 내가 넘어지는 것을 그녀가 봐서 유감이다.

연습문제 다음 직설법 문장은 가정법으로, 가정법 문장은 직설법으로 바꿔 쓰시오.

1 I'm sorry that I lost my watch.
  → I wish I _____.

2 I wish she had lent me her pen.
  → I'm sorry that she _____.

3 I'm sorry that I can't decide what to wear.
  → I wish I _____.

4 I wish Mark had not forgotten my birthday.
  → I'm sorry that Mark _____.

5 I'm sorry that you have to leave so soon.
  → I wish you _____.

6 I wish the field trip had not been canceled.
  → I'm sorry that the field trip _____.

7 I'm sorry that I don't have more cookies to eat.
  → I wish I _____.

8 I wish I had been able to solve the puzzle.
  → I'm sorry that I _____.

9 I'm sorry that I bought these sunglasses.
  → I wish I _____.

10 I wish I had done my homework last night.
  → I'm sorry that I _____.

기출로 적중 POINT 3 — as if + 가정법 과거/과거완료

정답 p.56

1. 「as if + 가정법 과거」는 '마치 ~인 것처럼'이라는 의미로 주절의 시제와 같은 시점의 사실과 반대되는 일을 가정한다.

   주어 + 동사 + as if + 주어 + 동사의 과거형 (be동사는 were)

   Dave talks **as if** he **were** a teacher. Dave는 마치 선생님인 것처럼 이야기한다.
   현재   현재의 사실과 반대되는 일
   → In fact, Dave **isn't** a teacher. 사실, Dave는 선생님이 아니다.

2. 「as if + 가정법 과거완료」는 '마치 ~이었던 것처럼'이라는 의미로 주절의 시제보다 앞선 시점의 사실과 반대되는 일을 가정한다.

   주어 + 동사 + as if + 주어 + had + p.p.

   Linda looks **as if** she **had not slept** well. Linda는 마치 잘 못 잤던 것처럼 보인다.
   현재   현재보다 앞선 과거의 사실과 반대되는 일
   → In fact, Linda **slept** well. 사실, Linda는 잘 잤다.

연습문제 | 우리말과 같도록 괄호 안의 말을 활용하여 가정법 문장을 완성하시오.

1 그 수업은 마치 지루한 것처럼 들린다. (be)
= The class sounds as if it _____ boring.

2 그 방은 마치 우리가 어제 페인트칠했던 것처럼 보인다. (paint)
= The room looks as if we _____ it yesterday.

3 나는 마치 열대 우림에 있는 것처럼 느낀다. (be)
= I feel as if I _____ in the rain forest.

4 마치 그가 모든 것을 아는 것처럼 보인다. (know)
= It seems as if he _____ everything.

5 Julie는 마치 벌써 그 영화를 봤던 것처럼 말한다. (watch)
= Julie talks as if she _____ the movie already.

6 그 로봇은 마치 사람인 것처럼 행동한다. (be)
= The robot acts as if it _____ a human.

7 Peter는 마치 한국에서 오랫동안 살았던 것처럼 보인다. (live)
= Peter appears as if he _____ in Korea for a long time.

서술형 대비 문제

A <보기>와 같이 각 인물들의 말에 나온 표현을 활용하여 가정법 문장을 완성하시오.

<보기>

Yunho

As I don't have enough money, I can't buy a nice laptop.

→ If I _had enough money_ , I _could buy a nice laptop_ .

---

1 **Emma**

As my feet aren't small, I can't wear these shoes.

→ If my feet _____ , I _____ .

2 **John**

I have a test, so I won't play with my friends.

→ If I _____ , I _____ .

3 **Becky**

The musical was too long, so I got sleepy.

→ If the musical _____ , I _____ .

4 **Ronald**

As I'm not in Italy, I can't visit the Colosseum.

→ If I _____ , I _____ .

5 **Suji**

As the library doesn't open on Sundays, I can't study there.

→ If the library _____ , I _____ .

6 **Tim**

As Charlie didn't bring his wallet, I lent him $20.

→ If Charlie _____ , I _____ .

7 **Amber**

As I told a lie to my parents, they were upset.

→ If I _____ , they _____ .

B 우리말과 같도록 괄호 안의 말을 알맞게 배열하시오.

1 내가 의사라면 좋을 텐데. (I, doctor, a, were)
= I wish _____.

2 오늘 따뜻하다면 좋을 텐데. (were, it, warm)
= I wish _____ today.

3 민호가 나의 조언을 들으면 좋을 텐데. (to, listen, advice, Minho, my, would)
= I wish _____.

4 내가 언젠가 그 배우를 만날 수 있다면 좋을 텐데. (could, I, the, meet, actor)
= I wish _____ someday.

5 내가 너와 함께 그 연극을 봤더라면 좋았을 텐데. (seen, play, had, I, the)
= I wish _____ with you.

6 나의 팀이 그 경기를 이겼더라면 좋았을 텐데. (game, my, the, won, team, had)
= I wish _____.

7 내가 너에게 나의 정원을 보여줄 수 있다면 좋을 텐데. (garden, I, could, you, my, show)
= I wish _____.

8 그가 나에게 그의 계획에 대해 말해줬더라면 좋았을 텐데. (had, his, about, plans, me, told, he)
= I wish _____.

C <보기>의 말을 활용하여 대화를 완성하시오.

<보기>	become an angel	finish the homework	not make a mistake	be a genius

1 *A*: Brad likes to talk about how smart he is.
B: Yeah. He acts as if he _____.

2 *A*: Chloe talks as if she _____ last night.
B: Really? I saw her doing her homework this morning.

3 *A*: Can you see Mandy wearing a Halloween costume?
B: I can. She looks as if she _____.

4 *A*: I wish George would stop complaining about everyone.
B: I agree. He sounds as if he _____ before.

중간·기말고사 실전 문제

1 우리말과 같도록 괄호 안의 말을 활용하여 빈칸에 쓰시오.

> 만약 내일 눈이 온다면, 나의 친구와 나는 눈사람을 만들 것이다. (snow)

= If it _____ tomorrow, my friend and I will make a snowman.

2 다음 중 밑줄 친 부분이 어법상 어색한 것은?

> If I knew about the rumor, I will tell you.
> ①   ②   ③
> Unfortunately, I don't know anything.
>   ④   ⑤

[3-4] 다음 빈칸에 들어갈 알맞은 것을 고르시오.

3

> If I _____ you, I would read this book.

① be   ② am
③ were   ④ will be
⑤ being

4

> If it were Saturday, I _____ my favorite TV show. But today is Thursday.

① watch   ② watched
③ can watch   ④ could watch
⑤ have watched

5 다음 대화의 빈칸에 공통으로 들어갈 알맞은 것은?

> *A*: What _____ you do if you were a magician?
> *B*: I _____ turn my little brother into a rabbit.

① will   ② would   ③ can
④ do   ⑤ did

6 다음 중 밑줄 친 부분이 어법상 어색한 것은?

① If you don't be quiet, you will wake the baby.
② If Maria weren't ill, she will go to school.
③ If I had owned a hamster, I would have named it Fluffy.
④ If Chris exercised regularly, he could become healthier.
⑤ If I had finished the race, I could have won a gold medal.

7 다음 글에서 어법상 어색한 부분을 찾아 쓰고 바르게 고쳐 쓰시오.

> If I had more time, I will visit more tourist sites in this city. However, I have to leave soon.

_____ → _____

[8-9] 다음 문장을 가정법 문장으로 바꿔 쓰시오.

8

As spiders don't have six legs, they are not insects.

→ If spiders _____ ,

_____ .

9

Jasmin didn't study hard, so she couldn't answer all the questions.

→ If Jasmin _____ ,

_____

_____ .

10 다음 문장을 직설법 문장으로 바르게 바꾼 것은?

If I were tall, I could join the basketball team.

① As I'm not tall, I can't join the basketball team.
② As I'm not tall, I couldn't join the basketball team.
③ As I wasn't tall, I can't join the basketball team.
④ As I'm tall, I couldn't join the basketball team.
⑤ As I'm tall, I can join the basketball team.

11 다음 중 어법상 <u>어색한</u> 것은?

① I wish you had replied to my text message.
② If you have arrived on time, I wouldn't have been upset.
③ He looks as if he had seen a ghost last night.
④ If the river weren't so polluted, many animals would live in it.
⑤ Joey talks as if he were the leader of our club.

12 다음 글의 빈칸에 들어갈 알맞은 것은?

I'm watching my sister swimming in the pool. I wish I _____ how to swim so that I could swim with her.

① know   ② knew
③ am knowing   ④ have known
⑤ had been known

13 다음 대화의 빈칸에 들어갈 말이 순서대로 짝지어진 것은?

A: I left my backpack on the subway. What should I do now?
B: If I _____ you, I _____ the lost and found.

*lost and found 분실물 보관소

① am – check
② am – would check
③ were – would check
④ were – would have checked
⑤ had been – would have checked

14 다음 두 문장의 의미가 같도록 빈칸에 알맞은 말을 쓰시오.

> I'm sorry that Joseph doesn't agree with me.
>
> = I wish Joseph _____ with me.

[15-16] 다음 우리말을 알맞게 영작한 것을 고르시오.

15

> 만약 그 라면이 맵지 않았더라면, 하나는 배탈이 나지 않았을 텐데.

① If the ramyeon weren't spicy, Hana will have a stomachache.
② If the ramyeon were spicy, Hana won't have a stomachache.
③ If the ramyeon had been spicy, Hana wouldn't have a stomachache.
④ If the ramyeon had not been spicy, Hana would have had a stomachache.
⑤ If the ramyeon had not been spicy, Hana wouldn't have had a stomachache.

16

> 내가 나의 가족과 보낼 더 많은 시간이 있다면 좋을 텐데.

① I wish I'll have more time to spend with my family.
② I wish I don't have more time to spend with my family.
③ I wish I had more time to spend with my family.
④ I wish I had had more time to spend with my family.
⑤ I wish I had not had more time to spend with my family.

17 다음 중 어법상 바른 것을 <u>모두</u> 고르시오.

① If my oven weren't broken, I could baked some pies.
② If I were your teacher, I wouldn't give you any homework this week.
③ If I had practiced harder, I would have performed on the stage much better.
④ If it had been sunny, we could go on a picnic tomorrow.
⑤ If she had listened to her doctor, she wouldn't be in the hospital then.

18 우리말과 같도록 괄호 안의 말을 활용하여 빈칸에 쓰시오.

> 내가 더 어렸을 때 중국어를 배웠더라면 좋았을 텐데. (learn)

= I wish I _____ _____ Chinese when I was younger.

19 다음 빈칸에 들어갈 말이 순서대로 짝지어진 것은?

> · I didn't take a shower in the morning. I wish I _____ a shower then.
> · Ms. Kim's homework is too difficult. I wish she _____ us easier homework from now on.

① take – will give
② took – would give
③ took – would have given
④ had taken – would give
⑤ had taken – would have given

20 다음 빈칸에 공통으로 들어갈 알맞은 것은?

· I wish I _____ in Alaska now.
· She behaves as if she _____ an adult.

① be ② is
③ were ④ have been
⑤ had been

21 다음 두 문장의 의미가 같도록 문장을 완성하시오.

I'm sorry that I didn't save money for an emergency.
= I wish _____
_____.

22 다음 빈칸에 들어갈 말로 어색한 것은?

I wish _____ last week.

① he had bought me a rose
② you had told me about the secret
③ I had not watched the scary movie alone
④ Luna had decided to visit me
⑤ I had Suho's phone number

23 다음 글의 빈칸에 들어갈 알맞은 것은?

I couldn't eat dinner at that restaurant because there weren't any tables. I wish I _____ a reservation earlier.

① make ② made
③ will make ④ had made
⑤ would make

24 다음 밑줄 친 부분을 바르게 고치지 못한 것은?

① I wish I have something to eat right now. (→ had had)
② It seems as if Samantha owns this place. (→ owned)
③ I wish I could sleep a little more yesterday. (→ could have slept)
④ I wish I am stronger than my older brother. (→ were)
⑤ Ken acts as if he had not seen me on the street now. (→ didn't see)

25 다음 두 문장의 의미가 같도록 빈칸에 알맞은 말을 쓰시오.

In fact, Bill is not a great singer.
= Bill talks as if _____ _____
_____ _____ _____.

26 다음 대화의 빈칸에 들어갈 말이 순서대로 짝지어진 것은?

A: You woke up too late! Hurry up, or you'll be late for school.
B: Oh, no. I wish I _____ to bed earlier last night. I have to catch the bus at 8:20.
A: You still have ten minutes. If you run fast enough, you _____ it.

① had gone – will miss
② went – will miss
③ had gone – won't miss
④ went – won't miss
⑤ had gone – would miss

CHAPTER 18
일치·화법·도치

일치   I **thought** that he **was** a doctor.   나는 그가 의사라고 생각했다.

화법   He said, "I'm not a doctor."   그는 "나는 의사가 아니야."라고 말했다.
      → He said **that he was** not a doctor.   그는 그가 의사가 아니라고 말했다.

도치   **On the table are some plates.**   식탁 위에 몇 개의 접시가 있다.

첫 번째 문장에서 주절의 과거시제 **thought**에 맞춰 종속절에도 과거시제 **was**를 썼어요. 이렇게 문장 안에서 시제를 맞추는 것을 **일치**라고 해요.

두 번째 문장처럼 그가 한 말을 큰따옴표("")를 사용하여 그대로 전달하는 것을 **직접 화법**이라고 하고, 세 번째 문장처럼 큰따옴표("") 없이 전달하는 사람의 입장에서 말하는 것을 **간접 화법**이라고 해요.

네 번째 문장에서 장소를 나타내는 부사구 **On the table**을 강조하기 위해 문장 맨 앞에 썼는데, 이때 「주어 + 동사」의 어순이 「동사 + 주어」로 바뀌는 것을 **도치**라고 해요.

기출로 적중 POINT

1-1 • 시제 일치

1-2 • 시제 일치의 예외

2   • 화법 전환: 평서문

3-1 • 화법 전환: 의문사가 있는 의문문

3-2 • 화법 전환: 의문사가 없는 의문문

4   • 도치

내신 100점 적중!
기출 출제율

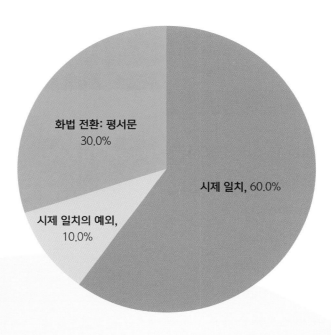

화법 전환: 평서문
30.0%

시제 일치, 60.0%

시제 일치의 예외,
10.0%

TOP 1 **시제 일치 (60%)**
주절의 시제에 따라 종속절의 시제를 일치시키는 문제가 자주 출제된다.

TOP 2 **화법 전환: 평서문 (30%)**
평서문의 직접 화법을 간접 화법으로 바꾸는 문제가 자주 출제된다.

TOP 3 **시제 일치의 예외 (10%)**
주절의 시제와 상관없이 종속절에 써야 하는 시제를 묻는 문제가 자주 출제된다.

시제 일치

1. **주절이 현재시제인 경우 종속절에는 의미에 따라 모든 시제를 쓸 수 있다.**

   I **think** that she **is** angry. 나는 그녀가 화났다고 생각한다.
   I **think** that she **was** angry. 나는 그녀가 화났었다고 생각한다.
   I **think** that she **will be** angry. 나는 그녀가 화날 것이라고 생각한다.

2. **주절이 과거시제인 경우 종속절에는 의미에 따라 과거시제나 과거완료시제를 쓴다.**

   I **knew** that Dan **lived** in California. 나는 Dan이 캘리포니아에 산다는 것을 알고 있었다.
   I **knew** that Dan **had lived** in California. 나는 Dan이 캘리포니아에 살았다는 것을 알고 있었다.
   └→ 과거완료시제는 「had + p.p.」의 형태로, 과거의 어느 시점에 발생한 일보다 더 이전에
      발생했던 일을 나타낸다.

   (Tip) 주절이 과거시제인 경우 종속절의 조동사도 과거형(would, could, might 등)을 쓴다.
   We **didn't know** that it (~~will~~, **would**) rain. 우리는 비가 올 것을 알지 못했다.
   They **hoped** that they (~~can~~, **could**) win the game. 그들은 그들이 그 경기를 이길 수 있기를 바랐다.

연습문제 A 밑줄 친 부분이 어법상 맞으면 O를 쓰고, 틀리면 바르게 고쳐 쓰시오.

1 I hope you will get better. → _____

2 He said that the room is too hot. → _____

3 We believe that we did our best. → _____

4 I thought that I may catch a cold. → _____

5 Yerin realized that she loses her keys. → _____

6 Jack said that I can borrow his bicycle. → _____

7 Noah told me that he had seen a ghost. → _____

8 I wondered why she won't answer her phone. → _____

연습문제 B 다음 문장을 과거시제로 바꿀 때 빈칸에 알맞은 말을 쓰시오.

1 I know that Yunho wants to be an actor.
   → I knew that Yunho _____ to be an actor.

2 I think that you will like the band's new album.
   → I thought that you _____ _____ the band's new album.

3 We believe that the quiz is too difficult.

→ We believed that the quiz _____ too difficult.

4 Carl says that he practices the cello a lot.

→ Carl said that he _____ the cello a lot.

5 Jacob hopes his parents will buy him a new computer.

→ Jacob hoped his parents _____ _____ him a new computer.

6 Mr. Jones thinks that he doesn't feel well.

→ Mr. Jones thought that he _____ _____ well.

7 Mom tells me that she will cook tomato pasta for dinner.

→ Mom told me that she _____ _____ tomato pasta for dinner.

8 Narae doesn't know that she has to apologize to me.

→ Narae didn't know that she _____ to apologize to me.

9 The man complains that he can hear noises from upstairs.

→ The man complained that he _____ _____ noises from upstairs.

10 Brian tells me that he finished reading the book.

→ Brian told me that he _____ _____ reading the book.

11 Jane promises that she will be more responsible.

→ Jane promised that she _____ _____ more responsible.

12 The speaker doesn't know that the audience is bored.

→ The speaker didn't know that the audience _____ bored.

13 Kate says that she may arrive late.

→ Kate said that she _____ _____ late.

14 My parents believe that I told them the truth.

→ My parents believed that I _____ _____ them the truth.

기출 적중문제 🎯

다음 글의 빈칸에 들어갈 말이 순서대로 짝지어진 것은?

> Yesterday, I was on a group tour in Bangkok. We went to a street market for lunch. The guide _____ us that we _____ something traditional.

① tells – will eat ② tells – would eat

③ told – eat ④ told – will eat

⑤ told – would eat

시제 일치의 예외

정답 p.58

1. 다음과 같은 경우에는 주절의 시제와 상관없이 종속절에 항상 현재시제를 쓴다.

현재의 습관이나 반복되는 일을 나타낼 때	Sarah **said** that she always **takes** a walk after lunch. Sarah는 그녀가 점심 식사 후에 항상 산책한다고 말했다.
일반적·과학적 사실을 말할 때	We **didn't know** that all birds **have** feathers. 우리는 모든 새가 깃털이 있다는 것을 알지 못했다. Ms. Park **taught** us that water **boils** at 100℃. 박 선생님은 우리에게 물이 섭씨 100도에서 끓는다는 것을 가르쳐주셨다.
속담·격언을 말할 때	Dad **told** me that haste **makes** waste. 아빠는 나에게 서두르면 일을 그르친다고 말씀하셨다. I **heard** that knowledge **is** power. 나는 아는 것이 힘이라고 들었다.

2. 다음과 같은 경우에는 주절의 시제와 상관없이 종속절에 항상 과거시제를 쓴다.

역사적 사실을 말할 때	I **learned** that the Second World War **ended** in 1945. 나는 제2차 세계 대전이 1945년에 끝났다는 것을 배웠다.

연습문제 | 다음 문장을 과거시제로 바꿀 때 빈칸에 알맞은 말을 써서 문장을 완성하시오.

1 Paula says that she swims every day.

→ Paula said that _____.

2 He tells me that light travels faster than sound.

→ He told me that _____.

3 Everyone knows that Beijing is the capital of China.

→ Everyone knew that _____.

4 She remembers that the Industrial Revolution started in the 1760s.

→ She remembered that _____.

5 Hyeri tells me that a friend in need is a friend indeed.

→ Hyeri told me that _____.

6 Ken says that he always drinks a cup of coffee in the morning.

→ Ken said that _____.

7 The kids learn that metal expands in hot weather.

→ The kids learned that _____.

POINT 2 화법 전환: 평서문

정답 p.58

평서문의 직접 화법은 다음과 같이 간접 화법으로 바꿀 수 있다.

직접 화법   She said, "I will watch the movie tonight."

     그녀는 "나는 오늘 밤에 그 영화를 볼 거야."라고 말했다.

간접 화법   She said (that) she would watch the movie that night.
          ①   ②   ③   ④   ⑤

     그녀는 그녀가 그날 밤에 그 영화를 볼 것이라고 말했다.

> ① 전달동사가 say인 경우 그대로 쓰고, say to인 경우 tell로 바꾼다.
> ② 콤마(,)와 큰따옴표(" ")를 없애고 접속사 that으로 두 절을 연결한다. 이때 that은 생략할 수 있다.
> ③ that절의 인칭대명사를 전달하는 사람의 입장에 맞게 바꾼다.
> ④ 전달동사가 현재시제인 경우 that절의 시제를 바꾸지 않고, 과거시제인 경우 과거시제나 과거완료시제로 바꾼다.
> ⑤ 지시대명사나 부사(구)를 전달하는 사람의 입장에 맞게 바꾼다.
>
> | | |
> |---|---|
> | this/these → that/those | here → there |
> | now → then | ago → before |
> | next → the following | last → the previous |
> | today → that day | tonight → that night |
> | yesterday → the previous day[the day before] | |
> | tomorrow → the next[following] day | |

Tom **said to** me, "**I need** to fix **my** phone **now**."

Tom은 나에게 "나는 지금 나의 전화기를 수리할 필요가 있어."라고 말했다.

→ Tom **told** me **(that)** **he needed** to fix **his** phone **then**.

     Tom은 나에게 그가 그때 그의 전화기를 수리할 필요가 있다고 말했다.

Yuna **said**, "**I enjoyed** watching **this** musical."   유나는 "나는 이 뮤지컬을 보는 것을 즐겼어."라고 말했다.

→ Yuna **said (that)** **she had enjoyed** watching **that** musical.

     유나는 그녀가 그 뮤지컬을 보는 것을 즐겼다고 말했다.

연습문제 A   다음 문장을 간접 화법으로 바꿀 때 빈칸에 알맞은 말을 써서 문장을 완성하시오.

1   He said to me, "I want a glass of cold water."

    → He _____ me that _____.

2   They said, "These paintings are amazing."

    → They _____ that _____.

3   My dad said, "I'm preparing breakfast now."

    → My dad _____ that _____.

4 Jenny said to me, "I will go to the dentist today."

→ Jenny _____ me that _____.

5 Daniel said to me, "Your dress looks very pretty."

→ Daniel _____ me that _____.

6 He said, "I can finish the science project tonight."

→ He _____ that _____.

7 Ms. Smith said, "I was satisfied with the meal."

→ Ms. Smith _____ that _____.

8 Alice said, "I will throw a party next week."

→ Alice _____ that _____.

9 Oliver said to me, "I graduated two years ago."

→ Oliver _____ me that _____.

연습문제 B   <보기>와 같이 다음 문장을 직접 화법으로 바꿀 때 빈칸에 알맞은 말을 써서 문장을 완성하시오.

> **<보기>**   Susie said that she didn't know my address.
>
>   → Susie said, *"I don't know your address."*

1 Jinho said that he wanted to join the book club.

→ Jinho said, _____

2 She told me that she was listening to K-pop then.

→ She said to me, _____

3 My brother said that he could fix the bicycle that day.

→ My brother said, _____

4 Mary told him that she would teach him math the next day.

→ Mary said to him, _____

5 Ron told me that he had had a car accident the previous week.

→ Ron said to me, _____

기출 적중문제 🎯

다음 문장을 간접 화법으로 바꿔 쓰시오.

> She said, "I will leave tomorrow."

→ _____

정답 p.58

기출로적중 POINT 3-1 화법 전환: 의문사가 있는 의문문

의문사가 있는 의문문의 직접 화법은 다음과 같이 간접 화법으로 바꿀 수 있다.

직접 화법   He said to me, "When does your class end?"
그는 나에게 "너의 수업은 언제 끝나니?"라고 말했다.

간접 화법   He asked me when my class ended.   그는 나에게 나의 수업이 언제 끝나는지 물었다.
　　　　　　　　①　　　②　　　　③

> ① 전달동사 say나 say to를 ask로 바꾼다.
> ② 콤마(,)와 큰따옴표(" ")를 없애고 의문사로 두 절을 연결한다.
> ③ 인칭대명사, 시제, 지시대명사, 부사(구)를 평서문의 화법 전환과 같은 방식으로 바꾸고, 「의문사 + 주어 + 동사」의 어순으로 쓴다. 이때 의문사가 주어인 경우 「의문사 + 동사」의 어순을 그대로 쓴다.

My friend **said to** me, "**Why are you** tired?"   나의 친구는 나에게 "너는 왜 피곤하니?"라고 말했다.
→ My friend **asked** me **why I was** tired.   나의 친구는 나에게 내가 왜 피곤한지 물었다.

Sam **said**, "**Who will do** the laundry?"   Sam은 "누가 빨래를 할 거니?"라고 말했다.
→ Sam **asked who would do** the laundry.   Sam은 누가 빨래를 할 것인지 물었다.

연습문제 | 다음 문장을 간접 화법으로 바꿀 때 빈칸에 알맞은 말을 써서 문장을 완성하시오.

1 Mark said to me, "How are you?"
　→ Mark asked me _____.

2 Emily said, "When does the store open?"
　→ Emily asked _____.

3 Mom said, "Why is the front door open?"
　→ Mom asked _____.

4 She said to me, "What do you want for Christmas?"
　→ She asked me _____.

5 He said, "Where can I buy a ticket?"
　→ He asked _____.

6 The teacher said, "Who is talking so loudly?"
　→ The teacher asked _____.

7 I said to Minsu, "When will you call me?"
　→ I asked Minsu _____.

8 The customer said, "What is the most popular dish?"
　→ The customer asked _____.

의문사가 없는 의문문의 직접 화법은 다음과 같이 간접 화법으로 바꿀 수 있다.

직접 화법   The woman said, "Do you need my help?"
그 여자는 "너는 나의 도움이 필요하니?"라고 말했다.

간접 화법   The woman asked if[whether] I needed her help.
                     ①   ②   ③
그 여자는 내가 그녀의 도움이 필요한지 물었다.

> ① 전달동사 say나 say to를 ask로 바꾼다.
> ② 콤마(,)와 큰따옴표(" ")를 없애고 if나 whether로 두 절을 연결한다.
> ③ 인칭대명사, 시제, 지시대명사, 부사(구)를 평서문의 화법 전환과 같은 방식으로 바꾸고, 「if[whether] + 주어 + 동사」의 어순으로 쓴다.

Jiho **said to** me, "**Can I borrow your** eraser?"
지호는 나에게 "내가 너의 지우개를 빌려도 되니?"라고 말했다.

→ Jiho **asked** me **if[whether]** **he could borrow my** eraser.
지호는 나에게 그가 나의 지우개를 빌려도 되는지 물었다.

The chef **said**, "**Was the food** delicious?"   그 요리사는 "음식이 맛있었나요?"라고 말했다.
→ The chef **asked if[whether]** **the food had been** delicious.
그 요리사는 음식이 맛있었는지 물었다.

연습문제 | 다음 문장을 간접 화법으로 바꿀 때 빈칸에 알맞은 말을 써서 문장을 완성하시오.

1 She said to me, "Are you ready to go out?"
  → She asked me _____.

2 My friend said to me, "Do you know the answer?"
  → My friend asked me _____.

3 The child said, "Will it snow tomorrow?"
  → The child asked _____.

4 Julie said to us, "Did you enjoy the concert?"
  → Julie asked us _____.

5 Kendal said to me, "Are you good at dancing?"
  → Kendal asked me _____.

6 Grandpa said to me, "Can you bring me the newspaper?"
  → Grandpa asked me _____.

POINT 4 도치

정답 p.58

부사(구)를 문장 맨 앞에 쓰고 주어와 동사의 순서를 바꿔 부사(구)의 의미를 강조할 수 있으며, 이와 같이 문장 안에서 어순이 바뀌는 것을 도치라고 한다.

❶ There/Here가 문장 맨 앞에 올 때: 「There/Here + 동사 + 주어」

The teacher comes here. 선생님이 여기로 오신다.

→ **Here comes the teacher.** 여기로 선생님이 오신다.

(Tip) 주어가 대명사인 경우 주어와 동사가 도치되지 않는다.
Here she comes. (O) 여기로 그녀가 온다.
Here comes she. (X)

❷ 장소나 방향을 나타내는 부사구가 문장 맨 앞에 올 때: 「장소나 방향을 나타내는 부사구 + 동사 + 주어」

The birds flew over the roof. 새들이 지붕 위로 날아갔다.

→ **Over the roof flew the birds.** 지붕 위로 새들이 날아갔다.

연습문제 괄호 안의 말을 알맞게 배열하시오.

1 Here _____ . (am, I)

2 There _____ on the table. (a vase, is)

3 On the lawn _____ with his dog. (a child, lies)

4 Under the tree _____ . (the man, sleeps)

5 There _____ on the subway this morning. (were, lots of people)

6 Here _____ . These are the sandwiches that you ordered. (are, they)

7 Behind the chair _____ . (a small cat, hid)

8 Here _____ . We'll be late if we miss it. (the bus, comes)

기출 적중문제

다음 밑줄 친 ⓐ~ⓔ 중 어법상 어색한 것을 찾아 기호를 쓰고 바르게 고쳐 쓰시오.

> *A*: There is a lion behind the tree.
>   ⓐ   ⓑ   ⓒ
> *B*: Oh, look! Here comes it.
>   ⓓ   ⓔ

____ → _____

Ⓐ 다음 문장의 밑줄 친 부분을 과거시제로 바꿔 완전한 문장을 쓰시오.

1 I <u>know</u> that Paul sings well.

→ _____

2 She <u>hopes</u> that Terry will keep his promise.

→ _____

3 We <u>learn</u> that we can't breathe underwater.

→ _____

4 I <u>hear</u> that Linda volunteers every month.

→ _____

5 I <u>think</u> that I have to go to the hospital.

→ _____

6 Mr. Lee <u>says</u> that Alexander Bell invented the telephone in 1876.

→ _____

7 Dad <u>tells</u> me that he may come home late.

→ _____

8 I <u>believe</u> that Eric doesn't know my phone number.

→ _____

9 Harry <u>is</u> sure that he turned off all the lights.

→ _____

Ⓑ 다음 대화를 간접 화법으로 바꿀 때 빈칸에 알맞은 말을 써서 문장을 완성하시오.

Ella ⟨ I need to learn how to swim.

I can teach you tomorrow. ⟩ Isaac

Jason ⟨ I will be back in 15 minutes.

I will wait for you here. ⟩ Sujin

1 Ella said that _____

_____ .

2 Isaac said that _____

_____ .

3 Jason said that _____

_____ .

4 Sujin said that _____

_____ .

Miso — I'm going to buy a new laptop today.

Where are you going to buy it? — Ryan

5 Miso said that _____

_____.

6 Ryan asked Miso _____

_____.

Mike — Do you want to watch this movie together?

I saw it last weekend. — Anna

7 Mike asked Anna _____

_____.

8 Anna said that _____

_____.

The chef — How is your steak?

It tastes really good. — Ms. Hall

9 The chef asked Ms. Hall _____

_____.

10 Ms. Hall said that _____

_____.

Gary — Can you speak Russian?

I can speak Russian a little. — Nina

11 Gary asked Nina _____

_____.

12 Nina said that _____

_____.

C 괄호 안의 말을 알맞게 배열하시오.

1 There _____ in our town. (a new mall, is)

2 Here _____. This is the picture you asked for. (is, it)

3 In the river _____. (live, a lot of fish)

4 There _____ at the back. (was, an empty seat)

5 Along the road _____. (ran, a few men)

6 Here _____ to Busan. (comes, the train)

7 Here _____ I borrowed from you. (some books, are)

8 Among the tall trees _____. (a cabin, stood)

9 There _____. Someone must be hurt. (an ambulance, goes)

10 Over the fence _____. (the white horse, jumped)

[1-2] 다음 빈칸에 들어갈 알맞은 것을 고르시오.

1

> My mom thought that my room _____ too dirty.

① be ② is
③ was ④ been
⑤ is being

2

> Copernicus discovered that the Earth _____ around the Sun.

① moves ② moved
③ has moved ④ was moving
⑤ would move

3 다음 중 밑줄 친 부분이 어법상 <u>어색한</u> 것은?

① We hoped that it <u>would be</u> sunny.
② I learned that the first computer <u>was</u> invented in the 1940s.
③ My brother didn't know that the Eiffel Tower <u>is</u> in Paris.
④ Samantha said that she <u>needs</u> to go to the dentist.
⑤ I wondered why Matt <u>had been</u> angry.

4 다음 문장을 간접 화법으로 바꿀 때 밑줄 친 부분이 어법상 어색한 것은?

> Cathy said, "I'm sleepy now."
> → Cathy <u>said</u> <u>that</u> <u>she</u> <u>is</u> sleepy <u>then</u>.
> ① ② ③ ④   ⑤

5 다음 문장을 과거시제로 바꿀 때 빈칸에 알맞은 말을 쓰시오.

> The hockey players believe that they can win the game easily.
> → The hockey players believed that they _____ _____ the game easily.

6 다음 빈칸에 들어갈 말이 순서대로 짝지어진 것은?

> · Dustin realized that his puppy _____ very hungry.
> · I heard that Yuri always _____ the piano at 3 P.M.

① is – practices
② is – was practicing
③ was – practices
④ was – was practicing
⑤ was – practiced

7 다음 문장을 간접 화법으로 바꿀 때 빈칸에 들어갈 알맞은 것은?

> Lily said to me, "I want to sit next to you on the bus."
> → Lily _____ on the bus.

① said me that I wanted to sit next to you
② said me that she wanted to sit next to me
③ told me that I want to sit next to me
④ told me that she wanted to sit next to you
⑤ told me that she wanted to sit next to me

8 다음 밑줄 친 @~ⓔ 중 어법상 어색한 것을 찾아 기호를 쓰고 바르게 고쳐 쓰시오.

My best friend said <u>that</u> she <u>will</u> <u>go</u> to
        ⓐ   ⓑ ⓒ

the amusement park <u>with</u> <u>me</u>.
                 ⓓ   ⓔ

_____ → _____

9 다음 문장을 간접 화법으로 바꿀 때 빈칸에 알맞은 말을 쓰시오.

He said, "My history report is due tomorrow."
→ He said that _____ history
report _____ due _____
_____ _____.

10 다음 중 직접 화법을 간접 화법으로 잘못 바꾼 것은?

① Bill said, "I like your jacket."
　→ Bill said that he liked my jacket.
② She said, "These cookies are tasty."
　→ She said that those cookies were tasty.
③ My parents said, "We're proud of you."
　→ My parents said that they were proud of me.
④ Jake said to me, "I'll call you today."
　→ Jake told me that he will call me that day.
⑤ The teacher said to us, "The field trip may be canceled."
　→ The teacher told us that the field trip might be canceled.

11 다음 문장을 간접 화법으로 바르게 바꾼 것은?

Evan said, "I can clean my room now."

① Evan said that he can clean my room now.
② Evan told that he can clean his room then.
③ Evan said that he could clean his room now.
④ Evan said that he could clean his room then.
⑤ Evan told that he could clean my room then.

12 다음 대화의 빈칸에 들어갈 말이 순서대로 짝지어진 것은?

A: Do you know where Hannah is?
B: I thought she _____ to the mall.
A: Actually, she told me that she _____ home instead. But I can't find her anywhere.
B: Oh, really? Why don't you call her?

① goes – will stay
② goes – would stay
③ went – will stay
④ went – would stay
⑤ would go – will stay

13

> Luke said to me, "Why are you crying?"
> → Luke asked me _____ .

① if I was crying   ② if I am crying
③ why I was crying   ④ why was I crying
⑤ why I am crying

14

> Minji said, "Can I use this pen?"
> → Minji asked _____ that pen.

① if she can use
② when she can use
③ when she could use
④ whether she can use
⑤ whether she could use

15 다음 직접 화법을 간접 화법으로 바꾼 문장에서 어법상 어색한 부분을 찾아 쓰고 바르게 고쳐 쓰시오.

> She said, "How does the movie end?"
> → She asked how the movie ends.

_____ → _____

16 다음 빈칸에 들어갈 알맞은 것은?

> Sumi asked her grandfather _____ he could give her some advice.

① as   ② if   ③ of
④ that   ⑤ which

17 다음 문장을 간접 화법으로 바르게 바꾼 것은?

> Hansu said to me, "Do you know how to get to the bank?"

① Hansu asks me if I know how to get to the bank.
② Hansu asked me if I knew how to get to the bank.
③ Hansu asked me if you knew how to get to the bank.
④ Hansu told me if I know how to get to the bank.
⑤ Hansu told me if you knew how to get to the bank.

18 우리말과 같도록 괄호 안의 말을 활용하여 문장을 완성하시오.

> 나의 엄마는 내가 어제 그녀에게 거짓말을 했다는 것을 알아내셨다. (lie to)

= My mom found out that I _____ yesterday.

19 다음 중 어법상 어색한 것은?

① Up the tree climbed the monkey.
② There are some cookies in the jar.
③ Below the mountain was the tunnel.
④ I should talk to Patrick. There comes he.
⑤ Here you are! I've looked everywhere for you.

20 다음 중 직접 화법을 간접 화법으로 잘못 바꾼 것의 개수는?

> ⓐ The police officer said, "Do you have your ID?"
> → The police officer asked if I had my ID.
> ⓑ Liam said, "Who plays tennis best?"
> → Liam asked played who tennis best.
> ⓒ I said to him, "Can you repair this machine?"
> → I asked him if I could repair that machine.
> ⓓ She said, "When will you show me your cat?"
> → She asked when I would show her my cat.
> ⓔ Jihoon said to me, "Were you a class president last year?"
> → Jihoon asked me if I was a class president the previous year.

① 없음   ② 1개   ③ 2개
④ 3개   ⑤ 4개

21 다음 문장을 직접 화법으로 바꿔 쓰시오.

> Maria said that she would go to bed before midnight.
>
> → _____
> _____

22 다음 중 밑줄 친 부분이 어법상 어색한 것은?

> Last summer, I visited South Korea and ①spent some time in a temple. I ②felt satisfied with the peaceful view. Unfortunately, I ③was the only guest that could speak Korean. So, the other guests asked me what the Buddhist monks ④were saying. I told them that I ⑤will translate the words, and they were very thankful.
>
> *Buddhist monk 스님
> *translate 통역하다

23 다음 문자 메시지의 밑줄 친 (A), (B)를 간접 화법으로 바꿀 때 빈칸에 알맞은 말을 써서 문장을 완성하시오.

Lena

> (A) I'm going to make an egg sandwich for dinner today. But we're out of eggs.
> 4:15

> Do you want me to stop by the supermarket?
> 4:19   Henry

Lena

> That would be nice.
> (B) Can you buy some eggs and a bottle of juice?
> 4:21

(A) Lena told Henry _____
_____ .

(B) Lena asked Henry _____
_____ .

2학년 교과서 대표 문법 한 눈에 보기

1 동아 (윤정미)

	LESSON	CH	POINT	PAGE
1	4형식(수여동사)	1	2	20
	both A and B	15	2	330
2	조동사 have to	4	5	87
	to부정사의 부사적 용법	6	4	130
3	수동태	5	1, 2	102, 104
	5형식(to부정사 목적격보어)	1	3-2	23
4	주격 관계대명사	16	2-1, 3	359, 364
	접속사 if	15	4-3	339
5	목적격 관계대명사	16	2-2, 3	361, 364
	5형식 (명사 목적격보어)	1	3-1	22
6	5형식(지각동사)	1	3-4	25
	so ~ that …	15	5	343
7	현재완료시제	3	5-1, 5-2, 5-3	62, 64, 66
	to부정사의 명사적 용법: It ~ to부정사	6	2-1	123
8	의문사가 있는 간접의문문	2	4-1	39
	because of	15	4-2	337

2 동아 (이병민)

	LESSON	CH	POINT	PAGE
1	to부정사의 형용사적 용법	6	3	128
	명령문 + and/or ~	15	1	328
2	현재완료시제	3	5-1, 5-2, 5-3	62, 64, 66
	5형식(to부정사 목적격보어)	1	3-2	23
3	수동태	5	1, 2	102, 104
	접속사 if	15	4-3	339
4	주격 관계대명사	16	2-1	359
	최상급 비교	13	4-1, 4-2	286, 288
5	to부정사의 명사적 용법: It ~ to부정사	6	2-1	123
	5형식(지각동사)	1	3-4	25
6	원급 비교: as + 원급 + as	13	2-1, 2-3	277, 280
	접속사 although	15	4-4	341
7	so ~ that …	15	5	343
	목적격 관계대명사	16	2-2, 3	361, 364
8	-thing + 형용사	11	2	233

3 천재 (이재영)

4 천재 (정사열)

11 지학사 (민찬규)

	LESSON	CH	POINT	PAGE
1	부정대명사 one/the other	10	5-3	216
	접속사 if	15	4-3	339
2	의문사 + to부정사	6	2-4	127
	주격 관계대명사	16	2-1, 3	359, 364
3	목적격 관계대명사	16	2-2, 3	361, 364
	5형식 (to부정사 목적격보어)	1	3-2	23
4	-thing + 형용사	11	2	233
	현재완료시제	3	5-1, 5-2, 5-3	62, 64, 66
5	수동태	5	1, 2	102, 104
	조동사가 있는 수동태		4	107
6	so ~ that …	15	5	343
	원급 비교: as + 원급 + as	13	2-1	277
7	to부정사의 명사적 용법: It ~ to부정사	6	2-1	123
	how come	2	2	36
8	5형식(사역동사)	1	3-3	24
	접속사 although	15	4-4	341

12 금성 (최인철)

	LESSON	CH	POINT	PAGE
1	접속사 if	15	4-3	339
	부가의문문	2	5	42
2	의문사 + to부정사	6	2-4	127
	so ~ that …	15	5	343
3	to부정사의 형용사적 용법	6	3	128
	동사를 강조하는 do	4	8	91
4	의문사가 있는 간접의문문	2	4-1	39
	수동태	5	1, 2	102, 104
5	enough to	6	6	133
	현재완료시제	3	5-1, 5-2, 5-3	62, 64, 66
6	주격 관계대명사	16	2-1, 3	359, 364
	to부정사의 명사적 용법: It ~ to부정사	6	2-1	123
7	목적격 관계대명사	16	2-2, 3	361, 364
	관계대명사 what		4	366
8	too ~ to	6	6	133
	가정법 과거	17	1-1	382

MEMO

최신 개정 교과서 완벽 반영

기출로적중 해커스 중학영문법

2학년

초판 8쇄 발행 2024년 10월 21일
초판 1쇄 발행 2020년 11월 4일

지은이	해커스 어학연구소
펴낸곳	㈜해커스 어학연구소
펴낸이	해커스 어학연구소 출판팀

주소	서울특별시 서초구 강남대로61길 23 ㈜해커스 어학연구소
고객센터	02-537-5000
교재 관련 문의	publishing@hackers.com
	해커스북 사이트(HackersBook.com) 고객센터 Q&A 게시판
동영상강의	star.Hackers.com

ISBN	978-89-6542-407-9 (53740)
Serial Number	01-08-01

**중고등영어 1위,
해커스북 HackersBook.com**

해커스북 중·고등

• 핵심만 담았다! **문법 암기리스트+단어 암기장 및 단어 암기장 MP3**
• 교과서 문법 포인트 학습이 쉬워지는 **2학년 교과서 대표 문법 한 눈에 보기**
• 서술형 시험을 완벽하게 대비할 수 있는 **영작/해석 워크시트**

한경비즈니스 선정 2020 한국품질만족도 교육(온·오프라인 중·고등영어) 부문 1위 해커스

| 해커스 중고등 교재 MAP |

나에게 맞는 교재 선택!

	초5	초6	예비중	중1	중2
문법			Hackers Grammar Smart Starter	Hackers Grammar Smart Level 1	Hackers Grammar Smart Level 2
				기출로 적중 해커스 중학영문법 1학년	기출로 적중 해커스 중학영문법 2학년
				해커스 중학영문법 중간·기말 대비 문제집 Level 1	해커스 중학영문법 중간·기말 대비 문제집 Level 2
서술형 구문				해커스 쓰기 자신감 Level 1	해커스 쓰기 자신감 Level 2
독해	Hackers Reading Smart Starter Level 1	Hackers Reading Smart Starter Level 2	Hackers Reading Smart Level 1	Hackers Reading Smart Level 2	Hackers Reading Smart Level 3
				Hackers Reading Ground Level 1	Hackers Reading Ground Level 2
				Hackers Reading Path Level 1	Hackers Reading Path Level 2
					해커스 첫수능 영어 기초독해
듣기				해커스 중학영어듣기 모의고사 24회 Level 1	해커스 중학영어듣기 모의고사 24회 Level 2
어휘			해커스 3연타 중학영단어		
				해커스 보카 중학 기초	해커스 보카 중학 필수
					해커스 보카 중학 숙어

	READING	LISTENING	VOCA
토플	HACKERS APEX READING for the TOEFL iBT Basic/Intermediate/ Advanced/Expert	HACKERS APEX LISTENING for the TOEFL iBT Basic/Intermediate/ Advanced/Expert	HACKERS APEX VOCA for the TOEFL iBT HACKERS VOCABULARY

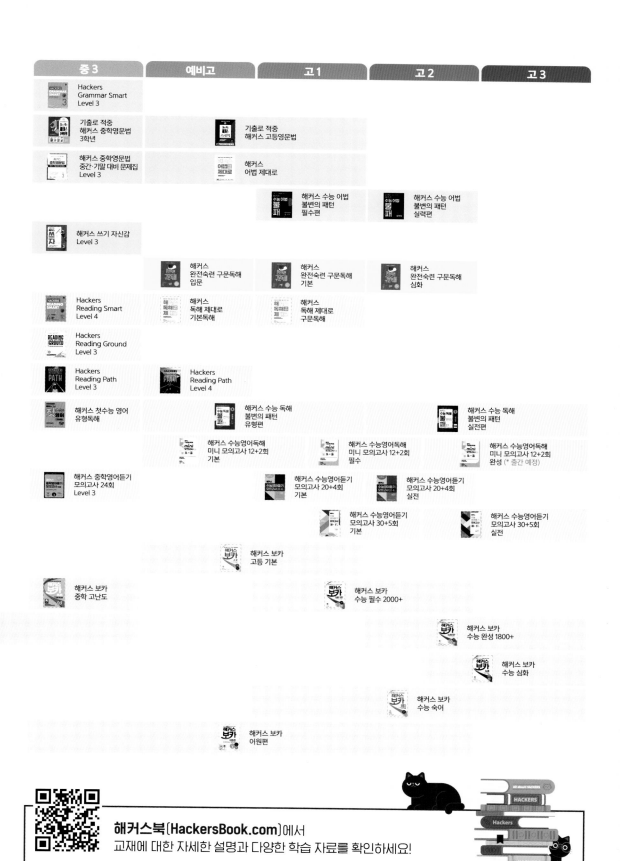

중3	예비고	고1	고2	고3
Hackers Grammar Smart Level 3				
기출로 적중 해커스 중학영문법 3학년	기출로 적중 해커스 고등영문법			
해커스 중학영문법 중간·기말 대비 문제집 Level 3	해커스 어법 제대로			
		해커스 수능 어법 불변의 패턴 필수편	해커스 수능 어법 불변의 패턴 실력편	
해커스 쓰기 자신감 Level 3				
	해커스 완전숙련 구문독해 입문	해커스 완전숙련 구문독해 기본	해커스 완전숙련 구문독해 심화	
Hackers Reading Smart Level 4	해커스 독해 제대로 기본독해	해커스 독해 제대로 구문독해		
Hackers Reading Ground Level 3				
Hackers Reading Path Level 3	Hackers Reading Path Level 4			
해커스 첫수능 영어 유형독해		해커스 수능 독해 불변의 패턴 유형편		해커스 수능 독해 불변의 패턴 실전편
	해커스 수능영어독해 미니 모의고사 12+2회 기본	해커스 수능영어독해 미니 모의고사 12+2회 필수		해커스 수능영어독해 미니 모의고사 12+2회 완성 (* 출간 예정)
해커스 중학영어듣기 모의고사 24회 Level 3		해커스 수능영어듣기 모의고사 20+4회 기본	해커스 수능영어듣기 모의고사 20+4회 실전	
		해커스 수능영어듣기 모의고사 30+5회 기본		해커스 수능영어듣기 모의고사 30+5회 실전
	해커스 보카 고등 기본			
해커스 보카 중학 고난도		해커스 보카 수능 필수 2000+		
			해커스 보카 수능 완성 1800+	
			해커스 보카 수능 심화	
		해커스 보카 수능 숙어		
	해커스 보카 어원편			

해커스북(HackersBook.com)에서
교재에 대한 자세한 설명과 다양한 학습 자료를 확인하세요!

최신 개정 교과서 완벽 반영

기출로적중

해커스
중학영문법

2학년

해커스 중학영문법이 특별한 이유!

1. 실제 중학교 내신 **기출문제 빅데이터 및 최신 개정 교과서** 완벽 반영

2. **단계별 문제풀이**를 통해 내신 시험에 확실하게 대비 가능

3. 문법 포인트 이해에 **필수적인 기초 문법**으로 체계적인 학습 시작

4. **워크북의 추가 문제**를 충분히 풀어보며 실력 완성

5. 내신 점수를 높여주는 **다양한 학습 자료** 제공

정가 **14,900** 원

53740

ISBN 978-89-6542-407-9

9 788965 424079

해커스북(HackersBook.com)에서
본 교재에 대한 다양한 추가 학습 자료를 이용하세요!

최신 개정 교과서 완벽 반영

기출로적중

해커스
중학영문법

- 중학 내신 기출 빅데이터 반영
- 실전·서술형 문제로 내신 완벽 대비

워크북

2학년

해커스 교재는
다릅니다

펼쳐 보면 느껴집니다

단 한 줄도 배움의 공백이 생기지 않도록
문장 한 줄마다 20년이 넘는
해커스의 영어교육 노하우를 담았음을

덮고 나면 확신합니다

수많은 선생님의 목소리와
정확한 출제 데이터 분석으로 꽉 찬
교재 한 권이면 충분함을

해커스북 중·고등
HackersBook.com

최신 개정 교과서 완벽 반영

기출로적중

해커스

중학영문법

2학년

이 책을 검토해주신 선생님들

강상훈 경기 평촌비상에듀학원 / **김가영** 서울 송정중학교 / **김원덕** 경기 올림피아드학원 / **박유정** 서울 반포중학교 / **박윤정** 경기 이지베스트학원

박은혜 서울 송파중학교 / **박정은** 서울 대청중학교 / **양세희** 서울 양세희수능영어학원 / **이계윤** 서울 씨앤씨학원 / **이유빈** 서울 잉글리쉬&매쓰매니저학원

이혜원 서울 대청중학교 / **정혜은** 서울 용곡중학교 / **최다빈** 서울 최강영어 / **최승복** 경기 오른어학원 / **최지영** 경기 다른영어학원

목차

목차

CHAPTER 1
문장의 형식

기출로 적중 POINT

POINT 1-1 1형식과 2형식

정답 p.61

연습문제 다음 밑줄 친 부분의 문장 성분을 <보기>에서 골라 쓰시오.

<보기> 주어 동사 주격 보어 수식어

1 The boys jumped on the bed.
  [   ] [   ] [   ]

2 Samuel became a lawyer.
  [   ] [   ] [   ]

3 The earthquake happened last week.
    [   ] [   ] [   ]

4 Jenny's mother is an English teacher.
    [   ] [   ] [   ]

5 The next bus should arrive soon.
    [   ] [   ] [   ]

6 The sweater feels soft.
    [   ] [   ] [   ]

7 The traffic light turned green.
      [   ] [   ][   ]

8 The concert will start in 30 minutes.
      [   ] [   ] [   ]

POINT 1-2 2형식: 감각동사

정답 p.61

연습문제 밑줄 친 부분이 어법상 맞으면 O를 쓰고, 틀리면 바르게 고쳐 완전한 문장을 쓰시오.

1 Your idea sounds greatly. → _____

2 This cupcake tastes like delicious. → _____

3 The garbage smells really bad. → _____

4 I feel awful about the accident. → _____

5 The muffin tastes chocolate. → _____

6 The blue flowers in the yard smell like good. → _____

7 Mr. White looks very upset today. → _____

8 All of the band's songs sounded wonderfully. → _____

연습문제 A 우리말과 같도록 괄호 안의 말을 알맞게 배열하시오.

1 그 아이는 나에게 많은 질문을 했다. (me, asked, many questions, the child)

= _____

2 그 농장은 치즈를 생산한다. (produces, the farm, cheese)

= _____

3 나는 거실에서 이상한 소리를 들었다. (in the living room, heard, a strange sound, I)

= _____

4 나의 할머니는 그녀의 식물에 물을 주신다. (her plants, my grandmother, waters)

= _____

5 나는 그에게 나의 주말 계획들을 말해줬다. (him, told, my weekend plans, I)

= _____

6 Jerry는 그의 누나에게 맛있는 핫도그를 만들어줬다. (a tasty hot dog, made, Jerry, his sister)

= _____

연습문제 B 다음 4형식 문장은 3형식으로, 3형식 문장은 4형식으로 바꿔 쓰시오.

1 Jake showed his photo album to me.

→ _____

2 May I ask you a favor?

→ _____

3 I gave some carrots to the horses.

→ _____

4 Can you find me the science textbook?

→ _____

5 The soccer player passed the ball to his teammate.

→ _____

6 My aunt bought me a new bicycle for Christmas.

→ _____

연습문제 A 다음 문장의 목적어에는 동그라미를 치고, 목적격 보어에는 밑줄을 치시오.

1 Did you find the math exam hard?

2 Please keep your room clean.

3 They made me the class president.

4 Exercising every day makes us healthy.

5 That muffler will keep your neck warm.

6 My mother calls me "angel face".

7 You need to keep the meat cool in the refrigerator.

8 This song made her a popular songwriter.

9 We called Jasmin the queen of golf.

10 Chris finds his new Chinese class too difficult.

11 Everyone found the instructions for the machine confusing.

연습문제 B 우리말과 같도록 괄호 안의 말을 알맞게 배열하시오.

1 Eric은 그 방송이 지루하다고 생각했다. (found, the show, Eric, boring)

= _____

2 사람들은 저 소방관을 영웅이라고 부른다. (call, people, that firefighter, a hero)

= _____

3 저 독특한 빌딩은 우리의 도시를 유명하게 만들었다. (famous, that unique building, our city, made)

= _____

4 그들은 Tom을 그들의 팀의 주장으로 만들었다. (made, of, Tom, the captain, their team, they)

= _____

5 나는 이 웹사이트가 유용하다고 생각한다. (this website, I, useful, find)

= _____

6 경찰관들은 마을을 안전하게 지킨다. (the village, the police officers, safe, keep)

= _____

7 우리는 우리의 선생님을 "Mr. Incredible"이라고 부른다. (we, our teacher, "Mr. Incredible", call)

= _____

8 그 숙제는 한 시간 동안 학생들을 바쁘게 했다. (for an hour, the students, kept, the homework, busy)

= _____

연습문제 A 우리말과 같도록 괄호 안의 말을 활용하여 문장을 완성하시오.

1 Kate는 나에게 그녀를 도와줄 것을 요청했다. (ask, help)

= Kate _____ .

2 너는 내가 체스 동아리에 가입하기를 원하니? (want, join the chess club)

= Do you _____ ?

3 경찰관은 그 여자에게 차를 즉시 멈추라고 명령했다. (order, stop the car)

= The police officer _____ immediately.

4 나는 그에게 제시간에 오라고 조언했다. (advise, be on time)

= I _____ .

5 나의 부모님은 내가 대학에 진학하기를 기대하신다. (expect, go to a university)

= My parents _____ .

6 판사는 그 남자가 집에 돌아가는 것을 허락했다. (allow, return home)

= The judge _____ .

7 Watson씨는 그녀의 남편에게 약간의 계란을 사라고 말하지 않았다. (tell, buy some eggs)

= Ms. Watson _____ .

연습문제 B 괄호 안에서 알맞은 것을 고르시오.

1 The teacher wanted us (listen / to listen) carefully.

2 Benny's behavior made me (angry / angrily).

3 Sophia asked her friend (to help / help) her with the science report.

4 The coach expected him (to exercise / exercise) more often.

5 His grandmother advised him (eat / to eat) more vegetables.

6 The doctor ordered the patient (take / to take) a long rest.

7 Jake didn't find the information (usefully / useful).

8 Mom asked me (to read / read) the recipe for her.

9 The boy didn't allow the dentist (to touch / touch) his teeth.

10 Her perfect math score made her (proud / proudly).

11 I always try to keep my room (neat / neatly).

12 I told him (go / to go) to bed early for the trip the next day.

연습문제 A 밑줄 친 부분이 어법상 맞으면 O를 쓰고, 틀리면 바르게 고쳐 완전한 문장을 쓰시오.

1 Doing yoga every morning makes you <u>feeling</u> fresh.

→ _____

2 The judge asked the people in the courtroom <u>to be</u> silent.

→ _____

3 My mom doesn't let me <u>to travel</u> by myself.

→ _____

4 Ms. Dale had us <u>to clean</u> the dirty shoes.

→ _____

5 I helped Dylan <u>to finish</u> his English assignment.

→ _____

6 The detective got the suspect <u>tell</u> the truth.

→ _____

7 Jason let his daughter <u>to play</u> with sand.

→ _____

8 The pilot told the passengers <u>wearing</u> a seat belt.

→ _____

연습문제 B 괄호 안에서 알맞은 것을 <u>모두</u> 고르시오.

1 That cat won't let us (touch / to touch) its belly.

2 Your new hairstyle makes you (look / to look) younger.

3 My parents got me (come / to come) home before 9 P.M.

4 Ms. Park had the plumber (repair / to repair) her kitchen sink.

5 I helped her (find / to find) her lost key.

6 Do you want me (close / to close) the window?

7 The teacher couldn't make the students (stop / to stop) talking.

8 The house owner let us (have / to have) a look around the house.

9 She had her brother (bring / to bring) her bag.

10 Could you help me (move / to move) this sofa?

11 I will get Harry (check / to check) our flight tickets.

12 James advised his children (brush / to brush) their teeth three times a day.

연습문제 A <보기>와 같이 다음 두 문장을 한 문장으로 연결하시오.

<보기> I saw the children. They were flying kites on the hill.
→ _I saw the children flying[fly]_ kites on the hill.

1 I saw a man. He was playing the trumpet in the park.
→ _____ the trumpet in the park.

2 I didn't hear Charles. He was coming into my room.
→ _____ into my room.

3 We watched the cat. It was chasing a mouse.
→ _____ a mouse.

4 Erica smelled the bread. It was burning in the kitchen.
→ _____ in the kitchen.

5 Paul listened to the woman. She was singing beautifully.
→ _____ beautifully.

6 Tom felt someone. Someone was touching him on the shoulder.
→ _____ him on the shoulder.

연습문제 B 괄호 안의 동사를 알맞은 형태로 바꿔 문장을 완성하시오.

1 I heard Benjamin _____ all day. (cough)

2 The horror movie made me _____. (scream)

3 Can you hear somebody _____ outside? (shout)

4 Tom had me _____ to Grace last night. (apologize)

5 Lisa doesn't allow her brother _____ her laptop. (use)

6 Fred felt something _____ above his head. (fly)

7 Have you watched a magician _____ magic tricks? (perform)

8 Did you see the horse _____ over the fence? (jump)

9 Emma asked her mother _____ some milk on the way home. (get)

10 Let your clothes _____ completely before you put them back on. (dry)

11 Reading many books will help you _____ your knowledge. (expand)

중간·기말고사 실전 문제

1 다음 빈칸에 들어갈 말로 <u>어색한</u> 것을 <u>모두</u> 고르시오.

> A: Did you see our new teacher?
> B: Yes, she looked _____.

① friendly ② scary ③ gently
④ lovely ⑤ gladly

2 다음 빈칸에 들어갈 알맞은 것은?

> The school doesn't allow the students
> _____ high heels.

① wear ② wore
③ wearing ④ to wear
⑤ are wearing

3 다음 중 어법상 바른 것을 <u>모두</u> 고르시오.

① Everyone expects Kim win the race.
② Lisa had her brother to fix her computer.
③ My father wants me to wash the dishes.
④ Brain asked me lending him a pencil.
⑤ The librarian told us to speak quietly.

4 다음 빈칸에 들어갈 말로 <u>어색한</u> 것은?

> The film director _____ me design
> the poster of the new movie.

① had ② let ③ helped
④ got ⑤ made

5 괄호 안의 말을 알맞게 배열하시오.

> Beth always makes funny jokes, so
> _____. (call, a
> comedian, I, her)

6 다음 우리말을 영작할 때 빈칸에 들어갈 알맞은 것은?

> 밖에 비가 오고 있었기 때문에 나는 너에게 우산을 가지고 가라고 조언했다.
> = I _____ an umbrella because it
>   was raining outside.

① advised you take
② advised take you
③ advised you to take
④ advised to take you
⑤ advised you taking

7 다음 빈칸에 들어갈 말로 <u>어색한</u> 것은?

> My parents and my sister came to the
> concert and _____ me playing the
> clarinet.

① watched ② saw
③ heard ④ listened to
⑤ had

8 우리말과 같도록 괄호 안의 말을 알맞게 배열하시오.

> 추운 날씨는 그 호수를 얼게 만들었다. (freeze,
> the, weather, the, cold, lake, made)

= _____

9 다음 빈칸에 들어갈 말로 어색한 것은?

> Kate's mother _____ her to clean her room before dinner.

① wanted　　　　② told
③ expected　　　④ made
⑤ asked

10 다음 중 어법상 어색한 것은?

① The car accident happened in front of the bank.
② The flowers in my garden grew fast.
③ Mark became angry after the fight.
④ People remained silently during the speech.
⑤ There weren't any empty seats on the bus.

11 다음 중 주어진 문장과 문장의 형식이 같은 것은?

> Emma kept the kitten warm with a blanket.

① The plane for London will depart soon.
② This medicine tastes really bad.
③ My uncle got me a job at his company.
④ The Internet makes our lives convenient.
⑤ Sam hoped to get a high score on the test.

12 다음 중 4형식 문장은 3형식으로, 3형식 문장은 4형식으로 바르게 바꾼 것은?

① George got me a birthday present.
　→ George got a birthday present to me.
② Diane read a story to the children.
　→ Diane read a story the children.
③ The waiter passed a menu to Liam.
　→ The waiter passed Liam to a menu.
④ Megan built Anna a snowman.
　→ Megan built a snowman for Anna.
⑤ The student asked the teacher a question.
　→ The student asked a question the teacher.

13 우리말과 같도록 괄호 안의 말을 알맞게 배열하시오.

> 나는 피자 한 조각을 위해 Jackson에게 5달러를 지불했다. (I, five dollars, Jackson, paid)

= _____ for a piece of pizza.

14 다음 빈칸에 들어갈 말이 순서대로 짝지어진 것은?

> · Mr. Porter will buy flowers _____ his wife on Valentine's Day.
> · Olivia asked a favor _____ her best friend last week.

① for – to　　② to – for　　③ for – of
④ to – of　　⑤ for – for

15 다음 중 어법상 바른 것끼리 묶인 것은?

ⓐ This chicken soup tastes great.
ⓑ I expected the package arrive today.
ⓒ The heavy rain sounded a waterfall.
ⓓ Mark smelled wood to burn in the fireplace.
ⓔ Many students in the class find Jeremy funny.
ⓕ The flight attendant helped the man to find his seat.

① ⓐ, ⓑ, ⓓ　　② ⓐ, ⓔ, ⓕ　　③ ⓑ, ⓒ, ⓕ
④ ⓑ, ⓓ, ⓔ　　⑤ ⓒ, ⓓ, ⓔ

16 다음 빈칸에 들어갈 말이 순서대로 짝지어진 것은?

· The coach advised the athletes _____ harder.
· I listened to the rain _____ on the trees.

① exercise –fall　　② exercising – to fall
③ to exercise – to fall　④ exercising – falling
⑤ to exercise – falling

17 우리말과 같도록 괄호 안의 말을 활용하여 빈칸에 알맞은 말을 쓰시오.

Sarah가 이 비밀을 알게 하지 마라. (let, know)

= _____ _____ _____ _____ this secret.

18 다음 중 밑줄 친 made의 쓰임이 나머지 넷과 다른 것은?

① The movie made the actor a star.
② The mountain climbing made Bill tired.
③ The lively music made everyone dance.
④ Honey bees made their nest in the roof.
⑤ The smell of the hamburger made me hungry.

19 다음 빈칸에 공통으로 들어갈 알맞은 것은?

· The children _____ mud cakes with water and dirt.
· My mother _____ me pick a dress to buy.
· Neal _____ his sister a cheese omelet.

① built　　② helped　　③ made
④ gave　　⑤ let

20 다음 중 어법상 어색한 것은?

① Brad let his brother ride his bike.
② The bus driver told me to show my ticket.
③ Ms. Johnson wants Joe make new friends.
④ My parents had me volunteer at the shelter.
⑤ Tanya helped her grandmother bake the pie.

21 <보기>와 같이 괄호 안의 말을 활용하여 문장을 완성하시오.

<보기>　The police officer ordered *the driver to stop the car* . (stop, the driver, the car)

(1) The police officer asked ＿＿＿＿＿

＿＿＿＿＿＿＿＿＿＿＿＿＿.

(the thief's appearance, describe, a woman)

(2) The police officer helped ＿＿＿＿

＿＿＿＿＿＿＿＿＿＿＿＿＿.

(an old lady, her wallet, find)

(3) The police officer got ＿＿＿＿＿

＿＿＿＿＿＿＿＿＿＿＿＿＿.

(his license, a man, show)

22 다음 중 문장의 형식이 같은 것끼리 묶인 것은?

ⓐ A rainbow appeared after the rain.
ⓑ Could you find my keys for me?
ⓒ There were a lot of people in the library.
ⓓ That beautiful beach made the city popular.
ⓔ I watched the sun rise from the horizon.
ⓕ The cloud looked like a dinosaur.
ⓖ The cat is sleeping on the couch.

① ⓐ, ⓒ, ⓕ　　② ⓐ, ⓒ, ⓖ　　③ ⓑ, ⓓ, ⓔ
④ ⓑ, ⓔ, ⓕ　　⑤ ⓓ, ⓔ, ⓖ

[23-24] 다음 두 문장을 한 문장으로 연결하시오.

23

My grandfather takes the medicine three times a day. The doctor had him do that.

→ The doctor ＿＿＿＿＿＿＿＿＿

＿＿＿＿＿＿＿＿＿＿＿＿＿.

24

I saw a puppy this morning. It was playing with a cat.

→ I ＿＿＿＿＿＿＿＿＿＿＿＿

＿＿＿＿＿＿＿＿＿＿＿＿＿.

25 다음 글의 밑줄 친 ⓐ~ⓔ 중 어법상 어색한 것을 찾아 기호를 쓰고 바르게 고쳐 쓰시오.

When I woke up on Saturday morning, I ⓐheard my dad cooking. The food ⓑsmelled nicely, so I went down to the kitchen. Dad was ⓒmaking pancakes for our family. I ⓓhelped him set the table. He ⓔasked me bring our family into the dining room. We all ate breakfast together.

(1) ＿＿＿　→　＿＿＿＿＿＿＿＿＿
(2) ＿＿＿　→　＿＿＿＿＿＿＿＿＿

CHAPTER 2
다양한 문장의 종류

기출로 적중 POINT

POINT 1

연습문제 **A** 다음 빈칸에 What이나 How 중 알맞은 것을 쓰시오.

1 _____ a lovely house!

2 _____ useful information it is!

3 _____ fast the ball rolls!

4 _____ brightly the sun shines!

5 _____ a delightful surprise!

6 _____ honorable the award is!

7 _____ an amazing invention!

8 _____ clever children they are!

9 _____ sweet these peaches smell!

10 _____ dark hair he has!

연습문제 **B** 다음 문장을 감탄문으로 바꿔 쓰시오.

1 She has a very friendly smile.

→ _____

2 That was a really easy puzzle.

→ _____

3 He thinks very creatively.

→ _____

4 The apples look very fresh.

→ _____

5 The advice is really practical.

→ _____

6 The lemon is very sour.

→ _____

7 The baby has really small feet.

→ _____

8 The man talks very quietly.

→ _____

POINT 2

연습문제 **A** 　우리말과 같도록 괄호 안의 말을 알맞게 배열하시오.

1 올해 무슨 일이 일어나게 될까? (this year, happen, what, will)

= _____

2 우리는 그 공원에 어떻게 갈 수 있니? (how, we, to the park, get, can)

= _____

3 너는 어젯밤에 어디에 있었니? (were, last night, you, where)

= _____

4 너는 왜 프랑스에서 공부하기로 결심했니? (did, decide, you, to study, why, in France)

= _____

5 Jerry는 어째서 항상 늦는 거니? (Jerry, how come, late, always, is)

= _____

6 너는 보통 저녁 식사 후에 무엇을 하니? (dinner, do, usually, after, do, you, what)

= _____

연습문제 **B** 　<보기>와 같이 알맞은 의문사를 활용하여 대화를 완성하시오.

> <보기>   *A*: *When is his birthday?*
>   *B*: His birthday is the twenty-fifth of November.

1 *A*: _____
    B: Dustin broke the window.

2 *A*: _____
    B: My phone number is 010-1234-5678.

3 *A*: _____
    B: I am upset because I lost my wallet.

4 *A*: _____
    B: I go to school by bus.

5 *A*: _____
    B: He is coming back to Korea next month.

6 *A*: _____
    B: You can find the cups on the top shelf.

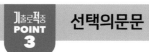
연습문제 A 우리말과 같도록 빈칸에 알맞은 말을 쓰시오.

1 너는 그 빨간 치마와 그 검은 드레스 중 어느 것을 샀니?

= _____ did you buy, the red skirt _____ the black dress?

2 너는 너의 고향에 고속 버스를 타고 갈 예정이니, 아니면 기차를 타고 갈 예정이니?

= _____ you going to your hometown by express bus _____ by train?

3 너는 사과와 오렌지 중 어느 것을 선호하니?

= _____ do you prefer, apple _____ orange?

4 그는 축구하는 것을 좋아하니, 아니면 농구하는 것을 좋아하니?

= _____ he like playing soccer _____ playing basketball?

5 우리는 토요일과 일요일 중에 언제 만나야 하니?

= _____ should we meet, Saturday _____ Sunday?

연습문제 B 자연스러운 대화가 되도록 질문과 대답을 연결하시오.

[1-6]

1 Is he from Spain or Italy?　　　　　　　　　　　·　　　　· ⓐ James.

2 Do you prefer reading books or watching movies?　·　　　　· ⓑ It's fiction.

3 Who sent this package, James or Helen?　　　　　·　　　　· ⓒ He is from Spain.

4 Is this story fiction or nonfiction?　　　　　　　·　　　　· ⓓ I prefer reading books.

5 Which do you like better, pasta or pizza?　　　　·　　　　· ⓔ On Thursday.

6 Did he go to the doctor on Tuesday or Thursday?　·　　　　· ⓕ I like pasta better.

[7-12]

7 Which do you prefer, chocolate or vanilla?　　　·　　　　· ⓐ He plays the violin.

8 Where did Emma travel, Vietnam or Thailand?　·　　　　· ⓑ A hamburger.

9 Will you eat a hamburger or a sandwich for lunch?　·　　　　· ⓒ Vietnam.

10 Did you make or buy this bracelet?　　　　　　·　　　　· ⓓ I prefer chocolate.

11 Does he play the cello or the violin?　　　　　·　　　　· ⓔ I think Minji can help us.

12 Who can help us, Minji or Jihee?　　　　　　·　　　　· ⓕ I bought it.

연습문제   <보기>와 같이 다음 두 문장을 한 문장으로 연결하시오.

> **<보기>**   Please tell me. + Where is the restroom?
>
> → *Please tell me where the restroom is.*

1   I don't know. + How much is this painting worth?

    → _____

2   Do you know? + What does this word mean?

    → _____

3   Can you tell me? + Where is the subway station?

    → _____

4   Do you think? + Why do we have to protect the environment?

    → _____

5   Do you believe? + How can you improve your communication skills?

    → _____

6   Can you remember? + What is his name?

    → _____

7   Can you tell me? + What made her so happy?

    → _____

8   Do you guess? + Where did you lose your passport?

    → _____

9   Please tell me. + How did you find out the answer to that problem?

    → _____

10   Do you imagine? + When will people live on Mars?

    → _____

11   I want to know. + How was the city of Pompeii destroyed?

    → _____

12   Do you think? + Where did they hide the evidence?

    → _____

13   I wonder. + Who invented the light bulb?

    → _____

14   Do you believe? + Who is telling the truth?

    → _____

연습문제 A 우리말과 같도록 괄호 안의 말을 알맞게 배열하시오.

1 너는 Jack이 개를 기르는지 아닌지 아니? (has, if, a, dog, Jack)

= Do you know _____ ?

2 저에게 제가 그 사건에 책임이 있는지 아닌지 말해주세요. (for, responsible, I, whether, am, incident, the)

= Please tell me _____ .

3 너는 그 쌍둥이들이 닮았는지 아닌지 기억하니? (whether, look, twins, the, alike)

= Do you remember _____ ?

4 나는 그가 나를 믿는지 아닌지 모른다. (if, trusts, me, he)

= I don't know _____ .

5 나는 Vivian이 너의 제안에 동의했는지 아닌지 확실하지 않다. (with, Vivian, if, agreed, suggestion, your)

= I'm not sure _____ .

6 나는 그가 아직 거기에서 일하는지 아닌지 궁금하다. (he, if, there, works, still)

= I wonder _____ .

7 너는 나에게 Lucas가 스페인어를 말하는지 아닌지 말해줄 수 있니? (Lucas, Spanish, whether, speaks)

= Can you tell me _____ ?

연습문제 B 다음 두 문장을 한 문장으로 연결하시오.

1 I'm not sure. + Will Kylie participate in this speech contest?

→ _____

2 Can you tell me? + Do we have class today?

→ _____

3 Do you know? + Did someone eat all the leftovers?

→ _____

4 I don't know. + Will James buy a new bag?

→ _____

5 I wonder. + Will it snow on Christmas Eve?

→ _____

6 Please tell me. + Did the cherry trees in Jejudo begin to bloom?

→ _____

7 I don't remember. + Does he like watching horror movies?

→ _____

연습문제 A 괄호 안에서 알맞은 것을 고르시오.

1 This isn't your jacket, (is / isn't) it?

2 Don't run in the hallway, (will / are) you?

3 She doesn't live in Seoul now, (does / doesn't) she?

4 He won't attend the meeting tomorrow, (will / won't) he?

5 Let's go to the swimming pool, (shall / don't) we?

6 The movie wasn't exciting, (was / wasn't) it?

7 Her handwriting is difficult to read, (is / isn't) it?

8 Turn the lights off, (will / aren't) you?

9 Jeremy tries to use eco-friendly products, (does / doesn't) he?

10 I'm good enough to win the dance contest, (am not / aren't) I?

연습문제 B 다음 빈칸에 알맞은 부가의문문을 쓰시오.

1 This book was quite interesting, _____?

2 Let's take a walk around the park, _____?

3 Minsu can read Chinese characters, _____?

4 Wash your hands right away, _____?

5 Koreans eat rice as their basic food, _____?

6 You had a cat when you were young, _____?

7 There are eight planets in the solar system, _____?

8 You didn't pay attention to the class, _____?

9 This pottery is made of clay, _____?

10 Dolphins are mammals, _____?

11 You can keep a secret for me, _____?

12 I'm younger than Liam, _____?

13 These eggs are fully boiled, _____?

14 The temperature in Africa is always over 20℃, _____?

15 Don't yell at each other, _____?

1 다음 중 어법상 <u>어색한</u> 것은?

① How can I buy a concert ticket?

② When did she graduate from high school?

③ What Michael is doing right now?

④ Who made these blueberry muffins?

⑤ Why did your grandfather call you?

2 우리말과 같도록 빈칸에 알맞은 말을 쓰시오.

> 너는 그룹으로 공부하는 것과 혼자 공부하는 것 중 어느 것을 선호하니?

= _____ do you prefer, studying in a group or studying alone?

[3-4] 다음 문장을 감탄문으로 바꿔 쓰시오.

3

> He is a really amazing soccer player.
>
> → _____

4

> The onions smell very bad.
>
> → _____

5 다음 빈칸에 들어갈 알맞은 것은?

> I'm not sure _____ these cookies contain peanuts.

① which ② what ③ whether

④ who ⑤ where

6 다음 두 문장을 한 문장으로 바르게 연결한 것은?

> Can you tell me? How did the accident happen?

① How can you tell me did the accident happen?

② How can you tell me the accident happened?

③ Can you tell me how did the accident happen?

④ Can you tell me if the accident happened?

⑤ Can you tell me how the accident happened?

7 다음 대화의 빈칸에 들어갈 알맞은 것은?

> A: You want to go to law school, _____?
>
> B: Actually, I haven't decided yet.

① don't I ② shall we

③ don't you ④ will you

⑤ didn't you

8 다음 중 밑줄 친 <u>what</u>의 쓰임이 나머지 넷과 <u>다른</u> 것은?

① <u>What</u> is your favorite type of movie?

② Do you know <u>what</u> Sophia's phone number is?

③ <u>What</u> caused the loud noise?

④ <u>What</u> a delicious meal that was!

⑤ Do you remember <u>what</u> the survey was about?

9 다음 (A)~(C)에 들어갈 말이 바르게 짝지어진 것은?

· These seats aren't for the disabled,
___(A)___ ?
· I'm singing well, ___(B)___ ?
· Give me some water, ___(C)___ ?

	(A)	(B)	(C)
①	are they	am I	will you
②	are these	am I	won't you
③	are they	aren't I	will you
④	are these	aren't I	won't you
⑤	are they	aren't I	won't you

10 다음 빈칸에 들어갈 말이 나머지 넷과 다른 것은?

① _____ brilliant your idea is!
② _____ heavily the rain fell!
③ _____ politely James behaved!
④ _____ crowded the store is!
⑤ _____ colorful socks you have!

11 다음 질문에 대한 대답으로 알맞은 것은?

A: How can I make a hotel reservation?
B: _____

① For three nights.
② We arrive on Friday.
③ You can call the hotel.
④ Find one near the beach.
⑤ Because we are going to Jeonju.

12 우리말과 같도록 괄호 안의 말을 알맞게 배열하시오.

나는 누가 벽에 저 그림을 그렸는지 모른다. (don't, drew, who, know, I, on the wall, that picture)

= _____
_____

13 다음 중 밑줄 친 부분이 어법상 바른 것은?

① Your brother is in trouble, doesn't he?
② This bread tastes really nice, doesn't this?
③ Let's go ice skating today, will you?
④ There was a fire in that building, wasn't it?
⑤ The two cultures have lots of things in common, don't they?

14 우리말과 같도록 주어진 <조건>에 맞게 영작하시오.

파리까지 비행은 정말 길었구나!

<조건>
1. 감탄문으로 쓰시오.
2. 7단어로 쓰시오.
3. the flight to Paris, long을 활용하시오.

= _____

15 다음 빈칸에 들어갈 말이 순서대로 짝지어진 것은?

> · I wonder _____ the sign represents.
> · Could you tell me _____ this film is based on a true story?

① when – if
② what – what
③ when – what
④ what – if
⑤ how – if

16 다음 대화의 빈칸에 들어갈 알맞은 것은?

> A: You said that you would clean your room today. But _____, have you?
> B: I was busy studying. I'll clean it now.

① you have cleaned your room
② you cleaned your room
③ you didn't clean your room
④ you haven't cleaned your room
⑤ you won't clean your room

17 다음 대답에 대한 질문으로 알맞은 것은?

> A: _____
> B: Because I like the city and its beautiful weather.

① Who made you choose to live in Madrid?
② When did you choose to live in Madrid?
③ Where did you choose to live in Madrid?
④ Why did you choose to live in Madrid?
⑤ How did you choose to live in Madrid?

[18-19] 다음 두 문장을 한 문장으로 연결하시오.

18

> I don't remember. What is the password for this website?
> → _____
> _____

19

> Do you know? Is the shopping mall open this Sunday?
> → _____
> _____

20 다음 대화의 빈칸에 들어갈 말이 순서대로 짝지어진 것은?

> A: Do you want to go to a café on Saturday afternoon?
> B: I'd like to, but I will be in Busan this weekend.
> A: Really? _____ are you going there?
> B: My brother is going to participate in a swimming competition. My family is going to watch it.
> A: I didn't know that your brother is a swimmer. _____ did he start swimming?
> B: About six years old. He's very talented.

① How – When
② When – How
③ Why – When
④ When – Why
⑤ Why – How

21 다음 중 어법상 바른 것을 <u>모두</u> 고르시오.

① What unique a color that building has!
② What helpful tips the book has!
③ What this store has friendly employees!
④ How early I woke up this morning!
⑤ How expensive are these earrings!

22 다음 글의 빈칸에 들어갈 알맞은 것은?

_____ It is made from a caterpillar cocoon. The caterpillar wraps itself in a soft material before it becomes a butterfly. This material is used to make silk.

*caterpillar 애벌레
*cocoon 고치

① Where do you know silk comes from?
② Why do you know silk comes from?
③ Do you know where does silk come from?
④ Do you know where silk comes from?
⑤ Do you know why silk comes from?

23 우리말과 같도록 주어진 <조건>에 맞게 영작하시오.

너는 왜 북극곰들이 하얀색이라고 생각하니?

<조건>
1. 간접의문문을 사용하시오.
2. 8단어로 쓰시오.
3. think, polar bears를 활용하시오.

= _____

24 다음 중 어법상 <u>어색한</u> 것끼리 묶인 것은?

ⓐ What a funny joke it is!
ⓑ You can speak German, can't you?
ⓒ I wonder how did the author imagine the mysterious story.
ⓓ Do you remember if William called us yesterday?
ⓔ How beautifully Beth played the piano!
ⓕ Do you imagine what the perfect holiday would be?
ⓖ Those pens belong to you, don't those?

① ⓐ, ⓒ, ⓓ ② ⓐ, ⓔ, ⓖ ③ ⓑ, ⓒ, ⓕ
④ ⓑ, ⓓ, ⓔ ⑤ ⓒ, ⓕ, ⓖ

25 다음 글의 밑줄 친 ⓐ~ⓔ 중 어법상 <u>어색한</u> 것을 찾아 기호를 쓰고 바르게 고쳐 쓰시오.

Do you know ⓐ<u>why do some birds travel</u> to different places before winter? ⓑ<u>What the purpose of their trips is</u> every year? It's because they need to move to new places with lots of food as the seasons change. Some birds travel great distances. ⓒ<u>What do you think the longest annual animal migration is</u>? It's the arctic tern's trip between Greenland and Antarctica. They travel 71,000 kilometers every year. That's an amazing distance, ⓓ<u>isn't it</u>? ⓔ<u>How</u> an interesting fact it is!

*tern 제비갈매기

(1) _____ → _____
(2) _____ → _____
(3) _____ → _____

CHAPTER 3
시제

기출로 적중 POINT

연습문제 괄호 안의 동사를 활용하여 현재시제 문장을 완성하시오.

1 A koala _____ most of its time sleeping. (spend)

2 A bad workman _____ his tools. (blame)

3 I'll take my umbrella if it _____ tomorrow. (rain)

4 The first train to Busan _____ at 9:00 A.M. (leave)

5 This laptop _____ to Larry. (belong)

6 He _____ two bottles of water every day. (drink)

7 Please answer the phone before it _____ twice. (ring)

8 The water pipe of my house often _____ in winter. (freeze)

POINT 2-1 과거시제

정답 p.65

연습문제 밑줄 친 부분이 어법상 맞으면 O를 쓰고, 틀리면 바르게 고쳐 완전한 문장을 쓰시오.

1 It <u>rains</u> a lot last week.

→ _____

2 My friends and I <u>play</u> baseball every weekend.

→ _____

3 Kevin <u>completed</u> his drawing yesterday.

→ _____

4 The Titanic <u>sinks</u> on April 15, 1912.

→ _____

5 Hangeul <u>was</u> invented in 1443.

→ _____

6 I <u>find</u> my grandmother's secret recipe a month ago.

→ _____

7 The first Olympic games <u>are</u> held in Greece in 1896.

→ _____

POINT 2-2 과거시제: 동사의 과거형과 과거분사형

정답 p.65

연습문제 다음 동사의 과거형과 과거분사형을 쓰시오.

1 attend	– _____ – _____	**2** enter	– _____ – _____
3 shut	– _____ – _____	**4** believe	– _____ – _____
5 stop	– _____ – _____	**6** run	– _____ – _____
7 hurt	– _____ – _____	**8** become	– _____ – _____
9 bring	– _____ – _____	**10** leave	– _____ – _____
11 overcome	– _____ – _____	**12** understand	– _____ – _____
13 mistake	– _____ – _____	**14** spread	– _____ – _____
15 study	– _____ – _____	**16** forget	– _____ – _____
17 choose	– _____ – _____	**18** lay	– _____ – _____
19 cost	– _____ – _____	**20** be	– _____ – _____

POINT 3 미래시제

정답 p.65

연습문제 괄호 안에서 알맞은 것을 고르시오.

1 Paul (searched / will search) online for information about art history tomorrow.

2 Many people (donated / will donate) money to the flood victims last summer.

3 I (buy / am going to buy) a new school uniform next weekend.

4 If you (feel / will feel) cold, please close the window.

5 We (did / will do) volunteer work at the nursing home next week.

6 My friends and I (went / are going to go) rafting tomorrow.

7 The oriental rugs (were / will be) popular in the 2000s.

8 Last year, she usually (fed / is going to feed) the cats living in the street.

9 The egg (hatched / is going to hatch) in a few days from now.

10 A group of scientists (left / will leave) for Antarctica the next Wednesday.

11 Oranges (have / will have) lots of vitamin C.

12 I (stopped / will stop) eating any food made of flour from now on.

연습문제 A 우리말과 같도록 괄호 안의 말을 활용하여 문장을 완성하시오.

1 너는 지금 너의 열쇠를 찾고 있니? (look)

= _____ for your key now?

2 그녀는 Julia가 전화했을 때 신문을 읽고 있었다. (read)

= _____ the newspaper when Julia called.

3 Betty는 꽃집에서 장미 냄새를 맡고 있다. (smell)

= _____ the roses at the flower shop.

4 너는 내일 머리를 자를 예정이니? (get)

= _____ a haircut tomorrow?

5 저것은 좋은 생각처럼 들린다. (sound)

= _____ like a good idea.

6 Kevin은 지금 Susie와 말다툼하고 있다. (argue)

= _____ with Susie now.

7 우리는 그때 거리에서 크리스마스 캐럴을 부르고 있었다. (sing)

= _____ a Christmas carol on the street at that time.

연습문제 B <보기>와 같이 괄호 안의 동사를 활용하여 대화를 완성하시오.

> **<보기>** *A*: Are you busy now?
>
> *B*: Yes. I _am cleaning_ my room. (clean)
>
> *A*: Why didn't you come to the mall with us?
>
> *B*: I _was doing_ yoga at that time. (do)

1 *A*: What were you doing last night?

B: I _____ with Sam on the phone. (chat)

2 *A*: What are the workers doing in the hall?

B: They _____ the walls. (paint)

3 *A*: Why did you come home late?

B: I _____ for my exams in the library. (prepare)

4 *A*: Did you have lunch already?

B: I _____ lunch now. (have)

연습문제 A　우리말과 같도록 괄호 안의 동사를 활용하여 현재완료시제 문장을 완성하시오.

1　우리는 유치원 때부터 친구였다. (be)

= _____ friends since kindergarten.

2　그 아이들은 전에 두리안을 먹어보지 않았다. (eat)

= _____ a durian before.

3　너는 Jackson에게서 약간의 편지를 받았니? (receive)

= _____ any letters from Jackson?

4　이 요구르트는 상했다. (go)

= _____ bad.

5　경찰은 아직 도둑을 찾지 못했다. (find)

= The police _____ the thief yet.

6　Tom은 얼마나 오래 한국어를 공부해왔니? (study)

= How long _____ Korean?

연습문제 B　<보기>와 같이 현재완료시제를 이용하여 다음 두 문장을 한 문장으로 연결하시오.

<보기>　David began to work at the bank ten months ago. He still works there.

→ David　*has worked at the bank for ten months*　.

1　Amy lost her ring. She still can't find her ring.

→ Amy _____ .

2　He borrowed my comic book two weeks ago. He still has my comic book.

→ He _____ .

3　My grandfather began to search for the treasure underwater in 1990. He still searches for it.

→ My grandfather _____ .

4　The organization started to fight against racism thirty years ago. It still fights against racism.

→ The organization _____ .

5　Yuna became a world famous ballerina in 2018. She is still a world famous ballerina.

→ Yuna _____ .

6　I began to write songs last winter. I still write songs.

→ I _____ .

연습문제 <보기>와 같이 우리말과 같도록 괄호 안의 말을 알맞게 배열하고 현재완료시제의 용법을 쓰시오.

<보기> 나의 아빠는 그의 전화기를 5년 동안 사용해오셨다. (has, dad, my, used)
= _My dad has used_ his phone for five years. [계속]

1 너희들은 전에 서로를 만난 적이 있니? (have, met, you)
= _____ each other before? [   ]

2 나의 오빠는 방금 그의 차를 세차했다. (washed, older, just, brother, has, my)
= _____ his car. [   ]

3 나는 이미 나의 수학 숙제를 완료했다. (have, completed, already, I)
= _____ my math homework. [   ]

4 이 지역에 일주일 동안 비가 세게 내렸다. (rained, hard, has, it)
= _____ in this region for a week. [   ]

5 그 가족은 그들의 여름 휴가로 하와이에 갔다. (the, has, family, gone)
= _____ to Hawaii for their summer vacation. [   ]

6 나는 '해리 포터' 시리즈를 읽어본 적이 없다. (read, never, I, have)
= _____ _Harry Potter_ series. [   ]

7 그녀는 식물을 키우는 것에 흥미를 잃었다. (lost, has, interest, she)
= _____ in growing plants. [   ]

8 나는 인도 카레를 맛본 적이 없다. (tasted, I, have, never)
= _____ Indian curry. [   ]

9 그 기업은 최근에 새 공장을 짓기 위해 땅을 구입했다. (bought, company, the, recently, has)
= _____ land to build a new factory. [   ]

10 한국 축구 팀은 월드컵에 참석하기 위해 러시아로 떠났다. (has, the, soccer team, Korean, left)
= _____ for Russia to attend the World Cup. [   ]

11 기술에서의 발전은 수백 년 동안 많은 이익으로 이끌었다. (in, led, have, technology, developments)
= _____ to many benefits for hundreds of years. [   ]

12 Johnson씨는 10년 동안 중학교에서 영어를 가르쳐왔다. (Ms. Johnson, taught, English, has)
= _____ at the middle school for ten years. [   ]

현재완료시제 vs. 과거시제

정답 p.66

연습문제 A 괄호 안의 동사를 활용하여 현재완료시제 또는 과거시제 문장을 완성하시오.

1 David _____ all over Europe since he was little. (travel)

2 Lisa _____ her eyes because the sun was too bright. (blink)

3 I _____ Polish and Russian since I was ten years old. (study)

4 Gabby _____ this phone case for me yesterday. (make)

5 We _____ in line to enter the concert hall for the past five hours. (wait)

6 Edward _____ a big fight with his friend last week. (have)

7 I _____ interested in drones since I first saw one. (be)

8 The fishing boat _____ to the bottom of the sea last night. (sink)

연습문제 B 밑줄 친 부분이 어법상 맞으면 O를 쓰고, 틀리면 바르게 고쳐 완전한 문장을 쓰시오.

1 It has been ten years since my grandfather passed away.

→ _____

2 The Second World War has ended in 1945.

→ _____

3 A number of people have moved to this city since it was developed.

→ _____

4 The price of oil went up since last month.

→ _____

5 Have you watched the comedy show on TV last night?

→ _____

6 The career counselor provided useful information since we first met.

→ _____

7 He has reported the incident to the police an hour ago.

→ _____

8 Financial fraud became more common since last year.

→ _____

중간·기말고사 실전 문제

1 다음 중 동사의 과거형과 과거분사형이 잘못된 것은?

① get – got – gotten
② try – tried – tried
③ spread – spread – spread
④ overcome – overcame – overcome
⑤ rise – rose – rose

2 다음 중 밑줄 친 부분이 어법상 바른 것은?

① A raccoon entered my house yesterday.
② Sunflowers have grew since July.
③ I saw a shooting star for the first time last night.
④ She begun to write the book in 1990.
⑤ Jessica and Matt have knew each other for a long time.

3 다음 두 문장의 의미가 같도록 빈칸에 알맞은 말을 쓰시오.

The next bus will arrive in 30 minutes.
= The next bus _____ _____
_____ _____ in 30
minutes.

4 다음 중 어법상 어색한 것은?

① The panda was born a month ago.
② I'll let you know if I find your phone.
③ A pineapple takes two years to grow.
④ Korea is famous for its textile industry in the 1970s.
⑤ The newspaper comes almost every day at 5 A.M.

5 다음 빈칸에 들어갈 알맞은 것은?

My family _____ in this apartment
since I was born.

① live   ② lives
③ lived   ④ is going to live
⑤ has lived

6 다음 중 어법상 어색한 것은?

① Jeff and his friends were playing baseball yesterday afternoon.
② Mina is participating in the piano contest tomorrow.
③ That painting is having positive energy.
④ I'm thinking of having some burritos for lunch.
⑤ My dog was digging in the ground to hide a bone when I came home.

7 다음 문장을 주어진 지시대로 바꿔 쓰시오.

Emily has been a Korean citizen since 2017.

(1) 부정문으로
→ _____

(2) 의문문으로
→ _____

8 괄호 안의 동사를 활용하여 질문에 대한 대답을 완성하시오.

> *A*: Did you see the pink sky last evening?
> *B*: Yes. It was really wonderful. The sky _____ pink around 7 P.M. (turn)

9 다음 중 어법상 바른 것은?

① Claire lived in Mokpo since she was born.
② Jessica has joined the orchestra last month.
③ The train station has been closed for over 50 years.
④ When have the accident happened?
⑤ We have gone on a field trip to a folk museum yesterday.

10 다음 중 밑줄 친 부분의 의미가 나머지 넷과 <u>다른</u> 것은?

① The concert <u>is going to</u> start at 9 P.M.
② The caterpillar <u>is going to</u> change into a butterfly soon.
③ Brenda <u>is going to</u> open her present now.
④ My family <u>is going to</u> the beach.
⑤ A typhoon <u>is going to</u> arrive at Jejudo tomorrow morning.

[11-12] 주어진 문장의 밑줄 친 부분과 용법이 같은 것을 고르시오.

11

> <u>Have</u> you ever <u>heard</u> of upcycling?

① I <u>haven't made</u> a decision yet.
② How long <u>have</u> you <u>studied</u> Egyptian art?
③ I <u>have</u> never <u>gone</u> bungee jumping.
④ We <u>haven't watched</u> the animated movie yet.
⑤ The cruise <u>has left</u> for Greece.

12

> A group of scientists <u>has</u> recently <u>discovered</u> an interesting fact about DNA.

① The model's success <u>has inspired</u> many people.
② The delivery <u>has</u> already <u>arrived</u> at my house.
③ Hannah <u>has been</u> to Norway twice.
④ My brother <u>has gone</u> to Seoul to find a job.
⑤ <u>Have</u> you <u>visited</u> the National Art Gallery before?

13 우리말과 같도록 괄호 안의 말을 활용하여 문장을 완성하시오.

> 대 피라미드는 수천 년 동안 서있어왔다. (stand, thousands of years)

= The Great Pyramid _____

_____.

14 다음 빈칸에 들어갈 알맞은 것을 <u>모두</u> 고르시오.

> Mr. Jackson knows a lot about Colombia. He has lived there _____.

① ten years ago ② last year
③ since 2000 ④ for five years
⑤ in 2007

15 다음 빈칸에 들어갈 말이 나머지 넷과 <u>다른</u> 것은?

① Canada has been a country _____ 1867.
② The weather has been very cold _____ Friday.
③ Neal has played guitar in a band _____ last year.
④ Chinese people have believed that red is lucky _____ a long time.
⑤ I have been a fan of the actor _____ I was ten years old.

[16-17] 현재완료시제를 이용하여 다음 두 문장을 한 문장으로 연결하시오.

16

> Michael lost a button of his jacket. He still cannot find it.
> → Michael _____
> _____.

17

> Samantha moved to Berlin in 2007. She still lives there.
> → Samantha _____.

18 다음 중 자연스럽지 <u>않은</u> 대화는?

① A: Have you taken out the garbage yet?
   B: No, I haven't yet. I'll do it now.
② A: Where did you go on your vacation?
   B: I went to China.
③ A: How long have you studied French?
   B: I have studied French for three years.
④ A: Have you ever eaten German sausage?
   B: Yes, I did. I have eaten it three times.
⑤ A: Did you make a wish on the full moon?
   B: Yes, I did. I wished I could win the lottery.

19 다음 대화의 밑줄 친 우리말과 같도록 괄호 안의 말을 활용하여 문장을 완성하시오.

> A: <u>너는 전에 문화적 차이를 경험해본 적이 있니?</u>
>   (experience, cultural differences)
> B: Yes, I had to take off my shoes when entering my friend's house in Korea.

= _____
before?

20 다음은 Ethan과 Natalie가 경험해본 것을 나타낸 표이다. 표를 보고 현재완료시제 문장을 완성하시오.

	Ethan	Natalie
bake pizza	X	O
travel to India	O	O

> Ethan hasn't baked pizza, but Natalie _____ before. Ethan and Natalie _____.

21 괄호 안의 동사를 활용하여 문장을 완성하시오.

Janet ⓐ_____(have) a pet parrot since last month. Last week, she ⓑ_____(decide) to teach it to talk. She taught it "hello." She said the same word over and over again. Her parrot finally ⓒ_____(say) "hello" to her.

22 다음 (A)~(C)에 들어갈 말이 바르게 짝지어진 것은?

· When the phone rang, I ___(A)___ TV.
· Percy Spencer ___(B)___ the microwave oven in 1946.
· Cameron ___(C)___ law in London since 2010.

	(A)	(B)	(C)
①	was watching	has invented	has studied
②	am watching	invented	has studied
③	was watching	invented	studied
④	am watching	has invented	studied
⑤	was watching	invented	has studied

23 다음 중 밑줄 친 부분이 어법상 <u>어색한</u> 것은?

The Summer Festival ①<u>is</u> a famous music festival. It ②<u>happens</u> every year in August. The first one ③<u>was</u> held in 1955. Many famous musicians ④ <u>performed</u> at this event since it started. Music fans hope the festival ⑤<u>will continue</u> for a long time.

24 다음 중 어법상 바른 것의 개수는?

ⓐ Isaac Newton has discovered gravity in 1687.
ⓑ The Grand Canyon was created millions of years ago.
ⓒ My brother was the captain of his soccer team since 2019.
ⓓ My dog chewed my mother's shoe yesterday.
ⓔ I haven't seen my best friend since she moved.
ⓕ World War I has ended on November 11, 1918.

① 1개　　　② 2개　　　③ 3개
④ 4개　　　⑤ 5개

25 다음 글의 밑줄 친 ⓐ~ⓔ 중 어법상 <u>어색한</u> 것을 찾아 기호를 쓰고 바르게 고쳐 쓰시오.

Have you heard of Cheonggyecheon? It is a small stream that ⓐ<u>flowed</u> through Seoul since 2005. Before that, a major road ⓑ<u>covered</u> the waterway. However, the mayor at the time thought the city ⓒ<u>is wasting</u> a valuable resource. So, he ⓓ<u>decides</u> to restore it. The stream has been so popular that the city ⓔ<u>is planning</u> to add more natural spaces in the city in the future.

*stream 하천

(1) _____ → _____
(2) _____ → _____
(3) _____ → _____

CHAPTER 4
조동사

연습문제 | 밑줄 친 부분이 어법상 맞으면 O를 쓰고, 틀리면 바르게 고쳐 쓰시오.

1　She will <u>spends</u> her summer vacation in Africa.　→ _____

2　People must not <u>violate</u> the law.　→ _____

3　Tony <u>cans</u> solve all the math questions.　→ _____

4　We will <u>can</u> arrive at the restaurant in ten minutes.　→ _____

5　Gina will <u>letting</u> you know if the schedule is changed.　→ _____

6　The country may <u>must</u> take military action.　→ _____

7　The elevator <u>wills</u> be repaired today.　→ _____

연습문제 | 우리말과 같도록 괄호 안의 말을 알맞게 배열하시오.

1　나는 캐나다 달러를 미국 달러로 교환할 수 있니? (exchange, I, can)

　= _____ Canadian dollars for US dollars?

2　나의 부탁을 들어주겠니? (do, you, could)

　= _____ me a favor?

3　Sam은 한국어를 전혀 말할 수 없다. (Sam, not, speak, can)

　= _____ Korean at all.

4　나는 구급차를 불러야 하니? (call, I, should)

　= _____ an ambulance?

5　너는 도움이 필요한 사람들을 무시하면 안 된다. (you, not, ignore, should)

　= _____ people in need.

6　그 선수는 내일 연습에 참여하지 않을 것이다. (will, participate, not, the, player)

　= _____ in the practice tomorrow.

7　너는 학교에서 장신구를 착용하면 안 된다. (wear, not, you, may)

　= _____ jewelry in school.

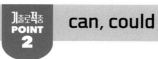

can, could

정답 p.67

연습문제 A | <보기>와 같이 다음 두 문장의 의미가 같도록 문장을 완성하시오.

> **<보기>** Surprisingly, snails can sleep for three years.
> = *Surprisingly, snails are able to sleep for three years.*
>
> Are you able to solve this riddle?
> = *Can you solve this riddle?*

1 I'm not able to manage this situation by myself.
= _____

2 Can I see stars with this telescope?
= _____

3 They couldn't go hiking because of the heavy rain.
= _____

4 Daniel wasn't able to believe the news.
= _____

5 He can write his name in Chinese.
= _____

6 Is she able to distinguish an imitation from an original?
= _____

연습문제 B | 밑줄 친 부분의 의미를 <보기>에서 골라 그 기호를 쓰시오.

> **<보기>** ⓐ 능력·가능 ⓑ 허가 ⓒ 요청 ⓓ 추측

1 <u>Can</u> I bring a guest to your birthday party? [　　　]
2 <u>Can</u> you help me with moving these boxes? [　　　]
3 He <u>can</u> do 100 push-ups in a row. [　　　]
4 <u>Could</u> you spell your surname for me? [　　　]
5 Sera <u>can't</u> be tired. She did not do anything today. [　　　]
6 You <u>can</u> have as many of these cupcakes as you want. [　　　]
7 The movie <u>can't</u> be based on a true story. [　　　]
8 The local police <u>couldn't</u> find the stolen car. [　　　]

Chapter 4 조동사 **45**

may, might

정답 p.67

연습문제 밑줄 친 부분이 허가, 약한 금지, 약한 추측 중 어떤 것을 나타내는지 쓰시오.

1 You <u>may</u> turn on the air conditioner.   [   ]

2 Paul <u>may not</u> like to speak in public.   [   ]

3 The students <u>may not</u> completely understand the lecture.   [   ]

4 You <u>may not</u> enter the teacher's office during the exam period.   [   ]

5 Hotel guests <u>may</u> use the fitness center for free.   [   ]

6 You <u>may</u> stay here longer if you want.   [   ]

7 The author's new novel <u>may not</u> satisfy every reader.   [   ]

8 The audience <u>may not</u> take pictures during the performance.   [   ]

9 My grandmother <u>may</u> like this flower vase.   [   ]

10 Chocolate candy <u>may</u> be poison to dogs.   [   ]

will, would I

정답 p.67

연습문제 우리말과 같도록 괄호 안의 말을 알맞게 배열하시오.

1 나에게 소금을 건네주겠니? (pass, will, you)

= _____ me the salt?

2 Tom은 곧 이집트로 떠날 것이다. (going, leave, to, Tom, is)

= _____ to Egypt soon.

3 나는 맨 먼저 편의점에 들를 것이다. (drop, will, I)

= _____ by the convenience store first.

4 따뜻한 날씨가 이번 주말 동안 계속될 것이다. (continue, will, weather, the, warm)

= _____ through this weekend.

5 저에게 약간의 차가운 물을 가져다주시겠어요? (you, bring, would)

= _____ me some cold water?

6 만약 네가 영수증을 가지고 있지 않다면 그 가게는 너에게 환불을 해주지 않을 것이다. (give, the, not, store, will)

= _____ you a refund if you don't have a receipt.

연습문제 | <보기>와 같이 다음 두 문장의 의미가 같도록 문장을 완성하시오.

<보기>   I want a warmer coat.
→ *I would like a warmer coat.*

I want to have some orange juice.
→ *I would like to have some orange juice.*

1 I want some sweet snacks.

→ _____

2 I want to have lunch with you tomorrow.

→ _____

3 Do you want to leave a message for him?

→ _____

4 I want a glass of water.

→ _____

5 Do you want some help?

→ _____

6 I want pancakes with maple syrup for breakfast.

→ _____

7 Do you want to read these magazines?

→ _____

8 Do you want some more sugar in your coffee?

→ _____

9 I want to be a doctor after I graduate from college.

→ _____

10 Do you want to live in a rural area?

→ _____

11 I want to hear some advice from you.

→ _____

12 Do you want ketchup with your fries?

→ _____

연습문제 **A** 밑줄 친 부분의 의미와 같은 것을 <보기>에서 골라 그 기호를 쓰시오.

<보기> ⓐ You must behave well in public places.
ⓑ That cat must be very clever.

1 This backpack must belong to Jacob. [   ]

2 You must take the medicine every day. [   ]

3 It must be over 40℃ outside. [   ]

4 There must be something wrong with the oven. [   ]

5 You must wear goggles and white gown in the laboratory. [   ]

6 All riders must wear helmets and other protective gears. [   ]

연습문제 **B** 우리말과 같도록 <보기>의 말과 괄호 안의 동사를 활용하여 문장을 완성하시오.

<보기>   must   can't   have to

1 학생들은 학교에서 교복을 입어야 한다. (wear)
= Students _____ a uniform at school.

2 너는 나에게서 어떤 것도 숨길 필요가 없다. (hide)
= You _____ anything from me.

3 그 등반가들은 눈보라가 없어질 때까지 기다려야 했다. (wait)
= The climbers _____ until the snowstorm disappeared.

4 이것이 정답일 리가 없다. (be)
= This _____ the correct answer.

5 너는 너의 시험에서 부정행위를 하면 안 된다. (cheat)
= You _____ on your test.

6 이 다이아몬드 반지는 매우 비싼 것임에 틀림없다. (be)
= This diamond ring _____ very expensive.

7 Julia는 다음 달에 그녀의 고향으로 돌아가야 한다. (go)
= Julia _____ back to her hometown next month.

POINT 6   should, had better

정답 p.68

연습문제   우리말과 같도록 괄호 안에서 알맞은 것을 고르시오.

1 너는 장학금을 받기 위해서 더 열심히 공부해야 한다.

= You (should / had better) study harder in order to get a scholarship.

2 나는 부를 행복과 동일시해서는 안 된다.

= I (should not / had better not) identify wealth with happiness.

3 너는 우리의 약속을 잊지 않는 것이 낫겠다.

= You (should not / had better not) forget our appointment.

4 우리는 지금 집을 떠나는 것이 낫다, 그렇지 않으면 우리는 비행기를 놓칠 것이다.

= We (should / had better) leave home now, or we'll miss the flight.

5 아이들은 어떤 낯선 사람들도 따라가면 안 된다.

= Children (should not / had better not) follow any strangers.

6 너는 똑같은 실수를 다시 하지 않는 것이 낫겠다.

= You (should not / had better not) make the same mistakes again.

7 너는 항상 너의 어머니의 충고를 들어야 한다.

= You (should / had better) always listen to your mother's advice.

8 Jenny는 다른 사람이 그녀에게 말하는 것을 기억하려고 노력해야 한다.

= Jenny (should / had better) try to remember what other people say to her.

9 너는 그 증상이 더 나빠지기 전에 진찰을 받는 것이 낫겠다.

= You (should / had better) see a doctor before the symptoms get worse.

10 만약 우리가 활력이 넘치고 싶다면 우리는 아침을 거르지 않는 것이 낫다.

= We (should not / had better not) skip breakfast if we want to be energetic.

11 그들은 선생님이 말할 때 수다를 떨지 말아야 한다.

= They (should not / had better not) chat when the teacher is talking.

12 부모는 그들의 아이들이 어릴 때 그들에게 올바른 식사 예절을 가르쳐야 한다.

= Parents (should / had better) teach their kids good table manners when they are young.

13 식당은 손님들에게 낮은 품질의 음식을 제공하지 않아야 한다.

= Restaurants (should not / had better not) provide low-quality food to customers.

14 너는 특히 날씨가 더울 때 많은 물을 마시는 게 낫다.

= You (should / had better) drink a lot of water, especially when the weather is hot.

used to, would

연습문제 A   우리말과 같도록 used to 또는 would와 괄호 안의 동사를 활용하여 빈칸에 쓰시오.

1   Maria는 전에는 많은 친구들이 있었다. (have)

= _____ many friends.

2   Brandon은 어렸을 때 여행을 많이 하곤 했다. (travel)

= _____ a lot when he was young.

3   나의 오빠는 매일 아침 공원 주변을 조깅하곤 했다. (jog)

= _____ around the park every morning.

4   전에는 그 길 끝에 경찰서가 있었다. (be)

= _____ a police station at the end of the street.

5   나는 풍경화를 그리는 데 나의 주말을 쓰곤 했다. (spend)

= _____ my weekends painting landscapes.

6   우리는 일요일마다 함께 쇼핑을 가곤 했다. (go)

= _____ shopping together every Sunday.

7   그는 20대였을 때는 유명한 가수였다. (be)

= _____ a famous singer when he was in his 20s.

8   Kevin은 운동하기 위해 주말마다 하이킹을 가곤 했다. (go)

= _____ hiking on the weekends to exercise.

9   Aria는 학교 갈 준비를 하기 위해 오전 여섯 시에 일어나는 데 익숙하다. (wake)

= _____ up at 6 A.M. to get ready for school.

10   그녀는 TV에서 축구 경기를 보느라 늦게까지 깨어있곤 했다. (stay)

= _____ up late watching soccer matches on TV.

연습문제 B   괄호 안에서 알맞은 것을 <u>모두</u> 고르시오.

1   We (used to / would) gather together at my place to hang out every Saturday.

2   I (used to / would) be short, but I am now the tallest student in my class.

3   He (used to / would) be an engineer in the 2010s.

4   She (used to / would) go camping with her parents on the weekends.

5   There (used to / would) be a gas station around the corner.

6   Ryan (used to / would) volunteer at a children's center on Tuesdays.

연습문제 밑줄 친 부분의 쓰임과 같은 것을 <보기>에서 골라 그 기호를 쓰시오.

<보기>　ⓐ Don't you enjoy playing table tennis?
　　　ⓑ Our family did live in Alaska for three years.
　　　ⓒ I have longer hair than Hailey does.

1 Do you often go mountain climbing? [　　　]

2 She ate more cookies than her sister did. [　　　]

3 I do like doing yoga in the morning. [　　　]

4 Some people do tend to ignore other's opinion. [　　　]

5 The woman's statements didn't agree with the facts. [　　　]

6 We do appreciate your interest in our new product. [　　　]

7 The cupboard door usually does not close tightly. [　　　]

8 Sara cooks as well as her mom does. [　　　]

9 I did see the famous actor at the Thai restaurant. [　　　]

10 Did you hear the mayor's speech on the radio this morning? – Yes, I did. [　　　]

11 Does this town always have many tourists? [　　　]

12 Unfortunately, our team leader doesn't show good leadership. [　　　]

13 Does that cheese smell terrible? – Yes, it does. [　　　]

14 Did you make these curtains by yourself? [　　　]

중간·기말고사 실전 문제

1 다음 중 어법상 바른 것은?

① No one cans travel to the past.

② May I have your attention, please?

③ Cars will can drive themselves someday.

④ Everyone in class musts follow the rules.

⑤ We should are grateful for having clean water.

2 다음 문장에서 틀린 부분을 바르게 고쳐 완전한 문장을 쓰시오.

> Sunglasses wills protect your eyes from the sun.
>
> → _____
>
> _____

3 다음 글의 빈칸에 들어갈 알맞은 것을 모두 고르시오.

> I _____ sing well when I was young. However, my voice is not very good now.

① can   ② am able to

③ couldn't   ④ could

⑤ was able to

4 다음 대화의 밑줄 친 부분과 의미가 같은 것은?

> A: Can I get a refund on this hat?
> B: Of course. Please show me the receipt.

① Should   ② Do   ③ Will

④ May   ⑤ Must

5 다음 우리말을 영작할 때 빈칸에 들어갈 알맞은 것은?

> 나를 위해 고구마 껍질을 벗겨주겠니?
>
> = _____ you peel the sweet potatoes for me?

① Do   ② Should   ③ Must

④ May   ⑤ Will

6 다음 중 어법상 바른 것은?

① I used to comparing myself with others.

② Can you suggest an idea for solving the air pollution problem?

③ Jason will can repair my computer today.

④ You don't may leave this building without my permission.

⑤ The police officers have to break the door down to enter the house last night.

7 다음 중 not이 들어갈 위치는?

> You ① had ② better ③ climb ④ the tall tree ⑤ because it is dangerous.

8 우리말과 같도록 괄호 안의 말을 활용하여 빈칸에 쓰시오.

> 판사는 모든 사건에 공평해야 한다. (be)

= A judge _____ _____ _____ fair in all cases.

9 다음 두 문장의 의미가 같도록 빈칸에 알맞은 말을 쓰세요.

Let me know if you want to go to the beach with us.
= Let me know if you _____ _____ _____ go to the beach with us.

10 다음 대화의 빈칸에 들어갈 알맞은 것은?

A: I'm sorry, but _____ this roller coaster. It's only for people over 160 cm tall.
B: OK. I'll go on another ride.

① you should ride
② you can ride
③ you won't ride
④ you can't ride
⑤ you don't have to ride

11 다음 문장을 부정문으로 바꿔 쓰시오.

There must be a problem with our Internet connection.

→ _____

_____

12 다음 대화의 밑줄 친 우리말과 같도록 괄호 안의 말을 활용하여 영작하시오.

A: I saw an injured kangaroo on the road. Can you tell me what to do?
B: 너는 119에 전화하는 것이 낫겠다. (call)

= _____

13 다음 중 밑줄 친 may의 의미가 나머지 넷과 다른 것은?

① May I use your phone for a second?
② You may eat anything in the refrigerator.
③ May I put my book in your locker?
④ You may be surprised when you hear the news.
⑤ You may play video games when you finish cleaning your room.

14 다음 빈칸에 들어갈 말이 순서대로 짝지어진 것은?

· I _____ the salmon salad, please.
· You _____ drive fast in a school zone.

① would like – should
② would like – should not
③ would like – need not
④ would like to – should
⑤ would like to – should not

15 주어진 문장의 밑줄 친 must와 의미가 다른 것은?

We must read good books to widen our vocabulary.

① I must leave for school every day at 7 A.M.
② We must not consider a rumor to be a fact.
③ Cyclists must follow regular traffic laws.
④ We must sit quietly on the bus.
⑤ Jeremy must be pleased with his good grades.

16 주어진 문장과 의미가 같은 것은?

> That was a popular snack, but the company stopped producing it.

① That may be a popular snack.
② That can't be a popular snack.
③ That must be a popular snack.
④ That was able to be a popular snack.
⑤ That used to be a popular snack.

17 다음 대화의 빈칸에 들어갈 알맞은 것을 <u>모두</u> 고르시오.

> *A*: Hi. Welcome to Sue Aquarium. How can I help you?
> *B*: I would like one adult ticket and two children's tickets.
> *A*: Okay, sir. How old are your children? You _____ pay for children under the age of 5.
> *B*: That's great! My twins are four years old.
> *A*: Then you only need one adult ticket. It's 20 dollars.

① have to   ② don't have to
③ must   ④ can't
⑤ need not

18 우리말과 같도록 괄호 안의 말을 활용하여 빈칸에 쓰시오.

> 나는 토요일마다 테니스 수업을 받곤 했다. (a tennis lesson, take)

= I _____ _____ _____
_____ _____ every Saturday.

19 우리말과 같도록 괄호 안의 말을 알맞게 배열하시오.

> 이것은 정문이어서, 너는 여기에 너의 자전거를 주차하지 않는 것이 낫겠다. (had, your bicycle, park, not, you, better, here)

= This is the gate, so _____
_____.

20 다음은 혜리와 도원이가 해야 하는 것을 나타낸 표이다. 표를 바르게 설명한 것은?

Hyeri	Dowon
• take a warm bath • fold the laundry • set the table for dinner	• feed the cat • fix the printer • wash the car

① Dowon has to fold the laundry.
② Dowon must not fix the printer.
③ Hyeri doesn't have to feed the cat.
④ Hyeri need not set the table for dinner.
⑤ Hyeri and Dowon don't need to wash the car.

21 다음 표지판을 보고 괄호 안의 말을 활용하여 문장을 완성하시오.

> You _____ in the library. (must, make noise)

22 주어진 문장의 밑줄 친 부분과 쓰임이 같은 것은?

Kelly <u>does</u> look like her twin sister.

① <u>Did</u> you see the lizard on the wall?
② This engine <u>doesn't</u> sound loud at all.
③ Will you <u>do</u> the dishes after finishing your meal?
④ Emily got as high a score as I <u>did</u> on the math test.
⑤ It <u>did</u> take only one minute for James to finish the difficult puzzle.

23 다음 (A)~(C)에 들어갈 말이 바르게 짝지어진 것은?

In many countries, a thumbs-up sign usually means *great* or *I agree*. However, if you give someone a thumbs-up sign in Greece or Iran, that person ___(A)___ get mad. That's because it is a rude gesture in those countries. Therefore, we ___(B)___ think that all cultures have the same ideas about gestures. We should be careful when using gestures and ___(C)___ use inappropriate gestures.

	(A)	(B)	(C)
①	might	may not	don't have to
②	should	should not	must not
③	may	should not	don't have to
④	should	may not	don't have to
⑤	may	should not	must not

24 다음은 나은이와 지훈이가 열두 살 때 할 수 있었던 것과 할 수 없었던 것을 나타낸 표이다. 표를 보고 빈칸에 알맞은 말을 쓰시오.

	Naeun	Jihun
do some magic tricks	O	O
watch English movies without subtitles	O	X

When Naeun and Jihun were twelve years old, they (A) _____ _____ _____ do some magic tricks. Naeun (B) _____ _____ _____ watch English movies without subtitles, but Jihun (C) _____ _____ _____ do it at that time.

25 다음 글의 빈칸에 들어갈 말로 <u>어색한</u> 것은?

Let me tell you the myth of Dangun. One day, a tiger and a bear ask the god, Hwanung, to make them people. The god tells them to stay in a cave for the next 100 days and to eat only garlic and mugwort. This is the only way for them to become humans. Therefore, the tiger and bear _____ leave the cave. After a few days, the tiger runs away. However, the patient bear eventually becomes a woman. She marries the god and has a child named Dangun. He founds the kingdom of Gojoseon.

*mugwort 쑥

① must not
② cannot
③ may not
④ should not
⑤ don't have to

CHAPTER 5
수동태

연습문제 A 밑줄 친 부분이 어법상 맞으면 O를 쓰고, 틀리면 바르게 고쳐 완전한 문장을 쓰시오.

1 Dishes are <u>wash</u> every day by Mom.

→ _____

2 The fence <u>painted</u> yesterday by Marcus.

→ _____

3 The picture of the flower was <u>took</u> by James.

→ _____

4 A cup of tea <u>was made</u> by Karen.

→ _____

5 Horror movies <u>love</u> by many people.

→ _____

6 The book *Jane Eyre* <u>was written</u> by Charlotte Bronte.

→ _____

7 My bag was <u>stole</u> by a tall man.

→ _____

연습문제 B 다음 능동태 문장은 수동태로, 수동태 문장은 능동태로 바꿔 쓰시오.

1 This restaurant offers great breakfasts.

→ _____

2 Sarah baked some chocolate chip cookies.

→ _____

3 North America was discovered by Columbus.

→ _____

4 Mom makes delicious pies.

→ _____

5 Many animals eat grass.

→ _____

6 Rachel found some blueberries.

→ _____

7 The mail is delivered every day by the mailman.

→ _____

연습문제 A 다음 능동태 문장은 수동태로, 수동태 문장은 능동태로 바꿔 쓰시오.

1 Harry answered Jenny's question.

→ _____

2 The funny movie was watched by us.

→ _____

3 The national museum is visited by many students.

→ _____

4 A car hit the tree.

→ _____

5 English and French are spoken by Canadians.

→ _____

6 My dad will read the newspaper.

→ _____

7 Willis Carrier invented the air conditioner.

→ _____

8 The company will release a new smart phone.

→ _____

연습문제 B 괄호 안에서 알맞은 것을 고르시오.

1 The copy machine (was fixed / will be fixed) the day after tomorrow.

2 The cake (was eaten / will be eaten) by Kate an hour ago.

3 The wall (was painted / will be painted) by John next Monday.

4 The window (was broken / will be broken) last month.

5 This car (was designed / will be designed) in 2000 by Korean company.

6 The kitchen (was cleaned / will be cleaned) tomorrow.

7 A new music album (was released / will be released) next month.

8 The radio (was fixed / will be fixed) yesterday by Kevin.

9 The telephone (was invented / will be invented) by Graham Bell.

10 The equation (was explained / will be explained) in the next class by the teacher.

수동태의 부정문과 의문문

정답 p.69

연습문제 | <보기>와 같이 다음 문장을 수동태의 부정문과 의문문으로 바꿔 쓰시오.

<보기>   They cleaned the bathroom floor.
→ *The bathroom floor wasn't[was not] cleaned by them.*
→ *Was the bathroom floor cleaned by them?*

1 They ate pasta and pizza.

→ _____

→ _____

2 Greg bought pencils and erasers.

→ _____

→ _____

3 Mr. Smith teaches math at school.

→ _____

→ _____

4 London held the Summer Olympics in 2016.

→ _____

→ _____

5 The cat scratched the delivery man's hand.

→ _____

→ _____

6 Kate wrote these mystery novels.

→ _____

→ _____

7 Steve Jobs designed the iPhone.

→ _____

→ _____

8 He planted those carrots.

→ _____

→ _____

9 Chinese people invented the toothbrush.

→ _____

→ _____

연습문제 A 우리말과 같도록 괄호 안의 말을 알맞게 배열하시오.

1 그 다이아몬드는 만져져서는 안 된다. (not, touched, be, should)

= The diamond _____.

2 지구는 보호되어야 한다. (be, must, protected)

= The earth _____.

3 그 피아노는 Mary에 의해 연주될 것이다. (played, will, Mary, be, by)

= The piano _____.

4 사용된 병은 재활용되어야 한다. (be, recycled, must)

= Used bottles _____.

5 동물들은 식당에 데리고 들어와 져서는 안 된다. (brought, be, not, may)

= Animals _____ in the restaurant.

6 스페인어는 Adam에 의해 말해질 수 있다. (spoken, Adam, be, can, by)

= Spanish _____.

7 호랑이는 정글에서 찾아질 수 없었다. (not, found, be, could)

= Tigers _____ in the jungle.

연습문제 B 다음 능동태 문장을 수동태로 바꿔 쓰시오.

1 You should carry this package carefully.

→ _____

2 You must keep this promise.

→ _____

3 We will eat the apple.

→ _____

4 Cindy must read this book.

→ _____

5 He may not finish the homework on time.

→ _____

6 People can visit the new theater now.

→ _____

연습문제 A 괄호 안에서 to, for, of 중 알맞은 것을 고르시오.

1 A funny story was told (to / for / of) me by my friend.

2 A complaint was sent (to / for / of) the store by a customer.

3 A special dinner was cooked (to / for / of) him by Karen.

4 These dishes were made (to / for / of) Kevin by Mr. Smith.

5 Pictures of the mountain were shown (to / for / of) Jeff.

6 Advice is given (to / for / of) Emma by Mr. Jones.

7 A favor was asked (to / for / of) her by her mom.

연습문제 B 다음 능동태 문장을 수동태로 바꿔 쓰시오.

1 My uncle bought me a pair of jeans.

→ A pair of jeans _____.

2 He showed me pictures of Mike's painting.

→ Pictures of Mike's painting _____.

3 Sally asked John a favor.

→ John _____.

4 Some people asked the actor autographs.

→ Autographs were _____.

5 She teaches middle school students Korean.

→ Korean _____.

6 The principal gave Alan a prize.

→ Alan _____.

7 Her mother bought her that hat.

→ That hat _____.

8 He wrote his grandpa a long letter.

→ A long letter _____.

9 A girl lent me a phone.

→ I _____.

10 Students asked Ms. Green some questions.

→ Some questions _____.

5형식 문장의 수동태

POINT **6**

정답 p.70

연습문제 다음 능동태 문장은 수동태로, 수동태 문장은 능동태로 바꿔 쓰시오.

1 Jake keeps the room so dirty.

→ _____

2 We heard him play the piano.

→ _____

3 My mom made me come home early.

→ _____

4 The cat is called Fluffy by the children.

→ _____

5 Sam was elected captain by the team.

→ _____

6 The boys were seen running outside in the rain by me.

→ _____

수동태 관용 표현

POINT **7**

정답 p.70

연습문제 다음 빈칸에 알맞은 전치사를 <보기>에서 골라 쓰시오.

<보기>   of   from   with   to   for   in   at

1 Bread is made _____ wheat.

2 Kate was satisfied _____ her grade.

3 The restaurant is known _____ its special dishes.

4 Sokcho is known _____ a lot of people as a vacation spot.

5 This t-shirt is made _____ cotton.

6 Everyone was surprised _____ the news.

7 The doughnut was filled _____ strawberry jam.

8 Jessica is interested _____ traveling to foreign countries.

9 Son Heung-min is known _____ his soccer skills.

10 The top of the mountain was covered _____ snow.

1 다음 중 어법상 <u>어색한</u> 것은?

① A lot of nice cars are made in Germany.

② A piece of paper was pinned to the curtain.

③ The bottle was opened by my brother.

④ The house was built next to a river.

⑤ Bart is confuse by the teacher's question.

2 다음 문장을 수동태로 바르게 바꾼 것은?

> Jane Austen wrote *Pride and Prejudice* in 1813.

① *Pride and Prejudice* written in 1813 by Jane Austen.

② *Pride and Prejudice* was write in 1813 by Jane Austen.

③ *Pride and Prejudice* is wrote in 1813 by Jane Austen.

④ *Pride and Prejudice* is written in 1813 by Jane Austen.

⑤ *Pride and Prejudice* was written in 1813 by Jane Austen.

3 우리말과 같도록 괄호 안의 말을 활용하여 빈칸에 쓰시오.

> 이 시장에서, 과일과 야채들은 농부에 의해 판매된다.
> (sell)

= At this market, fruits and vegetables

_____ _____ _____

farmers.

4 다음 문장을 수동태로 바꿔 쓰시오.

> David walks the dog every morning.
> → _____ every
> morning by David.

5 다음 중 어법상 바른 것끼리 묶인 것은?

> ⓐ Cars are produced at that factory next to the river.
> ⓑ The magazine articles were written by she.
> ⓒ The blue jeans with red belt are buying by the customer.
> ⓓ My laptop was borrowed by Jordan.
> ⓔ The coffee was serving by a waiter.

① ⓐ, ⓑ   ② ⓐ, ⓓ   ③ ⓑ, ⓒ

④ ⓒ, ⓔ   ⑤ ⓓ, ⓔ

6 다음 문장을 주어진 지시대로 바꿔 쓰시오.

> Carol painted the bookshelf.

(1) 수동태 부정문으로

→ _____

_____

(2) 수동태 의문문으로

→ _____

7 다음 문장을 수동태로 바꿀 때 빈칸에 들어갈 알맞은 것은?

> Paul gave Lisa a gift on her birthday.
> → A gift was given _____ Lisa on her birthday by Paul.

① to   ② for   ③ of
④ by   ⑤ from

8 다음 중 수동태 문장으로 바꿀 수 없는 것을 모두 고르시오.

① The weather became cold in December.
② My dog left its bone under the sofa.
③ Judy shook her head hard.
④ Harry broke the lamp on the table.
⑤ The blanket looks very soft and clean.

9 우리말과 같도록 괄호 안의 말을 활용하여 빈칸에 쓰시오.

> 이 요구르트는 냉장고에 보관되어야만 한다. (must, keep)

= This yogurt _____ _____ _____ in the refrigerator.

10 다음 중 문장의 태를 잘못 바꾼 것은?

① Mr. Grant translated the book.
   → The book was translated by Mr. Grant.
② The magician will perform a trick.
   → A trick will be performed by the magician.
③ The driver has parked the car.
   → The car is parked by the driver.
④ My uncle took this picture for me.
   → This picture was taken for me by my uncle.
⑤ The man will put the ring on the woman's finger.
   → The ring will be put on the woman's finger by the man.

11 우리말과 같도록 괄호 안의 말을 배열할 때 네 번째에 오는 것을 쓰시오.

> 도서관은 은행 옆에 지어질 것이다. (be, will, the, library, beside, the, built, bank)

→ _____

12 다음 문장에서 어법상 어색한 부분을 찾아 쓰고 바르게 고쳐 쓰시오.

> Paris is known to delicious food.

_____ → _____

13 괄호 안의 말을 활용하여 빈칸에 알맞은 말을 쓰시오.

> A quiz _____ to the class every week. (give)

14 다음 문장을 수동태로 바르게 바꾼 것을 모두 고르시오.

> The fans gave the actor flowers.

① The actor was given to flowers by the fans.
② The actor was given flowers by the fans.
③ Flowers were given the actor by the fans.
④ Flowers were given to the actor by the fans.
⑤ Flowers were given of the actor by the fans.

15 괄호 안의 말을 활용하여 빈칸에 알맞은 말을 쓰시오.

> The postcard _____ _____
> _____ Daniel yesterday by his
> uncle in Spain. (send)

16 다음 중 밑줄 친 부분이 어법상 어색한 것은?

① Your broken phone <u>will be repaired</u>.
② Music <u>should not be play</u> loudly at night.
③ Meat <u>can be eaten</u> without cooking.
④ Motorcycles <u>must not be driven</u> on the highway.
⑤ The new movie <u>might be released</u> next month.

17 우리말과 같도록 괄호 안의 말을 활용하여 빈칸에 쓰시오.

> Fred는 굉장한 농구선수로서 알려져 있다. (know)

= Fred _____ _____ _____
a great basketball player.

18 다음 빈칸에 들어갈 말이 나머지 넷과 <u>다른</u> 것은?

① The roads are covered _____ ice today.
② I hope you are pleased _____ the Christmas present.
③ The stadium was filled _____ soccer fans from around the world.
④ My grandpa is interested _____ history.
⑤ We were not satisfied _____ the customer service.

19 다음 중 어법상 <u>어색한</u> 것은?

① Kate was made to angry by the rude question.
② That old documentary was filmed in 1962.
③ The passengers were told to put on the seat belts.
④ A letter was sent to Tony by Rachel.
⑤ Pancakes were cooked for Mom by me.

20 다음 빈칸에 들어갈 말이 순서대로 짝지어진 것은?

> · Report cards were sent _____ the students' parents.
> · A favor was asked _____ me by Jackson.

① to - for   ② to - of   ③ of - to
④ for - to   ⑤ for - of

21 다음 빈칸에 들어갈 말이 순서대로 짝지어진 것은?

> · Mark is interested _____ learning science.
> · The politician is known _____ many citizens.

① in – to   ② in – with
③ with – for   ④ for – at
⑤ to – in

22 다음 중 밑줄 친 부분을 생략할 수 있는 것은?

① My bicycle was stolen <u>by someone</u>.
② The plants were not watered <u>by Greg</u>.
③ Paul was given a beautiful watch <u>by his grandfather</u>.
④ Amy was seen to leave the house <u>by her neighbor</u>.
⑤ The lost key was found <u>by the taxi driver</u>.

23 다음 중 어법상 바른 것의 개수는?

> ⓐ Were these mittens knitted by Samantha?
> ⓑ Did you bitten by a snake?
> ⓒ Was where this necklace purchased?
> ⓓ The dog wasn't allowed to jump on the sofa.
> ⓔ The mails not were sent by Mr. Davis.

① 1개   ② 2개   ③ 3개
④ 4개   ⑤ 5개

24 다음 빈칸에 to가 들어갈 수 <u>없는</u> 것은?

① The wolf was heard _____ howl at the moon.
② The boy was seen _____ climb the tree.
③ The people were made _____ stand in a line.
④ Minho was told _____ finish his bowl of vegetables.
⑤ Derek's puppy was named _____ Coco.

25 다음 대화의 밑줄 친 ⓐ~ⓔ 중 어법상 어색한 것을 찾아 기호를 쓰고 바르게 고쳐 쓰시오.

> A: Did you hear the news? Some dinosaur bones were found in China ⓐ<u>by</u> a farmer.
> B: What happened to the dinosaurs?
> A: They were ⓑ<u>bury</u> because of a volcano eruption. The bones were covered ⓒ<u>of</u> large rocks and volcanic ash.
> B: Wow. That's interesting.
> A: The bones stayed in the ground until they were ⓓ<u>discovered</u> by a farmer planting crops. Scientists are interested ⓔ<u>in</u> studying those bones.

(1) _____ → _____
(2) _____ → _____

CHAPTER 6
부정사

기출로 적중 POINT

연습문제 A | 밑줄 친 부분이 어법상 맞으면 O를 쓰고, 틀리면 바르게 고쳐 완전한 문장을 쓰시오.

1 My goal is to <u>reads</u> more good books.

→ _____

2 It is important to <u>study</u> politics.

→ _____

3 The teacher told us <u>run not to</u> in the hallway.

→ _____

4 I want to <u>returned</u> these small shoes.

→ _____

5 Jackson needs something <u>to drink</u>.

→ _____

6 Paris is a beautiful city to <u>visited</u>.

→ _____

7 We are happy <u>meet to</u> you.

→ _____

8 He tried very hard <u>to win</u> the race.

→ _____

연습문제 B | 밑줄 친 to부정사의 용법과 같은 것을 <보기>에서 골라 그 기호를 쓰시오.

<보기>　ⓐ I want <u>to eat</u> something spicy.
　　　　ⓑ She knows a lot of great places <u>to shop</u>.
　　　　ⓒ I turned on the radio <u>to listen</u> to songs.

1 I need <u>to buy</u> a blue shirt. [　　　]
2 There is nothing <u>to eat</u> in the kitchen. [　　　]
3 Paul was glad <u>to see</u> Jimin at the supermarket. [　　　]
4 Jamie's plan is <u>to travel</u> the world next year. [　　　]
5 They went to the library <u>to borrow</u> some books. [　　　]
6 He was the first person <u>to answer</u> the question. [　　　]
7 My dream is <u>to speak</u> four languages. [　　　]
8 Subin went to New York <u>to study</u> English. [　　　]

연습문제 A 다음 문장을 가주어 it을 사용한 문장으로 바꿔 쓰시오.

1 To wash your hands is necessary.

→ _____

2 To camp in the woods is exciting.

→ _____

3 To swim in this lake isn't safe.

→ _____

4 To remember the history is important.

→ _____

5 To see the stars in the cities is impossible.

→ _____

6 To apologize to my sister wasn't easy.

→ _____

7 To spend the winter in Hawaii is my dream.

→ _____

8 To fix my computer wasn't complicated.

→ _____

9 To play with fire is dangerous.

→ _____

연습문제 B 우리말과 같도록 괄호 안의 말을 알맞게 배열하시오.

1 한수의 꿈은 유명한 코미디언이 되는 것이다. (is, dream, become, Hansu's, to)

= _____ a famous comedian.

2 같이 노래를 부르는 것은 재미있었다. (sing, was, to, fun, it)

= _____ a song together.

3 나의 소망은 내년에 스페인에서 공부하는 것이다. (wish, to, is, my, study)

= _____ in Spain next year.

4 현대 사회에서 법을 지키는 것은 중요하다. (important, it, keep, to, the law, is)

= _____ in the modern society.

5 우리의 목표는 대기 오염을 줄이는 것이다. (reduce, goal, to, our, is)

= _____ the air pollution.

POINT 2-2

연습문제   우리말과 같도록 괄호 안의 말을 활용하여 문장을 완성하시오.

1 나는 내일까지 나의 자전거를 고칠 필요가 있다. (fix, need)
= _____ my bicycle by tomorrow.

2 우리는 오후에 화장실을 청소하기로 동의했다. (agree, clean)
= _____ the bathroom in the afternoon.

3 Jenny는 그 도시를 한번 더 방문하기를 바란다. (hope, visit)
= _____ the city one more time.

4 Henry는 이번 여름에 한국에 오기를 원한다. (want, come)
= _____ to Korea this summer.

5 Nancy는 더 이상 늦지 않기로 약속했다. (promise, be)
= _____ late anymore.

6 Eric은 뜨거운 코코아 한 잔을 마시기를 원한다. (would love, have)
= _____ a cup of hot cocoa.

7 Collins씨는 아침에 빨래를 하기로 결심했다. (decide, do)
= _____ the laundry in the morning.

8 그녀는 스스로 신발끈을 매는 것을 배웠다. (learn, tie)
= _____ the shoelaces by herself.

9 나는 John에게 나를 도와준 것에 대해 감사를 표하고 싶다. (thank, would like)
= _____ John for helping me.

10 Charlie는 산타클로스를 만나기를 바란다. (wish, meet)
= _____ the Santa Claus.

11 Sarah는 자전거를 사지 않기로 정했다. (choose, buy)
= _____ a bicycle.

12 우리 가족은 겨울에 태국에 가기로 계획한다. (plan, go)
= _____ to Thailand in winter.

13 그는 어제 그의 여동생을 돕기를 거부했다. (help, refuse)
= _____ his sister yesterday.

14 나는 생일 파티에서 나의 모든 친구들을 볼 수 있기를 기대한다. (expect, see)
= _____ all my friends at the birthday party.

연습문제 A 우리말과 같도록 괄호 안의 말을 활용하여 문장을 완성하시오.

1 나의 부모님은 내가 밖에서 노는 것을 허락하셨다. (allow, play)

= My parents _____ outside.

2 Keller 선생님은 나에게 역사를 공부하라고 조언했다. (advise, study)

= Ms. Keller _____ history.

3 그는 그들에게 그 상자들을 옮기라고 명령했다. (order, move)

= He _____ the boxes.

4 Sabrina는 그녀의 여동생이 조용히 하기를 원한다. (want, be)

= Sabrina _____ quiet.

5 나는 우리가 올림픽에서 금메달을 딸 것을 기대했다. (expect, win)

= I _____ the gold medal at the Olympic.

6 Ben은 John에게 그가 과학 과제를 하는 것을 도와달라고 요청했다. (ask, help)

= Ben _____ him with the science project.

7 의사는 나에게 매운 음식을 먹지 말라고 말했다. (tell, eat)

= The doctor _____ spicy food.

연습문제 B 밑줄 친 to부정사의 쓰임을 <보기>에서 골라 그 기호를 쓰시오.

> **<보기>** ⓐ 주어 ⓑ 주격 보어 ⓒ 목적어 ⓓ 목적격 보어

1 It is impossible to breathe in space. [   ]

2 My dream is to become a judge. [   ]

3 Kevin wants me to go to the library with him. [   ]

4 It is dangerous to hike in the dark. [   ]

5 The coach advised me not to eat fast food. [   ]

6 Her plan is to learn Korean this year. [   ]

7 I want to buy this black leather purse. [   ]

8 We hope to see our grandparents soon. [   ]

연습문제 A <보기>와 같이 우리말과 같도록 괄호 안의 말을 활용하여 문장을 완성하시오.

> <보기> 나는 오늘 무엇을 입을지 결정할 수 없다. (wear) = I can't decide _what to wear_ today.

1 우리는 휴일 동안 무엇을 할지 모른다. (do)

= We don't know _____ during the holiday.

2 Jason은 Mary에게 파리에서 어디를 방문할지 말해줬다. (visit)

= Jason told Mary _____ in Paris.

3 나는 인터넷에서 독일어를 어떻게 읽는지 배웠다. (read)

= I learned _____ German on Internet.

4 Green 선생님은 우리에게 언제 숙제를 제출할지 말해주셨니? (hand)

= Did Ms. Green tell us _____ in the homework?

5 Hailey는 나에게 히터를 어떻게 켜는지 물었다. (turn)

= Hailey asked me _____ on the heater.

6 너는 저녁으로 무엇을 준비할지 결정했니? (prepare)

= Did you decide _____ for the dinner?

7 이 불은 네가 언제 배터리를 교체해야 할지 보여줄 것이다. (change)

= This light will show you _____ the battery.

8 그는 나에게 바다에서 조개를 어디서 찾을지 가르쳐줬다. (find)

= He taught me _____ the clams in the ocean.

연습문제 B 다음 두 문장의 의미가 같도록 to부정사를 이용하여 문장을 완성하시오.

1 Could you show me how I should answer to the question?

= Could you show me _____?

2 I told Amy what she should buy for Kevin.

= I told Amy _____.

3 Many people learn how they should swim from their parents.

= Many people learn _____.

4 I asked the doctor when I should remove my wisdom tooth.

= I asked the doctor _____.

5 Some pigs know where they should find mushrooms.

= Some pigs know _____.

연습문제 A 괄호 안에서 알맞은 것을 고르시오.

1 Do you have a black pen (to write / to write with)?

2 Jack ordered something (to eat sweet / sweet to eat) at the café.

3 We have a lot of (homework to do / to do homework) for math class.

4 James needs (some time to sleep / sleep to some time).

5 The child has a cute doll (to play / to play with).

6 She found a comfortable chair (to sit on / on to sit).

7 We have many things (to talk about / about to talk) today.

8 He bought (a new computer to use / to use a new computer) in his room.

9 There is no water (to drink / drink to) in this glass bottle.

10 I will lend her a book (to read / to read with).

11 Kate is looking for something (to wear warm / warm to wear) in the closet.

12 The restaurant has many (things to eat / to eat things).

연습문제 B 우리말과 같도록 괄호 안의 말을 알맞게 배열하시오.

1 민수는 그를 도와줄 누구도 찾지 못했다. (to, anyone, help, couldn't find)
= Minsu _____ him.

2 나는 너에게 소개해줄 친구가 있다. (introduce, a friend, to, have)
= I _____ to you.

3 Sam은 닦을 약간의 더러운 신발들을 찾았다. (wash, found, some dirty shoes, to)
= Sam _____ .

4 그 경찰관은 함께 일할 파트너가 없다. (a partner, work with, doesn't have, to)
= That police officer _____ .

5 Tom은 살 아파트를 찾고 있다. (in, for, to, is searching, live, an apartment)
= Tom _____ .

6 나는 너에게 줄 특별한 무언가를 샀다. (to, something, bought, special, give)
= I _____ you.

7 싱크대에 요리할 약간의 야채가 있다. (are, to, some vegetables, there, cook)
= _____ in the sink.

연습문제 **A** | 밑줄 친 to부정사의 쓰임을 <보기>에서 골라 그 기호를 쓰시오.

<보기>   ⓐ 목적   ⓑ 형용사 수식   ⓒ 감정의 원인   ⓓ 판단의 근거   ⓔ 결과

1 The elephant lived to be 80 years old.   [   ]

2 Carl was excited to watch the new movie.   [   ]

3 The problem was hard to solve.   [   ]

4 Sally must be tired to sleep in class.   [   ]

5 Mr. Smith hurried to catch the bus.   [   ]

6 My older brother grew up to be a song writer.   [   ]

7 Linda must be sad to cry so much.   [   ]

8 He went to Spain to study architecture last year.   [   ]

9 The small earring was difficult to find.   [   ]

10 She was sad to hear the news about the accident.   [   ]

연습문제 **B** | 우리말과 같도록 괄호 안의 말을 활용하여 문장을 완성하시오.

1 나는 그 바이올린을 사기 위해 돈을 저축했다. (buy, the violin)
= I saved money _____.

2 Benny는 그녀의 할아버지를 방문해서 기뻤다. (glad, visit her grandfather)
= Benny was _____.

3 그녀는 자라서 간호사가 되었다. (grow up, be a nurse)
= She _____.

4 진수는 그의 시계를 잃어버려서 실망했다. (disappointed, lose his watch)
= Jinsu was _____.

5 나는 숙제를 하기 위해 나의 컴퓨터를 사용했다. (do, the homework)
= I used my computer _____.

6 Penny는 롤러코스터를 타게 되어 신이 났다. (excited, ride the roller coaster)
= Penny was _____.

7 이 러시아 소설은 이해하기에 어렵다. (difficult, understand)
= This Russian novel is _____.

8 David은 매주 보호소에서 봉사를 하다니 친절함에 틀림없다. (kind, volunteer)
= David must be _____ every week at the shelter.

to부정사의 의미상 주어

POINT 5

정답 p.73

연습문제 A 다음 빈칸에 to, for, of 중 알맞은 것을 쓰시오.

1 It is hard _____ me to sleep well at night.

2 It was nice _____ you to help the old man.

3 It was foolish _____ him to leave the umbrella on the train.

4 It was easy _____ him to pass the midterm exam.

5 It is impossible _____ me to walk faster than my brother.

6 It was brave _____ her to go hiking alone in the mountain.

7 It was rude _____ you to yell at the waiter.

8 Rufus wrote a letter to send _____ his friend in China.

9 It is hard _____ Nelson to speak French.

10 The puzzle was difficult _____ solve for children.

연습문제 B 우리말과 같도록 괄호 안의 말을 활용하여 문장을 완성하시오.

1 그가 우리를 위해 설거지를 하다니 친절하다. (kind, wash)
= It is _____ the dishes for us.

2 그가 입에 음식이 있는 채로 말하다니 예의 바르지 못했다. (polite, talk)
= It wasn't _____ with food in his mouth.

3 내가 나의 아버지와 체스를 두는 것은 재미있다. (fun, play)
= It is _____ chess with my father.

4 우리가 약간의 휴식을 취하는 것은 필수적이다. (necessary, get)
= It is _____ some rest.

5 내가 그 꽃병을 깨다니 부주의했다. (careless, break)
= It was _____ the vase.

6 내가 이 거대한 박스들을 나르는 것은 불가능하다. (impossible, carry)
= It is _____ these huge boxes.

7 내가 그 일을 완료하는 것은 어렵다. (hard, complete)
= It is _____ the work.

8 그가 모든 케이크를 먹다니 이기적이다. (selfish, eat)
= It is _____ the whole cake.

연습문제 다음 두 문장의 의미가 같도록 to부정사를 이용하여 문장을 완성하시오.

1 He is so smart that he can solve all the math problems.
   = He _____ .

2 Minha was so lucky that she could win the lottery.
   = Minha _____ .

3 The cat was so fat that it couldn't jump onto the sofa.
   = The cat _____ .

4 Ben is so tall that he can be a basketball player.
   = Ben _____ .

5 The bag is so light that I can hold it with one hand.
   = The bag_____ .

6 John is so funny that he can make anyone laugh.
   = John _____ .

7 You are so young that you can't watch that horror movie.
   = You _____ .

8 He is so rich that he can build a new house.
   = He _____ .

9 Jinho laughs so loud that everyone can hear him.
   = Jinho _____ .

10 The doughnut tasted so good that we could scream.
   = The doughnut _____ .

11 They were so busy that they couldn't have lunch at noon.
   = They _____ .

12 Paul was so tired that he couldn't exercise last night.
   = Paul _____ .

13 He studied so hard that he could pass the exam easily.
   = He _____ .

14 This soup is so salty that I can't eat it without water.
   = This soup _____ .

15 The cheetah ran so fast that we couldn't see it.
   = The cheetah _____ .

연습문제 A 밑줄 친 부분이 어법상 맞으면 O를 쓰고, 틀리면 바르게 고쳐 완전한 문장을 쓰시오.

1 I saw him <u>getting</u> on the bus.

→ _____

2 James helped me <u>to solve</u> the puzzle.

→ _____

3 Mom didn't let me <u>to go</u> to the rock concert.

→ _____

4 Our teacher made us <u>singing</u> in front of the class.

→ _____

5 Nathan saw someone <u>breaking</u> into Emily's house.

→ _____

6 We heard the neighbors <u>to yell</u> next door.

→ _____

7 I watched the children <u>play</u> on the field.

→ _____

8 Lauren had her sister <u>washing</u> her hands before dinner.

→ _____

연습문제 B 괄호 안의 동사를 알맞은 형태로 바꿔 문장을 완성하시오.

1 Cindy got me _____ the answers for the quiz. (check)

2 Liam heard someone _____ on the door. (knock)

3 He advised me _____ to Annie. (apologize)

4 Your story made me _____ sad. (feel)

5 I saw someone _____ the large apple tree. (climb)

6 Emily watched the orchestra _____ the classical music. (play)

7 She heard something _____ into the wall. (crash)

8 They asked Josh _____ them move the bookshelf. (help)

9 Our teacher made us _____ the math equation. (memorize)

10 Yuna smelled something _____ in the oven. (burn)

중간 · 기말고사 실전 문제

1 다음 빈칸에 들어갈 알맞은 것은?

> Beth plans _____ her grandparents tomorrow.

① visit   ② visits   ③ to visit
④ visiting   ⑤ visited

2 다음 빈칸에 들어갈 말로 <u>어색한</u> 것은?

> Robert _____ Dana take a picture in front of the statue.

① made   ② helped   ③ had
④ let   ⑤ wanted

3 다음 중 어법상 바른 것은?

① Greg expected getting a new phone for his birthday.
② The doctor told me eat more vegetables.
③ I am hoping starting college next year.
④ Anne has interesting something to tell us.
⑤ It is very important to wear a seat belt.

4 다음 문장에서 어법상 <u>어색한</u> 부분을 찾아 쓰고 바르게 고쳐 쓰시오.

> Brad agreed lending me his history textbook.

_____ → _____

5 다음 빈칸에 들어갈 말이 순서대로 짝지어진 것은?

> · Adam ordered the dog _____ barking.
> · My mother let me _____ outside.

① stop – play   ② stop – to play
③ to stop – play   ④ to stop – to play
⑤ stopping – play

6 다음 중 밑줄 친 to부정사의 용법이 나머지 넷과 <u>다른</u> 것은?

① <u>To bake</u> bread is very difficult.
② I would like <u>to watch</u> a movie tonight.
③ It is fun <u>to act</u> a role in a play.
④ Brian decided <u>to help</u> Jane fix her radio.
⑤ Lucy went to a pharmacy <u>to buy</u> some medicine.

7 다음 글의 밑줄 친 우리말 (A)와 같도록 주어진 <조건>에 맞게 빈칸에 알맞은 말을 쓰시오.

> (A) <u>미술 대회에서 우승하는 것은 Sarah의 목표였다.</u> Fortunately, the judges chose her painting as the winner. She felt very proud and happy.

<조건>
1. 가주어 it을 사용하시오.
2. goal, win first prize를 포함하시오.

= _____ _____

_____ _____

_____ in the art

contest.

8 다음 중 밑줄 친 부분이 어법상 어색한 것은?

① Danny was scared to ride the horse.

② The teacher gave me a pencil to write.

③ It was pleasure to meet new friends.

④ Let me get you a chair to sit on.

⑤ The lawyer advised me to sign the paper.

[9-10] 다음 글을 읽고 주어진 질문에 답하시오.

Wendy,

I have exciting news ⓐto share. I'm going to Portland next weekend to visit you. I want to have lots of fun with you, but (A) I don't know what to do. Maybe you have some ideas. Please e-mail me back soon.

Sincerely, Rachel

9 위 글의 밑줄 친 ⓐ의 용법과 다른 것은?

① Mike's plan was to take the bus to the bank.

② Here is the closet to hang your clothes.

③ Ms. Kim gave me an interesting book to read.

④ There is some beef to cook on the table.

⑤ She gave the baby a toy to play with.

10 위 글의 밑줄 친 (A)와 의미가 같도록 빈칸에 알맞은 말을 쓰시오.

= I don't know _____ _____

_____ _____

11 우리말과 같도록 괄호 안의 말을 알맞게 배열하시오.

여기 너의 건강을 나아지게 할 약간의 조언들이 있다.
(improve, tips, your, a few, health, to)

= Here are _____

_____ .

12 다음 빈칸에 들어갈 말이 나머지 넷과 다른 것은?

① It was kind _____ him to lend me his cell phone.

② It was exciting _____ me to meet my favorite actor.

③ It is easy _____ Mandy to wake up early.

④ It was tiring _____ her to clean the house.

⑤ It is dangerous _____ children to play on the street.

13 다음 빈칸에 들어갈 말이 순서대로 짝지어진 것은?

· Jenny has many friends to talk _____.

· Do you have a piece of paper to write _____.

① with – to   ② on – with

③ at – on   ④ to – on

⑤ to – with

14 다음 빈칸에 알맞은 말을 넣어 대화를 완성하시오.

A: It is nice _____ James to bring you flowers.

B: Yes. They are very beautiful.

[15-16] 다음 글을 읽고 주어진 질문에 답하시오.

Do you like amusement parks? I love to go to amusement parks ⓐto ride roller coasters. They are my favorite rides. When you ride on a roller coaster, you move very quickly. In addition, you will sometimes be upside-down. But don't get scared. (A) 롤러코스터는 너를 안전하게 유지해 줄 안전벨트를 가지고 있다. (seat belts, keep) Why don't you try a roller coaster soon?

15 위 글의 밑줄 친 ⓐ의 쓰임과 같은 것을 모두 고르시오.

① We were happy to volunteer at the shelter.

② Kate must be angry to yell at Jake.

③ The mountain is too high to climb in an hour.

④ Neal bought some eggs to cook pancakes.

⑤ Monkeys use their tails to hang from branches.

16 위 글의 밑줄 친 우리말 (A)와 같도록 괄호 안의 말을 활용하여 문장을 완성하시오.

= Roller coasters _____

_____.

17 우리말과 같도록 괄호 안의 말을 배열할 때 세 번째에 오는 것을 쓰시오.

Jane은 할 흥미로운 무언가를 제안했다. (something, do, Jane, to, interesting, suggested)

→ _____

18 다음 중 어법상 어색한 것은?

① Chloe had her brother clean his room.

② Did you see the car drive through the tunnel?

③ The man helped me find my wallet.

④ Jack lets his puppy sleeping on his bed.

⑤ I heard the fire alarm ringing.

19 다음 빈칸에 들어갈 말이 나머지 넷과 다른 것은?

① The scissors are sharp _____ to cut anything.

② My father's jacket is _____ big for me to wear.

③ I was _____ excited to sleep on Christmas Eve.

④ The sand was _____ hot to walk on.

⑤ Sam is _____ young to go to school.

20 다음 대화에 나온 표현을 활용하여 빈칸에 알맞은 말을 쓰시오.

> *Jason*: It's really warm today. Could you turn on the fan, please?
> *Peter* : Sure. There you go.

→ Jason asked Peter _____

_____ _____ _____

_____ .

[21-22] 다음 대화를 읽고 주어진 질문에 답하시오.

> *Brad*: Is Dave going to the movies with us?
> *Sara* : Yes. (A) <u>그는 어디서 그를 만날지 말하기 위해 전화했다.</u> (meet) He will be in the theater lobby.
> *Brad*: OK. I'm really excited ⓐ<u>to watch</u> this movie.
> *Sara* : Me, too. It should be great.

21 위 대화의 밑줄 친 우리말 (A)와 같도록 괄호 안의 말을 활용하여 빈칸에 쓰시오.

= He called to tell _____ _____

_____ _____ .

22 위 대화의 밑줄 친 ⓐ의 용법과 같은 것은?

① My father told me <u>to wash</u> my hands.
② Lynn was surprised <u>to see</u> the large spider.
③ It is easy <u>to peel</u> an apple with that knife.
④ Our family rented a house <u>to live</u> in.
⑤ Eric chose not <u>to visit</u> the Museum of Art.

[23-24] 다음 두 문장의 의미가 같도록 문장을 완성하시오.

23

> My brother is so strong that he can lift me over his head.
> = My brother is _____
>
> _____ .

24

> The music was so loud that I couldn't talk to the waiter.
> = The music was _____
>
> _____ .

25 다음 밑줄 친 to부정사의 용법이 같은 것끼리 묶인 것은?

> ⓐ You should call the hotel <u>to make</u> a reservation.
> ⓑ Our plan was <u>to study</u> three hours every day.
> ⓒ It is hard <u>to see</u> stars in the cities.
> ⓓ Jamie was scared <u>to hear</u> the news about the earthquake.
> ⓔ The boy climbed the tree <u>to pick</u> a peach.
> ⓕ There were many kinds of cheese <u>to eat</u> in the refrigerator.

① ⓐ, ⓑ, ⓕ   ② ⓐ, ⓓ, ⓔ   ③ ⓑ, ⓒ, ⓓ
④ ⓑ, ⓓ, ⓕ   ⑤ ⓒ, ⓔ, ⓕ

CHAPTER 7
동명사

기출로 적중 POINT

연습문제 A 우리말과 같도록 괄호 안의 동사를 활용하여 빈칸에 알맞은 말을 쓰시오.

1 책을 읽는 것은 중요하다. (read)

= _____ books is important.

2 그는 수영하는 것을 잘한다. (swim)

= He is good at _____ .

3 그녀의 직업은 건물을 디자인하는 것이다. (design)

= Her job is _____ buildings.

4 Jenny는 오후 4시에 수학을 공부하기 시작했다. (study)

= Jenny started _____ math at 4 P.M.

5 노래자랑 대회에서 우승을 한 것은 나를 자랑스럽게 만들었다. (win)

= _____ at the singing contest made me proud.

6 George는 학교에 자전거를 타고 가는 것을 좋아하지 않는다. (ride)

= George doesn't like _____ bike to school.

연습문제 B 밑줄 친 동명사의 쓰임과 같은 것을 <보기>에서 골라 그 기호를 쓰시오.

<보기> ⓐ Making new friends is sometimes difficult.
ⓑ My hobby is watching funny videos online.
ⓒ It began raining heavily in the afternoon.
ⓓ We're looking forward to seeing each other.

1 Ben is used to eating dinner alone. [   ]

2 Exercising regularly is good for your health. [   ]

3 Speaking in English always makes me nervous. [   ]

4 My goal is becoming the class president. [   ]

5 Sarah enjoys eating kimchi. [   ]

6 The dog started chasing the black cat. [   ]

7 Thank you for listening to my presentation. [   ]

8 Josh is good at playing the flute. [   ]

9 My dream is studying abroad for a year. [   ]

10 Sending a letter to your grandmother is a good idea. [   ]

연습문제 다음 두 문장의 의미가 같도록 동명사를 이용하여 문장을 완성하시오.

1 It is fun to build a snowman in winter.

= _____ fun.

2 Rick's hobby is to collect the sea shells on the beach.

= Rick's hobby _____ .

3 It is exciting to play video games with friends.

= _____ exciting.

4 It makes me nervous to act on the stage.

= _____ me nervous.

5 Erica's job is to paint the wall.

= Erica's job _____ .

6 It is interesting to talk to new people.

= _____ interesting.

7 Adam's plan is to visit France this weekend.

= Adam's plan _____ .

8 The salesperson's goal is to sell more products to the customers.

= The salesperson's goal _____ .

9 It is difficult to wake up early in the morning.

= _____ difficult.

10 It is really dangerous to drive at night.

= _____ really dangerous.

11 My favorite activity is to plant flowers in the garden.

= My favorite activity _____ .

12 Emma's dream is to teach English.

= Emma's dream _____ .

연습문제 우리말과 같도록 괄호 안의 말을 활용하여 문장을 완성하시오.

1 Thomas는 새로운 언어를 배우는 것을 즐긴다. (enjoy, learn)

= _____ new languages.

2 Kate는 대통령의 초상화를 그리는 것을 끝냈다. (finish, draw)

= _____ the portrait of the president.

3 나는 패스트푸드를 먹는 것을 피할 것이다. (avoid, have)

= _____ fast food.

4 우리는 우리의 꿈을 이루려고 노력하는 것을 포기하지 않았다. (give up, try)

= _____ to achieve our dreams.

5 Mike는 치과에 가는 것을 미뤘다. (postpone, go)

= _____ to the dentist.

6 Emily는 휴가를 가는 것에 대해 생각하는 것을 계속했다. (keep, think)

= _____ about going on a vacation.

7 James는 그의 친구에게 그의 노트북을 빌려주는 것을 꺼리지 않았다. (mind, lend)

= _____ his laptop to his friend.

8 Sarah는 어젯밤에 그 창문을 깬 것을 부인했다. (deny, break)

= _____ the window last night.

9 그들은 화요일마다 야구하는 것을 연습한다. (practice, play)

= _____ baseball every Tuesday.

10 우리는 그 연극이 시작했을 때 말하는 것을 멈췄다. (stop, talk)

= _____ when the play started.

11 그는 이 컴퓨터를 사는 것을 제안한다. (suggest, buy)

= _____ this computer.

12 그 팀은 그 프로젝트에 착수하는 것을 연기했다. (put off, work)

= _____ on the project.

13 나는 유명한 배우가 되는 것을 상상할 수 있다. (imagine, become)

= _____ a famous actor.

14 우리는 환경을 보호하기 위해 집에서 플라스틱을 사용하는 것을 그만뒀다. (quit, use)

= _____ plastics in the house to protect the environment.

POINT 3-2 · 동명사와 to부정사를 모두 목적어로 쓰는 동사 Ⅰ

정답 p.75

연습문제 괄호 안의 동사를 동명사나 to부정사 형태로 바꿔 문장을 완성하시오.

1 Mary doesn't avoid _____ difficult work. (do)

2 The baby started _____ at 2 A.M. (cry)

3 William hopes _____ the college in England. (enter)

4 Tim would like _____ his friend to camping. (bring)

5 Do you prefer _____ healthy food? (have)

6 Chloe continued _____ up early on Saturdays. (wake)

7 The coach suggested _____ the uniform. (change)

8 We love _____ about each other. (joke)

9 Dad began _____ about the old times. (talk)

10 Jack promised _____ biting his nails. (stop)

POINT 3-3 · 동명사와 to부정사를 모두 목적어로 쓰는 동사 Ⅱ

정답 p.75

연습문제 우리말과 같도록 괄호 안의 말을 활용하여 문장을 완성하시오.

1 Barry는 한 시간 전에 빨래를 한 것을 잊었다. (forget, do)
= Barry _____ the laundry an hour ago.

2 그녀는 잃어버린 펜을 서랍에서 찾는 것을 멈췄다. (stop, look)
= She _____ for the lost pen in the drawer.

3 수업에 당신의 노트북을 가져올 것을 기억하세요. (remember, bring)
= Please _____ your laptop to the class.

4 그는 테이블 위에 있던 마지막 도넛을 먹은 것을 후회한다. (regret, eat)
= He _____ the last doughnut on the table.

5 Sam은 그가 달아나기 전에 그 도둑을 잡으려고 노력했다. (try, catch)
= Sam _____ the thief before he ran away.

6 나는 프랑스에 있는 나의 친구에게 편지를 보낼 것을 잊었다. (forget, send)
= I _____ the letter to my friend in France.

연습문제 A 우리말과 같도록 괄호 안의 말을 활용하여 문장을 완성하시오.

1 Irene은 그녀의 개가 웅덩이에 뛰어들지 못하게 했다. (dog, jump)

= Irene _____ into the puddle.

2 아이들은 다음 주에 캠핑 가는 것을 기대하고 있다. (go)

= The children are _____ camping next week.

3 Owen은 아침 식사를 거르는 데 익숙하다. (skip)

= Owen _____ breakfast.

4 너는 새로운 것을 시도하는 것을 무서워하면 안된다. (try)

= You shouldn't _____ new things.

5 그는 그의 친구들에게 거짓말하는 것을 잘한다. (lie)

= He _____ to his friends.

6 John은 당황스러웠기 때문에 침대 밑에 숨고 싶었다. (hide)

= John _____ under the bed because he was embarrassed.

7 집에 돌아오자마자, 그는 에어컨을 켰다. (come)

= _____ back home, he turned on the air conditioner.

8 Edmund Hillary는 1952년에 에베레스트산을 등반하는 데 성공했다. (climb)

= Edmund Hillary _____ Mount Everest in 1952.

연습문제 B 다음 빈칸에 알맞은 전치사를 <보기>에서 골라 쓰시오.

<보기> in   to   for   of   by

1 The students were interested _____ discussing the political issues.

2 Hana was tired _____ listening to the same song repeatedly.

3 Thank you _____ inviting me to the dinner.

4 We thought _____ asking Mom for help.

5 Sorry _____ wasting your time today.

6 Fred got used _____ making speech in public.

7 You can get a refund _____ writing down your account.

기출로 작중 해커스 중학영문법 2학년 워크북

연습문제 | 우리말과 같도록 괄호 안의 말을 알맞게 배열하시오.

1 그 새로운 식당은 시도할 가치가 있었다. (trying, worth, was)

= The new restaurant _____ .

2 Paul은 지금 그의 방을 청소하느라 바쁘다. (busy, room, cleaning, his, is)

= Paul _____ right now.

3 너의 개와 산책을 하는 게 어때? (taking, about, walk, what, a)

= _____ with your dog?

4 Amy는 수업에 집중하는 데 어려움을 겪었다. (concentrating, trouble, had)

= Amy _____ on the class.

5 우리는 그 연극을 위해 연습하는 데 충분한 시간을 쓸 수 없었다. (time, couldn't, enough, practicing, spend)

= We _____ for the play.

6 그 소년들은 겨울마다 산에 스키를 타러 간다. (skiing, boys, the, go)

= _____ in the mountain every winter.

7 나는 그의 농담에 웃지 않을 수 없었다. (help, not, laughing, could)

= I _____ at his joke.

8 과거에 대해 불평해도 소용없다. (use, complaining, no, it's)

= _____ about the past.

[1-2] 다음 빈칸에 들어갈 알맞은 것을 고르시오.

1

> Cameron's hobby is _____ pictures of imaginary animals.

① draw   ② draws   ③ drawing
④ drew   ⑤ drawn

2

> Samantha hates _____ up early on weekends.

① wake   ② woke   ③ waking
④ woken   ⑤ to waking

3 우리말과 같도록 괄호 안의 말을 활용하여 빈칸에 쓰시오.

> 야채를 먹지 않는 것은 건강 문제를 초래할 수 있다.
> (eat)

= _____ _____ vegetables can cause health problems.

4 다음 중 어법상 어색한 것은?

① Did the thief deny stealing your phone?
② Sarah wants to play the violin well.
③ You must stop running in the classroom.
④ I don't like taking the bus to school.
⑤ We postponed to go on a trip next week.

5 다음 글의 빈칸에 들어갈 말이 순서대로 짝지어진 것은?

> On Sunday, Brad felt very bored. He was tired of _____ TV. His father suggested _____ baseball in the park. But then it started raining. So, Brad had to stay home and watch TV.

① to watch – playing
② watching – to play
③ watching – playing
④ watch – to play
⑤ watch – playing

6 다음 대화의 빈칸에 들어갈 알맞은 것은?

> A: Did you enjoy your vacation in Hawaii?
> B: Yes. It was amazing. I will never forget _____ in the warm ocean.

① swim   ② swam   ③ to swim
④ swimming   ⑤ to swimming

7 주어진 문장의 밑줄 친 부분과 쓰임이 다른 것은?

> The snow kept falling last night.

① Knitting a muffler with my grandmother was fun.
② Steve regrets arguing with his best friend.
③ The kitten is sleeping under the table.
④ My dream is starting a vegan restaurant.
⑤ The doctor succeeded in discovering the vaccine.

8 다음 빈칸에 들어갈 말로 <u>어색한</u> 것은?

> Jason _____ singing with his friends on the stage.

① liked
② practiced
③ remembers
④ wants
⑤ quit

9 다음 대화의 빈칸에 들어갈 말이 순서대로 짝지어진 것은?

> A: I regret _____ at my brother an hour ago. He broke my glasses, and I was so angry.
> B: How about _____ to him? Tell him you didn't mean to hurt his feelings.
> A: I will. Thank you for your advice.

① to yell – to apologize
② yelling – apologizing
③ to yell – apologized
④ yelling – to apologize
⑤ to yell – apologizing

10 <보기>와 같이 다음 두 문장을 한 문장으로 연결하시오.

> <보기> Raymond closed the door. He forgot it.
> → *Raymond forgot closing the door.*

> Jared visited the Grand Canyon during the trip. He remembers it.
>
> → _____
> _____

11 우리말과 같도록 괄호 안의 말을 활용하여 빈칸에 쓰시오.

> 클래식 음악을 듣는 것은 내가 쉬는 것을 돕는다.
> (classical music, help)

= _____ _____

_____ _____ me relax.

12 다음 빈칸에 들어갈 말이 순서대로 짝지어진 것은?

> · You shouldn't swim for an hour after _____ a meal.
> · I found the information about blue whales by _____ the Internet.

① to eat – to search
② eating – to search
③ eat – searching
④ to eat – searching
⑤ eating – searching

13 다음 중 어법상 바른 것의 개수는?

> ⓐ Adam imagined to live in a huge castle.
> ⓑ Avoid talking when you have a sore throat.
> ⓒ We finished do the puzzle at three in the morning.
> ⓓ Jess continued to sharpen the pencil.
> ⓔ The boy denied breaking the vase.

① 1개
② 2개
③ 3개
④ 4개
⑤ 5개

14 다음 글의 빈칸에 공통으로 들어갈 알맞은 것은?

> It was not worth _____ to fix my old computer. On _____ to fix it, smoke came out of it. Now, it completely stopped working.

① try   ② trying   ③ to try
④ tried   ⑤ to trying

15 다음 문장에서 어법상 어색한 부분을 찾아 쓰고 바르게 고쳐 쓰시오.

> The jacket looked good on me. I couldn't help to buy it.

_____ → _____

16 다음 대화의 (A)~(C)에 들어갈 말이 바르게 짝지어진 것은?

> *Kyle*: What did you decide ___(A)___ up as for Halloween?
> *Kim* : I haven't made up my mind yet. Any ideas?
> *Kyle*: What about being a vampire or a pirate?
> *Kim* : I prefer ___(B)___ a vampire costume.
> *Kyle*: That's great. Then I suggest ___(C)___ on a cape.
> *Kim* : Good idea!

	(A)	(B)	(C)
①	to dress	wear	putting
②	to dress	wearing	putting
③	dressing	wearing	putting
④	dressing	wearing	to put
⑤	to dress	to wear	to put

17 다음 밑줄 친 ⓐ~ⓔ 중 어법상 어색한 것을 찾아 기호를 쓰고 바르게 고쳐 쓰시오.

> · His hobby is ⓐwatching old movies.
> · Why do you keep ⓑturn off the air conditioner?
> · Brushing your teeth ⓒprevent cavities.
> · Victor is nervous about ⓓgoing to high school.
> · I don't mind ⓔto open the window.

(1) _____ → _____
(2) _____ → _____
(3) _____ → _____

18 다음 두 문장의 의미가 같도록 빈칸에 알맞은 말을 쓰시오.

> It is interesting to learn about the planets in our solar system.
> = _____ _____ _____ _____ in our solar system is interesting.

19 다음 중 짝지어진 두 문장의 의미가 다른 것은?

① The puppy began to bark at the big dog.
   = The puppy began barking at the big dog.
② The gardener tried to move the large rock by himself.
   = The gardener tried moving the large rock by himself.
③ George loves to ski in the winter.
   = George loves skiing in the winter.
④ The bird continued singing for an hour.
   = The bird continued to sing for an hour.
⑤ Jane will start to make lunch soon.
   = Jane will start making lunch soon.

20 다음 우리말을 영작할 때 빈칸에 들어갈 알맞은 것은?

> 그 법은 운전자가 학교 앞에 차를 세우지 못하게 한다.
> = The law prevents drivers from _____ in front of schools.

① park ② parks ③ parked
④ to park ⑤ parking

21 다음 밑줄 친 부분의 쓰임이 같은 것끼리 묶인 것은?

> ⓐ My sister is worried about <u>taking</u> the midterm exam.
> ⓑ John and Paul hate <u>being</u> late to their classes.
> ⓒ <u>Winning</u> the marathon has been my dream for a long time.
> ⓓ Ollie's part-time job is <u>delivering</u> pizzas.
> ⓔ The doctor's suggestion was <u>drinking</u> some hot tea.

① ⓐ, ⓑ ② ⓐ, ⓒ ③ ⓑ, ⓓ
④ ⓒ, ⓓ ⑤ ⓓ, ⓔ

22 우리말과 같도록 괄호 안의 말을 활용하여 문장을 완성하시오.

> Joseph은 어제 처음으로 파스타를 요리해봤다.
> (try, cook pasta)

= Joseph _____ for the first time yesterday.

23 다음 우리말을 알맞게 영작한 것은?

> 나는 이 싼 지갑을 산 것을 후회하지 않는다.

① I don't regret to buy this cheap purse.
② I don't regret bought this cheap purse.
③ I don't regret buy this cheap purse.
④ I don't regret to buying this cheap purse.
⑤ I don't regret buying this cheap purse.

24 다음 대화의 빈칸에 들어갈 알맞은 것은?

> *A*: These library books are due today.
> _____
> *B*: OK. I will drop them off after school.

① Don't forget to return them.
② Forget to return them.
③ Remember returning them.
④ Don't forget returning them.
⑤ Don't remember to return them.

25 다음 중 어법상 <u>어색한</u> 것끼리 묶인 것은?

> ⓐ Making new friends is hard for some people.
> ⓑ Studying history help us to understand the past.
> ⓒ Fred avoids to use paper towels at home.
> ⓓ Do you want to go camping this weekend?
> ⓔ Carl's goal is joining the school's volleyball team.

① ⓐ, ⓑ ② ⓐ, ⓔ ③ ⓑ, ⓒ
④ ⓒ, ⓓ ⑤ ⓓ, ⓔ

CHAPTER 8
분사

기출로 적중 POINT

연습문제 A 다음 문장의 분사에 동그라미를 치고, 분사가 수식하거나 보충 설명하는 부분에 밑줄을 치시오.

1 I couldn't find my lost wallet.

2 The movie was boring to watch.

3 The baby was sleeping all day.

4 The store is closed for a week from tomorrow.

5 Did they have the elevator fixed?

6 The birds were hiding in the tree.

7 The book written by Bernard Werber is on the table.

8 She looked worried because she couldn't find her keys.

연습문제 B 밑줄 친 부분의 쓰임과 같은 것을 <보기>에서 골라 그 기호를 쓰시오.

> <보기>   ⓐ Don't touch the <u>boiling</u> water.
>   ⓑ The rules of the game sounds <u>confusing</u>.

1 I saw a <u>flashing</u> light through the window.　　　[　　　]

2 She looked <u>tired</u> after studying all night.　　　[　　　]

3 I bought a <u>used</u> camera from him.　　　[　　　]

4 She saw Jerry <u>dancing</u> alone in the classroom.　　　[　　　]

5 He stood <u>looking</u> at the picture.　　　[　　　]

6 Dad got the refrigerator <u>repaired</u>.　　　[　　　]

7 I heard an <u>interesting</u> fact about snails.　　　[　　　]

8 She seemed <u>amazed</u> by what James told her.　　　[　　　]

연습문제 A 괄호 안에서 알맞은 것을 고르시오.

1 The girl (wearing / worn) a pink shirt is pretty.

2 I was (cooking / cooked) in the kitchen with Mike.

3 The book was (writing / written) by Virginia Woolf.

4 The news was (shocking / shocked) to everyone.

5 The leaves (falling / fallen) from the tree are on the road.

6 The girl (reading / read) a book on the sofa is Emily.

7 Have you played the game (calling / called) Snakes and Ladders?

8 You can see dolphins (swimming / swum) in the ocean.

9 Fredrick's arms were (breaking / broken) in the accident.

10 This car was (making / made) in Germany.

연습문제 B 괄호 안의 동사를 알맞은 형태로 바꿔 빈칸에 쓰시오.

1 I can't read this sign _____ in Chinese. (write)

2 The musical *Cats* is _____ by many people. (love)

3 Sam bought a wallet _____ in France. (make)

4 We took a walk to see the _____ sun. (rise)

5 Is that girl _____ on the bench your sister? (sit)

6 There is a man _____ on the stage. (sing)

7 She has a cat _____ Fluffy. (name)

8 This bag is _____ by Virgil Abloh. (design)

9 The Statue of Liberty was _____ in 1884. (build)

10 Jenny is _____ a delicious dish for her mom. (cook)

11 Have you ever _____ the song written by him? (hear)

12 Kevin went to the museum to see a picture _____ by Monet. (paint)

연습문제 A 괄호 안의 동사를 알맞은 형태로 바꿔 빈칸에 쓰시오.

1 (satisfy)　① This restaurant's food is _____.
　　　　　　　② All the customers are _____.

2 (tire)　① A long day in school is _____ for students.
　　　　　② Staying in school all day makes students _____.

3 (bore)　① Ms. Brown's class is _____.
　　　　　② _____ students can't concentrate on the class.

4 (embarrass)　① His grade on the math exam was _____.
　　　　　　　② He was _____ by his grade on the math exam.

5 (confuse)　① The puzzle was _____.
　　　　　　② The puzzle made the child _____.

6 (depress)　① We heard the _____ news on TV.
　　　　　　② We were _____ by the news.

7 (move)　① Martin Luther King's speech was very _____.
　　　　　② Many people were _____ by Martin Luther King's speech.

8 (surprise)　① The birthday party was _____.
　　　　　　② I was _____ by the birthday party.

연습문제 B 밑줄 친 부분이 어법상 맞으면 O를 쓰고, 틀리면 바르게 고쳐 완전한 문장을 쓰시오.

1 Is your friend <u>interesting</u> in Korean history?
　→ _____

2 The trip to the amusement park was <u>excited</u>.
　→ _____

3 The scientists are <u>shocking</u> about the melting glaciers.
　→ _____

4 I was <u>tired</u> because of the long walk back home.
　→ _____

5 Cameron's grade made his mother <u>disappointed</u>.
　→ _____

6 Kevin was deeply <u>touching</u> by his brother's present.
　→ _____

POINT 4

연습문제 **A**　밑줄 친 부분의 쓰임이 현재분사인지 동명사인지 쓰시오.

1　I am <u>going</u> to Spain for my summer vacation.　[　　　]

2　The girl <u>standing</u> in the middle is my daughter.　[　　　]

3　I'm planning to buy a new tent and a <u>sleeping</u> bag.　[　　　]

4　His hobby is <u>skateboarding</u> in the park.　[　　　]

5　I saw a boy <u>crying</u> in front of my house.　[　　　]

6　She heard dogs <u>barking</u> across the street.　[　　　]

7　<u>Studying</u> science is difficult for many students.　[　　　]

8　He enjoys <u>playing</u> online games with his friends.　[　　　]

9　Yura is <u>reading</u> a mystery novel.　[　　　]

10　The explanation sounded <u>confusing</u> to me.　[　　　]

연습문제 **B**　우리말과 같도록 괄호 안의 말을 알맞게 배열하시오.

1　나는 나무에 달린 배를 봤다. (hanging, a, tree, the, on, pear)
= I saw _____.

2　Tony는 그의 할아버지께 지팡이를 사드렸다. (stick, a, bought, walking, Tony)
= _____ for his grandfather.

3　꽃에 물을 주고 있는 그 남자는 키가 매우 컸다. (flowers, watering, the, the, man)
= _____ was very tall.

4　우리는 하늘에서 빛나는 보름달을 보기 위해 불을 껐다. (in, full moon, sky, the, the, shining)
= We turned off the light to see _____.

5　수업에 오기 전에 너의 무용화를 신어라. (dancing, on, shoes, your, put)
= _____ before coming to class.

6　James는 지금 그의 개에게 먹이를 주고 있다. (feeding, James, his, is, dog)
= _____ now.

7　수영하고 있는 돌고래들을 봐라. 그것들은 매우 아름답다. (swimming, the, at, dolphins, look)
= _____. They are very beautiful.

8　호랑이를 사냥하는 것은 많은 나라에서 불법이다. (is, tigers, illegal, hunting)
= _____ in many countries.

연습문제 다음 두 문장의 의미가 같도록 분사구문을 이용하여 영작하시오. (단, 부사절의 접속사를 생략하시오.)

1 When he saw me, he ran away.

= _____

2 As she is too tired, she did not go out with her family.

= _____

3 Because I felt dizzy, I went to bed early.

= _____

4 After Kate talked to the teacher, she felt much better.

= _____

5 As she did not study for the exam, she failed it.

= _____

6 Because he woke up late, he had to skip breakfast.

= _____

7 Because she did not know the way back home, she cried.

= _____

8 When I looked up, I saw birds flying over the bridge.

= _____

9 When I stayed in Canada, I became friends with John.

= _____

10 As I didn't see the doctor, I couldn't buy the medicine.

= _____

11 While I read the book, I fell asleep.

= _____

12 Because he felt cold, he turned on the heater.

= _____

13 Because they didn't have money, they had to walk back to the hotel.

= _____

14 While he walked down the street, he met his teacher.

= _____

기출로 적중 해카스 중학영문법 2학년 워크북

연습문제 A 우리말과 같도록 괄호 안의 말을 활용하여 문장을 완성하시오.

1 나는 강을 따라 걸으면서, 나의 문제들에 대해 생각했다. (walk along the river)

= _____, I thought about my problems.

2 그는 고기를 먹지 않기 때문에, 샐러드 한 그릇을 주문했다. (eat meat)

= _____, he ordered a bowl of salad.

3 그녀는 일찍 일어났기 때문에, 조깅하러 나갔다. (get up early)

= _____, she went out for jogging.

4 Mary는 친구에게 전화를 걸면서, 화장실로 걸어 들어갔다. (call her friend)

= _____, Mary walked into the bathroom.

5 나는 은행에 도착한 후에, 돈을 인출하기 위해 현금지급기를 사용했다. (arrive at the bank)

= _____, I used the ATM to withdraw money.

6 나는 비록 피곤하지만, 나의 방을 청소할 수 있다. (be tired)

= Though _____, I can clean my room.

7 나는 내일 학교에 가지 않기 때문에, 정오까지 잘 것이다. (go to school tomorrow)

= _____, I will sleep untill noon.

8 Thomas는 충분히 나이가 들었기 때문에, 그 영화를 혼자 볼 수 있었다. (be old enough)

= _____, Thomas could watch the movie alone.

연습문제 B 다음 문장의 밑줄 친 부분을 분사구문으로 바꿔 쓰시오.

1 Because he ate too much, he had a stomachache.

= _____, he had a stomachache.

2 As he called my name, he came into the classroom.

= _____, he came into the classroom.

3 After she passed the exam, she became a doctor.

= _____, she became a doctor.

4 When I feel lonely, I talk to my friends.

= _____, I talk to my friends.

5 Because she was so sick, she could not come to school.

= _____, she could not come to school.

중간·기말고사 실전 문제

[1-2] 다음 빈칸에 들어갈 알맞은 것을 고르시오.

1

> After a few weeks, the police found the
> _____ bicycle.

① steal   ② stole

③ stealing   ④ stolen

⑤ steals

2

> The new animated movie was very
> _____ .

① excite   ② excites

③ exciting   ④ excited

⑤ to exciting

3 다음 중 밑줄 친 부분이 어법상 바른 것은?

① The chef uses freezing vegetables for the soup.

② Have a seat in the chair painting blue.

③ Kelly watched the artist drawn the portrait.

④ I took a picture of snow fallen from the sky.

⑤ The tree was covered with shining light bulbs.

4 우리말과 같도록 괄호 안의 말을 활용하여 빈칸에 쓰시오.

> Harry는 영화 세트장으로 사용된 집을 방문했다.
> (use)

= Harry visited the house _____ as a movie set.

5 다음 (A)~(C)에 들어갈 말이 바르게 짝지어진 것은?

> *Martin*: Did you hear the lady ___(A)___ opera in the subway station this morning?
>
> *Ella*   : Yes. I was really ___(B)___ by her voice.
>
> *Martin*: So was I. She is one of the most ___(C)___ vocalists I've ever heard.

	(A)	(B)	(C)
①	sang	fascinating	amazed
②	sang	fascinated	amazing
③	singing	fascinating	amazed
④	singing	fascinated	amazing
⑤	singing	fascinating	amazing

[6-7] 분사를 이용하여 다음 두 문장을 한 문장으로 연결하시오.

6

> The pie was on the table. It was baked by my mother.
> → The pie _____ was on the table.

7

> The lady is a nurse. She is taking our temperature.
> → The lady _____ is a nurse.

8 다음 중 밑줄 친 부분이 어법상 어색한 것은?

① Jake repaired the broken watch by himself.
② The poem written by Emily Dickinson was very touching.
③ Who is that man standing over there?
④ I bought this fried chicken from that store.
⑤ The bird flown around the bush has beautiful feather.

9 다음 문장을 분사구문을 이용하여 바꿔 쓰시오.

When I wash my hands, I use liquid soap.
= _____, I use liquid soap.

10 다음 대화의 빈칸에 들어갈 말이 순서대로 짝지어진 것은?

A: What did you do last weekend?
B: I went to the amusement park. There was a Halloween haunted house. It was very _____.
A: Wow. You sound like you were really _____.

① shock – surprising
② shocking – surprised
③ shocked – surprising
④ shocking – surprising
⑤ shocked – surprised

11 다음 중 어법상 어색한 것의 개수는?

ⓐ Carol was confused by the directions in the cook book.
ⓑ He found the book really bored.
ⓒ The closet was full of fascinated clothes.
ⓓ Everyone has experienced an embarrassing moment.
ⓔ Bad weather can make people feel depressing.

① 1개 ② 2개 ③ 3개
④ 4개 ⑤ 5개

12 우리말과 같도록 괄호 안의 말을 활용하여 빈칸에 쓰시오.

그는 음악을 들은 후에, 춤을 추기 시작했다. (hear the music)

= _____ _____ _____
_____ _____, he started to dance.
= _____ _____ _____, he started to dance.

13 다음 문장의 밑줄 친 부분을 분사구문으로 바꿔 쓰시오.

Because she didn't know the way, she couldn't go to the stadium.
= _____, she couldn't go to the stadium.

14 다음 중 밑줄 친 부분의 쓰임이 나머지 넷과 다른 것은?

① We have a <u>writing</u> class at 11 A.M. every morning.
② I wanted to buy a <u>coloring</u> book.
③ My grandmother has to use <u>reading</u> glasses.
④ Do you have any <u>sleeping</u> bag that I can borrow?
⑤ I saw some horses <u>running</u> in the field.

15 다음 (A)~(C)에 들어갈 말이 바르게 짝지어진 것은?

· Are you ____(A)____ about the field trip next week?
· The book contains many ____(B)____ short stories.
· My father had his car ____(C)____ this morning.

	(A)	(B)	(C)
①	exciting	moving	cleaned
②	excited	moved	cleaning
③	exciting	moved	cleaning
④	excited	moving	cleaned
⑤	exciting	moved	cleaned

16 우리말과 같도록 괄호 안의 말을 활용하여 빈칸에 쓰시오.

Alfred Nobel은 그의 발명품이 무기로 사용되었기 때문에 충격받았다. (shock)

= Alfred Nobel was _____ because his inventions were used as weapons.

17 다음 밑줄 친 부분의 쓰임이 같은 것끼리 묶인 것은?

ⓐ There are some birds <u>sitting</u> in the tree.
ⓑ Don't stop <u>working</u> toward your goal.
ⓒ Sandy's dream is <u>visiting</u> Europe.
ⓓ Ryan is <u>filming</u> a nature documentary.
ⓔ Please answer the <u>ringing</u> phone.

① ⓐ, ⓑ, ⓒ   ② ⓐ, ⓒ, ⓓ   ③ ⓐ, ⓓ, ⓔ
④ ⓑ, ⓒ, ⓔ   ⑤ ⓑ, ⓓ, ⓔ

18 다음 문장을 분사구문을 이용하여 바꿔 쓸 때 빈칸에 들어갈 알맞은 것은?

While I checked my essay, I noticed some errors.
= _____, I noticed some errors.

① Check my essay
② Checks my essay
③ Checked my essay
④ Checking my essay
⑤ I checked my essay

19 다음 두 문장을 한 문장으로 연결할 때 빈칸에 들어갈 알맞은 것은?

Ben saw a boy and a girl. They were sharing an ice cream.
→ Ben saw a boy and a girl _____ an ice cream.

① shares   ② to share
③ sharing   ④ shared
⑤ be shared

20 주어진 문장의 밑줄 친 부분과 쓰임이 같은 것은?

> Lena felt sorry for the crying cat, so she gave it some tuna.

① I found a red dress hanging in the closet.
② You should start working harder to finish your homework.
③ My mother purchased running shoes to run a marathon.
④ Eating nutritious food is the key to staying healthy.
⑤ It's difficult to learn a language without spending enough time to study.

21 다음 빈칸에 들어갈 말이 순서대로 짝지어진 것은?

> · _____ on the beach, I watched the boats sail by.
> · Is this _____ umbrella yours?

① Sat – broken
② Sitting – broken
③ Sat – breaking
④ Sitting – breaking
⑤ Sit – broken

22 다음 밑줄 친 부분과 바꿔 쓸 수 있는 것은?

> Being angry, I sat down and slowly counted to ten.

① As I was angry
② And I was angry
③ When I am angry
④ Before I was angry
⑤ Although I am angry

[23-24] 우리말과 같도록 괄호 안의 말을 활용하여 빈칸에 쓰시오.

23

> 약간의 우유도 없었기 때문에, Kevin은 슈퍼마켓에 갔다. (have, any milk)

= _____ _____ _____

_____, Kevin went to the supermarket.

24

> 선생님은 교실 앞에 팔짱을 낀 채로 서 있었다. (her arms, fold)

= The teacher stood in front of the class

_____ _____ _____

_____ .

25 다음 글의 밑줄 친 ⓐ~ⓔ 중 어법상 어색한 것을 찾아 기호를 쓰고 바르게 고쳐 쓰시오.

> When Vanessa woke up, she was really ⓐconfusing. She heard someone ⓑcalling her name, but it sounded far away. She decided to respond. With a ⓒshaking voice she said, "Yes?" ⓓAnswered her, the other person said "It's me, Melanie! You called me." Vanessa realized that she accidentally dialed her friend's phone while she was ⓔslept.

(1) _____ → _____
(2) _____ → _____
(3) _____ → _____

CHAPTER 9
명사와 관사

기출로 적중 POINT

연습문제 A 다음 명사의 종류를 <보기>에서 골라 그 기호를 쓰시오.

<보기> ⓐ 보통명사   ⓑ 집합명사   ⓒ 고유명사   ⓓ 추상명사   ⓔ 물질명사

1 happiness [   ]   **2** sand [   ]   **3** computer [   ]

4 Rachel [   ]   **5** money [   ]   **6** oxygen [   ]

7 audience [   ]   **8** butter [   ]   **9** knowledge [   ]

10 France [   ]   **11** confidence [   ]   **12** trophy [   ]

13 dust [   ]   **14** spoon [   ]   **15** October [   ]

16 peace [   ]   **17** team [   ]   **18** student [   ]

19 water [   ]   **20** America [   ]   **21** advice [   ]

22 phone [   ]   **23** friend [   ]   **24** group [   ]

25 grape [   ]   **26** salt [   ]   **27** carrot [   ]

28 family [   ]   **29** gasoline [   ]   **30** Friday [   ]

연습문제 B 괄호 안에서 알맞은 것을 고르시오.

1 I need (an egg / egg) for the science project.

2 The organization is looking for more (volunteer / volunteers).

3 If you have (a question / question), please raise your hand.

4 Can you get me two bottles of (orange juice / orange juices)?

5 Jenny did not want to lend Kate any (money / moneys).

6 We were excited to climb (Hallasan / Hallasans).

7 My (family / families) is the most important thing in my life.

8 Do you want (a sugar / sugar) in your coffee?

9 You can get more (information / informations) on our website.

10 (A giraffe / Giraffe) has a very long neck and legs.

11 Eight (team / teams) are competing in the tournament.

12 (A January / January) is the first month of the year.

셀 수 있는 명사의 복수형

정답 p.78

연습문제 A 다음 명사의 복수형을 쓰시오.

1 wolf   – _____

2 man   – _____

3 monkey   – _____

4 tooth   – _____

5 potato   – _____

6 piano   – _____

7 leaf   – _____

8 box   – _____

9 child   – _____

10 country   – _____

11 panda   – _____

12 volcano   – _____

13 lady   – _____

14 salmon   – _____

15 cliff   – _____

16 key   – _____

17 foot   – _____

18 book   – _____

19 fish   – _____

20 ox   – _____

21 baby   – _____

22 mouse   – _____

23 address   – _____

24 enemy   – _____

연습문제 B 밑줄 친 부분이 어법상 맞으면 O를 쓰고, 틀리면 바르게 고쳐 쓰시오.

1 The classroom has four <u>window</u>. → _____

2 I need three <u>shelfs</u> to put my books on. → _____

3 You have to brush your <u>tooths</u> three times a day. → _____

4 She bought some <u>flowers</u> for her mother's birthday. → _____

5 I saw some <u>ladyes</u> chatting under the tree. → _____

6 The government faced lots of <u>problem</u>. → _____

7 He saw some <u>childs</u> playing soccer in the field. → _____

8 They organized many <u>activities</u> for students. → _____

9 Look at those yellow <u>tomatos</u> over there. → _____

10 Some <u>goose</u> were swimming in the lake. → _____

11 There are a few <u>churchs</u> in the town. → _____

12 The cars waited for the two <u>deers</u> to cross the road. → _____

연습문제 A 우리말과 같도록 괄호 안의 말을 활용하여 문장을 완성하시오. (단, 숫자는 영어로 쓰시오.)

1 우리는 커피 세 컵을 주문했다. (coffee, cup)

= We ordered _____.

2 나는 오늘 아침에 우유 한 잔을 마셨다. (milk, glass)

= I drank _____ this morning.

3 그 여자는 그녀의 아들의 생일파티를 위해 탄산음료 50캔을 샀다. (soda, can)

= The woman bought _____ for her son's birthday party.

4 너는 케이크 한 조각을 원하니? (cake, piece)

= Would you like _____?

5 Max는 그의 에세이를 출력하기 위해 종이 일곱 장을 사용했다. (paper, sheet)

= Max used _____ to print out his essay.

6 Pamela는 저녁으로 수프 한 그릇을 먹었다. (soup, bowl)

= Pamela ate _____ for dinner.

7 요리법에 따르면, 너는 반죽에 설탕 다섯 스푼을 넣어야 한다. (sugar, spoonful)

= According to the recipe, you should add _____ to the dough.

8 지호는 초콜릿 바 하나를 그의 남동생과 나눠 가졌다. (chocolate, bar)

= Jiho shared _____ with his little brother.

9 Hazel은 그녀의 샌드위치에 햄 두 장을 추가했다. (ham, slice)

= Hazel added _____ to her sandwich.

연습문제 B 괄호 안에서 알맞은 것을 고르시오.

1 Luke asked me to bring two (cans / sheets) of paint to his house.

2 I bought three (bar / bars) of soap at the market.

3 Five loaves of (bread / breads) cost only 15 dollars in this bakery.

4 Can you help me move a (piece / loaf) of furniture to the garage?

5 My mom likes to start the day with a (cup / cups) of tea.

6 I heard a (sheet / piece) of information about the incident.

7 Please get the player a (bottle / bottles) of water right now.

8 The boy saw his dad put a bar of (gold / golds) in the safe.

연습문제 A 밑줄 친 부분이 어법상 맞으면 O를 쓰고, 틀리면 바르게 고쳐 완전한 문장을 쓰시오.

1 Charlie found a <u>four-leaves</u> clover in his grandmother's garden.

→ _____

2 Sarah went to Africa for a <u>three-months</u> volunteer program.

→ _____

3 I bought three <u>pairs of jeans</u> at a flea market.

→ _____

4 It is annoying that I cannot find the other <u>sock</u>.

→ _____

5 He is trying to knit a <u>gloves</u> for his girlfriend.

→ _____

6 Kelly picked up a <u>hundred-dollars</u> bill on the street.

→ _____

7 The shoe company donated 200 <u>pairs of sneaker</u> for the poor.

→ _____

8 She lost <u>a pair of shoes</u> while playing in the ocean.

→ _____

연습문제 B 다음 문장의 밑줄 친 부분과 동격인 부분에 밑줄을 치시오.

1 <u>This man</u>, Mr. Choi, is my homeroom teacher.

2 Who is this girl in the picture? - That is <u>my sister</u>, Suzy.

3 I'm against <u>the idea</u> that students should wear a school uniform.

4 <u>The rumor</u> that Kate and James fought with each other turned out to be true.

5 <u>His mother</u>, Jennifer, is a world-famous actress.

6 I love <u>Adele</u>, a Grammy Award-winning artist.

7 <u>The doctor's advice</u> that I should take a rest was very helpful.

8 <u>Your two-year-old son</u>, Andrew, is so adorable.

9 Did you hear <u>the announcement</u> that the graduation ceremony has been postponed?

10 <u>The fact</u> that Mozart composed his first opera when he was twelve years old is amazing.

연습문제 우리말과 같도록 괄호 안의 말을 활용하여 문장을 완성하시오.

1 그 여자들의 가방은 매우 비싸게 보인다. (the women, bags)

= _____ look very expensive.

2 그 콘서트장의 입구에서 만나자. (the concert hall, the entrance)

= Let's meet at _____.

3 나에게 오늘의 날씨를 말해주겠니? (today, weather)

= Can you tell me _____?

4 Green 선생님이 유라를 교무실로 불렀다. (room, the teachers)

= Mr. Green called Yura to _____.

5 그녀는 어머니의 날에 그녀의 엄마를 위해 장미꽃 한 다발을 샀다. (Mother, Day)

= She bought a bunch of roses for her mom on _____.

6 그 학생들의 태도는 매우 긍정적이다. (the students, attitude)

= _____ is very positive.

7 그 산의 꼭대기는 항상 눈으로 덮여 있다. (the mountain, the top)

= _____ is always covered with snow.

연습문제 다음 빈칸에 a나 an 중 알맞은 것을 쓰고, 필요하지 않으면 X를 쓰시오.

1 I take a swimming class three times _____ week.

2 Sofia wanted to study in France for _____ year.

3 _____ cat can jump from a very tall place.

4 I like to watch _____ fireworks on New Year's Day.

5 Emily tries to stretch at least once _____ hour every day.

6 I'm planning to buy _____ used computer this weekend.

7 I take _____ vitamin C every day.

8 Can I borrow _____ eraser from you?

연습문제 | 다음 문장의 밑줄 친 부분을 바르게 고쳐 쓰시오.

1 My mom buys groceries twice <u>the week</u>. → _____

2 It's too hot and humid in here. Let's open <u>window</u>. → _____

3 I read a book. <u>Book</u> was about Amazon Rainforest. → _____

4 Where did you learn how to play <u>a piano</u>? → _____

5 It took Kevin <u>the day</u> to complete his science project. → _____

6 Do you know where <u>a park</u> in this photo is? → _____

7 He bought <u>expensive watch</u> for his dad. → _____

8 Charles and I graduated from <u>same university</u>. → _____

9 I think that Beethoven is <u>a greatest composer</u>. → _____

10 <u>Moon</u> rotates around the Earth. → _____

POINT 6-3

관사를 쓰지 않는 경우

정답 p.79

연습문제 | 알맞은 관사와 괄호 안의 말을 활용하여 문장을 완성하시오. (단, 관사가 필요하지 않으면 쓰지 마시오.)

1 Jeremy enjoys playing _____ with his friends on weekends. (soccer)

2 My mother made a hotel reservation by _____. (phone)

3 Do you know that you can get to the museum by _____? (bus)

4 Mr. Wilson has _____. (daughter)

5 Kenny loves listening to Amy play _____. (flute)

6 It takes about _____ to go to Incheon from Seoul. (hour)

7 Traveling by _____ was the most exciting experience. (plane)

8 Where do you want to go for _____ today? (lunch)

9 My seven-year-old brother is going to go to _____ next year. (school)

10 The lawyer went to _____ to visit his client. (prison)

중간 · 기말고사 실전 문제

1 다음 중 명사의 종류가 서로 <u>다른</u> 것끼리 짝지어진 것은?

① building, radio, koala
② luck, danger, knowledge
③ group, energy, news
④ January, Paris, Friday
⑤ band, family, club

2 다음 중 명사의 복수형이 바른 것은?

① zoo – zooes   ② cliff – clives
③ tooth – tooths   ④ donkey – donkeys
⑤ sandwich – sandwichs

3 다음 빈칸에 들어갈 알맞은 것을 <u>모두</u> 고르시오.

Emma bought a _____ for her mother at the market.

① tulip   ② rice   ③ melon
④ flour   ⑤ sunglasses

4 다음 우리말을 알맞게 영작한 것은?

① 우유 한 잔 = a glass of milks
② 빵 세 덩어리 = three loaf of bread
③ 충고 한 마디 = a slice of advice
④ 물 다섯 병 = five bottles of water
⑤ 밥 두 공기 = two bowl of rices

5 다음 중 밑줄 친 부분이 어법상 바른 것은?

① Many <u>sheeps</u> on the hill are eating the grass.
② One of the <u>dishs</u> fell off the shelf.
③ There are hundreds of <u>coines</u> in my piggy bank.
④ Our dog gave birth to three <u>puppyes</u> last night.
⑤ <u>Giraffes</u> have the highest blood pressure among animals.

6 다음 빈칸에 공통으로 들어갈 알맞은 것은?

· Peter took _____ bread out of the loaf.
· The detective got _____ information from the newspaper.

① a glass of   ② a slice of
③ a sheet of   ④ a loaf of
⑤ a piece of

7 다음 중 어법상 <u>어색한</u> 것은?

① Do you play the guitar well?
② Jinsu takes a taekwondo class three times a week.
③ The Sun is one of many stars.
④ Could you turn down the volume?
⑤ Make sure not to make a same mistake.

8 다음 글의 빈칸에 들어갈 알맞은 것은?

> Did you see lots of _____ over there?

① group ② peach ③ person
④ ox ⑤ fish

[9-10] 우리말과 같도록 괄호 안의 명사를 활용하여 문장을 완성하시오. (단, 숫자는 영어로 쓰시오.)

9

> 저에게 케이크 네 조각과 주스 두 병을 주시겠어요?
> (cake, juice)

= Can you give me _____
  and _____, please?

10

> 모든 사람은 다음 미술 수업에 가위 한 자루를 가지고
> 와야 한다. (scissor)

= Everyone has to bring _____
  to the next art class.

11 다음 중 어법상 바른 것은?

① I wish you a good luck.
② James can't eat any food containing peanuts.
③ The rainforest gives the planet a lot of oxygens.
④ I've just heard an exciting news about our field trip.
⑤ Some rude students show little respects for their teachers.

12 다음 빈칸에 들어갈 말이 순서대로 짝지어진 것은?

> · I only ate two _____ of pizza and my brother ate the rest.
> · We need to buy a _____ of paint to finish painting the wall.

① pieces – can ② slices – cup
③ piece – cup ④ slice – can
⑤ bars – cups

13 다음 <보기> 중 빈칸에 들어갈 수 있는 것의 개수는?

> <보기> Boston museum zebras
>   butter problems mosquito

> Is there a _____ near here?

① 1개 ② 2개 ③ 3개
④ 4개 ⑤ 5개

14 다음 중 밑줄 친 부분의 쓰임이 나머지 넷과 다른 것은?

① Mr. Patel, our English teacher, is from Toronto.
② If you buy it now, you can get a discount.
③ Have you heard of chorizo, the Mexican sausage?
④ We, professional dancers, are proud of our performance.
⑤ She is watching *Panda Land*, her favorite TV show.

[15-16] 다음 문장에서 <u>틀린</u> 부분을 바르게 고쳐 완전한 문장을 쓰시오.

15

> We stayed in a five-stars hotel in Berlin.
>
> → _____

16

> We bought twenty slices of hams for the party.
>
> → _____
> _____

17 다음 중 어법상 <u>어색한</u> 것을 <u>모두</u> 고르시오.

① I need to put a spoonful of salt into the soup.
② The waiter is carrying two cup of coffees.
③ John got seven pairs of socks for Christmas.
④ There is a bar of soap next to the sink.
⑤ Could you hand over three sheets of papers to her?

18 주어진 문장의 밑줄 친 부분과 의미가 같은 것은?

> How often do you use a train <u>a</u> month?

① Are you looking for <u>a</u> towel?
② Jane doesn't have <u>a</u> sister.
③ <u>A</u> golden retriever is a type of dog.
④ I saw <u>a</u> man walking in the street.
⑤ Take this medicine once <u>a</u> day.

19 다음 빈칸에 the가 들어갈 수 있는 것은?

① We're going to the museum by _____ train tomorrow.
② Erin's mother makes _____ breakfast for her every day.
③ I hope we can play _____ hockey during PE class today.
④ My brother Tony goes to _____ college in New York.
⑤ Some reporters went to _____ hospital to interview the injured actor.

[20-21] 우리말과 같도록 괄호 안의 말을 활용하여 문장을 완성하시오.

20

> 그 과학자들은 그 동물들의 행동을 흥미롭다고 생각했다. (the animals, behavior)

= The scientists found _____ interesting.

21

> 영국의 모양은 용처럼 보인다. (the United Kingdom, the shape)

= _____ looks like a dragon.

22 다음 중 밑줄 친 부분이 어법상 어색한 것끼리 묶인 것은?

ⓐ I would like a bowl of cereal for breakfast.
ⓑ My dog chewed a shoe in front of the door.
ⓒ Sarah bought five pairs of jean at the mall.
ⓓ Four bands will play at the concert.
ⓔ You should drink eight glasses of waters a day.
ⓕ The thieves stole thousands of bars of golds from the safe.

① ⓐ, ⓑ, ⓒ   ② ⓐ, ⓓ, ⓔ   ③ ⓐ, ⓒ, ⓕ
④ ⓑ, ⓓ, ⓔ   ⑤ ⓒ, ⓔ, ⓕ

23 다음 (A)~(C)에 들어갈 말이 바르게 짝지어진 것은?

· The envelope contained five ___(A)___ bills.
· Cheetahs have many ___(B)___ on their fur.
· The room is filled with much ___(C)___ .

	(A)	(B)	(C)
①	ten-dollar	spot	smoke
②	ten-dollars	spot	smoke
③	ten-dollar	spots	smoke
④	ten-dollars	spots	smokes
⑤	ten-dollar	spots	smokes

24 다음 글의 밑줄 친 ⓐ~ⓔ를 바르게 고치지 못한 것은?

We decided to go on a trip last weekend. We went to South Beach ⓐby the train. When we got to ⓑa beach, it started to rain heavily. We were so disappointed. We decided to go to ⓒrestaurant to make other plans. We all ordered a drink and ⓓthe slice of pie. While we were eating, ⓔa rain stopped. We were all happy!

① ⓐ by the train → by a train
② ⓑ a beach → the beach
③ ⓒ restaurant → a restaurant
④ ⓓ the slice of pie → a slice of pie
⑤ ⓔ a rain → the rain

25 다음 글의 밑줄 친 ⓐ~ⓔ 중 어법상 어색한 것을 찾아 기호를 쓰고 바르게 고쳐 쓰시오.

Have you tasted ⓐsalmons before? They are really tasty. How about salmon ⓑeggs? These are called roe. They are bright orange and look like tiny ⓒball. If you haven't tried them, you should. Just put a few spoonfuls on a ⓓslice of bread. This is one of ⓔthe best fish dishes.

(1) _____ → _____
(2) _____ → _____

CHAPTER 10
대명사

기출로 적중 POINT

연습문제 A 다음 빈칸에 문장의 밑줄 친 부분을 대신하는 알맞은 인칭대명사를 쓰시오.

1 I have to walk _____ dog every morning.

2 Jamie bought two pairs of jeans, but _____ were too tight.

3 Kate did not lend James _____ notebook.

4 Ethan and I were talking in class, so the teacher scolded _____.

5 I bought a new phone yesterday. _____ is made by Samsung.

6 The café is known for _____ special latte.

7 Tall swimmers can swim faster with _____ long legs and arms.

8 Where is Bill? Did _____ come to school today?

9 James seems to be sick. I'll take _____ to the doctor soon.

10 Don't even try to eat my cookies. They are all _____.

11 Claire and Tim went to see a movie last Saturday. _____ had a lot of fun.

12 The drama was so exciting that I watched _____ two times.

13 Have you seen my new earrings? I can't find _____ anywhere.

연습문제 B 우리말과 같도록 괄호 안의 인칭대명사를 알맞은 형태로 바꿔 빈칸에 쓰시오.

1 (I) ① 나의 자전거는 고장 났다. = _____ bicycle is broken.
       ② 너는 나의 것을 고칠 수 있니? = Can you fix _____?

2 (you) ① 이것은 너의 침대니? = Is this _____ bed?
        ② 너의 것은 아주 편하다. = _____ is really comfortable.

3 (he) ① 그의 양말은 검은색이다. = _____ socks are black.
       ② 그 검은 것들은 그의 것이다. = The black ones are _____.

4 (she) ① 그녀의 전화기는 계속 울린다. = _____ phone keeps ringing.
        ② 저 전화기는 그녀의 것이다. = That phone is _____.

5 (we) ① 사진 속의 그 새끼 고양이들은 우리의 것이다. = The kittens in the photo are _____.
       ② 누군가 우리의 새끼 고양이들의 사진을 찍었다. = Someone took a photo of _____ kittens.

6 (they) ① 빨간 지붕이 있는 그 집은 그들의 것이다. = The house with the red roof is _____.
        ② 그들의 집은 빨간 지붕을 가지고 있다. = _____ house has a red roof.

연습문제 A 다음 빈칸에 알맞은 재귀대명사를 쓰고 생략할 수 있으면 O, 생략할 수 없으면 X를 쓰시오.

1 I _____ wrote this essay. [   ]

2 Kate cut _____ when she sliced the onions. [   ]

3 He _____ made the waffles for breakfast. [   ]

4 She thought of _____ as a great actress. [   ]

5 Barry likes the sneakers _____. [   ]

6 Yujin introduced _____ to her new classmates. [   ]

7 We should all be proud of _____. [   ]

8 She looked at _____ in the mirror. [   ]

9 I consider _____ a diligent student. [   ]

10 The movie _____ was worth watching. [   ]

연습문제 B 우리말과 같도록 <보기>의 말을 활용하여 문장을 완성하시오.

<보기>	enjoy oneself	help oneself to
	by oneself	make oneself at home
	talk to oneself	think to oneself

1 우리는 축제에 가서 즐거운 시간을 보냈다.

= We went to the festival and _____.

2 식탁 위에 당신이 원하는 어떤 것이든 마음껏 드세요.

= Please _____ anything you want on the table.

3 너는 방금 전에 혼잣말을 했니?

= Were you _____ just now?

4 나의 여동생은 혼자서 전구를 바꿀 수 있다.

= My younger sister can change the light bulb _____.

5 나는 "얼마나 좋은 날인가!"라고 혼자 생각했다.

= I _____, "What a great day!"

6 그 주인은 손님들에게 그들이 머무르는 동안 편히 쉬라고 말했다.

= The host told the guests to _____ during their stay.

POINT 3

연습문제 A 괄호 안에서 알맞은 것을 고르시오.

1 (This / These) seats are already taken.

2 (This / These) way is a shortcut.

3 (That / Those) are real flowers.

4 (That / Those) robots are hard to assemble.

5 (That / Those) painting was painted by Picasso.

6 (This / These) toilet is out of order now.

7 (This / These) is the best moment in my life.

8 (This / These) are my parents' wedding photos.

9 Your smile is as beautiful as (that / those) of the Mona Lisa.

10 How long did it take to build (that / those) buildings?

연습문제 B 밑줄 친 부분의 쓰임과 같은 것을 <보기>에서 골라 그 기호를 쓰시오.

<보기>   ⓐ <u>This</u> is the new middle school in my town.
           ⓑ Did you make <u>those</u> wooden toys by yourself?

1 <u>These</u> are my closest colleagues.   [   ]

2 <u>This</u> is my father's hometown.   [   ]

3 <u>That</u> painter has a unique drawing style.   [   ]

4 The kid accidently broke <u>that</u> vase.   [   ]

5 <u>That</u> is one of the tallest mountains in the world.   [   ]

6 <u>That</u> is the point of the article.   [   ]

7 Why don't you try <u>those</u> earrings?   [   ]

8 <u>These</u> plates have a pretty floral pattern.   [   ]

9 <u>This</u> bibimbap tastes really good.   [   ]

10 <u>Those</u> are the books written by Bernard Werber.   [   ]

연습문제 **A** <보기>와 같이 다음 문장을 가주어 it을 사용한 문장으로 바꿔 쓰시오.

> <보기>   To stare at the sun is hard.
> → *It is hard to stare at the sun.*

1 To change my name was not easy.

→ _____

2 To learn Chinese is difficult.

→ _____

3 To swim in this river is dangerous.

→ _____

4 To lose the game was disappointing.

→ _____

5 To get used to the new environment was very hard.

→ _____

6 To meet with people from different cultures is always fun.

→ _____

연습문제 **B** 밑줄 친 it의 쓰임과 같은 것을 <보기>에서 골라 그 기호를 쓰시오.

> <보기>   ⓐ I bought vitamin D for you. Make sure to take it every morning.
> ⓑ It is dark outside, so you'd better stay home.
> ⓒ It would be amazing to travel to space.

1 Is it September 7 today?   [   ]
2 Will it be raining heavily tomorrow?   [   ]
3 I have a puppy. It is two months old.   [   ]
4 It is already 11:30 P.M. You should go to bed now.   [   ]
5 It is important to apply sunscreen when we go out.   [   ]
6 It is a relaxing song to listen to when you feel tired.   [   ]
7 It is surprising that he won first place in the contest.   [   ]
8 It is certain that the president will visit our town next week. [   ]
9 Do you think this hair color is appropriate for school? – Yes, I think it is.   [   ]

연습문제 밑줄 친 부분을 one, ones, it, them 중 하나로 고쳐 쓰시오.

1 These shoes are too small. I need bigger <u>them</u>.   → _____

2 There are some pies on the table. Mom baked <u>it</u>.   → _____

3 <u>Ones</u> should not judge a book by its cover.   → _____

4 Ms. Jones sent you a letter. Did you read <u>one</u>?   → _____

5 When did you borrow these books? - I borrowed <u>it</u> a week ago.   → _____

6 Amy's umbrella was gone, so she bought a new <u>it</u>.   → _____

7 I just hung some pictures on the wall. Have you seen <u>ones</u>?   → _____

8 Jacob ate two big oranges and three small <u>them</u>.   → _____

9 Dad's car is broken. He is planning to buy a new <u>it</u> soon.   → _____

10 Where did you get this camera from? – I got <u>one</u> from the electronics store.   → _____

11 Would you like to have some blueberries? I picked <u>ones</u> at the farm.   → _____

12 I wanted green olives for my recipe, but the store only had black <u>one</u>.   → _____

연습문제 괄호 안에서 알맞은 것을 고르시오.

1 I need to buy (some / any) balloons for the party.

2 There isn't (some / any) pizza left.

3 He would never hurt (someone / anyone).

4 She was hanging out with (some / any) friends.

5 (Someone / Anyone) knocked on his door.

6 Could you bring me (some / any) water?

7 Are there (some / any) further questions?

8 There is (something / anything) strange about this house.

9 These cherries taste really sweet. Would you like (some / any)?

10 The hunters couldn't see (something / anything) in the dark woods.

부정대명사: another, other

정답 p.81

연습문제 A 다음 빈칸에 알맞은 말을 <보기>에서 한 번씩만 골라 쓰시오.

<보기> one ones another the other the others some

1 Many people are on the subway. _____ are reading books. Others are looking at their phones.

2 There are ten questions. Five questions are correct, and _____ are incorrect.

3 James lost his favorite shirt. He will buy the same _____.

4 Mark is feeling very sorry for his fault. Let's give him _____ chance.

5 Metal spoons are stronger than wooden _____.

6 There are two coats on the chair. One is mine. _____ is my sister's.

연습문제 B 우리말과 같도록 괄호 안의 말을 활용하여 문장을 완성하시오.

1 나는 열 개의 사과가 있다. 몇몇은 썩었고, 나머지 전부는 싱싱하다. (be, rotten, fresh)
= I have ten apples. _____, and _____.

2 나의 반에 30명의 학생들이 있다. 몇몇은 안경을 쓰고, 나머지 전부는 안경을 쓰지 않는다. (wear, glasses)
= There are 30 students in my class. _____, and
_____.

3 많은 사람들이 해변에 있다. 몇몇은 서핑을 즐기고, 다른 사람들은 수영을 즐긴다. (enjoy, surfing, swimming)
= Many people are on the beach. _____, and
_____.

4 나는 두 명의 외국인 친구가 있다. 하나는 러시아 출신이고, 나머지 하나는 브라질 출신이다. (be, from Russia, from Brazil)
= I have two foreign friends. _____, and _____.

5 사람들은 다양한 색깔을 좋아한다. 몇몇은 밝은 색깔을 좋아하고, 다른 사람들은 어두운 색깔을 좋아한다. (like, bright colors, dark colors)
= People like various colors. _____, and _____.

6 나는 세 명의 형제가 있다. 한 명은 변호사이고, 다른 하나는 의사이고, 나머지 하나는 건축가이다. (be, a lawyer, a doctor, an architect)
= I have three brothers. _____, _____, and
_____.

연습문제 **A** 우리말과 같도록 괄호 안의 말을 활용하여 문장을 완성하시오.

1 Emily와 Amy 둘 다 전에 싱가포르에 가본 적이 있다. (Emily and Amy)

= _____ have been to Singapore before.

2 모든 아이들은 퍼레이드를 보는 것을 기대하고 있다. (the kids)

= _____ are looking forward to seeing the parade.

3 우리 각각은 다른 외모를 가지고 있다. (us)

= _____ has a different appearance.

4 나의 학교의 모든 학생은 박 선생님을 좋아한다. (student)

= _____ in my school likes Mr. Park.

5 그 모든 세균이 인체에 해로운 것은 아니다. (the germs)

= _____ are harmful to the human body.

6 정답 각각은 30점의 가치가 있다. (correct answer)

= _____ is worth 30 points.

연습문제 **B** 밑줄 친 부분이 어법상 맞으면 O를 쓰고, 틀리면 바르게 고쳐 완전한 문장을 쓰시오.

1 Not all dogs <u>is</u> gentle.

→ _____

2 Both my parents <u>wants</u> me to become a doctor.

→ _____

3 All of the information <u>were</u> helpful.

→ _____

4 Each of the students <u>have</u> a student ID card.

→ _____

5 Everybody in this room <u>enjoy</u> watching musicals.

→ _____

6 Not every oil <u>is</u> bad for your health.

→ _____

7 Each item <u>were</u> carefully checked.

→ _____

8 Every person <u>are</u> entitled to the freedom of expression.

→ _____

연습문제 A 다음 대화의 빈칸에 알맞은 말을 <보기>에서 한 번씩만 골라 쓰시오.

<보기> who   whose   whom   what   which

1 *A*: With _____ does your daughter usually hang out?
  B: She usually hangs out with her best friend, Yeji.

2 *A*: _____ purse is this?
  B: I think it's Jenny's.

3 *A*: _____ are you going to do this weekend?
  B: I'm going to watch a volleyball match at the stadium.

4 *A*: _____ is the author of *The Great Gatsby*?
  B: It's Scott Fitzgerald.

5 *A*: _____ do you like better, romance films or action films?
  B: I like action films better.

연습문제 B 우리말과 같도록 괄호 안의 말을 알맞게 배열하시오.

1 누구의 이름이 목록에 있니? (whose, is, on the list, name)
 = _____

2 그들은 지금 무엇에 대해 이야기하고 있니? (they, talking about, are, what, now)
 = _____

3 그 사진에서 너의 옆에 서 있는 여자는 누구니? (the woman, who, standing, is, in the picture, next to you)
 = _____

4 너는 커피와 녹차 중 어느 것을 마시기를 원하니? (which, you, do, want, to, drink, or, coffee, green tea)
 = _____

5 미나는 무슨 종류의 꽃을 좋아하니? (kind of flowers, what, Mina, like, does)
 = _____

6 그는 누구와 함께 박물관에 가니? (with, is, he, whom, to the museum, going)
 = _____

7 Lisa는 무엇을 가장 좋아하니? (most, like, Lisa, what, does)
 = _____

8 너는 재즈와 클래식 음악 중 어느 것을 선호하니? (jazz, or, you, do, prefer, classical music, which)
 = _____

1 다음 대화의 빈칸에 들어갈 말이 순서대로 짝지어진 것은?

> A: Excuse me. Is this _____ umbrella?
> B: Yes, it's _____. There is my name on it.
> A: Sorry. It looks exactly like my umbrella.

① you – my
② your – my
③ your – mine
④ yours – my
⑤ yours – mine

2 다음 중 밑줄 친 부분을 생략할 수 있는 것을 모두 고르시오.

① Why don't we paint the house underline{ourselves}?
② Please be careful not to burn yourself.
③ I want to express myself better.
④ The melody itself isn't good, but the lyrics are good.
⑤ Mr. Park felt ashamed of himself for his mistakes.

3 다음 글의 빈칸에 들어갈 알맞은 것은?

> Congratulations on your victory in the final soccer match! As your coach, I am so proud of you. All of you should be proud of _____.

① you
② your
③ yourself
④ yourselves
⑤ ourselves

4 다음 중 밑줄 친 it의 쓰임이 나머지 넷과 다른 것은?

① Is it winter in Australia now?
② It is bright outside.
③ Can you tell me where it is?
④ It is already 10 P.M.
⑤ It is especially cold in the morning.

5 다음 글에서 어법상 어색한 부분을 찾아 쓰고 바르게 고쳐 쓰시오.

> Eyebrows have two functions. One is to protect our eyes from dirt, and other is to express emotions.

_____ → _____

6 우리말과 같도록 재귀대명사를 이용하여 빈칸에 알맞은 말을 쓰시오.

> 수업 중에 혼잣말을 하는 것을 멈춰주겠니?

= Can you stop _____ _____
_____ during class?

7 다음 빈칸에 들어갈 말이 순서대로 짝지어진 것은?

> · Shelly baked some cupcakes and gave _____ to her classmates.
> · This shirt is too big for me. Do you have a smaller _____?

① them - it
② them - one
③ them - ones
④ ones - it
⑤ ones - one

8 다음 빈칸에 들어갈 말이 순서대로 짝지어진 것은?

> · _____ of the water on the table was wiped up.
> · _____ children are interested in folk music.

① Each – Every　　② All – Every
③ Both – All　　④ All – Both
⑤ Each – All

9 우리말과 같도록 괄호 안의 말을 활용하여 문장을 완성하시오.

> 너 자신을 돌아보는 것은 중요하다. (important, reflect)

= It _____ on yourself.

10 다음 (A)~(C)에 들어갈 말이 바르게 짝지어진 것은?

> A traffic light consists of three colors. __(A)__ is red, and it means "stop." __(B)__ is yellow, and it is a warning signal. The other is green, which means "go." On the other hand, a crosswalk light consists of only two colors. One is red, and __(C)__ is green.

	(A)	(B)	(C)
①	Ones	Another	others
②	Ones	Other	the other
③	One	Another	the others
④	One	Other	the others
⑤	One	Another	the other

11 주어진 문장의 밑줄 친 it과 쓰임이 같은 것을 모두 고르시오.

> It is my father's birthday today.

① It is April 1.
② It is Jessica's laptop.
③ It is good to read many books.
④ It is far from here to the library.
⑤ It is certain that I turned off the lights in the living room.

12 다음 빈칸에 공통으로 들어갈 알맞은 것은?

> · _____ prefer reading paper newspaper, and others prefer reading online.
> · Kelly sent me _____ pictures of her new kitten.

① One[one]　　② Some[some]
③ Ones[ones]　　④ Any[any]
⑤ The other[the other]

13 다음 대화의 빈칸에 알맞은 말을 <보기>에서 한 번씩만 골라 쓰시오.

> <보기>　who　what　which

(1) A: _____ of these bags is yours?
　　B: The one on the right.

(2) A: _____ wants to solve this puzzle with me?
　　B: I do.

(3) A: _____ does FYI mean?
　　B: It means "for your information."

14 다음 빈칸에 들어갈 말이 순서대로 짝지어진 것은?

> · Each runner _____ given a different
>   number during the race.
> · Every house on the block _____ the
>   same style.

① were – have   ② was – have
③ were – has   ④ was – has
⑤ be – have

15 다음 대화의 빈칸에 들어갈 말이 순서대로 짝지어진 것은?

> A: It's been a long time. Please make
>   _____ at home. Would you like to
>   have _____ hot tea?
> B: Thanks. It's so kind of you.

① you – some   ② you – any
③ yourself – some ④ your – some
⑤ yourself – any

16 다음 글의 빈칸에 들어갈 말이 순서대로 짝지어진 것은?

> Our family has two pets. One is a small
> kitten, and _____ is a large dog.
> They love to play with _____, even
> though they are very different sizes.

① another – one another
② other – one another
③ the other – one another
④ another – each other
⑤ the other – each other

17 다음 중 밑줄 친 these의 쓰임이 나머지 넷과 다른 것은?

① Are these your new glasses?
② Have you ever tried these before?
③ Can I have some more of these?
④ I really like these shoes.
⑤ These are the books I told you about.

18 다음 빈칸에 알맞은 말을 <보기>에서 한 번씩만 골라 쓰시오.

> <보기>   this   that   those

(1) The cost of repairing the car is as high
    as _____ of buying a new one.

(2) I just found _____ wallet. Do you
    know whose it is?

(3) _____ boxes are really heavy. Can
    you help me move them?

19 다음 중 밑줄 친 부분이 어법상 어색한 것끼리 묶인 것은?

> ⓐ All of the researchers in the lab was
>   wearing a white coat.
> ⓑ Each person has a different opinion
>   of the movie.
> ⓒ Both of the paths lead to the
>   mountaintop.
> ⓓ Every runner don't finish the
>   marathon.
> ⓔ Each of the rooms have a view of the
>   ocean.

① ⓐ, ⓑ, ⓔ   ② ⓐ, ⓒ, ⓓ   ③ ⓐ, ⓓ, ⓔ
④ ⓑ, ⓒ, ⓓ   ⑤ ⓑ, ⓒ, ⓔ

20 다음 빈칸에 another가 들어갈 수 <u>없는</u> 것은?

① I bought a novel yesterday, and I bought _____ today.
② I lost my library card. Can I get _____?
③ I don't have a muffler, but I need _____.
④ This road is closed, so we must find _____ way.
⑤ This window won't open. Is there _____ one in this house?

21 다음 밑줄 친 it의 쓰임이 같은 것끼리 묶인 것은?

> ⓐ <u>It</u> is fun to read cartoons.
> ⓑ <u>It</u> isn't easy to fix that machine.
> ⓒ I saw a picture that you drew. <u>It</u> was fantastic.
> ⓓ <u>It</u> is only 500 meters to the Chinese restaurant.
> ⓔ <u>It</u> was sad that I lost my favorite bracelet.

① ⓐ, ⓑ, ⓔ
② ⓐ, ⓒ, ⓓ
③ ⓐ, ⓒ, ⓔ
④ ⓑ, ⓒ, ⓓ
⑤ ⓑ, ⓓ, ⓔ

22 다음 중 밑줄 친 부분이 어법상 바른 것은?

① Are there other <u>method</u> to pay?
② Julie bought five bowls. Some are made of wood, and <u>the other</u> are made of glass.
③ I have ten pairs of sneakers, but I want to buy new <u>them</u>.
④ I have visited two countries in Europe. One is Germany, and <u>other</u> is Switzerland.
⑤ I have tried three Vietnamese dishes. One was sweet, another was sour, and <u>the other</u> was salty.

23 다음 대화의 빈칸에 들어갈 알맞은 것은?

> *A*: With _____ did you go skiing last weekend?
> *B*: My friend, Adam.

① who
② what
③ which
④ whom
⑤ whose

24 다음 밑줄 친 ⓐ~ⓔ 중 어법상 어색한 것을 찾아 기호를 쓰고 바르게 고쳐 쓰시오.

> · My mom ⓐ<u>myself</u> repaired the roof.
> · The song in ⓑ<u>themselves</u> is great.
> · I made a chocolate cake for ⓒ<u>him</u>.
> · Why can't you do it ⓓ<u>yourself</u>?
> · People usually introduce ⓔ<u>them</u> when they first meet.

(1) _____ → _____
(2) _____ → _____
(3) _____ → _____

25 다음 글의 밑줄 친 it과 쓰임이 <u>다른</u> 것을 <u>모두</u> 고르시오.

> Tourism is the main source of money for many developing countries. However, <u>it</u> is damaging the local environment. So, the governments must find a way to protect nature.
>
> *tourism 관광업

① I like listening to others. <u>It</u> is my strength.
② <u>It</u> is too hot and humid this summer.
③ Put <u>it</u> in the closet by the door.
④ <u>It</u> is rude to ask too many personal questions.
⑤ <u>It</u> was a rewarding experience.

CHAPTER 11
형용사

연습문제 A <보기>와 같이 다음 문장을 바꿔 쓰시오.

> **<보기>** The sofa is comfortable. → It *is a comfortable sofa* .

1 This dictionary is old. → This _____.

2 The room is spacious. → It _____.

3 That pattern is simple but unique. → That is _____.

4 This necklace is very expensive. → This is _____.

5 The boy was confident. → He was _____.

6 This needle is sharp. → This is _____.

7 That product was popular. → That was _____.

연습문제 B 우리말과 같도록 <보기>에서 알맞을 말을 골라 쓰시오.

> **<보기>** afraid   pleased   sleeping   asleep   living   alive   lonely   alike

1 나는 무대에서 춤을 출 때 살아있다고 느낀다.

= I feel _____ when I dance on the stage.

2 저 자고 있는 아기는 나의 조카 Jason이다.

= That _____ baby is my nephew, Jason.

3 Grace와 그녀의 언니는 닮아 보이지 않는다.

= Grace and her older sister do not look _____.

4 재호는 치과에 가는 것을 무서워한다.

= Jaeho is _____ of going to the dentist.

5 나는 외롭다고 느낄 때 그림을 그린다.

= I draw paintings when I feel _____.

6 이 노래는 항상 나를 기쁘게 만든다.

= This song always makes me _____.

7 희정이는 소파에서 잠들었다.

= Heejung has fallen _____ on the sofa.

8 물은 살아있는 생명체에게 필수적이다.

= Water is essential for _____ creatures.

연습문제 A 괄호 안의 형용사를 알맞은 곳에 넣어 완전한 문장을 쓰시오.

1 Do you know anyone? (brave)

→ _____

2 She told us something. (exciting)

→ _____

3 Someone helped my grandma at the train station. (kind)

→ _____

4 I don't have anything to wear for the wedding. (suitable)

→ _____

5 There is nothing in this store. (special)

→ _____

6 Did the thief steal anything? (valuable)

→ _____

7 We can learn things when we talk to other people. (new)

→ _____

8 Have you met anybody like that actor? (attractive)

→ _____

연습문제 B 괄호 안에서 알맞은 것을 고르시오.

1 I have (something surprising / surprising something) to tell you.

2 There are lots of (things delicious / delicious things) on the menu.

3 Is there (anything interesting / interesting anything) to do?

4 (Something bad / Bad something) has just happened to John.

5 (Someone tall / Tall someone) passed us.

6 There are many (things useful / useful things) in his bag.

7 We should be grateful for every (thing little / little thing).

8 Please give me (something cold / cold something) to drink.

9 There is (something strange / strange something) about his story.

10 Think carefully before doing (anything important / important anything).

연습문제 **A** <보기>와 같이 다음 문장을 바꿔 쓰시오.

<보기> Kelly donated money for poor people.
→ *Kelly donated money for the poor.*

1 Rich people should share what they have.

→ _____

2 The campaign is targeted at young people.

→ _____

3 Audrey Hepburn helped poor people in Africa.

→ _____

4 It is usually hard for disabled people to find jobs.

→ _____

5 Unemployed people tend to be very depressed.

→ _____

6 The school teaches blind people how to read and write.

→ _____

7 The charity gives out free foods to homeless people.

→ _____

8 There is a care center in my neighborhood for old people.

→ _____

9 Masks make it difficult for deaf people to communicate.

→ _____

연습문제 **B** 괄호 안에서 알맞은 것을 고르시오.

1 (A / The) wise usually make the right decisions.

2 Some dogs are trained to help (the blind / the blinds).

3 The young (need / needs) more jobs.

4 (Does / Do) the rich donate more money than others?

5 The injured (gets / get) enough rest to recover.

6 Many volunteers gathered to help (the disabled / the disableds).

연습문제 A 다음 기수는 서수로, 서수는 기수로 바꿔 쓰시오. (단, 영어로 쓰시오.)

1	one	→ _____	**2**	twenty	→ _____
3	eleventh	→ _____	**4**	four	→ _____
5	ninety	→ _____	**6**	twenty-one	→ _____
7	one hundredth	→ _____	**8**	eighty	→ _____
9	thirty-seventh	→ _____	**10**	fifty-fifth	→ _____
11	seventy-second	→ _____	**12**	three	→ _____
13	tenth	→ _____	**14**	forty-four	→ _____
15	sixty-one	→ _____	**16**	twelfth	→ _____
17	seventeenth	→ _____	**18**	fifty	→ _____
19	twenty-nine	→ _____	**20**	sixty-six	→ _____

연습문제 B 우리말과 같도록 괄호 안의 말을 활용하여 문장을 완성하시오.

1 그녀의 첫째 아들은 곧 결혼한다. (son)

= Her _____ is getting married soon.

2 오늘은 그 회사의 스무 번째 기념일이다. (anniversary)

= Today is the _____ of the company.

3 그 여행 그룹의 세 번째 여행지는 불국사였다. (destination)

= The _____ of the tour group was Bulguksa.

4 그들의 계획은 천 그루의 나무를 심는 것이다. (tree)

= Their plan is to plant _____ .

5 나의 부모님은 서로를 삼십 년 전에 만났다. (year)

= My parents met each other _____ ago.

6 민지의 남동생은 5학년이다. (grade)

= Minji's younger brother is in the _____ .

7 이 건물에는 스물 두 개의 층이 있다. (floor)

= There are _____ in the building.

8 그 저녁의 네 번째 코스는 구운 생선이었다. (course)

= The _____ of the dinner was roasted fish.

연습문제 우리말과 같도록 문장을 완성하시오. (단, 숫자는 영어로 쓰시오.)

1 나는 벌써 물의 3분의 2를 마셨다.

= I already drank _____ of the water.

2 하루에 세 번 식후에 그 약을 복용하세요.

= Please take the medicine _____ a day after each meal.

3 그 그랜드 피아노는 그 전자 피아노보다 열 배 더 비싸다.

= The grand piano is _____ as expensive as the electronic piano.

4 사람들은 하루의 4분의 1을 자는 데 써야 한다.

= People should spend _____ of a day sleeping.

5 그 수프에 3분의 1 스푼의 소금을 넣어라.

= Put _____ spoons of salt into the soup.

6 오직 그 반의 8분의 5만 학교에 도착했다.

= Only _____ of the class arrived at school.

7 우리는 그 캠핑장까지 1과 5분의 3킬로미터를 더 가야 한다.

= We have to go _____ more kilometers to the campsite.

8 나는 지수네 집에 한 번 가봤다.

= I've been to Jisu's house _____.

연습문제 다음 연도와 날짜를 영어로 바르게 읽었으면 O를 쓰고, 틀리게 읽었으면 바르게 고쳐 쓰시오.

1 5월 25일 → May twenty-fives → _____

2 1999년 → nineteen ninety-nine → _____

3 1800년대 → the eighteen hundred → _____

4 9월 3일 → September the three → _____

5 6월 22일 → June twenty-second → _____

6 1750년대 → the seventeen fifty → _____

연습문제 A 괄호 안에서 many와 much 중 알맞은 것을 고르시오.

1 Make as (many / much) copies as you need.

2 How (many / much) money did we use?

3 (Many / Much) insects are considered harmful.

4 Don't eat too (many / much) food, or you will have a stomachache.

5 I haven't finished (many / much) homework yet.

6 We don't have (many / much) information about our new coach.

7 Malaria is very common in (many / much) tropical countries.

8 How (many / much) sugar do you want in your tea?

9 There are (many / much) unsolved mysteries in the world.

10 Alice doesn't have (many / much) free time.

연습문제 B 다음 문장의 밑줄 친 부분을 many나 much로 바꿔 완전한 문장을 쓰시오.

1 I didn't get plenty of sleep last night.

→ _____

2 Garlic is a basic ingredient in lots of Korean dishes.

→ _____

3 A number of dolphins can dive to depths of 200 meters.

→ _____

4 Did she speak with lots of enthusiasm?

→ _____

5 Many teenagers don't have a lot of economic knowledge.

→ _____

6 Does it take lots of time to change old habits?

→ _____

7 We have worked together on a number of projects.

→ _____

8 There are lots of historical sites in Europe.

→ _____

연습문제 A 괄호 안에서 알맞은 말을 골라 빈칸에 쓰시오.

1 (a few / a little)
  ① Only _____ leaves were left on the branch.
  ② Add _____ olive oil to the salad.

2 (few / little)
  ① She has _____ interest in politics.
  ② It may take _____ hours to cool down.

3 (a few / a little)
  ① I felt _____ drops of rain.
  ② Mix the eggs with _____ flour.

4 (few / little)
  ① _____ people know that it's my birthday.
  ② There is _____ water left in the bottle.

5 (a few / a little)
  ① _____ cushions are on the bed.
  ② You should save _____ money each week.

6 (few / little)
  ① They had _____ time to prepare for the presentation.
  ② There are _____ stores still open in the town.

연습문제 B 우리말과 같도록 <보기>의 말과 괄호 안의 명사를 활용하여 문장을 완성하시오.

| <보기> a few   a little   few   little   many   much |

1 Amy는 학교에 약간의 친구들이 있다. (friend)
= Amy has _____ at school.

2 지금 물리학을 배우는 학생들은 거의 없다. (student)
= _____ learn physics now.

3 그 책상은 많은 공간을 차지한다. (space)
= The desk takes up _____.

4 우리 할머니는 어렸을 때 교육을 받을 기회가 거의 없었다. (chance)
= My grandmother had _____ for education when she was young.

5 나는 그 남자에게 나의 핫초코에 약간의 휘핑크림을 올려달라고 요청했다. (whipped cream)
= I asked the man to put _____ on my hot chocolate.

6 내일은 비가 거의 오지 않을 것으로 예상된다. (rain)
= _____ is expected to fall tomorrow.

7 많은 일자리들은 금융위기 동안 사라졌다. (job)
= _____ were lost during the financial crisis.

연습문제 다음 빈칸에 some이나 any 중 알맞은 것을 쓰시오.

1 Volcanoes can erupt at _____ time.

2 Would you like to add _____ sugar to your coffee?

3 Do you have _____ problems here?

4 If you have _____ questions, please e-mail us.

5 You can withdraw money from _____ ATM in this town.

6 Can you give me _____ advice on solving this problem?

7 _____ form of cheating is not allowed.

8 Ms. Moore has _____ expensive jewelry.

9 Have _____ more vegetables.

10 Can you see _____ errors in my essay?

11 The museum has _____ works of modern art.

12 Does your family have _____ pets?

13 He is so tired because he didn't get _____ sleep last night.

14 We stopped by the shop to buy _____ apples.

15 Call the front desk, and ask them to bring us _____ clean towels.

1 주어진 문장의 밑줄 친 형용사와 용법이 같은 것을 모두 고르시오.

> That fish on the beach looks <u>alive</u>.

① My dad works for a <u>global</u> company.
② I feel <u>confident</u> about tomorrow's exam.
③ A kilt is a <u>traditional</u> Scottish clothing item.
④ Our house has a <u>wooden</u> fence.
⑤ The movie made the children <u>afraid</u>.

2 다음 대화에서 어법상 어색한 부분을 찾아 쓰고 바르게 고쳐 쓰시오.

> *A*: Did you do fun anything during the holidays?
> *B*: No. I just stayed home and rested.

_____ → _____

3 다음 빈칸에 들어갈 알맞은 것은?

> There are _____ tickets left for the concert. Therefore, they will be sold out soon.

① few   ② many   ③ a little
④ little   ⑤ much

4 다음 밑줄 친 부분과 바꿔 쓸 수 있는 것을 모두 고르시오.

> The hotel has <u>plenty of</u> rooms available.

① many   ② much   ③ little
④ a few   ⑤ a number of

5 다음 중 영어로 바르게 읽은 것끼리 묶인 것은?

> ⓐ 91 → ninety-first
> ⓑ $5\frac{7}{9}$ → five and seven-ninths
> ⓒ 1990년대 → the nineteen nineties
> ⓓ 9월 3일 → the three of September
> ⓔ $\frac{1}{3}$ → a thirds
> ⓕ 12th → twelveth
> ⓖ 2020년 → two thousand twenty

① ⓐ, ⓒ, ⓕ   ② ⓐ, ⓓ, ⓖ   ③ ⓑ, ⓒ, ⓖ
④ ⓑ, ⓔ, ⓖ   ⑤ ⓓ, ⓔ, ⓕ

6 우리말과 같도록 괄호 안의 말을 배열할 때 여섯 번째에 오는 것을 쓰시오.

> 너는 도전적인 무언가를 찾고 있니? (are, something, for, you, looking, challenging)

→ _____

7 다음 빈칸에 들어갈 말로 어색한 것은?

> There are _____ tools in the garage.

① a lot of   ② a few
③ a number of   ④ a little
⑤ lots of

8 다음 빈칸에 들어갈 말이 순서대로 짝지어진 것은?

· I don't see _____ here.
· All I want now is _____ sleep.

① anyone familiar – a few
② anyone familiar – a little
③ familiar anyone – a little
④ familiar anyone – a few
⑤ anyone familiar – few

9 다음 중 어법상 바른 것을 <u>모두</u> 고르시오.

① We saw some ducks in the river.
② Chad isn't wearing some shoes.
③ Do you have any brothers or sisters?
④ Would you like any peanuts?
⑤ If you need some help, please ask me.

[10-11] 다음 대화의 밑줄 친 우리말과 같도록 문장을 완성하시오. (단, 숫자는 영어로 쓰시오.)

10

A: How many times do you go to the gym in a week?
B: <u>나는 거기에 일주일에 세 번 가.</u>

= I go there _____ a week.

11

A: When is your parents' anniversary?
B: <u>8월 31일이야.</u>

= It's _____.

12 다음 중 어법상 <u>어색한</u> 것은?

① Jackson is afraid of spiders.
② I thought of a possible solution to the problem.
③ Peter is alone in his bedroom.
④ I'm so glad to see you again.
⑤ My awake brother is sitting on the sofa.

13 다음 두 문장의 의미가 같도록 문장을 완성하시오.

Injured people at the scene of the car accident were taken to the hospital in an ambulance.
= _____ at the scene of the car accident were taken to the hospital in an ambulance.

14 다음 (A)~(C)에 들어갈 말이 바르게 짝지어진 것은?

Amy: I'm bored these days. What should I do?
Alex: Trying __(A)__ might help. Do you have __(B)__ hobbies?
Amy: Not really. I usually just play with my __(C)__ kittens.

	(A)	(B)	(C)
①	something new	any	three
②	new something	some	three
③	something new	some	third
④	something new	any	third
⑤	new something	any	three

Chapter 11 형용사 **145**

15 다음 중 어법상 어색한 것은?

① Is there anyone tall in your family?
② The old have the same chances to achieve their goals as the young.
③ There was useful nothing in the video.
④ The unemployed need help from the government.
⑤ My friend works with a charity for the blind.

16 다음 빈칸에 들어갈 말이 순서대로 짝지어진 것은?

The beach was crowded as _____ tourists visited it on the weekend. Some city officials were worried that lots of trash would be left on the beach. However, only _____ trash was found after the weekend. Most people took their trash home.

① many – a little   ② much – a little
③ many – much   ④ much – much
⑤ many – a few

17 다음 중 밑줄 친 부분이 어법상 바른 것은?

① Exposure to too <u>many</u> sun is harmful.
② <u>A few</u> snow fell during the night.
③ It required <u>few</u> effort to move the chairs.
④ That clock tower has been a meeting place for <u>many</u> years.
⑤ We heard that Spain has <u>much</u> places to visit.

18 다음 빈칸에 a little이 들어갈 수 <u>없는</u> 것은?

① _____ evidence of UFOs has been found.
② Here's _____ information about the contest.
③ I gained _____ weight over the summer.
④ You can hear _____ noise from the cars in the streets.
⑤ John runs _____ kilometers every day.

19 다음 중 어법상 어색한 것을 <u>모두</u> 고르시오.

① Thousands of person are waiting outside the concert hall.
② The inventor is trying to think of something useful for our lives.
③ You say things silly all the time.
④ They deliver food to poor families once a week.
⑤ We take a test about ten times a year.

20 다음 글의 밑줄 친 우리말과 같도록 문장을 완성하시오.

Many guests were at the wedding when we arrived. <u>그러나, 우리가 떠날 때는 손님들이 거의 없었다.</u>

= However, there were _____ when we left.

21 다음 중 어법상 바른 것은?

① One year has 365th days.

② The new soccer stadium has sixty-five thousands seats.

③ The ancient pyramids took thousands of worker to build.

④ Millions of stars shine in the sky every night.

⑤ Hundred of people danced in the street.

22 다음 밑줄 친 부분과 공통으로 바꿔 쓸 수 있는 것은?

· A few sandwiches are left in the fridge.
· Would you like to wear a little perfume?

① many ② much ③ some
④ any ⑤ a number of

23 다음 중 어법상 어색한 것의 개수는?

ⓐ This news won't attract much interest.
ⓑ There is few milk left in the bottle.
ⓒ We have many technology to make our lives easier.
ⓓ Mt. Everest is so high that few climbers have reached the top.
ⓔ The rainforest provides the earth with plenty of oxygen.

① 1개 ② 2개 ③ 3개
④ 4개 ⑤ 5개

24 다음 (A)~(C)에 들어갈 말이 바르게 짝지어진 것은?

· Your directions were perfect, so we had ___(A)___ difficulty finding your house.
· Mary is very popular, and she has ___(B)___ friends.
· I have had ___(C)___ problems with my phone lately but nothing serious.

	(A)	(B)	(C)
①	little	many	a little
②	a little	much	few
③	a little	few	a little
④	little	many	a few
⑤	few	any	few

25 다음 글의 밑줄 친 ⓐ~ⓔ 중 어법상 어색한 것을 찾아 기호를 쓰고 바르게 고쳐 쓰시오.

I heard ⓐinteresting something recently. When a man was scuba diving, he saw ⓑsome wood on the bottom of the sea. He became ⓒcurious, so he collected it. He took it to an expert, and the expert told him that it was from an old ship. The man decided to go back and dive the ⓓtwo time. This time, he found ⓔa few gold coins.

(1) _____ → _____
(2) _____ → _____

CHAPTER 12
부사

기출로 적중 POINT

연습문제 **A** 다음 문장의 밑줄 친 부사가 수식하는 부분에 밑줄을 치시오.

1 It was <u>too</u> cold yesterday.

2 The coach wants his players to practice <u>hard</u>.

3 This article is <u>very</u> interesting.

4 <u>Luckily</u>, she managed to pass the exam.

5 The ending of this movie is <u>really</u> difficult to understand.

6 Jenna usually eats meals <u>slowly</u>.

7 Her handwriting is <u>incredibly</u> nice.

8 The patient responded to the medicine <u>extremely</u> quickly.

9 <u>Unfortunately</u>, Tim got in a car accident.

10 They lived together in the countryside <u>happily</u>.

연습문제 **B** 우리말과 같도록 <보기>에서 알맞은 말을 한 번씩만 골라 쓰시오.

<보기> basically   terribly   carefully   surprisingly   wisely   loudly   rudely   finally

1 Sam은 크게 말해서, 그의 말을 듣는 것이 쉬웠다.
= Sam spoke _____ , so it was easy to hear him.

2 그 소년은 항상 어른들에게 너무 무례하게 말한다.
= The boy always talks too _____ to elders.

3 마침내, 그의 삶에 좋은 무언가가 일어났다.
= _____ , something good happened in his life.

4 그녀는 그 화병을 조심스럽게 아래층으로 옮겼다.
= She moved the vase _____ down the stairs.

5 그 기말고사는 놀랄만큼 쉬웠다.
= The final exam was _____ easy.

6 Melanie는 창의적으로 생각함으로써 지혜롭게 문제를 해결했다.
= Melanie _____ solved the problem by thinking creatively.

7 저희가 불편을 끼친 것에 대해 너무 죄송합니다.
= We're _____ sorry for causing inconvenience.

8 기본적으로, 청소년들은 그들의 부모와 다르다.
= _____ , teenagers are different from their parents.

연습문제 A 다음 형용사를 부사로 바꿔 쓰시오.

1 dramatic → _____

2 careful → _____

3 lucky → _____

4 good → _____

5 different → _____

6 rare → _____

7 full → _____

8 polite → _____

9 busy → _____

10 happy → _____

11 real → _____

12 comfortable → _____

13 heavy → _____

14 serious → _____

15 athletic → _____

16 special → _____

17 sudden → _____

18 practical → _____

19 lazy → _____

20 generous → _____

21 angry → _____

22 true → _____

23 dull → _____

24 responsible → _____

25 proper → _____

26 energetic → _____

연습문제 B 괄호 안의 말을 알맞은 형태로 바꿔 빈칸에 쓰시오.

1 The baby smiled _____. (happy)

2 Listen to the announcement _____. (careful)

3 Your voice sounds _____. (strange)

4 _____, the power went out. (sudden)

5 Mangoes grow _____ in tropical regions. (good)

6 He refused David's invitation _____. (polite)

7 _____, nothing can last forever. (sad)

8 Amy wasn't _____ aware of her problems. (full)

9 Camila plays the violin _____ well. (fantastic)

10 She kept biting her nails _____. (nervous)

형용사와 형태가 같은 부사

정답 p.86

연습문제 | 다음 중 밑줄 친 부분의 품사가 나머지 둘과 다른 것을 고르시오.

1 ① He came home <u>late</u> yesterday.
② It gets colder and colder in the <u>late</u> fall.
③ Don't drink too much water <u>late</u> at night.

2 ① We can see the top of the <u>high</u> mountain.
② He kicked the ball <u>high</u> into the air.
③ The temperature is so <u>high</u>.

3 ① The game was <u>pretty</u> exciting.
② What a <u>pretty</u> cat!
③ The ending was <u>pretty</u> obvious.

4 ① She has <u>long</u> blonde hair.
② The employees often work <u>long</u> hours.
③ Turtles are known for living <u>long</u>.

5 ① Life is hard <u>enough</u> as it is.
② Is six bottles of soda <u>enough</u> for the party?
③ He studied <u>enough</u> to pass the exam.

6 ① He is a <u>fast</u> typist.
② This is a very <u>fast</u> car.
③ Children grow up so <u>fast</u>.

7 ① Lauren goes to bed <u>early</u>.
② She left <u>early</u> to avoid traffic.
③ I received an <u>early</u> reply from the university.

8 ① She worked <u>hard</u> all her life.
② He tried <u>hard</u> to ignore the bad comments.
③ This is a <u>hard</u> wooden chair.

-ly가 붙으면 의미가 달라지는 부사

정답 p.86

연습문제 | 괄호 안에서 알맞은 말을 골라 빈칸에 쓰시오.

1 (late / lately) ① Jeremy was reading _____ at night.
② Have you seen any changes _____?

2 (high / highly) ① Raise your hands _____ if you have any questions.
② We _____ recommend you to join our chess club.

3 (hard / hardly) ① I'm trying _____ to remember her name.
② There is _____ any time to waste.

4 (close / closely) ① She heard someone following _____ behind her.
② Smell and taste are _____ connected.

5 (near / nearly) ① Emily's homework is _____ done.
② As the storm drew _____, the community became nervous.

연습문제 A 괄호 안의 빈도부사를 알맞은 곳에 넣어 완전한 문장을 쓰시오.

1 Do you buy things online? (sometimes)

→ _____

2 He will forgive me for what I said. (never)

→ _____

3 My daughter has an afternoon nap at 2 P.M. (usually)

→ _____

4 The author's writing style is the same. (always)

→ _____

5 You should wash your hands. (often)

→ _____

6 Miranda agrees on Kate's idea. (rarely)

→ _____

7 My father and I are at home on weekdays. (seldom)

→ _____

연습문제 B 다음 표를 보고 빈칸에 알맞은 빈도부사를 <보기>에서 골라 쓰시오.

<보기>   always   often   seldom   never

How often do you exercise at the gym?							
	Mon	Tue	Wed	Thu	Fri	Sat	Sun
Charlie	O	O	X	O	O	O	X
Jenny	O	O	O	O	O	O	O
Mike	X	X	X	X	X	X	X
Gina	X	X	X	X	X	O	X

1 Charlie _____ exercises at the gym.

2 Jenny _____ exercises at the gym.

3 Mike _____ exercises at the gym.

4 Gina _____ exercises at the gym.

연습문제 | 우리말과 같도록 <보기>에서 알맞은 말을 골라 쓰시오.

<보기> already still yet

1 나는 이미 그 감독의 새 영화를 봤다.

= I've _____ seen the director's new film.

2 그는 이미 어디로 갈지 정했니?

= Has he decided where to go _____?

3 나는 아직 나의 실험 보고서를 끝내지 못했다.

= I _____ haven't finished my lab paper.

4 그 벽의 페인트는 아직 마르지 않았다.

= The paint on the wall has not dried _____.

5 너는 아직 산타클로스가 존재한다고 믿니?

= Do you _____ believe that Santa Claus exists?

6 그 선수는 벌써 이번 시즌에 두 번의 홈런을 쳤니?

= Has the player _____ hit two home runs this season?

7 인종차별주의는 아직 많은 사회에 뿌리 깊게 박혀 있다.

= Racism is _____ deeply rooted in many societies.

POINT 4-2 **다양한 부사:** too, either

정답 p.86

연습문제 | 다음 빈칸에 too나 either를 넣어 대화를 완성하시오.

1 A: I jog every day.   B: I jog every day, _____.

2 A: Sarah enjoys baking cookies.   B: I enjoy baking cookies, _____.

3 A: Ben won't accept your apologies.   B: Anne won't accept your apologies, _____.

4 A: Catherine has never been to Busan.   B: I have never been to Busan, _____.

5 A: I don't like his attitude.   B: I don't like his attitude, _____.

6 A: Eunhye can't eat peanuts.   B: I can't eat peanuts, _____.

7 A: I voted for James to be our team captain.   B: I voted for him, _____.

정답 p.86

연습문제 A 다음 빈칸에 so나 neither를 넣어 괄호 안의 말을 활용하여 대화를 완성하시오.

1 A: I am a hardworking student.

B: _____ (I)

2 A: I decided what to study in college.

B: _____ (I)

3 A: She is worried about the science quiz.

B: _____ (he)

4 A: Minsu didn't spread the rumors about her.

B: _____ (I)

5 A: She won't take an exam tomorrow.

B: _____ (I)

6 A: Jay has a special talent for dancing.

B: _____ (Minju)

7 A: I can't get used to waking up early.

B: _____ (I)

8 A: The library is easily accessible by bus.

B: _____ (the cinema)

9 A: Ms. Kwon needs some legal advice.

B: _____ (Mr. Johnson)

연습문제 B 다음 대화의 빈칸에 알맞은 말을 <보기>에서 한 번씩만 골라 쓰시오.

<보기>　too　either　so　neither

1 A: I've lived in this town for a long time.

B: _____ have I.

2 A: My brother scored a goal during the match.

B: James scored a goal during the match, _____.

3 A: Subin can't really understand what the man is saying.

B: Minjun can't really understand what the man is saying, _____.

4 A: He couldn't complete a full marathon.

B: _____ could Manny.

연습문제 A 우리말과 같도록 <보기>의 말을 활용하여 문장을 완성하시오.

<보기>	turn on	take off	pick up	wake up
	give up	write down	put off	turn in

1 만약 당신이 덥다고 느껴지면, 에어컨을 켜세요.

= Please _____ the air conditioner if you feel hot.

2 그는 그의 숙제를 제시간에 제출했니?

= Did he _____ his homework on time?

3 그녀는 쉽게 그녀의 꿈을 포기할 수 없었다.

= She couldn't _____ her dreams easily.

4 당신의 신발을 벗고 안으로 들어오세요.

= Please _____ your shoes and come inside.

5 너는 그것을 잊어버리기 전에 그의 전화번호를 적는 것이 낫겠다.

= You had better _____ his phone number before you forget it.

6 Dan은 그의 여동생을 깨우려고 노력하고 있다.

= Dan is trying to _____ his little sister.

7 그녀는 땅에 있는 그 카드를 줍기 위해 몸을 구부렸다.

= She bent down to _____ the card from the ground.

8 그들은 그들의 결혼식을 내년으로 미뤄야 했다.

= They had to _____ their wedding until next year.

연습문제 B 밑줄 친 부분이 어법상 맞으면 O를 쓰고, 틀리면 바르게 고쳐 쓰시오.

1 Promise to give the money back to us. → _____

2 Why don't you look up it in the dictionary? → _____

3 Can I try on these jeans? → _____

4 Sally is looking the moon at. → _____

5 I put my uniform on before going to work. → _____

6 All of you have to hand in them by tomorrow. → _____

연습문제 A   밑줄 친 부분을 Where, When, Why, How 중 하나로 고쳐 쓰시오.

1   A: <u>When</u> are you from?   B: I'm from South Korea.

→ _____

2   A: <u>How</u> is the best time to call you?   B: Around noon will be the best.

→ _____

3   A: <u>How</u> did you kiss on her cheek?   B: Because it is a French way of greeting.

→ _____

4   A: <u>Why</u> did you get the scar on your hand?   B: I accidentally poured hot water on my hand.

→ _____

5   A: <u>Where</u> are you going to pay me back?   B: I'll pay you back tomorrow.

→ _____

6   A: <u>How</u> are they planning to travel?   B: They're planning to travel to Busan.

→ _____

7   A: <u>When</u> is Mr. Brown doing?   B: He is doing great.

→ _____

8   A: <u>Where</u> are you in such a hurry?   B: Because I woke up late and the bus is coming soon.

→ _____

연습문제 B   <보기>의 말을 활용하여 대화를 완성하시오.

<보기>	How tall	How big	How long	How far
	How old	How often	How many	How much

1   A: _____ is your dog?   B: It's five years old.

2   A: _____ is the Nile River?   B: It's around 6,700 km long.

3   A: _____ do you go swimming?   B: I go swimming three times a week.

4   A: _____ moons does Jupiter have?   B: It has around 76 moons.

5   A: _____ is that hat?   B: It's 8,000 won.

6   A: _____ is the bus stop from here?   B: It's just a few blocks away.

7   A: _____ is South Korea?   B: Its population is similar to that of Kenya.

8   A: _____ is your sister?   B: She's about 165cm tall.

중간·기말고사 실전 문제

1 다음 중 짝지어진 관계가 나머지 넷과 <u>다른</u> 것은?

① simple – simply
② good – well
③ dull – dully
④ cost – costly
⑤ specific – specifically

2 다음 중 어법상 <u>어색한</u> 것은?

① Surprisingly, few people attended the ceremony.
② The pottery looks really unique.
③ The food at the restaurant was incredible good.
④ My three-year-old nephew learns languages really fast.
⑤ Peter had to drive carefully along the narrow road.

3 다음 중 밑줄 친 long의 쓰임이 나머지 넷과 <u>다른</u> 것은?

① What <u>long</u> hair you have!
② Did you wait <u>long</u> for the bus?
③ It's a <u>long</u> journey to Chile.
④ A <u>long</u> time ago, dinosaurs used to live on earth.
⑤ There is a <u>long</u> line of people outside the restaurant.

4 괄호 안의 말을 알맞게 배열하시오.

> A: How is your laptop?
> B: It's great. _____
> _____ with it. (any problems, had, rarely, I, have)

5 다음 (A)~(C)에 들어갈 말이 바르게 짝지어진 것은?

> · I am ____(A)____ sorry for hurting your feelings earlier.
> · Show me the ____(B)____ way to make a taco.
> · John ____(C)____ comes to class on time.

	(A)	(B)	(C)
①	truly	proper	hardly
②	true	properly	hardly
③	truly	proper	hard
④	true	properly	hard
⑤	truly	properly	hard

6 다음 빈칸에 공통으로 들어갈 알맞은 것은?

> · Could you pick _____ your trash?
> · Try your best and never give _____.

① on
② off
③ down
④ up
⑤ out

7 다음 빈칸에 either가 들어갈 수 <u>없는</u> 것은?

① I can't believe the news, _____.
② My aunt is a nurse, _____.
③ They aren't members of our club, _____.
④ I won't be in class tomorrow, _____.
⑤ Steve doesn't have a bicycle, _____.

8 우리말과 같도록 괄호 안의 말을 활용하여 문장을 완성하시오.

> Hall씨는 토론 동안 그녀의 의견을 논리적으로 주장했다. (argue, opinion, logical)

= Ms. Hall _____ during the debate.

9 다음 대화의 빈칸에 들어갈 알맞은 것은?

> *Dad*: Tom and Ava, did you clean your rooms yet?
> *Tom*: Yes, I did.
> *Ava* : ＿＿＿＿＿＿＿ Look at how clean mine is now.

① Neither I did.　② So I did.
③ Neither did I.　④ So did I.
⑤ Neither didn't I.

10 다음 중 어법상 바른 것은?

① I have been always a fan of K-pop.
② Real facts hardly are mentioned in the news article.
③ You can hear sometimes the owl at night.
④ She often has been in the hospital recently.
⑤ The convenience store never closes.

11 다음 빈칸에 들어갈 말이 순서대로 짝지어진 것은?

> ·We cannot ＿＿＿＿ make it to the meeting on time.
> ·I ＿＿＿＿ recommend the new sushi restaurant on Main Street.

① possibly – highly　② possible – high
③ possible – highly　④ possibly – high
⑤ possibility – highly

12 다음 빈칸에 공통으로 들어갈 알맞은 의문부사를 쓰시오.

> ·＿＿＿＿ do I spell your last name?
> ·＿＿＿＿ is your grandmother these days?

13 다음 표를 보고 <보기>의 빈도부사를 활용하여 문장을 완성하시오.

How often do you go cycling?					
	Mon	Tue	Wed	Thu	Fri
Noah	O	X	O	X	X
Liam	X	X	X	X	O
Amy	O	O	O	O	O

<보기>　sometimes　hardly　always

(1) Noah ＿＿＿＿＿＿＿＿＿＿
　　on weekdays.
(2) Liam ＿＿＿＿＿＿＿＿＿＿
　　on weekdays.
(3) Amy ＿＿＿＿＿＿＿＿＿＿
　　on weekdays.

14 다음 중 어법상 어색한 것끼리 묶인 것은?

> ⓐ I wanted to watch TV, so I turned it on.
> ⓑ My sweater is really itchy, so I can't wait to take off it.
> ⓒ The police are trying to find out the truth.
> ⓓ Give me your assignments, and I'll hand them in for you.
> ⓔ We put off the picnic because the weather was bad.
> ⓕ I don't know the restaurant's address, but I'll look up it.
> ⓖ Kate took the skirt into the fitting room and tried on it.

① ⓐ, ⓑ, ⓒ　② ⓐ, ⓒ, ⓕ　③ ⓑ, ⓓ, ⓔ
④ ⓑ, ⓕ, ⓖ　⑤ ⓒ, ⓓ, ⓖ

15

A: _____ did you throw away your shoes?

B: I threw them away because they were old.

16

A: _____ did John injure his arm?

B: He hurt it last weekend.

17 주어진 문장의 밑줄 친 enough와 쓰임이 같은 것은?

He isn't tall enough to ride the roller coaster.

① Are there enough plates for everyone?

② I have enough information to write my essay.

③ Nate didn't get enough sleep last night.

④ The weather is not windy enough for us to fly a kite.

⑤ Jinho hopes to receive enough votes to become the student president.

18 우리말과 같도록 괄호 안의 말을 알맞게 배열하시오.

나는 나의 결정에 대해 전적으로 확신했다. (my decision, about, sure, was, absolutely, I)

= _____

19 다음 빈칸에 알맞은 말을 <보기>에서 한 번씩만 골라 쓰시오.

<보기> already still yet

(1) I have _____ booked my plane ticket.

(2) Steven _____ hasn't returned my phone call.

(3) Have you talked to Monica _____?

20 다음 (A)~(C)에 들어갈 말이 바르게 짝지어진 것은?

· ___(A)___, it has rained a lot in my hometown.

· The sign has some ___(B)___ descriptions of the museum's art.

· The two eagles flew ___(C)___ into the sky.

	(A)	(B)	(C)
①	Lately	general	high
②	Lately	general	highly
③	Late	general	highly
④	Lately	generally	highly
⑤	Late	generally	high

21 다음 중 어법상 어색한 것을 모두 고르시오.

① Actually, the store is already closed for the night.

② We worked very hard on our project.

③ Why don't you sit close to me?

④ I will serious consider your advice.

⑤ Hotels have been near empty because of the bad economy.

22 다음 중 어법상 바른 것끼리 묶인 것은?

ⓐ Put on your coat before you go outside.
ⓑ Why don't you wake up her now?
ⓒ Have you never seen this movie before?
ⓓ We cannot buy usually fresh fish at this market.
ⓔ Did often you watch cartoons on TV when you were younger?
ⓕ When you finish reading the book, please give it back to Jihyun.
ⓖ The sun will harm you if your eyes look it at.

① ⓐ, ⓑ, ⓒ   ② ⓐ, ⓒ, ⓕ   ③ ⓑ, ⓓ, ⓔ
④ ⓑ, ⓕ, ⓖ   ⑤ ⓒ, ⓓ, ⓖ

23 다음 글의 빈칸에 들어갈 말이 순서대로 짝지어진 것은?

_____ do you take naps? These days, a lot of people think they are too busy to sleep during the day. However, a short nap can help us improve our performance. So, _____ should we take naps? According to the research, the best time is in the early afternoon between 1 P.M. and 3 P.M.

① How many – when
② How often – why
③ How often – when
④ How much – where
⑤ How many – where

24 다음 중 어법상 <u>어색한</u> 것의 개수는?

ⓐ Luckily, Ben found his lost wallet.
ⓑ The children were total happy about their Christmas gifts.
ⓒ The deer quickly disappeared into the forest.
ⓓ The fireworks were pretty amazing last night.
ⓔ Sumin is not enough old to remember the 2002 World Cup.

① 1개   ② 2개   ③ 3개
④ 4개   ⑤ 5개

25 다음 글의 밑줄 친 ⓐ~ⓔ 중 어법상 <u>어색한</u> 것을 찾아 기호를 쓰고 바르게 고쳐 쓰시오.

ⓐ<u>How many</u> times do you check your smartphone? These days, smartphones seem to be ⓑ<u>extreme important</u> to people. Researchers say that people ⓒ<u>check usually</u> their smartphones 90 times a day. Nearly 60 percent of college students are ⓓ<u>highly</u> addicted to their phones. What about you? Would you ⓔ<u>give up</u> your smartphone?

(1) _____ → _____
(2) _____ → _____

기출로 작중 해카스 중학영문법 2학년 워크북

CHAPTER 13
비교구문

기출로 적중 POINT

연습문제 다음 형용사나 부사의 비교급과 최상급을 쓰시오.

1 low – _____ – _____

2 noisy – _____ – _____

3 bright – _____ – _____

4 cold – _____ – _____

5 popular – _____ – _____

6 funny – _____ – _____

7 slow – _____ – _____

8 kind – _____ – _____

9 simple – _____ – _____

10 pretty – _____ – _____

11 heavy – _____ – _____

12 boring – _____ – _____

13 active – _____ – _____

14 famous – _____ – _____

15 dry – _____ – _____

16 high – _____ – _____

17 lucky – _____ – _____

18 poor – _____ – _____

19 exactly – _____ – _____

20 safe – _____ – _____

연습문제 다음 중 원급 – 비교급 – 최상급 형태가 잘못된 것을 고르시오.

1 ① badly – worse – worst
② curious – more curious – most curious
③ hot – hoter – hotest

2 ① strange – stranger – strangest
② useless – more useless – most useless
③ nice – more nice – most nice

3 ① quickly – quicklier – quickliest
② little – less – least
③ far – further – furthest

4 ① late – latter – lastest
② wet – wetter – wettest
③ new – newer – newest

5 ① old – elder – eldest
② thick – thicker – thickest
③ beautiful – beautifuler – beautifulest

6 ① far – farther – farthest
② tired – tireder – tiredest
③ shocking – more shocking – most shocking

7 ① young – younger – youngest
② ill – iller – illest
③ slowly – more slowly – most slowly

8 ① creative – more creative – most creative
② messy – messier – messiest
③ good – well – best

원급 비교: as + 원급 + as

POINT 2-1

정답 p.88

연습문제 A 우리말과 같도록 괄호 안의 말을 알맞게 배열하시오.

1 이 책은 공책만큼 얇다. (a notebook, thin, as, is, this book, as)

= _____

2 Kevin은 그의 형제들만큼 많이 먹는다. (Kevin, as, his brothers, do, eats, as, much)

= _____

3 이 낡은 컴퓨터는 새 컴퓨터만큼 잘 작동한다. (this old computer, as, works, the new one, well, as)

= _____

4 영어 시험은 수학 시험만큼 어렵지 않았다. (the math exam, not, as, difficult, as, the English exam, was)

= _____

5 이 담요는 저것만큼 부드럽지 않다. (as, as, soft, is, that one, this blanket, not)

= _____

6 그녀는 스페인어를 모국어 사용자만큼 유창하게 말한다. (Spanish, she, as, a native speaker, fluently, as, speaks)

= _____

연습문제 B <보기>와 같이 다음 세 문장의 의미가 같도록 문장을 완성하시오.

> **<보기>** This apple is not as red as that apple.
> = *That apple is redder than this apple.*
> = *This apple is less red than that apple.*

1 That watermelon is not as sweet as this cherry.

= _____

= _____

2 This necklace is not as expensive as that ring.

= _____

= _____

3 The train is not as fast as the plane.

= _____

= _____

4 Seoul's temperature is not as high as Daegu's temperature.

= _____

= _____

기출로 적중 해커스 중학영문법 2학년 워크북

원급 비교: as + 원급 + as + 주어 + can[could]

정답 p.88

연습문제 다음 두 문장의 의미가 같도록 문장을 완성하시오.

1 They jumped as hard as they could.
= They jumped _____.

2 We need to finish writing this paper as quickly as possible.
= We need to finish writing this paper _____.

3 He tried to speak as loudly as he could.
= He tried to speak _____.

4 Dad promised to repair my bicycle as soon as possible.
= Dad promised to repair my bicycle _____.

5 Please answer these survey questions as honestly as you can.
= Please answer these survey questions _____.

6 George drew the bear as realistically as possible.
= George drew the bear _____.

원급 비교: 배수사 + as + 원급 + as

정답 p.88

연습문제 우리말과 같도록 괄호 안의 말을 활용하여 문장을 완성하시오. (단, 형태를 바꾸지 마시오.)

1 이 전화기는 저것보다 네 배 더 무겁다. (heavier)
= This phone is _____ that one.

2 나의 엄마는 나보다 세 배 더 나이 드셨다. (older)
= My mom is _____ me.

3 평균적인 사람은 개보다 일곱 배 더 오래 산다. (longer)
= An average human lives _____ a dog.

4 새끼 판다는 그것의 어미보다 900배 더 작다. (smaller)
= A panda cub is _____ its mother.

5 지구는 태양보다 333,000배 더 가볍다. (lighter)
= The Earth weighs _____ the Sun.

6 미국은 한국보다 약 99배 더 크다. (bigger)
= The United States is about _____ South Korea.

POINT 3-1 비교급 비교: 비교급 + than

정답 p.88

연습문제 A | <보기>와 같이 괄호 안의 말을 활용하여 다음 두 문장을 한 문장을 바꿔 쓰시오.

<보기>　Jane arrived at school at 8:10. Mary arrived at school at 8:45.

→ Jane _arrived at school earlier than Mary_ . (early)

1 Kate is 160 cm. Molly is 170 cm.

→ Kate _____ . (short)

2 My bag is 3kg. Her bag is 2kg.

→ My bag _____ . (heavy)

3 Jisu's dog can do five tricks. Lisa's dog can do two tricks.

→ Jisu's dog _____ . (many tricks)

4 A gazelle can run 97 km per hour. A horse can run 88 km per hour.

→ A gazelle _____ . (fast)

5 Gangwon-do is -10℃. Seoul is -2.5℃.

→ Gangwon-do _____ . (cold)

6 Sam made five million won. Jane made two million won.

→ Sam _____ . (much money)

연습문제 B | 괄호 안에서 알맞은 것을 모두 고르시오.

1 This plate is (pretty / prettier) than that one.

2 Chocolate is (much / more) sweeter than a banana.

3 This test is (very / even) harder than I thought.

4 Hong Kong is (much / more) crowded than Seoul.

5 This car is (far / even) more expensive than that one.

6 Snails move (a lot / even) slower than sloths.

7 Kate has a very (large / larger) phone.

8 Giraffes are (tall / taller) than elephants.

9 It's (far / still) colder in Korea than Vietnam.

10 Josh cooks (a lot / very) better than his mother.

연습문제 A 우리말과 같도록 괄호 안의 말을 활용하여 문장을 완성하시오.

1 나는 뉴욕에 오래 머무르면 머무를수록 그 장소를 더 좋아했다. (long, much)

= _____ I stayed in New York, _____ I liked the place.

2 우리가 산을 높이 올라가면 올라갈수록 더 추워진다. (high, cold)

= _____ we go up the mountain, _____ it gets.

3 너는 자주 운동하면 운동할수록 더 건강해질 것이다. (often, healthy)

= _____ you exercise, _____ you will become.

4 비가 세게 오면 올수록 호수는 더 깊어졌다. (heavily, deep)

= _____ it rained, _____ the lake got.

5 너는 많이 연습하면 연습할수록 피아노를 더 잘 연주할 것이다. (much, well)

= _____ you practice, _____ you will play the piano.

6 우리가 더 멀리 가면 갈수록 건물들은 더 작아 보였다. (far, small)

= _____ we went, _____ the buildings looked.

연습문제 B <보기>와 같이 다음 문장을 「the + 비교급, the + 비교급」을 이용하여 바꿔 쓰시오.

> **<보기>** If we arrive sooner, we will get better seats.
>
> → *The sooner we arrive, the better seats we will get.*

1 As I studied longer, I got more tired.

→ _____

2 If the storm is more violent, it will be more dangerous.

→ _____

3 If the roads get icier, they become harder to drive on.

→ _____

4 As Ben thought about the interview more, he got more nervous.

→ _____

5 If I have more friends, I will be happier.

→ _____

6 As Carl grew taller, his pants became shorter.

→ _____

연습문제 우리말과 같도록 괄호 안의 말을 활용하여 문장을 완성하시오.

1 Smith씨의 건강은 점점 더 나빠지고 있다. (get, bad)

= Mr. Smith's health _____.

2 지구 온난화 때문에, 봄이 점점 더 짧아지고 있다. (get, short)

= Due to global warming, spring _____.

3 가지가 점점 더 커지고 있다. (grow, large)

= The eggplant _____.

4 요즘 일자리를 찾는 것은 점점 더 힘들어지고 있다. (get, hard)

= Finding jobs _____ these days.

5 그 비행기는 하늘로 점점 더 높이 날았다. (fly, high)

= The plane _____ into the sky.

6 그 이야기는 점점 더 흥미로워지고 있다. (get, interesting)

= The story _____.

7 그 비누는 내가 사용할수록 점점 더 작아졌다. (get, small)

= The soap _____ as I used it.

8 K-pop은 점점 더 인기 있어지고 있다. (become, popular)

= K-pop _____.

9 Tiffany의 한국어는 점점 더 좋아지고 있다. (get, good)

= Tiffany's Korean _____.

10 그들은 점점 더 피곤해지고 있다. (get, tired)

= They _____.

11 그 별은 점점 더 밝게 빛나고 있다. (shine, bright)

= The star _____.

12 그녀는 그의 무례한 행동에 점점 더 짜증이 나고 있었다. (become, irritated)

= She _____ by his rude behavior.

13 여름이 다가오면서, 낮이 점점 더 길어졌다. (become, long)

= As summer approached, the days _____.

연습문제 A　우리말과 같도록 괄호 안의 말을 활용하여 문장을 완성하시오.

1 토론토는 캐나다에서 가장 안전한 도시이다. (safe city, Canada)

= Toronto is _____.

2 세계에서 가장 오래된 나무는 캘리포니아에 있다. (old tree, the world)

= _____ is in California.

3 Molly는 그녀의 반에서 최고의 학생이다. (good student, her class)

= Molly is _____.

4 양쯔강은 중국에서 가장 긴 강이다. (long river, China)

= The Yangtze river is _____.

5 러시아는 아시아에서 가장 큰 나라이다. (big country, Asia)

= Russia is _____.

6 우정은 내 삶에서 가장 중요한 것이다. (important thing, my life)

= Friendship is _____.

연습문제 B　괄호 안의 말을 활용하여 문장을 완성하시오.

1 Love is _____ than hatred. (strong)

2 This is _____ lipstick in the store. (expensive)

3 Emily is _____ child in her family. (young)

4 James speaks Korean _____ than Michael. (well)

5 Saturday is _____ day of the week for Suji. (relaxing)

6 Music is as _____ as the human race. (old)

7 Your cookie looks _____ than my muffin. (large)

8 Thomas was walking down the street very _____. (slowly)

9 This cushion is as _____ as a sponge. (soft)

10 That restaurant makes _____ pizza in town. (good)

POINT 4-2

연습문제 우리말과 같도록 괄호 안의 말을 활용하여 영작하시오.

1 Paul은 내가 본 사람 중에서 가장 똑똑한 사람들 중 한 명이다. (Paul, smart person)

= _____ I've ever seen.

2 알버트 아인슈타인은 역사상 가장 위대한 과학자들 중 한 명이다. (Albert Einstein, great scientist)

= _____ in history.

3 부르즈 할리파는 세상에서 가장 높은 건물들 중 하나이다. (Burj Khalifa, tall building)

= _____ in the world.

4 비엔나는 유럽에서 여행하기에 가장 좋은 도시들 중 한 곳이다. (Vienna, good city)

= _____ to travel in Europe.

5 김은 한국에서 가장 흔한 성들 중 하나이다. (Kim, common last name)

= _____ in Korea.

POINT 4-3 최상급 비교: 원급과 비교급을 이용한 최상급 표현   정답 p.89

연습문제 다음 문장들의 의미가 같도록 문장을 완성하시오.

1 This question is the hardest one on the quiz.

= No _____ is _____ as this one on the quiz.

= No _____ is _____ than this one on the quiz.

= This one is _____ any _____ on the quiz.

= This one is _____ all the _____ on the quiz.

2 Mount Everest is the highest mountain in the world.

= No _____ is _____ as Mount Everest in the world.

= No _____ is _____ than Mount Everest in the world.

= Mount Everest is _____ any _____ in the world.

= Mount Everest is _____ all the _____ in the world.

3 Health is the most important thing in life.

= No _____ is _____ as health in life.

= No _____ is _____ than health in life.

= Health is _____ any _____ in life.

= Health is _____ all the _____ in life.

중간·기말고사 실전 문제

1 다음 중 원급 – 비교급 – 최상급 형태가 잘못된 것을 <u>모두</u> 고르시오.

① strange – stranger – strangest
② lonely – more lonely– most lonely
③ serious – more serious – most serious
④ far – farther – furthest
⑤ gladly – more gladly – most gladly

2 다음 중 밑줄 친 부분이 어법상 어색한 것은?

Let me <u>introduce</u> you to <u>one</u> of
        ①   ②
<u>most</u> <u>famous</u> <u>places</u> in Korea.
  ③   ④   ⑤

3 다음 빈칸에 들어갈 말이 순서대로 짝지어진 것은?

· Tim was not _____ tired as the other runners.
· The moon is brighter _____ the stars.

① as – as
② so – as
③ than – so
④ so – than
⑤ than – than

4 우리말과 같도록 괄호 안의 말을 알맞게 배열하시오.

Brian의 개는 나의 것보다 네 배 더 나이가 많다.
(older, mine, four times, Brian's dog, than, is)

= _____

[5-7] 다음 빈칸에 들어갈 알맞은 것을 고르시오.

5

My sister was as _____ as a bee.

① busy
② busier
③ more busy
④ busiest
⑤ most busy

6

The life of a cactus is often _____ than 300 years.

① long
② longer
③ more long
④ the longest
⑤ the most long

7

Who is _____ person in your family?

① diligenter
② more diligent
③ the diligentest
④ most diligent
⑤ the most diligent

8 다음 중 어법상 어색한 것을 <u>모두</u> 고르시오.

① She sang as beautifully as she could.
② That building is the tallest in the city.
③ Lions are slower than cheetahs.
④ Martin is so smart as his brother.
⑤ Your phone was even expensive than mine.

9 다음 빈칸에 들어갈 말이 순서대로 짝지어진 것은?

Sara is a _____ talented artist, but Gina is a _____ more talented artist than Sara.

① much – far
② much – still
③ very – far
④ very – very
⑤ even – very

10 다음 문장에서 어법상 어색한 부분을 찾아 쓰고 바르게 고쳐 쓰시오.

Dolphins are the more intelligent of all sea animals.

_____ → _____

11 다음 글의 밑줄 친 (A)를 비교급 문장으로 바꿔 쓰시오.

Many people eat fruits because they think they are healthy. For example, some fruits have a lot of Vitamin C. However, (A) fruits are not as healthy as vegetables. This is because fruits often contain a lot of sugar, but vegetables usually don't.

→ However, vegetables _____

_____ .

12 다음 중 어법상 바른 것은?

① Be sure to study as more as you can this weekend.
② That house is the largest in the six houses on this street.
③ Venus is the most bright planet in the sky.
④ Greg is the funniest person in my English class.
⑤ My last vacation was better one I have ever taken.

[13-14] 다음 두 문장의 의미가 같도록 빈칸에 알맞은 말을 쓰시오.

13

Chris is stronger than any other player on the tennis team.
= Chris is _____ _____
_____ on the tennis team.

14

Thai food is spicier than Italian food.
= Italian food is _____
_____ _____ _____
Thai food.

15 다음은 세 종류의 나무를 비교하는 표이다. 다음 표를 잘못 설명한 것은?

나무	Apple trees	Baobab trees	Giant Sequoia trees
높이	10m	25m	76m
수명	100 years	1000 years	3000 years

① Giant Sequoia trees can live the longest of all.
② Apple trees don't live as long as Giant Sequoia trees.
③ Baobab trees grow as tall as Giant Sequoia trees.
④ Giant Sequoia trees grow the tallest of the three.
⑤ Baobab trees grow taller than apple trees.

16 다음 문장과 의미가 같은 것은?

> Minho's grades aren't as good as Nina's grades.

① Minho's grades are better than Nina's grades.
② Nina's grades aren't better than Minho's grades.
③ Nina's grades are better than Minho's grades.
④ Nina's grades aren't as good as Minho's grades.
⑤ Minho's grades are the best of all the students.

17 다음 두 문장의 의미가 같도록 문장을 완성하시오.

> If a pillow is softer, it is usually more comfortable.
> = _____ a pillow is, _____ it usually is.

18 다음 중 어법상 어색한 것은?

① That was the strangest book I've ever read.
② Jane is one of the friendliest people in our neighborhood.
③ Tony tries to exercise as often as possible.
④ The wind is getting stronger and stronger.
⑤ The many money Jake earned, the happy he became.

19 다음 두 문장의 의미가 같도록 비교급을 이용하여 문장을 완성하시오.

> The blue whale is the largest animal on the planet.
> = No other _____
> _____ the blue whale on the planet.

20 다음은 세 종류의 과일을 비교하는 표이다. 괄호 안의 말을 활용하여 문장을 완성하시오.

	Apple	Grapefruit	Pear
Cost	$1	$2	$4
Weight	100 grams	200 grams	150 grams

(1) The grapefruit is _____ _____ of the three. (heavy)

(2) The apple is _____ _____ the grapefruit. (cheap)

(3) No other fruit is _____ _____ as the pear. (expensive)

21 다음 두 문장의 의미가 같도록 빈칸에 알맞은 말을 쓰시오.

Read the direction on the board as carefully as possible.
= Read the direction on the board _____ _____ _____ _____ _____.

22 괄호 안의 말을 활용하여 다음 두 문장을 한 문장으로 바꿔 쓰시오.

· The desk is 50 kilograms.
· The book shelf is 45 kilograms.

→ The book shelf is _____ the desk. (heavy)

23 다음 빈칸에 들어갈 말이 순서대로 짝지어진 것은?

_____ you practice the piano before the concert, _____ you will feel.

① More – more confident
② The more – the more confident
③ The more – the most confident
④ The most – the more confident
⑤ The most – the most confident

24 다음 대화에서 어법상 <u>어색한</u> 부분을 찾아 쓰고 바르게 고쳐 쓰시오.

A: Bali was one of the most beautiful place I have ever visited.
B: I hope I can travel there someday.

_____ → _____

25 다음 중 어법상 바른 것의 개수는?

ⓐ Brad is the smartest student in all.
ⓑ War and Peace is one of the longest books I have ever read.
ⓒ The less you sleep, the worse you will feel.
ⓓ Salad is much healthier than pizza.
ⓔ As I got older, I became more and more interested in the world news.

① 1개   ② 2개   ③ 3개
④ 4개   ⑤ 5개

해커스북 중·고등
www.HackersBook.com

CHAPTER 14
전치사

기출로 적중 POINT

시간 전치사 I

POINT 1-1

정답 p.90

연습문제 다음 빈칸에 at, on, in 중 알맞은 것을 쓰시오.

1 My brother was born _____ 2002.

2 Let's meet in front of the pool _____ 3 o'clock.

3 We are going to play soccer _____ Saturday.

4 Machines didn't exist _____ the past.

5 Mom drinks a cup of coffee _____ the morning.

6 Jenny has lunch with her classmate _____ Tuesdays.

7 I get up _____ 6 A.M. every morning.

8 These pots were made _____ the 18th century.

9 We always go to my grandma's _____ the beginning of the year.

10 People eat turkey _____ Thanksgiving Day.

시간 전치사 II

POINT 1-2

정답 p.90

연습문제 괄호 안에서 알맞은 전치사를 고르시오.

1 This bakery has been open (since / from) 1999.

2 This report must be finished (by / until) 8 P.M. today.

3 The government is raising the tax on cigarettes (from / since) next month.

4 Her dream is to become a marine biologist (after / from) graduation.

5 I have studied English (by / since) the second grade in elementary school.

6 All athletes must arrive at the stadium (by / until) seven.

7 Remember to turn the gas off (since / before) leaving the house.

8 The female duck sits on the eggs (until / from) the eggs hatch.

9 Guests are not allowed in the museum (after / by) 9 P.M.

10 Please wash your hands (before / since) eating anything.

11 Franklin Roosevelt was the president of the US (from / by) 1933 to 1945.

12 I lived in Toronto (until / from) I was 19, and then I moved back to Korea.

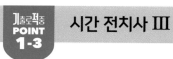

정답 p.90

연습문제 for와 during 중 다음 빈칸에 들어갈 전치사가 나머지 둘과 <u>다른</u> 것을 고르시오.

1
① Jimmy swam _____ 30 minutes.
② It rains a lot _____ the summer.
③ I haven't seen him _____ weeks.

2
① Sarah has been sick _____ two days.
② Ben waited for Sam _____ an hour.
③ Bears rarely wake up _____ the winter.

3
① Many jobs were lost _____ the Great Depression.
② Everyone enjoyed themselves _____ the festival.
③ They have been married _____ more than ten years.

4
① Jenny and Minji has been best friends _____ years.
② Many people moved out of Ireland _____ the famine.
③ I'm usually in class _____ the day.

5
① The audiences clapped _____ 15 minutes.
② The box was damaged _____ the delivery.
③ Jisu has learned German _____ almost a year.

6
① Emily played the piano _____ five years.
② Please do not talk _____ the exam.
③ John prepared for the dinner _____ four hours.

7
① Many people died _____ the world wars.
② I took a long nap _____ the daytime.
③ We lived in this building _____ 18 years.

8
① She just stood there _____ a long time.
② The river dried up _____ the drought.
③ The baby cried _____ a while.

9
① Amy is staying in France _____ three weeks.
② They walked a lot _____ their tour.
③ Many banks went bankrupt _____ the recession.

10
① You should not talk _____ the movie.
② Bats hunt for food _____ the nighttime.
③ Kate thought about the topic _____ a second.

11
① Van Gogh's works were not widely appreciated _____ his lifetime.
② The song continued _____ five hours.
③ Messi has played soccer _____ more than 20 years.

12
① He was injured badly _____ the accident.
② George has been a doctor _____ 30 years.
③ Don't use your phone _____ the lecture.

13
① Adam slept _____ the history class.
② I have to go outside _____ a minute to throw out the trash.
③ Doris was absent _____ a week because she visited her cousin in England.

14
① They watched the rain fall _____ the storm.
② Some people left _____ his speech.
③ James stayed in the hospital _____ a month.

POINT 2-1 장소 전치사: at, on, in I

정답 p.90

연습문제 우리말과 같도록 괄호 안에서 at, on, in 중 알맞은 것을 고르시오.

1 Kelly는 그녀가 가장 좋아하는 포스터를 거실 벽에 걸었다.
= Kelly hung her favorite poster (at / on / in) the living room wall.

2 버스 정류장에 긴 줄이 있었다.
= There was a long line (at / on / in) the bus stop.

3 그 고양이는 모든 사람이 떠날 때까지 Jeff의 방 안에 숨어 있었다.
= The cat was hiding (at / on / in) Jeff's room until everyone left.

4 John은 새들이 나는 것을 보기 위해 잔디 위에 누웠다.
= John laid (at / on / in) the grass to watch the birds fly.

5 Jennifer는 10월까지 베를린에 머무를 것이다.
= Jennifer is going to stay (at / on / in) Berlin until October.

6 그녀는 모퉁이에서 30분 동안 Sam을 기다려왔다.
= She has waited for Sam (at / on / in) the corner for half an hour.

POINT 2-2 장소 전치사: at, on, in II

정답 p.90

연습문제 다음 빈칸에 at, on, in 중 알맞은 것을 쓰시오.

1 Let's look up this word _____ the dictionary.

2 Teenagers likes to chat _____ the Internet.

3 Can you pick me up _____ the way to the station?

4 There were many cars _____ the road today.

5 The girl _____ a yellow T-shirt is my little sister.

6 Octopus lives deep down _____ the ocean.

7 The marathon runners stood _____ the starting line.

8 Jennifer lost her phone while she was _____ Rome.

9 Shouldn't you be _____ school right now?

10 The dog was lying _____ the middle of the room.

POINT 3 위치 전치사

정답 p.90

연습문제 우리말과 같도록 빈칸에 알맞은 전치사를 <보기>에서 골라 쓰시오.

<보기> in front of   over   next to   under   among

1 프랑스는 독일 바로 옆에 있다.

= France is right _____ Germany.

2 그 고양이는 밖으로 나가기 위해 대문 밑으로 그것의 몸을 비집었다.

= The cat squeezed its body _____ the gate to go outside.

3 태양이 도시 위에 빛나고 있다.

= The sun is shining _____ the city.

4 날씨가 추웠기 때문에, 그들은 캠프파이어 앞에 모였다.

= As it was cold, they gathered _____ the camp fire.

5 그녀는 나무들 사이에 사슴 한 마리가 달리는 것을 봤다.

= She saw a deer running _____ the trees.

POINT 4 방향 전치사

정답 p.91

연습문제 우리말과 같도록 빈칸에 알맞은 전치사를 <보기>에서 골라 쓰시오.

<보기> through   to   into   along   over

1 Jane과 나는 함께 아쿠아리움에 갔다.

= Jane and I went _____ the aquarium together.

2 그들은 공이 울타리를 넘어 날아가는 것을 지켜봤다.

= They watched the ball fly _____ the fence.

3 그는 잘못하여 그의 열쇠를 호수 안으로 빠트렸다.

= He accidentally dropped his key _____ the lake.

4 그 개는 온종일 창문을 통해 밖을 보는 데 썼다.

= The dog spent all day looking outside _____ the window.

5 도시를 더 좋아 보이게 만들기 위해, 그 시장은 길을 따라 나무를 심기로 결정했다.

= To make the city look better, the mayor decided to plant trees _____ the road.

연습문제 우리말과 같도록 빈칸에 알맞은 전치사를 <보기>에서 골라 쓰시오.

<보기> with   without   by   about   like   as   for   against

1 저를 위해 문을 잡아주시겠어요?

= Could you hold the door _____ me?

2 그 축구팀은 챔피언 결정전에서 자신들의 라이벌과 경기를 했다.

= The soccer team played _____ its rival in the championship game.

3 그의 여름 방학 동안, John은 조부모님과 함께 지냈다.

= During his summer vacation, John stayed _____ his grandparents.

4 우리는 비행기를 타고 제주도에 갈 것이다.

= We are going to Jejudo _____ plane.

5 Luke는 그의 지갑 없이 집을 나섰다.

= Luke left the house _____ his wallet.

6 '엘리제를 위하여'는 베토벤에 의해 작곡되었다.

= *Für Elise* was composed _____ Beethoven.

7 그들은 Morgan씨가 그들을 아기처럼 대했기 때문에 화났다.

= They were angry because Mr. Morgan treated them _____ babies.

8 Mike는 언젠가 노벨상을 타는 것에 대해 꿈꾼다.

= Mike dreams _____ winning a Noble Prize someday.

9 그는 자신의 손을 비누와 물로 씻었다.

= He washed his hands _____ soap and water.

10 너는 베이킹소다를 사용함으로써 세제를 만들 수 있다.

= You can make detergent _____ using baking soda.

11 Kevin은 불고기와 김밥과 같은 한국 음식을 좋아한다.

= Kevin loves Korean food _____ bulgogi and gimbap.

12 Jackson씨는 22년 동안 상담사로 일해왔다.

= Mr. Jackson has worked _____ a counselor for 22 years.

전치사 관용 표현: 형용사 + 전치사

정답 p.91

연습문제 괄호 안에서 알맞은 전치사를 고르시오.

1 Drinking a cup of coffee everyday is good (at / for) your health.

2 Mady's voice is similar (to / of) her mother's.

3 Jimmy is bad (from / at) making important decisions.

4 She was afraid (of / with) upsetting her parents.

5 Not everyone is good (at / for) math.

6 The magic show was finally ready (in / for) the audience.

7 Jenny is curious (about / to) everything and everyone.

8 Amy was late (for / of) the doctor's appointment.

9 Portuguese is different (to / from) Spanish.

10 This bakery is famous (about / for) its chocolate croissant.

11 Watching too much TV is bad (for / at) children's eyes.

12 I was proud (of / to) my brother when he won the singing contest.

13 After watching the documentary, she felt sorry (to / for) the wild animals.

14 William Blake's poetry is full (of / for) admiration to the nature.

전치사 관용 표현: 동사 + 전치사

정답 p.91

연습문제 괄호 안에서 알맞은 전치사를 고르시오.

1 Lions and tigers belong (to / from) the cat family.

2 Please wait (for / to) the traffic lights to change behind the yellow line.

3 I am old enough to take care (in / of) myself.

4 My dad listens (to / in) the radio on his way to work.

5 Fred is looking (about / for) his glasses under the bed.

6 Thank you (to / for) sending me this postcard.

7 How much did you spend (on / from) snacks today?

8 Jonathan looked (at / from) himself in the mirror.

9 Andrew laughed (in / at) his own foolish mistake.

10 You never know when you will run (at / into) a celebrity.

1 다음 빈칸에 들어갈 알맞은 것은?

> Our basketball team practices from
> 9 A.M. _____ 11 A.M. every Saturday.

① at   ② since   ③ to
④ for   ⑤ on

2 다음 우리말을 영작할 때 빈칸에 들어갈 알맞은 전치사는?

> Ginny는 서울에서 15년 동안 살았다.
> = Ginny has lived in Seoul _____ 15
>   years.

① during   ② for   ③ from
④ since   ⑤ on

3 우리말과 같도록 빈칸에 알맞은 말을 쓰시오.

> 나는 어제 나의 할아버지와 전화로 이야기를 했다.

= I talked to my grandfather _____
_____ _____ yesterday.

4 다음 중 밑줄 친 부분이 어법상 어색한 것은?

① My older sister works in New York City.
② Put the bacon at the hot frying pan.
③ A lot of olives are grown in Spain.
④ There is a small bird on the branch.
⑤ I met some friends at the entrance of the
   library.

5 우리말과 같도록 빈칸에 알맞은 전치사를 쓰시오.

> 그 기차는 긴 터널을 통해서 갔다.

= The train went _____ a long tunnel.

6 다음 빈칸에 공통으로 들어갈 알맞은 것은?

> · The essay must be turned in _____
>   Tuesday.
> · The fastest way to get to the museum
>   is _____ taxi.

① during   ② to   ③ at
④ by   ⑤ on

7 다음 빈칸에 들어갈 전치사가 같은 것끼리 묶인 것은?

> · The shopping cart is full ⓐ_____
>   vegetables.
> · Jack is very different ⓑ_____ me.
> · Italy is famous ⓒ_____ its amazing
>   food.
> · David was sorry ⓓ_____ breaking
>   the glasses.
> · My classmate is good ⓔ_____
>   drawing pictures.

① ⓐ, ⓑ   ② ⓐ, ⓔ   ③ ⓑ, ⓒ
④ ⓒ, ⓓ   ⑤ ⓓ, ⓔ

8 다음 빈칸에 들어갈 말이 순서대로 짝지어진 것은?

> · The architect was proud ___(A)___ his building design.
> · The woman left the room ___(B)___ a sound.
> · Lewis woke up ___(C)___ dawn to watch the sun rise.

	(A)	(B)	(C)
①	of	for	in
②	as	without	at
③	as	without	on
④	of	like	in
⑤	of	without	at

9 주어진 문장의 @에 들어갈 전치사가 다음 빈칸에 들어갈 전치사와 <u>다른</u> 것을 고르시오.

> We plan to attend the film festival
> @_____ Busan.

① Over a billion people live _____ China.
② Tom is waiting _____ the corner for the bus.
③ Put the milk _____ the refrigerator.
④ I had to stand _____ line to order a burger.
⑤ The thief got _____ the car and drove away.

10 다음 빈칸에 들어갈 말로 <u>어색한</u> 것은?

> Michael's party will be held on _____.

① Sunday morning ② his birthday
③ December 15   ④ 7 o'clock
⑤ Saturday

11 주어진 문장의 밑줄 친 <u>by</u>와 의미가 같은 것은?

> The postcard was sent <u>by</u> my cousin.

① We traveled <u>by</u> train through Eastern Europe.
② You can only pay <u>by</u> cash at that store.
③ We enjoyed the cake baked <u>by</u> Natalie.
④ Anna goes to school <u>by</u> bus every day.
⑤ Can you finish practicing the violin by 2 P.M.?

12 다음 대화의 빈칸에 들어갈 말이 순서대로 짝지어진 것은?

> A: Excuse me. Could you give me directions to the National Bank?
> B: Sure. Go _____ this subway station through Exit 6.
> A: OK. Then what?
> B: Walk across the street. The National Bank is the largest building _____ the hospital and the post office.
> A: Thanks so much for your help.

① out of – between   ② into – between
③ out of – among   ④ into – among
⑤ into – out of

13 다음 빈칸에 들어갈 말이 순서대로 짝지어진 것은?

> · Did you knit these mittens _____ your mother?
> · We can go _____ the restaurant from here.

① for - to   ② for - for   ③ to- to
④ to - at   ⑤ at - to

14 우리말과 같도록 빈칸에 알맞은 전치사를 쓰시오.

> 학생들은 그들의 나라의 역사에 대해 배웠다.

= The students learned _____ their country's history.

15 다음 빈칸에 들어갈 알맞은 것은?

> Stacy bumped _____ her science teacher at the supermarket on Sunday.

① into   ② around   ③ across
④ out of   ⑤ as

16 다음 밑줄 친 ⓐ~ⓔ 중 어법상 어색한 것을 찾아 기호를 쓰고 바르게 고쳐 쓰시오.

> Today, I was late ⓐfor school. I was afraid ⓑfor getting in trouble. But as I arrived ⓒto school, I knew that something was wrong. The school wasn't full ⓓof students. Then I realized that it was Saturday. I felt sorry ⓔat myself.

(1) _____ → _____
(2) _____ → _____
(3) _____ → _____

17 다음 중 밑줄 친 like의 쓰임이 나머지 넷과 다른 것은?

① Her house looks like an old castle.
② I have brown hair like my father's.
③ Jenna's perfume smells like flowers.
④ Dianne is acting like a two-year-old baby.
⑤ They like watching horror movies.

18 다음 중 어느 빈칸에도 들어갈 수 없는 것은?

> **<How to Build a Campfire>**
>
> 1. Dig a small hole ⓐ_____ the fire.
> 2. Pick up some large rocks ⓑ_____ the ground, and place them around the hole.
> 3. Put some paper ⓒ_____ the hole.
> 4. Stack small pieces of wood ⓓ_____ top of the paper.
> 5. Use a match to light the wood and paper ⓔ_____ fire.
>
> *stack 쌓다

① for   ② in   ③ on
④ from   ⑤ about

19 다음 중 밑줄 친 부분이 어법상 어색한 것은?

> A: Beth, have you finished your history report yet?
> B: No. It's not due ①by Friday.
> A: Friday? That's a relief. I thought that I had to submit it ②on Wednesday.
> B: Why don't we go ③to the library together? We can find some books ④for our report topics.
> A: That's a good idea. I'll meet you there ⑤in 30 minutes.

20 다음 중 밑줄 친 부분이 어법상 어색한 것은?

① Sarah was <u>against</u> the new class rule.

② We ate lunch from noon <u>to</u> 2 P.M.

③ The birds return <u>for</u> the island every winter.

④ I enjoy team sports <u>like</u> baseball and soccer.

⑤ Bora read a book <u>about</u> a monster in Scotland.

21 다음 빈칸에 공통으로 들어갈 알맞은 것은?

> · There was a woman _____ a dog in the park.
> · I cleaned the floor _____ a mop.

① at   ② with   ③ on

④ for   ⑤ to

22 다음 글의 빈칸에 들어갈 말이 순서대로 짝지어진 것은?

> The Veryovkina Cave in Georgia is the deepest cave on the planet. Explorers looked _____ the bottom of this cave for many years. It was finally discovered in 2018. The bottom of the cave is over two kilometers _____ the surface of the earth.

① for – above   ② for – below

③ at – above   ④ to – below

⑤ to – over

23 다음 글의 빈칸에 들어갈 말이 순서대로 짝지어진 것은?

> On Saturday, Kyle decided to visit Namsan. The top of this mountain is _____ Seoul. So, Kyle had a great view of the city. He ate lunch at a picnic table _____ some trees. It was a perfect day.

① under – among   ② among – between

③ above – among   ④ under – between

⑤ above – over

24 다음 중 어법상 어색한 것은?

① Peter spent $1,000 in a new computer.

② The first snow usually comes in December.

③ You should thank your grandmother for the gift.

④ Our family will go on a vacation next week.

⑤ Everyone laughed at Benny's funny joke.

25 다음은 유리의 교실 책상 배치도이다. 빈칸에 알맞은 말을 쓰시오.

Black board		
Paul	Yuri	Mary
Kate	Ben	Jieun
James	Liam	Suho

> Yuri sits ⓐ_____ Ben in the classroom. James sits ⓑ_____ Liam. Suho sits ⓒ_____ Jieun.

해커스북 중·고등
www.HackersBook.com

CHAPTER 15
접속사

기출로 적중 POINT

연습문제 A <보기>에서 가장 알맞은 접속사를 골라 다음 두 문장을 한 문장으로 연결하시오.

<보기> and   but   or   so

1 Daniel is handsome. + He is generous.
→ Daniel is handsome _____ generous.

2 History textbooks are boring. + They are useful.
→ History textbooks are boring _____ useful.

3 Do you want some soda? + Do you want some water?
→ Do you want some soda _____ water?

4 It is sunny today. + We decided to go on a picnic.
→ It is sunny today, _____ we decided to go on a picnic.

5 Minsu likes playing computer games. + Sohee likes playing computer games.
→ Minsu _____ Sohee like playing computer games.

6 Rachel enjoys painting. + She is not good at it.
→ Rachel enjoys painting, _____ she is not good at it.

연습문제 B <보기>와 같이 다음 문장을 명령문으로 바꿔 쓰시오.

<보기> If you take this medicine, you'll feel better.
　　　 → *Take this medicine, and you'll feel better.*

1 If you clean your room, your mom will be very happy.
→ _____

2 If you don't keep your promises, other people won't trust you.
→ _____

3 If you leave now, you'll arrive at school on time.
→ _____

4 If you wear gloves, your hands will feel warm.
→ _____

5 If you don't eat breakfast, you'll get hungry later.
→ _____

6 If you walk just two blocks, you'll see the bank.
→ _____

연습문제 A 우리말과 같도록 괄호 안의 말을 활용하여 문장을 완성하시오.

1 나는 그 신발과 그 모자 둘 다 사기를 원했다. (the shoes, the hat)

= I wanted to buy _____.

2 이 책은 재미있지도 유익하지도 않다. (interesting, informative)

= This book is _____.

3 나의 남동생이나 나 둘 중 하나는 설거지를 해야 한다. (my brother, I)

= _____ have to wash the dishes.

4 헬렌 켈러는 들을 수도 볼 수도 없었지만 다섯 개의 언어를 배웠다. (hear, see)

= Helen Keller could _____, but she learned five languages.

5 아마추어와 프로 둘 다 이 대회에 참가할 수 있다. (amateurs, professionals)

= _____ can participate in this competition.

6 저 드레스는 아름다울 뿐만 아니라 편하기도 하다. (beautiful, comfortable)

= That dress is _____.

7 레오나르도 다빈치는 유명한 예술가였을 뿐만 아니라 위대한 과학자였다. (a famous artist, a great scientist)

= Leonardo da Vinci was _____.

연습문제 B 괄호 안에서 알맞은 것을 고르시오.

1 Not only Jisu but also Mina (is / are) good at playing the violin.

2 Both Paul and Nina (likes / like) K-pop music.

3 Not only Kevin but also Peter (is / are) interested in Korean history.

4 Neither Nancy nor Jack (has / have) been to New York.

5 Vegetables as well as brown rice (is / are) good for your health.

6 Both tomatoes and strawberries (is / are) fruits.

7 Not only coffee but also tea (contains / contain) large amount of caffeine.

8 Neither the chair nor the sofa (is / are) comfortable to sit on.

9 Naomi as well as Scarlet (enjoys / enjoy) watching action movies.

10 Either Italy or Germany (is / are) going to win the World Cup.

11 Both Tom and Wendy (wants / want) to drink some hot tea.

명사절을 이끄는 접속사: that

정답 p.92

연습문제 A 우리말과 같도록 괄호 안의 말을 알맞게 배열하시오.

1 사람들은 날씨가 그들의 기분에 영향을 준다고 믿는다. (affects, believe, their mood, that, the weather)

= People _____.

2 우리가 서로를 믿는 것은 중요하다. (important, is, trust, we, each other, that)

= It _____.

3 그 사실은 캐나다가 두 번째로 큰 나라라는 것이다. (Canada, country, is, is, second, the, that, largest)

= The fact _____.

4 나는 더 많은 사람들이 자원 봉사를 하기를 바란다. (will, more, hope, volunteer, that, people)

= I _____.

연습문제 B 다음 중 밑줄 친 that의 쓰임이 나머지 둘과 다른 것을 고르시오.

1 ① It is surprising <u>that</u> the building is still under construction.
② He met <u>that</u> girl at his friend's birthday party.
③ Have you read <u>that</u> article?

2 ① The truth is <u>that</u> I am not good at sewing.
② Kate told me <u>that</u> she didn't finish her homework.
③ <u>That</u> is Jenny's scarf on the table.

명사절을 이끄는 접속사: if, whether

정답 p.93

연습문제 <보기>와 같이 다음 문장을 괄호 안의 접속사를 활용하여 바꿔 쓰시오.

<보기> Does this store open on Sundays? → I wonder _if this store opens on Sundays_ . (if)

1 Did I make her upset?

→ I wanted to know _____. (if)

2 Can you meet me after school?

→ Please tell me _____. (whether)

3 Is the movie based on a true story?

→ I'm not sure _____. (whether)

4 Can dolphins and whales breathe underwater?

→ She wants to know _____. (if)

연습문제 A 괄호 안에서 알맞은 것을 고르시오.

1 I read a magazine (while / until) I was waiting for the bus.

2 Linda will have dinner before the movie (starts / will start).

3 Yunho went back home (as soon as / until) he got the phone call.

4 What do you usually do (as / when) you have free time?

5 You need to soak the sweater (before / after) you wash it.

6 She ran into her friend (until / as) she walked down the street.

7 She will continue working (until / while) she is 65 years old.

8 I fell asleep (while / before) the teacher was giving a lecture.

9 Please sweep the floor while I (will do / do) the laundry.

10 The store was open (until / since) it was 10 P.M. yesterday.

연습문제 B 다음 빈칸에 가장 알맞은 말을 <보기>에서 골라 쓰시오.

<보기>	after you live for five years	since I was five years old
	while his mom was taking a nap	when they are asleep
	as he heard his grandfather's story	as soon as the passengers are all seated
	before they go to bed	

1 My family has lived in this city _____.

2 Many people grind their teeth _____.

3 You can apply for the US citizenship _____.

4 Jonathan went to the store _____.

5 They always watch the news _____.

6 The bus will leave _____.

7 Dennis felt touched _____.

연습문제 A <보기>와 같이 다음 문장을 괄호 안의 접속사를 활용하여 바꿔 쓰시오.

<보기> She worked out hard, so she was exhausted.
→ *She was exhausted since she worked out hard.* (since)

1 I was sleepy, so I took a short nap.
→ _____ (because)

2 The hotels were too expensive, so Pete chose to stay in a hostel.
→ _____ (since)

3 She needed some fresh air, so she opened the window.
→ _____ (since)

4 The weather was bad, so our flight was canceled.
→ _____ (because)

5 It is very cold in the Arctic, so polar bears need body fat to keep themselves warm.
→ _____ (as)

6 We practiced a lot, so we won the dance competition.
→ _____ (because)

7 The shirt was sold out, so she couldn't buy it.
→ _____ (since)

연습문제 B because와 because of 중 다음 빈칸에 들어갈 말이 나머지 둘과 다른 것을 고르시오.

1 ① Everyone likes Sam _____ he is friendly.
② You should drive carefully today _____ the fog.
③ I can't drink soda _____ a toothache.

2 ① The painter became famous _____ her unique style.
② The light was out _____ the heavy rain.
③ They couldn't buy the TV _____ it was too expensive.

3 ① My dog wagged its tail _____ it saw me.
② I forgot to bring my key _____ I was in a hurry.
③ She studied until late at night _____ the math exam.

4 ① The boy went to see a doctor _____ he hurt his back.
② The view is not good _____ the air pollution.
③ She stopped reading the novel _____ she had to go to bed.

연습문제 A   <보기>와 같이 우리말과 같도록 괄호 안의 말을 활용하여 문장을 완성하시오.

<보기> 만약 네가 창문을 닫지 않는다면, 너무 추울 것이다. (close the window)

= *If you don't close the window* , it will be too cold.

= *Unless you close the window* , it will be too cold.

1 만약 네가 그의 조언을 듣지 않는다면, 너는 후회할 것이다. (take his advice)

= _____ , you'll regret it.

= _____ , you'll regret it.

2 만약 네가 약속을 지킬 수 없다면, 약속해서는 안 된다. (can keep a promise)

= _____ , you shouldn't make it.

= _____ , you shouldn't make it.

3 만약 비가 오지 않는다면, 야구 경기는 취소되지 않을 것이다. (rain)

= _____ , the baseball game won't be canceled.

= _____ , the baseball game won't be canceled.

4 만약 네가 19살이 아니라면, 너는 이 영화를 혼자 볼 수 없다.(be 19 years old)

= _____ , you can't watch this movie alone.

= _____ , you can't watch this movie alone.

5 만약 우리가 우리의 환경을 보호하지 않는다면, 미래 세대는 황무지에 살 것이다. (protect our environment)

= _____ , future generations will live in a wasteland.

= _____ , future generations will live in a wasteland.

연습문제 B   괄호 안에서 알맞은 것을 고르시오.

1 (If / Unless) you don't hand in your essay on time, you cannot get an A.

2 (If / Unless) you put on sunscreen, you will get a sunburn.

3 Remember to turn off the light (if / unless) you are the last person to leave the room.

4 We will miss the train unless we (get / will get) to the station by 3 P.M.

5 Unless she (does / will do) it herself, she will not be satisfied with it.

6 (If / Unless) you have any questions, you can always ask me.

7 If you (visit / will visit) your grandparents tomorrow, they will be very happy.

8 Derek will be late for school (if / unless) he leaves home now.

연습문제 | 우리말과 같도록 괄호 안의 말을 알맞게 배열하시오.

1 비록 Katie는 피곤했지만 잠이 들지 못했다. (was, although, tired, Katie)

= ＿＿＿＿＿＿＿＿＿＿＿＿＿＿＿＿＿, she couldn't fall asleep.

2 비록 그 남자는 매우 나이가 많을지라도 꽤 힘이 세다. (though, was, man, old, even, very, that)

= ＿＿＿＿＿＿＿＿＿＿＿＿＿＿＿＿＿, he is quite strong.

3 비록 나는 아침을 먹지 않지만 낮 동안 배고프다고 느끼지 않는다. (I, eat, though, don't, breakfast)

= ＿＿＿＿＿＿＿＿＿＿＿＿＿＿＿＿＿, I don't feel hungry during the day.

4 비록 이미 9월일지라도 날씨는 여전히 덥고 습하다. (even, September, already, though, it's)

= The weather is still hot and humid ＿＿＿＿＿＿＿＿＿＿＿＿＿＿＿＿＿.

5 비록 그것은 작지만 Jessie의 방은 잘 꾸며져 있다. (it, small, although, is)

= Jessie's room is well decorated ＿＿＿＿＿＿＿＿＿＿＿＿＿.

6 비록 문법이 어려울지라도, 너는 그것을 공부하는 것을 포기하면 안 된다. (though, grammar, hard, even, is)

= ＿＿＿＿＿＿＿＿＿＿＿＿＿＿＿＿＿, you shouldn't give up studying it.

7 비록 아일랜드어가 공용어지만 아일랜드에서는 영어가 더 널리 사용된다. (official, the, Irish, though, language, is)

= English is more widely spoken in Ireland ＿＿＿＿＿＿＿＿＿＿＿＿＿＿＿.

기출로적중 POINT 4-5 부사절을 이끄는 접속사: as의 다양한 의미　　　정답 p.93

연습문제 | 밑줄 친 as의 의미를 <보기>에서 골라 그 기호를 쓰시오.

| <보기> ⓐ ~하고 있을 때　ⓑ ~하기 때문에　ⓒ ~ 대로　ⓓ ~할수록　ⓔ ~으로서 |

1 As she was too tired, she went to bed early.　[　　]

2 As I was washing the dishes, I broke my favorite cup.　[　　]

3 I can't go to the concert as all tickets are sold out.　[　　]

4 My brother got home as we were having dinner.　[　　]

5 As the boy practiced the piano, he got better.　[　　]

6 The project was completed yesterday as it was planned.　[　　]

7 As a chef, the man knows everything about food.　[　　]

8 She fell asleep as she was reading a book.　[　　]

POINT 5 — so that / so ~ that …

정답 p.93

연습문제 우리말과 같도록 괄호 안의 말을 알맞게 배열하시오.

1 선생님은 그것이 눈에 띄도록 그 공지를 빨간 펜으로 썼다. (so, would, stand out, it, that)
= The teacher wrote the notice in red pen _____.

2 나의 아빠는 너무 바빠서서 나와 놀아줄 시간이 없었다. (didn't, he, so, time to play, that, busy, have, with me)
= My dad was _____.

3 과학자들은 약을 찾기 위해 수년 동안 그 병을 연구했다. (they, find, so, could, a medication, that)
= Scientists studied the disease for years _____.

4 나는 나의 엄마에게 선물을 사드릴 수 있도록 많은 돈을 모았다. (so, I, could, that, a present, buy, my mom)
= I saved a lot of money _____.

5 그 소파는 너무 무거워서 그녀는 그것을 혼자서 옮길 수 없다. (heavy, that, so, can't, move, she, it)
= The sofa is _____ by herself.

6 너의 어린 여동생이 잠을 잘 수 있도록 너의 목소리를 낮춰라. (that, can, your baby sister, so, sleep)
= Lower your voice _____.

7 그의 청바지는 너무 커서 그는 벨트를 착용해야 한다. (that, wear, so, to, needs, big, he, a belt)
= His jeans are _____.

8 Ben은 그것을 더 잘 이해하기 위해 그 기사를 두 번 읽었다. (could, he, that, understand, better, it, so)
= Ben read the article twice _____.

POINT 6 — 접속부사

정답 p.93

연습문제 빈칸에 알맞은 말을 <보기>에서 골라 쓰시오.

<보기>	however	for example	in addition	on the other hand	therefore

1 Liam has many things to do. _____, he has to cook dinner and water the plants.

2 Jamie was about to go out for a walk. _____, it started to rain.

3 She speaks Spanish very well. _____, she can speak French fluently.

4 David didn't go to school yesterday. _____, he didn't hear about the science project.

5 I like listening to rap music. _____, my twin sister likes listening to classical music.

중간·기말고사 실전 문제

1 다음 빈칸에 들어갈 알맞은 것을 고르시오.

> It was a surprise _____ Chris became our new class president.

① and   ② so   ③ that
④ or   ⑤ if

2 다음 두 문장의 의미가 같도록 문장을 완성하시오. (단, as를 반드시 포함하시오.)

> Not only monkeys but also gorillas live in the jungle.
> = _____ live in the jungle.

3 다음 두 문장의 의미가 같도록 빈칸에 알맞은 접속사를 쓰시오.

> Evan won't say if he is coming on the trip or not.
> = Evan won't say _____ he is coming on the trip or not.

4 다음 빈칸에 들어갈 접속사가 나머지 넷과 <u>다른</u> 것은?

① Exercise every day, _____ you will stay healthy.
② Wake up early, _____ you won't be late for school again.
③ Bring an umbrella, _____ you'll get wet because of the rain.
④ Be nice to people, _____ you will make many friends.
⑤ Use this coupon, _____ you'll get a discount on that jacket.

5 다음 중 밑줄 친 that을 생략할 수 있는 것을 <u>모두</u> 고르시오.

① Who left <u>that</u> knife in the sink?
② I hope <u>that</u> it doesn't rain tomorrow.
③ Neal couldn't believe <u>that</u> Anne won the lottery.
④ A beaver built <u>that</u> dam in the river.
⑤ Is <u>that</u> the movie you wanted to watch?

6 다음 글의 빈칸에 들어갈 말이 순서대로 짝지어진 것은?

> My sister wants to be a doctor _____ a lawyer when she grows up. This will be difficult, _____ she will have to study hard in school. I hope she achieves her dream.

① so – or   ② or – so   ③ and – or
④ so – so   ⑤ or – but

7 다음 밑줄 친 부분을 바르게 고친 것끼리 묶인 것은?

> ⓐ Both Jiho and I <u>am</u> playing video games. (→ is)
> ⓑ My brother is either eating lunch or <u>to clean</u> the kitchen right now. (→ clean)
> ⓒ David hopes to neither work nor <u>studying</u> on his vacation. (→ study)
> ⓓ The nurse as well as the doctors <u>are</u> helping the patient. (→ is)

① ⓐ, ⓑ   ② ⓐ, ⓒ   ③ ⓑ, ⓒ
④ ⓑ, ⓓ   ⑤ ⓒ, ⓓ

8 알맞은 접속사를 이용하여 다음 두 문장을 한 문장으로 연결하시오.

> He was in New York. He visited the Empire State Building then.
> → _____ he was in New York, he visited the Empire State Building.

[9-10] 다음 두 문장의 의미가 같도록 빈칸에 알맞은 접속사를 쓰시오.

9

> She isn't strong enough, so she can't lift this chair.
> = She can't lift this chair _____ she isn't strong enough.

10

> If we don't buy tickets, we can't enter the museum.
> = _____ we buy tickets, we can't enter the museum.

11 우리말과 같도록 괄호 안의 말을 알맞게 배열하시오.

> 비록 날씨가 매우 춥지만, Matt는 코트를 입지 않았다. (the, very, weather, although, cold, is)

= _____, Matt did not wear a coat.

12 다음 빈칸에 들어갈 말이 순서대로 짝지어진 것은?

> · The vase was broken _____ Ollie accidentally hit it with his bat.
> · I find this sofa very comfortable _____ its soft cushions.

① because – because of
② because – because
③ since – because
④ because of – because of
⑤ because of – because

13 다음 중 어법상 어색한 것의 개수는?

> ⓐ I'll buy a ticket when I'll arrive at the theater.
> ⓑ Unless you'll get up now, we will eat breakfast without you.
> ⓒ David never takes a taxi if a bus is in service.
> ⓓ He'll be tired after he runs with his dog.
> ⓔ Jennifer can watch TV if she will finish her homework.

① 없음   ② 1개   ③ 2개
④ 3개   ⑤ 4개

14 우리말과 같도록 주어진 <조건>에 맞게 영작하시오.

> 이 소설은 길 뿐만 아니라 지루하기도 하다.

> **<조건>**
> 1. this novel, not, long, boring을 활용하시오.
> 2. 9단어로 쓰시오.

= _____

15 다음 밑줄 친 부분과 바꿔 쓸 수 있는 것은?

> Mindy bought a bicycle to ride in the park.

① to that she could ride it in the park
② so that she could ride it in the park
③ so that she couldn't ride it in the park
④ so she could that ride it in the park
⑤ so she couldn't that ride it in the park

16 다음 두 문장의 의미가 같도록 문장을 완성하시오.

> If you go to bed early, you will get a good sleep.
> = Go to bed early, _____
> _____ .

17 주어진 문장의 밑줄 친 as와 의미가 같은 것은?

> My brother collects comic books as a hobby.

① Martin hurt his arm as he was playing tennis.
② Call me later as I am busy right now.
③ The snow started falling as I left the apartment.
④ Bora watched TV as Junho prepared dinner.
⑤ Jenny made some popcorn as a snack.

18 다음 중 밑줄 친 since의 의미가 나머지 넷과 다른 것은?

① We can't go to the beach since the storm is coming.
② Maria has planted trees every year since she was a child.
③ Mike bought me dinner since it was my birthday.
④ Lisa can't talk on the phone since she is driving.
⑤ I didn't go to the swimming pool since my legs were broken.

19 주어진 문장의 밑줄 친 if와 쓰임이 같은 것은?

> That glass will break if you drop it on the ground.

① Do you know if Peter enjoys eating hot dogs?
② You should ask if we can make campfires here.
③ Did you decide if you will go to Spain?
④ I'm not sure if it will be sunny on the weekend.
⑤ Mark feels bored if he doesn't play video games.

20 다음 (A)~(C)에 들어갈 말이 바르게 짝지어진 것은?

> My older brother has visited many countries. ___(A)___, he went to Venezuela last year. I want to travel like him. ___(B)___, I am too young now. Therefore, I will plan my trips for the future. ___(C)___ I get older, I will travel the world.

	(A)	(B)	(C)
①	For example	However	When
②	For example	Besides	If
③	For example	However	Until
④	Therefore	Besides	If
⑤	Therefore	However	When

21 다음 빈칸에 들어갈 알맞은 것을 <u>모두</u> 고르시오.

> Candice was _____ her friends after school.

① too busy to meet
② too busy that she could meet
③ such busy that she couldn't meet
④ so busy to she could meet
⑤ so busy that she couldn't meet

22 「so ~ that ...」 구문을 이용하여 다음 두 문장을 한 문장으로 연결하시오.

> Ryan's birthday party was fun. I stayed longer than I planned.
>
> → _____
>
>   _____

23 다음 중 밑줄 친 <u>when</u>의 쓰임이 나머지 넷과 <u>다른</u> 것은?

① The car made a strange noise <u>when</u> Dad started it.
② Raymond moved to Busan <u>when</u> he was a child.
③ Do you know <u>when</u> the department store will open?
④ Sam was worried <u>when</u> he saw his friend crying.
⑤ I like to add pineapple as a topping <u>when</u> I order pizza.

[24-25] 다음 글을 읽고 주어진 질문에 답하시오.

> There are many advantages to children playing team sports. It provides them with a chance to exercise. ⓐ_____, they can learn about teamwork. There are disadvantages, though. For example, they won't have as much time to study ⓑ_____ sports.

24 위 글의 빈칸 ⓐ에 들어갈 알맞은 것을 고르시오.

① Finally   ② In addition
③ Therefore   ④ However
⑤ On the other hand

25 위 글의 빈칸 ⓑ에 들어갈 가장 알맞은 것은?

① if they play
② if they will play
③ if they played
④ unless they won't play
⑤ unless they don't play

CHAPTER 16
관계사

연습문제 A 다음 문장의 선행사에는 동그라미를 치고, 관계대명사에는 밑줄을 치시오.

1 I really liked the pictures which Somi took.

2 Jenny is the girl whose hair is red.

3 That is the tree which we planted three years ago.

4 I have never met the people who live next door.

5 Whitcomb L. Judson is the man who invented the zipper.

6 Jinsu is wearing the glasses that his mother bought for him.

7 This is a documentary which is about the World War II.

8 Steven has a dog whose name is Max.

9 Ocarina is a musical instrument which was created by the Chinese people.

10 Mr. Sawyer is the teacher that likes to play soccer.

연습문제 B 밑줄 친 부분이 어법상 맞으면 O를 쓰고, 틀리면 바르게 고쳐 완전한 문장을 쓰시오.

1 I have a cat who likes to sleep on my bed.

→ _____

2 Isaac Newton was a great scientist whom many people respect.

→ _____

3 Amy has an aunt which is a famous actress.

→ _____

4 This is a book whom is about the tale of Robin Hood.

→ _____

5 This is the police officer who found the missing child.

→ _____

6 Millet is an artist who paintings are held at the gallery.

→ _____

7 She met the people which lived upstairs.

→ _____

8 Jennifer is my friend which I can tell everything.

→ _____

연습문제 A 관계대명사를 이용하여 다음 두 문장을 한 문장으로 연결하시오. (단, that은 쓰지 마시오.)

1 A frog is an animal. It lives both on land and in water.

→ _____

2 The room was dirty. It was not cleaned for a week.

→ _____

3 The police caught the girl. The girl stole Tim's wallet.

→ _____

4 Mr. Morgan bought a car. It was made in Germany.

→ _____

5 *Hamlet* is a play. It is about Prince Hamlet's revenge.

→ _____

6 James fought with the boys. They made fun of his hair.

→ _____

7 The monitor is not working. It is on Jake's table.

→ _____

8 Dolphins are mammals. They can't breathe underwater.

→ _____

연습문제 B 다음 중 밑줄 친 who의 쓰임이 나머지 둘과 다른 것을 고르시오.

1 ① The man <u>who</u> was on TV show became popular.
    ② <u>Who</u> is your new English teacher?
    ③ Amy is the girl <u>who</u> can play the piano well.

2 ① Josh has a friend <u>who</u> lives in New Zealand.
    ② <u>Who</u> ate the last piece of this cake?
    ③ He is not sure <u>who</u> took his bag.

3 ① She is the teacher <u>who</u> can help us.
    ② We didn't learn <u>who</u> invented the telephone.
    ③ Dan is the person <u>who</u> you should go ask the question.

4 ① Is he the man <u>who</u> lives in this building?
    ② Dora is the student <u>who</u> used to bully Jack.
    ③ Do you know <u>who</u> sent us this postcard?

5 ① Did you see <u>who</u> broke our window?
    ② Do you know <u>who</u> left the letter here?
    ③ Penny is my cousin <u>who</u> is a doctor.

6 ① I wonder <u>who</u> didn't come to the meeting yesterday.
    ② Jenny remembers the woman <u>who</u> yelled at her.
    ③ I know the man <u>who</u> fixed this elevator.

연습문제 A 관계대명사를 이용하여 다음 두 문장을 한 문장으로 연결하시오. (단, that은 쓰지 마시오.)

1 Look at the new backpack. I bought it yesterday.
→ Look at _____.

2 This is the girl. Jared met her at the library.
→ This is _____.

3 I still remember the surprise party. My friends organized it three years ago.
→ I still remember _____.

4 I can smell the food. My neighbors are cooking it.
→ I can smell _____.

5 This is the picture book. Penny gave it to her nephew on his birthday.
→ This is _____.

6 Someone stole Jenny's bag. Her mom made it for her.
→ Someone stole _____.

7 Ben never found his phone. He lost it in the movie theater.
→ Ben never found _____.

8 Birds collect tree branches. They will use them to make their nest.
→ Birds collect _____.

연습문제 B 우리말과 같도록 괄호 안의 말을 알맞게 배열하시오.

1 햄버거는 내가 그 식당에서 주문한 음식이다. (I, dish, ordered, the, at, which, restaurant, the)
= A hamburger is _____.

2 너는 우리가 교회에서 만났던 Ms. Taylor를 기억하니? (whom, church, we, Ms. Taylor, met, at)
= Do you remember _____?

3 그는 우리가 TV 광고에서 본 남자다. (man, saw, whom, TV commercial, we, in, the, the)
= He is _____.

4 내가 일년에 두 번 방문하는 나의 조부모님은 뉴질랜드에 사신다. (who, visit, a, grandparents, my, year, twice, I)
= _____ live in New Zealand.

5 Jenny가 오늘 산 꽃들은 정말 아름답다. (which, bought, the, Jenny, flowers, today)
= _____ are so beautiful.

6 *Yellow-Red-Blue*는 칸딘스키에 의해 그려진 그림이다. (Kandinsky, a painting, was, by, which, painted)
= *Yellow-Red-Blue* is _____.

연습문제 A 관계대명사를 이용하여 다음 두 문장을 한 문장으로 연결하시오.

1 Paul gave me a teddy bear. Its ears are huge.

→ Paul gave me _____.

2 Tom has a parrot. Its feathers are blue and red.

→ Tom has _____.

3 He is wearing a jacket. Its zipper is broken.

→ He is wearing _____.

4 A cactus is a plant. Its stems store water.

→ A cactus is _____.

5 She is the girl. Her handwriting is the best in our class.

→ She is _____.

6 Golf is a game. Its aim is to hit a very small ball into a hole far away.

→ Golf is _____.

7 J.K. Rowling is a famous author. Her books were translated into many languages.

→ J.K. Rowling is _____.

연습문제 B 밑줄 친 부분의 쓰임과 같은 것을 <보기>에서 골라 그 기호를 쓰시오.

> <보기> ⓐ Gustave Eiffel is the man <u>who</u> designed the Eiffel Tower.
> ⓑ I'm using the computer <u>which</u> Kevin fixed yesterday.
> ⓒ She lives in the building <u>whose</u> roof is green.

1 Mike is a boy <u>who</u> speaks Korean fluently. [   ]

2 This is the house <u>whose</u> walls are red. [   ]

3 This is the music <u>which</u> I like most. [   ]

4 Beavers are animals <u>which</u> live in rivers. [   ]

5 Jenny has a brother <u>whose</u> wife is a lawyer. [   ]

6 Tom broke the laptop <u>which</u> he borrowed from Carl. [   ]

7 I'm eating egg sandwich <u>which</u> was made by my dad. [   ]

8 The police chased the driver <u>who</u> was driving too fast. [   ]

연습문제 A 관계대명사 that을 이용하여 다음 두 문장을 한 문장으로 연결하고, that과 바꿔 쓸 수 있는 말을 <u>모두</u> 쓰시오.

1 Peter is the boy. I met him on the subway.

→ Peter is _____.   → _____

2 He bought her a hairpin. It is small but useful.

→ He bought her _____.   → _____

3 John is my colleague. He has dinner with me once a week.

→ John is _____.   → _____

4 She is the woman. We saw her in the park two days ago.

→ She is _____.   → _____

5 I took a picture of the tree. It was 150 years old.

→ I took a picture of _____.   → _____

6 Mother Teresa was a nun. She was respected by many people.

→ Mother Teresa was _____.   → _____

7 Mr. Smith is the teacher. He taught me how to play the guitar.

→ Mr. Smith is _____.   → _____

8 Please move your things. They are underneath the table.

→ Please move _____.   → _____

연습문제 B 다음 중 밑줄 친 that의 쓰임이 나머지 둘과 <u>다른</u> 것을 고르시오.

1 ① This is the food <u>that</u> Jenny enjoys eating.
② It is surprising <u>that</u> female lion does most of the hunting.
③ A bullfrog is the only animal <u>that</u> never sleeps.

2 ① She is the nicest person <u>that</u> I've ever met.
② Matt was glad <u>that</u> he could go home.
③ The company needs somebody <u>that</u> can speak Chinese.

3 ① Edmund Hillary is the first man <u>that</u> climbed the Mt. Everest.
② Is this the bus <u>that</u> goes to the Seoul Station?
③ It is true <u>that</u> the earth is round.

4 ① I'm sorry <u>that</u> you are so sick.
② This is the best restaurant <u>that</u> Ben has ever visited.
③ The girl <u>that</u> is dancing on the stage is my sister.

연습문제 A 우리말과 같도록 괄호 안의 말을 활용하여 문장을 완성하시오.

1 나는 네가 말한 것을 이해할 수 없었다. (say)

= I couldn't understand _____.

2 네가 너의 일기장에 쓴 것을 내가 봐도 되니? (write in your diary)

= May I look at _____?

3 지수는 나에게 그녀의 주머니 안에 있던 것을 보여줬다. (be in her pocket)

= Jisu showed me _____.

4 하나는 James가 주말에 하고 싶었던 것을 기억할 수 없다. (want to do on the weekend)

= Hana cannot remember _____.

5 그녀의 친절함은 그녀를 다른 모든 사람과 구별해 주는 것이었다. (differentiate her from everyone else)

= Her kindness was _____.

6 Sam이 가장 원하는 것은 그의 아버지가 그를 자랑스러워하는 것이다. (want the most)

= _____ is for his father to be proud of him.

7 그 실험의 결과는 그들이 예상했던 것과 달랐다. (expect)

= The result of the experiment was different from _____.

연습문제 B 다음 빈칸에 what이나 which 중 알맞은 것을 쓰시오.

1 _____ we're looking at is the Statue of Liberty.

2 I ate all the cookies _____ my mom baked yesterday.

3 _____ I like most about this book is its ending.

4 Mr. Anderson is excited to read _____ his grandson wrote in the letter.

5 The thing _____ Kevin hates most is waking up early on Sunday.

6 Animals _____ live in cold places have more fur than others.

7 _____ he got from his friends was a gift card.

8 The tree _____ she planted last year grew taller than the house.

연습문제 A 다음 문장에서 생략된 부분을 넣어 완전한 문장을 쓰시오.

1 Penny is the girl everyone loves.

→ _____

2 The pasta made by Mom is always delicious.

→ _____

3 A gram is a unit used to measure mass.

→ _____

4 *A Farewell to Arms* is a novel written by Hemmingway.

→ _____

5 Ben interviewed a man working in the government in the past.

→ _____

6 Kelly likes the purse John bought for her.

→ _____

7 The man standing in front of the entrance is my dad.

→ _____

8 The house built 20 years ago is still in good shape.

→ _____

연습문제 B 다음 중 밑줄 친 부분을 생략할 수 <u>없는</u> 것을 고르시오.

1 ① Heaven helps those <u>who</u> help themselves.
② This is the poem <u>which</u> she wrote.

2 ① This is the piano <u>which</u> I own.
② I am looking for the person <u>who</u> spread this rumor.

3 ① I read the book <u>which</u> she gave to me.
② My brother has a toy <u>which</u> is broken.

4 ① I bought the same watch <u>that</u> Kate has.
② He knows a boy <u>who</u> runs really fast.

5 ① Fruits <u>which</u> are sold in the convenience store are expensive.
② I know someone <u>who</u> can help us.

6 ① I collect coins <u>that</u> are from different countries.
② Jenny is the prettiest girl <u>that</u> I know.

7 ① Emily ate the bread <u>which</u> she brought.
② I bought a skirt <u>which</u> was the perfect fit for me.

8 ① He was hit by a man <u>who was</u> riding the bike.
② Tim has a new pillow <u>that</u> is big and soft.

전치사 + 관계대명사

정답 p.96

연습문제 <보기>와 같이 관계대명사를 이용하여 다음 두 문장을 한 문장으로 연결하시오. (단, 관계대명사는 생략하지 마시오.)

> <보기>　Nancy is my neighbor. I speak to her every day.
> → _Nancy is my neighbor who[whom/that] I speak to every day._
> → _Nancy is my neighbor to whom I speak every day._

1 I ordered the ratatouille. This restaurant is famous for it.

→ _____

→ _____

2 This is papyrus. Ancient Egyptians used to write on it.

→ _____

→ _____

3 The boy is my cousin. Jenny is playing with him.

→ _____

→ _____

4 This is the sofa. Mr. Smith talked about it last night.

→ _____

→ _____

관계부사

정답 p.96

연습문제 밑줄 친 부분이 어법상 맞으면 O를 쓰고, 틀리면 바르게 고쳐 완전한 문장을 쓰시오.

1 China is the country when Minho spent his childhood.

→ _____

2 Let me show you how to make kimchi.

→ _____

3 Do you know how she was so mad at us?

→ _____

4 1991 is the year where the Cold War ended.

→ _____

중간 · 기말고사 실전 문제

1 다음 빈칸에 들어갈 알맞은 것은?

> Jane is wearing the scarf _____ her mother gave her.

① who ② which ③ what
④ whom ⑤ whose

2 다음 빈칸에 들어갈 말이 순서대로 짝지어진 것은?

> · Kevin picked up a bag _____ was thrown in the trash can.
> · The policeman chased the person _____ robbed the bank.

① who – who ② who – that
③ which – which ④ that – who
⑤ that – which

3 다음 문장에서 어법상 어색한 부분을 찾아 쓰고 바르게 고쳐 쓰시오.

> That map is that I found in the treasure chest.

_____ → _____

4 다음 중 어법상 바른 것은?

① This is the apartment who Jerry lives.
② It was Jenna that called to ask me a question last night.
③ We stayed at a hotel what was close to the ocean.
④ Nate is an artist whose paints pictures.
⑤ Look at the girl and the dog which are running in the field.

5 다음 빈칸에 공통으로 들어갈 알맞은 것은?

> · Erica ate the pasta _____ the chef specially cooked.
> · I know _____ the weather will be nice tomorrow.
> · There was a man _____ was wearing a yellow raincoat.

① which ② who ③ whom
④ whose ⑤ that

6 다음 중 밑줄 친 that의 쓰임이 나머지 넷과 다른 것은?

① The necklace that Mary wore was beautiful.
② The people that I met at the art class were interesting.
③ The book that you saw on the Internet was sold out.
④ Brad is the mechanic that fixed my car.
⑤ Alice is the student that the teacher called.

7 다음 두 문장을 한 문장으로 바르게 연결한 것을 모두 고르시오.

> Danny is the musician. He is playing the drums.

① Danny is the musician who is playing the drums.
② Danny is the musician who playing the drums.
③ Danny is the musician whom is playing the drums.
④ Danny is the musician playing the drums.
⑤ Danny the musician is playing the drums.

8 주어진 문장의 밑줄 친 that과 쓰임이 같은 것은?

> The poem that you wrote was beautiful.

① Please open that door for me.
② I heard that Max is moving to Chicago next year.
③ Buy the watch that has the leather strap.
④ Jared saw that Owen was crossing the street.
⑤ Martin bought that at the farmer's market.

9 다음 중 어느 빈칸에도 들어갈 수 없는 것은?

> · Sarah showed us the picture _____ she took on her vacation.
> · Molly is the girl _____ hair is red.
> · Do you know the person _____ made him so angry?

① which   ② that   ③ what
④ whose   ⑤ who

10 다음 빈칸에 that이 들어갈 수 없는 것은?

① The Earth is the only planet in our solar system _____ has life.
② I found a lost puppy _____ has brown and white fur.
③ The man _____ is standing over there is my uncle.
④ Jake saw the car _____ color was green.
⑤ Will you show me everything _____ you bought at the store?

11 다음 대화의 빈칸에 들어갈 알맞은 것은?

> A: Do you know a place _____ we can have a picnic?
> B: Yes. There is a park near my house.

① where   ② when   ③ how
④ why   ⑤ what

12 주어진 문장의 밑줄 친 who와 쓰임이 같은 것은?

> Josh is the student who won the essay contest.

① Who turned on the air conditioner with the window open?
② We need to decide who the president of our class will be.
③ A mayor is the person who represents the town.
④ Do you remember who you met at the bookstore?
⑤ Please tell me who will be my partner for the history project.

13 다음 자동차 평가표를 보고 관계대명사를 이용하여 문장을 완성하시오.

<Car Review: Delta S5>

Reviewer	Review
Dan005	This car has many safety features.
Lee_A	Its seats are very comfortable.

(1) The Delta S5 is a car _____
_____ .

(2) The Delta S5 is a car _____
_____ .

[14-16] 알맞은 관계대명사를 이용하여 다음 두 문장을 한 문장으로 연결하시오.

14

> George made a new friend. She lives next to his house.

→ _____

_____

15

> Kate called her neighbor. His car was parked in front of her house.

→ _____

_____

16

> There are a soldier and an eagle. They are looking down the hill.

→ _____

_____

18 다음 중 어법상 어색한 것을 모두 고르시오.

① Ms. Lee is the woman who volunteer at the shelter regularly.

② There is the person who sang at the park last night.

③ This is the museum in which Salvador Dali's paintings are displayed.

④ The bear ate the fish that it caught in the river.

⑤ We went to the amusement park what was full of children.

19 다음 빈칸에 들어갈 알맞은 것을 모두 고르시오.

> Kate moved _____ that were in her room to the living room.

① the bed　　　　② the boxes
③ the bookshelf　④ the computer
⑤ the desk and chair

17 다음 중 밑줄 친 부분을 생략할 수 있는 것은?

① Basketball is a sport that is very exciting.

② That is the building which was built last year.

③ Mr. Parker is the doctor whom I met yesterday.

④ They are the band members that won the talent show.

⑤ Fleming is the scientist who discovered penicillin.

20 다음 중 밑줄 친 what의 쓰임이 나머지 넷과 다른 것은?

① What I need right now is a hot cup of coffee.

② I'm not sure what his name is.

③ A sandwich is what I made for lunch today.

④ What Paul said was very surprising.

⑤ Lisa told me what she wants for her birthday.

21 다음 빈칸에 공통으로 들어갈 알맞은 말을 쓰시오.

· Neil Armstrong is the first person _____ walked on the moon.
· Something _____ scared the little girl is hiding in that room.
· The boy and the dogs _____ are drawn in the picture look excited.

22 주어진 <조건>에 맞게 다음 두 문장을 한 문장으로 연결하시오.

Boston is the city. I was born in that city in 2002.

<조건>
1. 관계부사를 이용하세요.
2. the city를 활용하세요.

→ _____

23 다음 중 밑줄 친 부분을 생략할 수 있는 것의 개수는?

ⓐ Mr. Williams is a doctor <u>who</u> has a lot of experience.
ⓑ Gino's sells the pizza <u>that</u> I eat every Tuesday.
ⓒ The dancers <u>who</u> are performing on the stage are amazing.
ⓓ The redwood is a giant tree <u>which</u> grows in California.
ⓔ Please pick up the clothes <u>that are</u> lying on the floor.

① 없음   ② 1개   ③ 2개
④ 3개   ⑤ 4개

24 다음 우리말을 알맞게 영작한 것은?

Bill이 굽고 있던 쿠키들은 맛있는 냄새가 났다.

① The cookies that Bill was baking smelled delicious.
② Bill was baking cookies what smelled delicious.
③ Bill that the cookies was baking smelled delicious.
④ Bill that was baking the cookies smelled delicious.
⑤ The cookies that was baking Bill smelled delicious.

25 다음은 Chris의 가족의 오늘 일정이다. <보기>와 같이 관계대명사를 이용하여 문장을 완성하시오.

Member	Schedule
Mom	She mopped the floor at 10 A.M.
Dad	He will cook dinner at 7 o'clock.
Jenny	She is walking the dog now.
Chris	Dad asked him to help him cook dinner.

<보기> Mom is the family member _____

(1) Dad is the family member _____
_____.

(2) Jenny is the family member _____
_____.

(3) Chris is the family member _____
_____.

CHAPTER 17
가정법

연습문제 A 밑줄 친 부분이 어법상 맞으면 O를 쓰고, 틀리면 바르게 고쳐 쓰시오.

1 If I were taller, I <u>can</u> join the basketball team. → _____

2 If it <u>rained</u> tomorrow, we will cancel the field trip. → _____

3 If you <u>soak</u> the bottle in water, the label will peel off easily. → _____

4 If I were rich, I would <u>bought</u> that red car. → _____

5 If he <u>had</u> more time, he would exercise more. → _____

6 If you <u>searched</u> more carefully, you will find your lost earrings. → _____

7 If you <u>keep</u> the food in the fridge, it can last longer. → _____

8 If Laura <u>came</u> back, I will give you a call. → _____

연습문제 B 다음 문장을 가정법 문장으로 바꿔 쓰시오.

1 As I'm not in California, I can't meet you.

= _____

2 As Jack is sleepy, he can't focus in class.

= _____

3 As Mariah doesn't know how to drive, we won't go out to the lake this weekend.

= _____

4 As the chairs are too heavy, Kelly can't move them by herself.

= _____

5 As I don't have enough money, I won't help more people.

= _____

6 As she doesn't remember Kelly's address, she can't give it to you.

= _____

7 As Michael doesn't have a jacket, he will buy a new one.

= _____

8 As the weather is so cold, I won't go outside for a walk.

= _____

연습문제 우리말과 같도록 괄호 안의 말을 활용하여 문장을 완성하시오.

1 만약 내가 속초에 살았더라면, 나는 매일 해변에 갔을 텐데. (live, go)

= If I _____ in Sokcho, I _____ to the beach every day.

2 만약 Sam이 피곤하지 않았더라면, 그는 우리와 함께 축구를 했을 텐데. (be, play)

= If Sam _____ tired, he _____ soccer with us.

3 만약 Jake가 Amy를 보러 가지 않았더라면, 그녀는 그에게 선물을 줄 수 없었을 텐데. (go, give)

= If Jake _____ to see Amy, she _____ him the present.

4 만약 그가 더 열심히 훈련했더라면, 그는 금메달을 딸 수 있었을 텐데. (train, win)

= If he _____ harder, he _____ the gold medal.

5 만약 콘서트가 더 신났더라면, 그녀는 그렇게 일찍 떠나지 않았을 텐데. (be, leave)

= If the concert _____ more exciting, she _____ so soon.

6 만약 내가 숙제를 더 일찍 끝냈더라면, 나는 잘 시간이 더 많았을 텐데. (finish, have)

= If I _____ my homework earlier, I _____ more time to sleep.

7 만약 그 카메라가 비싸지 않았더라면, Jack은 그것을 샀을 텐데. (be, buy)

= If the camera _____ expensive, Jack _____ it.

8 만약 그가 그의 직장을 관뒀더라면, 그는 그 자신의 음식점을 열었을 텐데. (quit, open)

= If he _____ his job, he _____ his own restaurant.

9 만약 그가 돕기 위해 오지 않았더라면, 우리는 이 상자들을 제시간에 다 옮길 수 없었을 텐데. (come, move)

= If he _____ to help, we _____ these boxes on time.

10 만약 내가 시간이 더 있었더라면, 나는 모든 정답을 적었을 텐데. (have, write)

= If I _____ more time, I _____ down all the answers.

11 만약 Fred가 오늘 일찍 일어났더라면, 그는 버스를 놓치지 않았을 텐데. (wake, miss)

=If Fred _____ up early today, he _____ the bus.

12 만약 Jenny가 그렇게 긴장하지 않았더라면, 그녀는 그에게 이야기를 했을 텐데. (be, talk)

= If Jenny _____ so nervous, she _____ to him.

13 만약 Dan이 차를 가지고 있었더라면, 그는 그의 개를 그와 함께 데리고 갔을 텐데. (have, take)

= If Dan _____ a car, he _____ his dog with him.

14 만약 내가 그의 생일인 것을 알았더라면, 나는 그에게 전화했을 텐데. (know, call)

= If I _____ it was his birthday, I _____ him.

연습문제 A 괄호 안에서 알맞은 것을 고르시오.

1 I wish this shirt (is / were) on sale.

2 I wish I (have not / had not) said those words to Sam.

3 I wish he (would / will) pay attention to what I say.

4 I wish this actress (would / will) star in more movies.

5 I wish I (know / knew) the answer to everything.

6 I wish the people upstairs (would / will) stop making loud noises at night.

7 I wish I (could / can) make money by doing what I like.

8 I wish Sam (would not / will not) leave Korea so soon.

연습문제 B 다음 문장을 I wish를 사용한 가정법 문장으로 바꿔 쓰시오.

1 I'm sorry that I can't read more books.

→ _____

2 I'm sorry that I'm not as strong as superman.

→ _____

3 I'm sorry that he won't throw out some of his clothes.

→ _____

4 I'm sorry that I can't return this TV.

→ _____

5 I'm sorry that our team won't win the championship.

→ _____

6 I'm sorry that I don't have much food to eat.

→ _____

7 I'm sorry that your parents can't come to see you perform.

→ _____

8 I'm sorry that I'm not good at playing the violin.

→ _____

9 I'm sorry that my mother won't let me make my own decisions.

→ _____

10 I'm sorry that we don't have another day to finish this project.

→ _____

기출로 작중 POINT 2-2 | I wish + 가정법 과거완료

정답 p.98

연습문제 | 우리말과 같도록 괄호 안의 말을 활용하여 I wish를 사용한 가정법 문장을 완성하시오.

1 내가 첫 버스를 타기 위해 더 일찍 집을 떠났더라면 좋았을 텐데. (leave)

= _____ home earlier to catch the first bus.

2 내가 이 문제를 어떻게 풀지 알았더라면 좋았을 텐데. (know)

= _____ how to solve this question.

3 할아버지가 우리와 함께 여기에 계셔서 나의 여동생이 결혼하는 것을 보셨더라면 좋았을 텐데. (be)

= _____ here with us to see my sister get married.

4 내가 돈을 낭비하지 않고 더 많은 돈을 모았더라면 좋았을 텐데. (save)

= _____ more money without wasting it.

5 내가 그 어리석은 실수를 하는 것을 그가 보지 않았더라면 좋았을 텐데. (see)

= _____ me make that foolish mistake.

6 내가 어렸을 때 공부를 더 열심히 했더라면 좋았을 텐데. (study)

= _____ harder when I was younger.

기출로 작중 POINT 3 | as if + 가정법 과거/과거완료

정답 p.98

연습문제 | 다음 문장을 as if를 사용한 가정법 문장으로 바꿔 쓰시오.

1 In fact, Jack isn't a chef.

→ Jack talks _____.

2 In fact, James didn't see the suspect.

→ James acts _____.

3 In fact, Sarah didn't study Korean for a long time.

→ Sarah sounds _____.

4 In fact, Peter wasn't sick last night.

→ Peter looks _____.

5 In fact, the house isn't repaired.

→ The house looks _____.

6 In fact, he doesn't sing well.

→ He acts _____.

중간·기말고사 실전 문제

1 다음 중 밑줄 친 부분이 어법상 어색한 것은?

> If Greg <u>had</u> some money, he <u>will lend</u> it
> ①   ②   ③
> to me. However, he doesn't <u>have</u> <u>any</u>
>   ④   ⑤
> money now.

2 우리말과 같도록 괄호 안의 말을 활용하여 빈칸에 쓰시오.

> 만약 이 컴퓨터가 세일 중이라면, 나는 나의 남동생을 위해 그것을 살 것이다. (be)

= If this computer _____ on sale, I would buy it for my brother.

[3-4] 다음 빈칸에 들어갈 알맞은 것을 고르시오.

3

> If I _____ a billionaire, I would buy a huge house with a swimming pool.

① be   ② am   ③ were
④ will be   ⑤ being

4

> If it were sunny, we _____ to the beach together. But it's raining right now.

① go   ② went   ③ can go
④ could go   ⑤ have gone

5 다음 중 밑줄 친 부분이 어법상 어색한 것은?

① If you study hard, you <u>will pass</u> the English test tomorrow.
② If the mountain weren't so high, I <u>will climb</u> it easily.
③ If Ken had called me, I <u>would have invited</u> him to dinner.
④ If my dad worked less, he <u>could spend</u> more time with us.
⑤ If I had woken up earlier, I <u>could have gone</u> to the gym before school.

6 다음 대화의 빈칸에 공통으로 들어갈 알맞은 것은?

> *A*: Where _____ you live if you could choose a country?
> *B*: I _____ live in France because I love French food.

① will   ② would   ③ had
④ do   ⑤ did

7 다음 글에서 어법상 어색한 부분을 찾아 쓰고 바르게 고쳐 쓰시오.

> If I had a puppy, I will name it Coco. However, I don't have one.

_____ → _____

8 다음 문장을 직설법 문장으로 바르게 바꾼 것은?

> If the museum were open, we could visit it in the afternoon.

① As the museum isn't open, we can't visit it in the afternoon.
② As the museum isn't open, we couldn't visit it in the afternoon.
③ As the museum wasn't open, I can't visit it in the afternoon.
④ As the museum is open, I can visit it in the afternoon.
⑤ As the museum is open, I couldn't visit it in the afternoon.

[9-10] 다음 문장을 가정법 문장으로 바꿔 쓰시오.

9

> As dolphins are mammals, they feed milk to their babies.

→ If dolphins _____
_____.

10

> Patricia didn't wash the dishes, so she couldn't use the dishes for dinner.

→ If Patricia _____
_____.

11 다음 중 어법상 <u>어색한</u> 것은?

① I wish Sally had invited Josh to her party.
② If I have looked under the couch, I would have found my wallet.
③ Miranda's bicycle looked as if it had not been ridden at all.
④ If the dog weren't so big, I would pet it.
⑤ My brother acts as if he were a better student than me.

12 다음 글의 빈칸에 들어갈 알맞은 것은?

> I'm waiting for my father to take me to the mall. I wish I _____ my driver's license so that I could drive there myself.

① have   ② had
③ am having   ④ have had
⑤ had been having

13 다음 대화의 빈칸에 들어갈 말이 순서대로 짝지어진 것은?

> A: My science project is due tomorrow, but I don't have enough time to finish it.
> B: If I _____ in your situation, I _____ the teacher to give you more time.

① am - ask
② were - would ask
③ were - would have asked
④ had been - would ask
⑤ had been - would have asked

14 우리말과 같도록 괄호 안의 말을 활용하여 빈칸에 쓰시오.

> 내가 없는 동안 배관공이 싱크대를 고쳤더라면 좋았을 텐데. (fix)

= I wish the plumber _____ _____ the sink while I was gone.

15 다음 두 문장의 의미가 같도록 빈칸에 알맞은 말을 쓰시오.

> I'm sorry that I don't know Lisa's phone number.
> = I wish I _____ Lisa's phone number.

16 다음 빈칸에 들어갈 말이 순서대로 짝지어진 것은?

> · I gave my dog a cookie this morning.
>   I wish I _____ my dog the cookie then.
> · I can't speak English better than Miso.
>   I wish I _____ English better than Miso now.

① don't give - can speak
② didn't give - could speak
③ didn't give - could have spoken
④ had not given - could speak
⑤ had not given - could have spoken

17 다음 두 문장의 의미가 같도록 문장을 완성하시오.

> I'm sorry that James left Korea last year.
> = I wish _____.

[18-19] 다음 우리말을 알맞게 영작한 것을 고르시오.

18

> 만약 지진이 일어나지 않았더라면, 그 빌딩은 무너지지 않았을 텐데.

① If the earthquake didn't happen, the building will collapse.
② If the earthquake happened, the building won't collapse.
③ If the earthquake had happened, the building wouldn't collapse.
④ If the earthquake had not happened, the building would have collapsed.
⑤ If the earthquake had not happened, the building wouldn't have collapsed.

19

> Maria가 나에게 전화하기로 한 그녀의 약속을 지켰더라면 좋았을 텐데.

① I wish Maria will keep her promise to call me.
② I wish Maria don't keep her promise to call me.
③ I wish Maria had kept her promise to call me.
④ I wish Maria have kept her promise to call me.
⑤ I wish Maria had not kept her promise to call me.

20 다음 글의 빈칸에 들어갈 알맞은 것은?

I couldn't watch the movie at the theater because it was too scary. I wish I _____ much braver.

① am   ② were   ③ will be
④ had been   ⑤ would be

21 다음 빈칸에 공통으로 들어갈 알맞은 것은?

· Brian acts as if he _____ very popular.
· I wish I _____ an astronaut now.

① be   ② is
③ were   ④ has been
⑤ had been

22 다음 중 어법상 바른 것을 모두 고르시오.

① If the lake were frozen, we could gone ice skating.
② If I were a president, I would make more holidays.
③ If Mason had entered the marathon, he would have won.
④ If the water had been warmer, I could swim in the ocean.
⑤ If Tommy had taken a taxi, he wouldn't be late then.

23 다음 두 문장의 의미가 같도록 빈칸에 알맞은 말을 쓰시오.

In fact, this necklace isn't expensive.
= This necklace looks as if _____ _____ _____.

24 다음 대화의 빈칸에 들어갈 말이 순서대로 짝지어진 것은?

A: Why is Nathan mad at you?
B: I borrowed his laptop without asking him. I wish I _____ his permission first.
A: Don't worry. If you apologize, he _____ you.

① had gotten – won't forgive
② got – will forgive
③ had gotten – will forgive
④ got – won't forgive
⑤ had gotten – would forgive

25 다음 밑줄 친 부분을 바르게 고치지 못한 것은?

① I wish I can drink some water now.
(→ could have drunk)
② It looks as if a million people come to the park today. (→ came)
③ I wish I am a more talented singer.
(→ were)
④ I wish we could meet the mayor yesterday. (→ could have met)
⑤ Sam acts as if he didn't study for the test, yesterday. (→ had not studied)

CHAPTER 18
일치·화법·도치

기출로적중 POINT 1-1 시제 일치

정답 p.100

연습문제 | 괄호 안에서 알맞은 것을 모두 고르시오.

1 I believe that Kate (is / will be) a doctor.

2 We all know that Jenny (is / was) the best athlete in our school.

3 I thought that Patrick (will / would) fail the exam.

4 We want to share how people (stay / stayed) calm in stressful situations.

5 I heard that Alaska (becomes / became) the 49th US state in 1866.

6 Helen thought that her sister (may not / might not) be at home then.

7 Mike promised that he (will / would) take good care of his hamster.

8 Mom told me that she (can / could) teach me her secret recipe.

9 She wondered why no one (come / came) to school today.

10 Everyone believed that our team (will / would) win the game.

기출로적중 POINT 1-2 시제 일치의 예외

정답 p.100

연습문제 | 다음 문장의 밑줄 친 부분을 과거시제로 바꿔 완전한 문장을 쓰시오.

1 I hear that the early bird catches the worm.

→ _____

2 Mr. Jones tells us that the Olympic gold medals are not made entirely out of gold.

→ _____

3 Ben doesn't know that there are eight planets in our solar system.

→ _____

4 The taxi driver tells us that there are many tourist attractions in this town.

→ _____

5 We remember that the Korean War started in 1950.

→ _____

6 I know that 0°C is equal to 32°F.

→ _____

7 Mr. Cooper teaches us that an ant lives up to two or three years.

→ _____

연습문제 | 다음 직접 화법은 간접 화법으로, 간접 화법은 직접 화법으로 바꿀 때 빈칸에 알맞은 말을 써서 문장을 완성하시오.

1 She said, "I want to order a cup of coffee."
→ She _____ .

2 Tom told me that he wanted me to help him clean the classroom.
→ Tom _____

3 The doctor said, "You should come to the hospital tomorrow."
→ The doctor _____

4 John said, "I'm going to participate in the charity event next week."
→ John _____ .

5 He told me that he had gone to the bank the day before.
→ He _____

6 Mr. Taylor told me that he wanted me to join the soccer team.
→ Mr. Taylor _____

7 Olivia told me that she would go to the new café with me.
→ Olivia _____

8 Ms. Jones said, "I can visit your house tomorrow."
→ Ms. Jones _____

9 Jonathan said, "I need to borrow your dictionary now."
→ Jonathan _____ .

10 Sam told me that he had enjoyed watching the magic show.
→ Sam _____

11 Mom said, "It's too late for you to go out alone."
→ Mom _____ .

12 Steve said that he could eat this turkey all by himself.
→ Steve _____

13 Hana told me that she had fought with Jihye the previous week.
→ Hana _____

14 The mailman said that he would bring me the letters the next day.
→ The mailman _____

연습문제 A 다음 문장을 간접 화법으로 바꿀 때 빈칸에 알맞은 말을 써서 문장을 완성하시오.

1 Sally said to me, "Where can I go to fix my phone?"

→ Sally _____ .

2 She said, "What will you get Ben for his 20th birthday?"

→ She _____ .

3 John said, "Who ate all the cookies in the cookie jar?"

→ John _____ .

4 Sarah said, "How did you get the huge bump on your forehead?"

→ Sarah _____ .

5 He said to me, "Where can I get more information about the summer camp?"

→ He _____ .

6 Rachel said to me, "How quickly can you make the presentation slides?"

→ Rachel _____ .

7 The teacher said to us, "Where do you want to go for the field trip?"

→ The teacher _____ .

연습문제 B 다음 직접 화법을 간접 화법으로 바꾼 문장에서 어법상 어색한 부분을 찾아 바르게 고쳐 완전한 문장을 쓰시오.

1 He said to me, "When will you do the laundry?"

→ He asked me when I will do the laundry.

→ _____

2 Ben said to me, "Who do you admire the most?"

→ Ben asked me who I admire the most.

→ _____

3 Kevin said to me, "What do you think is the smallest thing in the world?"

→ Kevin asked me what I think was the smallest thing in the world.

→ _____

4 The police said to me, "Who was here yesterday?"

→ The police asked me who was there the previous day.

→ _____

화법 전환: 의문사가 없는 의문문

정답 p.100

연습문제 다음 문장을 간접 화법으로 바꿀 때 빈칸에 알맞은 말을 써서 문장을 완성하시오.

1 The police officer said to me, "Did you see the accident?"
→ The police officer _____.

2 Jenny said to me, "Do you know what the largest living thing on Earth is?"
→ Jenny _____.

3 Lucas said to me, "Have you been to Japan?"
→ Lucas _____.

4 Peter said to me, "Will this money be enough to buy the dress?"
→ Peter _____.

5 Sarah said to me, "Can you pick me up at the airport tomorrow?"
→ Sarah _____.

6 Tom said to me, "Do you know that there is a place called Pig Beach?"
→ Tom _____.

7 The waiter said to me, "Will you have some more water?"
→ The waiter _____.

8 She said to me, "Are you familiar with the rules of hockey?"
→ She _____.

도치

정답 p.100

연습문제 괄호 안에서 알맞은 것을 고르시오.

1 There (some milk is / is some milk) left in the bottle.

2 Over the tree (flew the bird / the bird flew).

3 Into the water (jumped the otter / the otter jumped).

4 Here (the book is / is the book) you asked for.

5 In the field (stood the cow / the cow stood).

6 Hide! Here (come they / they come).

7 There (are three apples / three apples are) on the table.

8 Under the table (hid the child / the child hid).

기출로 작중 해커스 중학영문법 2학년 워크북

중간·기말고사 실전 문제

[1-3] 다음 빈칸에 들어갈 알맞은 것을 고르시오.

1

> David felt that the watch _____ too expensive.

① be   ② is   ③ was
④ been   ⑤ is being

2

> Teacher taught us that dolphins _____ for almost 40 years.

① live   ② lived   ③ were living
④ have lived   ⑤ would live

3

> Everyone knows that Hangeul _____ invented by King Sejong in 1443.

① be   ② is   ③ was
④ has been   ⑤ will be

4 다음 중 밑줄 친 부분이 어법상 어색한 것은?

① The hikers thought that it <u>would be</u> hard to climb the mountain.
② We learned that dinosaurs <u>existed</u> on earth millions of years ago.
③ Jamie told me that kangaroos never <u>stop growing</u>.
④ Kate said that she <u>wants</u> to travel around the world.
⑤ Luke wondered why Mary <u>couldn't come</u> to his birthday party.

5 다음 문장을 간접 화법으로 바꿀 때 빈칸에 들어갈 알맞은 것은?

> Michael said to me, "I need to borrow your textbook for math class."
> → Michael _____ for math class.

① said me that I needed to borrow your textbook
② said me that he needed to borrow my textbook
③ told me that I need to borrow my textbook
④ told me that he needed to borrow my textbook
⑤ told me that he needed to borrow your textbook

6 다음 밑줄 친 ⓐ~ⓔ 중 어법상 어색한 것을 찾아 기호를 쓰고 바르게 고쳐 쓰시오.

> Josh told Bora <u>that</u> he <u>will</u> <u>help</u> her
>   ⓐ   ⓑ   ⓒ
> <u>wash</u> the dishes <u>after</u> dinner.
> ⓓ   ⓔ

_____ → _____

7 다음 문장을 과거시제로 바꿀 때 빈칸에 알맞은 말을 쓰시오.

> We hope that we will have time to take pictures together.
> → We hoped that we _____ _____ time to take pictures together.

8 다음 중 직접 화법을 간접 화법으로 잘못 바꾼 것은?

① My father said, "I bought you a new skateboard."
→ My father said that he bought me a new skateboard.

② The police officer said, "You cannot park your car here."
→ The police officer said that I could not park my car there.

③ Leo said, "Your paintings are amazing."
→ Leo said that my paintings were amazing.

④ The security guard said to us, "The art museum is closed now."
→ The security guard told us that the art museum was closed then.

⑤ The neighbor said to me, "I will look after your dog tomorrow."
→ The neighbor told me that he will look after my dog the following day.

9 다음 대화의 빈칸에 들어갈 말이 순서대로 짝지어 진 것은?

A: Who is the class president in John's class?
B: I heard that Beth _____ yesterday.
A: Really? Mark must be upset, then.
B: Right. He told me that he _____ disappointed if he wasn't chosen.

① is elected – will be
② is elected – would be
③ was elected – will be
④ was elected – would be
⑤ would be elected – will be

10 다음 문장을 간접 화법으로 바꿀 때 밑줄 친 부분이 어법상 어색한 것은?

Danny said, "I'm cooking now."
→ Danny said that he is cooking then.
　　　　①　②　③④　　　　⑤

11 다음 중 밑줄 친 부분이 어법상 어색한 것은?

Yesterday, my school held a science fair and ①invited all of the students' parents to attend. Mom was working that day, but Dad ②came. My classmate and I ③did a project on volcanoes. I hoped that we ④will win first prize, but we didn't. However, my father said that my project ⑤was amazing, so I felt very proud.

12 다음 문장을 간접 화법으로 바르게 바꾼 것은?

The teacher said, "I will collect your essays now."

① The teacher said that she will collect your essays now.
② The teacher told that she will collect our essays then.
③ The teacher said that she would collect our essays now.
④ The teacher told that she would collect your essays then.
⑤ The teacher said that she would collect our essays then.

[13-14] 다음 문장을 간접 화법으로 바꿀 때 빈칸에 들어갈 알맞은 것을 고르시오.

13

Hannah said to me, "When can we wear a costume?"
→ Hannah asked me _____ a costume.

① if we can wear   ② if we could wear
③ when we wear   ④ when we can wear
⑤ when we could wear

14

Brandon said, "Can I borrow your phone?"
→ Brandon asked _____ my phone.

① if he can borrow
② when he can borrow
③ when he could borrow
④ whether he can borrow
⑤ whether he could borrow

15 다음 빈칸에 들어갈 말이 순서대로 짝지어진 것은?

· Steven knew that his parents _____ angry about his math grade.
· Carla told me that she _____ swimming lessons every week.

① are – takes
② are – was taking
③ were – takes
④ were – took
⑤ were – was taking

16 다음 직접 화법을 간접 화법으로 바꾼 문장에서 어법상 어색한 부분을 찾아 쓰고 바르게 고쳐 쓰시오.

The chef said, "How do you like your eggs?"
→ The chef asked how I like my eggs.

_____ → _____

17 다음 문장을 간접 화법으로 바꿀 때 빈칸에 알맞은 말을 쓰시오.

Owen said, "My little sister is sick today."
→ Owen said that _____ little sister _____ sick _____ .

18 우리말과 같도록 괄호 안의 말을 활용하여 문장을 완성하시오.

Jason은 그의 여동생이 지난주에 그의 컴퓨터를 고장 냈다는 것을 알게 됐다. (break)

= Jason learned that his sister _____ _____ last week.

19 다음 문장을 간접 화법으로 바르게 바꾼 것은?

The waiter said to me, "Are you ready to order?"

① The waiter asks me if I was ready to order.
② The waiter asked me if you are ready to order.
③ The waiter asked me if I was ready to order.
④ The waiter told me if I was ready to order.
⑤ The waiter told me if you were ready to order.

20 다음 빈칸에 들어갈 알맞은 것은?

> Jane asked Jeff _____ he could do her a favor.

① if ② of ③ for
④ that ⑤ which

21 다음 중 어법상 <u>어색한</u> 것은?

① At the bus station waited the passengers.
② There are many students in the library.
③ Across the street is the National Bank.
④ We should find a box. Here one is.
⑤ I can't see my friends. There they are!

22 다음 문자 메시지의 밑줄 친 (A), (B)를 간접 화법으로 바꿀 때 빈칸에 알맞은 말을 써서 문장을 완성하시오.

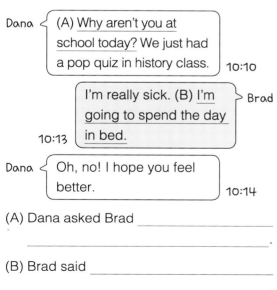

Dana (A) Why aren't you at school today? We just had a pop quiz in history class. 10:10

I'm really sick. (B) I'm going to spend the day in bed. Brad
10:13

Dana Oh, no! I hope you feel better. 10:14

(A) Dana asked Brad _____

_____ .

(B) Brad said _____

_____ .

23 다음 문장을 직접 화법으로 바꿔 쓰시오.

> Mr. Lee said that he would buy a new running machine that day.
>
> → _____
>
> _____

24 다음 문장을 간접 화법으로 바꿔 쓰시오.

> Thomas said to Jenny, "Do you have time to play a board game?"
>
> → _____
>
> _____

25 다음 중 직접 화법을 간접 화법으로 <u>잘못</u> 바꾼 것의 개수는?

> ⓐ The receptionist said, "Do you have an appointment?"
> → The receptionist asked if I had an appointment.
> ⓑ Paul said, "Which book is the most interesting?"
> → Paul asked is which book the most interesting.
> ⓒ Mark said to us, "Was the dinner I cooked last night delicious?"
> → Mark asked us if the dinner he had cooked the previous night had been delicious.
> ⓓ I said to the man, "Can you hold the door for me?"
> → I asked the man if I could hold the door for him.

① 없음 ② 1개 ③ 2개
④ 3개 ⑤ 4개

MEMO

나에게 맞는 교재 선택!

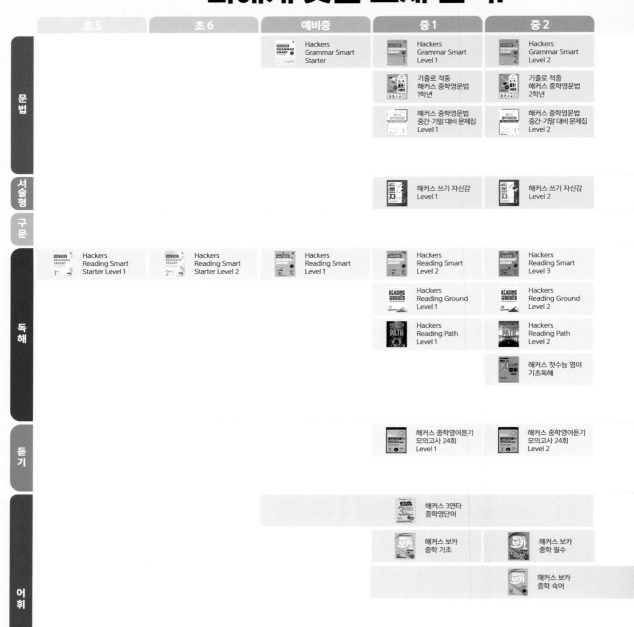

	초5	초6	예비중	중1	중2
문법			Hackers Grammar Smart Starter	Hackers Grammar Smart Level 1	Hackers Grammar Smart Level 2
				기출로 적중 해커스 중학영문법 1학년	기출로 적중 해커스 중학영문법 2학년
				해커스 중학영문법 중간·기말 대비 문제집 Level 1	해커스 중학영문법 중간·기말 대비 문제집 Level 2
서술형 구문				해커스 쓰기 자신감 Level 1	해커스 쓰기 자신감 Level 2
독해	Hackers Reading Smart Starter Level 1	Hackers Reading Smart Starter Level 2	Hackers Reading Smart Level 1	Hackers Reading Smart Level 2	Hackers Reading Smart Level 3
				Hackers Reading Ground Level 1	Hackers Reading Ground Level 2
				Hackers Reading Path Level 1	Hackers Reading Path Level 2
					해커스 첫수능 영어 기초독해
듣기				해커스 중학영어듣기 모의고사 24회 Level 1	해커스 중학영어듣기 모의고사 24회 Level 2
어휘			해커스 3연타 중학영단어		
				해커스 보카 중학 기초	해커스 보카 중학 필수
					해커스 보카 중학 숙어

	READING	LISTENING	VOCA
토플	HACKERS APEX READING for the TOEFL iBT — Basic/Intermediate/Advanced/Expert	HACKERS APEX LISTENING for the TOEFL iBT — Basic/Intermediate/Advanced/Expert	HACKERS APEX VOCA for the TOEFL iBT — HACKERS VOCABULARY

중3	예비고	고1	고2	고3
Hackers Grammar Smart Level 3				
기출로 적중 해커스 중학영문법 3학년	기출로 적중 해커스 고등영문법			
해커스 중학영문법 중간·기말 대비 문제집 Level 3	해커스 어법 제대로			
		해커스 수능 어법 불변의 패턴 필수편	해커스 수능 어법 불변의 패턴 실력편	
해커스 쓰기 자신감 Level 3				
	해커스 완전숙련 구문독해 입문	해커스 완전숙련 구문독해 기본	해커스 완전숙련 구문독해 심화	
Hackers Reading Smart Level 4	해커스 독해 제대로 기본독해	해커스 독해 제대로 구문독해		
Hackers Reading Ground Level 3				
Hackers Reading Path Level 3	Hackers Reading Path Level 4			
해커스 첫수능 영어 유형독해		해커스 수능 독해 불변의 패턴 유형편		해커스 수능 독해 불변의 패턴 실전편
	해커스 수능영어독해 미니 모의고사 12+2회 기본	해커스 수능영어독해 미니 모의고사 12+2회 필수		해커스 수능영어독해 미니 모의고사 12+2회 완성 (* 출간 예정)
해커스 중학영어듣기 모의고사 24회 Level 3		해커스 수능영어듣기 모의고사 20+4회 기본	해커스 수능영어듣기 모의고사 20+4회 실전	
		해커스 수능영어듣기 모의고사 30+5회 기본	해커스 수능영어듣기 모의고사 30+5회 실전	
	해커스 보카 고등 기본			
해커스 보카 중학 고난도		해커스 보카 수능 필수 2000+		
			해커스 보카 수능 완성 1800+	
			해커스 보카 수능 심화	
	해커스 보카 수능 숙어			
	해커스 보카 어원편			

해커스북(HackersBook.com)에서
교재에 대한 자세한 설명과 다양한 학습 자료를 확인하세요!

최신 개정 교과서 완벽 반영

기출로적중

해커스
중학영문법

2학년

워크북

최신 개정 교과서 완벽 반영

기출로 적중
해커스
중학영문법

2학년

해설집

이 책을 검토해주신 선생님들

강상훈 경기 평촌비상에듀학원 / **김가영** 서울 송정중학교 / **김원덕** 경기 올림피아드학원 / **박유정** 서울 반포중학교 / **박윤정** 경기 이지베스트학원

박은혜 서울 송파중학교 / **박정은** 서울 대청중학교 / **양세희** 서울 양세희수능영어학원 / **이계윤** 서울 씨앤씨학원 / **이유빈** 서울 잉글리쉬&매쓰매니저학원

이혜원 서울 대청중학교 / **정혜은** 서울 용곡중학교 / **최다빈** 서울 최강영어 / **최승복** 경기 오른어학원 / **최지영** 경기 다른영어학원

CHAPTER 1
문장의 형식
p.18

POINT 1-1 1형식과 2형식

연습문제
1	1형식	**2**	2형식	**3**	1형식	**4**	2형식
5	2형식	**6**	1형식	**7**	1형식	**8**	2형식
9	2형식	**10**	1형식	**11**	2형식	**12**	1형식
13	1형식						

POINT 1-2 2형식: 감각동사

연습문제
1	strong	**2**	salty	**3**	looks like
4	fresh	**5**	felt like	**6**	amazing
7	tastes like	**8**	nervous	**9**	smell like
10	friendly	**11**	feels		

기출 적중문제

정답 The story sounds like a lie.
해설 감각동사 뒤에 명사가 올 때는 「감각동사 + like + 명사」의 형태로 쓴다.

POINT 2 3형식과 4형식

연습문제 A
1 loves modern art
2 built the birds a house
3 asked me my opinion
4 finished the science project
5 sent Rachel some Korean snacks
6 read her grandmother the newspaper

연습문제 B
1 I lent my cell phone to her.
2 Josh gave me a box of cookies.
3 We made a birthday card for Sandra.
4 Can you bring me an umbrella?
5 Jinsu sent a package to his best friend.
6 I will get a bottle of water for you.
7 The journalist asked some questions of the president.

기출 적중문제

정답 ②
해설 · 「sell + 직접 목적어 + to + 간접 목적어」
· 「buy + 직접 목적어 + for + 간접 목적어」

POINT 3-1 5형식: 명사나 형용사를 목적격 보어로 쓰는 동사

연습문제
1	warm	**2**	me the captain
3	easy	**4**	me a liar
5	the garden clean	**6**	her a celebrity
7	interesting		

기출 적중문제

정답 People call this food a kebab.
해설 5형식: 「주어 + 동사 + 목적어 + 목적격 보어」

POINT 3-2 5형식: to부정사를 목적격 보어로 쓰는 동사

연습문제
1 asked Adam to have
2 expected him to come
3 want me to apologize
4 ordered them to open
5 allowed me to play
6 told her to join
7 advised Amy to brush

기출 적중문제

정답 ④
해설 study → to study

POINT 3-3 5형식: 사역동사

연습문제
1	watch	**2**	paint
3	stop	**4**	to take
5	find, to find	**6**	explain
7	put, to put	**8**	sleep

정답 ③, ⑤

해설 목적격 보어 자리에 동사원형(sweep)이 왔으므로 목적격 보어 자리에 to부정사가 오는 expected와 준사역동사 got 은 쓸 수 없다.

POINT 3-4 5형식: 지각동사

 연습 문제

1 heard the dog bark
2 watched a man dancing
3 felt the ground shaking
4 smell something burning
5 listened to her whisper
6 saw his son drawing
7 watched a snake climb

정답 The teacher heard someone laugh[laughing] out loud in the classroom.

해설 「hear + 목적어 + 동사원형/V-ing형」

서술형 대비 문제

Ⓐ
1 short
2 O
3 open
4 sounds
5 fresh
6 looks like
7 O
8 O
9 quiet

Ⓑ
1 made toys for the baby
2 lend me your dictionary
3 read a fairy tale to her son
4 sold us fresh watermelons
5 get a lunch box for Kevin
6 taught them an important lesson
7 asked some questions of her teacher
8 tell her the real reason

Ⓒ
1 eat some fruit
2 to open the window
3 skip breakfast
4 to pick up the laundry

Ⓓ
1 Claire to finish her homework
2 Yumi playing[play] the violin
3 John (to) find his smartphone
4 Alex sending[send] a text message
5 me sing a song in front of my classmates
6 his friends taking[take] a walk

중간·기말고사 실전 문제

1 ③   2 ②, ④ 3 ①   4 ⑤   5 ④
6 made the leaves fall   7 ②, ⑤
8 Jiwoo gives the cats some food   9 ④
10 ③   11 we call him Mozart   12 ⑤
13 ③   14 ④   15 ④   16 ④   17 ③
18 ⑤   19 ③   20 ④   21 ④   22 Mark
throw out some garbage   23 Ruby getting[get]
on the bus   24 ⑤   25 ③   26 ②
27 (1) to water the plants (2) walk the dog (3) (to)
move a closet   28 (1) ⓑ → tasted delicious
(2) ⓔ → made her feel happy

1   ③ sourly → sour

2   감각동사의 주격 보어 자리에는 형용사만 오므로 부사 nicely와 sadly는 쓸 수 없다.

3   ·「teach + 직접 목적어 + to + 간접 목적어」
     ·「ask + 직접 목적어 + of + 간접 목적어」

4   ⑤ felt like → felt

5   「expect + 목적어 + to부정사」

6   「make + 목적어 + 동사원형」

7   ① make → to make
     ③ studying → to study
     ④ to tell → tell

8   4형식: 「주어 + 동사 + 간접 목적어(~에게) + 직접 목적어(~을)」

9   목적격 보어 자리에 V-ing형(making)이 왔으므로 목적격 보어 자리에 동사원형이 오는 사역동사 made는 쓸 수 없다.

10   목적격 보어 자리에 동사원형(do)이 왔으므로 목적격 보어 자리에 to부정사가 오는 준사역동사 get은 쓸 수 없다.

11   5형식: 「주어 + 동사 + 목적어 + 목적격 보어」

12   「allow + 목적어 + to부정사」

13   「let + 목적어 + 동사원형」

14   ④ busily → busy

15   주어진 문장과 ④: 5형식
     ①: 4형식   ②: 2형식   ③: 3형식   ⑤: 1형식

16   목적격 보어 자리에 to부정사(to come)가 왔으므로 목적격 보어 자리에 동사원형이 오는 사역동사 had는 쓸 수 없다.

17   ③ make → to make

18   ·「allow + 목적어 + to부정사」
     ·「hear + 목적어 + 동사원형/V-ing형」

19   ·「show + 직접 목적어 + to + 간접 목적어」
     ·「advise + 목적어 + to부정사」

20 ⓐ to smile → smile[smiling]
ⓒ cried → cry[crying]
ⓔ to touch → touch[touching]

21 ④의 kept는 목적어를 필요로 하는 3형식 동사이고, ①②③⑤의 kept는 목적어와 목적격 보어를 필요로 하는 5형식 동사이다.

22 「make + 목적어 + 동사원형」

23 「see + 목적어 + 동사원형/V-ing형」

24 · 목적어와 목적격 보어를 필요로 하는 5형식 사역동사 made
· 간접 목적어와 직접 목적어를 필요로 하는 4형식 수여동사 made
· 목적어를 필요로 하는 3형식 동사 made

25 ① for → to
② the truth me → me the truth
④ for breakfast → breakfast
⑤ for → of

26 ⓑⓔ: 5형식
ⓐ: 1형식   ⓒ: 4형식   ⓓ: 3형식   ⓕ: 2형식

27 (1) 「ask + 목적어 + to부정사」
(2) 「have + 목적어 + 동사원형」
(3) 「help + 목적어 + 동사원형/to부정사」

28 (1) 감각동사의 주격 보어 자리에는 형용사(delicious)만 온다.
(2) 사역동사의 목적격 보어 자리에는 동사원형(feel)이 온다.

CHAPTER 2
다양한 문장의 종류
p.34

POINT 1 감탄문

 연습문제 A

1 What	**2** How	**3** How
4 What	**5** How	**6** What
7 How	**8** What	**9** What
10 How		

 연습문제 B

1 How lovely (your kittens are)!
2 How comfortable (the chair is)!
3 What a low voice (Jinho has)!
4 What delicious strawberries (they are)!
5 How lucky (I was)!
6 What a wonderful time (we had)!
7 How carefully she drove!
8 What beautiful weather (it is)!
9 How long turtles live!
10 How nice (the bread smells)!
11 What helpful advice (this is)!
12 What an exciting game (that was)!

기출 적중문제

정답 ③
해설 ③ What   ①②④⑤ How

POINT 2 의문사 의문문

 연습문제 A

1 When does this bus leave?
2 What happened last night?
3 Who will be our homeroom teacher?
4 How was your first day at school?
5 Where is Brandon going now?
6 What do you want for lunch?
7 How come he lost his bag?
8 Who made her cry?
9 Where can we find the toilet?
10 How did Mr. Johnson get the information?
11 Why should I apologize to Linda?
12 When did you move to Busan?

 연습문제 B

1 ⓓ	**2** ⓐ	**3** ⓕ	**4** ⓑ
5 ⓔ	**6** ⓒ		

정답 what do you like about Korean culture
해설 일반동사가 있는 의문사 의문문: 「의문사 + do/does/did +
주어 + 동사원형 ~?」

POINT 3 선택의문문

 연습문제 A
1 Are, or   2 Which, or
3 When, or   4 Do, or

연습문제 B
1 ⓓ   2 ⓖ   3 ⓐ   4 ⓕ
5 ⓑ   6 ⓒ   7 ⓔ

POINT 4-1 의문사가 있는 간접의문문

 연습문제 A
1 who she is
2 when the bank opens
3 when the next train will arrive
4 where I can find the library
5 who took my bike
6 when the dinosaurs disappeared
7 why Jason is so upset
8 how the movie ends

연습문제 B
1 What do you think the dog is eating?
2 When do you believe we can take a break?
3 What do you guess the next song will be?
4 Who do you think is telling a lie?
5 Where do you believe you lost your bag?
6 Why do you imagine he acted rudely?

기출 적중문제
정답 (1) I don't know when the concert starts.
　　(2) How do you think she got a high score?
해설 (1) 의문사가 있는 간접의문문: 「의문사 + 주어 + 동사」
　　(2) 간접의문문을 포함하는 문장의 동사가 think이므로 간접
　　의문문의 의문사(How)를 문장 맨 앞에 쓴다.

POINT 4-2 의문사가 없는 간접의문문

 연습문제
1 if[whether] Anna can ride a bike
2 if[whether] you have a pet
3 if[whether] Kenny will buy a new wallet
4 if[whether] Alex is at home
5 if[whether] they are[they're] playing outside
6 if[whether] it will rain tomorrow
7 if[whether] James came to school last Friday

정답 if[whether] she can eat
해설 의문사가 없는 간접의문문: 「if[whether] + 주어 + 동사」

POINT 5 부가의문문

 연습문제 A
1 was it   2 can't they   3 doesn't he
4 aren't I   5 isn't it   6 didn't you
7 will you   8 are there   9 won't they
10 shall we

 연습문제 B
1 No, I didn't.   2 Yes, they can.
3 No, he doesn't.   4 No, they aren't.
5 Yes, it will.

기출 적중문제
정답 ②
해설 앞 문장의 동사가 긍정을 나타내는 일반동사(called)이므로
부정의 부가의문문 didn't she를 쓴다.

서술형 대비 문제

Ⓐ
1 What   2 O
3 O   4 aren't I
5 the stars shine   6 doesn't he
7 O   8 or
9 a beautiful smile   10 isn't it

Ⓑ
1 Where was Angela's smartphone?
2 What is your favorite subject?
3 Who wrote this novel?
4 When will the plane land?
5 How can I make chocolate brownies?
6 Why did Jacob look sad?

Ⓒ
1 Can you tell me what you are doing?
2 Do you know who broke the mirror?
3 When do you think we will[we'll] meet Yuna again?
4 I want to know where he put the knife.
5 I wonder if[whether] Jenny likes this restaurant.
6 Why do you believe they were so shocked?
7 Please tell me how I can get to the bus station.
8 I don't remember if[whether] I turned off the light.

Ⓓ
1 doesn't she / Yes, she does

중간·기말고사 실전 문제

1 ③　　**2** ②　　**3** Which　　**4** ③
5 ⑤　　**6** ⑤　　**7** ②　　**8** ③　　**9** ④
10 ③　　**11** What an excellent dancer (she is)!
12 How sweet (this orange juice tastes)!　　**13** ②
14 ④　　**15** ④　　**16** when your birthday is
17 ⑤　　**18** ④　　**19** How big the concert hall is!
20 ⑤　　**21** ②　　**22** ⑤　　**23** ④　　**24** ③, ④
25 ④　　**26** ⑤　　**27** Please tell me how you
became a soccer player.　　**28** I'm not sure
if[whether] it will be sunny tomorrow.　　**29** ②
30 I wonder where Junsu parked　　**31** When
do you believe we should go　　**32** ⑤
33 Who do you think will win the race?　　**34** ③
35 ⑤　　**36** (1) ⓐ → What is your plan　(2) ⓑ →
why they like Busan　(3) ⓔ → don't you

1 What 감탄문: 「What + (a/an) + 형용사 + 명사 + (주어 + 동사)!」

2 ② How your trip to Busan was? → How was your trip to Busan?

3 여름과 겨울 중 어느 것(Which)을 더 좋아하는지 묻고 있으므로 or를 사용하여 상대방의 선택을 묻는 선택의문문이다.

4 앞 문장의 동사가 긍정을 나타내는 일반동사(have)이므로 부정의 부가의문문 don't you를 쓴다.

5 · '그는 언제 결혼하기를 원하니?'라는 의미이므로 When(언제)을 쓴다.
· '어린이날은 언제니?'라는 의미이므로 When(언제)을 쓴다.

6 '너는 그 도둑이 마스크를 쓰고 있었는지 아닌지 기억하니?'라는 의미이므로 의문사가 없는 간접의문문을 이끄는 whether를 쓴다.

7 의문사가 있는 간접의문문: 「의문사 + 주어 + 동사」

8 빈칸 뒤에 「형용사 + 주어 + 동사!」가 나오는 감탄문이므로 How를 쓴다.

9 청유문의 부가의문문: 「shall we?」

10 ③ is Ms. Park → Ms. Park is

11 What 감탄문: 「What + (a/an) + 형용사 + 명사 + (주어 + 동사)!」

12 How 감탄문: 「How + 형용사/부사 + (주어 + 동사)!」

13 명령문의 부가의문문: 「will you?」

14 ④: 감탄문에 쓰인 what
①②③⑤: 의문문에 쓰인 의문사 what

15 ④: What　　①②③⑤: How

16 의문사가 있는 간접의문문: 「의문사 + 주어 + 동사」

17 (A) I'm으로 시작하는 문장의 부가의문문 aren't I를 쓴다.
(B) 앞 문장의 동사가 부정을 나타내는 조동사(won't)이므로 긍정의 부가의문문 will he를 쓴다.
(C) 「There + be동사」 구문의 부가의문문의 주어로는 there를 쓴다. 앞 문장의 동사가 긍정을 나타내는 be동사(were)이므로 부정의 부가의문문 weren't there를 쓴다.

18 How(어떻게)로 묻고 있으므로 방법에 해당하는 구체적인 정보로 대답한다.

19 How 감탄문: 「How + 형용사 + (주어 + 동사)!」

20 부가의문문에 대답할 때는 대답의 내용이 긍정이면 Yes로 답한다.

21 '나는 온라인으로 쇼핑했어.'라고 대답했으므로 쇼핑몰에서 쇼핑했는지, 아니면 온라인으로 쇼핑했는지 묻는 선택의문문에 대한 대답이다.

22 ① was that → was it
② shall we → will you
③ isn't he → is he
④ aren't these → aren't they

23 · '너는 네가 너의 개에게 먹이를 줬는지 아닌지 기억하니?'라는 의미이므로 의문사가 없는 간접의문문을 이끄는 if를 쓴다.
· '누가 이 소포를 보냈는지 나에게 말해줄 수 있니?'라는 의미이므로 who(누구)를 쓴다.

24 ① huge a → a huge
② they are sharp scissors → sharp scissors they are
⑤ tastes this cookie → this cookie tastes

25 · 빈칸 뒤에 「형용사 + 명사!」가 나오는 감탄문이므로 What을 쓴다.
· '너의 삶에서 가장 중요한 것은 무엇이니?'라는 의미이므로 What(무엇)을 쓴다.

26 '지난주에.'라고 대답했으므로 When(언제)으로 물어야 한다.

27 의문사가 있는 간접의문문: 「의문사 + 주어 + 동사」

28 의문사가 없는 간접의문문: 「if[whether] + 주어 + 동사」

29 첫 번째 빈칸: '너와 너의 친구들은 어디에 갈 거니?'라는 의미이므로 Where(어디에)를 쓴다.
두 번째 빈칸: '그 전시회의 주제는 무엇이니?'라는 의미이므로 What(무엇)을 쓴다.

30 의문사가 있는 간접의문문: 「의문사 + 주어 + 동사」

31 간접의문문을 포함하는 문장의 동사가 believe이므로 간접의문문의 의문사(when)를 문장 맨 앞에 쓴다.

32 ⓐ cheap a → a cheap

ⓑ is my phone → my phone is

ⓓ you visited → did you visit

33 의문사가 있는 간접의문문은 「의문사 + 주어 + 동사」의 형태이다. 간접의문문을 포함하는 문장의 동사가 think이므로 간접의문문의 의문사(who)를 문장 맨 앞에 쓴다.

34 웨딩드레스가 흰색인 이유를 설명하고 있으므로 why(왜)를 쓴다. 의문사가 있는 간접의문문은 「의문사 + 주어 + 동사」의 형태이다.

35 부가의문문으로 「did you?」를 썼으므로 앞 문장의 동사는 부정을 나타내는 일반동사의 과거형을 쓴다.

36 (1) be동사가 있는 의문사 의문문: 「의문사 + be동사 + 주어 ~?」

(2) 의문사가 있는 간접의문문: 「의문사 + 주어 + 동사」

(3) 앞 문장의 동사가 긍정을 나타내는 일반동사(want)이므로 부정의 부가의문문 don't you를 쓴다.

CHAPTER 3
시제

p.54

POINT 1 현재시제

1	exercises	**2**	rises	**3**	is
4	rings	**5**	leaves	**6**	has
7	belongs	**8**	catches	**9**	sings
10	work	**11**	arrives	**12**	ride

POINT 2-1 과거시제

1	Was	**2**	sent	**3**	found
4	broke	**5**	is	**6**	reads
7	held	**8**	was	**9**	go
10	met	**11**	rained	**12**	went
13	was				

기출 적중문제

정답 ④

해설 eats → ate

POINT 2-2 과거시제: 동사의 과거형과 과거분사형

1	started	**2**	improved
3	stopped	**4**	tried
5	listened	**6**	played
7	believed	**8**	chatted
9	enjoyed	**10**	remembered
11	carried	**12**	shopped
13	invented	**14**	agreed
15	entered	**16**	studied

1	grew – grown	**2**	heard – heard
3	threw – thrown	**4**	made – made
5	ran – run	**6**	became – become
7	spent – spent	**8**	laid – laid
9	ate – eaten	**10**	slept – slept
11	cost – cost	**12**	had – had
13	was/were – been	**14**	read – read
15	left – left	**16**	built – built
17	let – let	**18**	shut – shut
19	wrote – written	**20**	kept – kept
21	broke – broken	**22**	rose – risen
23	took – taken	**24**	thought – thought
25	did – done	**26**	spread – spread

27	saw – seen	28	fed – fed
29	knew – known	30	found – found
31	brought – brought	32	hurt – hurt
33	forgot – forgotten	34	drove – driven

POINT 3 미래시제

1 They will[They'll] watch a baseball game together
2 The sky is going to be clear
3 Peter will bake a cake for Sally's birthday
4 A strong typhoon is going to hit the city
5 Luke will not[won't] invite me to his house
6 Will you and your brother call your grandparents
7 The restaurant is going to move to a new location
8 What is Mr. Jenkins going to cook for breakfast

POINT 4 진행시제

A	1	was jogging	2	are, studying
	3	wasn't arguing	4	is leaving
	5	was taking	6	are waiting
	7	are making	8	is, arriving
	9	were planning	10	are learning
	11	are visiting	12	was watering

B	1	know	2	O	3	has
	4	O	5	smell	6	loves
	7	O	8	O	9	are having
	10	O				

POINT 5-1 현재완료시제

A	1	has forgotten	2	has been
	3	have had	4	has played
	5	has lost	6	has risen
	7	have worked		

B
1 We have not[haven't] been to Dokdo before.
2 Have they lost their bags and passports?
3 Joshua has not[hasn't] seen a rainbow.
4 Have you told your parents about the problem?
5 I have not[haven't] tried the recipe for onion soup.
6 Has Tina run a marathon recently?

C
1 It has rained a lot
2 We have known each other
3 Has Mr. Collins worked as a pilot
4 I have not watched new movies
5 What have the students broken
6 Woomin has not been to the dentist

POINT 5-2 현재완료시제의 용법

A	1	Have, fallen	2	has gone
	3	have visited	4	has, done
	5	has broken	6	hasn't left
	7	have, been	8	have caused

B	1	ⓒ	2	ⓐ	3	ⓓ	4	ⓑ
	5	ⓐ	6	ⓒ	7	ⓑ	8	ⓓ
	9	ⓑ	10	ⓐ				

POINT 5-3 현재완료시제 vs. 과거시제

A	1	has studied	2	snowed
	3	left	4	bought
	5	haven't read	6	did you clean
	7	had	8	has lived
	9	Have you known	10	cooked

11 went, haven't seen

B
1	arrived	2	Has, been
3	have, planted	4	hasn't been
5	moved	6	has used
7	visited	8	haven't talked

C
1	O	2	has practiced
3	opened	4	O
5	didn't go	6	won
7	O	8	wrote
9	did you take	10	O
11	graduated	12	saw

기출 적중문제

정답 ①, ⑤

해설 현재완료시제는 특정한 과거 시점을 나타내는 표현과 함께 쓸 수 없다.

서술형 대비 문제

A
1 Water freezes at 0°C.
2 A cat ran into my house yesterday.
3 The restaurant is going to close soon.
4 Fred goes to the café every Wednesday.
5 They participated in the singing contest two weeks ago.
6 We were nervous when our first game started.
7 I will visit the website to find out more information.

B
1 are eating ice cream
2 was wrapping a gift
3 was waiting for her mother

C
1 has saved money for two months
2 has taken this medicine since 2006
3 have practiced taekwondo since last month
4 has gone to the beach
5 has lived in Sydney since 2009
6 has played chess since last spring
7 has lost her new bracelet
8 have been in this city for three days

D
ⓐ came ⓑ left ⓒ am ⓓ have visited
ⓔ have been ⓕ will go[am going to]

중간·기말고사 실전 문제

1 ⑤	2 ③	3 ③	4 ④	5 has, departed

6 ③　7 ②　8 ⑤　9 went
10 ④, ⑤　11 is going to visit　12 ⑤　13 ④
14 ④　15 ①, ⑤　16 ②　17 ②　18 Columbus landed in North America in 1492.
19 ③　20 ③　21 Have you heard this song
22 ③　23 ⑤　24 (1) Anne and Diana haven't[have not] been friends since 2015.　(2) Have Anne and Diana been friends since 2015?
25 ②　26 ④　27 ②, ④　28 ④
29 hasn't[has not] ridden a horse, have visited Vietnam　30 ③　31 ⑤　32 ④　33 They were playing baduk　34 have lived in London since 2012　35 has worked at the restaurant for five years　36 has gone to Russia
37 (1) ⓑ → decided (2) ⓒ → has spent　38 has grown corn for 20 years　39 ⓐ have volunteered ⓑ baked ⓒ wrote 40 ④　41 ③
42 Many students haven't[have not] solved the riddle.　43 ③　44 (1) ⓐ → have lived (2) ⓓ → have　45 ④, ⑤　46 (A) went to soccer practice (B) will go shopping

1 ⑤ teach – taught – taught

2 ③ mistake – mistook – mistaken

3 ① heared → heard
② broken → broke
④ have drinked → have drunk
⑤ has drove → has driven

4 현재완료시제 문장이므로 write의 과거형인 wrote가 아닌 과거분사형 written을 쓴다.

5 현재완료시제: 「have/has + p.p.」

6 ③ writes → wrote

7 last weekend는 과거시제와 주로 함께 쓰이는 부사(구)이다.

8 since는 현재완료시제와 주로 함께 쓰이는 표현이다.

9 과거시제로 묻고 있으므로 과거시제로 답한다.

10 ① will study → studied
② was listening → is listening
③ Is → Was

11 미래시제는 「will + 동사원형」이나 「be going to + 동사원형」의 형태이다.

12 ·'나는 네가 나에게 문자 메시지를 보냈을 때 자고 있었다.'라는 의미이므로 과거진행시제를 쓴다.
·in 1969는 과거시제와 주로 함께 쓰이는 부사(구)이다.

13 ④ drank → has drunk

14 ④ will be → is (시간이나 조건을 나타내는 부사절에서는 미래시제 대신 현재시제를 쓴다.)

15 현재진행시제는 미래를 나타내는 부사(구)와 주로 함께 쓰여 예정된 가까운 미래의 일을 나타낼 수 있다.

16 last month(지난달에)는 과거시제와 주로 함께 쓰이는 부사(구)이다.

17 ② is having → has (소유의 의미를 나타내는 have는 진행형으로 쓸 수 없다.)

18 in 1492는 과거시제와 주로 함께 쓰이는 부사(구)이다.

19 ③: 현재진행시제 ①②④⑤: 미래시제

20 첫 번째 빈칸: last May는 과거시제와 주로 함께 쓰이는 부사(구)이다.
두 번째 빈칸: 현재완료시제 문장에서 빈칸 뒤에 일이 지속된 기간을 나타내는 three months가 왔으므로 for를 쓴다.

21 과거부터 현재까지의 경험을 나타내는 현재완료시제 문장이다. 현재완료시제의 의문문은 「Have/Has + 주어 + p.p. ~?」의 형태이다.

22 주어진 문장과 ③: 계속 ①: 경험 ②⑤: 완료 ④: 결과

23 주어진 문장과 ⑤: 경험 ①: 계속 ②: 완료 ③④: 결과

24 (1) 현재완료시제의 부정문: 「have/has + not + p.p.」
(2) 현재완료시제의 의문문: 「Have/Has + 주어 + p.p. ~?」

25 (A) '나는 어떤 소리를 들었을 때 TV를 보고 있었다.'라는 의미이므로 과거진행시제를 쓴다.
(B) 어제 발생한 일을 나타내고 있으므로 과거시제를 쓴다.
(C) since는 현재완료시제와 주로 함께 쓰이는 표현이다.

26 ④ for ①②③⑤ since

27 현재완료시제는 특정한 과거 시점을 나타내는 표현과 함께 쓸 수 없다.

28 ④: 현재진행시제가 미래를 나타내는 부사구(tomorrow afternoon)와 함께 쓰여 예정된 가까운 미래의 일을 나타내고 있다.
①②③⑤: 현재진행시제가 현재 진행되고 있는 동작을 나타내고 있다.

29 첫 번째 빈칸: Iris는 말을 타본 적이 없다고 했으므로 hasn't[has not] ridden a horse를 쓴다.
두 번째 빈칸: Alex와 Iris는 베트남에 가본 적이 있다고 했으므로 have visited Vietnam을 쓴다.

30 '너는 개를 길러본 적이 있니?'라는 질문에 '하지만 나는 전에 이구아나를 길러본 적이 있어.'라고 했으므로 '아니, 없어.'라는 의미의 부정의 대답으로 답해야 한다. 현재완료시제의 의문문에 대한 부정의 대답은 「No, 주어 + have/has + not.」의 형태이다.

31 (A)와 ⑤: 경험 ①: 결과 ②④: 완료 ③: 계속

32 ① knew → have known

33 과거진행시제로 묻고 있으므로 과거진행시제로 답한다. your father and brother는 인칭대명사 they로 바꿔 쓸 수 있다.

34 Jane과 Jim이 2012년에 런던으로 이사했고 아직도 계속 런던에 살고 있으므로 현재완료시제와 since(~ 이후로)를 쓴다.

35 Martin이 5년 전에 그 식당에서 일하기 시작했고 아직도 계속 그곳에서 일하고 있으므로 현재완료시제와 for(~ 동안)를 쓴다.

36 유미가 러시아로 갔고 그 결과 지금 여기에 없으므로 현재완료시제를 쓴다.

37 (1) A few years ago는 과거시제와 주로 함께 쓰이는 부사(구)이다.
(2) since는 현재완료시제와 주로 함께 쓰이는 표현이다.

38 Smith씨가 20년 전에도 옥수수를 재배했고 지금도 계속 옥수수를 재배하고 있으므로 현재완료시제와 for(~ 동안)를 쓴다.

39 ⓐ since는 현재완료시제와 주로 함께 쓰이는 표현이다.
ⓑ last weekend는 과거시제와 주로 함께 쓰이는 부사(구)이다.
ⓒ 지난주에 발생한 일을 나타내고 있으므로 과거시제를 쓴다.

40 현재완료시제의 의문문에 대한 부정의 대답: 「No, 주어 + have/has + not.」

41 ⓑ have read → read
ⓓ since → for
ⓔ have you met → did you meet

42 과거부터 현재까지 계속되는 일을 나타내는 현재완료시제 문장이다. 현재완료시제의 부정문은 「have/has + not + p.p.」의 형태이다.

43 ① is → was
② will have → had
④ had → has
⑤ visited → have visited

44 (1) 현재완료시제: 「have/has + p.p.」
(2) 소유의 의미를 나타내는 have는 진행형으로 쓸 수 없다.

45 ④ will have → had
⑤ wanted → have wanted

46 (A) Julie는 화요일인 어제(yesterday) 축구 연습에 갔으므로 과거시제를 쓴다.
(B) Julie는 목요일인 내일(tomorrow) 쇼핑하러 갈 것이므로 미래시제를 쓴다.

---

② have they built → did they build
③ has visited → visited
⑤ have found → found

POINT 1-1 조동사의 쓰임

 연습문제

1 recycle		**2** may	
3 wear		**4** can	
5 will be able to		**6** make	
7 return		**8** may have to	
9 be		**10** will	

기출 적중문제

정답 ③

해설 ① is → be
② can → be able to
④ musts → must
⑤ needed → need

POINT 1-2 조동사가 있는 부정문과 의문문

연습문제

1 Mr. Davis cannot[can't] drive
2 Should I wear
3 We may not have
4 Can Jimin run
5 She will not[won't] be
6 Will Gary and Mindy get
7 You should not[shouldn't] use

기출 적중문제

정답 This math problem may not be easy.
해설 조동사가 있는 부정문: 「조동사 + not + 동사원형」

POINT 2 can, could

 연습문제 A

1 Tony is able to bake
2 Amy wasn't[was not] able to find
3 Are you able to hear
4 Mr. Clark isn't[is not] able to see
5 They weren't[were not] able to sleep
6 Is she able to tell
7 My little brother is able to read
8 We aren't[are not] able to meet

 연습문제 B

1 ⓐ	**2** ⓒ	**3** ⓑ	**4** ⓐ
5 ⓓ	**6** ⓒ	**7** ⓐ	**8** ⓑ
9 ⓓ	**10** ⓒ	**11** ⓑ	**12** ⓓ

기출 적중문제

정답 ④

해설 ④: 요청   ①②③⑤: 허가

POINT 3 may, might

 연습문제

1 ⓐ	**2** ⓑ	**3** ⓑ	**4** ⓐ
5 ⓐ	**6** ⓐ	**7** ⓑ	**8** ⓑ
9 ⓑ	**10** ⓐ	**11** ⓑ	**12** ⓑ
13 ⓐ	**14** ⓐ	**15** ⓑ	**16** ⓐ

기출 적중문제

정답 ③

해설 ③: 허가   ①②④⑤: 약한 추측

POINT 4-1 will, would I

연습문제 A

1 They're[They are] going to travel
2 My father isn't[is not] going to buy
3 Is Kevin going to visit
4 The survey is going to take
5 Are your brothers going to wash

연습문제 B

1 We will plant	**2** They won't allow
3 Will you put	**4** I will read
5 Would you call	

POINT 4-2 will, would II

연습문제

1 Would you like	**2** I would like to
3 Would you like to	**4** Would you like
5 Would you like to	**6** Would you like
7 I would like to	**8** I would like
9 I would like to	

기출 적중문제

정답 Would you like to go to the concert together?
해설 「would like to + 동사원형」 '~하기를 원하다'

POINT 5 must, have to

 연습문제 A

1 must	**2** must	**3** must not
4 can't	**5** must	**6** must not
7 must	**8** must	

B

1 must[have to] respect
2 must not leave
3 had to take
4 will have to change
5 don't have to worry
6 must[has to] take
7 had to help
8 doesn't have to pay
9 will have to participate

기출 적중문제

정답 ③, ④
해설 불필요(~할 필요가 없다)의 의미를 나타내는 don't have to 나 need not을 쓴다.

POINT 6 should, had better

1 We should save
2 You shouldn't fall
3 He'd better take
4 Should I invite
5 We'd better ask
6 You'd better not believe

기출 적중문제

정답 You had better not put your bag here.
해설 had better의 부정형: had better not

POINT 7 used to, would

1 used to have
2 would play
3 used to be
4 am used to living
5 would bring

기출 적중문제

정답 Becky used to[would] do yoga
해설 과거의 반복적인 습관(~하곤 했다)을 나타내는 used to나 would를 쓴다.

POINT 8 do

1 ⓑ   2 ⓐ   3 ⓒ   4 ⓒ
5 ⓑ   6 ⓐ

기출 적중문제

정답 sing
해설 do는 동사 앞에서 동사를 강조할 때 쓰고 전체 문장이 'Jessica does sing very well.'이므로 세 번째에 오는 것은 sing이다.

서술형 대비 문제

Ⓐ
1 be
2 Can you peel
3 O
4 O
5 might
6 will not[won't] be
7 have to
8 would like to travel
9 O
10 eat

Ⓑ
1 We can see
2 My uncle used to be
3 I will[I'll] lose
4 Can I have
5 Mia should clean
6 The students will perform
7 You should speak

Ⓒ
1 could rain
2 had better wear
3 would like to visit
4 must be
5 used to meet
6 may not borrow

Ⓓ
1 You don't have to knock.
2 That car must be expensive.
3 Would you like my help?
4 This lemonade does taste sour.
5 They may miss their train.
6 The movie can't be a true story.
7 Our city is going to hold the event in the fall.
8 Noah was not able to go to school yesterday.

중간·기말고사 실전 문제

1 ⑤   2 ⑤   3 The plane will take off in a minute.   4 ③   5 ④   6 ①   7 ④
8 ④   9 ②   10 ①   11 ③   12 ④
13 ③   14 has to wear   15 ④   16 ①
17 This tree must be old.   18 ④   19 ④
20 ③   21 would like   22 ②
23 You'd[You had] better drink hot tea.   24 ④
25 ⑤   26 ④   27 ③   28 we had better not be noisy   29 ③   30 ④   31 ③   32 ⑤
33 must not take a picture   34 There can't be a problem with my phone.   35 would play the flute   36 was able to, were not able to
37 You will[You'll] be able to win the first prize in the singing contest.

1 조동사 뒤에는 동사원형이 온다.

2 ⑤ wills → will

3 조동사 뒤에는 동사원형이 온다.

4 had better의 부정형: had better not

5 약한 추측(~일지도 모른다)의 의미를 나타내는 might를 쓴다.

6 can과 may는 허가(~해도 된다)의 의미를 나타낸다.

7 충고·의무(~해야 한다)의 의미를 나타내는 should의 부정형인 should not을 쓴다.

8 능력·가능(~할 수 있다)의 의미를 나타내는 can의 과거형인 could를 쓴다.

9 요청(~해주겠니?)의 의미를 나타내는 Will을 쓴다.

10 약한 추측(~일지도 모른다)의 의미를 나타내는 may를 쓴다.

11 ① biting → bite
② don't may → may not
④ must → have to
⑤ have → had

12 don't have to = need not

13 과거의 상태(전에는 ~이었다)를 나타내는 used to를 쓴다.

14 의무(~해야 한다)의 의미를 나타내는 has to를 쓴다.

15 의무(~해야 한다)의 의미를 나타내는 must를 쓴다.

16 주어진 문장과 ⑤: 동사를 강조하는 do
①: 일반동사의 의문문에 쓰이는 do
②: 일반동사의 부정문에 쓰이는 do
③: 일반동사 do   ④: 대동사 do

17 강한 추측(~임에 틀림없다)의 의미를 나타내는 must를 쓴다.

18 허가(~해도 된다)의 의미를 나타내는 can의 부정형인 can't를 쓴다.

19 ·「would like to + 동사원형」 '~하기를 원하다'
·충고·의무(~해야 한다)의 의미를 나타내는 should의 부정형인 should not을 쓴다.

20 과거의 상태(전에는 ~이었다)를 나타내는 used to를 쓴다.

21 「want + 명사」=「would like + 명사」

22 couldn't = wasn't able to

23 강한 충고(~하는 것이 낫다)의 의미를 나타내는 had better를 쓴다.

24 ④: 약한 추측   ①②③⑤: 허가

25 ·의무(~해야 한다)의 의미를 나타내는 must를 쓴다.
·강한 추측(~임에 틀림없다)의 의미를 나타내는 must를 쓴다.

26 '당신은 이 엘리베이터를 타면 안 됩니다.'라는 의미이므로 '~할 필요가 없다'라는 의미의 don't have to는 쓸 수 없다.

27 ③: 「be used to + V-ing」 '~하는 데 익숙하다'
①②④⑤: '~하곤 했다'

28 had better의 부정형: had better not

29 must = have to '~해야 한다'
must not '~하면 안 된다'
don't have to = don't need to '~할 필요가 없다'

30 ④: 강한 추측   주어진 문장과 ①②③⑤: 의무

31 '너는 그녀가 아름다운 미소를 가지고 있다고 생각하지 않니?'라는 질문에 'Yes, she does.'라는 긍정의 내용으로 답했으므로 대동사 does는 동사구 has a beautiful smile의 반복을 피하기 위해 쓰였다.

32 (A) 약한 추측(~일지도 모른다)의 의미를 나타내는 may를 쓴다.
(B) 의무(~해야 한다)의 의미를 나타내는 have to를 쓴다.
(C) 강한 금지(~하면 안 된다)의 의미를 나타내는 must not을 쓴다.

33 사진을 찍으면 안 된다는 표지판이므로 강한 금지(~하면 안 된다)의 의미를 나타내는 must not을 쓴다.

34 강한 추측을 나타내는 must의 부정: can't(~일 리가 없다)

35 과거의 반복적인 습관(~하곤 했다)을 나타내는 would를 쓴다.

36 첫 번째 빈칸: 시우는 초등학생 때 자전거를 탈 수 있었으므로 능력·가능(~할 수 있다)의 의미를 나타내는 was able to를 쓴다.
두 번째 빈칸: 시우와 지안이는 초등학생 때 중국어를 말할 수 없었으므로 were not able to를 쓴다.

37 will be able to '~할 수 있을 것이다'

CHAPTER 5
수동태

p.102

POINT 1 수동태 문장 만드는 법

 연습문제 **A**

1	spoken	2	taken
3	cleaned	4	drawn
5	are loved	6	raised
7	returned	8	discovered
9	are eaten	10	tastes

 연습문제 **B**

1	are made	2	is sung
3	are invited	4	are written
5	are grown	6	is visited
7	are produced	8	are read
9	are shown	10	is delivered

 연습문제 **C**

1 The sofa was moved by Junho.
2 A beautiful poem was written by Gina.
3 Old coins are collected by Albus.
4 Some apple pies were baked by Ms. Miller.
5 Shrimps are eaten by many kinds of sea animals.
6 A wedding dress was worn by my mother.

기출 적중문제

정답 saw → was seen
해설 수동태의 동사는 「be + p.p.」의 형태이므로 was seen을 쓴다.

POINT 2 수동태의 시제

 연습문제 **A**

1 The class president is picked
2 Howard lost the watch
3 Some trees will be planted
4 My friend wrote this essay
5 Maria will visit the history museum
6 Plastic bottles are recycled
7 A delicious meal has been prepared
8 Many Koreans respect King Sejong
9 The fence will be painted
10 The plates were put
11 The house has been built
12 Cindy and her brothers have broken the chair

 연습문제 **B**

1	was broken	2	will be released
3	will be finished	4	was cooked
5	have been made	6	was decorated

 기출 적중문제

정답 ③
해설 ① burns → burned
　　　② fix → fixed
　　　④ practiced → practices
　　　⑤ finishing → finished

POINT 3 수동태의 부정문과 의문문

연습문제

1 wasn't bitten
2 Are, understood
3 aren't read
4 How was, made
5 By whom was, invented

 기출 적중문제

정답 Was the door locked
해설 의문사가 없는 수동태의 의문문: 「be동사 + 주어 + p.p. ~?」

POINT 4 조동사가 있는 수동태

연습문제

1	can be opened	2	may be sent
3	should be put	4	will not be fixed
5	Should, be kept	6	Can, be predicted
7	must not be hunted		

기출 적중문제

정답 The sweater must be washed
해설 조동사가 있는 수동태: 「조동사 + be + p.p.」

POINT 5 4형식 문장의 수동태

 연습문제 **A**

1	to	2	to	3	for	4	for
5	to	6	for	7	of	8	to

 연습문제 **B**

1 was shown the pictures of cats by Jenny / were shown to Matt by Jenny
2 were made for me by Emma
3 are given helpful advice by Jonathan / is given to people by Jonathan
4 was bought for Joseph by her
5 was sent a text message by my friend / was sent to me by my friend
6 was asked a favor by the old man / was asked of him by the old man
7 are taught English by Sophia / is taught to children by Sophia

정답 ④

해설 4형식 문장을 직접 목적어가 주어인 수동태 문장으로 바꿀 때 간접 목적어 앞에 to/for/of 중 하나를 쓰며, build는 전치사 for를 쓰는 동사이다.

POINT 6 5형식 문장의 수동태

연습문제

1 The building is kept clean by Mr. Smith.
2 He is called Teddy by his friends.
3 I'm[I am] expected to come home early by my parents.
4 Some children were heard to laugh by Nina.
5 She was elected the leader by the members.
6 Suho was made to stay at home by her.
7 I was advised to study harder by my teacher.

POINT 7 수동태 관용 표현

연습문제

| **1** from | **2** with | **3** in | **4** of |
| **5** with | **6** for | **7** to | **8** at |

정답 was filled with tools

해설 be filled with '~으로 가득 차 있다'

서술형 대비 문제

 A

1 him	**2** O
3 presented	**4** canceled
5 broken	**6** O
7 be rented	**8** been used
9 O	**10** held

B
1 The plant should be watered by you.
2 Were the onions sliced by him?
3 The information wasn't[was not] provided by the journalist.
4 Those documents will be copied by James.
5 The bicycle wasn't[was not] damaged by the children.
6 Were the earrings found under the bed by Beth?
7 This medicine must be taken by the flu patients.

C
1 Someone was heard to sneeze by Jiho.

2 My father bought me a guitar.
3 She made Luke shop for groceries.
4 Some questions were asked of us by the police officer.
5 Her fans call her Sunny.
6 A digital camera was lent to me by Benjamin.

D
1 ⓐ disappointed at[by] ⓑ filled with
ⓒ made of ⓓ pleased with
2 ⓐ interested in ⓑ covered with
ⓒ surprised at ⓓ known to

중간·기말고사 실전 문제

1 caught **2** ① **3** ④ **4** This singer is loved by many teenagers. **5** ⑤
6 are purchased by **7** ④ **8** My teeth are brushed **9** ④ **10** ③
11 (1) The shirt wasn't[was not] washed last night by Jason. (2) Was the shirt washed last night by Jason?
12 ②, ⑤ **13** ② **14** ①, ③ **15** can be watched
16 ② **17** learned **18** ② **19** ③
20 of → with **21** was built **22** are held **23** ②, ④ **24** ④ **25** was shown to
26 ④ **27** ① **28** ② **29** is interested in
30 ⑤ **31** ② **32** She was elected vice president **33** ② **34** ⑤ **35** ②, ⑤
36 Was, broken **37** (1) ⓐ → discovered (2) ⓑ → were robbed **38** ③ **39** ④ **40** A bathroom is called a loo by British people. **41** ②

1 수동태의 동사는 「be + p.p.」의 형태이므로 catch의 과거분사형인 caught을 쓴다.

2 ① respect → respected

3 축구공이 차는 것이 아니라 차이는 것이므로 수동태를 쓴다. 수동태의 동사는 「be + p.p.」의 형태이고 주어 A soccer ball은 단수이므로 was kicked를 쓴다.

4 가수가 사랑하는 것이 아니라 사랑받는 것이므로 수동태를 쓴다. 수동태의 동사는 「be + p.p.」의 형태이고 주어 This singer는 3인칭 단수이므로 is loved를 쓴다.

5 과거시제 수동태의 동사는 「was/were + p.p.」의 형태이고 주어 *Alice in Wonderland*는 단수이므로 was written을 쓴다.

6 수동태의 동사는 「be + p.p.」의 형태이고 주어 beach towels는 3인칭 복수이므로 are purchased를 쓴다. 행위자는 「by + 목적격」의 형태이므로 by를 쓴다.

7 손님들이 환영하는 것이 아니라 환영받는 것이므로 수동태를 쓴

다. 수동태의 동사는 「be + p.p.」의 형태이고 주어 The guests 는 복수이므로 were greeted를 쓴다.

8 수동태의 동사는 「be + p.p.」의 형태이고 주어 My teeth는 3인 칭 복수이므로 are brushed를 쓴다.

9 ④ have written → have been written (현재완료시제의 수동태: 「have/has been + p.p.」)

10 ⓐ he → him
ⓓ wearing → worn
ⓔ uses → is used

11 (1) 수동태의 부정문: 「be동사 + not + p.p.」
(2) 의문사가 없는 수동태의 의문문: 「be동사 + 주어 + p.p. ~?」

12 ① located → is located
③ make → made
④ bite → was bitten

13 4형식 문장을 직접 목적어가 주어인 수동태 문장으로 바꿀 때 간 접 목적어 앞에 to/for/of 중 하나를 쓰며, cook은 전치사 for를 쓰는 동사이다.

14 ①③: go와 sound는 목적어를 가지지 않는 동사이므로 수동태 로 쓸 수 없다.

15 조동사가 있는 수동태: 「조동사 + be + p.p.」

16 ② is → was (과거시제의 수동태: 「was/were + p.p.」)

17 미래시제의 수동태는 「will be + p.p.」의 형태이고 전체 문장이 'Chinese will be learned by Mark.'이므로 네 번째에 오는 것은 learned이다.

18 '오늘 오후에 쿠키를 구울 것이다'라는 미래의 의미이므로 미래시 제의 수동태인 「will be + p.p.」를 쓴다.

19 목적어가 두 개(us, art)인 4형식 문장이므로 두 개의 수동태 문장 을 만들 수 있다. 직접 목적어가 주어인 수동태 문장은 간접 목적 어 앞에 to/for/of 중 하나를 쓰며, teach는 전치사 to를 쓰는 동 사이다.

20 be covered with '~으로 덮여 있다'

21 N서울타워가 짓는 것이 아니라 지어진 것이므로 수동태를 쓴다. 주어 The N Seoul Tower는 단수이고 in 1969는 과거를 나타 내는 부사구이므로 과거시제 was built를 쓴다.

22 대통령 선거가 여는 것이 아니라 열리는 것이므로 수동태를 쓴다. 주어 Presidential elections는 3인칭 복수이고 now는 현재를 나타내는 부사구이므로 현재시제 are held를 쓴다.

23 목적어가 두 개(Lisa, a free ticket)인 4형식 문장이므로 두 개 의 수동태 문장을 만들 수 있다. 직접 목적어가 주어인 수동태 문 장은 간접 목적어 앞에 to/for/of 중 하나를 쓰며, give는 전치사 to를 쓰는 동사이다.

24 새에게 먹이를 주면 안 된다는 표지판이므로 '~하면 안 된다'라는 의미의 must not을 쓴다. 조동사가 있는 수동태는 「조동사 + be + p.p.」의 형태이다.

25 가족 앨범이 보여주는 것이 아니라 보이는 것이므로 수동태를 쓴 다. 주어 The family album은 단수이고 last weekend는 과 거를 나타내는 부사구이므로 과거시제 was shown을 쓴다. 4형 식 문장을 직접 목적어가 주어인 수동태 문장으로 바꿀 때 간접 목 적어 앞에 to/for/of 중 하나를 쓰며, show는 전치사 to를 쓰는 동사이다.

26 ④ may not be leave → may not be left

27 be known for '~으로 유명하다'

28 ① be → were
③ sent → be sent
④ I → me
⑤ bring → brought

29 be interested in '~에 흥미가 있다'

30 ⑤ to   ①②③④ with

31 ② to neat → neat

32 목적격 보어가 명사(vice president)인 5형식 수동태 문장에서 는 목적격 보어를 「be동사 + p.p.」 뒤에 그대로 쓴다.

33 · lend는 간접 목적어 앞에 전치사 to를 쓰는 동사이다.
· ask는 간접 목적어 앞에 전치사 of를 쓰는 동사이다.

34 ⑤ 목적격 보어가 명사인 5형식 수동태 문장에서는 목적격 보어를 「be동사 + p.p.」 뒤에 그대로 쓴다.

35 ②⑤: 4형식 문장을 직접 목적어가 주어인 수동태 문장으로 바꿀 때 간접 목적어 앞에 to/for/of 중 하나를 쓰며, give와 tell은 전 치사 to를 쓰는 동사이다.

36 의문사가 없는 수동태의 의문문: 「be동사 + 주어 + p.p. ~?」

37 (1) 의문사가 있는 수동태의 의문문: 「의문사 + be동사 + 주어 + p.p. ~?」
(2) 무덤은 도둑질하는 것이 아니라 도둑맞는 것이므로 수동태 를 쓴다.

38 · be surprised at '~에 놀라다'
· be made from '~으로 만들어지다(재료 성질이 변함)'

39 ④: 행위자가 일반인이거나 중요하지 않을 때는 「by + 목적격」을 생략할 수 있다.

40 목적격 보어가 명사인 5형식 문장을 수동태로 바꿀 때는 목적격 보어를 「be동사 + p.p.」 뒤에 그대로 쓴다.

41 ⓑ did → was
ⓒ Was how → How was
ⓔ not are → aren't[are not]

CHAPTER 6
부정사

p.122

POINT 1　to부정사의 형태와 용법

 연습문제

1	to learn	**2**	to study	**3**	visit
4	to drink	**5**	not to sleep	**6**	buy
7	not to waste	**8**	not to tell	**9**	To get

기출 적중문제

정답 ③

해설 ① catch → to catch
　　 ② to going → to go
　　 ④ stay not to → not to stay
　　 ⑤ to called → to call

POINT 2-1　명사적 용법: 주어와 주격 보어로 쓰이는 to부정사

 연습문제 **A**

1 It is important to study history.
2 It is hard to travel to the moon.
3 It isn't[is not] safe to swim in this river.
4 It was confusing to use that machine.
5 It is necessary to brush your teeth.
6 It is exciting to play online games.
7 It wasn't[was not] difficult to climb this mountain.
8 It is my dream to spend the summer in Europe.
9 It is Junsu's hobby to collect stamps.
10 It is impossible to predict our future.

 연습문제 **B**

1 Katie's wish is to travel
2 His dream was to become
3 It is fun to watch
4 The chef's goal is to open
5 Her hobby was to play
6 His job is to protect
7 It is good to eat
8 My mom's advice was to drink
9 It is important to believe
10 My plan is to study

기출 적중문제

정답 ②

해설 ②: 보어　①③④⑤: 주어

POINT 2-2　명사적 용법: to부정사를 목적어로 쓰는 동사

 연습문제

1 wishes to find
2 agreed to lend
3 chose not to purchase
4 would love to go
5 need to sleep
6 hope to make
7 learn to walk
8 decided not to take

기출 적중문제

정답 answering → to answer

해설 refuse는 to부정사를 목적어로 쓰는 동사이므로 to answer를 쓴다.

POINT 2-3　명사적 용법: to부정사를 목적격 보어로 쓰는 동사

 연습문제

1 to turn down the volume
2 to use his cell phone
3 to close the window
4 to study with her today
5 not to play the piano at night

기출 적중문제

정답 tell me to be careful

해설 '나에게 조심하라고 말씀하신다'라는 의미이므로 동사 tell(말하다)의 목적어로 me를 쓴다. tell은 to부정사를 목적격 보어로 쓰는 동사이므로 to be careful을 쓴다.

POINT 2-4　명사적 용법: 의문사 + to부정사

연습문제

1	what to do	**2**	where to put
3	how to solve	**4**	when to hold
5	where to visit		

기출 적중문제

정답 how to get to city hall

해설 '나에게 시청에 어떻게 가는지 말해줄 수 있니?'라는 의미이므로 「how + to부정사」(어떻게 ~할지)를 쓴다.

POINT 3　형용사적 용법

 연습문제 **A**

1 brought a cup of coffee to drink
2 need some time to rest

3 have anything to eat
4 want a new computer to use
5 have many books to read
6 is looking for someone smart to solve
7 found three flowers to plant
8 is the best season to swim
9 have a lot of homework to do
10 bought something nice to wear
11 knows many tourist sites to visit

 연습문제 **B**
1 bought a house to live in
2 met new friends to talk to
3 recommended a song to listen to
4 a piece of paper to write on
5 isn't any chair to sit on

기출 적중문제
정답 ⑤
해설 write → write with

POINT 4 부사적 용법

 연습문제 **A**
1	to buy groceries	2	not safe to drink
3	grew up to be	4	comfortable to wear
5	difficult to read	6	to ask me something

 연습문제 **B**
1 was sad to hear the bad news
2 must be clever to repair computers
3 were excited to win the first prize
4 can't be honest to tell many lies
5 was surprised to see me in the market

 연습문제 **C**
1	ⓐ	2	ⓒ	3	ⓑ	4	ⓔ
5	ⓓ	6	ⓐ				

기출 적중문제
정답 ④
해설 주어진 문장과 ④: 목적
①: 판단의 근거 ②: 결과 ③: 감정의 원인
⑤: 형용사 수식

POINT 5 to부정사의 의미상 주어

 연습문제 **A**
1	for	2	of	3	of	4	of
5	for						

 연습문제 **B**
1 for me to understand
2 of her to ask
3 for us to follow
4 of him to lose

5 for cats to jump

POINT 6 too ~ to, enough to

 연습문제 **A**
1 too hot to play
2 strong enough to move
3 too hungry to concentrate
4 kind enough to help
5 hard enough to pass
6 too slow to win
7 too spicy for me to eat
8 brave enough to catch
9 too ill to go
10 large enough for us to throw

 연습문제 **B**
1 is so smart that he can be a doctor
2 is too sleepy to read the book
3 is small enough to fit in my bag
4 was so sour that I couldn't[could not] drink it
5 was too tired to walk home
6 is so funny that she can make me laugh
7 is sharp enough to cut everything
8 is so long that she can't[cannot] wear it

기출 적중문제
정답 ③
해설 「too + 형용사/부사 + to부정사」는 「so + 형용사/부사 + that + 주어 + can't + 동사원형」으로 바꿔 쓸 수 있고 배열한 부분이 'so boring that children couldn't watch it'이므로 다섯 번째에 오는 것은 couldn't이다.

POINT 7 원형부정사

연습문제
1	play, playing	2	feel
3	sing, singing	4	break, breaking
5	wash, to wash	6	get
7	borrow	8	burn, burning
9	write	10	shake, shaking

기출 적중문제
정답 ①
해설 make는 원형부정사를 목적격 보어로 쓰는 사역동사이므로 fall을 쓴다.

서술형 대비 문제

 Ⓐ
1	O	2	to wear

3 how to bake		**4** to drink	
5 for		**6** O	
7 is		**8** O	
9 It		**10** to sit on	

(B)
1 It is exciting to plan a trip.
2 It is wonderful to listen to his songs.
3 It is convenient to shop online.
4 It is my dream to become an astronaut.
5 It is dangerous to ride a bike without a helmet.
6 It was impossible to find an empty seat on the subway.
7 It is not wise to spend too much time on computer games.

(C)
1 is not safe to eat
2 refused to talk about the problem
3 needs a notebook to write in
4 lived to be 200 years old
5 does not have time to sleep
6 were surprised to see the shooting star
7 pass me something fun to read
8 use their trunks to communicate

(D)
1 is too young to drive a car
2 was so generous that he could forgive me
3 was so expensive that I couldn't[could not] buy it
4 is good enough to play in the major leagues
5 is so hard that I can't[cannot] chew it

중간·기말고사 실전 문제

1 ④ **2** ② **3** It, to finish the report
4 buying → to buy **5** ④ **6** ④ **7** ③
8 He told me not to expect a miracle. **9** ⑤
10 It is impossible to live without water. **11** ③
12 ① **13** what I should say **14** some
ways to protect your eyes **15** surprised to
receive a letter **16** ⑤ **17** ② **18** ①, ⑤
19 has sharp teeth to grab the animal **20** ②
21 to speak more slowly **22** ④ **23** a new
doll to play with **24** poisonous enough to kill
people **25** too dark for me to read the magazine
26 ② **27** to finish his homework **28** how to
speak English **29** ② **30** ③ **31** us
32 delicious **33** ④ **34** ② **35** of you
36 when to move **37** ④ **38** ①

1 want는 to부정사를 목적어로 쓰는 동사이므로 to get을 쓴다.

2
① lose → to lose
③ having → to have
④ leaves → leave
⑤ That → It

3 to부정사가 주어로 쓰일 때 주어 자리에 가주어 it을 쓰고 진주어 to부정사(구)를 뒤로 보낼 수 있다.

4 decide는 to부정사를 목적어로 쓰는 동사이므로 to buy를 쓴다.

5 목적격 보어로 원형부정사(swim)가 왔으므로 to부정사를 목적격 보어로 쓰는 allow는 쓸 수 없다.

6
① buying → to buy
② study → to study
③ heavy to something → something heavy to
⑤ speaking → to speak

7
· ask는 to부정사를 목적격 보어로 쓰는 동사이므로 to wait를 쓴다.
· make는 원형부정사를 목적격 보어로 쓰는 동사이므로 wash를 쓴다.

8 tell은 to부정사를 목적격 보어로 쓰는 동사이고, to부정사의 부정형은 「not to + 동사원형」이다.

9 ⑤: 부사적 용법 ①②③④: 명사적 용법

10 to부정사가 주어로 쓰일 때 주어 자리에 가주어 it을 쓰고 진주어 to부정사(구)를 뒤로 보낼 수 있다.

11 ③ to live → to live in

12 ①: 명사적 용법
밑줄 친 부분과 ②③④⑤: 형용사적 용법

13 「의문사 + to부정사」는 「의문사 + 주어 + should + 동사원형」으로 바꿔 쓸 수 있다.

14 '보호할 방법들'이라는 의미로 명사 ways를 수식하는 형용사적 용법의 to부정사를 쓴다.

15 '편지를 받아서 놀랐다'라는 의미로 감정의 원인을 나타내는 부사적 용법의 to부정사를 쓴다.

16 ⑤ laughing → laugh (make는 원형부정사를 목적격 보어로 쓰는 사역동사이다.)

17
· to부정사가 수식하는 명사 nests가 전치사의 목적어이고, '새들은 살 둥지를 짓는다.'라는 의미이므로 전치사 in을 쓴다.
· to부정사가 수식하는 명사 fork가 전치사의 목적어이고, '나는 먹을 포크가 필요하다.'라는 의미이므로 전치사 with를 쓴다.

18 밑줄 친 부분과 ①⑤: 목적(부사적 용법)
②: 감정의 원인(부사적 용법)
③: 형용사 수식(부사적 용법)
④: 판단의 근거(부사적 용법)

19 '붙잡을 이빨'이라는 의미로 명사 teeth를 수식하는 형용사적 용법의 to부정사를 쓴다.

20 · '나의 고양이는 식탁 위에 뛰어 오르기에 너무 무겁다.'라는 의미이므로 「too + 형용사/부사 + to부정사」(…하기에 너무 ~한)에서 too를 쓴다.
· 'Luna는 누구와 이야기하기에 너무 속상했다.'라는 의미이므로 「too + 형용사/부사 + to부정사」(…하기에 너무 ~한)에서 too를 쓴다.

21 ask는 to부정사를 목적격 보어로 쓰는 동사이므로 to speak를 쓴다.

22 주어진 문장과 ④: 형용사적 용법
①②: 부사적 용법   ③⑤: 명사적 용법

23 to부정사가 수식하는 명사 doll이 전치사의 목적어이므로 to부정사 뒤에 전치사 with를 쓴다.

24 「so + 형용사/부사 + that + 주어 + can + 동사원형」은 「형용사/부사 + enough + to부정사」로 바꿔 쓸 수 있다.

25 「so + 형용사/부사 + that + 주어 + can't + 동사원형」은 「too + 형용사/부사 + to부정사」로 바꿔 쓸 수 있다.

26 ⓐⓒⓓ: 형용사적 용법
ⓑ: 명사적 용법   ⓔ: 부사적 용법

27 '숙제를 끝내서 기뻤다'라는 의미로 감정의 원인을 나타내는 부사적 용법의 to부정사를 쓴다.

28 '어떻게 ~할지'라는 의미의 「how + to부정사」를 쓴다.

29 밑줄 친 부분과 ②: 감정의 원인(부사적 용법)
①④: 목적(부사적 용법)
③: 판단의 근거(부사적 용법)
⑤: 결과(부사적 용법)

30 ③ for → of (의미상 주어가 사람의 성격을 나타내는 형용사 뒤에 쓰일 때는 「of + 목적격」의 형태로 쓴다.)

31 to부정사가 주어로 쓰일 때 주어 자리에 가주어 it을 쓰고 진주어 to부정사(구)를 뒤로 보낼 수 있고, 의미상 주어는 「for + 목적격」의 형태로 쓴다. 전체 문장이 'It is important for us to respect others.'이므로 다섯 번째에 오는 것은 us이다.

32 -thing으로 끝나는 대명사(something)가 형용사와 to부정사의 수식을 동시에 받을 때는 「-thing + 형용사 + to부정사」의 형태로 쓴다. 전체 문장이 'He will cook something delicious to eat.'이므로 다섯 번째에 오는 것은 delicious이다.

33 ④ of   ①②③⑤ for

34 「형용사/부사 + enough + to부정사」는 「so + 형용사/부사 + that + 주어 + can + 동사원형」으로 바꿔 쓸 수 있다.

35 의미상 주어가 사람의 성격을 나타내는 형용사(foolish) 뒤에 쓰일 때는 「of + 목적격」의 형태로 쓴다.

36 '언제 ~할지'라는 의미의 「when + to부정사」를 쓴다.

37 ④ too   ①②③⑤ enough

38 ⓐⓑⓕ: 부사적 용법
ⓒⓓ: 명사적 용법   ⓔ: 형용사적 용법

CHAPTER 7
동명사
p.146

POINT 1 동명사의 형태와 쓰임

연습문제

1	ⓒ	2	ⓐ	3	ⓒ	4	ⓑ
5	ⓓ	6	ⓑ	7	ⓐ	8	ⓓ

기출 적중문제

정답 Go → Going[To go]
해설 주어 자리이므로 명사 역할을 하는 동명사 Going이나 to부정사 To go를 쓴다.

POINT 2 주어와 보어로 쓰이는 동명사

연습문제

1 Watching a magic show is
2 collecting movie posters
3 Exercising regularly is
4 Breaking old habits is
5 meeting my favorite actor
6 Exploring a new city is
7 reading more books this year

기출 적중문제

정답 Having good friends is important.
해설 주어 자리이므로 명사 역할을 하는 동명사 Having을 쓴다. 주어로 쓰인 동명사는 항상 단수 취급하므로 is를 쓴다.

POINT 3-1 동명사를 목적어로 쓰는 동사

연습문제
A

1	enjoy listening	2	denied hiding
3	decide to move	4	avoid taking
5	put off going	6	finished writing
7	stopped working	8	want to visit
9	kept thinking	10	need to play
11	imagine living	12	give up exercising
13	quit wasting	14	expect to stay
15	suggested eating	16	practices playing

연습문제
B

1	doing	2	to taste	3	O
4	to keep	5	riding	6	going
7	O	8	O	9	smoking
10	winning				

정답 ③

해설 going → to go (wish는 to부정사를 목적어로 쓰는 동사이다.)

POINT 3-2 동명사와 to부정사를 모두 목적어로 쓰는 동사 Ⅰ

1 waiting, to wait	2 using
3 to see	4 crying, to cry
5 to do	6 doing, to do
7 waking, to wake	8 speaking
9 spending, to spend	10 meeting
11 studying, to study	12 working, to work

정답 ③

해설 첫 번째 빈칸: like는 동명사와 to부정사를 모두 목적어로 쓰는 동사이므로 making이나 to make를 쓴다.
두 번째 빈칸: enjoy는 동명사를 목적어로 쓰는 동사이므로 making을 쓴다.

POINT 3-3 동명사와 to부정사를 모두 목적어로 쓰는 동사 Ⅱ

A
1 remember turning	2 forget to lock
3 try ordering	4 regretted fighting
5 tried to finish	6 Remember to buy
7 regret to tell	8 forget seeing

B
1 sharing	2 walking
3 to turn	4 meeting
5 drawing	6 to calm
7 spending	8 visiting
9 using	10 to brush

정답 ⑤

해설 to hide → hiding ('~한 것을 기억하다'라는 의미이므로 동사 remember 뒤에 동명사를 쓴다.)

POINT 4-1 동명사 관용 표현 Ⅰ

A
1 look forward to seeing
2 are afraid of failing
3 is bad at remembering
4 by exercising
5 thanked Sam for taking

---

6 are good at climbing
7 was sorry for[about] forgetting
8 felt like eating
9 thought of growing
10 On seeing
11 is tired of living
12 kept[prevented] me from focusing
13 is interested in learning
14 succeeded in inventing

B
1 swimming	2 carrying	3 using
4 doing	5 arriving	6 studying
7 solving	8 talking	

정답 by recycling plastic bottles

해설 '~함으로써'라는 의미의 「by + V-ing」를 쓴다.

POINT 4-2 동명사 관용 표현 Ⅱ

1 was busy doing
2 had trouble following
3 spent three hours writing
4 It's no use repairing
5 is worth buying
6 goes fishing
7 cannot help respecting[cannot but respect]

정답 wear → wearing

해설 '~하는 게 어때?'라는 의미의 「How about + V-ing ~?」를 쓴다.

서술형 대비 문제

A
1 Touching[To touch] a spider
2 becoming[to become] a violinist
3 playing badminton
4 taking[to take] a nap
5 to plant flowers
6 Eating[To eat] chocolate cake

B
1 is	2 O
3 getting[to get]	4 O
5 not having	6 Playing[To play]

C
1 watching	2 following
3 to visit	4 drinking
5 holding	6 to stay

7 dancing   8 to order
9 walking   10 to buy
11 borrowing

(D) 1 has trouble sleeping
2 looking forward to traveling
3 is interested in learning
4 am tired of listening
5 spend lots of money developing
6 are used to living
7 thanked Jamie for preparing

중간·기말고사 실전 문제

1 ⑤   2 ④   3 ②   4 Not wearing
5 ⑤   6 ③   7 ③, ④ 8 ④   9 ③
10 ③   11 ②   12 ③   13 ⑤
14 Emily will never forget seeing the Queen of England. 15 ④   16 Learning a new language takes   17 ④   18 (1) being[to be] a fashion designer (2) designing[to design] new clothes (3) drawing pictures, knitting sweaters   19 It's no use arguing about the problem. 20 ③   21 ③
22 playing   23 to have → having 24 feel → feeling   25 ①   26 (1) ⓑ → living (2) ⓒ → helps (3) ⓓ → visiting   27 ④
28 Washing your hands, is   29 ⑤   30 ②
31 ③   32 trying to put out 33 ④   34 ⑤
35 What do you say to taking   36 cannot help wondering   37 ⑤

1 주어 자리이므로 명사 역할을 하는 동명사 Climbing을 쓴다.

2 보어 자리이므로 명사 역할을 하는 동명사 writing을 쓴다.

3 enjoy는 동명사를 목적어로 쓰는 동사이므로 drinking을 쓴다.

4 '안전벨트를 매지 않는 것'이라는 의미이므로 주어 자리에 동명사를 쓴다. 동명사의 부정형은 동명사 앞에 not을 쓴다.

5 ⑤ to clean → cleaning

6 첫 번째 빈칸: imagine은 동명사를 목적어로 쓰는 동사이므로 flying을 쓴다.
두 번째 빈칸: '~하는 것을 생각하다'라는 의미의 「think of + V-ing」를 쓴다.

7 continue는 동명사와 to부정사를 모두 목적어로 쓰는 동사이므로 searching이나 to search를 쓴다.

8 '나는 나의 남동생에게 산타클로스가 존재하지 않는다고 말한 것을 후회해.'라는 의미이므로 동사 regret 뒤에 동명사 telling을 쓴다.

9 ③ to take → taking

10 ③: 진행형의 V-ing   주어진 문장과 ①②④⑤: 동명사

11 동명사 swimming이 목적어이므로 to부정사를 목적어로 쓰는 plan은 쓸 수 없다.

12 첫 번째 빈칸: '네가 나갈 때 너의 우산을 가지고 가는 것을 잊지 마.'라는 의미이므로 동사 forget 뒤에 to부정사 to take를 쓴다.
두 번째 빈칸: '~에 대해 …에게 감사하다'라는 의미의 「thank … for + V-ing」를 쓴다.

13 ⑤ to join → joining

14 'Emily는 영국의 여왕을 본 것을 결코 잊지 않을 것이다.'라는 의미이므로 동사 forget 뒤에 동명사 seeing을 쓴다.

15 ④: 진행형의 V-ing   ①②③⑤: 동명사

16 주어 자리이므로 명사 역할을 하는 동명사 Learning을 쓴다. 주어로 쓰인 동명사는 항상 단수 취급하므로 takes를 쓴다.

17 ・전치사(without)의 목적어 자리이므로 동명사 asking을 쓴다.
・'~하는 데 성공하다'라는 의미의 「succeed in + V-ing」를 쓴다.

18 (1) 보어 자리이므로 명사 역할을 하는 동명사 being이나 to부정사 to be를 쓴다.
(2) like는 동명사와 to부정사를 모두 목적어로 쓰는 동사이므로 designing이나 to design을 쓴다.
(3) '~하는 것을 잘하다'라는 의미의 「be good at + V-ing」를 쓴다.

19 '~해도 소용없다'라는 의미의 「It's no use + V-ing」를 쓴다.

20 ・'~하는 것에 싫증이 나다'라는 의미의 「be tired of + V-ing」를 쓴다.
・postpone은 동명사를 목적어로 쓰는 동사이므로 moving을 쓴다.

21 ⓐ to steal → stealing
ⓒ take → taking[to take]

22 첫 번째 빈칸: love는 동명사와 to부정사를 모두 목적어로 쓰는 동사이므로 playing이나 to play를 쓴다.
두 번째 빈칸: '~하는 것을 잘하다'라는 의미의 「be good at + V-ing」를 쓴다.

23 '~하는 게 어때?'라는 의미의 「What about + V-ing ~?」를 쓴다.

24 '~하지 않을 수 없다'라는 의미의 「cannot help + V-ing」를 쓴다.

25 (A): plan은 to부정사를 목적어로 쓰는 동사이므로 to get을 쓴다.
(B): '~하는 데 어려움을 겪다'라는 의미의 「have trouble + V-ing」를 쓴다.
(C): suggest는 동명사를 목적어로 쓰는 동사이므로 buying을 쓴다.

26 (1) imagine은 동명사를 목적어로 쓰는 동사이므로 living을 쓴다.
(2) 주어로 쓰인 동명사는 항상 단수 취급하므로 helps를 쓴다.
(3) '~하는 것을 기대하다'라는 의미의 「look forward to + V-ing」를 쓴다.

27 첫 번째 빈칸: '~하고 싶다'라는 의미의 「feel like + V-ing」를 쓴다.
두 번째 빈칸: '~하자마자'라는 의미의 「on + V-ing」를 쓴다.

28 주어 자리에 가주어 it이 쓰인 문장이므로 주어 자리에 동명사 Washing이 쓰인 문장으로 바꿔 쓸 수 있다.

29 「stop + to부정사」는 '~하기 위해 멈추다'라는 의미이고, 「stop + 동명사」는 '~하는 것을 멈추다'라는 의미이다.

30 '~하는 데 어려움을 겪다'라는 의미의 「have trouble + V-ing」를 쓴다.

31 ⓑⓓ: 보어   ⓐ: 전치사의 목적어   ⓒ: 주어
ⓔ: 동사의 목적어

32 '~하려고 노력하다'라는 의미이므로 동사 try 뒤에 to부정사 to put out을 쓴다.

33 '~한 것을 기억하다'라는 의미이므로 동사 remember 뒤에 동명사 calling을 쓴다.

34 내일 등산을 갈 계획이라는 말에 추울 것이라고 들었다고 했으므로 '너의 재킷을 가지고 가는 것을 잊지 마.'라는 말이 적절하다. '~할 것을 잊다'라는 의미이므로 동사 forget 뒤에 to부정사 to take를 쓴다.

35 '~하는 게 어때?'라는 의미의 「How about + V-ing ~?」는 「What do you say to + V-ing ~?」로 바꿔 쓸 수 있다.

36 '~하지 않을 수 없다'라는 의미의 「cannot but + 동사원형」은 「cannot help + V-ing」로 바꿔 쓸 수 있다.

37 ⓓ to break → breaking
ⓔ require → requires

CHAPTER 8
분사

p.166

POINT 1   분사의 형태와 쓰임

 연습문제

1 ⓐ	**2** ⓑ	**3** ⓐ	**4** ⓐ
5 ⓐ	**6** ⓐ	**7** ⓑ	**8** ⓐ
9 ⓑ	**10** ⓑ	**11** ⓐ	**12** ⓑ
13 ⓑ			

POINT 2   현재분사와 과거분사

연습문제 A

1 crying baby   **2** broken toy
3 frozen lake
4 fish swimming in the lake
5 sleeping boy   **6** ringing alarm
7 singing bird
8 cake covered with strawberry cream

연습문제 B

1 called	**2** sitting	**3** flying
4 made	**5** arrived	**6** rising
7 built	**8** turned	**9** filled
10 walking	**11** wearing	**12** damaged

기출 적중문제

정답   painting → painted
해설   명사 house를 수식하고 명사와의 관계가 수동이므로 과거분사 painted를 쓴다.

POINT 3   감정을 나타내는 분사

 연습문제 A

1 exciting	**2** depressed
3 amazing	**4** interesting
5 disappointed	**6** fascinating
7 touching	**8** shocked

연습문제 B

1 ① moving		② moved
2 ① tired		② tiring
3 ① shocking		② shocked
4 ① embarrassing		② embarrassed
5 ① bored		② boring
6 ① disappointed		② disappointing
7 ① satisfied		② satisfying
8 ① surprising		② surprised
9 ① confusing		② confused

POINT 4 현재분사 vs. 동명사

연습
문제
A

1 ⓑ	2 ⓐ	3 ⓐ	4 ⓐ
5 ⓑ	6 ⓑ	7 ⓐ	8 ⓑ
9 ⓑ	10 ⓐ	11 ⓐ	12 ⓑ

연습
문제
B

1 That singing girl is my classmate.
2 Where are your running shoes?
3 Her hobby is drawing cartoons.
4 I need some drinking water.
5 The bee is resting on a flower.
6 The chef is cooking a steak.
7 We have to keep walking forward.
8 I heard him yelling at someone.
9 Can you catch a flying butterfly?
10 Ken dove into the swimming pool.
11 The barking dog made people scared.
12 Learning new languages is fun.

POINT 5-1 분사구문 만드는 법

연습
문제

1 Looking out the window
2 Feeling sick
3 Eating breakfast
4 Being too short
5 Not having much time
6 Talking to his friend
7 Waiting in line
8 Not knowing what to do

POINT 5-2 분사구문의 다양한 의미

연습
문제
A

1 Running up the stairs
2 Being so depressed
3 Reaching the bank
4 Climbing the mountain
5 Not having enough money
6 Sitting on the beach
7 Reading a book
8 Studying hard

9 locking the door
10 Standing on the hill

연습
문제
B

1 Because I felt sleepy
2 When she took a walk
3 After he graduated from university
4 and we arrived in Hong Kong at noon

서술형 대비 문제

A

1 He had his shirt washed.
2 Sehun's new pink hair looks shocking.
3 O
4 Gina was pleased with her final grades.
5 Who is that man taking pictures?
6 I need to fix my broken computer.
7 Terry sleeps with the window closed.
8 Luke got me cheese made in France.
9 O
10 I want to raise a talking parrot.

B

1 ⓐ exciting   ⓑ amazed
  ⓒ touching   ⓓ fascinated
2 ⓐ interesting   ⓑ disappointed
  ⓒ boring   ⓓ tired

C

1 we watched a movie / Watching a movie
2 I didn't have a pen / Not having a pen
3 I saw a spider / Seeing a spider
4 she had a headache / Having a headache
5 they jogged together / Jogging together
6 she let the bird out / letting the bird out
7 he was tall / Being tall
8 I cleaned my room / Cleaning my room
9 he waited to buy a ticket / waiting to buy a ticket

중간·기말고사 실전 문제

| 1 ② | 2 ④ | 3 ④ | 4 ④ | 5 ④ |

6 held   7 ③, ⑤   8 ⑤   9 hidden by my dog   10 checking our IDs   11 ④

12 disappointed   13 ⑤   14 ②   15 Not

knowing the answer **16** with the door locked

17 ④　　**18** ②　　**19** ④　　**20** Not having her

wallet　　**21** ④　　**22** ②　　**23** Having some free

time　　**24** ②　　**25** ④　　**26** ③　　**27** ②

28 ③　　**29** ②　　**30** ①　　**31** ②　　**32** ③

33 After she entered the room / Entering the room

34 ③　　**35** Go → Going　　**36** ②

37 (1) ⓐ → bored (2) ⓓ → Following (3) ⓔ → injured

---

1 명사 girl을 수식하고 명사와의 관계가 능동이므로 현재분사 wearing을 쓴다.

2 목적어 the window를 보충 설명하고 목적어와의 관계가 수동이므로 과거분사 broken을 쓴다.

3 The price of the new smartphone은 감정을 일으키는 주체이므로 현재분사 shocking을 쓴다.

4 ① fallen → falling
② turning→ turned
③ making → made
⑤ satisfied → satisfying

5 (A): 목적어 the woman을 보충 설명하고 목적어와의 관계가 능동이므로 현재분사 playing을 쓴다.
(B): I는 감정을 느끼는 대상이므로 과거분사 moved를 쓴다.
(C): Her performance는 감정을 일으키는 주체이므로 현재분사 fascinating을 쓴다.

6 목적어 a concert를 보충 설명하고 목적어와의 관계가 수동이므로 과거분사 held를 쓴다.

7 The students는 감정을 느끼는 대상이므로 '~한 감정을 일으키는'의 의미인 현재분사 pleasing과 disappointing은 쓸 수 없다.

8 ① tiring → tired
② disappointed → disappointing
③ touching → touched
④ confused → confusing

9 과거분사 hidden이 전치사구(by my dog)와 함께 구를 이루어 쓰였으므로 명사 shoes 뒤에서 명사를 수식한다.

10 현재분사 checking이 목적어(our IDs)와 함께 구를 이루어 쓰였으므로 명사 man 뒤에서 명사를 수식한다.

11 ④ made → making

12 My family and I는 감정을 느끼는 대상이므로 과거분사 disappointed를 쓴다.

13 ・명사 dolphins를 수식하고 명사와의 관계가 능동이므로 현재분사 living을 쓴다.
・목적어 his bike를 보충 설명하고 목적어와의 관계가 수동이므로 과거분사 repaired를 쓴다.

14 (A): 명사 view를 수식하고 명사와의 관계가 능동이므로 현재분사 amazing을 쓴다.

(B): 명사 activities를 수식하고 명사와의 관계가 능동이므로 현재분사 exciting을 쓴다.
(C): you는 감정을 느끼는 대상이므로 과거분사 interested를 쓴다.

15 이유를 나타내는 분사구문이고, 분사구문의 부정형은 분사 앞에 not을 붙여 만들므로 Not knowing the answer를 쓴다.

16 '…가 ~한 채로'는 「with + 명사 + 분사」의 형태로 쓰고, 명사 door와의 관계가 수동이므로 과거분사 locked를 쓴다.

17 주어진 문장과 ④: 현재분사　　①②③⑤: 동명사

18 ・명사 students를 수식하고 명사와의 관계가 능동이므로 현재분사 studying을 쓴다.
・명사 people을 수식하고 명사와의 관계가 능동이므로 현재분사 waiting을 쓴다.

19 ④ pulling → pulled

20 접속사 Because와 주어 she를 생략하고 동사 didn't have를 Not having으로 바꾼다.

21 ④: 현재분사　　①②③⑤: 동명사

22 첫 번째 빈칸: it은 감정을 일으키는 주체이므로 현재분사 amazing을 쓴다.
두 번째 빈칸: You는 감정을 느끼는 대상이므로 과거분사 excited를 쓴다.

23 접속사 When과 주어 I를 생략하고 동사 had를 Having으로 바꾼다.

24 ⓐⓑⓔ: 현재분사　　ⓒⓓ: 동명사

25 접속사 While과 주어 I를 생략하고 동사 watched를 Watching으로 바꾼다.

26 목적어 Ryan and Emily를 보충 설명하고 목적어와의 관계가 능동이므로 현재분사 arguing을 쓴다.

27 ② depressed → depressing

28 주어진 문장과 ③: 현재분사　　①②④⑤: 동명사

29 ・'나는 기차를 기다리면서, 만화책을 읽었다.'라는 의미의 분사구문이므로 Waiting을 쓴다.
・명사 car를 수식하고 명사와의 관계가 수동이므로 parked를 쓴다.

30 '나는 목이 말랐기 때문에, 차가운 물 세 컵을 마셨다.'라는 의미이므로 이유를 나타내는 As I was thirsty를 쓴다.

31 ②: 현재분사　　①③④⑤: 동명사

32 ⓑ excited → exciting
ⓒ amazed → amazing
ⓔ satisfying → satisfied

33 첫 번째 문장: '~한 후에'라는 의미의 접속사 After를 쓰고, 문장의 시제가 과거이므로 entered를 쓴다.
두 번째 문장: 접속사 After와 주어 she를 생략하고 동사 entered를 Entering으로 바꾼다.

34 접속사 Because와 주어 he를 생략하고 동사 has를 Having으로 바꾼다.

35 '나는 나의 방 안으로 들어가면서, 불을 켰다.'라는 의미의 분사구문이므로 Going을 쓴다.

36 ⓐ confused → confusing
ⓒ knitting → knitted

37 (1) He는 감정을 느끼는 대상이므로 과거분사 bored를 쓴다.
(2) '그는 소음을 따라갔을 때, 부상을 입은 새를 발견했다.'라는 의미의 분사구문이므로 Following을 쓴다.
(3) 명사 bird를 수식하고 명사와의 관계가 수동이므로 과거분사 injured를 쓴다.

CHAPTER 9
명사와 관사

p.186

POINT 1 셀 수 있는 명사와 셀 수 없는 명사

연습문제 A

1	O	2	X	3	O	4	X
5	X	6	O	7	O	8	X
9	X	10	X	11	O	12	X
13	X	14	X	15	O	16	X
17	O	18	X				

연습문제 B

1	①	2	③	3	③	4	①
5	②	6	②				

연습문제 C

1	chairs	2	a question
3	orange juice	4	money
5	Hallasan	6	family
7	sugar	8	information
9	An elephant	10	teams
11	December		

기출 적중문제

정답 ③
해설 trashes → trash

POINT 2 셀 수 있는 명사의 복수형

연습문제 A

1	bottles	2	cities	3	watches
4	mice	5	potatoes	6	friends
7	oxen	8	geese	9	deer
10	brushes	11	tomatoes	12	women
13	dishes	14	bicycles	15	roofs
16	keys	17	photos	18	zoos
19	knives	20	dolphins	21	sheep
22	activities	23	cameras	24	lives
25	babies	26	radios	27	feet
28	memories	29	buses	30	neighbors
31	shelves	32	cliffs		

연습문제 B

1	men	2	children	3	girls
4	pianos	5	heroes	6	town
7	temple	8	teeth	9	Leaves
10	ring	11	videos	12	thieves
13	universities	14	address	15	roofs

기출 적중문제

정답 ③
해설 deer - deer

POINT 3 셀 수 없는 명사의 수량 표현

연습문제 A
1 seven glasses of water
2 a slice of cake
3 three spoonfuls of salt
4 two bowls of salad

연습문제 B
1	cup	2	slices
3	gold	4	spoonfuls
5	rice	6	loaves of bread
7	glass	8	slices
9	piece	10	sheets of paper
11	pieces of furniture	12	cans
13	bottles of milk	14	cup

기출 적중문제

정답 two loaves of bread, a bowl of soup

해설 첫 번째 빈칸: 셀 수 없는 명사 bread는 단위명사 loaf로 수량을 나타내고, 복수형은 loaves를 쓴다.
두 번째 빈칸: 셀 수 없는 명사 soup는 단위명사 bowl로 수량을 나타낸다.

POINT 4 명사 관련 표현

연습문제 A
1 a pair of sunglasses
2 three-month vacation
3 Five pairs of red socks
4 two-door car
5 ten pairs of new sneakers
6 three-room house
7 a glove
8 five-year-old brother
9 four pairs of shorts
10 twenty-dollar bill
11 a pair of scissors

연습문제 B
1 Nabi
2 Teresa
3 Paul likes Karen
4 the best soccer player
5 I should read more books
6 the climate is changing
7 one of the world's most famous paintings
8 the flight has been canceled

기출 적중문제

정답 ③

해설 eleven-months-old baby → eleven-month-old baby

POINT 5 명사의 소유격

연습문제
1 Sally's dolls
2 women's restroom
3 the color of the flag
4 Parents' Day
5 the top of the mountain
6 yesterday's newspaper
7 the soldier's uniform
8 animals' behavior
9 the title of this movie
10 five pounds' weight

POINT 6-1 부정관사 a(n)의 쓰임

연습문제
1	ⓐ	2	ⓒ	3	ⓑ	4	ⓐ
5	ⓑ	6	ⓒ	7	ⓑ	8	ⓐ
9	ⓒ	10	ⓐ				

POINT 6-2 정관사 the의 쓰임

연습문제
1	The	2	the	3	a	4	the
5	the	6	a	7	the	8	the
9	the	10	an	11	The		

POINT 6-3 관사를 쓰지 않는 경우

연습문제
1	X	2	a	3	the	4	X
5	the	6	a	7	The	8	X
9	the	10	X	11	X	12	the
13	X	14	X				

서술형 대비 문제

(A)
1	tomatoes	2	sheep
3	O	4	leaves
5	three-volume	6	pictures
7	geese	8	Children's Day
9	luck	10	O
11	O	12	furniture
13	O	14	two-week

(B)
1 ⓐ a ⓑ A ⓒ the ⓓ X ⓔ an ⓕ X
2 ⓐ X ⓑ the ⓒ the ⓓ a ⓔ X ⓕ the

1 ⓐ a bottle of orange juice
  ⓑ three slices[pieces] of pizza
  ⓒ two loaves of bread
  ⓓ a pair of sunglasses
  ⓔ five cans of coke
2 ⓐ two glasses of milk
  ⓑ four slices[pieces] of cake
  ⓒ a bar of chocolate
  ⓓ two sheets[pieces] of paper
  ⓔ a pair of shorts

중간·기말고사 실전 문제

1 ② **2** ④ **3** ③, ⑤ **4** ⑤ **5** ③
6 ② **7** ② **8** ③ **9** ②
10 a pair of socks **11** two loaves of bread
12 ② **13** ④ **14** ③ **15** ⑤ **16** Daniel is a 15-year-old boy. **17** They asked for seven glasses of orange juice. **18** my grandparents' house **19** The shape of the umbrella **20** ③
21 ③ **22** ② **23** a bowl of cereal, two slices [pieces] of bread **24** three bottles of ink, a can of paint **25** ⑤ **26** (1) ⓐ → children (2) ⓓ → sandwiches

1 ① knife – knives
  ③ foot – feet
  ④ baby – babies
  ⑤ mouse – mice

2 ④: tree는 보통명사, peace는 추상명사, juice는 물질명사이다.
  ①: 집합명사 ②: 고유명사 ③: 보통명사 ⑤: 추상명사

3 pear와 egg는 셀 수 있는 명사이므로 단수일 때는 앞에 a(n)을 붙인다.

4 ① slice → slices
  ② soaps → soap
  ③ sheet → piece
  ④ cup of coffees → cups of coffee

5 수를 나타내는 형용사 many와 함께 쓸 수 있는 것은 셀 수 있는 명사의 복수형이므로 deer의 복수형인 deer를 쓴다.

6 ② oxes → oxen

7 · 셀 수 없는 명사 cake는 단위명사 slice나 piece로 수량을 나타낸다.
  · 셀 수 없는 명사 paper는 단위명사 sheet나 piece로 수량을 나타낸다.

8 ③ a → the (악기 이름 앞에는 정관사 the를 쓴다.)

9 hat과 pencil case는 셀 수 있는 명사의 단수형이므로 a와 함께 쓸 수 있다.

10 한 쌍이 짝을 이루는 명사 sock은 항상 복수형(socks)으로 쓰고, a pair of를 활용하여 수량을 나타낸다.

11 셀 수 없는 명사 bread는 단위명사 loaf(덩어리)로 수량을 나타내고, 복수형은 loaves를 쓴다.

12 ① A knowledge → Knowledge
  ③ an air → air
  ④ milks → milk
  ⑤ informations → information

13 · 셀 수 없는 명사 chocolate은 단위명사 bar로 수량을 나타내고, 복수형은 bars를 쓴다.
  · 셀 수 없는 명사 soup는 단위명사 bowl로 수량을 나타낸다.

14 ⓑ five cans of sodas → five cans of soda
  ⓒ a pair of scissor → a pair of scissors

15 주어진 문장과 ⑤: ~마다(per)
  ①②④: 하나의(one) ③: 종족 전체를 대표할 때

16 하이픈(-)으로 연결되어 명사를 꾸미는 「숫자 + 단위명사」의 단위명사는 항상 단수형으로 쓰므로 15-year-old를 쓴다.

17 셀 수 없는 명사 orange juice의 복수형은 단위명사 glass에 -(e)s를 붙여 만들므로 seven glasses of orange juice를 쓴다.

18 사람을 나타내며 -s로 끝나는 복수명사(grandparents)의 소유격은 명사에 -'를 붙여 만들므로 my grandparents' house를 쓴다.

19 무생물을 나타내는 명사(umbrella)의 소유격은 주로 「of + 명사」로 나타내므로 The shape of the umbrella를 쓴다.

20 ③: 부사절 뒤에 쓰는 콤마(,) ①②④⑤: 동격 콤마(,)

21 (A) 하이픈(-)으로 연결되어 명사를 꾸미는 「숫자 + 단위명사」의 단위명사는 항상 단수형으로 쓰므로 month를 쓴다.
  (B) 수를 나타내는 형용사 many와 함께 쓸 수 있는 것은 셀 수 있는 명사의 복수형이므로 bookstores를 쓴다.
  (C) 셀 수 없는 명사 dust는 앞에 a(n)을 붙일 수 없고 복수형으로도 쓸 수 없으므로 dust를 쓴다.

22 ② 빈칸 뒤의 capital city가 전치사구(of France)의 수식을 받고 있으므로 정관사 the를 쓴다.
  ① 빈칸 뒤의 장소(church)가 본래의 목적(예배)으로 쓰였으므로 관사를 쓰지 않는다.
  ③ 과목 이름(math) 앞에는 관사를 쓰지 않는다.
  ④ 「by + 교통수단」에서 교통수단(subway) 앞에는 관사를 쓰지 않는다.
  ⑤ 식사 이름(dinner) 앞에는 관사를 쓰지 않는다.

23 첫 번째 빈칸: 셀 수 없는 명사 cereal은 단위명사 bowl로 수량을 나타낸다.
  두 번째 빈칸: 셀 수 없는 명사 bread는 단위명사 slice/piece (조각)로 수량을 나타내고, 복수형은 slices/pieces를 쓴다.

24 첫 번째 빈칸: 셀 수 없는 명사 ink는 단위명사 bottle로 수량을 나타내고, 복수형은 bottles를 쓴다.

두 번째 빈칸: 셀 수 없는 명사 paint는 can으로 수량을 나타낸다.

25 ⑤ the taxi → taxi (「by + 교통수단」에서 교통수단(taxi) 앞에는 관사를 쓰지 않는다.)

26 (1) 셀 수 있는 명사(child)는 복수일 때 복수형으로 써야 하므로 children을 쓴다.

(2) 수를 나타내는 형용사 a few와 함께 쓸 수 있는 것은 셀 수 있는 명사의 복수형이므로 sandwiches를 쓴다.

CHAPTER 10
대명사

POINT 1 인칭대명사

연습문제 A

1 You		**2** My		**3** us	
4 their		**5** me		**6** her	
7 my		**8** me		**9** Its	
10 your		**11** her		**12** He	
13 It		**14** we		**15** them	
16 him					

연습문제 B

1 My, mine	**2** your, Yours
3 his, his	**4** her, Hers
5 ours, our	**6** theirs, Their

기출 적중문제

정답 ③

해설 첫 번째 빈칸: 빈칸 뒤에 소유의 대상이 되는 명사 first class 가 왔으므로 소유격 your를 쓴다.

두 번째 빈칸: 앞에서 언급된 (your) first class(너의 첫 번째 수업)를 대신하고 있으므로 3인칭 단수 주격 it을 쓴다.

POINT 2 재귀대명사

연습문제 A

1 himself	**2** her
3 herself	**4** me
5 themselves	**6** myself
7 us	**8** ourselves

연습문제 B

1 X	**2** O	**3** X	**4** O
5 O	**6** X	**7** X	

연습문제 C

1 talks to himself
2 helped themselves to
3 by herself
4 enjoy yourselves
5 made ourselves at home
6 thought to myself
7 in itself
8 for himself

기출 적중문제

정답 ①, ⑤

해설 ①⑤: 강조 용법(생략 가능)
②③④: 재귀 용법(생략 불가능)

메인북 정답 및 해설 l **Chapter 10** 대명사 **29**

POINT 3 지시대명사

연습문제 A
1 those　2 that　3 This
4 these

연습문제 B
1 ⓐ　2 ⓑ　3 ⓑ　4 ⓐ
5 ⓑ　6 ⓐ　7 ⓐ　8 ⓑ

연습문제 C
1 that　2 those　3 that
4 those　5 those

기출 적중문제
정답 ④
해설 ④: 지시대명사　①②③⑤: 지시형용사

POINT 4 it의 다양한 쓰임

연습문제 A
1 isn't hard to make a snowman
2 is important to keep your promises
3 is sad that our journey ends tomorrow
4 is useful to know some scientific facts
5 is impossible to predict the future
6 is surprising that you remember my address
7 is healthy to eat an apple every day
8 is interesting that baby seals can't swim

연습문제 B
1 ⓑ　2 ⓐ　3 ⓑ　4 ©
5 ⓐ　6 ©　7 ©　8 ⓑ
9 ⓐ　10 ©　11 ⓑ　12 ⓐ

기출 적중문제
정답 ④
해설 주어진 문장과 ④: 가주어 it　①③: 비인칭 주어 it
②⑤: 대명사 it

POINT 5-1 부정대명사: one

연습문제
1 one　2 them　3 ones
4 it　5 ones　6 one
7 ones　8 them　9 one
10 it　11 one　12 One
13 them

POINT 5-2 부정대명사: some, any

연습문제
1 some　2 some
3 any　4 any
5 some　6 some

7 any　8 some
9 any　10 some
11 something　12 anybody
13 Someone　14 something
15 anything　16 Someone

POINT 5-3 부정대명사: another, other

연습문제 A
1 others　2 another
3 other　4 another

연습문제 B
1 One, the other
2 Some, the others
3 One, another, the other
4 Some, others

기출 적중문제
정답 One, the other
해설 「one ~, the other -」'(둘 중) 하나는 ~, 나머지 하나는 -'

POINT 5-4 부정대명사: all, both, each, every

연습문제 A
1 All the students have to wear a uniform.
2 Both the cars are made in Germany.
3 Each of the girls has a different hobby.
4 All of the money was stolen by the thief.
5 Animals can communicate with one another.
6 Not every Korean likes spicy food.
7 Each hockey team is preparing for the final match.
8 The Earth and the Moon pull each other.
9 Everybody was playing a board game.
10 Not all fat is bad for your health.

연습문제 B
1 are　2 was　3 knows
4 need　5 are　6 grows
7 looks　8 was　9 is
10 sends

기출 적중문제
정답 ③
해설 cost → costs

POINT 6 의문대명사

연습문제 A
1 Who　2 Which　3 Whose
4 What　5 whom

연습문제 B

1	What	**2**	Which
3	Whose	**4**	Who[Whom]
5	Who	**6**	whom
7	Which	**8**	What

연습문제 C

1 Which restaurant do you recommend?
2 Which hotel will your family book?
3 What subject does Semi like to study?
4 What flower did Eric give to Samantha?
5 Which hero do you like in the movie?

기출 적중문제

정답 (1) Which (2) Who (3) What
해설 (1) 정해진 범위 안에서의 선택을 묻고 있고 빈칸 뒤에 명사 (shirt)가 있으므로 의문형용사 Which를 쓴다.
　　(2) '누가 너에게 어떻게 자전거를 타는지 가르쳐줬니?'라는 의미이므로 의문대명사 Who를 쓴다.
　　(3) '너는 저녁 식사 후에 무엇을 할 거니?'라는 의미이므로 의문대명사 What을 쓴다.

서술형 대비 문제

A

1	himself	**2**	ourselves
3	herself	**4**	itself
5	themselves	**6**	herself
7	myself	**8**	himself
9	yourself[yourselves]		

B
1 It will be cold
2 It wasn't my idea
3 It was very dark
4 It is important to eat breakfast
5 It is true that pets are good friends
6 It is easy to catch a cold
7 It is September 12
8 It was disappointing that my team lost the game

C
1 One is a handbag, the other is a backpack
2 Some are brown, the others are gray
3 One is a jacket, another is a coat, the other is a skirt
4 Some are pears, others are melons
5 One is sleeping, the other is sitting
6 Some are baseballs, the others are basketballs
7 One is happiness, another is love, the other is health

D

1	children	**2**	O
3	were	**4**	passenger

5	O	**6**	was
7	class	**8**	these postcards
9	my hands		

중간·기말고사 실전 문제

1	②	**2**	②	**3**	④	**4**	①, ③
5	yourself	**6**	③	**7**	④	**8**	④
9	②	**10**	⑤	**11**	Which	**12**	④
13	④	**14**	④, ⑤	**15**	other → the other		
16	enjoyed ourselves			**17**	④	**18**	③
19	③	**20**	②	**21**	⑤	**22**	③	**23**	①, ④
24	①	**25**	④	**26**	⑤	**27**	②, ⑤	**28**	is

28 important to recycle plastics **29** ③ **30** ④
31 (1) this (2) that (3) These **32** ② **33** ④
34 ②, ④ **35** Some are playing the violin, the others are playing

1 첫 번째 빈칸: 빈칸 뒤에 소유의 대상이 되는 명사 phone이 왔으므로 소유격 your를 쓴다.
　　두 번째 빈칸: '너의 것'이라는 의미의 소유대명사 yours를 쓴다.

2 ②: 대명사 it　①③④⑤: 비인칭 주어 it

3 ① that → those
　　② These → This
　　③ him → his
　　⑤ those → that

4 ①③: 강조 용법(생략 가능)　②④⑤: 재귀 용법(생략 불가능)

5 동사 cut의 목적어가 주어 You와 같은 대상이므로 재귀대명사 yourself를 쓴다.

6 「one ~, the other -」'(둘 중) 하나는 ~, 나머지 하나는 -'

7 「some ~, others -」'(여럿 중) 몇몇은 ~, 다른 것들은 -'

8 '몇몇 사람들은 많은 사람들 앞에서 그들 자신에 대해 이야기하는 것을 불편하게 느낀다.'라는 의미이므로 재귀대명사 themselves를 쓴다.

9 ① you → yourself
　　③ myself → themselves
　　④ me → myself
　　⑤ themselves → itself

10 · 빈칸 뒤에 단수 동사(is)가 왔으므로 단수 취급하는 「each of + 복수명사(the potatoes)」를 쓴다.
　　· 빈칸 뒤에 복수 동사(were)가 왔으므로 복수 취급하는 「all + 복수명사(the stores)」를 쓴다.

11 정해진 범위 안에서의 선택을 묻고 있고 빈칸 뒤에 명사(cake)가 있으므로 의문형용사 Which를 쓴다.

12 앞에서 언급된 명사(balloon)와 같은 종류의 불특정한 사물을 가리키고 있으므로 부정대명사 one을 쓴다.

13 · 「all + 복수명사」는 복수 취급하므로 were를 쓴다.
· 「each + 단수명사」는 단수 취급하므로 has를 쓴다.

14 주어진 문장과 ④⑤: 가주어 it
①: 비인칭 주어 it　　②③: 대명사 it

15 「one ~, the other -」 '(둘 중) 하나는 ~, 나머지 하나는 -'

16 「enjoy oneself」 '즐거운 시간을 보내다'

17 ⓑⓒⓔ: 대명사 it　　ⓐ: 비인칭 주어 it　　ⓓ: 가주어 it

18 · 앞에서 언급된 특정한 대상(a letter)을 가리키고 있으므로 it을 쓴다.
· 앞에서 언급된 복수명사(gloves)와 같은 종류의 불특정한 사물을 가리키고 있으므로 부정대명사 ones를 쓴다.

19 ③: 앞에서 언급된 명사(car)와 같은 종류의 불특정한 사물을 가리키고 있으므로 부정대명사 one을 쓴다.

20 ② author → authors

21 첫 번째 빈칸: 「help oneself to」 '~을 마음껏 먹다'
두 번째 빈칸: 요청을 나타내는 의문문이므로 some을 쓴다.

22 · 「some ~, others -」 '(여럿 중) 몇몇은 ~, 다른 사람들은 -'
· '약간의 질문들'이라는 의미이고 긍정문이므로 some을 쓴다.

23 주어진 문장과 ①④: 강조 용법　　②③⑤: 재귀 용법

24 「one ~, another -, the other …」 '(셋 중) 하나는 ~, 다른 하나는 -, 나머지 하나는 …'

25 ④: '너는 누구와 함께 극장에 갔니?'라는 의미이고 빈칸 앞에 전치사(With)가 있으므로 whom을 쓴다.

26 ① likes → like
② have → has
③ eats → eat
④ was → were

27 주어진 문장과 ②⑤: 지시형용사
①③④: 지시대명사

28 to부정사구가 문장의 주어로 쓰였을 때는 주로 주어 자리에 가주어 it을 쓰고 진주어를 뒤로 보낸다.

29 첫 번째 빈칸: 「one ~, the other -」 '(둘 중) 하나는 ~, 나머지 하나는 -'
두 번째 빈칸: 두 명의 남동생들이 서로 싸운다고 했으므로 '(둘 사이에) 서로'라는 의미의 each other를 쓴다.

30 ⓒ yourself → himself
ⓔ him → himself

31 (1) 가까이 있는 단수의 사물(a phone)을 가리키고 있으므로 this를 쓴다.
(2) 비교 표현에서 앞에 나온 단수명사(The population)의 반복을 피하기 위해 사용했으므로 that을 쓴다.
(3) 가까이 있는 복수의 사물(laptops)를 수식하고 있으므로

These를 쓴다.

32 '너는 누구에게 그 소포를 보낼 거니?'라는 의미이고 빈칸 앞에 전치사(To)가 있으므로 whom을 쓴다.

33 ④ another → the other

34 ②: 비인칭 주어 it　④: 가주어 it
주어진 문장과 ①③⑤: 대명사 it

35 「some ~, the others -」 '(여럿 중) 몇몇은 ~, 나머지 전부는 -'

CHAPTER 11
형용사

p.232

POINT 1 형용사의 용법

A
1 is a round stone
2 was an amazing musical
3 is a shiny diamond
4 is an old and broken car
5 is a clever boy
6 was a rich and famous singer

B
1	alike	2	live	3	scared
4	alive	5	sleeping		

POINT 2 -thing/-body/-one + 형용사

1 Would you like to have something sweet?
2 Have you ever met anyone famous?
3 Nothing special happened last night.
4 My mother met somebody kind at the post office.
5 He couldn't find anything wrong with his computer.
6 We can learn new things when we travel abroad.
7 There was somebody funny at Mina's birthday party.

기출 적중문제

정답 sticky something → something sticky
해설 -thing으로 끝나는 대명사(something)를 수식할 때는 형용사(sticky)가 대명사 뒤에 온다.

POINT 3 the + 형용사

A
1 The young should listen to their parents.
2 We did some volunteer work for the poor.
3 Many charities offer free meals to the homeless.
4 The school trains guide dogs for the blind.
5 They took care of the injured at the hospital.

B
1	The	2	are	3	use
4	Do	5	have	6	the blind

POINT 4-1 수사: 기수와 서수

A
1	ninth	2	fourth
3	ten	4	thirty-first
5	twenty-second	6	seventieth
7	eightieth	8	thirty-three
9	a[one] hundred	10	sixty-two
11	eleventh	12	eighteen
13	seventy-fifth	14	one thousandth
15	fifty-nine	16	forty

B
1 three daughters, third daughter
2 fifty guests, fiftieth guest
3 six dishes, sixth dish
4 twenty-five floors, twenty-fifth floor
5 twelve colored pencils, twelfth colored pencil

C
1	Millions of dollars	2	Four thousand days
3	hundreds of flowers	4	thousands of years
5	a[one] million trees		

기출 적중문제

정답 Thousands of koalas live in Australia.
해설 「thousands + of + 복수명사」 '수천의 ~'

POINT 4-2 수사: 분수, 배수, 횟수

1 one-quarter[a quarter/one-fourth/a fourth]
2	once	3	twice
4	five-sixths	5	three and two-thirds
6	five times	7	four times
8	Two-ninths		

POINT 4-3 수사: 연도와 날짜

1 nineteen fifty-eight
2 July (the) fifteenth[the fifteenth of July]
3 November (the) thirty-first[the thirty-first of November]
4 twelve sixty-five
5 the nineteen nineties
6 two thousand (and) seven
7 January (the) first[the first of January]
8 the fourteen hundreds
9 September (the) fourth[the fourth of September]

정답 　June (the) twenty-third[the twenty-third of June]

해설 　6월 23일 → June (the) twenty-third[the twenty-third of June]

POINT 5-1 　수량형용사: many, much, a lot of

1	many	**2**	much	**3**	many
4	much	**5**	many	**6**	Many
7	much	**8**	many	**9**	much
10	much	**11**	much	**12**	many
13	much	**14**	many	**15**	much

연습
문제
B

1 My neighbor has many flowers in her garden.
2 Is there much water in the bottle?
3 You should eat many vegetables.
4 We don't have much time to get ready.
5 Do you save much money every month?
6 Many soldiers fought for peace.
7 She made many friends on her trip to Europe.
8 Alex's mentor didn't give him much advice.
9 Did you have much fun at the summer camp?
10 There were many problems with the new machine.

정답 　many → much[a lot of/lots of/plenty of]

해설 　bread는 셀 수 없는 명사이므로 셀 수 없는 명사와 함께 쓰는 much[a lot of/lots of/plenty of]를 쓴다.

POINT 5-2 　수량형용사: (a) few, (a) little

연습
문제
A

1	Few	**2**	little	**3**	a little
4	a few	**5**	a little	**6**	a few
7	a few	**8**	few	**9**	a little
10	A few				

1	A few birds	**2**	few coins
3	little rice	**4**	a little flour
5	few frogs	**6**	a little ketchup
7	Few tourists	**8**	a few dollars
9	little help		

정답 　③, ⑤

해설 　① a few → a little
　　② a little → a few
　　④ a few → a little

POINT 5-3 　수량형용사: some, any

1	Some	**2**	any	**3**	any
4	some	**5**	some	**6**	any
7	some	**8**	any	**9**	some
10	any	**11**	any		

서술형 대비 문제

Ⓐ
1 O
2 hundreds of beautiful beaches
3 The twenty-fifth
4 O
5 the nineteen-twenties
6 O
7 some
8 any
9 millions of lives
10 one-third[a third]

Ⓑ
1 dirty thing
2 anybody strange
3 anything spicy
4 someone interested
5 nobody famous
6 something new
7 nothing useful
8 somebody creative

Ⓒ
1	many ways	**2**	a little courage
3	much damage	**4**	A few children
5	few chances	**6**	many insects
7	a little sleep	**8**	much trash
9	little rain	**10**	a few mistakes

중간·기말고사 실전 문제

1 ③ 　**2** ⑤ 　**3** different anything → anything different 　**4** ③ 　**5** ①, ⑤
6 the disabled 　**7** ⑤ 　**8** famous
9 ④ 　**10** ② 　**11** ② 　**12** ③ 　**13** ④
14 ③ 　**15** four times 　**16** July (the) twenty-fifth[the twenty-fifth of July] 　**17** ① 　**18** ④
19 ④ 　**20** ③ 　**21** ② 　**22** little water
23 ④ 　**24** ④ 　**25** ①, ②

1 　③: 서술적 용법 　①②④⑤: 한정적 용법

2 ⑤ live → alive

3 -thing으로 끝나는 대명사(anything)를 수식할 때는 형용사(different)가 대명사 뒤에 온다.

4 tea는 셀 수 없는 명사이고 '나는 약간의 차를 마신 후에 따뜻하게 느꼈다.'라는 의미이므로 a little(약간의)을 쓴다.

5 fish는 셀 수 있는 명사의 복수형이므로, '많은(a lot of)'이라는 의미이며 셀 수 있는 명사와 함께 쓰는 many와 a number of를 쓴다.

6 「the + 형용사」(~한 사람들) = 「형용사 + people」

7 첫 번째 빈칸: people은 셀 수 있는 명사의 복수형이므로 셀 수 있는 명사와 함께 쓰는 Many를 쓴다.
두 번째 빈칸: friends는 셀 수 있는 명사의 복수형이고 '약간의 친구들이 병원에 있는 그를 방문했다.'라는 의미이므로 a few(약간의)를 쓴다.

8 -one으로 끝나는 대명사(anyone)를 수식할 때는 형용사(famous)가 대명사 뒤에 오고 전체 문장이 'Have you met anyone famous before?'이므로 다섯 번째에 오는 것은 famous이다.

9 ① some → any
② any → some
③ some → any
⑤ some → any

10 · -thing으로 끝나는 대명사(nothing)를 수식할 때는 형용사(important)가 대명사 뒤에 온다.
· salt는 셀 수 없는 명사이므로 셀 수 없는 명사와 함께 쓰는 a little을 쓴다.

11 ② new someone → someone new

12 ⓐ eighty-second → eighty-two
ⓒ nineteen fifty-ones → nineteen fifty-one
ⓓ the twelve of November → the twelfth of November [November (the) twelfth]
ⓔ one-fourths → one-fourth[a fourth/one-quarter/a quarter]

13 children은 셀 수 있는 명사의 복수형이므로 셀 수 없는 명사와 함께 쓰는 a little은 쓸 수 없다.

14 ③: cream은 셀 수 없는 명사이므로 셀 수 있는 명사와 함께 쓰는 a few를 쓸 수 없다.

15 '한 번, 두 번'을 제외한 횟수는 「기수 + times」로 나타내므로 four times를 쓴다.

16 7월 25일 → July (the) twenty-fifth[the twenty-fifth of July]

17 (A) -thing으로 끝나는 대명사(something)를 수식할 때는 형용사(sweet)가 대명사 뒤에 온다.
(B) 권유를 나타내는 의문문에는 some을 쓴다.
(C) '초콜릿 두 개'라는 의미이므로 기수인 two를 쓴다.

18 ④ special something → something special

19 ① many → much
② few → little
③ little → few
⑤ a few → a little

20 ① million → millions
② thousands → thousand
④ eight → eighth
⑤ customer → customers

21 ⓒ a little → a few
ⓓ many → much

22 water(물)는 셀 수 없는 명사이므로 little(거의 없는)과 함께 쓴다.

23 essays는 셀 수 있는 명사의 복수형이고 advice는 셀 수 없는 명사이므로 셀 수 있는 명사, 셀 수 없는 명사 모두와 함께 쓸 수 있는 some을 쓴다. any는 긍정문과 요청을 나타내는 의문문에 쓸 수 없다.

24 (A) sleep은 셀 수 없는 명사이고 '위층이 너무 시끄러웠기 때문에 준수는 어젯밤에 거의 잠을 자지 못했다.'라는 의미이므로 little(거의 없는)을 쓴다.
(B) languages는 셀 수 있는 명사의 복수형이고 'Joe는 여러 나라에서 살아와서 많은 언어를 말할 수 있다.'라는 의미이므로 many(많은)를 쓴다. any는 긍정문에 쓸 수 없다.
(C) tomatoes는 셀 수 있는 명사의 복수형이고 '우리는 토마토 소스를 만들기 위해 약간의 토마토가 필요하다.'라는 의미이므로 a few(약간의)를 쓴다.

25 ③ famously → famous
④ any → some
⑤ meaningful something → something meaningful

CHAPTER 12
부사

p.252

POINT 1 부사의 쓰임

 연습문제

1	arrived	2	clean
3	flew	4	the bus came on time
5	fast	6	told
7	talked	8	sure
9	spends	10	quickly
11	answered	12	hastily
13	the soccer team won the championship		
14	drove	15	wrong

POINT 2-1 부사의 형태

 연습문제 A

1	nicely	2	finally
3	carefully	4	easily
5	gently	6	wisely
7	strangely	8	luckily
9	sadly	10	clearly
11	lazily	12	differently
13	perfectly	14	well
15	fully	16	really
17	busily	18	politely
19	heavily	20	comfortably
21	safely	22	certainly
23	noisily	24	seriously
25	truly	26	angrily
27	suddenly	28	simply
29	responsibly	30	quietly
31	energetically	32	horribly
33	bravely	34	sincerely
35	properly	36	fantastically
37	dully	38	specially
39	nervously	40	possibly

연습문제 B

	①	②
1	heavy	heavily
2	gentle	gently
3	Basically	basic
4	good	well
5	true	truly
6	fully	full
7	really	real

기출 적중문제

정답 fix the car easily
해설 '쉽게'라는 의미의 부사 easily를 쓴다.

POINT 2-2 형용사와 형태가 같은 부사

연습문제

1	①	2	②	3	①	4	②
5	②	6	①	7	①	8	②

기출 적중문제

정답 the sofa comfortable enough
해설 enough가 형용사(comfortable)를 수식하는 부사로 쓰였으므로 형용사 뒤에 온다.

POINT 2-3 -ly가 붙으면 의미가 달라지는 부사

 연습문제

1	lately	2	high	3	hardly
4	near	5	closely	6	late
7	highly	8	nearly	9	close
10	hard				

기출 적중문제

정답 ④
해설 hardly → hard

POINT 3 빈도부사

 연습문제 A

1	sometimes	2	often
3	never	4	always
5	usually	6	seldom[rarely/hardly]
7	never	8	usually
9	seldom[rarely/hardly]		

연습문제 B

1 I seldom drink soda.
2 The restaurant is always busy on Friday night.
3 What do you usually buy online?
4 You can often see rainbows after heavy rain.
5 It is hardly possible to swim across the river.
6 The café will always be open during the holiday.
7 This word is rarely used in modern English.
8 I have never been to the movie theater alone.
9 I sometimes hear the birds singing in the morning.
10 Lightning hardly hits in the same place twice.

기출 적중문제

정답 He usually plays computer games
해설 빈도부사(usually)는 일반동사(plays) 앞에 온다.

POINT 4-1 다양한 부사: already, still, yet

연습문제

1 still	2 yet	3 already
4 already	5 yet	6 already
7 yet	8 still	9 still

POINT 4-2 다양한 부사: too, either

연습문제

1 too	2 either	3 too
4 either	5 too	6 too
7 either	8 too	9 either
10 either	11 too	12 too
13 either	14 too	

POINT 4-3 다양한 부사: so, neither

연습문제

1 So is Michael.	2 Neither does he.
3 So can she.	4 So am I.
5 Neither can I.	6 So will Rachel.
7 So does she.	8 Neither was I.
9 So will Luke.	10 Neither is he.
11 So does Yeri.	12 Neither will I.
13 Neither did I.	14 Neither was he.

POINT 5 타동사 + 부사

연습문제 A

1 wake up	2 Hand[Turn] in
3 give up	4 write down
5 put on	6 pick up
7 find out	8 take off
9 turn off	10 put off

연습문제 B

1 give it up
2 try on these sunglasses
3 find it out, find the truth out
4 give them back
5 wake me up
6 turn off the heater
7 Look at me
8 take off our caps
9 look up the words, look them up
10 turned it on
11 hand in the document
12 throw away my clothes, throw them away

POINT 6 의문부사

연습문제 A

1 Where	2 How	3 When
4 Why	5 Where	6 Why
7 How	8 When	

연습문제 B

1 often	2 big	3 much
4 old	5 tall	6 often
7 many	8 much	9 long
10 far	11 many	

서술형 대비 문제

 A

1 carefully	2 late
3 hardly	4 comfortable
5 truly	6 enough
7 freely	8 Clearly
9 terrible	10 highly
11 quietly	

 B

1 Vitamin C is often helpful to prevent a cold.
2 How long is the Nile in Africa?
3 Do women usually live longer than men?
4 How often does your sister clean her room?
5 Brian has never eaten Greek food before.
6 We sometimes play soccer during our lunch hour.
7 Traveling in space has always been my dream.

C

1 already	2 still	3 yet
4 So	5 either	6 Neither
7 too		

D

1 Let's put it off until next week.
2 Can I try them on in the fitting room?
3 The journalists found them out finally.
4 My mother gave it up last year.
5 I always wake him up in the morning.

6 You don't have to turn it off now.
7 Daniel felt chilly, so he put it on.

중간·기말고사 실전 문제

1 ⑤	**2** ③, ⑤	**3** ④	**4** How	**5** ①
6 ③	**7** ②, ④	**8** ④	**9** ③	**10** Where
11 when	**12** ④	**13** ③	**14** ④	**15** ④
16 ③	**17** (1) yet (2) already (3) still		**18** ①	
19 ④	**20** (1) always goes jogging (2) sometimes goes jogging (3) seldom goes jogging			**21** ③
22 ③, ④				

1 ⑤: 명사 – 형용사   ①②③④: 형용사 – 부사

2 ③ clear → clearly
⑤ good → well

3 · turn on '~을 켜다'
· try on '~을 입어보다/신어보다'

4 · '나는 어떻게 은행에 갈 수 있니?'라는 의미이므로 방법을 묻는 How를 쓴다.
· '너의 부모님은 요즘 어떻게 지내시니?'라는 의미이므로 상태를 묻는 How를 쓴다.

5 (A) 주어 You의 보어로 쓰여 주어를 보충 설명하고 있으므로 형용사 responsible(책임이 있는)을 쓴다.
(B) '거의'라는 의미의 부사 nearly를 쓴다.
(C) '가까이'라는 의미의 부사 close를 쓴다.

6 ③: 부사   ①②④⑤: 형용사

7 ① lately → late
③ polite → politely
⑤ high → highly

8 ④: 부정문에 대한 동의를 나타낼 때는 either를 쓴다.

9 ① always is → is always
② can see rarely → can rarely see
④ see sometimes → sometimes see
⑤ usually has been → has usually been

10 발리에 갔다고 대답했으므로 장소를 묻는 Where를 쓴다.

11 한 달 전에 그것을 샀다고 대답했으므로 시간이나 날짜를 묻는 when을 쓴다.

12 · '동등하게'라는 의미의 부사 equally를 쓴다.
· '가까이'라는 의미의 부사 near를 쓴다.

13 부정문에 대한 동의를 나타내고 있고 앞 문장에 일반동사의 과거형(didn't spill)이 쓰였으므로 「Neither + did + 주어」를 쓴다.

14 ④: 형용사   ①②③⑤: 부사

15 ⓒ took off it → took it off
ⓓ wake up her → wake her up

16 첫 번째 빈칸: '너는 1년 동안 얼마나 많은 책을 읽니?'라는 의미이므로 개수를 묻는 How many를 쓴다.
두 번째 빈칸: '우리는 왜 책을 읽어야 하니?'라는 의미이므로 이유를 묻는 why를 쓴다.

17 (1) 주로 의문문 맨 뒤에서 '이미, 벌써'라는 의미로 쓰이는 yet을 쓴다.
(2) 의문문에서 '벌써'라는 의미로 쓰여 놀라움을 나타내는 already를 쓴다.
(3) 부정어(doesn't) 앞에서 '아직, 여전히'라는 의미로 쓰이는 still을 쓴다.

18 (A) 주어 I의 보어로 쓰여 주어를 보충 설명하고 있으므로 형용사 lucky(운이 좋은)를 쓴다.
(B) '면밀히'라는 의미의 부사 closely를 쓴다.
(C) '큰 소리로'라는 의미의 부사 loudly를 쓴다.

19 ⓐ hugely → huge
ⓒ enough early → early enough
ⓓ international → internationally

20 (1) 찬호는 평일에 다섯 번 조깅하러 가므로 always(항상)를 쓴다. 빈도부사는 일반동사 앞에 온다.
(2) 지희는 평일에 두 번 조깅하러 가므로 sometimes(때때로, 가끔)를 쓴다.
(3) 예림이는 평일에 한 번 조깅하러 가므로 seldom(거의 ~않다)을 쓴다.

21 ⓑ give back it → give it back
ⓓ Do often you → Do you often

22 ③ ride always → always ride
④ complete → completely

POINT 1-1 규칙 변화

1 smarter, smartest
2 hotter, hottest
3 bigger, biggest
4 louder, loudest
5 more beautiful, most beautiful
6 nicer, nicest
7 more easily, most easily
8 greater, greatest
9 stranger, strangest
10 healthier, healthiest
11 more helpful, most helpful
12 darker, darkest
13 younger, youngest
14 thinner, thinnest
15 more serious, most serious
16 hungrier, hungriest
17 cheaper, cheapest
18 longer, longest
19 more expensive, most expensive
20 more quickly, most quickly
21 warmer, warmest
22 fewer, fewest
23 more interesting, most interesting
24 stronger, strongest
25 scarier, scariest
26 sweeter, sweetest
27 more important, most important
28 wider, widest
29 more tired, most tired
30 lonelier, loneliest
31 more useless, most useless
32 wetter, wettest
33 more boring, most boring
34 tastier, tastiest
35 closer, closest
36 more gladly, most gladly

POINT 1-2 불규칙 변화

1 more, most
2 worse, worst
3 elder
4 less, least
5 better, best
6 more, most

7 farther
8 worse, worst
9 better, best
10 last
11 oldest
12 worse, worst
13 later
14 furthest

정답 ③, ⑤
해설 ③ safely – more safely – most safely
　　　 ⑤ good – better – best

POINT 2-1 원급 비교: as + 원급 + as

A
1 as cold as
2 as often as
3 not as[so] dry as
4 as light as
5 as sweet as
6 not as[so] difficult as
7 as late as
8 not as[so] dirty as
9 not as[so] polite as
10 as early as
11 as quickly as
12 not as[so] low as

B
1 hotter than / less hot than
2 heavier than / less heavy than
3 higher than / less high than
4 more delicious than / less delicious than

정답 ⓓ → bright
해설 '…만큼'이라는 의미의 as가 있고 '그녀의 눈은 별들만큼 밝
　　　 다.'라는 의미이므로 원급 bright를 쓴다.

POINT 2-2 원급 비교: as + 원급 + as + 주어 + can[could]

1 as much as possible
2 as neatly as she could
3 as safely as he could
4 as quickly as possible
5 as closely as possible
6 as soon as you can
7 as loudly as they can
8 as honestly as possible

정답 as soon as I could

해설 '…가 할 수 있는 한 ~한/하게'라는 의미의 「as + 원급 + as + 주어 + could」를 쓴다.

POINT 2-3 원급 비교: 배수사 + as + 원급 + as

1 seven times as long as
2 ten times lighter than
3 1,500 times as heavy as
4 eight times older than
5 three times as large as
6 200 times higher than
7 five times as far as

정답 This book is twice as thick as that one.

해설 '…보다 -배 더 ~한/하게'라는 의미의 「배수사 + as + 원급 + as」를 쓴다.

POINT 3-1 비교급 비교: 비교급 + than

연습문제 A

1 brighter than	2 more interesting than
3 slower than	4 sooner than
5 colder than	6 tastier than
7 softer than	8 more nervous than
9 sadder than	10 more exciting than
11 busier than	12 more important than

연습문제 B

1 younger than	2 taller than
3 heavier than	4 older than
5 faster than	6 more expensive than
7 more, than	

연습문제 C

| 1 very | 2 higher | 3 even |
| 4 more | 5 a lot | 6 safer |

정답 ③

해설 ① more stronger → stronger
② as → than
④ loud → louder
⑤ very → much[even/still/far/a lot]

POINT 3-2 비교급 비교: the + 비교급, the + 비교급

연습문제 A

1 The deeper, the darker
2 The harder, the better
3 The more heavily, the wetter
4 The more often, the healthier
5 The colder, the more depressed
6 The more popular, the more
7 The louder, the more
8 The longer, the angrier
9 The warmer, the more beautiful
10 The higher, the farther
11 The more, the more

연습문제 B

1 The earlier Emma goes to bed, the longer she can sleep.
2 The emptier the box got, the lighter it became.
3 The cloudier it got, the more disappointed John felt.
4 The more I thought about the test, the more nervous I got.
5 The more free time I have, the more relaxed I feel.
6 The more crowded the restaurant is, the noisier it becomes.
7 The more famous the actor became, the busier he got.
8 The more friends you invite to the party, the more exciting it will be.
9 The more often you exercise, the stronger you will become.
10 The less packaging the item has, the cheaper it is.

정답 The more I practiced, the better I played the cello.

해설 '나는 연습하면 할수록 첼로를 더 잘 연주했다.'라고 했으므로 '~하면 할수록 더 …하다'라는 의미의 「the + 비교급, the + 비교급」을 쓴다.

POINT 3-3 비교급 비교: 비교급 + and + 비교급

1 brighter and brighter
2 shorter and shorter
3 bigger and bigger
4 more and more exciting
5 faster and faster
6 smarter and smarter
7 redder and redder
8 tighter and tighter

9   more and more popular
10 better and better
11 higher and higher

POINT 4-1 최상급 비교: the + 최상급

A
1 the shortest	2 the heaviest
3 the fastest	4 the most expensive
5 the longest	6 the largest

B
1 the biggest country in Asia
2 the most dangerous animal in the jungle
3 the softest chair in our house
4 the most delicious pizza in this town
5 the most important thing in my life
6 the best singer of all my friends
7 the most beautiful beach in Korea
8 the most colorful season of the four
9 the most excellent artwork in the gallery

▶ 기출 적중문제
정답 ⑤
해설 첫 번째 빈칸: '벌새는 세상에서 가장 작은 새이다.'라는 의미
이므로 최상급 the smallest를 쓴다.
두 번째 빈칸: 빈칸 뒤에 장소나 범위를 나타내는 명사(the
world)가 있으므로 in을 쓴다.

POINT 4-2 최상급 비교: one of the + 최상급 + 복수명사

1 one of the longest rivers
2 one of the best cities
3 one of the most common last names
4 one of the saddest movies
5 one of the greatest artists
6 one of the most scientific writing systems
7 one of the most serious problems

▶ 기출 적중문제
정답 ③, ⑤
해설 ③ funnier → the funniest
    ⑤ day → days

POINT 4-3 최상급 비교: 원급과 비교급을 이용한 최상급 표현

1 No (other) bridge, as[so] long as / No (other)
bridge, longer than / longer than any other
bridge / longer than all the other bridges
2 No (other) planet, as[so] bright as / No (other)
planet, brighter than / brighter than any other
planet / brighter than all the other planets
3 No (other) place, as[so] mysterious as / No
(other) place, more mysterious than / more
mysterious than any other place / more
mysterious than all the other places

서술형 대비 문제

A
1 best		2 O	
3 as[so] cold as		4 O	
5 the toughest			
6 much[even/still/far/a lot]			
7 in		8 smart	

B
1 the shortest	2 taller than
3 as young as	4 older than
5 the cheapest	

6 four times as expensive as[four times more
   expensive than]
7 thicker than
8 thinner than

C
1 smaller than	2 the largest
3 as[so] big as	4 the coldest
5 hotter than	

D
1 better and better
2 one of the healthiest vegetables
3 The hotter, the more
4 more and more useful
5 The harder, the more confused
6 as early as possible
7 one of the finest houses
8 as often as you can

중간·기말고사 실전 문제

1 ④	2 ③	3 ③	4 ④	5 ①
6 ②	7 ⑤	8 ⓓ → better	9 ②	

10 Bora finished her homework as quickly as she could. **11** Judy's hair is three times longer than mine. **12** ①, ⑤ **13** ④ **14** as cheap as **15** are faster than bicycles **16** the most diligent student **17** as[so] smart as **18** more → most **19** ⑤ **20** ③, ⑤ **21** ③ **22** ② **23** The longer, the colder **24** ④ **25** The larger, the harder **26** (1) the tallest (2) as[so] short as (3) younger than (4) as[so] old as **27** ④ **28** house is more luxurious than **29** ④ **30** as clearly as you can **31** closer and closer **32** ⑤ **33** ⑤ **34** The Internet is one of the greatest inventions **35** ② **36** novel → novels **37** ① **38** ③ **39** ②, ④

1 ④ strange – stranger – strangest

2 ③ late – latter – last 또는 late – later – latest

3 ③ most popular → the most popular

4 · '광주는 서울만큼 붐비지 않는다.'라는 의미의 원급 비교이므로 as를 쓴다. 부정문인 경우 as 대신 so를 쓸 수 있다.
· '멜론은 체리보다 더 크다.'라는 의미의 비교급 비교이므로 than을 쓴다.

5 '이 상자들은 돌만큼 무겁다.'라는 의미이므로 원급 heavy를 쓴다.

6 '고래는 돌고래보다 더 깊게 잠수할 수 있다.'라는 의미이므로 비교급 deeper를 쓴다.

7 '누가 너의 나라에서 가장 유명한 배우이니?'라는 의미이므로 최상급 the most famous를 쓴다.

8 'Luna는 나보다 훨씬 더 춤을 잘 춘다'라는 의미이므로 비교급 better를 쓴다.

9 ②: 판다는 개보다 더 무거우므로 '개는 판다보다 더 무겁다.'는 적절하지 않다.

10 '…가 할 수 있는 한 ~한/하게'라는 의미의 「as + 원급 + as + 주어 + could」를 쓴다.

11 '…보다 -배 더 ~한/하게'라는 의미의 「배수사 + 비교급 + than」을 쓴다.

12 ① as → than
⑤ beautiful → more beautiful

13 첫 번째 빈칸: 빈칸 뒤에 원급(good)이 있으므로 원급을 강조하는 very를 쓴다.
두 번째 빈칸: 빈칸 뒤에 비교급(better)이 있으므로 비교급을 강조하는 far 또는 still을 쓴다.

14 장갑과 스카프의 가격이 같으므로 원급 비교 as cheap as를 쓴다.

15 '자전거는 자동차만큼 빠르지 않다.'라는 의미의 문장은 '자동차는 자전거보다 더 빠르다.'로 바꿔 쓸 수 있다.

16 「비교급 + than any other + 단수명사」는 「the + 최상급」으로 바꿔 쓸 수 있다.

17 '원숭이는 개보다 더 똑똑하다.'라는 의미의 문장은 '개는 원숭이 만큼 똑똑하지 않다.'로 바꿔 쓸 수 있다.

18 '수학은 모든 것 중에서 가장 어려운 과목이다.'라는 의미이므로 최상급 the most difficult를 쓴다.

19 '우리가 더 크게 말할수록 우리의 선생님은 더 화가 나셨다.'라는 의미의 문장이므로 '~하면 할수록 더 …하다'라는 의미의 「the + 비교급, the + 비교급」을 쓴다.

20 ①: 컴퓨터 B가 가장 비싸므로 '컴퓨터 A는 가장 비싼 컴퓨터이 다.'는 적절하지 않다.
②: 컴퓨터 B가 컴퓨터 A보다 더 새것이므로 '컴퓨터 B는 컴퓨터 A보다 더 오래됐다.'는 적절하지 않다.
④: 컴퓨터 A가 가장 오래됐으므로 '컴퓨터 C는 모든 것 중에서 가장 오래됐다.'는 적절하지 않다.

21 ③ many → more, happy → happier

22 주어진 문장과 ②: '훨씬' (비교급 강조)
①③④⑤: '많은' (수량형용사)

23 '~하면 할수록 더 …하다'라는 의미의 「the + 비교급, the + 비교급」을 쓴다.

24 ④: '조깅은 건강해지는 가장 쉬운 방법들 중 하나이다.'

25 '만약 집이 더 크다면, 그것을 청소하는 것은 더 어렵다.'라는 의미의 문장이므로 '~하면 할수록 더 …하다'라는 의미의 「the + 비교급, the + 비교급」을 쓴다.

26 (1) Charlie는 가장 키가 크므로 the tallest를 쓴다.
(2) Brad는 Diana만큼 키가 작지 않으므로 as[so] short as 를 쓴다.
(3) Brad는 다른 어떤 학생들보다 더 어리므로 younger than 을 쓴다.
(4) 다른 어떤 학생도 Diana만큼 나이가 많지 않으므로 as[so] old as를 쓴다.

27 · '이것은 도시에서 가장 좋은 호텔들 중 하나이다.'라는 의미이므 로 「one of the + 최상급 + 복수명사」를 쓴다.
· '그는 한국에서 다른 어떤 코미디언보다 더 웃기다.'라는 의미이 므로 비교급 funnier를 쓴다.

28 「the + 최상급」은 「No other + 단수명사 ~ 비교급 + than」으 로 바꿔 쓸 수 있다.

29 ⓔ more and more sweet → sweeter and sweeter

30 「as + 원급 + as + possible」은 「as + 원급 + as + 주어 + can」으로 바꿔 쓸 수 있다.

31 '점점 더 ~한/하게'라는 의미의 「비교급 + and + 비교급」을 쓴 다.

32 '가장 ~한'이라는 의미의 「the + 최상급」을 쓴다. interesting의 최상급은 the most interesting이다.

33 ① most tasty → tastiest

② in → of
③ gloomier → gloomiest
④ more → much

34 '가장 ~한 것들 중 하나'라는 의미의 「one of the + 최상급 + 복수명사」를 쓴다.

35 '우리는 많이 재활용하면 할수록 환경을 덜 훼손한다.'라는 의미이므로 '~하면 할수록 더 …하다'라는 의미의 「the + 비교급, the + 비교급」을 쓴다.

36 '가장 ~한 것들 중 하나'는 「one of the + 최상급 + 복수명사」의 형태이므로 복수명사 novels를 쓴다.

37 빈칸 뒤에 비교급(more dangerous)이 있으므로 비교급을 강조하는 a lot/even/much/far를 쓴다. very는 원급을 강조한다.

38 '이 새 신발은 저 오래된 신발만큼 편하지 않다.'라는 의미의 문장은 '저 오래된 신발은 이 새 신발보다 더 편하다.'로 바꿔 쓸 수 있다.

39 ① best → well
③ longer → long
⑤ strong → stronger

POINT 1-1 시간 전치사 I

연습문제

1 in	**2** at	**3** on	**4** in
5 in	**6** on	**7** at	**8** on
9 on			

POINT 1-2 시간 전치사 II

연습문제 A

1 ① after ② Before
2 ① before ② after
3 ① Before ② After
4 ① After ② before

연습문제 B

1 until **2** since **3** by
4 From **5** until **6** from
7 since **8** by **9** until
10 since **11** from

기출 적중문제

정답 ②

해설 (A): '10월 이후로, 학생들은 장기자랑을 준비해왔다.'라는 의미이므로 특정 시점부터 어떤 행동이나 상황이 계속되는 것을 나타내는 전치사 Since(~ 이후로)를 쓴다.
(B): 날짜(December 5) 앞에는 전치사 on을 쓴다.
(C): '표는 12월 4일까지 판매될 것이다.'라는 의미이므로 특정 시점까지 어떤 행동이나 상황이 계속되는 것을 나타내는 전치사 until(~까지)을 쓴다.

POINT 1-3 시간 전치사 III

연습문제 A

1 for **2** during **3** during
4 during **5** for **6** during
7 for **8** for **9** for
10 during

연습문제 B

1 by Wednesday
2 from June 12 to June 15
3 since last night
4 before putting
5 until this Friday
6 in the 20th century
7 during the performance
8 after the earthquake

9　at the end of the year
10　for three days
11　before 10 o'clock
12　until tomorrow
13　for a while
14　after watching

기출 적중문제

정답　①
해설　첫 번째 빈칸: 숫자를 포함한 기간 표현(an hour) 앞이므로
전치사 for(~ 동안)를 쓴다.
두 번째 빈칸: 특정 기간을 나타내는 명사(the speech) 앞
이므로 전치사 during(~ 동안)을 쓴다.

POINT 2-1　장소 전치사: at, on, in Ⅰ

연습문제
| **1** at | **2** on | **3** in | **4** on |
| **5** on | **6** at | **7** on | **8** in |

기출 적중문제

정답　at, on, in
해설　첫 번째 빈칸: 하나의 지점(the bus stop) 앞에는 전치사 at
을 쓴다.
두 번째 빈칸: '그녀는 벤치 위에 앉아 있다'라는 의미이므로
표면에 접촉한 상태를 나타내는 전치사 on(~ 위에)을 쓴다.
세 번째 빈칸: 공간의 내부(her basket) 앞에는 전치사 in을
쓴다.

POINT 2-2　장소 전치사: at, on, in Ⅱ

연습문제
1 on	**2** at	**3** in	**4** at
5 in	**6** in	**7** in	**8** on
9 in	**10** on	**11** in	**12** in
13 in	**14** on	**15** in	**16** on
17 at	**18** on	**19** in	**20** in
21 on	**22** in	**23** on	**24** at
25 on	**26** in	**27** in	

기출 적중문제

정답　④
해설　· 자연환경(the river) 앞에는 전치사 in을 쓴다.
· 인쇄물(the picture) 앞에는 전치사 in을 쓴다.
· 공간의 내부(the building) 앞에는 전치사 in을 쓴다.

POINT 3　위치 전치사

연습문제
1 under	**2** over	**3** next to
4 near	**5** beside	**6** below
7 among	**8** in front of	**9** between
10 by	**11** above	**12** behind

기출 적중문제

정답　⑤
해설　'나의 개는 항상 나의 엄마와 나 사이에서 자려고 노력한
다.'라는 의미이고 my mom and me는 둘이므로 전치사
between((둘) 사이에)을 쓴다.

POINT 4　방향 전치사

연습문제
1 down	**2** into	**3** over
4 across	**5** for	**6** out of
7 to	**8** around	**9** through
10 up	**11** from	**12** along

기출 적중문제

정답　for
해설　leave와 함께 쓰여 가고자 하는 방향을 나타내고 있으므로
전치사 for(~으로)를 쓴다.

POINT 5　기타 전치사

연습문제 A
| **1** about | **2** with | **3** without |
| **4** as | **5** with | **6** by |

연습문제 B
1 for	**2** with	**3** against
4 with	**5** by	**6** like
7 by	**8** on	

기출 적중문제

정답　⑤
해설　· 'Brenda는 어제 그녀의 친구들과 함께 점심을 먹었다.'라
는 의미이므로 전치사 with(~와 함께)를 쓴다.
· '너는 유리 렌즈를 이용해서 불을 피울 수 있다.'라는 의미이
므로 전치사 with(~을 이용해서)를 쓴다.
· '큰 여행 가방을 가진 그 남자는 피곤하게 보인다.'라는 의
미이므로 전치사 with(~을 가진)를 쓴다.

POINT 6-1　전치사 관용 표현: 형용사 + 전치사

연습문제
| **1** for | **2** at | **3** for[about] |
| **4** for | **5** for | **6** of |

7 to	**8** of	**9** about	

기출 적중문제

정답 ⑤

해설 be different from '~과 다르다'

POINT 6-2 전치사 관용 표현: 동사 + 전치사

연습 문제

1 into	**2** to	**3** to	**4** for
5 at	**6** on	**7** for	**8** for
9 of	**10** at		

기출 적중문제

정답 ③

해설 · laugh at '~을 보고/듣고 웃다'
· look at '~을 보다'

서술형 대비 문제

Ⓐ
1 for	**2** in	**3** by
4 on	**5** since	**6** at
7 as	**8** during	**9** about
10 by	**11** with	**12** against

Ⓑ
1 about	**2** for[about]	**3** to
4 for	**5** into	**6** of
7 of		

Ⓒ
ⓐ on	ⓑ next to	ⓒ out of
ⓓ for	ⓔ at	ⓕ in
ⓖ across	ⓗ between	ⓘ in front of
ⓙ with	ⓚ up	ⓛ into
ⓜ above		

중간·기말고사 실전 문제

1 ⑤	**2** ②	**3** on the Internet	**4** across
5 ③	**6** ②	**7** ①	**8** ③ **9** ②
10 ②	**11** ①	**12** ⑤	**13** ④ **14** ②
15 ②	**16** ④	**17** ⑤	**18** ③ **19** ③
20 (1) in (2) beside (3) into		**21** without	
22 ③	**23** ④	**24** ①	**25** ⓐ without
ⓑ against ⓒ by ⓓ as ⓔ for		**26** (1) ⓐ → at	
(2) ⓒ → for (3) ⓓ → from		**27** out of	**28** ④
29 ①	**30** in front of, behind		**31** ①

32 ③	**33** ③	**34** (1) ⓑ → to (2) ⓓ → of		
35 ③	**36** ③	**37** ③	**38** ②	**39** ②
40 ②	**41** ①	**42** ④	**43** The dog is	
waiting for its owner		**44** ①		

1 날짜(May 15) 앞에는 전치사 on을 쓴다.

2 특정 기간을 나타내는 명사(the day) 앞이므로 전치사 during (~동안)을 쓴다.

3 통신수단(the Internet) 앞에는 전치사 on을 쓴다.

4 '~을 가로질러'라는 의미의 전치사 across를 쓴다.

5 · '너는 다음 주 월요일까지 도서관 책을 반납해야 한다.'라는 의미이므로 정해진 시점까지 어떤 행동이나 상황이 완료되는 것을 나타내는 전치사 by(~까지)를 쓴다.
· '사람들은 배를 타고 독도를 방문할 수 있다.'라는 의미이므로 전치사 by(~을 타고)를 쓴다.

6 · 'Cam은 그의 열쇠들을 책상 위에서 찾았다.'라는 의미이므로 표면에 접촉한 상태를 나타내는 전치사 on(~ 위에)을 쓴다.
· on the way home '집으로 가는 길에'

7 · 연도(1945) 앞에는 전치사 in을 쓴다.
· '두 섬들 사이에 있는 다리는 지난달에 지어졌다.'라는 의미이고 two islands는 둘이므로 전치사 between((둘) 사이에)을 쓴다.

8 'Julie는 정오부터 2시 30분까지 요리 수업을 듣는다.'라는 의미이므로 「from ~ to …」(~부터 …까지)를 쓴다.

9 ② at → on

10 · look for '~을 찾다'
· '나는 항상 핫도그를 케첩과 함께 먹는다.'라는 의미이므로 전치사 with(~와 함께)를 쓴다.

11 ⓐⓑ for ⓒ of ⓓ into ⓔ about

12 ⑤ above → up

13 ④ at ①②③⑤ in

14 ②: 소녀가 두 개의 그네 옆에 서 있으므로 '소녀는 두 개의 그네 사이에 서 있다.'는 적절하지 않다.

15 첫 번째 빈칸: '나는 그것을 너의 장난감 상자 안의 다른 인형들 사이에서 봤다고 생각했어.'라는 의미이고 맥락상 the other dolls는 셋 이상이므로 전치사 among((셋 이상) 사이에)을 쓴다.
두 번째 빈칸: '너는 너의 침대 아래를 확인했니?'라는 의미이므로 전치사 under(~ 아래에)를 쓴다.

16 '~처럼'이라는 의미의 전치사 like를 쓴다.

17 주어진 문장과 ⑤: '~을 위해'
①: '~에 찬성하여' ②④ '~ 동안' ③ '~으로'

18 ③: 아침·오후·저녁(the morning) 앞에는 전치사 in을 쓴다.

19 · '저에게 서울역으로 어떻게 가는지 말해주시겠어요?'라는 의미이고 get과 함께 쓰여 도착 지점을 나타내고 있으므로 전치사

to(~으로)를 쓴다.
· '그는 축구 팀에 참가하기 위해 런던으로 떠났다.'라는 의미이고 leave와 함께 쓰여 가고자 하는 방향을 나타내고 있으므로 전치사 for(~으로)를 쓴다.

20 (1) 약간의 편지들이 우체통 안에 있으므로 전치사 in(~ 안에)을 쓴다.
(2) 자전거가 우체통 옆에 세워져 있으므로 전치사 beside(~ 옆에)를 쓴다.
(3) 아이가 정원 안으로 들어가고 있으므로 전치사 into(~ 안으로)를 쓴다.

21 '~ 없이'라는 의미의 전치사 without을 쓴다.

22 ③ in   ①②④⑤ by

23 · 'Nina는 파란 머리카락을 가진 남자를 봤다.'라는 의미이므로 전치사 with(~을 가진)를 쓴다.
· '네가 먹기 전에 숟가락을 이용해서 수프를 저어라.'라는 의미이므로 전치사 with(~을 이용해서)를 쓴다.

24 (A): 'George는 화요일까지 서울에 머무를 것이다.'라는 의미이므로 특정 시점까지 어떤 행동이나 상황이 계속되는 것을 나타내는 전치사 until(~까지)을 쓴다.
(B): be proud of '~을 자랑스러워하다'
(C): 'Jenny는 지금 누구와도 함께 놀기를 원하지 않는다.'라는 의미이므로 전치사 with(~과 함께)를 쓴다.

25 ⓐ: '나는 처음으로 나의 부모님 없이 제주도에 계신 나의 이모를 방문할 거야.'라는 의미이므로 전치사 without(~ 없이)을 쓴다.
ⓑ: '그들은 그것에 반대하지 않으셨어?'라는 의미이므로 전치사 against(~에 반대하여)를 쓴다.
ⓒ: '너는 거기에 비행기를 타고 가니?'라는 의미이므로 전치사 by(~을 타고)를 쓴다.
ⓓ: '나는 학생으로서 할인을 받을 수 있어.'라는 의미이므로 전치사 as(~으로서)를 쓴다.
ⓔ: '나는 그들이 학생들을 위해 할인을 제공하는 것을 알지 못했어.'라는 의미이므로 전치사 for(~을 위해)를 쓴다.

26 (1) be good at '~을 잘하다'
(2) be famous for '~으로 유명하다'
(3) be different from '~과 다르다'

27 '~ 밖으로'라는 의미의 전치사 out of를 쓴다.

28 ④: 동사 like   ①②③⑤: 전치사 like

29 ⓐⓑ in   ⓒ on   ⓓ for   ⓔ from

30 첫 번째 빈칸: Hannah가 Adam 앞에 앉아 있으므로 전치사 in front of(~ 앞에)를 쓴다.
두 번째 빈칸: 'Hannah는 Adam 앞에 앉아 있었다'는 'Adam은 Hannah 뒤에 앉아 있었다'와 같은 의미이므로 전치사 behind(~ 뒤에)를 쓴다.

31 (A): on one's way to the supermarket '슈퍼마켓으로 가는 길에'
(B): be full of '~으로 가득 차 있다'

(C): 시점(night) 앞에는 전치사 at을 쓴다.

32 ③ from → to

33 laugh at '~을 보고/듣고 웃다'

34 (1) be similar to '~과 비슷하다'
(2) be afraid of '~을 무서워하다'

35 첫 번째 빈칸: '폼페이는 오랫동안 화산재 아래에 묻혀있었다.'라는 의미이므로 전치사 under(~ 아래에)를 쓴다.
두 번째 빈칸: spend 시간/돈 on '~에 시간/돈을 쓰다'

36 '아침에 나의 방 안으로 너무 많은 햇빛이 들어온다.'라는 의미이므로 전치사 into(~ 안으로)를 쓴다.

37 첫 번째 빈칸: 기념일(Mom's birthday) 앞에는 전치사 on을 쓴다.
두 번째 빈칸: '나는 이미 그녀를 위해 마을에 있는 좋은 식당을 예약했어.'라는 의미이므로 전치사 for(~을 위해)를 쓴다.

38 · run into '~을 우연히 만나다'
· take care of '~을 돌보다'
· be ready for '~에 준비가 되다'
· be famous for '~으로 유명하다'
· be bad at '~을 못하다'

39 첫 번째 빈칸: '두 개의 나라 사이를 이동하는 것'이라는 의미이고 the two countries는 둘이므로 전치사 between((둘) 사이에)을 쓴다.
두 번째 빈칸: '영국 해협 아래에 수중 터널이 있다'라는 의미이므로 전치사 below(~(보다) 아래에)를 쓴다.

40 · belong to '~에 속하다'
· listen to '~을 듣다'

41 ① to → for

42 첫 번째 빈칸: 특정 기간을 나타내는 명사(the winter) 앞이므로 전치사 during(~ 동안)을 쓴다.
두 번째 빈칸: '캐나다와 멕시코 사이에 있는 미국'이라는 의미이고 Canada and Mexico는 둘이므로 전치사 between((둘) 사이에)을 쓴다.

43 wait for '~을 기다리다'

44 ① until → by

CHAPTER 15
접속사

p.328

POINT 1 등위접속사

1	and	2	or	3	but
4	so	5	and	6	but
7	order	8	and	9	but
10	strong	11	or	12	doing

1 and you'll feel better
2 and you can get a good grade
3 or you'll miss the train
4 and you'll get healthier
5 or the baby will wake up
6 or you'll catch a cold
7 or you'll fall down the stairs
8 and he'll forgive you
9 or you'll be late for school

기출 적중문제

정답 but my sister broke it
해설 '하지만'이라는 의미의 but을 쓴다.

POINT 2 상관접속사

1	or	2	and	3	but (also)
4	nor	5	Both	6	neither
7	Either	8	not only	9	Either
10	and	11	not only	12	nor

1	both, and	2	Not only, but also
3	Neither, nor	4	as well as
5	either, or	6	not only, but also
7	both, and	8	as well as

1	is	2	is	3	are
4	are	5	are	6	is

기출 적중문제

정답 a headache as well as a sore throat
해설 not only A but also B(A뿐만 아니라 B도)는 B as well as A로 바꿔 쓸 수 있다.

POINT 3-1 명사절을 이끄는 접속사: that

1	ⓒ	2	ⓐ	3	ⓑ	4	ⓒ
5	ⓒ	6	ⓑ	7	ⓐ	8	ⓒ

1 I guess that this scarf is yours.
2 I hope that I can finish the report on time.
3 He knows that I want to be an astronaut.
4 I think that science is the easiest subject.
5 Everyone says that Patrick is a genius.
6 I thought that you had dinner with your friends.
7 I didn't know that Jessie called me last night.
8 I believe that laughing is good for our health.

1	ⓒ	2	ⓑ	3	ⓐ	4	ⓒ
5	ⓑ	6	ⓐ				

기출 적중문제

정답 ④
해설 ④: 지시형용사 ①②③⑤: 명사절 접속사

POINT 3-2 명사절을 이끄는 접속사: if, whether

1 whether I should wait in line (or not)
2 if you turned the lights off (or not)
3 whether Nate will join our soccer team (or not)
4 if monkeys are smarter than parrots (or not)
5 whether you can speak Korean (or not)
6 if Emily likes red roses (or not)
7 whether we have[we've] met each other before (or not)

기출 적중문제

정답 if[whether] it will rain tomorrow
해설 '~인지 아닌지'라는 의미의 if/whether를 쓴다.

POINT 4-1 부사절을 이끄는 접속사: 시간

1	when	2	since	3	While
4	as	5	As soon as		

1 until I find helpful information
2 while she eats dinner
3 after you take this medicine
4 when he is ready
5 before he fell asleep
6 as soon as I buy a hat
7 since he had surgery
8 as I was going to the library

정답 ④

해설 · '내가 불을 켜기 전에 매우 어두웠다.'라는 의미이므로
before(~하기 전에)를 쓴다.
· 시간을 나타내는 부사절에서는 미래시제 대신 현재시제를
쓰므로 blow를 쓴다.

POINT 4-2 부사절을 이끄는 접속사: 이유

연습문제 A
1 He arrived late because he missed the bus.
2 I drank two bottles of water because I was thirsty.
3 The boat isn't moving because the wind is too weak.
4 She couldn't ride the roller coaster because she wasn't tall enough.
5 There were many car accidents because the roads were icy.
6 He ordered pizza because he didn't want to cook.

연습문제 B
1 since it's too expensive
2 As you are sleepy
3 because she is kind to others
4 As you lied to me
5 Since the movie was great
6 because I'm too busy

연습문제 C
1 because of　2 because of
3 because　4 because of
5 because　6 because of
7 because　8 because of
9 because　10 because

기출 적중문제
정답 ②
해설 ② because of　①③④⑤ because

POINT 4-3 부사절을 이끄는 접속사: 조건

연습문제 A
1 unless you apologize to your friend
2 If you don't[do not] wear a sweater
3 Unless you take notes now
4 If the store isn't[is not] too far away
5 unless we protect their habitat
6 If you don't[do not] have a visa
7 Unless you exercise regularly
8 Unless you try your best
9 Unless you are over 20
10 If I don't[do not] go to the library

연습문제 B
1 Unless　2 O　3 if
4 unless　5 O　6 stop
7 is　8 O　9 mix

기출 적중문제
정답 ③, ⑤
해설 '만약 ~하지 않는다면'이라는 의미의 unless와 if ~ not을 쓴다. unless는 not과 함께 쓰지 않는다.

POINT 4-4 부사절을 이끄는 접속사: 양보

연습문제 A
1 Even though the watch is expensive
2 though he didn't have much time
3 Though I made a big mistake
4 Although Yuna and Yujin are twins
5 Though he plays hockey well
6 even though the food is delicious
7 Although we did our best

기출 적중문제
정답 Although[Though] I had an umbrella
해설 '비록 ~이지만'이라는 의미의 Although/Though를 쓴다.

POINT 4-5 부사절을 이끄는 접속사: as의 다양한 의미

연습문제 A
1 ⓐ　2 ⓑ　3 ⓒ　4 ⓑ
5 ⓔ　6 ⓓ　7 ⓒ　8 ⓔ
9 ⓐ　10 ⓓ

기출 적중문제
정답 ②
해설 ②: '~하기 때문에'　①③④⑤: '~할수록'

POINT 5 so that / so ~ that …

연습문제 A
1 so that I could keep warm
2 so that he can get healthy
3 so that she could do well in her school play
4 so that I can make the tea sweeter
5 so that you can get a good grade
6 so that we can save the environment
7 so that I could check for new messages
8 so that he could wake up early

연습문제 B
1 so heavy that I can't lift it
2 so hungry that he ate the whole pie

3 so bright that people shouldn't look at it directly

4 so boring that everyone fell asleep

5 so heavily that we had to cancel our picnic

6 so difficult that many people can't understand it

7 so quickly that I couldn't catch it

8 so wise that we respect him very much

정답 ①

해설 '그 책은 너무 유명해져서 영화로 만들어졌다.'라는 의미이므로 「so + 형용사 + that …」(너무 ~해서 …한)을 쓴다.

POINT 6 접속부사

연습 문제

1 On the other hand **2** However

3 Therefore **4** For example

5 Besides **6** In addition

정답 ②

해설 '경기를 이기는 것은 중요하다. 그러나, 공정하게 경기하는 것은 훨씬 더 중요하다.'라는 의미이므로 However(그러나)를 쓴다.

서술형 대비 문제

Ⓐ
1 that I lost my key
2 if Sally is sick
3 that Paul can't go to the festival
4 whether you will visit Korea again
5 that pigs are smart animals
6 that I didn't bring my homework
7 that he enjoyed staying here
8 if Ottawa is the capital of Canada

Ⓑ
1 or **2** have **3** O
4 rains **5** but (also) **6** dancing
7 O **8** is **9** watch

Ⓒ
1 before you eat your sandwich
2 until they are red
3 while he was playing football
4 since I was very young
5 as soon as I came home
6 though it is very expensive

---

7 so that they can hear better

8 as he studied the wrong chapter

9 when I called her

10 if you like modern art

Ⓓ
1 so small that Eric can't wear it
2 so heavily that Bill can't go outside
3 so hot that Minha can't eat it

중간·기말고사 실전 문제

1 ④ **2** but it is uncomfortable **3** ①

4 ④ **5** ①, ④ **6** Green as well as blue

7 ④ **8** ②, ⑤ **9** whether **10** ⑤

11 ② **12** ④ **13** that I lied to him **14** ③

15 whether Sujin will like my gift **16** When

17 ③ **18** because[since/as]

19 Unless **20** will see → sees **21** ④

22 ① **23** or you'll be late **24** He eats dinner after he helps his mom prepare dinner. / He eats dinner before he brushes his teeth. **25** ④

26 ③ **27** It is not only hot but also humid.

28 ⑤ **29** ③ **30** ① **31** so that he could finish early **32** and they'll[they will] understand **33** ② **34** ② **35** Even though she has many cookies **36** so loud that I can't hear **37** ① **38** ③ **39** ④

40 ④ **41** ① **42** ② **43** The room was so hot that I turned the air conditioner on. **44** ②

45 so excited that he can't fall asleep **46** ①, ⑤

47 ④ **48** (1) You'll save much energy if you unplug unused devices. (2) Please don't play the piano because it is after 10 o'clock. (3) I haven't talked to Mina since we fought last month. **49** After she writes in her diary **50** ②

---

1 '나는 나의 친구와 함께 스케이트장에 갔고, 우리는 같이 스케이트를 탔어.'라는 의미이므로 and(그리고)를 쓴다.

2 '하지만'이라는 의미의 but을 쓴다.

3 첫 번째 빈칸: '나의 할머니의 생신이 곧 다가오고 있어서, 나는 그녀를 방문하기로 계획하고 있다.'라는 의미이므로 so(그래서)를 쓴다.
두 번째 빈칸: '나는 그녀의 마을로 버스 또는 기차로 갈 수 있다.'라는 의미이므로 or(또는)를 쓴다.

4 ④ is → are (B as well as A 뒤에 오는 동사는 B에 수일치시킨다.)

5 '비록 표의 가격은 높았지만, 그 뮤지컬은 훌륭했다.'라는 의미이므로 Although/Though(비록 ~이지만)를 쓴다.

6 not only A but also B(A뿐만 아니라 B도)는 B as well as A 로 바꿔 쓸 수 있다.

7 ⓐ am → are (both A and B 뒤에는 항상 복수동사를 쓴다.)
ⓒ to go → go

8 ②⑤: 명사절 접속사 (that절이 문장 안에서 목적어로 쓰였을 때 that을 생략할 수 있다.)
①: 지시대명사　③④: 지시형용사

9 if/whether는 '~인지 아닌지'라는 의미로, 명사절을 이끈다.

10 that은 문장 안에서 주어로 쓰이는 명사절을 이끈다. 이때 주로 주어 자리에 가주어 it을 쓰고 진주어 that절을 뒤로 보낸다.

11 '만약 네가 컴퓨터를 사용하고 있지 않다면, 너는 그것을 꺼야 한다.'라는 의미이므로 If(만약 ~한다면)를 쓴다.

12 ④: 지시형용사　①②③⑤: 명사절 접속사

13 'Jacob은 내가 그에게 거짓말했다고 생각한다.'라는 의미이다. that은 문장 안에서 목적어로 쓰이는 명사절을 이끈다.

14 ③ or　①②④⑤ and

15 '나는 수진이가 나의 선물을 좋아할지 아닌지 궁금해하고 있다.'라는 의미이므로 whether(~인지 아닌지)를 쓴다.

16 '그는 15살이었을 때 이미 세 개의 언어를 말할 수 있었다.'라는 의미이므로 When(~할 때)을 쓴다.

17 '~하자마자'라는 의미의 as soon as를 쓴다.

18 '우리는 충분히 나이가 들지 않아서'라는 의미는 '우리는 충분히 나이가 들지 않았기 때문에'라는 의미를 나타내므로 '~하기 때문에'라는 의미의 because/since/as를 쓴다.

19 if ~ not(만약 ~하지 않는다면)은 unless로 바꿔 쓸 수 있다.

20 조건을 나타내는 부사절에서는 미래시제 대신 현재시제를 쓰므로 sees를 쓴다.

21 ④: '~한 이후로'　①②③⑤: '~하기 때문에'

22 ・빈칸 뒤에 절(he didn't come to school today)이 있으므로 because/since(~하기 때문에)를 쓴다.
・빈칸 뒤에 명사구(her fancy jewelry)가 있으므로 because of(~ 때문에)를 쓴다.

23 「명령문 + or ~」 '···해라, 그렇지 않으면 ~'

24 Tim은 7:45에 그의 엄마가 저녁 식사를 준비하시는 것을 도와드린 후에(after) 8:15에 저녁을 먹는다. Tim은 9:00에 그의 이를 닦기 전에(before) 8:15에 저녁을 먹는다.

25 ⓐ I'll → I
ⓓ you'll → you
ⓔ will drink → drinks

26 ・'만약 내가 태국에 간다면, 두리안을 먹어볼 것이다.'라는 의미이므로 If(만약 ~한다면)를 쓴다.
・'너는 네가 현관을 잠갔는지 아닌지 기억하니?'라는 의미이므로 if(~인지 아닌지)를 쓴다.

27 'A뿐만 아니라 B도'라는 의미의 not only A but also B를 쓴다.

28 주어진 문장은 '공휴일이기 때문에 오늘은 가게들이 문을 열지 않는다.'라는 의미이므로 because(~하기 때문에)를 쓴다. ⑤는 'Olivia가 우유로 가득 차 있는 잔을 깼기 때문에 바닥이 젖었다.'라는 의미이므로 because를 쓴다.
① When　② until　③ and　④ that

29 '그녀는 매일 운동했기 때문에 많은 체중을 감량했다.'라는 의미이므로 because(~하기 때문에)를 쓴다.

30 ①: 전치사　②③④⑤: 부사절 접속사

31 '~할 수 있도록'이라는 의미의 so that을 쓴다.

32 '···해라, 그러면 ~'이라는 의미의 「명령문 + and ~」를 쓴다.

33 since/because는 '~하기 때문에'라는 의미로, 이유를 나타내는 부사절을 이끈다.

34 주어진 문장과 ②: '~하기 때문에'
①③: '~하고 있을 때, ~하면서'　④: '~할수록'　⑤: '~으로서'(전치사)

35 even though(비록 ~일지라도)는 양보를 나타내는 부사절을 이끈다.

36 '음악이 너무 커서 나는 너를 들을 수 없다.'라는 의미이므로 「so + 형용사 + that ···」(너무 ~해서 ···한)을 쓴다.

37 '금속으로 만들어진 것들은 더운 날씨에서 팽창한다. 예를 들어, 다리와 철도선은 여름 동안 팽창한다.'라는 의미이므로 For example(예를 들어)을 쓴다.

38 '만약 병이 열리지 않는다면, 그것을 뜨거운 물에 넣어봐라.'라는 의미이므로 If a jar doesn't open을 쓴다. unless는 not과 함께 쓰지 않는다.

39 '그 버스는 너무 붐벼서 진호는 탈 수 없었다.'라는 의미이므로 「so + 형용사 + that ···」(너무 ~해서 ···한)을 쓴다.

40 (A) '지난 주말에, 나의 친구들과 나는 들판에서 축구를 하기를 원했다. 그러나, 비가 퍼붓기 시작했다.'라는 의미이므로 However(그러나)를 쓴다.
(B) '우리는 젖기를 원하지 않았다. 그러므로, 우리는 대신에 체육관에서 농구를 했다.'라는 의미이므로 Therefore(그러므로)를 쓴다.
(C) '만약 비가 오지 않는다면 우리는 이번 주말에 축구를 하기로 약속했다.'라는 의미이므로 if(만약 ~한다면)를 쓴다. unless는 not과 함께 쓰지 않는다.

41 목적을 나타내는 to부정사는 부사절 접속사 so that을 이용하여 바꿔 쓸 수 있다.

42 첫 번째 빈칸: '서해에는 수백 개의 섬이 있다. 반면에, 동해에는 섬들이 많이 없다.'라는 의미이므로 On the other hand(반면에)를 쓴다.
두 번째 빈칸: '반면에, 동해에는 섬들이 많이 없다. 게다가, 서쪽 해안은 진흙투성이인 해변들이 있지만 동쪽 해안은 모래로 뒤덮인 것들이 있다.'라는 의미이므로 In addition(게다가)을 쓴다.

43 「so + 형용사 + that …」(너무 ~해서 …한)은 결과를 나타낸다.

44 ②: 의문사　①③④⑤: 부사절 접속사

45 '민수는 너무 신이 나서 잠들 수 없다.'라는 의미이므로 「so + 형용사 + that …」(너무 ~해서 …한)을 쓴다.

46 '너무 ~해서 …할 수 없는'이라는 의미의 「so 형용사 that 주어 can't」와 「too ~ to」를 쓴다.

47 주어진 문장과 ④: 부사절 접속사　①②③⑤: 명사절 접속사

48 (1) '만약 네가 사용하지 않는 장치들의 플러그를 뽑는다면 너는 많은 에너지를 절약할 것이다.'
(2) '10시가 지났기 때문에 피아노를 치지 마세요.'
(3) '나는 우리가 지난달에 싸운 이후로 미나와 이야기하지 않았다.'

49 '그녀는 자기 전에 그녀의 일기를 쓴다.'라는 의미는 '그녀는 그녀의 일기를 쓴 후에 잔다.'라는 의미를 나타내므로 '~한 후에'라는 의미의 After를 쓴다.

50 if ~ not(만약 ~하지 않는다면)은 unless로 바꿔 쓸 수 있다. unless는 not과 함께 쓰지 않는다.

CHAPTER 16
관계사

p.358

POINT 1　관계대명사의 역할과 종류

1 선행사: a woman, 관계대명사: who
2 선행사: the bread, 관계대명사: which
3 선행사: a postcard, 관계대명사: which
4 선행사: the door, 관계대명사: whose
5 선행사: the man, 관계대명사: who
6 선행사: some tomatoes, 관계대명사: which
7 선행사: a singer, 관계대명사: whose
8 선행사: the girl, 관계대명사: whom
9 선행사: the snowman, 관계대명사: that
10 선행사: a train, 관계대명사: which
11 선행사: the bench, 관계대명사: which
12 선행사: the same jacket, 관계대명사: that

POINT 2-1　주격 관계대명사

1 My dad got me a doll which has blue eyes.
2 I know the man who delivers milk every morning.
3 I have a watch which was made in Switzerland.
4 The lamp which is on the table is not working.
5 Jimmy drank the orange juice which was in the fridge.
6 Ms. Lee scolded the boys who talked during class.
7 We bought a new sofa which fits in our living room.
8 A trophy was given to the woman who won the contest.

1 who	**2** leaves	**3** which
4 has	**5** which	**6** hunt
7 which	**8** are	**9** which
10 who		

1 ⓐ	**2** ⓑ	**3** ⓐ	**4** ⓐ
5 ⓑ	**6** ⓑ	**7** ⓑ	**8** ⓐ
9 ⓐ			

정답 ④

해설 ① who → which
② which → who
③ who → which
⑤ which → who

POINT 2-2 목적격 관계대명사

 연습문제 A

1 who[whom] I trust
2 which I want to try
3 which my father is making
4 who[whom] I know well
5 who[whom] I respect very much
6 which we can use
7 which were already used
8 who[whom] we saw at the gallery
9 which we planted five years ago
10 who[whom] I met at the gym

 연습문제 B

1 the boy who[whom] I like
2 an e-mail which Clara sent
3 the book which he read
4 The printer which I use
5 The students who[whom] we saw
6 the man who[whom] she met
7 the medicine which Alexander Fleming discovered
8 the hotdog which he sells
9 food which they will eat
10 The firefighter who[whom] we saw
11 The pencil which she found
12 his backpack which he left

기출 적중문제
정답 a lot of activities which we enjoyed
해설 두 번째 문장은 첫 번째 문장의 a lot of activities에 대해 보충 설명하고 있고, 두 번째 문장의 them이 목적어 역할을 하고 있으므로 사물을 선행사로 하는 목적격 관계대명사 which를 쓴다.

POINT 2-3 소유격 관계대명사

 연습문제

1 whose hair is white
2 whose son is a lawyer
3 whose voice sounds amazing
4 whose phone is missing
5 whose books are popular among teens
6 whose brake is broken

7 whose leaves are very large
8 whose house has five rooms
9 whose test scores are over 90
10 whose director won three awards
11 whose baby cries too much at night

POINT 3 관계대명사 that

 연습문제 A

1 which 2 which
3 who, whom 4 who
5 who 6 which
7 who, whom 8 who

 연습문제 B

1 Elena wants something that she can eat quickly.
2 The beaver is the only animal that builds dams.
3 Is this the last bus that goes to Gangnam?
4 Kelly bought the same watch that I purchased online.
5 Cameron sat on the first chair that he saw.
6 There is somebody that is knocking on the door.
7 There are some cows and a farmer that are resting under the tree.

 연습문제 C

1 ⓐ 2 ⓑ 3 ⓑ 4 ⓐ
5 ⓐ 6 ⓑ

기출 적중문제
정답 ③
해설 ③: 명사절 접속사 ①②④⑤: 관계대명사

POINT 4 관계대명사 what

 연습문제

1 what 2 which 3 which
4 what 5 What 6 What
7 which 8 which 9 which
10 what 11 what 12 What
13 what

기출 적중문제
정답 What Leonard needs
해설 관계대명사 what은 '~한 것'이라는 의미로 선행사를 포함하고 있다.

POINT 5 관계대명사의 생략

연습
문제
A

1	whom	**2**	who is	**3**	which is
4	that	**5**	that	**6**	that was
7	which	**8**	which is	**9**	that
10	who is				

연습
문제
B

1	O	**2**	O	**3**	X	**4**	O
5	X	**6**	O	**7**	O	**8**	X
9	O						

연습
문제
C

1 The house Charlie bought
2 the pictures you took
3 the girl I met
4 the novels written by Mr. Brown
5 the same joke he told
6 The mushroom I found
7 The celebrity I interviewed
8 that student eating a hamburger
9 The man looking at the map
10 the people in the burning house

기출 적중문제
정답 ①, ④
해설 목적격 관계대명사와 「주격 관계대명사 + be동사」는 생략할 수 있다.

POINT 6 전치사 + 관계대명사

연습
문제

1 This is the toy mouse which[that] my cat plays with.
   This is the toy mouse with which my cat plays.
2 I know the man who[whom/that] you were speaking to.
   I know the man to whom you were speaking.
3 I visited the Opera House which[that] Sydney is famous for.
   I visited the Opera House for which Sydney is famous.

기출 적중문제
정답 ⓑ → which
해설 전치사 바로 뒤에는 관계대명사 that을 쓸 수 없다.

POINT 7 관계부사

연습
문제
A

1	when	**2**	why	**3**	when
4	where	**5**	how	**6**	where

연습
문제
B

1 where Monet lived
2 how you can solve the problem
3 why she quit drinking soda
4 when we plant trees
5 how he built the robot
6 where coffee beans grow
7 when he graduated from middle school
8 why glaciers are melting
9 where I eat lunch every day
10 when the Korean War ended
11 how my grandma cooked the soup
12 why you were late for school

기출 적중문제
정답 the park where they play baseball
해설 선행사(the park)가 장소를 나타내므로 관계부사 where를 쓴다.

서술형 대비 문제

(A)
1 who filmed popular movies
2 whose color is orange
3 which was drawn by Picasso
4 which I played yesterday
5 whose tail is long and black
6 who[whom] everyone can trust

(B)
1 the wallet that I lost
2 what your parents say
3 the only bus that goes
4 What you need
5 a muffler that will keep
6 what he read
7 The dinosaur that Eric drew
8 What surprised me

(C)
1 The horse which[that] I rode yesterday was gentle.
2 I tried to catch the ball which[that] was rolling down the stairs.
3 Frank read a book which[that] was written in 1999.
4 I want to be a class president who[whom/that] everyone likes.
5 I miss my friend who[whom/that] I met at summer camp last year.
6 The Korean alphabet which[that] King Sejong invented is called Hangeul.
7 The passenger who[that] is sitting behind me keeps kicking my seat.

Ⓓ **1** ⓐ where　　　ⓑ when
　　ⓒ which[that]　ⓓ who[that]
2 ⓐ who[that]　　ⓑ which[that]
　　ⓒ how　　　　ⓓ why

중간·기말고사 실전 문제

1 ④　**2** ④　**3** ④　**4** ③　**5** ⑤
6 whom → who[that]　**7** ③　**8** ②, ⑤
9 ⑤　**10** my friend who[that] helps　**11** ②
12 why　**13** ③　**14** ④　**15** ①, ④　**16** ⑤
17 ③　**18** (1) which[that] all family members can
watch together　(2) whose special effects are
amazing　**19** ⑤　**20** I borrowed a pen whose
color was blue.　**21** We should help the child
who[that] lost her cat.　**22** ④　**23** What I
need is to exercise every day.　**24** ⑤　**25** ②
26 ③　**27** ①　**28** that　**29** ②, ③　**30** is
the city which I want to visit　**31** Jason is the
astronaut about whom I told you.　**32** ②
33 ⑤　**34** This park is the place where I usually
take a walk.　**35** (1) who[that] was talking to
Jamie on the phone　(2) who[whom/that] Martha went
to see　(3) who[that] was cooking dinner

1 선행사(the pancake)가 사물이므로 관계대명사 which를 쓴다.

2 · 선행사(the can)가 사물이므로 관계대명사 which나 that을 쓴다.
· 선행사(the man)가 사람이므로 관계대명사 who나 that을 쓴다.

3 두 번째 문장은 첫 번째 문장의 the new Mexican dish에 대해 보충 설명하고 있고, 두 번째 문장의 It이 주어 역할을 하고 있으므로 사물을 선행사로 하는 주격 관계대명사 which를 쓴다.

4 ① which → who[that]
② what → who[that]
④ who → which[that]
⑤ whose → which[that]

5 · 선행사(yoga lessons)가 사물이므로 관계대명사 which나 that을 쓴다.
· '~이라는 것'이라는 의미로 동사 believe의 목적어인 명사절을 이끄는 명사절 접속사 that을 쓴다.
· 선행사(a person)가 사람이므로 관계대명사 who나 that을 쓴다.

6 선행사(the man)가 사람이므로 주격 관계대명사는 who나 that을 쓴다. whom은 목적격 관계대명사로만 쓰인다.

7 ③: 주격 관계대명사　①②④⑤: 목적격 관계대명사

8 관계대명사절의 동사가 복수동사(were)이므로 선행사는 복수명사 the lamps와 the old books를 쓴다.

9 주어진 문장과 ⑤: 관계대명사
①: 지시형용사　②④: 명사절 접속사　③: 지시대명사

10 선행사(my friend)가 사람이므로 관계대명사 who나 that을 쓰고, 선행사가 단수명사이므로 관계대명사절의 동사는 단수동사 helps를 쓴다.

11 선행사(the time)가 시간을 나타내므로 관계부사 when을 쓴다.

12 선행사(the reason)가 이유를 나타내고 「전치사 + 관계대명사」는 관계부사로 바꿔 쓸 수 있으므로 관계부사 why를 쓴다.

13 ③ score → scores

14 ④ whose (빈칸 뒤에 선행사 the house가 소유하는 대상인 명사 roof가 있으므로 소유격 관계대명사 whose를 쓴다.)

15 두 번째 문장은 첫 번째 문장의 the boy에 대해 보충 설명하고 있고, 두 번째 문장의 He가 주어 역할을 하고 있으므로 사람을 선행사로 하는 주격 관계대명사 who를 쓴다. 「주격 관계대명사 + be동사」는 생략할 수 있다.

16 ⑤: 관계대명사　①②③④: 명사절 접속사

17 · 선행사(potatoes)가 사물이므로 관계대명사 which나 that을 쓴다.
· 빈칸 뒤에 선행사(a new student)가 소유하는 대상인 명사(name)가 있으므로 소유격 관계대명사 whose를 쓴다.
· 선행사(a new worker)가 사람이므로 관계대명사 who나 that을 쓴다.

18 (1) 첫 번째 평가의 the movie가 목적어 역할을 하고 있으므로 사물을 선행사로 하는 목적격 관계대명사 which나 that을 쓴다.
(2) 두 번째 평가의 The movie's가 소유격의 역할을 하고 있으므로 소유격 관계대명사 whose를 쓴다.

19 ⑤: 의문사　①②③④: 관계대명사

20 두 번째 문장은 첫 번째 문장의 a pen에 대해 보충 설명하고 있고, 두 번째 문장의 Its가 소유격의 역할을 하고 있으므로 소유격 관계대명사 whose를 쓴다.

21 두 번째 문장은 첫 번째 문장의 the child에 대해 보충 설명하고 있고, 두 번째 문장의 She가 주어 역할을 하고 있으므로 사람을 선행사로 하는 주격 관계대명사 who나 that을 쓴다.

22 ④: 주격 관계대명사 (주격 관계대명사는 생략할 수 없다.)
①②③⑤: 목적격 관계대명사

23 관계대명사 what은 '~한 것'이라는 의미로 선행사를 포함하고 있다.

24 '진수가 들고 있던 그 사전'이라고 했으므로 선행사는 the dictionary이고, 선행사가 사물이므로 관계대명사 which를 쓴다.

25 ⓐ blooms → bloom
   ⓑ which → who[that]
   ⓓ what → which[that]

26 주어진 문장과 ③: 관계대명사   ①②④⑤: 의문사

27 ①: 목적격 관계대명사는 생략할 수 있다.

28 · 선행사(the greatest author)에 최상급이 포함되어 있으므로 관계대명사 that을 쓴다.
   · 선행사(The girl and the unicorn)에 사람과 동물이 포함되어 있으므로 관계대명사 that을 쓴다.
   · 선행사(The only thing)에 the only가 포함되어 있으므로 관계대명사 that을 쓴다.

29 ② the way how → how[the way]
   ③ cook → cooks

30 '파리는 내가 언젠가 방문하기를 원하는 도시이다.'라는 상황이므로 선행사는 the city이다.

31 전치사 바로 뒤에는 관계대명사 who를 쓸 수 없다.

32 ⓐⓔ: 목적격 관계대명사와 「주격 관계대명사 + be동사」는 생략할 수 있다.

33 (A): 선행사(the teacher)가 사람이므로 관계대명사 who를 쓴다.
   (B): 선행사(my classmate)가 단수명사이므로 관계대명사절의 동사는 단수동사 does를 쓴다.
   (C): 선행사(the chocolate croissants)가 사물이므로 관계대명사 which나 that을 쓴다.

34 두 번째 문장은 첫 번째 문장의 the place에 대해 보충 설명하고 있고, 선행사(the place)가 장소를 나타내므로 관계부사 where를 쓴다.

35 (1) Chloe는 전화로 Jamie와 이야기하고 있던 소녀이고, 선행사(the girl)가 사람이므로 주격 관계대명사 who나 that을 쓴다.
   (2) 민준이는 Martha가 보러 간 소년이고, 선행사(the boy)가 사람이므로 목적격 관계대명사 who/whom/that을 쓴다.
   (3) Bill은 저녁 식사를 요리하고 있던 소년이고, 선행사(the boy)가 사람이므로 주격 관계대명사 who나 that을 쓴다.

CHAPTER 17
가정법

p.382

POINT 1-1 가정법 과거

연습문제 **A**

1 were, would travel
2 knew, would tell
3 were, would apologize
4 weren't, could buy
5 won, would buy
6 had, wouldn't walk
7 invited, would visit
8 were, could go
9 spoke, could have

연습문제 **B**

1 If I weren't sick, I could go to school today.
2 If Lisa weren't shy, she would talk to strangers.
3 If I had a brother or a sister, I wouldn't be lonely.
4 If the suitcase weren't heavy, he could carry it.
5 If the wind didn't blow, I wouldn't feel chilly.
6 If you knew how to ski, we could ski together.
7 If the air conditioner worked, this room wouldn't be hot.
8 If the concert tickets weren't sold out, I wouldn't be disappointed.

기출 적중문제

정답 am tired, I can't play soccer with you
해설 현재의 사실과 반대되는 일을 가정하는 가정법 과거 문장이므로 '나는 피곤하기 때문에, 너와 함께 축구를 할 수 없다.'라는 직설법 문장으로 바꿔 쓸 수 있고, 이때 현재시제를 쓴다.

POINT 1-2 가정법 과거완료

연습문제

1 had known
2 wouldn't have dropped
3 would have missed
4 had arrived
5 had been
6 wouldn't have fallen
7 had come
8 would have finished
9 had not been
10 could have gone
11 had not forgotten

POINT 2-1   I wish + 가정법 과거

연습문제

1	were	**2**	could win
3	didn't close	**4**	knew
5	could see	**6**	didn't feel
7	would fall	**8**	could go
9	sold	**10**	had
11	would write	**12**	spent

기출 적중문제

정답 could go

해설 '~하면 좋을 텐데'라는 의미로 현재 이룰 수 없거나 실현 가능성이 매우 작은 일을 소망하고 있으므로 「I wish + 가정법 과거」를 쓴다.

POINT 2-2   I wish + 가정법 과거완료

연습문제

1 had not lost my watch
2 didn't lend me her pen
3 could decide what to wear
4 forgot my birthday
5 didn't have to leave so soon
6 was canceled
7 had more cookies to eat
8 wasn't able to solve the puzzle
9 had not bought these sunglasses
10 didn't do my homework last night

POINT 3   as if + 가정법 과거/과거완료

연습문제

1	were	**2**	had painted
3	were	**4**	knew
5	had watched	**6**	were
7	had lived		

서술형 대비 문제

(A)
1 were small, could wear these shoes
2 didn't have a test, would play with my friends
3 had not been too long, wouldn't have gotten sleepy
4 were in Italy, could visit the Colosseum
5 opened on Sundays, could study there
6 had brought his wallet, wouldn't have lent him $20

7 had not told a lie to my parents, wouldn't have been upset

(B)
1 I were a doctor
2 it were warm
3 Minho would listen to my advice
4 I could meet the actor
5 I had seen the play
6 my team had won the game
7 I could show you my garden
8 he had told me about his plans

(C)
1 were a genius
2 had finished the homework
3 became an angel
4 had not made a mistake

중간·기말고사 실전 문제

1 snows   **2** ③   **3** ③   **4** ④
5 ②   **6** ②   **7** will → would   **8** had six legs, they would be insects   **9** had studied hard, she could have answered all the questions
10 ①   **11** ②   **12** ②   **13** ③
14 agreed   **15** ⑤   **16** ③   **17** ②, ③
18 had learned   **19** ④   **20** ③   **21** I had saved money for an emergency   **22** ⑤
23 ④   **24** ①   **25** he were a great singer
26 ③

1 조건문은 현재나 미래에 일어날 수 있는 상황을 나타내며, 조건문에서는 미래를 나타내더라도 현재시제를 쓴다.

2 ③ will tell → would tell

3 현재의 사실과 반대되는 일을 가정하고 있으므로 가정법 과거를 쓰고, 가정법 과거에서 if절의 be동사는 주어에 상관없이 were를 쓴다.

4 현재의 사실과 반대되는 일을 가정하고 있으므로 주절에는 「주어 + 조동사의 과거형(could) + 동사원형」을 쓴다.

5 현재의 사실과 반대되는 일을 가정하고 있으므로 주절에는 조동사의 과거형 would를 쓴다.

6 ② will go → would go

7 현재의 사실과 반대되는 일을 가정하고 있으므로 주절에는 조동사의 과거형 would를 쓴다.

8 현재의 사실과 반대되는 일을 가정하는 가정법 과거 「If + 주어 + 동사의 과거형 ~, 주어 + 조동사의 과거형 + 동사원형 …」으로 바꿔 쓸 수 있다.

9 과거의 사실과 반대되는 일을 가정하는 가정법 과거완료 「If + 주어 + had + p.p. ~, 주어 + 조동사의 과거형 + have + p.p. …」로 바꿔 쓸 수 있다.

10 현재의 사실과 반대되는 일을 가정하는 가정법 과거 문장이므로 '나는 키가 크지 않기 때문에, 농구팀에 가입할 수 없다.'라는 직설법 문장으로 바꿔 쓸 수 있고, 이때 현재시제를 쓴다.

11 ② have arrived → had arrived

12 현재 이룰 수 없거나 실현 가능성이 매우 작은 일을 소망하는 「I wish + 가정법 과거」를 써야 하므로 knew를 쓴다.

13 현재의 사실과 반대되는 일을 가정하고 있으므로 가정법 과거 「If + 주어 + 동사의 과거형 ~, 주어 + 조동사의 과거형 + 동사원형 …」을 쓴다.

14 현재 이룰 수 없거나 실현 가능성이 매우 작은 일을 소망하는 「I wish + 가정법 과거」로 바꿔 쓸 수 있으므로 agreed를 쓴다.

15 '만약 ~했더라면 …했을 텐데'의 의미로 과거의 사실과 반대되는 일을 가정하는 가정법 과거완료이므로 「If + 주어 + had + p.p. ~, 주어 + 조동사의 과거형 + have + p.p. …」를 쓴다.

16 '~하면 좋을 텐데'라는 의미로 현재 이룰 수 없거나 실현 가능성이 매우 작은 일을 소망하고 있으므로 「I wish + 가정법 과거」를 쓴다.

17 ① baked → bake
④ had been → were
⑤ be → have been

18 '~했더라면 좋았을 텐데'라는 의미로 과거에 이루지 못한 일을 소망하는 「I wish + 가정법 과거완료」를 써야 하므로 had learned를 쓴다.

19 ・과거에 이루지 못한 일을 소망하는 「I wish + 가정법 과거완료」를 써야 하므로 had taken을 쓴다.
・현재 이룰 수 없거나 실현 가능성이 매우 작은 일을 소망하는 「I wish + 가정법 과거」를 써야 하므로 would give를 쓴다.

20 ・현재 이룰 수 없거나 실현 가능성이 매우 작은 일을 소망하는 「I wish + 가정법 과거」를 써야 하므로 were를 쓴다.
・주절의 시제(현재시제)와 같은 시점의 사실과 반대되는 일을 가정하는 「as if + 가정법 과거」를 써야 하므로 were를 쓴다.

21 과거에 이루지 못한 일을 소망하는 「I wish + 가정법 과거완료」로 바꿔 쓸 수 있다.

22 last week는 과거를 나타내는 부사구이므로 과거에 이루지 못한 일을 소망하는 「I wish + 가정법 과거완료」를 쓴다.

23 과거에 이루지 못한 일을 소망하는 「I wish + 가정법 과거완료」를 써야 하므로 had made를 쓴다.

24 ① had had → had

25 주절의 시제(현재시제)와 같은 시점의 사실과 반대되는 일을 가정하는 「as if + 가정법 과거」로 바꿔 쓸 수 있다.

26 첫 번째 빈칸: 과거에 이루지 못한 일을 소망하는 「I wish + 가정법 과거완료」를 써야 하므로 had gone을 쓴다.

두 번째 빈칸: 현재나 미래에 일어날 수 있는 상황을 나타내는 조건문을 써야 하므로 won't miss를 쓴다.

CHAPTER 18
일치·화법·도치

p.396

POINT 1-1 시제 일치

연습문제 A

1	O	**2**	was[had been]
3	O	**4**	might
5	lost[had lost]	**6**	could
7	O	**8**	wouldn't[would not]

연습문제 B

1	wanted	**2**	would like
3	was	**4**	practiced
5	would buy	**6**	didn't feel
7	would cook	**8**	had
9	could hear	**10**	had finished
11	would be	**12**	was
13	might arrive	**14**	had told

기출 적중문제

정답 ⑤

해설 어제 일어난 일이므로 주절에는 과거시제 told를 쓴다. 주절이 과거시제이므로 종속절에는 조동사의 과거형 would를 쓴다.

POINT 1-2 시제 일치의 예외

연습문제

1 she swims every day
2 light travels faster than sound
3 Beijing is the capital of China
4 the Industrial Revolution started in the 1760s
5 a friend in need is a friend indeed
6 he always drinks a cup of coffee in the morning
7 metal expands in hot weather

POINT 2 화법 전환: 평서문

연습문제 A

1 told, he wanted a glass of cold water
2 said, those paintings were amazing
3 said, he was preparing breakfast then
4 told, she would go to the dentist that day
5 told, my dress looked very pretty
6 said, he could finish the science project that night
7 said, she had been satisfied with the meal
8 said, she would throw a party the following week
9 told, he had graduated two years before

연습문제 B

1 "I want to join the book club."
2 "I'm[I am] listening to K-pop now."
3 "I can fix the bicycle today."
4 "I'll[I will] teach you math tomorrow."
5 "I had a car accident last week."

기출 적중문제

정답 She said (that) she would leave the next[following] day.

해설 전달동사 say는 그대로 쓰고, 전달동사가 과거시제이므로 종속절의 현재형 will을 과거형 would로 바꾼다. 전달하는 사람의 입장에 맞게 부사 tomorrow를 the next[following] day로 바꾼다.

POINT 3-1 화법 전환: 의문사가 있는 의문문

연습문제

1 how I was
2 when the store opened
3 why the front door was open
4 what I wanted for Christmas
5 where he could buy a ticket
6 who was talking so loudly
7 when he would call me
8 what the most popular dish was

POINT 3-2 화법 전환: 의문사가 없는 의문문

연습문제

1 if[whether] I was ready to go out
2 if[whether] I knew the answer
3 if[whether] it would snow the next[following] day
4 if[whether] we had enjoyed the concert
5 if[whether] I was good at dancing
6 if[whether] I could bring him the newspaper

POINT 4 도치

연습문제

1	I am	**2**	is a vase
3	lies a child	**4**	sleeps the man
5	were lots of people	**6**	they are
7	hid a small cat	**8**	comes the bus

정답 ⓔ → it comes

해설 There/Here가 문장 맨 앞에 올 때 주어가 대명사인 경우 주어와 동사가 도치되지 않는다.

서술형 대비 문제

Ⓐ
1 I knew that Paul sang well.
2 She hoped that Terry would keep his promise.
3 We learned that we can't breathe underwater.
4 I heard that Linda volunteers every month.
5 I thought that I had to go to the hospital.
6 Mr. Lee said that Alexander Bell invented the telephone in 1876.
7 Dad told me that he might come home late.
8 I believed that Eric didn't know my phone number.
9 Harry was sure that he had turned off all the lights.

Ⓑ
1 she needed to learn how to swim
2 he could teach her the next[following] day
3 he would be back in 15 minutes
4 she would wait for him there
5 she was going to buy a new laptop that day
6 where she was going to buy it
7 if[whether] she wanted to watch that movie together
8 she had seen it the previous weekend
9 how her steak was
10 it tasted really good
11 if[whether] she could speak Russian
12 she could speak Russian a little

Ⓒ
1 is a new mall
2 it is
3 live a lot of fish
4 was an empty seat
5 ran a few men
6 comes the train
7 are some books
8 stood a cabin
9 goes an ambulance
10 jumped the white horse

중간·기말고사 실전 문제

1 ③ **2** ① **3** ④ **4** ④ **5** could win **6** ③ **7** ⑤ **8** ⓑ → would **9** his, was, the next[following] day **10** ④ **11** ④ **12** ④ **13** ③ **14** ⑤ **15** ends → ended **16** ② **17** ② **18** had lied to her **19** ④ **20** ④ **21** Maria said, "I'll[I will] go to bed before midnight." **22** ⑤ **23** (that) she was going to make an egg sandwich for dinner that day / if [whether] he could buy some eggs and a bottle of juice

1 주절이 과거시제이므로 종속절에는 과거시제 was를 쓴다.

2 과학적 사실을 말할 때는 주절의 시제와 상관없이 종속절에 항상 현재시제를 쓰므로 현재시제 moves를 쓴다.

3 ④ needs → needed[had needed]

4 전달동사가 과거시제이므로 종속절의 현재시제 am을 과거시제 was로 바꾼다.

5 주절이 현재시제에서 과거시제로 바뀌었으므로 종속절도 조동사의 과거형 could를 쓴다.

6 · 첫 번째 빈칸: 주절이 과거시제이므로 종속절에는 과거시제 was를 쓴다.
· 두 번째 빈칸: 현재의 습관이나 반복되는 일을 나타낼 때는 주절의 시제와 상관없이 종속절에 항상 현재시제를 쓰므로 현재시제 practices를 쓴다.

7 전달동사 say to는 tell로 바꾸고, 전달동사가 과거시제이므로 종속절의 현재시제 want를 과거시제 wanted로 바꾼다. 전달하는 사람의 입장에 맞게 인칭대명사 I를 she로 바꾸고 you를 me로 바꾼다.

8 주절이 과거시제이므로 종속절에는 조동사의 과거형 would를 쓴다.

9 전달동사가 과거시제이므로 종속절의 현재시제 is를 과거시제 was로 바꾼다. 전달하는 사람의 입장에 맞게 인칭대명사 my를 his로 바꾸고 부사 tomorrow를 the next[following] day로 바꾼다.

10 ④ will → would

11 전달동사 say는 그대로 쓰고, 전달동사가 과거시제이므로 종속절의 현재형 can을 과거형 could로 바꾼다. 전달하는 사람의 입장에 맞게 인칭대명사 my를 his로 바꾸고 부사 now를 then으로 바꾼다.

12 첫 번째 빈칸: 주절이 과거시제이므로 종속절에는 과거시제 went를 쓴다.
두 번째 빈칸: 주절이 과거시제이므로 종속절에는 조동사의 과거형 would를 쓴다.

13 의문사가 있는 의문문의 간접 화법은 의문사(why)로 주절과 종

속절을 연결하고, 종속절을 「의문사 + 주어 + 동사」의 어순으로 쓴다. 전달동사가 과거시제이므로 종속절의 현재시제 are ~ crying을 과거시제 was crying으로 바꾸고, 전달하는 사람의 입장에 맞게 인칭대명사 you를 I로 바꾼다.

14 의문사가 없는 의문문의 간접 화법은 if나 whether로 주절과 종속절을 연결하고, 전달동사가 과거시제이므로 종속절의 현재형 Can을 과거형 could로 바꾼다. 전달하는 사람의 입장에 맞게 인칭대명사 I를 she로 바꾼다.

15 전달동사가 과거시제이므로 종속절의 현재시제 ends를 과거시제 ended로 바꾼다.

16 의문사가 없는 의문문의 간접 화법은 if나 whether로 주절과 종속절을 연결한다.

17 전달동사 say to는 ask로 바꾸고, 전달동사가 과거시제이므로 종속절의 현재시제 Do ~ know를 과거시제 knew로 바꾼다. 전달하는 사람의 입장에 맞게 인칭대명사 you를 I로 바꾼다.

18 주절이 과거시제이고, 내가 거짓말을 한 것은 나의 엄마가 알아낸 시점보다 더 이전에 발생한 일이므로 과거완료시제 had lied to her를 쓴다.

19 ④ comes he → he comes

20 ⓑ played who → who played
ⓒ I → he
ⓔ was → had been

21 전달동사 say는 그대로 쓰고, 전달동사가 과거시제라서 종속절에 과거형 would가 쓰였으므로 현재형 will을 쓴다. Maria의 입장에 맞게 인칭대명사 she를 I로 바꾼다.

22 ⑤ will translate → would translate

23 (A) 전달동사가 과거시제이므로 종속절의 현재시제 am을 과거시제 was로 바꾸고, 전달하는 사람의 입장에 맞게 인칭대명사 I를 she로 바꾸고 부사 today를 that day로 바꾼다.
(B) 의문사가 없는 의문문의 간접 화법은 if나 whether로 주절과 종속절을 연결하고, 종속절을 「if[whether] + 주어 + 동사」의 어순으로 쓴다. 전달동사가 과거시제이므로 종속절의 현재형 Can을 과거형 could로 바꾼다. 전달하는 사람의 입장에 맞게 인칭대명사 you를 he로 바꾼다.

CHAPTER 1
문장의 형식
p.8

POINT 1-1 1형식과 2형식

1	주어, 동사, 수식어	**2**	주어, 동사, 주격 보어
3	주어, 동사, 수식어	**4**	주어, 동사, 주격 보어
5	주어, 동사, 수식어	**6**	주어, 동사, 주격 보어
7	주어, 동사, 주격 보어	**8**	주어, 동사, 수식어

POINT 1-2 2형식: 감각동사

1 Your idea sounds great.
2 This cupcake tastes delicious.
3 O
4 O
5 The muffin tastes like chocolate.
6 The blue flowers in the yard smell good.
7 O
8 All of the band's songs sounded wonderful.

POINT 2 3형식과 4형식

1 The child asked me many questions.
2 The farm produces cheese.
3 I heard a strange sound in the living room.
4 My grandmother waters her plants.
5 I told him my weekend plans.
6 Jerry made his sister a tasty hot dog.

1 Jake showed me his photo album.
2 May I ask a favor of you?
3 I gave the horses some carrots.
4 Can you find the science textbook for me?
5 The soccer player passed his teammate the ball.
6 My aunt bought a new bicycle for me for Christmas.

POINT 3-1 5형식: 명사나 형용사를 목적격 보어로 쓰는 동사

1 목적어: the math exam, 목적격 보어: hard
2 목적어: your room, 목적격 보어: clean
3 목적어: me, 목적격 보어: the class president
4 목적어: us, 목적격 보어: healthy
5 목적어: your neck, 목적격 보어: warm
6 목적어: me, 목적격 보어: "angel face"
7 목적어: the meat, 목적격 보어: cool
8 목적어: her, 목적격 보어: a popular songwriter
9 목적어: Jasmin, 목적격 보어: the queen of golf
10 목적어: his new Chinese class, 목적격 보어: too difficult
11 목적어: the instructions for the machine, 목적격 보어: confusing

1 Eric found the show boring.
2 People call that firefighter a hero.
3 That unique building made our city famous.
4 They made Tom the captain of their team.
5 I find this website useful.
6 The police officers keep the village safe.
7 We call our teacher "Mr. Incredible".
8 The homework kept the students busy for an hour.

POINT 3-2 5형식: to부정사를 목적격 보어로 쓰는 동사

1 asked me to help her
2 want me to join the chess club
3 ordered the woman to stop the car
4 advised him to be on time
5 expect me to go to a university
6 allowed the man to return home
7 didn't tell her husband to buy some eggs

1	to listen	**2**	angry	**3**	to help
4	to exercise	**5**	to eat	**6**	to take
7	useful	**8**	to read	**9**	to touch
10	proud	**11**	neat	**12**	to go

POINT 3-3 5형식: 사역동사

연습문제 A

1 Doing yoga every morning makes you feel fresh.
2 O
3 My mom doesn't let me travel by myself.
4 Ms. Dale had us clean the dirty shoes.
5 O
6 The detective got the suspect to tell the truth.
7 Jason let his daughter play with sand.
8 The pilot told the passengers to wear a seat belt.

연습문제 B

1	touch	2	look
3	to come	4	repair
5	find, to find	6	to close
7	stop	8	have
9	bring	10	move, to move
11	to check	12	to brush

POINT 3-4   5형식: 지각동사

연습문제 A

1 I saw a man playing[play].
2 I didn't hear Charles coming[come].
3 We watched the cat chasing[chase].
4 Erica smelled the bread burning[burn].
5 Paul listened to the woman singing[sing].
6 Tom felt someone touching[touch].

연습문제 B

1	cough[coughing]	2	scream
3	shout[shouting]	4	apologize
5	to use	6	fly[flying]
7	perform[performing]	8	jump[jumping]
9	to get	10	dry
11	expand[to expand]		

중간·기말고사 실전 문제

1 ③, ⑤ 2 ④ 3 ③, ⑤ 4 ④ 5 I call her a comedian 6 ③ 7 ⑤ 8 The cold weather made the lake freeze. 9 ④
10 ④ 11 ④ 12 ④ 13 I paid Jackson five dollars 14 ③ 15 ② 16 ⑤
17 Don't let Sarah know 18 ④ 19 ③
20 ③ 21 (1) a woman to describe the thief's appearance (2) an old lady (to) find her wallet (3) a man to show his license 22 ② 23 had my grandfather take the medicine three times a day 24 saw a puppy playing[play] with a cat this morning 25 (1) ⓑ → smelled nice (2) ⓔ → asked me to bring

---

1 감각동사의 주격 보어 자리에는 형용사만 오므로 부사 gently와 gladly는 쓸 수 없다.

2 「allow + 목적어 + to부정사」

3 ① win → to win
  ② to fix → fix
  ④ lending → to lend

4 목적격 보어 자리에 동사원형(design)이 왔으므로 목적격 보어 자리에 to부정사가 오는 준사역동사 got은 쓸 수 없다.

5 5형식: 「주어 + 동사 + 목적어 + 목적격 보어」

6 「advise + 목적어 + to부정사」

7 목적격 보어 자리에 현재분사(playing)가 왔으므로 목적격 보어 자리에 동사원형이 오는 사역동사 had는 쓸 수 없다.

8 「make + 목적어 + 동사원형」

9 목적격 보어 자리에 to부정사(to clean)가 왔으므로 목적격 보어 자리에 동사원형이 오는 사역동사 made는 쓸 수 없다.

10 ④ silently → silent

11 주어진 문장과 ④: 5형식
  ①: 1형식   ②: 2형식   ③: 4형식   ⑤: 3형식

12 ① to → for
  ② a story the children → the children a story
  ③ to a menu → a menu
  ⑤ the teacher → of the teacher

13 4형식: 「주어 + 동사 + 간접 목적어(~에게) + 직접 목적어(~을)」

14 ·「buy + 직접 목적어 + for + 간접 목적어」
   ·「ask + 직접 목적어 + of + 간접 목적어」

15 ⓑ arrive → to arrive
   ⓒ a waterfall → like a waterfall
   ⓓ to burn → burn[burning]

16 ·「advise + 목적어 + to부정사」
   ·「listen to + 목적어 + 동사원형/V-ing형」

17 「let + 목적어 + 동사원형」

18 ④의 make는 목적어를 필요로 하는 3형식 동사이고, ①②③⑤의 make는 목적어와 목적격 보어를 필요로 하는 5형식 동사이다.

19 ·목적어를 필요로 하는 3형식 동사 made
   ·목적어와 목적격 보어를 필요로 하는 5형식 사역동사 made
   ·간접 목적어와 직접 목적어를 필요로 하는 4형식 수여동사 made

20 ③ make → to make

21 (1) 「ask + 목적어 + to부정사」
   (2) 「help + 목적어 + 동사원형/to부정사」
   (3) 「get + 목적어 + to부정사」

22 ⓐⓒⓖ: 1형식

ⓑ: 3형식　ⓓⓔ: 5형식　ⓕ: 2형식

23 「have + 목적어 + 동사원형」

24 「see + 목적어 + 동사원형/V-ing형」

25 (1) 감각동사 smell의 주격 보어 자리에는 형용사(nice)만 온다.
(2) 5형식 동사 ask의 목적격 보어 자리에는 to부정사(to bring)가 온다.

CHAPTER 2
다양한 문장의 종류
p.20

POINT 1 감탄문

1 What	**2** What	**3** How
4 How	**5** What	**6** How
7 What	**8** What	**9** How
10 What		

1 What a friendly smile (she has)!
2 What an easy puzzle (that was)!
3 How creatively he thinks!
4 How fresh (the apples look)!
5 How practical (the advice is)!
6 How sour (the lemon is)!
7 What small feet (the baby has)!
8 How quietly the man talks!

POINT 2 의문사 의문문

1 What will happen this year?
2 How can we get to the park?
3 Where were you last night?
4 Why did you decide to study in France?
5 How come Jerry is always late?
6 What do you usually do after dinner?

1 Who broke the window?
2 What is your phone number?
3 Why are you upset?
4 How do you go to school?
5 When is he coming back to Korea?
6 Where can I find the cups?

POINT 3 선택의문문

1 Which, or	**2** Are, or	**3** Which, or
4 Does, or	**5** When, or	

1 ⓒ	**2** ⓓ	**3** ⓐ	**4** ⓑ
5 ⓕ	**6** ⓔ	**7** ⓓ	**8** ⓒ
9 ⓑ	**10** ⓕ	**11** ⓐ	**12** ⓔ

POINT 4-1 의문사가 있는 간접의문문

연습문제

1 I don't know how much this painting is worth.
2 Do you know what this word means?
3 Can you tell me where the subway station is?
4 Why do you think we have to protect the environment?
5 How do you believe you can improve your communication skills?
6 Can you remember what his name is?
7 Can you tell me what made her so happy?
8 Where do you guess you lost your passport?
9 Please tell me how you found out the answer to that problem.
10 When do you imagine people will live on Mars?
11 I want to know how the city of Pompeii was destroyed.
12 Where do you think they hid the evidence?
13 I wonder who invented the light bulb.
14 Who do you believe is telling the truth?

POINT 4-2 의문사가 없는 간접의문문

연습문제 A

1 if Jack has a dog
2 whether I am responsible for the incident
3 whether the twins look alike
4 if he trusts me
5 if Vivian agreed with your suggestion
6 if he still works there
7 whether Lucas speaks Spanish

연습문제 B

1 I'm not sure if[whether] Kylie will participate in this speech contest.
2 Can you tell me if[whether] we have class today?
3 Do you know if[whether] someone ate all the leftovers?
4 I don't know if[whether] James will buy a new bag.
5 I wonder if[whether] it will[it'll] snow on Christmas Eve.
6 Please tell me if[whether] the cherry trees in Jejudo began to bloom.
7 I don't remember if[whether] he likes watching horror movies.

POINT 5 부가의문문

연습문제 A

1 is
2 will
3 does
4 will
5 shall
6 was
7 isn't
8 will
9 doesn't
10 aren't

연습문제 B

1 wasn't it
2 shall we
3 can't he
4 will you
5 don't they
6 didn't you
7 aren't there
8 did you
9 isn't it
10 aren't they
11 can't you
12 aren't I
13 aren't they
14 isn't it
15 will you

중간·기말고사 실전 문제

1 ③ **2** Which **3** What an amazing soccer player (he is)! **4** How bad (the onions smell)! **5** ③ **6** ⑤ **7** ③ **8** ④ **9** ③ **10** ⑤ **11** ③ **12** I don't know who drew that picture on the wall. **13** ⑤ **14** How long the flight to Paris was! **15** ④ **16** ④ **17** ④ **18** I don't remember what the password for this website is. **19** Do you know if[whether] the shopping mall is open this Sunday? **20** ③ **21** ②, ④ **22** ④ **23** Why do you think polar bears are white? **24** ⑤ **25** (1) ⓐ → why some birds travel (2) ⓑ → What is the purpose of their trips (3) ⓔ → What

1 ③ Michael is → is Michael

2 그룹으로 공부하는 것과 혼자 공부하는 것 중 어느 것(Which)을 선호하는지 묻고 있으므로 or를 사용하여 상대방의 선택을 묻는 선택의문문이다.

3 What 감탄문: 「What + (a/an) + 형용사 + 명사 + (주어 + 동사)!」

4 How 감탄문: 「How + 형용사 + (주어 + 동사)!」

5 '나는 이 쿠키들이 땅콩을 포함하는지 아닌지 확실히 알지 못한다.'라는 의미이므로 의문사가 없는 간접의문문을 이끄는 whether를 쓴다.

6 의문사가 있는 간접의문문: 「의문사 + 주어 + 동사」

7 앞 문장의 동사가 긍정을 나타내는 일반동사(want)이므로 부정의 부가의문문 don't you를 쓴다.

8 ④: 감탄문에 쓰인 what
①②③⑤: 의문문에 쓰인 의문사 what

9 (A) 앞 문장의 동사가 부정을 나타내는 be동사(aren't)이므로 긍정의 부가의문문 are they를 쓴다.

(B) I'm으로 시작하는 문장이므로 부가의문문 aren't I를 쓴다.

(C) 앞 문장이 명령문이므로 명령문의 부가의문문 will you를 쓴다.

10 ⑤: What   ①②③④: How

11 How(어떻게)로 묻고 있으므로 방법에 해당하는 구체적인 정보로 대답한다.

12 간접의문문의 주어가 의문사인 경우: 「의문사 + 동사」

13 ① doesn't he → isn't he
② doesn't this → doesn't it
③ will you → shall we
④ wasn't it → wasn't there

14 How 감탄문: 「How + 형용사 + (주어 + 동사)!」

15 · '나는 그 표지판이 무엇을 나타내는지 궁금하다.'라는 의미이므로 what(무엇)을 쓴다.
· '이 영화가 실화에 바탕을 두었는지 아닌지 저에게 말해주시겠어요?'라는 의미이므로 의문사가 없는 간접의문문을 이끄는 if를 쓴다.

16 부가의문문으로 have you?를 썼으므로 앞 문장의 동사는 부정을 나타내는 일반동사의 현재완료형을 쓴다.

17 '나는 그 도시와 그것의 아름다운 날씨를 좋아하기 때문이야.'라고 대답했으므로 Why(왜)로 묻는다.

18 의문사가 있는 간접의문문: 「의문사 + 주어 + 동사」

19 의문사가 없는 간접의문문: 「if[whether] + 주어 + 동사」

20 첫 번째 빈칸: '너는 그곳에 왜 갈 거니?'라는 의미이므로 Why(왜)를 쓴다.
두 번째 빈칸: '그는 언제 수영을 시작했니?'라는 의미이므로 When(언제)을 쓴다.

21 ① unique a → a unique
③ What this store has friendly employees! → What friendly employees this store has!
⑤ are these earrings → these earrings are

22 실크가 어디서 생겨나는지를 설명하고 있으므로 where(어디서)를 쓴다. 의문사가 있는 간접의문문은 「의문사 + 주어 + 동사」의 형태이다.

23 의문사가 있는 간접의문문은 「의문사 + 주어 + 동사」의 형태이다. 간접의문문을 포함하는 문장의 동사가 think이므로 간접의문문의 의문사(why)를 문장 맨 앞에 쓴다.

24 ⓒ how did the author imagine → how the author imagined
ⓕ Do you imagine what → What do you imagine
ⓖ don't those → don't they

25 (1) 의문사가 있는 간접의문문: 「의문사 + 주어 + 동사」
(2) be동사가 있는 의문사 의문문: 「의문사 + be동사 + 주어 ~?」
(3) What 감탄문: 「What + (a/an) + 형용사 + 명사 + (주어 + 동사)!」

CHAPTER 3
시제
p.32

POINT 1   현재시제

1	spends	2	blames	3	rains
4	leaves	5	belongs	6	drinks
7	rings	8	freezes		

POINT 2-1   과거시제

1 It rained a lot last week.
2 O
3 O
4 The Titanic sank on April 15, 1912.
5 O
6 I found my grandmother's secret recipe a month ago.
7 The first Olympic games were held in Greece in 1896.

POINT 2-2   과거시제: 동사의 과거형과 과거분사형

1	attended, attended	2	entered, entered
3	shut, shut	4	believed, believed
5	stopped, stopped	6	ran, run
7	hurt, hurt	8	became, become
9	brought, brought	10	left, left
11	overcame, overcome		
12	understood, understood		
13	mistook, mistaken	14	spread, spread
15	studied, studied	16	forgot, forgotten
17	chose, chosen	18	laid, laid
19	cost, cost	20	was/were, been

POINT 3   미래시제

1	will search	2	donated
3	am going to buy	4	feel
5	will do	6	are going to go
7	were	8	fed
9	is going to hatch	10	will leave
11	have	12	will stop

POINT 4 진행시제

연습문제 A
1 Are you looking
2 She was reading
3 Betty is smelling
4 Are you getting[Are you going to get]
5 That sounds
6 Kevin is arguing
7 We were singing

연습문제 B
1 was chatting
2 are painting
3 was preparing
4 am having

POINT 5-1 현재완료시제

연습문제 A
1 We have been
2 The kids have not[haven't] eaten
3 Have you received
4 This yogurt has gone
5 have not[haven't] found
6 has Tom studied

연습문제 B
1 has lost her ring
2 has had my comic book for two weeks
3 has searched for the treasure underwater since 1990
4 has fought against racism for thirty years
5 has been a world famous ballerina since 2018
6 have written songs since last winter

POINT 5-2 현재완료시제의 용법

연습문제
1 Have you met, 경험
2 My older brother has just washed, 완료
3 I have already completed, 완료
4 It has rained hard, 계속
5 The family has gone, 결과
6 I have never read, 경험
7 She has lost interest, 결과
8 I have never tasted, 경험
9 The company has recently bought, 완료
10 The Korean soccer team has left, 결과
11 Developments in technology have led, 계속
12 Ms. Johnson has taught English, 계속

POINT 5-3 현재완료시제 vs. 과거시제

연습문제 A
1 has traveled
2 blinked
3 have studied
4 made
5 have waited
6 had

7 have been
8 sank

연습문제 B
1 O
2 The Second World War ended in 1945.
3 O
4 The price of oil has gone up since last month.
5 Did you watch the comedy show on TV last night?
6 The career counselor has provided useful information since we first met.
7 He reported the incident to the police an hour ago.
8 Financial fraud has become more common since last year.

중간·기말고사 실전 문제

1 ⑤
2 ③
3 is going to arrive
4 ④
5 ⑤
6 ③
7 (1) Emily hasn't[has not] been a Korean citizen since 2017. (2) Has Emily been a Korean citizen since 2017?
8 turned
9 ③
10 ④
11 ③
12 ②
13 has stood for thousands of years
14 ③, ④
15 ④
16 has lost a button of his jacket
17 has lived in Berlin since 2007
18 ④
19 Have you experienced cultural differences
20 has baked pizza, have traveled to India
21 ⓐ has had ⓑ decided ⓒ said
22 ⑤
23 ④
24 ③
25 (1) ⓐ → has flowed (2) ⓒ → was wasting (3) ⓓ → decided

1 ⑤ rise - rose - risen

2 ① enterred → entered
  ② have grew → have grown
  ④ begun → began
  ⑤ have knew → have known

3 미래시제는 「will + 동사원형」이나 「be going to + 동사원형」의 형태이다.

4 ④ is → was

5 since는 현재완료시제와 주로 함께 쓰이는 표현이다.

6 ③ is having → has (소유의 의미를 나타내는 have는 진행형으로 쓸 수 없다.)

7 (1) 현재완료시제의 부정문: 「have/has + not + p.p.」
  (2) 현재완료시제의 의문문: 「Have/Has + 주어 + p.p. ~?」

8 과거시제로 묻고 있으므로 과거시제로 답한다.

9 ① lived → has lived
  ② has joined → joined

④ have the accident happened → did the accident happen

⑤ has gone → went

10 ④: 현재진행시제   ①②③⑤: 미래시제

11 주어진 문장과 ③: 경험   ①④: 완료   ②: 계속   ⑤: 결과

12 주어진 문장과 ②: 완료   ①④: 결과   ③⑤: 경험

13 과거부터 현재까지 계속되는 일을 나타내는 현재완료시제 문장이다. 현재완료시제의 긍정문은 「have/has + p.p.」의 형태이다.

14 since와 for는 현재완료시제와 주로 함께 쓰이는 표현이다.

15 ④: for   ①②③⑤: since

16 Michael은 그의 재킷의 단추를 잃어버렸고 아직도 그것을 찾지 못하였으므로 현재완료시제를 쓴다.

17 Samantha는 베를린에 2007년에 이사했고 아직도 거기에 살고 있으므로 현재완료시제를 쓴다.

18 ④ did → have

19 과거부터 현재까지의 경험을 나타내는 현재완료시제 문장이다. 현재완료시제의 의문문은 「Have/Has + 주어 + p.p. ~?」의 형태이다.

20 첫 번째 빈칸: Natalie는 피자를 구워본 적이 있다고 했으므로 has baked pizza를 쓴다.
두 번째 빈칸: Ethan과 Natalie는 인도를 여행해본 적이 있다고 했으므로 have traveled to India를 쓴다.

21 ⓐ since는 현재완료시제와 주로 함께 쓰이는 표현이다.
ⓑ Last week은 과거시제와 주로 함께 쓰이는 부사구이다.
ⓒ 지난주에 발생한 일을 나타내고 있으므로 과거시제를 쓴다.

22 (A) '전화가 울렸을 때 나는 TV를 보고 있었다.'라는 의미이므로 과거진행시제를 쓴다.
(B) 역사적 사실을 말하고 있으므로 과거시제를 쓴다.
(C) since는 현재완료시제와 주로 함께 쓰이는 표현이다.

23 ④ performed → have performed

24 ⓐ has discovered → discovered
ⓒ was → has been
ⓕ has ended → ended

25 (1) since는 현재완료시제와 주로 함께 쓰이는 표현이다.
(2) 과거의 특정 시점에 진행되고 있던 일을 나타내고 있으므로 과거진행시제를 쓴다.
(3) 과거의 일을 나타내고 있으므로 과거시제를 쓴다.

CHAPTER 4
조동사
p.44

POINT 1-1   조동사의 쓰임

1 spend	2 O	3 can
4 be able to	5 let	6 have to
7 will		

POINT 1-2   조동사가 있는 부정문과 의문문

1 Can I exchange
2 Could you do
3 Sam cannot speak
4 Should I call
5 You should not ignore
6 The player will not participate
7 You may not wear

POINT 2   can, could

연습문제 A
1 I can't[cannot] manage this situation by myself.
2 Am I able to see stars with this telescope?
3 They weren't[were not] able to go hiking because of the heavy rain.
4 Daniel couldn't[could not] believe the news.
5 He is able to write his name in Chinese.
6 Can she distinguish an imitation from an original?

연습문제 B

1 ⓑ	2 ⓒ	3 ⓐ	4 ⓒ
5 ⓓ	6 ⓑ	7 ⓓ	8 ⓐ

POINT 3   may, might

1 허가	2 약한 추측	3 약한 추측
4 약한 금지	5 허가	6 허가
7 약한 추측	8 약한 금지	9 약한 추측
10 약한 추측		

POINT 4-1   will, would I

1 Will you pass
2 Tom is going to leave

3 I will drop

4 The warm weather will continue

5 Would you bring

6 The store will not give

POINT 4-2 will, would Ⅱ

1 I would like some sweet snacks.

2 I would like to have lunch with you tomorrow.

3 Would you like to leave a message for him?

4 I would like a glass of water.

5 Would you like some help?

6 I would like pancakes with maple syrup for breakfast.

7 Would you like to read these magazines?

8 Would you like some more sugar in your coffee?

9 I would like to be a doctor after I graduate from college.

10 Would you like to live in a rural area?

11 I would like to hear some advice from you.

12 Would you like ketchup with your fries?

POINT 5 must, have to

연습 문제 A

1 ⓑ   **2** ⓐ   **3** ⓑ   **4** ⓑ

5 ⓐ   **7** ⓐ

연습 문제 B

1 must[have to] wear   **2** don't have to hide

3 had to wait   **4** can't be

5 must not cheat   **6** must be

7 must[has to] go

POINT 6 should, had better

연습 문제

1 should   **2** should not

3 had better not   **4** had better

5 should not   **6** had better not

7 should   **8** should

9 had better   **10** had better not

11 should not   **12** should

13 should not   **14** had better

POINT 7 used to, would

연습 문제 A

1 Maria used to have

2 Brandon used to[would] travel

3 My brother used to[would] jog

4 There used to be

5 I used to[would] spend

6 We used to[would] go

7 He used to be

8 Kevin used to[would] go

9 Aria is used to waking

10 She used to[would] stay

연습 문제 B

1 used to, would   **2** used to

3 used to   **4** used to, would

5 used to   **6** used to, would

POINT 8 do

연습 문제

1 ⓐ   **2** ⓒ   **3** ⓑ   **4** ⓑ

5 ⓐ   **6** ⓑ   **7** ⓐ   **8** ⓒ

9 ⓑ   **10** ⓒ   **11** ⓐ   **12** ⓐ

13 ⓒ   **14** ⓐ

중간·기말고사 실전 문제

1 ②   **2** Sunglasses will protect your eyes from the sun.   **3** ④, ⑤   **4** ④   **5** ⑤   **6** ②

7 ③   **8** has to be   **9** would like to

10 ④   **11** There can't be a problem with our Internet connection.   **12** You had better call 119.   **13** ④   **14** ②   **15** ⑤   **16** ⑤

17 ②, ⑤   **18** would take a tennis lesson   **19** you had better not park your bicycle here   **20** ③

21 must not make noise   **22** ⑤   **23** ⑤

24 (A) were able to (B) was able to (C) wasn't able to   **25** ⑤

1 ① cans → can

  ③ will can → will be able to

  ④ musts → must

  ⑤ are → be

2 조동사는 주어의 인칭이나 수에 따라 형태가 변하지 않는다.

3 could = was/were able to (능력·가능)

4 can과 may는 허가(~해도 된다)의 의미를 나타낸다.

5 요청(~해주겠니?)의 의미를 나타내는 Will을 쓴다.

6 ① comparing → compare

  ③ will can → will be able to

  ④ don't may → may not

  ⑤ have to → had to

7 had better의 부정형: had better not

8 의무(~해야 한다)의 의미를 나타내는 has to를 쓴다.

9 「want to + 동사원형」 = 「would like to + 동사원형」

10 능력·가능(~할 수 있다)을 나타내는 can의 부정형 can't를 쓴다.

11 강한 추측을 나타내는 must의 부정: can't(~일 리가 없다)

12 강한 충고(~하는 것이 낫다)의 의미를 나타내는 had better를 쓴다.

13 ④: 약한 추측 ①②③⑤: 허가

14 · 「would like + 명사」 '~을 원하다'
· 충고·의무(~해야 한다)의 의미를 나타내는 should의 부정형 should not을 쓴다.

15 ⑤: 강한 추측 주어진 문장과 ①②③④: 의무

16 과거의 상태(전에는 ~이었다)를 나타내는 used to를 쓴다.

17 '다섯 살 아래의 아이들은 지불할 필요가 없다.'라는 의미이므로 don't have to와 need not을 쓴다.

18 과거의 반복적인 습관(~하곤 했다)을 나타내는 would를 쓴다.

19 had better의 부정형: had better not

20 must = have to '~해야 한다'
must not '~하면 안 된다'
don't have to = don't need to = need not '~할 필요가 없다'

21 도서관에서 소음을 내면 안 된다는 표지판이므로 강한 금지(~하면 안 된다)의 의미를 나타내는 must not을 쓴다.

22 주어진 문장과 ⑤: 동사를 강조하는 do
①: 일반동사의 의문문에 쓰이는 do
②: 일반동사의 부정문에 쓰이는 do
③: 일반동사 do ④: 대동사 do

23 (A) 약한 추측(~일지도 모른다)의 의미를 나타내는 may를 쓴다.
(B) 충고·의무(~해야 한다)의 의미를 나타내는 should의 부정형 should not을 쓴다.
(C) 강한 금지(~하면 안 된다)의 의미를 나타내는 must not을 쓴다.

24 (A) 나은이와 지훈이는 초등학생 때 약간의 마술을 할 수 있었으므로 능력·가능(~할 수 있다)의 의미를 나타내는 were able to를 쓴다.
(B) 나은이는 초등학생 때 자막 없이 영어로 된 영화를 볼 수 있었으므로 was able to를 쓴다.
(C) 지훈이는 초등학생 때 자막 없이 영어로 된 영화를 볼 수 없었으므로 wasn't able to를 쓴다.

25 '호랑이와 곰은 동굴 밖으로 나가면 안 된다'라는 의미이므로 '~할 필요가 없다'라는 의미의 don't have to는 쓸 수 없다.

CHAPTER 5
수동태
p.58

POINT 1 수동태 문장 만드는 법

연습문제 A

1 Dishes are washed every day by Mom.
2 The fence was painted yesterday by Marcus.
3 The picture of the flower was taken by James.
4 O
5 Horror movies are loved by many people.
6 O
7 My bag was stolen by a tall man.

연습문제 B

1 Great breakfasts are offered by this restaurant.
2 Some chocolate chip cookies were baked by Sarah.
3 Columbus discovered North America.
4 Delicious pies are made by Mom.
5 Grass is eaten by many animals.
6 Some blueberries were found by Rachel.
7 The mailman delivers mail every day.

POINT 2 수동태의 시제

연습문제 A

1 Jenny's question was answered by Harry.
2 We watched the funny movie.
3 Many students visit the national museum.
4 The tree was hit by a car.
5 Canadians speak English and French.
6 The newspaper will be read by my dad.
7 The air conditioner was invented by Willis Carrier.
8 A new smart phone will be released by the company.

연습문제 B

1	will be fixed	**2**	was eaten
3	will be painted	**4**	was broken
5	was designed	**6**	will be cleaned
7	will be released	**8**	was fixed
9	was invented	**10**	will be explained

POINT 3 수동태의 부정문과 의문문

연습문제

1 Pasta and pizza weren't[were not] eaten by them.
Were pasta and pizza eaten by them?
2 Pencils and erasers weren't[were not] bought

by Greg.
Were pencils and erasers bought by Greg?

3 Math isn't[is not] taught by Mr. Smith at school.
Is math taught by Mr. Smith at school?

4 The Summer Olympics weren't[were not] held in 2016 by London.
Were the Summer Olympics held in 2016 by London?

5 The deliveryman's hand wasn't[was not] scratched by the cat.
Was the deliveryman's hand scratched by the cat?

6 These mystery novels weren't[were not] written by Kate.
Were these mystery novels written by Kate?

7 The iPhone wasn't[was not] designed by Steve Jobs.
Was the iPhone designed by Steve Jobs?

8 Those carrots weren't[were not] planted by him.
Were those carrots planted by him?

9 The toothbrush wasn't[was not] invented by Chinese people.
Was the toothbrush invented by Chinese people?

POINT 4 조동사가 있는 수동태

 연습문제 A
1 should not be touched
2 must be protected
3 will be played by Mary
4 must be recycled
5 may not be brought
6 can be spoken by Adam
7 could not be found

 연습문제 B
1 This package should be carried carefully by you.
2 This promise must be kept by you.
3 The apple will be eaten by us.
4 This book must be read by Cindy.
5 The homework may not be finished on time by him.
6 The new theater can be visited now by people.

POINT 5 4형식 문장의 수동태

 연습문제 A

1	to	2	to	3	for
4	for	5	to	6	to
7	of				

 연습문제 B
1 was bought for me by my uncle
2 were shown to me by him
3 was asked a favor by Sally
4 asked of the actor by some people
5 is taught to middle school students by her
6 was given a prize by the principal
7 was bought for her by her mother
8 was written to his grandpa by him
9 was lent a phone by a girl
10 were asked of Ms. Green by students

POINT 6 5형식 문장의 수동태

 연습문제
1 The room is kept so dirty by Jake.
2 He was heard to play the piano by us.
3 I was made to come home early by my mom.
4 The children call the cat Fluffy.
5 The team elected Sam captain.
6 I saw the boys running outside in the rain.

POINT 7 수동태 관용 표현

 연습문제

1	from	2	with	3	for
4	to	5	of	6	at
7	with	8	in	9	for
10	with				

중간·기말고사 실전 문제

1 ⑤ 2 ⑤ 3 are sold by 4 The dog is walked 5 ② 6 (1) The bookshelf wasn't[was not] painted by Carol. (2) Was the bookshelf painted by Carol? 7 ① 8 ①, ⑤ 9 must be kept 10 ③ 11 be 12 to → for 13 is given 14 ②, ④ 15 was sent to 16 ② 17 is known as 18 ④ 19 ① 20 ② 21 ① 22 ① 23 ② 24 ⑤ 25 (1) ⓑ → buried (2) ⓒ → with

1 ⑤ confuse → confused

2 능동태의 시제가 과거이면 수동태의 동사는 「was/were + p.p.」의 형태이고, 주어 Pride and Prejudice는 단수이므로 was written을 쓴다.

3 수동태의 동사는 「be + p.p.」의 형태이고 주어 fruits and vegetables는 복수이므로 are sold를 쓴다. 행위자는 「by + 목적격」의 형태이므로 by를 쓴다.

4 수동태의 동사는 「be + p.p.」의 형태이고 주어 The dog는 단수이므로 is walked를 쓴다.

5 ⓑ she → her
ⓒ buying → bought
ⓔ serving → served

6 (1) 수동태의 부정문: 「be동사 + not + p.p.」
(2) 의문사가 없는 수동태의 의문문: 「be동사 + 주어 + p.p. ~?」

7 4형식 문장을 직접 목적어가 주어인 수동태 문장으로 바꿀 때 간접 목적어 앞에 to/for/of 중 하나를 쓰며, give는 전치사 to를 쓰는 동사이다.

8 ①⑤: become과 look은 목적어를 가지지 않는 동사이므로 수동태로 쓸 수 없다.

9 조동사가 있는 문장의 수동태: 「조동사 + be + p.p.」

10 ③ is → has been

11 미래시제의 수동태는 「will be + p.p.」의 형태이고 'The library will be built beside the bank.'이므로 네 번째에 오는 것은 be이다.

12 be known for '~으로 유명하다'

13 수동태의 동사는 「be + p.p.」의 형태이므로 is given을 쓴다.

14 4형식 문장은 간접 목적어와 직접 목적어를 주어로 하는 두 개의 수동태 문장을 만들 수 있다. 직접 목적어가 주어인 수동태 문장으로 바꿀 때 간접 목적어 앞에 to/for/of 중 하나를 쓰며, give는 전치사 to를 쓰는 동사이다.

15 엽서가 보내는 것이 아니라 보내지는 것이므로 수동태를 쓴다. 4형식 문장을 직접 목적어가 주어인 수동태 문장으로 바꿀 때 간접 목적어 앞에 to/for/of 중 하나를 쓰며, send는 전치사 to를 쓰는 동사이다.

16 ② should not be play → should not be played

17 be known as '~으로서 알려져 있다'

18 ④ in ①②③⑤ with

19 ① made to angry → made angry

20 · 4형식 문장을 직접 목적어가 주어인 수동태 문장으로 바꿀 때 send는 간접 목적어 앞에 전치사 to를 쓰는 동사이다.
· 4형식 문장을 직접 목적어가 주어인 수동태 문장으로 바꿀 때 ask는 간접 목적어 앞에 전치사 of를 쓰는 동사이다.

21 · be interested in '~에 흥미가 있다'
· be known to '~에게 알려져 있다'

22 ①: 행위자가 일반인이거나 중요하지 않을 때는 「by + 목적격」을 생략할 수 있다.

23 ⓑ Did → Were
ⓒ Was where → Where was
ⓔ not were → were not[weren't]

24 ⑤ : 목적격 보어가 명사인 5형식 문장을 수동태로 바꿀 때는 목적

격 보어를 「be동사 + p.p.」 뒤에 그대로 쓴다.

25 (1) 일반동사의 수동태: 「be동사 + p.p.」
(2) be covered with '~으로 덮여 있다'

CHAPTER 6
부정사

p.70

POINT 1 to부정사의 형태와 용법

A

1 My goal is to read more good books.
2 O
3 The teacher told us not to run in the hallway.
4 I want to return these small shoes.
5 O
6 Paris is a beautiful city to visit.
7 We are happy to meet you.
8 O

B

| 1 | ⓐ | 2 | ⓑ | 3 | ⓒ | 4 | ⓐ |
| 5 | ⓒ | 6 | ⓑ | 7 | ⓐ | 8 | ⓒ |

POINT 2-1 명사적 용법: 주어와 주격 보어로 쓰이는 to부정사

A

1 It is necessary to wash your hands.
2 It is exciting to camp in the woods.
3 It isn't[is not] safe to swim in this lake.
4 It is important to remember the history.
5 It is impossible to see the stars in the cities.
6 It wasn't[was not] easy to apologize to my sister.
7 It is my dream to spend the winter in Hawaii.
8 It wasn't[was not] complicated to fix my computer.
9 It is dangerous to play with fire.

B

1 Hansu's dream is to become
2 It was fun to sing
3 My wish is to study
4 It is important to keep the law
5 Our goal is to reduce

POINT 2-2 명사적 용법: to부정사를 목적어로 쓰는 동사

A

1 I need to fix
2 We agreed to clean
3 Jenny hopes to visit
4 Henry wants to come
5 Nancy promised not to be

6 Eric would love to have
7 Mr. Collins decided to do
8 She learned to tie
9 I would like to thank
10 Charlie wishes to meet
11 Sarah chose not to buy
12 Our family plans to go
13 He refused to help
14 I expect to see

POINT 2-3 명사적 용법: to부정사를 목적격 보어로 쓰는 동사

A

1 allowed me to play
2 advised me to study
3 ordered them to move
4 wants her sister to be
5 expected us to win
6 asked John to help
7 told me not to eat

B

| 1 | ⓐ | 2 | ⓑ | 3 | ⓓ | 4 | ⓐ |
| 5 | ⓓ | 6 | ⓑ | 7 | ⓒ | 8 | ⓒ |

POINT 2-4 명사적 용법: 의문사 + to부정사

A

1	what to do	2	where to visit
3	how to read	4	when to hand
5	how to turn	6	what to prepare
7	when to change	8	where to find

B

1 how to answer to the question
2 what to buy for Kevin
3 how to swim from their parents
4 when to remove my wisdom tooth
5 where to find mushrooms

POINT 3 형용사적 용법

A

1	to write with	2	sweet to eat
3	homework to do	4	some time to sleep
5	to play with	6	to sit on
7	to talk about	8	a new computer to use
9	to drink	10	to read
11	warm to wear	12	things to eat

B

1 couldn't find anyone to help
2 have a friend to introduce
3 found some dirty shoes to wash

4 doesn't have a partner to work with
5 is searching for an apartment to live in
6 bought something special to give
7 There are some vegetables to cook

11 were too busy to have lunch at noon
12 was too tired to exercise last night
13 studied hard enough to pass the exam easily
14 is too salty for me to eat without water
15 ran too fast for us to see

POINT 4 부사적 용법

1 ⓔ 2 ⓒ 3 ⓑ 4 ⓓ
5 ⓐ 6 ⓔ 7 ⓓ 8 ⓐ
9 ⓑ 10 ⓒ

1 (in order) to buy the violin
2 glad to visit his grandfather
3 grew up to be a nurse
4 disappointed to lose his watch
5 (in order) to do my homework
6 excited to ride the roller coaster
7 difficult to understand
8 kind to volunteer

POINT 5 to부정사의 의미상 주어

1 for 2 of 3 of
4 for 5 for 6 of
7 of 8 to 9 for
10 to

1 kind of him to wash
2 polite of him to talk
3 fun for me to play
4 necessary for us to get
5 careless of me to break
6 impossible for me to carry
7 hard for me to complete
8 selfish of him to eat

POINT 6 too ~ to, enough to

1 is smart enough to solve all the math problems
2 was lucky enough to win the lottery
3 was too fat to jump onto the sofa
4 is tall enough to be a basketball player
5 is light enough for me to hold with one hand
6 is funny enough to make anyone laugh
7 are too young to watch that horror movie
8 is rich enough to build a new house
9 laughs loud enough for everyone to hear
10 tasted good enough for us to scream

POINT 7 원형부정사

1 O
2 O
3 Mom didn't let me go to the rock concert.
4 Our teacher made us sing in front of the class.
5 O
6 We heard the neighbors yell[yelling] next door.
7 O
8 Lauren had her sister wash her hands before dinner.

1 to check 2 knock[knocking]
3 to apologize 4 feel
5 climb[climbing] 6 play[playing]
7 crash[crashing] 8 to help
9 memorize 10 burn[buring]

중간·기말고사 실전 문제

1 ③ 2 ⑤ 3 ⑤ 4 lending → to lend 5 ③ 6 ⑤ 7 It was Sarah's goal to win first prize 8 ② 9 ① 10 what I should do 11 a few tips to improve your health 12 ① 13 ④ 14 of 15 ④, ⑤
16 have seat belts to keep you safe
17 something 18 ④ 19 ① 20 to turn on the fan 21 where to meet him 22 ②
23 strong enough to lift me over his head
24 too loud for me to talk to the waiter 25 ②

1 plan은 to부정사를 목적어로 쓰는 동사이다.

2 want는 to부정사를 목적격 보어로 쓰는 동사이다.

3 ① getting → to get
② eat → to eat
③ starting → to start
④ interesting something → something interesting

4 agree는 to부정사를 목적어로 쓰는 동사이므로 to lend를 쓴다.

5 · order는 to부정사를 목적격 보어로 쓰는 동사이므로 to stop 을 쓴다.
· let은 원형부정사를 목적격 보어로 쓰는 동사이므로 play를 쓴다.

6 ⑤: 부사적 용법 ①②③④: 명사적 용법

7 to부정사가 주어로 쓰일 때 주어 자리에 가주어 it을 쓰고 진주어 to부정사(구)를 뒤로 보낼 수 있다.

8 ② to write → to write with

9 ①: 명사적 용법 밑줄 친 ⓐ와 ②③④⑤: 형용사적 용법

10 「의문사 + to부정사」는 「의문사 + 주어 + should + 동사원형」으로 바꿔 쓸 수 있다.

11 '나아지게 할 약간의 조언들'이라는 의미로 명사 a few tips를 수식하는 형용사적 용법의 to부정사를 쓴다.

12 ① of   ②③④⑤ for

13 · to부정사가 수식하는 명사 friends가 전치사의 목적어이고, '이야기할 많은 친구'라는 의미이므로 전치사 to를 쓴다.
· to부정사가 수식하는 명사 paper가 전치사의 목적어이고, '쓸 약간의 종이'라는 의미이므로 전치사 on을 쓴다.

14 사람의 성격을 나타내는 형용사(nice)가 쓰일 때 의미상 주어를 「of + 목적격」의 형태로 쓴다.

15 밑줄 친 ⓐ와 ④⑤: 목적(부사적 용법)
①: 감정의 원인(부사적 용법)
②: 판단의 근거(부사적 용법)
③: 형용사 수식(부사적 용법)

16 '유지해 줄 안전벨트'라는 의미로 명사 seat belts를 수식하는 형용사적 용법의 to부정사를 쓴다.

17 -thing으로 끝나는 대명사(something)가 형용사와 to부정사의 수식을 동시에 받을 때 「-thing + 형용사 + to부정사」의 형태로 쓴다. 전체 문장이 'Jane suggested something interesting to do.'이므로 세 번째에 오는 것은 something이다.

18 ④ sleeping → sleep

19 ① enough   ②③④⑤ too

20 ask는 to부정사를 목적격 보어로 쓰는 동사이므로 to turn을 쓴다.

21 '어디서 ~할지'라는 의미의 「where + to부정사」를 쓴다.

22 밑줄 친 ⓐ와 ②: 부사적 용법
①③⑤: 명사적 용법   ④: 형용사적 용법

23 「so + 형용사/부사 + that + 주어 + can + 동사원형」은 「형용사/부사 + enough + to부정사」로 바꿔 쓸 수 있다.

24 「so + 형용사/부사 + that + 주어 + can't + 동사원형」은 「too + 형용사/부사 + to부정사」로 바꿔 쓸 수 있다.

25 ⓐⓓⓔ: 부사적 용법
ⓑⓒ: 명사적 용법   ⓕ: 형용사적 용법

POINT 1 동명사의 형태와 쓰임

연습문제 **A**

1	Reading	**2**	swimming	**3**	designing
4	studying	**5**	Winning	**6**	riding

연습문제 **B**

1	ⓓ	**2**	ⓐ	**3**	ⓐ	**4**	ⓑ
5	ⓒ	**6**	ⓒ	**7**	ⓓ	**8**	ⓓ
9	ⓑ	**10**	ⓐ				

POINT 2 주어와 보어로 쓰이는 동명사

연습문제

1 Building a snowman in winter is
2 is collecting the sea shells on the beach
3 Playing video games with friends is
4 Acting on the stage makes
5 is painting the wall
6 Talking to new people is
7 is visiting France this weekend
8 is selling more products to the customers
9 Waking up early in the morning is
10 Driving at night is
11 is planting flowers in the garden
12 is teaching English

POINT 3-1 동명사를 목적어로 쓰는 동사

연습문제

1 Thomas enjoys learning
2 Kate finished drawing
3 I will avoid having
4 We didn't[did not] give up trying
5 Mike postponed going
6 Emily kept thinking
7 James didn't[did not] mind lending
8 Sarah denied breaking
9 They practice playing
10 We stopped talking
11 He suggests buying
12 The team put off working
13 I can imagine becoming
14 We quit using

POINT 3-2 동명사와 to부정사를 모두 목적어로 쓰는 동사 I

1	doing	**2**	crying[to cry]
3	to enter	**4**	to bring
5	having[to have]	**6**	waking[to wake]
7	changing	**8**	joking[to joke]
9	talking[to talk]	**10**	to stop

POINT 3-3 동명사와 to부정사를 모두 목적어로 쓰는 동사 II

1	forgot doing	**2**	stopped looking
3	remember to bring	**4**	regrets eating
5	tried to catch	**6**	forgot to send

POINT 4-1 동명사 관용 표현 I

1 kept[prevented] her dog from jumping
2 looking forward to going
3 is used to skipping
4 be afraid of trying
5 is good at lying
6 felt like hiding
7 On coming
8 succeeded in climbing

1	in	**2**	of	**3**	for
4	of	**5**	for	**6**	to
7	by				

POINT 4-2 동명사 관용 표현 II

1 was worth trying
2 is busy cleaning his room
3 What about taking a walk
4 had trouble concentrating
5 couldn't spend enough time practicing
6 The boys go skiing
7 could not help laughing
8 It's no use complaining

중간·기말고사 실전 문제

1 ③	**2** ③	**3** Not eating		**4** ⑤
5 ③	**6** ④	**7** ③	**8** ④	**9** ②

10 Jared remembers visiting the Grand Canyon during the trip. **11** Listening to classical music helps **12** ⑤ **13** ③ **14** ② **15** to buy → buying **16** ② **17** (1) ⓑ → turning (2) ⓒ → prevents (3) ⓔ → opening **18** Learning about the planets **19** ② **20** ⑤ **21** ⑤ **22** tried cooking pasta **23** ⑤ **24** ① **25** ③

1 보어 자리이므로 명사 역할을 하는 동명사 drawing을 쓴다.

2 목적어 자리이므로 명사 역할을 하는 동명사 waking을 쓴다.

3 '야채를 먹지 않는 것'이라는 의미이므로 주어 자리에 동명사를 쓰고 동명사의 부정형은 동명사 앞에 Not을 쓴다.

4 ⑤ to go → going

5 첫 번째 빈칸: '~하는 것에 싫증이 나다'라는 의미의 「be tired of + V-ing」를 쓴다.
두 번째 빈칸: suggest는 동명사를 목적어로 쓰는 동사이므로 playing을 쓴다.

6 '나는 그 따뜻한 바다에서 수영했던 것을 절대 잊지 못할 거야.'라는 의미이므로 동사 forget 뒤에 동명사 swimming을 쓴다.

7 ③: 진행형의 V-ing   주어진 문장과 ①②④⑤: 동명사

8 동명사 singing이 목적어이므로 동명사를 목적어로 쓰는 동사 like, practice, remember, quit을 쓴다. want는 to부정사를 목적어로 쓰는 동사이다.

9 첫 번째 빈칸: '나는 한 시간 전에 나의 남동생에게 소리지른 것을 후회해.'라는 의미이므로 동사 regret 뒤에 동명사 yelling을 쓴다.
두 번째 빈칸: '~하는 게 어때?'라는 의미의 「How about + V-ing」를 쓴다.

10 'Jared는 그 여행 동안 그랜드 캐년을 방문한 것을 기억한다.'라는 의미이므로 동사 remember 뒤에 동명사 visiting을 쓴다.

11 주어 자리이므로 명사 역할을 하는 동명사 Listening을 쓴다. 주어로 쓰인 동명사는 항상 단수 취급하므로 단수동사 helps를 쓴다.

12 ·전치사(after)의 목적어 자리이므로 동명사 eating을 쓴다.
·「by + V-ing」 ~함으로써

13 ⓐ to live → living
ⓒ do → doing

14 첫 번째 빈칸: 「be worth + V-ing」 '~할 가치가 있다'
두 번째 빈칸: 「on + V-ing」 '~하자마자'

15 '~하지 않을 수 없다'라는 의미의 「cannot help + V-ing」를 쓴다.

16 (A) decide는 to부정사를 목적어로 쓰는 동사이므로 to dress를 쓴다.

(B) prefer는 동명사를 목적어로 쓰는 동사이므로 wearing을 쓴다.

(C) suggest는 동명사를 목적어로 쓰는 동사이므로 putting을 쓴다.

17 (1) keep은 동명사를 목적어로 쓰는 동사이므로 turning을 쓴다.

(2) 주어로 쓰인 동명사는 항상 단수 취급하므로 단수동사 prevents를 쓴다.

(3) mind는 동명사를 목적어로 쓰는 동사이므로 opening을 쓴다.

18 주어 자리에 가주어 it이 쓰인 문장이다. 이때 주어 자리에 동명사 Learning이나 to부정사 To learn이 쓰인 문장으로 바꿔 쓸 수 있다.

19 「try + 동명사」는 '(시험 삼아) ~해보다'라는 의미이고, 「try + to부정사」는 '~하려고 노력하다'라는 의미이다.

20 「prevent … from + V-ing」…가 ~하지 못하게 하다

21 ⓓⓔ: 보어 ⓐ: 전치사의 목적어 ⓑ: 동사의 목적어
ⓒ: 주어

22 '(시험 삼아) ~해보다'라는 의미이므로 동사 try 뒤에 동명사 cooking을 쓴다.

23 '~한 것을 후회하다'라는 의미이므로 동사 regret 뒤에 동명사 buying을 쓴다.

24 도서관 책들의 반납 기한이 오늘이라고 했으므로 '그것들을 반납하는 것을 잊지 마.'라는 말이 적절하다. '~할 것을 잊다'라는 의미이므로 동사 forget 뒤에 to부정사 to return을 쓴다.

25 ⓑ help → helps
ⓒ to use → using

CHAPTER 8
분사

p.98

POINT 1 분사의 형태와 쓰임

1 분사: lost, 수식: wallet
2 분사: boring, 보충 설명: The movie
3 분사: sleeping, 보충 설명: The baby
4 분사: closed, 보충 설명: The store
5 분사: fixed, 보충 설명: the elevator
6 분사: hiding, 보충 설명: The birds
7 분사: written, 수식: The book
8 분사: worried, 보충 설명: She

1 ⓐ **2** ⓑ **3** ⓐ **4** ⓑ
5 ⓑ **6** ⓑ **7** ⓐ **8** ⓑ

POINT 2 현재분사와 과거분사

1 wearing **2** cooking **3** written
4 shocking **5** fallen **6** reading
7 called **8** swimming **9** broken
10 made

1 written **2** loved **3** made
4 rising **5** sitting **6** singing
7 named **8** designed **9** built
10 cooking **11** heard **12** painted

POINT 3 감정을 나타내는 분사

1 ① satisfying ② satisfied
2 ① tiring ② tired
3 ① boring ② Bored
4 ① embarrassing ② embarrassed
5 ① confusing ② confused
6 ① depressing ② depressed
7 ① moving ② moved
8 ① surprising ② surprised

1 Is your friend interested in Korean history?
2 The trip to the amusement park was exciting.
3 The scientists are shocked about the melting glaciers.
4 O
5 O
6 Kevin was deeply touched by his brother's present.

POINT 4 현재분사 vs. 동명사

연습문제 A

1 현재분사	2 현재분사	3 동명사
4 동명사	5 현재분사	6 현재분사
7 동명사	8 동명사	9 현재분사
10 현재분사		

연습문제 B

1 a pear hanging on the tree
2 Tony bought a walking stick
3 The man watering the flowers
4 the full moon shining in the sky
5 Put on your dancing shoes
6 James is feeding his dog
7 Look at the swimming dolphins
8 Hunting tigers is illegal

POINT 5-1 분사구문 만드는 법

연습문제

1 Seeing me, he ran away.
2 Being too tired, she did not go out with her family.
3 Feeling dizzy, I went to bed early.
4 Talking to the teacher, she felt much better.
5 Not studying for the exam, she failed it.
6 Waking up late, he had to skip breakfast.
7 Not knowing the way back home, she cried.
8 Looking up, I saw birds flying over the bridge.
9 Staying in Canada, I became friends with John.
10 Not seeing the doctor, I couldn't buy the medicine.
11 Reading the book, I fell asleep.
12 Feeling cold, he turned on the heater.
13 Not having money, they had to walk back to the hotel.
14 Walking down the street, he met his teacher.

POINT 5-2 분사구문의 다양한 의미

연습문제 A

1 Walking along the river
2 Not eating meat
3 Getting up early
4 Calling her friend
5 Arriving at the bank
6 being tired
7 Not going to school tomorrow
8 Being old enough

연습문제 B

1 Eating too much
2 Calling my name

3 Passing the exam
4 Feeling lonely
5 Being so sick

중간·기말고사 실전 문제

1 ④ 2 ③ 3 ⑤ 4 used 5 ④
6 baked by my mother temperature 7 taking our 8 ⑤ 9 Washing my hands 10 ② 11 ③ 12 After he heard the music, Hearing the music 13 Not knowing the way 14 ⑤ 15 ④ 16 shocked
17 ③ 18 ④ 19 ③ 20 ① 21 ②
22 ① 23 Not having any milk 24 with her arms folded 25 (1) ⓐ → confused (2) ⓓ → Answering (3) ⓔ → sleeping

1 명사 bicycle을 수식하고 명사와의 관계가 수동이므로 과거분사 stolen을 쓴다.

2 The new animated movie는 감정을 일으키는 주체이므로 현재분사 exciting을 쓴다.

3 ① freezing → frozen
② painting → painted
③ drawn → drawing
④ fallen → falling

4 명사 house를 수식하고 명사와의 관계가 수동이므로 과거분사 used를 쓴다.

5 (A) 목적어 the lady와 목적격 보어의 관계가 능동이므로 현재분사 singing을 쓴다.
(B) I는 감정을 느끼는 주체이므로 과거분사 fascinated를 쓴다.
(C) vocalists는 감정을 일으키는 주체이므로 현재분사 amazing을 쓴다.

6 과거분사 baked가 전치사구(by my mother)와 함께 구를 이루어 쓰였으므로 명사 pie 뒤에서 명사를 수식한다.

7 현재분사 taking이 목적어(our temperature)와 함께 구를 이루어 쓰였으므로 명사 lady 뒤에서 명사를 수식한다.

8 ⑤ flown → flying

9 접속사 When과 주어 I를 생략하고 동사 wash를 Washing으로 바꾼다.

10 첫 번째 빈칸: It은 감정을 일으키는 주체이므로 현재분사 shocking을 쓴다.
두 번째 빈칸: You는 감정을 느끼는 주체이므로 과거분사 surprised를 쓴다.

11 ⓑ bored → boring
ⓒ fascinated → fascinating
ⓔ depressing → depressed

12 첫 번째 문장: '~한 후에'라는 의미의 접속사 After를 쓰고 문장의 시제가 과거이므로 heard를 쓴다.
두 번째 문장: 접속사 After와 주어 he를 생략하고 동사 heard를 Hearing으로 바꾼다.

13 접속사 Because와 주어 she를 생략하고 동사 didn't know를 Not knowing으로 바꾼다.

14 ⑤: 현재분사   ①②③④: 동명사

15 (A) you는 감정을 느끼는 주체이므로 과거분사 excited를 쓴다.
(B) short stories는 감정을 일으키는 주체이므로 현재분사 moving을 쓴다.
(C) 목적어 his car와 목적격 보어의 관계가 수동이므로 과거분사 cleaned를 쓴다.

16 Alfred Nobel은 감정을 느끼는 주체이므로 과거분사 shocked를 쓴다.

17 ⓐⓓⓔ: 현재분사   ⓑⓒ: 동명사

18 접속사 While과 주어 I를 생략하고 동사 checked를 Checking으로 바꾼다.

19 목적어 a boy and a girl을 보충 설명하고 목적어와의 관계가 능동이므로 현재분사 sharing을 쓴다.

20 주어진 문장과 ①: 현재분사   ②③④⑤: 동명사

21 · '나는 해변에 앉아서, 보트가 지나가는 것을 봤다.'라는 의미의 분사구문이므로 Sitting을 쓴다.
· 명사 umbrella를 수식하고 명사와의 관계가 수동이므로 broken을 쓴다.

22 '나는 화가 났기 때문에, 앉아서 천천히 열까지 세었다.'라는 의미이므로 이유를 나타내는 As I was angry를 쓴다.

23 이유를 나타내는 분사구문이고, 분사구문의 부정형은 분사 앞에 not을 붙여 만들므로 Not having any milk를 쓴다.

24 '…가 ~한 채로'는 「with + 명사 + 분사」의 형태로 쓰고, 명사 her arms와 분사의 관계가 수동이므로 과거분사 folded를 쓴다.

25 (1) she는 감정을 느끼는 주체이므로 과거분사 confused를 쓴다.
(2) '그녀에게 대답하며, 그 다른 사람이 "나야, Melanie!"라고 말했다.'라는 의미의 분사구문이므로 Answering을 쓴다.
(3) 주어 she를 보충 설명하고 주어와의 관계가 능동이므로 현재분사 sleeping을 쓴다.

CHAPTER 9
명사와 관사
p.110

POINT 1 셀 수 있는 명사와 셀 수 없는 명사

연습문제 A

1 ⓓ	2 ⓔ	3 ⓐ	4 ⓒ
5 ⓔ	6 ⓔ	7 ⓑ	8 ⓔ
9 ⓓ	10 ⓒ	11 ⓓ	12 ⓐ
13 ⓔ	14 ⓐ	15 ⓒ	16 ⓓ
17 ⓑ	18 ⓐ	19 ⓔ	20 ⓒ
21 ⓓ	22 ⓐ	23 ⓐ	24 ⓑ
25 ⓐ	26 ⓔ	27 ⓐ	28 ⓑ
29 ⓔ	30 ⓒ		

연습문제 B

1 an egg	2 volunteers	3 a question
4 orange juice	5 money	6 Hallasan
7 family	8 sugar	9 information
10 A giraffe	11 teams	12 January

POINT 2 셀 수 있는 명사의 복수형

연습문제 A

1 wolves	2 men	3 monkeys
4 teeth	5 potatoes	6 pianos
7 leaves	8 boxes	9 children
10 countries	11 pandas	12 volcanoes
13 ladies	14 salmon	15 cliffs
16 keys	17 feet	18 books
19 fish	20 oxen	21 babies
22 mice	23 addresses	24 enemies

연습문제 B

1 windows	2 shelves	3 teeth
4 O	5 ladies	6 problems
7 children	8 O	9 tomatoes
10 geese	11 churches	12 deer

POINT 3 셀 수 없는 명사의 수량 표현

연습문제 A

1 three cups of coffee
2 a glass of milk
3 50 cans of soda
4 a piece of cake
5 seven sheets of paper
6 a bowl of soup
7 five spoonfuls of sugar
8 a bar of chocolate
9 two slices of ham

1 cans   **2** bars   **3** bread
4 piece   **5** cup   **6** piece
7 bottle   **8** gold

POINT 4 명사 관련 표현

연습문제
A

1 Charlie found a four-leaf clover in his grandmother's garden.
2 Sarah went to Africa for a three-month volunteer program.
3 O
4 O
5 He is trying to knit a pair of gloves for his girlfriend.
6 Kelly picked up a hundred-dollar bill on the street.
7 The shoe company donated 200 pairs of sneakers for the poor.
8 O

연습문제
B

1 Mr. Choi
2 Suzy
3 students should wear a school uniform
4 Kate and James fought with each other
5 Jennifer
6 a Grammy Award-winning artist
7 I should take a rest
8 Andrew
9 the graduation ceremony has been postponed
10 Mozart composed his first opera when he was twelve years old

POINT 5 명사의 소유격

연습문제

1 The women's bags
2 the entrance of the concert hall
3 today's weather
4 the teachers' room
5 Mother's Day
6 The students' attitude
7 The top of the mountain

POINT 6-1 부정관사 a(n)의 쓰임

연습문제

1 a   **2** a   **3** A   **4** X
5 an   **6** a   **7** X   **8** an

POINT 6-2 정관사 the의 쓰임

연습문제

1 a week   **2** the window
3 The book   **4** the piano
5 a day   **6** the park
7 an expensive watch   **8** the same university
9 the greatest composer
10 The moon

POINT 6-3 관사를 쓰지 않는 경우

연습문제

1 soccer   **2** phone   **3** bus
4 a daughter   **5** the flute   **6** an hour
7 plane   **8** lunch   **9** school
10 the prison

중간·기말고사 실전 문제

1 ③   **2** ④   **3** ①, ③   **4** ④   **5** ⑤
6 ⑤   **7** ⑤   **8** ⑤   **9** four slices [pieces] of cake, two bottles of juice   **10** a pair of scissors   **11** ②   **12** ①   **13** ②
14 ②   **15** We stayed in a five-star-hotel in Berlin.
16 We bought twenty slices of ham for the party.
17 ②, ⑤   **18** ⑤   **19** ⑤   **20** the animals' behavior   **21** The shape of the United Kingdom
22 ⑤   **23** ③   **24** ①   **25** (1) ⓐ → salmon (2) ⓒ → balls

1 ③: group은 집합명사, energy는 물질명사, news는 추상명사이다.
   ①: 보통명사 ②: 추상명사 ④: 고유명사 ⑤: 집합명사

2 ① zooes – zoos
   ② clives – cliffs
   ③ tooths – teeth
   ⑤ sandwichs – sandwiches

3 tulip과 melon은 셀 수 있는 명사의 단수형이므로 a와 함께 쓸 수 있다.

4 ① milks → milk
   ② loaf → loaves
   ③ slice → piece
   ⑤ two bowl of rices → two bowls of rice

5 ① sheeps → sheep
   ② dishs → dishes
   ③ coines → coins
   ④ puppyes → puppies

6 · 셀 수 없는 명사 bread는 단위명사 slice나 piece로 수량을 나타낸다.
· 셀 수 없는 명사 information은 단위명사 sheet나 piece로 수량을 나타낸다.

7 ⑤ a → the

8 수를 나타내는 형용사 lots of와 함께 쓸 수 있는 것은 셀 수 있는 명사의 복수형이므로 fish의 복수형인 fish를 쓴다.

9 첫 번째 빈칸: 셀 수 없는 명사 cake는 단위명사 slice/piece로 수량을 나타내고, 복수형은 slices/pieces를 쓴다.
두 번째 빈칸: 셀 수 없는 명사 juice는 단위명사 bottle로 수량을 나타내고, 복수형은 bottles를 쓴다.

10 한 쌍이 짝을 이루는 명사 scissor는 항상 복수형(scissors)으로 쓰고, a pair of를 활용하여 수량을 나타낸다.

11 ① a good luck → good luck
③ oxygens → oxygen
④ an exciting news → exciting news
⑤ respects → respect

12 · 셀 수 없는 명사 pizza는 단위명사 piece로 수량을 나타내고, 복수형은 pieces를 쓴다.
· 셀 수 없는 명사 paint는 단위명사 can으로 수량을 나타낸다.

13 museum과 mosquito는 셀 수 있는 명사의 단수형이므로 a와 함께 쓸 수 있다.

14 ②: 부사절 뒤에 쓰는 콤마(,)　①③④⑤: 동격 콤마(,)

15 하이픈(-)으로 연결되어 명사를 꾸미는 「숫자 + 단위명사」의 단위 명사는 항상 단수형으로 쓰므로 five-star hotel을 쓴다.

16 셀 수 없는 명사 ham의 복수형은 단위명사 slice에 -(e)s를 붙여 만들므로 twenty slices of ham을 쓴다.

17 ② two cup of coffees → two cups of coffee
⑤ papers → paper

18 주어진 문장과 ⑤: ~마다(per)
①②④: 하나의(one)　③: 종족 전체를 대표할 때

19 ⑤ 빈칸 뒤의 hospital이 본래의 목적(의료)으로 쓰이지 않았으므로 정관사 the를 쓴다.
① 「by + 교통수단」에서 교통수단(train) 앞에는 관사를 쓰지 않는다.
② 식사 이름 앞에는 관사를 쓰지 않는다.
③ 운동 이름 앞에는 관사를 쓰지 않는다.
④ 빈칸 뒤의 장소(college)가 본래의 목적(학습)으로 쓰였으므로 관사를 쓰지 않는다.

20 생물을 나타내며 -s로 끝나는 복수명사(animals)의 소유격은 명사에 '를 붙여 만들므로 the animal's behavior를 쓴다.

21 무생물을 나타내는 명사(the United Kingdom)의 소유격은 주로 「of + 명사」로 나타내므로 The shape of the United Kingdom을 쓴다.

22 ⓒ jean → jeans

ⓔ waters → water
ⓕ golds → gold

23 (A) 하이픈(-)으로 연결되어 명사를 꾸미는 「숫자 + 단위명사」의 단위명사는 항상 단수형으로 쓰므로 ten-dollar를 쓴다.
(B) 수를 나타내는 형용사 many와 함께 쓸 수 있는 것은 셀 수 있는 명사의 복수형이므로 spots를 쓴다.
(C) 셀 수 없는 명사 smoke는 앞에 a(n)을 붙일 수 없고 복수형으로도 쓸 수 없으므로 smoke를 쓴다.

24 ⓐ by a train → by train

25 (1) salmon은 단수형과 복수형이 같으므로 salmon을 쓴다.
(2) 셀 수 있는 명사(ball)는 복수일 때 복수형으로 써야 하므로 balls를 쓴다.

CHAPTER 10
대명사

p.122

POINT 1 인칭대명사

1	my	2	they	3	her
4	us	5	It	6	its
7	their	8	he	9	him
10	mine	11	They	12	it
13	them				

1 ① My ② mine
2 ① your ② Yours
3 ① His ② his
4 ① Her ② hers
5 ① ours ② our
6 ① theirs ② Their

POINT 2 재귀대명사

1 myself, O
2 herself, X
3 himself, O
4 herself, X
5 themselves, O
6 herself, X
7 ourselves, X
8 herself, X
9 myself, X
10 itself, O

1 enjoyed ourselves
2 help yourself to
3 talking to yourself
4 by herself
5 thought to myself
6 make themselves at home

POINT 3 지시대명사

1	These	2	This	3	Those
4	Those	5	That	6	This
7	This	8	These	9	that
10	those				

1	ⓐ	2	ⓐ	3	ⓑ	4	ⓑ
5	ⓐ	6	ⓐ	7	ⓑ	8	ⓑ
9	ⓑ	10	ⓐ				

POINT 4 it의 다양한 쓰임

1 It was not[wasn't] easy to change my name.
2 It is difficult to learn Chinese.
3 It is dangerous to swim in this river.
4 It was disappointing to lose the game.

5 It was very hard to get used to the new environment.
6 It is always fun to meet with people from different cultures.

1	ⓑ	2	ⓑ	3	ⓐ	4	ⓑ
5	ⓒ	6	ⓐ	7	ⓒ	8	ⓒ
9	ⓐ						

POINT 5-1 부정대명사: one

1	ones	2	them	3	One
4	it	5	them	6	one
7	them	8	ones	9	one
10	it	11	them	12	ones

POINT 5-2 부정대명사: some, any

1	some	2	any	3	anyone
4	some	5	Someone	6	some
7	any	8	something	9	some
10	anything				

POINT 5-3 부정대명사: another, other

1	Some	2	the others	3	one
4	another	5	ones	6	The other

1 Some are rotten, the others are fresh
2 Some wear glasses, the others don't wear glasses
3 Some enjoy surfing, others enjoy swimming
4 One is from Russia, the other is from Brazil
5 Some like bright colors, others like dark colors
6 One is a lawyer, another is a doctor, the other is an architect

POINT 5-4 부정대명사: all, both, each, every

1 Both Emily and Amy
2 All (of) the kids
3 Each of us
4 Every student
5 Not all (of) the germs
6 Each correct answer

1 Not all dogs are gentle.
2 Both my parents want me to become a doctor.
3 All of the information was helpful.
4 Each of the students has a student ID card.

5 Everybody in this room enjoys watching musicals.

6 O

7 Each item was carefully checked.

8 Every person is entitled to the freedom of expression.

POINT 6 의문대명사

1 whom **2** Whose **3** What
4 Who **5** Which

1 Whose name is on the list?

2 What are they talking about now?

3 Who is the woman standing next to you in the picture?

4 Which do you want to drink, coffee or green tea?

5 What kind of flowers does Mina like?

6 Whom is he going to the museum with?[With whom is he going to the museum?]

7 What does Lisa like most?

8 Which do you prefer, jazz or classical music?

중간·기말고사 실전 문제

1 ③ **2** ①, ④ **3** ④ **4** ③ **5** other
→ the other **6** talking to yourself
7 ② **8** ④ **9** is important to reflect
10 ⑤ **11** ①, ④ **12** ② **13** (1) Which (2)
Who (3) What **14** ④ **15** ③ **16** ⑤
17 ④ **18** (1) that (2) this (3) Those **19** ③
20 ③ **21** ① **22** ⑤ **23** ④ **24** (1) ⓐ
→ herself (2) ⓑ → itself (3) ⓔ → themselves
25 ②, ④

1 첫 번째 빈칸: 빈칸 뒤에 소유의 대상이 되는 명사 umbrella가 왔
으므로 소유격 your를 쓴다.
두 번째 빈칸: '나의 것'이라는 의미의 소유대명사 mine을 쓴다.

2 ①④: 강조 용법(생략 가능) ②③⑤: 재귀 용법(생략 불가능)

3 '여러분 모두 여러분 자신을 자랑스러워해야 합니다.'라는 의미이
므로 재귀대명사 yourselves를 쓴다.

4 ③: 대명사 it ①②④⑤: 비인칭 주어 it

5 「one ~, the other -」'(둘 중) 하나는 ~, 나머지 하나는 -'

6 「talk to oneself」: 혼잣말하다

7 · 앞에서 언급된 특정한 대상(some cupcakes)을 가리키고 있

으므로 them을 쓴다.
· 앞에서 언급된 단수명사(shirt)와 같은 종류의 불특정한 사물을
가리키고 있으므로 부정대명사 one을 쓴다.

8 · 빈칸 뒤에 물질명사(water)가 왔으므로 「All of + ~」를 쓴다.
· 빈칸 뒤에 복수명사(children)가 왔으므로 Both를 쓴다.

9 to부정사구가 문장의 주어로 쓰였을 때는 주로 주어 자리에 가주
어 it을 쓰고 진주어를 뒤로 보낸다.

10 「One ~, another -, the other …」'(셋 중) 하나는 ~, 다른 하
나는 ~, 나머지 하나는 …'

11 주어진 문장과 ①④: 비인칭 주어 it
②: 대명사 it ③⑤: 가주어 it

12 · 「some ~, others -」'(여럿 중) 몇몇은 ~, 다른 사람들은 -'
· '약간의 사진들'이라는 의미이고 긍정문이므로 some을 쓴다.

13 (1) '이 가방 중 어떤 것이 너의 것이니?'라는 의미이므로 Which
를 쓴다.
(2) '누가 나와 함께 이 퍼즐을 풀기를 원하니?'라는 의미이므로
Who를 쓴다.
(3) 'FYI가 무슨 뜻이니?'라는 의미이므로 What을 쓴다.

14 · 「each + 단수명사」는 단수 취급하므로 was를 쓴다.
· 「every + 단수명사」는 단수 취급하므로 has를 쓴다.

15 첫 번째 빈칸: 「make oneself at home」'(집에서처럼) 편히 쉬
다'
두 번째 빈칸: 권유를 나타내는 의문문이므로 some을 쓴다.

16 첫 번째 빈칸: 「one ~, the other -」'(둘 중) 하나는 ~, 나머지
하나는 -'
두 번째 빈칸: '(둘 사이에) 서로'라는 의미의 each other를 쓴다.

17 ④: 지시형용사 these ①②③⑤: 지시대명사 these

18 (1) 비교 표현에서 앞에 나온 단수명사(The cost)의 반복을 피하
기 위해 사용했으므로 that을 쓴다.
(2) 가까이 있는 단수의 사물(wallet)을 수식하고 있으므로 this
를 쓴다.
(3) 멀리 있는 복수의 사물(boxes)을 수식하고 있으므로 Those
를 쓴다.

19 ⓐ was → were
ⓓ don't → doesn't
ⓔ have → has

20 ③ 앞에서 언급된 명사(muffler)와 같은 종류의 불특정한 사물을
가리키고 있으므로 부정대명사 one을 쓴다.

21 ⓐⓑⓔ: 가주어 it ⓒ: 대명사 it ⓓ: 비인칭 주어 it

22 ① method → methods
② the other → the others
③ them → ones
④ other → the other

23 '너는 지난 주말에 누구와 함께 스키 타러 갔니?'라는 의미이고 빈
칸 앞에 전치사(With)가 있으므로 whom을 쓴다.

24 (1) '나의 엄마는 스스로 지붕을 고치셨다.'라는 의미이므로 재귀대명사 herself를 쓴다.

(2) '노래 그 자체가 좋다.'라는 의미이므로 재귀대명사 itself를 쓴다.

(3) '사람들은 보통 처음 만났을 때 그들 자신을 소개한다.'라는 의미이므로 재귀대명사 themselves를 쓴다.

25 ②: 비인칭 주어 it   ④: 가주어 it
주어진 문장과 ①③⑤: 대명사 it

CHAPTER 11
형용사

p.136

POINT 1   형용사의 용법

1 is an old dictionary
2 is a spacious room
3 a simple but unique pattern
4 a very expensive necklace
5 a confident boy
6 a sharp needle
7 a popular product

1 alive	**2** sleeping	**3** alike
4 afraid	**5** lonely	**6** pleased
7 asleep	**8** living	

POINT 2   -thing/-body/-one + 형용사

1 Do you know anyone brave?
2 She told us something exciting.
3 Someone kind helped my grandma at the train station.
4 I don't have anything suitable to wear for the wedding.
5 There is nothing special in this store.
6 Did the thief steal anything valuable?
7 We can learn new things when we talk to other people.
8 Have you met anybody attractive like that actor?

1 something surprising	**2** delicious things
3 anything interesting	**4** Something bad
5 Someone tall	**6** useful things
7 little thing	**8** something cold
9 something strange	**10** anything important

POINT 3   the + 형용사

1 The rich should share what they have.
2 The campaign is targeted at the young.
3 Audrey Hepburn helped the poor in Africa.
4 It is usually hard for the disabled to find jobs.
5 The unemployed tend to be very depressed.
6 The school teaches the blind how to read and

write.

7 The charity gives out free foods to the homeless.

8 There is a care center in my neighborhood for the old.

9 Masks make it difficult for the deaf to communicate.

1	The	2	the blind	3	need
4	Do	5	get	6	the disabled

POINT 4-1 수사: 기수와 서수

연습문제 A

1	first	2	twentieth	3	eleven
4	fourth	5	ninetieth	6	twenty-first
7	one hundred	8	eightieth	9	thirty-seven
10	fifty-five	11	seventy-two	12	third
13	ten	14	forty-fourth	15	sixty-first
16	twelve	17	seventeen	18	fiftieth
19	twenty-ninth	20	sixty-sixth		

연습문제 B

1	first son	2	twentieth anniversary
3	third destination	4	a thousand trees
5	thirty years	6	fifth grade
7	twenty-two floors	8	fourth course

POINT 4-2 수사: 분수, 배수, 횟수

연습문제

1 two-thirds
2 three times
3 ten times
4 one-quarter[a quarter/one-fourth/a fourth]
5 one-third[a third]
6 five-eighths
7 one and three-fifths
8 once

POINT 4-3 수사: 연도와 날짜

연습문제

1 May (the) twenty-fifth[the twenty-fifth of May]
2 O
3 the eighteen hundreds
4 September (the) third[third of September]
5 O
6 the seventeen fifties

POINT 5-1 수량형용사: many, much, a lot of

연습문제 A

1	many	2	much	3	Many
4	much	5	much	6	much
7	many	8	much	9	many
10	much				

연습문제 B

1 I didn't get much sleep last night.
2 Garlic is a basic ingredient in many Korean dishes.
3 Many dolphins can dive to depths of 200 meters.
4 Did she speak with much enthusiasm?
5 Many teenagers don't have much economic knowledge.
6 Does it take much time to change old habits?
7 We have worked together on many projects.
8 There are many historical sites in Europe.

POINT 5-2 수량형용사: (a) few, (a) little

연습문제 A

1	① a few ② a little	2	① little ② few
3	① a few ② a little	4	① Few ② little
5	① A few ② a little	6	① little ② few

연습문제 B

1	a few friends	2	Few students
3	much space	4	few chances
5	a little whipped cream	6	Little rain
7	Many jobs		

POINT 5-3 수량형용사: some, any

연습문제

1	any	2	some	3	any
4	any	5	any	6	some
7	Any	8	some	9	some
10	any	11	some	12	any
13	any	14	some	15	some

중간·기말고사 실전 문제

1	②, ⑤	2	fun anything → anything fun	3	①
4	①, ⑤	5	③	6	challenging	7	④
8	②	9	①, ③	10	three times
11	August (the) thirty-first[the thirty-first of August]
12	⑤	13	The injured	14	①	15	③
16	①	17	④	18	⑤	19	①, ③	20	few

guests   **21** ④   **22** ③   **23** ②   **24** ④
25 (1) ⓐ → something interesting (2) ⓓ → second

1 주어진 문장과 ②⑤: 서술적 용법 ①③④: 한정적 용법

2 -thing으로 끝나는 대명사(anything)를 수식할 때는 형용사 (fun)가 명사 뒤에 온다.

3 ticket은 셀 수 있는 명사이고 '콘서트 표들이 거의 없다.'라는 의미이므로 few(거의 없는)를 쓴다.

4 rooms는 셀 수 있는 명사의 복수형이므로, '많은(plenty of)'이 라는 의미이며 셀 수 있는 명사와 함께 쓰는 many와 a number of를 쓴다.

5 ⓐ ninety-first → ninety-one
ⓓ the three of September → the third of September [September (the) third]
ⓔ a thirds → a third[one third]
ⓕ twelveth → twelfth

6 -thing으로 끝나는 대명사(something)를 수식할 때는 형용사(challenging)가 대명사 뒤에 오고 전체 문장이 'Are you looking for something challenging?'이므로 여섯 번째에 오는 것은 challenging이다.

7 tools는 셀 수 있는 명사의 복수형이므로 셀 수 없는 명사와 함께 쓰는 a little은 쓸 수 없다.

8 · -one으로 끝나는 대명사(anyone)를 수식할 때는 형용사(familiar)가 대명사 뒤에 온다.
· sleep은 셀 수 없는 명사이므로 셀 수 없는 명사와 함께 쓰는 a little을 쓴다.

9 ② some → any
④ any → some
⑤ some → any

10 '한 번, 두 번'을 제외한 횟수는 「기수 + times」로 나타내므로 three times를 쓴다.

11 8월 31일 → August (the) thirty-first[the thirty-first of August]

12 ⑤ 형용사 awake는 서술적 용법으로만 쓰이므로 명사(brother)를 앞에서 수식할 수 없다.

13 「the + 형용사」(~한 사람들) = 「형용사 + people」

14 (A) -thing으로 끝나는 대명사(something)를 수식할 때는 형용사(new)가 대명사 뒤에 온다.
(B) 의문문이므로 any를 쓴다.
(C) '세 마리의 고양이'라는 의미이므로 정수인 three를 쓴다.

15 ③ useful nothing → nothing useful

16 첫 번째 빈칸: tourists는 셀 수 있는 명사의 복수형이므로 셀 수 있는 명사와 함께 쓰는 many를 쓴다.
두 번째 빈칸: trash는 셀 수 없는 명사이고 '주말 후에 오직 약간의 쓰레기만 발견되었다.'라는 의미이므로 a little(약간의)을 쓴다.

17 ① many → much
② A few → A little
③ few → little
⑤ much → many

18 ⑤ kilometer는 셀 수 있는 명사이므로 셀 수 없는 명사와 함께 쓰는 a little을 쓸 수 없다.

19 ① Thousands of person → Thousands of people
③ things silly → silly things

20 guest(손님)는 셀 수 있는 명사이므로 few(거의 없는)와 함께 쓴다.

21 ① 365th → 365
② thousands → thousand
③ worker → workers
⑤ Hundred → Hundreds

22 sandwiches는 셀 수 있는 명사의 복수형이고 perfume은 셀 수 없는 명사이므로 셀 수 있는 명사의 복수형, 셀 수 없는 명사 모두와 함께 쓸 수 있는 some을 쓴다. any는 긍정문과 권유를 나타내는 의문문에 쓸 수 없다.

23 ⓑ few → little
ⓒ many → much

24 (A) difficulty는 셀 수 없는 명사이고 '당신의 길 안내가 완벽해서 우리가 당신의 집을 찾는 데 어려움이 거의 없었다.'라는 의미이므로 little(거의 없는)을 쓴다.
(B) friends는 셀 수 있는 명사의 복수형이고 'Mary는 인기가 매우 많아서 그녀는 많은 친구가 있다.'라는 의미이므로 many (많은)를 쓴다. any는 긍정문에 쓸 수 없다.
(C) problems는 셀 수 있는 명사의 복수형이고 '나는 최근에 나의 전화기에 약간의 문제가 있었지만 심각한 것은 없다.'라는 의미이므로 a few(약간의)를 쓴다.

25 (1) -thing으로 끝나는 대명사(something)를 수식할 때는 형용사(interesting)가 대명사 뒤에 온다.
(2) '두 번째'라는 의미이므로 서수인 second를 쓴다.

CHAPTER 12
부사

p.150

POINT 1 부사의 쓰임

 연습문제 A

1 cold	2 practice	3 interesting
4 she managed to pass the exam		
5 difficult	6 eats	7 nice
8 quickly	9 Tim got in a car accident	
10 lived		

 연습문제 B

1 loudly	2 rudely	3 Finally
4 carefully	5 surprisingly	6 wisely
7 terribly	8 Basically	

POINT 2-1 부사의 형태

연습문제 A

1 dramatically	2 carefully	3 luckily
4 well	5 differently	6 rarely
7 fully	8 politely	9 busily
10 happily	11 really	12 comfortably
13 heavily	14 seriously	15 athletically
16 specially	17 suddenly	18 practically
19 lazily	20 generously	21 angrily
22 truly	23 dully	24 responsibly
25 properly	26 energetically	

연습문제 B

1 happily	2 carefully	3 strange
4 Suddenly	5 well	6 politely
7 Sadly	8 fully	9 fantastically
10 nervously		

POINT 2-2 형용사와 형태가 같은 부사

 연습문제

1 ②	2 ②	3 ②	4 ③
5 ②	6 ③	7 ③	8 ③

POINT 2-3 -ly가 붙으면 의미가 달라지는 부사

연습문제

1 ① late ② lately	2 ① high ② highly
3 ① hard ② hardly	4 ① close ② closely
5 ① nearly ② near	

POINT 3 빈도부사

 연습문제 A

1 Do you sometimes buy things online?
2 He will never forgive me for what I said.
3 My daughter usually has an afternoon nap at 2 P.M.
4 The author's writing style is always the same.
5 You should often wash your hands.
6 Miranda rarely agrees on Kate's idea.
7 My father and I are seldom at home on weekdays.

연습문제 B

1 often	2 always	3 never
4 seldom		

POINT 4-1 다양한 부사: already, still, yet

 연습문제

1 already	2 yet	3 still
4 yet	5 still	6 already
7 still		

POINT 4-2 다양한 부사: too, either

연습문제

1 too	2 too	3 either
4 either	5 either	6 either
7 too		

POINT 4-3 다양한 부사: so, neither

연습문제 A

1 So am I.	2 So did I.
3 So is he.	4 Neither did I.
5 Neither will I.	6 So does Minju.
7 Neither can I.	8 So is the cinema.
9 So does Mr. Johnson.	

연습문제 B

1 So	2 too	3 either
4 Neither		

POINT 5 타동사 + 부사

 연습문제 A

1 turn on	2 turn in	3 give up
4 take off	5 write down	6 wake up
7 pick up	8 put off	

 연습문제 B

1 O
2 Why don't you look it up in the dictionary?

3 O

4 Sally is looking at the moon.

5 O

6 All of you have to hand them in by tomorrow.

POINT 6 의문부사

연습문제 A

1 Where	**2** When	**3** Why
4 How	**5** When	**6** Where
7 How	**8** Why	

연습문제 B

1 How old	**2** How long	**3** How often
4 How many	**5** How much	**6** How far
7 How big	**8** How tall	

중간·기말고사 실전 문제

1 ④ **2** ③ **3** ② **4** I have rarely had any problems **5** ① **6** ④ **7** ② **8** argued her opinion logically **9** ④ **10** ⑤ **11** ① **12** How **13** (1) sometimes goes cycling (2) hardly goes cycling (3) always goes cycling **14** ④ **15** Why **16** When **17** ④ **18** I was absolutely sure about my decision. **19** (1) already (2) still (3) yet **20** ① **21** ④, ⑤ **22** ② **23** ③ **24** ② **25** (1) ⓑ → extremely important (2) ⓒ → usually check

1 ④: 명사 – 형용사 ①②③⑤: 형용사 – 부사

2 ③ incredible → incredibly

3 ②: 부사 ①③④⑤: 형용사

4 빈도부사는 조동사(have) 뒤에 위치한다.

5 (A) '정말로'라는 의미의 부사 truly를 쓴다.
(B) '적절한'이라는 의미의 형용사 proper를 쓴다.
(C) '거의 ~않다'라는 의미의 부사 hardly를 쓴다.

6 · pick up '~을 줍다'
· give up '~을 포기하다'

7 ② 긍정문에 대한 동의를 나타낼 때는 too를 쓴다.

8 동사(argued)를 꾸미는 부사 logically(논리적으로)를 쓴다.

9 긍정문에 대한 동의를 나타내고 있고 앞 문장에 일반동사의 과거형(did)이 쓰였으므로 「So + did + 주어」를 쓴다.

10 ① been always → always been
② hardly are → are hardly
③ can hear sometimes → can sometimes hear
④ often has → has often

11 · '도저히'라는 의미의 부사 possibly를 쓴다.
· '매우'라는 의미의 부사 highly를 쓴다.

12 · '너의 성의 철자를 어떻게 쓰니?'라는 의미이므로 방법을 묻는 How를 쓴다.
· '너의 할머니는 요즘 어떠시니?'라는 의미이므로 상태를 묻는 How를 쓴다.

13 (1) Noah는 평일에 두 번 자전거 타러 가므로 sometimes(때때로)를 쓴다. 빈도부사는 일반동사 앞에 온다.
(2) Liam은 평일에 한 번 자전거 타러 가므로 hardly(거의 ~않다)를 쓴다.
(3) Ava는 평일에 다섯 번 자전거 타러 가므로 always(항상)를 쓴다.

14 ⓑ take off it → take it off
ⓕ look up it → look it up
ⓖ tried on it → tried it on

15 그것들이 낡았기 때문에 버렸다고 대답했으므로 이유를 묻는 Why를 쓴다.

16 지난 주말에 다쳤다고 대답했으므로 시간이나 날짜를 묻는 When을 쓴다.

17 주어진 문장과 ④: 부사 ①②③⑤: 형용사

18 부사 absolutely는 형용사 sure를 수식한다.

19 (1) '이미'라는 의미의 already를 쓴다.
(2) 부정어(hasn't) 앞에서 '아직, 여전히'라는 의미로 쓰이는 still을 쓴다.
(3) 주로 의문문 맨 뒤에서 '이미, 벌써'라는 의미로 쓰이는 yet을 쓴다.

20 (A) '최근에'라는 의미의 부사 Lately를 쓴다.
(B) '일반적인'이라는 의미의 형용사 general을 쓴다.
(C) '높게'라는 의미의 부사 high를 쓴다.

21 ④ serious → seriously
⑤ near → nearly

22 ⓑ wake up her → wake her up
ⓓ buy usually → usually buy
ⓔ Did often you → Did you often
ⓖ look it at → look at it

23 첫 번째 빈칸: '너는 얼마나 자주 낮잠을 자니?'라는 의미이므로 빈도를 묻는 How often을 쓴다.
두 번째 빈칸: '우리는 언제 낮잠을 자야 하니?'라는 의미이므로 시간이나 날짜를 묻는 when을 쓴다.

24 ⓑ total → totally
ⓔ enough old → old enough

25 (1) '극도로'라는 의미의 부사 extremely를 쓴다.
(2) 빈도부사(usually)는 일반동사(check) 앞에 온다.

CHAPTER 13
비교구문

p.164

POINT 1-1 규칙 변화 I

1	lower – lowest	2	noisier – noisiest
3	brighter – brightest	4	colder – coldest
5	more popular – most popular		
6	funnier – funniest		
7	slower – slowest	8	kinder – kindest
9	simpler – simplest	10	prettier – prettiest
11	heavier – heaviest		
12	more boring – most boring		
13	more active – most active		
14	more famous – most famous		
15	drier - driest	16	higher – highest
17	luckier – luckiest	18	poorer –poorest
19	more exactly – most exactly		
20	safer – safest		

POINT 1-2 불규칙 변화

1	③	2	③	3	①	4	①
5	③	6	②	7	②	8	③

POINT 2-1 원급 비교: as + 원급 + as

1 This book is as thin as a notebook.
2 Kevin eats as much as his brothers do.
3 This old computer works as well as the new one.
4 The English exam was not as difficult as the math exam.
5 This blanket is not as soft as that one.
6 She speaks Spanish as fluently as a native speaker.

1 This cherry is sweeter than that watermelon.
   That watermelon is less sweet than this cherry.
2 That ring is more expensive than this necklace.
   This necklace is less expensive than that ring.
3 The plane is faster than the train.
   The train is less fast than the plane.
4 Daegu's temperature is higher than Seoul's temperature.
   Seoul's temperature is less high than Daegu's temperature.

POINT 2-2 원급 비교: as + 원급 + as + 주어 + can[could]

1 as hard as possible
2 as quickly as we can
3 as loudly as possible
4 as soon as he could
5 as honestly as possible
6 as realistically as he could

POINT 2-3 원급 비교: 배수사 + as + 원급 + as

1 four times heavier than
2 three times older than
3 seven times longer than
4 900 times smaller than
5 333,000 times lighter than
6 99 times bigger than

POINT 3-1 비교급 비교: 비교급 + than

1 is shorter than Molly
2 is heavier than her bag
3 can do more tricks than Lisa's dog
4 can run faster than a horse
5 is colder than Seoul
6 made more money than Jane

1	prettier	2	much	3	even
4	more	5	far / even	6	a lot / even
7	large	8	taller	9	far / still
10	a lot				

POINT 3-2 비교급 비교: the + 비교급, the + 비교급

1 The longer, the more
2 The higher, the colder
3 The more often, the healthier
4 The more heavily, the deeper
5 The more, the better
6 The farther, the smaller

1 The longer I studied, the more tired I got.
2 The more violent the storm is, the more dangerous it will be.
3 The icier the roads get, the harder they become to drive on.

4 The more Ben thought about the interview, the more nervous he got.

5 The more friends I have, the happier I will be.

6 The taller Carl grew, the shorter his pants became.

POINT 3-3 비교급 비교: 비교급 + and + 비교급

1 is getting worse and worse
2 is getting shorter and shorter
3 is growing larger and larger
4 is getting harder and harder
5 flew higher and higher
6 is getting more and more interesting
7 got smaller and smaller
8 is becoming more and more popular
9 is getting better and better
10 are getting more and more tired
11 is shining brighter and brighter
12 was becoming more and more irritated
13 became longer and longer

POINT 4-1 최상급 비교: the + 최상급

연습
문제
A

1 the safest city in Canada
2 The oldest tree in the world
3 the best student in her class
4 the longest river in China
5 the biggest country in Asia
6 the most important thing in my life

연습
문제
B

1	stronger	2	the most expensive
3	the youngest	4	better
5	the most relaxing	6	old
7	larger	8	slowly
9	soft	10	the best

POINT 4-2 최상급 비교: one of the + 최상급 + 복수 명사

1 Paul is one of the smartest people
2 Albert Einstein is one of the greatest scientists
3 Burj Khalifa is one of the tallest buildings
4 Vienna is one of the best cities
5 Kim is one of the most common last names

POINT 4-3 최상급 비교: 원급과 비교급을 이용한 최상급 표현

1 (other) question, as[so] hard
(other) question, harder
harder than, other question
harder than, other questions

2 (other) mountain, as[so] high
(other) mountain, higher
higher than, other mountain
higher than, other mountains

3 (other) thing, as[so] important
(other) thing, more important
more important than, other thing
more important than, other things

중간·기말고사 실전 문제

1 ②, ④ 2 ③ 3 ④ 4 Brian's dog is four times older than mine. 5 ① 6 ② 7 ⑤ 8 ④, ⑤ 9 ③ 10 more → most 11 are healthier than fruits 12 ④ 13 the strongest player 14 not as[so] spicy as 15 ③ 16 ③ 17 The softer, the more comfortable 18 ⑤ 19 animal is larger than 20 (1) the heaviest (2) cheaper than (3) as[so] expensive 21 as carefully as you can 22 not as[so] heavy as 23 ② 24 place → places 25 ④

1 ② lonely – lonelier – loneliest
④ far – farther – farthest

2 ③ most famous → the most famous

3 · 'Tim은 나머지 달리기 선수들만큼 지치지 않았다.'라는 의미이므로 '…만큼'이라는 의미의 as 또는 so를 쓴다. 부정문일 경우 as 대신 so를 쓸 수 있다.
· '달은 별들보다 더 밝다.'라는 의미이므로 '…보다'라는 의미의 than을 쓴다.

4 「배수사 + 비교급 + than」'…보다 -배 더 ~한/하게'

5 '…만큼'이라는 의미의 as가 있고 '나의 여동생은 벌만큼 바쁘다.'라는 의미이므로 원급 busy를 쓴다.

6 '…보다'라는 의미의 than이 있고 '선인장의 수명은 보통 300년보다 더 길다.'라는 의미이므로 비교급 longer를 쓴다.

7 비교 범위를 나타내는 in your family가 있고 '누가 너의 가족에서 가장 부지런하니?'라는 의미이므로 최상급 the most diligent를 쓴다.

8 ④ so → as

⑤ expensive → more expensive

9 첫 번째 빈칸: 빈칸 뒤에 원급(talented)이 있으므로 원급을 강조하는 very를 쓴다.

두 번째 빈칸: 빈칸 뒤에 비교급(more talented)이 있으므로 비교급을 강조하는 far 또는 still을 쓴다.

10 비교 범위를 나타내는 of all see animals가 있고 '돌고래는 바다 동물 중에서 가장 똑똑하다.'라는 의미이므로 최상급 the most intelligent를 쓴다.

11 '과일은 채소만큼 건강에 좋지 않다.'라는 의미의 문장은 '채소는 과일보다 건강에 더 좋다.'로 바꿔 쓸 수 있다.

12 ① more → much

② in → of

③ most bright → brightest

⑤ better → the best

13 「비교급 + than any other + 단수명사」는 「the + 최상급」으로 바꿔 쓸 수 있다.

14 「비교급 + than」은 「not + as[so] + 원급 + as」로 바꿔 쓸 수 있다.

15 ③ Giant Sequoia 나무가 가장 높이 자란다고 했으므로 'Baobab 나무는 Giant Sequoia 나무만큼 높이 자란다.'는 적절하지 않다.

16 '민호의 성적은 Nina의 성적만큼 좋지 않다.'라는 의미의 문장은 'Nina의 성적은 민호의 성적보다 더 좋다.'로 바꿔 쓸 수 있다.

17 '~하면 할수록 더 …하다'라는 의미의 「the + 비교급, the + 비교급」을 쓴다.

18 ⑤ many → more, happy → happier

19 「the + 최상급」은 「No other + 단수명사 ~ 비교급 + than」으로 바꿔 쓸 수 있다.

20 (1) 자몽은 셋 중에서 가장 무겁다고 했으므로 the heaviest를 쓴다.

(2) 사과는 자몽보다 더 싸다고 했으므로 cheaper than을 쓴다.

(3) 어떤 과일도 배만큼 비싸지 않다고 했으므로 as[so] expensive as를 쓴다.

21 「as + 원급 + as + possible」은 「as + 원급 + as + 주어 + can」으로 바꿔 쓸 수 있다.

22 책장은 책상만큼 무겁지 않다고 했으므로 not as[so] heavy as를 쓴다.

23 '네가 콘서트 전에 피아노 연습을 하면 할수록 너는 더 자신감 있게 느낄 것이다.'라고 했으므로 '~하면 할수록 더 …하다'라는 의미의 「the + 비교급, the + 비교급」을 쓴다.

24 '가장 ~한 것들 중 하나'는 「one of the + 최상급 + 복수명사」의 형태로 써야 하므로 복수명사 places를 쓴다.

25 ⓐ in → of

CHAPTER 14
전치사

p.178

POINT 1-1 시간 전치사 Ⅰ

연습문제	**1** in	**2** at	**3** on
	4 in	**5** in	**6** on
	7 at	**8** in	**9** at
	10 on		

POINT 1-2 시간 전치사 Ⅱ

연습문제	**1** since	**2** by	**3** from
	4 after	**5** since	**6** by
	7 before	**8** until	**9** after
	10 before	**11** from	**12** until

POINT 1-3 시간 전치사 Ⅲ

연습문제	**1** ②	**2** ③	**3** ③	**4** ①
	5 ②	**6** ②	**7** ③	**8** ②
	9 ①	**10** ③	**11** ①	**12** ②
	13 ①	**14** ③		

POINT 2-1 장소 전치사: at, on, in Ⅰ

연습문제	**1** on	**2** at	**3** in
	4 on	**5** in	**6** at

POINT 2-2 장소 전치사: at, on, in Ⅱ

연습문제	**1** in	**2** on	**3** on
	4 on	**5** in	**6** in
	7 at	**8** in	**9** at
	10 in		

POINT 3 위치 전치사

연습문제	**1** next to	**2** under	**3** over
	4 in front of	**5** among	

POINT 4 방향 전치사

연습문제

1 to	**2** over	**3** into
4 through	**5** along	

POINT 5 기타 전치사

연습문제

1 for	**2** against	**3** with
4 by	**5** without	**6** by
7 like	**8** about	**9** with
10 by	**11** like	**12** as

POINT 6-1 전치사 관용 표현: 형용사 + 전치사

연습문제

1 for	**2** to	**3** at
4 of	**5** at	**6** for
7 about	**8** for	**9** from
10 for	**11** for	**12** of
13 for	**14** of	

POINT 6-2 전치사 관용 표현: 동사 + 전치사

연습문제

1 to	**2** for	**3** of
4 to	**5** for	**6** for
7 on	**8** at	**9** at
10 into		

중간·기말고사 실전 문제

1 ③	**2** ②	**3** on the phone	**4** ②
5 through	**6** ④	**7** ④	**8** ⑤
9 ②	**10** ④	**11** ③	**12** ①	**13** ①
14 about	**15** ①	**16** (1) ⓑ → of (2) ⓒ → at	
(3) ⓔ → for	**17** ⑤	**18** ⑤	**19** ①
20 ③	**21** ②	**22** ②	**23** ③	**24** ①
25 ⓐ in front of ⓑ next to[by/beside] ⓒ behind			

1 '우리 농구팀은 토요일마다 오전 9시부터 오전 11시까지 연습한다.'라는 의미이므로 「from ~ to …」(~부터 …까지)를 쓴다.

2 기간을 나타내는 명사(15 years) 앞이므로 '~동안'이라는 의미의 전치사 for를 쓴다.

3 통신수단(the phone) 앞에는 전치사 on을 쓴다.

4 ② at → on

5 '~을 통해서'라는 의미의 전치사 through를 쓴다.

6 · '그 에세이는 화요일까지 제출되어야 한다.'라는 의미이므로 정해진 시점까지 어떤 행동이나 상황이 완료되는 것을 나타내는 전치사 by(~까지)를 쓴다.
· '박물관에 도착하는 가장 빠른 방법은 택시를 타고 가는 것이다.'라는 의미이므로 전치사 by(~을 타고)를 쓴다.

7 ⓒⓓ for   ⓐ of   ⓑ from   ⓔ at

8 (A): be proud of '~을 자랑스러워하다'
(B): '그 여자는 소리 없이 방을 떠났다.'라는 의미이므로 전치사 without(~ 없이)을 쓴다.
(C): 시점(dawn) 앞에는 전치사 at을 쓴다.

9 ② at   주어진 문장의 ⓐ와 ①③④⑤ in

10 ④ 시각(7 o'clock) 앞에는 전치사 at을 쓴다.

11 주어진 문장과 ③: '~에 의해'   ①④: '~을 타고'   ②: '~로'
⑤: '~까지'

12 첫 번째 빈칸: '6번 출구를 통해 이 지하철역 밖으로 나가세요.'라는 의미이므로 전치사 out of(~ 밖으로)를 쓴다.
두 번째 빈칸: '국립 은행은 병원과 우체국 사이에 가장 큰 건물이에요.'라는 의미이고 the hospital and the post office는 둘이므로 전치사 between(~ 사이에)을 쓴다.

13 · '너는 너의 어머니를 위해 이 장갑들을 떴니?'라는 의미이므로 전치사 for(~를 위해)를 쓴다.
· '우리는 여기서부터 음식점까지 갈 수 있다.'라는 의미이므로 전치사 to(~까지)를 쓴다.

14 '~에 대해'라는 의미의 전치사 about을 쓴다.

15 bump into '~를 우연히 만나다'

16 (1) be afraid of '~을 무서워하다'
(2) 장소(school) 앞에는 전치사 at을 쓴다.
(3) be sorry for '~에 대해 미안해하다'

17 ⑤: 동사 like   ①②③④: 전치사 like

18 ⓓⓔ on   ⓐ for   ⓑ from   ⓒ in

19 ① by → until

20 ③ for → to

21 · '공원에 개를 가진 한 명의 여자가 있었다.'라는 의미이므로 전치사 with(~을 가진)를 쓴다.
· '나는 걸레로 바닥을 청소했다.'라는 의미이므로 전치사 with(~을 이용해서)를 쓴다.

22 첫 번째 빈칸: look for '~을 찾다'
두 번째 빈칸: '동굴의 밑부분은 지구의 표면보다 2킬로미터가 넘는 곳보다 아래에 있다.'라는 의미이므로 전치사 below(~(보다) 아래에)를 쓴다.

23 첫 번째 빈칸: '이 산의 정상은 서울보다 위에 있다.'라는 의미이므로 전치사 above(~ (보다) 위에)를 쓴다.
두 번째 빈칸: '그는 몇 그루의 나무 사이에 있는 소풍용 테이블에

서 점심을 먹었다.'라는 의미이고 some trees는 셋 이상이므로 전치사 among(~(셋 이상) 사이에)을 쓴다.

24 ① in → on

25 첫 번째 빈칸: '~ 앞에'라는 의미의 전치사 in front of를 쓴다.
두 번째 빈칸: '~ 옆에'라는 의미의 전치사 next to/by/beside를 쓴다.
세 번째 빈칸: '~ 뒤에'라는 의미의 전치사 behind를 쓴다.

CHAPTER 15
접속사

p.190

POINT 1-1 등위접속사

| **1** and | **2** but | **3** or |
| **4** so | **5** and | **6** but |

1 Clean your room, and your mom will be very happy.
2 Keep your promises, or other people won't trust you.
3 Leave now, and you'll arrive at school on time.
4 Wear gloves, and your hands will feel warm.
5 Eat breakfast, or you'll get hungry later.
6 Walk just two blocks, and you'll see the bank.

POINT 2 상관접속사

1 both the shoes and the hat
2 neither interesting nor informative
3 Either my brother or I
4 neither hear nor see
5 Both amateurs and professionals
6 not only beautiful but (also) comfortable [comfortable as well as beautiful]
7 not only a famous artist but (also) a great scientist[a great scientist as well as a famous artist]

1 is	**2** like	**3** is
4 has	**5** are	**6** are
7 contains	**8** is	**9** enjoys
10 is	**11** want	

POINT 3-1 명사절을 이끄는 접속사: that

1 believe that the weather affects their mood
2 is important that we trust each other
3 is that Canada is the second largest country
4 hope that more people will volunteer

| **1** ① | **2** ③ |

POINT 3-2 명사절을 이끄는 접속사: if, whether

1 if I made her upset
2 whether you can meet me after school
3 whether the movie is based on a true story
4 if dolphins and whales can breathe under water

POINT 4-1 부사절을 이끄는 접속사: 시간

A

1	while	2	starts	3	as soon as
4	when	5	before	6	as
7	until	8	while	9	do
10	until				

B

1 since I was five years old
2 when they are asleep
3 after you live for five years
4 while his mom was taking a nap
5 before they go to bed
6 as soon as the passengers are all seated
7 as he heard his grandfather's story

POINT 4-2 부사절을 이끄는 접속사: 이유

A

1 I took a short nap because I was so sleepy.
2 Pete chose to stay in a hostel since the hotels were too expensive.
3 She opened the window since she needed some fresh air.
4 Our flight was canceled because the weather was bad.
5 Polar bears need body fat to keep themselves warm as it is very cold in the Arctic.
6 We won the dance competition because we practiced a lot.
7 She couldn't buy the shirt since it was sold out.

B

1	①	2	③	3	③	4	②

POINT 4-3 부사절을 이끄는 접속사: 조건

A

1 If you don't take his advice /
Unless you take his advice
2 If you can't keep a promise /
Unless you can keep a promise

---

3 If it doesn't rain /
Unless it rains
4 If you aren't 19 years old /
Unless you are 19 years old
5 If we don't protect our environment /
Unless we protect our environment

B

1	If	2	Unless	3	if
4	get	5	does	6	If
7	visit	8	unless		

POINT 4-4 부사절을 이끄는 접속사: 양보

1 Although Katie was tired
2 Even though that man was very old
3 Though I don't eat breakfast
4 even though it's already September
5 although it is small
6 Even though grammar is hard
7 though Irish is the official language

POINT 4-5 부사절을 이끄는 접속사: as의 다양한 의미

1	ⓑ	2	ⓐ	3	ⓑ	4	ⓐ
5	ⓓ	6	ⓒ	7	ⓔ	8	ⓐ

POINT 5 so that / so ~ that …

1 so that it would stand out
2 so busy that he didn't have time to play with me
3 so that they could find a medication
4 so that I could buy my mom a present
5 so heavy that she can't move it
6 so that your baby sister can sleep
7 so big that he needs to wear a belt
8 so that he could understand it better

POINT 6 접속부사

A

1	For example	2	However
3	In addition	4	Therefore
5	On the other hand		

1 ③　**2** Gorillas as well as monkeys
3 whether　**4** ③　**5** ②, ③ **6** ②
7 ⑤　**8** When **9** because[since / as]
10 Unless　**11** Although the weather is
very cold **12** ①　**13** ④　**14** This novel is not
only long but also boring.　**15** ②
16 and you will get a good sleep　**17** ⑤
18 ②　**19** ⑤　**20** ①　**21** ①, ⑤ **22** Ryan's
birthday party was so fun that I stayed longer than I
planned.　**23** ③　**24** ②　**25** ①

1 명사절 접속사 that은 문장 안에서 주어로 쓰이는 명사절을 이끈다. 이때 주로 주어 자리에 가주어 it을 쓰고 진주어 that절을 뒤로 보낸다.

2 not only A but also B(A뿐만 아니라 B도)는 B as well as A로 바꿔 쓸 수 있다.

3 if와 whether는 '~인지 아닌지'라는 의미로, 명사절을 이끈다.

4 ③ or　①②④⑤ and

5 ②③: 명사절 접속사 (that절이 문장 안에서 목적어로 쓰였을 때 that을 생략할 수 있다.)
①④: 지시형용사　⑤: 지시대명사

6 첫 번째 빈칸: '나의 여동생은 그녀가 자라면 의사 또는 변호사가 되기를 원한다.'라는 의미이므로 or(또는)를 쓴다.
두 번째 빈칸: '이것은 어려울 것이어서, 그녀는 학교에서 공부를 열심히 해야 할 것이다.'라는 의미이므로 so(그래서)를 쓴다.

7 ⓐ is → are (both A and B 뒤에는 항상 복수동사를 쓴다.)
ⓑ clean → cleaning

8 '그는 뉴욕에 있었을 때 Empire State 빌딩을 방문했다.'라는 의미이므로 When(~할 때)을 쓴다.

9 '그녀는 충분히 힘이 세지 않아서'라는 의미는 '그녀는 충분히 힘이 세지 않기 때문에'라는 의미를 나타내므로 '~이기 때문에'라는 의미의 because/since/as를 쓴다.

10 if ~ not(만약 ~하지 않는다면)은 unless로 바꿔 쓸 수 있다.

11 although(비록 ~이지만)는 양보를 나타내는 부사절을 이끈다.

12 · 빈칸 뒤에 절(Ollie accidentally hit it with his bat)이 있으므로 because/since(~하기 때문에)를 쓴다.
· 빈칸 뒤에 명사구(its soft cushions)가 있으므로 because of(~ 때문에)를 쓴다.

13 ⓐ I'll arrive → I arrive
ⓑ you'll get up → you get up
ⓔ she will finish → she finishes

14 'A뿐만 아니라 B도'라는 의미의 not only A but also B를 쓴다.

15 목적을 나타내는 to부정사는 부사절 접속사 so that을 이용하여

나타낼 수 있다.

16 「명령문 + and ~」'~해라, 그러면 ~'

17 주어진 문장과 ⑤: ~으로서　①③④: ~하고 있을 때
②: ~하기 때문에

18 ②: '~한 이후로'　①③④⑤: '~하기 때문에'

19 주어진 문장과 ⑤: 부사절 접속사　①②③④: 명사절 접속사

20 (A) '나의 형은 많은 나라를 방문했다. 예를 들어, 그는 작년에 베네수엘라에 갔다.'라는 의미이므로 For example(예를 들어)을 쓴다.
(B) '나도 그처럼 여행하기를 원한다. 그러나, 나는 지금 너무 어리다.'라는 의미이므로 However(그러나)를 쓴다.
(C) '내가 나이가 더 들었을 때, 나는 세계를 여행할 것이다.'라는 의미이므로 When(~할 때)을 쓴다.

21 '너무 ~해서 …할 수 없는'이라는 의미의 「so ~ that … can't」와 「too ~ to」를 쓴다.

22 「so + 형용사 + that …」(너무 ~해서 …한)은 결과를 나타낸다.

23 ③: 의문사　①②④⑤: 부사절 접속사

24 '그것은 그들에게 운동할 기회를 제공한다. 게다가, 그들은 팀워크에 대해 배울 수 있다.'라는 의미이므로 In addition(게다가)을 쓴다.

25 '그들이 스포츠를 한다면 공부할 시간이 많지 않을 것이다.'라는 의미이므로 if they play를 쓴다. unless는 not과 함께 쓰지 않는다.

CHAPTER 16
관계사

p.204

POINT 1 관계대명사의 역할과 종류

1 선행사: the pictures, 관계대명사: which
2 선행사: the girl, 관계대명사: whose
3 선행사: the tree, 관계대명사: which
4 선행사: the people, 관계대명사: who
5 선행사: the man, 관계대명사: who
6 선행사: the glasses, 관계대명사: that
7 선행사: a documentary, 관계대명사: which
8 선행사: a dog, 관계대명사: whose
9 선행사: a musical instrument, 관계대명사: which
10 선행사: the teacher, 관계대명사: that

1 I have a cat which[that] likes to sleep on my bed.
2 O
3 Amy has an aunt who[that] is a famous actress.
4 This is a book which[that] is about the tale of Robin Hood.
5 O
6 Millet is an artist whose paintings are held at the gallery.
7 She met the people who[that] lived upstairs.
8 Jennifer is my friend who[whom/that] I can tell everything.

POINT 2-1 주격 관계대명사

1 A frog is an animal which lives both on land and in water.
2 The room which was not cleaned for a week was dirty.
3 The police caught the girl who stole Tim's wallet.
4 Mr. Morgan bought a car which was made in Germany.
5 *Hamlet* is a play which is about Prince Hamlet's revenge.
6 James fought with the boys who made fun of his hair.
7 The monitor which is on Jake's table is not working.
8 Dolphins are mammals which can't breathe underwater.

| | 1 ② | 2 ① | 3 ② | 4 ③ |
| B | 5 ③ | 6 ① | | |

POINT 2-2 목적격 관계대명사

1 the new backpack which I bought yesterday
2 the girl who[whom] I met at the library
3 the surprise party which my friends organized three years ago
4 the food which my neighbors are cooking
5 the picture book which Penny gave to her nephew on his birthday
6 Jenny's bag which her mom made for her
7 his phone which he lost in the movie theater
8 tree branches which they will use to make their nest

1 the dish which I ordered at the restaurant
2 Ms. Taylor whom we met at church
3 the man whom we saw in the TV commercial
4 My grandparents who I visit twice a year
5 The flowers which Jenny bought today
6 a painting which was painted by Kandinsky

POINT 2-3 소유격 관계대명사

1 a teddy bear whose ears are huge
2 a parrot whose feathers are blue and red
3 a jacket whose zipper is broken
4 a plant whose stems store water
5 the girl whose handwriting is the best in our class
6 a game whose aim is to hit a very small ball into a hole far away
7 a famous author whose books were translated into many languages

| | 1 ⓐ | 2 ⓒ | 3 ⓑ | 4 ⓐ |
| B | 5 ⓒ | 6 ⓑ | 7 ⓐ | 8 ⓐ |

POINT 3 관계대명사 that

1 the boy that I met on the subway
   who, whom
2 a hairpin that is small but useful
   which
3 my colleague that has dinner with me once a week

who

4 the woman that we saw in the park two days ago
who, whom

5 the tree that was 150 years old
which

6 a nun that was respected by many people
who

7 the teacher that taught me how to play the guitar
who

8 your things that are underneath the table
which

| 1 | ② | 2 | ② | 3 | ③ | 4 | ① |

POINT 4 관계대명사 what

1 what you said
2 what you wrote in your diary
3 what was in her pocket
4 what James wanted to do on the weekend
5 what differentiated her from everyone else
6 What Sam wants the most
7 what they expected

| 1 | What | 2 | which | 3 | What | 4 | what |
| 5 | which | 6 | which | 7 | What | 8 | which |

POINT 5 관계대명사의 생략

1 Penny is the girl who[whom/that] everyone loves.
2 The pasta which[that] is made by Mom is always delicious.
3 A gram is a unit which[that] is used to measure mass.
4 *A Farewell to Arms* is a novel which[that] is written by Hemmingway.
5 Ben interviewed a man who[that] was working in the government in the past.
6 Kelly likes the purse which[that] John bought for her.
7 The man who[that] is standing in front of the entrance is my dad.
8 The house which[that] was built 20 years ago is still in good shape.

| 1 | ① | 2 | ② | 3 | ② | 4 | ② |

| 5 | ② | 6 | ① | 7 | ② | 8 | ② |

POINT 6 전치사 + 관계대명사

1 I ordered the ratatouille which[that] this restaurant is famous for.
I ordered the ratatouille for which this restaurant is famous.

2 This is papyrus which[that] ancient Egyptians used to write on.
This is papyrus on which ancient Egyptians used to write.

3 The boy who[whom/that] Jenny is playing with is my cousin.
The boy with whom Jenny is playing is my cousin.

4 This is the sofa which[that] Mr. Smith talked about last night.
This is the sofa about which Mr. Smith talked last night.

POINT 7 관계부사

1 China is the country where Minho spent his childhood.
2 O
3 Do you know why she was so mad at us?
4 1991 is the year when the Cold War ended.

중간·기말고사 실전 문제

1	②	2	④	3	that → what	4	②
5	⑤	6	④	7	①, ④	8	③
9	③	10	④	11	①	12	③	13 (1)

which[that] has many safety features (2) whose seats are very comfortable **14** George made a new friend who[that] lives next to his house.
15 Kate called her neighbor whose car is parked in front of her house. **16** There are a soldier and an eagle that are looking down the hill. **17** ③
18 ①, ⑤ **19** ②, ⑤ **20** ② **21** that
22 Boston is the city where I was born in 2002.
23 ③ **24** ① **25** (1) who[that] will cook dinner at 7 o'clock (2) who [that] is walking the dog now (3) who[whom/that] dad asked to help him cook dinner

1 선행사(the scarf)가 사물이므로 관계대명사 which를 쓴다.

2 ・선행사(a bag)가 사물이므로 관계대명사 which나 that을 쓴다.
 ・선행사(the person)가 사람이므로 관계대명사 who나 that을 쓴다.

3 선행사가 없으므로 선행사를 포함하는 관계대명사 what을 쓴다.

4 ① who → where[in which]
 ③ what → which[that]
 ④ whose → who[that]
 ⑤ which → that

5 ・선행사(the pasta)가 사물이므로 관계대명사 which나 that을 쓴다.
 ・'~이라는 것'이라는 의미로 동사 know의 목적어 역할을 하는 명사절 접속사 that을 쓴다.
 ・선행사(a man)가 사람이므로 관계대명사 who나 that을 쓴다.

6 ④: 주격 관계대명사 　①②③⑤: 목적격 관계대명사

7 두 번째 문장은 첫 번째 문장의 Danny에 대해 보충 설명하고 있고, 두 번째 문장의 He가 주어 역할을 하고 있으므로 사람을 선행사로 하는 주격 관계대명사 who를 쓴다. 「주격 관계대명사 + be동사」는 생략할 수 있다.

8 주어진 문장과 ③: 관계대명사 　①: 지시형용사
 ②④: 명사절 접속사 　⑤: 지시대명사

9 ・선행사(the picture)가 사물이므로 관계대명사 which나 that을 쓴다.
 ・빈칸 뒤에 선행사(the girl)가 소유하는 대상이 되는 명사(hair)가 있으므로 관계대명사 whose를 쓴다.
 ・선행사(the person)가 사람이므로 관계대명사 who나 that을 쓴다.

10 ④ whose (빈칸 뒤에 선행사가 소유하는 대상이 되는 명사가 있으므로 관계대명사 whose를 쓴다.)

11 선행사(a place)가 장소를 나타내므로 관계부사 where를 쓴다.

12 주어진 문장과 ③: 관계대명사 　①②④⑤: 의문사

13 (1) 'This car has many safety features.'는 a car에 대해 보충 설명하고 있고, This car가 주어 역할을 하고 있으므로 사물을 선행사로 하는 주격관계대명사 which나 that을 쓴다.
 (2) 'Its seats are very comfortable.'은 a car에 대해 보충 설명하고 있고, seats는 a car가 소유하는 대상이 되는 명사이므로 소유격 관계대명사 whose를 쓴다.

14 두 번째 문장은 첫 번째 문장의 a new friend에 대해 보충 설명하고 있고, 두 번째 문장의 She가 주어 역할을 하고 있으므로 사람을 선행사로 하는 주격 관계대명사 who나 that을 쓴다.

15 두 번째 문장은 첫 번째 문장의 her neighbor에 대해 보충 설명하고 있고, 두 번째 문장의 his가 소유격의 역할을 하고 있으므로 소유격 관계대명사 whose를 쓴다.

16 두 번째 문장은 첫 번째 문장의 a soldier and an eagle에 대

해 보충 설명하고 있고, 두 번째 문장의 They가 주어 역할을 하고 있으므로 사람과 동물을 선행사로 하는 주격 관계대명사 that을 쓴다.

17 ③: 목적격 관계대명사 (목적격 관계대명사는 생략할 수 있다.)
 ①②④⑤: 주격 관계대명사

18 ① volunteer → volunteers
 ⑤ what → which[that]

19 관계대명사절의 동사가 복수동사(were)이므로 선행사는 복수명사 the boxes와 the desk and chair를 쓴다.

20 ②: 의문사 　①③④⑤: 관계대명사

21 ・선행사(the first person)에 서수가 포함되어 있으므로 관계대명사 that을 쓴다.
 ・선행사(Something)에 -thing이 포함되어 있으므로 관계대명사 that을 쓴다.
 ・선행사(The boy and the dogs)에 사람과 동물이 포함되어 있으므로 관계대명사 that을 쓴다.

22 두 번째 문장은 첫 번째 문장의 the city에 대해 보충 설명하고 있고, 선행사(the city)가 장소를 나타내므로 관계부사 where를 쓴다.

23 ⓑ: 목적격 관계대명사 　ⓔ: 「주격 관계대명사 + be동사」 (목적격 관계대명사와 「주격 관계대명사 + be동사」는 생략할 수 있다.)
 ⓐⓒⓓ: 주격 관계대명사

24 'Bill이 굽고 있던 쿠키들'이라고 했으므로 선행사는 the cookies이고, 선행사가 사물이므로 관계대명사 that을 쓴다. 'Bill이 굽고 있던'이라고 했으므로 Bill was baking을 관계대명사절에 쓴다.

25 (1) 아빠는 7시 정각에 저녁 식사를 요리할 가족 구성원이고, 선행사(the family member)가 사람이므로 주격 관계대명사 who나 that을 쓴다.
 (2) Jenny는 지금 개를 산책시키고 있는 가족 구성원이고, 선행사(the family member)가 사람이므로 주격 관계대명사 who나 that을 쓴다.
 (3) Chris는 아빠가 그가 저녁 식사를 요리하는 것을 도와달라고 부탁한 가족 구성원이고, 선행사(the family member)가 사람이므로 목적격 관계대명사 who/whom/that을 쓴다.

POINT 1-1 가정법 과거

1	could	2	rains	3	O
4	buy	5	O	6	search
7	O	8	comes		

1 If I were in California, I could meet you.
2 If Jack weren't sleepy, he could focus in class.
3 If Mariah knew how to drive, we would go out to the lake this weekend.
4 If the chairs weren't too heavy, Kelly could move them by herself.
5 If I had enough money, I would help more people.
6 If she remembered Kelly's address, she could give it to you.
7 If Michael had a jacket, he wouldn't buy a new one.
8 If the weather weren't so cold, I would go outside for a walk.

POINT 1-2 가정법 과거완료

1 had lived, would have gone
2 had not been, would have played
3 had not gone, couldn't have given
4 had trained, could have won
5 had been, wouldn't have left
6 had finished, would have had
7 had not been, would have bought
8 had quit, would have opened
9 had not come, couldn't have moved
10 had had, would have written
11 had woken, wouldn't have missed
12 had not been, would have talked
13 had had, would have taken
14 had known, would have called

POINT 2-1 I wish + 가정법 과거

1	were	2	had not	3	would
4	would	5	knew	6	would
7	could	8	would not		

1 I wish I could read more books.
2 I wish I were as strong as superman.
3 I wish he would throw out some of his clothes.
4 I wish I could return this TV.
5 I wish our team would win the championship.
6 I wish I had much food to eat.
7 I wish your parents could come to see you perform.
8 I wish I were good at playing the violin.
9 I wish my mother would let me make my own decisions.
10 I wish we had another day to finish this project.

POINT 2-2 I wish + 가정법 과거완료

1 I wish I had left
2 I wish I had known
3 I wish grandpa had been
4 I wish I had saved
5 I wish he had not seen
6 I wish I had studied

POINT 3 as if + 가정법 과거/과거완료

1 as if he were a chef
2 as if he had seen the suspect
3 as if she had studied Korean for a long time
4 as if he had been sick last night
5 as if it were repaired
6 as if he sang well

중간·기말고사 실전 문제

1	③	2	were	3	③	4	④	5	②
6	②	7	will → would			8	①		

9 weren't mammals, they wouldn't feed milk to their babies   10 had washed the dishes, she could have used the dishes for dinner 11 ②   12 ②
13 ②   14 had fixed   15 knew 16 ④
17 James had not left Korea last year   18 ⑤
19 ③   20 ④   21 ③   22 ②, ③ 23 it were expensive   24 ③   25 ①

1   ③ will lend → would lend

2   현재의 사실과 반대되는 일을 가정하고 있으므로 가정법 과거를 쓰고, 가정법 과거에서 if절의 be동사는 주어에 상관없이 were를 쓴다.

3 현재의 사실과 반대되는 일을 가정하고 있으므로 가정법 과거를 쓰고, 가정법 과거에서 if절의 be동사는 주어에 상관없이 were를 쓴다.

4 현재의 사실과 반대되는 일을 가정하고 있으므로 주절에는 「주어 + 조동사의 과거형(could) + 동사원형」을 쓴다.

5 ② will climb → would climb

6 현재의 사실과 반대되는 일을 가정하고 있으므로 주절에는 조동사의 과거형 would를 쓴다.

7 현재의 사실과 반대되는 일을 가정하고 있으므로 주절에는 조동사의 과거형 would를 쓴다.

8 현재의 사실과 반대되는 일을 가정하는 가정법 과거 문장은 '박물관이 열지 않았기 때문에, 우리는 오후에 그곳을 방문할 수 없다.' 라는 직설법 문장으로 바꿔 쓸 수 있고, 이때 현재시제를 쓴다.

9 현재의 사실과 반대되는 일을 가정하는 가정법 과거 「If + 주어 + 동사의 과거형 ~, 주어 + 조동사의 과거형 + 동사원형 …」으로 바꿔 쓸 수 있다.

10 과거의 사실과 반대되는 일을 가정하는 가정법 과거완료 「If + 주어 + had + p.p. ~, 주어 + 조동사의 과거형 + have + p.p. …」로 바꿔 쓸 수 있다.

11 ② have looked → had looked

12 현재 이룰 수 없거나 실현 가능성이 매우 적은 일을 소망하는 「I wish + 가정법 과거」를 써야 하므로 had를 쓴다.

13 현재의 사실과 반대되는 일을 가정하고 있으므로 가정법 과거 「If + 주어 + 동사의 과거형 ~, 주어 + 조동사의 과거형 + 동사원형 …」을 쓴다.

14 '~했더라면 좋았을 텐데'라는 의미로 과거에 이루지 못한 일을 소망하는 「I wish + 가정법 과거완료」를 써야 하므로 had fixed를 쓴다.

15 현재 이룰 수 없거나 실현 가능성이 매우 적은 일을 소망하는 「I wish + 가정법 과거」로 바꿔 쓸 수 있으므로 knew를 쓴다.

16 ・과거에 이루지 못한 일을 소망하는 「I wish + 가정법 과거완료」를 써야 하므로 had not given을 쓴다.
・현재 이룰 수 없거나 실현 가능성이 매우 적은 일을 소망하는 「I wish + 가정법 과거」를 써야 하므로 could speak을 쓴다.

17 과거에 이루지 못한 일을 소망하는 「I wish + 가정법 과거완료」로 바꿔 쓸 수 있으므로 James had not left Korea last year를 쓴다.

18 '만약 ~했더라면 …했을 텐데'의 의미로 과거의 사실과 반대되는 일을 가정하는 가정법 과거완료이므로 「If + 주어 + had + p.p. ~, 주어 + 조동사의 과거형 + have + p.p. …」를 쓴다.

19 '~했더라면 좋았을 텐데'라는 의미로 과거에 이루지 못한 일을 소망하는 「I wish + 가정법 과거완료」를 쓴다.

20 과거에 이루지 못한 일을 소망하는 「I wish + 가정법 과거완료」를 써야 하므로 had been을 쓴다.

21 ・주절의 시제(현재시제)와 같은 시점의 사실과 반대되는 일을 가정하는 「as if + 가정법 과거」를 써야 하므로 were를 쓴다.
・현재 이룰 수 없거나 실현 가능성이 매우 적은 일을 소망하는 「I wish + 가정법 과거」를 써야 하므로 were를 쓴다.

22 ① gone → go
④ had been → were
⑤ be → have been

23 주절의 시제(현재시제)와 같은 시점의 사실과 반대되는 일을 가정하는 「as if + 가정법 과거」로 바꿔 쓸 수 있으므로 it were expensive를 쓴다.

24 첫 번째 빈칸: 과거에 이루지 못한 일을 소망하는 「I wish + 가정법 과거완료」를 써야 하므로 had gotten을 쓴다.
두 번째 빈칸: 현재나 미래에 일어날 수 있는 상황을 나타내는 단순 조건문을 써야 하므로 will forgive를 쓴다.

25 ① could have drunk → could drink

POINT 1-1 시제 일치

1 is, will be	**2** is, was	**3** would
4 stay, stayed	**5** became	**6** might not
7 would	**8** could	**9** came
10 would		

POINT 1-2 시제 일치의 예외

1 I heard that the early bird catches the worm.

2 Mr. Jones told us that the Olympic gold medals are not made entirely out of gold.

3 Ben didn't know that there are eight planets in our solar system.

4 The taxi driver told us that there were many tourist attractions in this town.

5 We remembered that the Korean War started in 1950.

6 I knew that 0°C is equal to 32°F.

7 Mr. Cooper taught us that an ant lives up to two or three years.

POINT 2 화법 전환: 평서문

1 said (that) she wanted to order a cup of coffee

2 said to me, "I want you to help me clean the classroom."

3 said (that) I should come to the hospital the next[following] day

4 said (that) he was going to participate in the charity event the following week

5 said to me, "I went to the bank yesterday."

6 said to me, "I want you to join the soccer team."

7 said to me, "I will[I'll] go to the new café with you."

8 said (that) she could visit my house the next[following] day

9 said (that) he needed to borrow my dictionary then

10 said to me, "I enjoyed watching the magic show."

11 said (that) it was too late for me to go out alone

12 said, "I can eat this turkey all by myself."

13 said to me, "I fought with Jihye last week."

14 said, "I will[I'll] bring you the letters tomorrow."

POINT 3-1 화법 전환: 의문사가 있는 의문문

1 asked me where she could go to fix her phone

2 asked what I would get Ben for his 20th birthday

3 asked who had eaten all the cookies in the cookie jar

4 asked how I had gotten the huge bump on my forehead

5 asked me where he could get more information about the summer camp

6 asked me how quickly I could make the presentation slides

7 asked us where we wanted to go for the field trip

1 He asked me when I would do the laundry.

2 Ben asked me who I admired the most.

3 Kevin asked me what I thought was the smallest thing in the world.

4 The police asked me who had been there the previous day.

POINT 3-2 화법 전환: 의문사가 없는 의문문

1 asked me if[whether] I had seen the accident

2 asked me if[whether] I knew what the largest living thing on Earth was

3 asked me if[whether] I had been to Japan

4 asked me if[whether] that money would be enough to buy the dress

5 asked me if[whether] I could pick her up at the airport the next[following] day

6 asked me if[whether] I knew that there was a place called Pig Beach

7 asked me if[whether] I would have some more water

8 asked me if[whether] I was familiar with the rules of hockey

POINT 4 도치

1 is some milk	**2** flew the bird
3 jumped the otter	**4** is the book

5 stood the cow		6 they come	
7 are three apples		8 hid the child	

중간·기말고사 실전 문제

1 ③ **2** ① **3** ③ **4** ④ **5** ④
6 ⓑ → would **7** would have **8** ⑤
9 ④ **10** ④ **11** ④ **12** ⑤ **13** ⑤
14 ⑤ **15** ③ **16** like → liked **17** his,
was, that day **18** had broken his computer
19 ③ **20** ① **21** ④ **22** (A) why he wasn't
at school that day (B) (that) he was going to spend
the day in bed **23** Mr. Lee said, "I'll[I will] buy
a new running machine today." **24** Thomas asked
Jenny if she had time to play a board game.
25 ③

1 주절이 과거시제이므로 종속절에는 과거시제 was를 쓴다.

2 과학적 사실을 말할 때는 주절의 시제와 상관없이 종속절에 항상 현재시제를 쓰므로 현재시제 live를 쓴다.

3 역사적 사실을 말할 때는 주절의 시제와 상관없이 종속절에 항상 과거시제를 쓰므로 과거시제 was를 쓴다.

4 ④ wants → wanted

5 전달동사 say to는 tell로 바꾸고, 전달동사가 과거시제이므로 종속절의 현재시제 need를 과거시제 needed로 바꾼다. 전달하는 사람의 입장에 맞게 인칭대명사 I를 he로 바꾸고 your를 my로 바꾼다.

6 주절이 과거시제이므로 종속절에는 조동사의 과거형 would를 쓴다.

7 주절이 현재시제에서 과거시제로 바뀌었으므로 종속절도 조동사의 과거형 would를 쓴다.

8 ⑤ will → would

9 첫 번째 빈칸: 주절이 과거시제이므로 종속절에는 과거시제 was elected를 쓴다.
두 번째 빈칸: 주절이 과거시제이므로 종속절에는 조동사의 과거형을 포함한 would be를 쓴다.

10 전달동사가 과거시제이므로 종속절의 현재시제 is를 과거시제 was로 바꾼다.

11 ④ will win → would win

12 전달동사 say는 그대로 쓰고, 전달동사가 과거시제이므로 종속절의 현재형 will을 과거형 would로 바꾼다. 전달하는 사람의 입장에 맞게 인칭대명사 your를 our로 바꾸고 부사 now를 then으로 바꾼다.

13 의문사가 있는 의문문의 간접 화법은 의문사(when)로 주절과 종속절을 연결하고, 종속절을 「의문사 + 주어 + 동사」의 어순으로

쓴다. 전달동사가 과거시제이므로 종속절의 현재시제 can wear를 과거시제 could wear로 바꾼다.

14 의문사가 없는 의문문의 간접 화법은 if나 whether로 주절과 종속절을 연결하고, 전달동사가 과거시제이므로 종속절의 현재형 Can을 과거형 could로 바꾼다. 전달하는 사람의 입장에 맞게 인칭대명사 I를 he로 바꾼다.

15 첫 번째 빈칸: 주절이 과거시제이므로 종속절에는 과거시제 were를 쓴다.
두 번째 빈칸: 현재의 습관이나 반복되는 일을 나타낼 때는 주절의 시제와 상관없이 종속절에 항상 현재시제를 쓰므로 현재시제 takes를 쓴다.

16 전달동사가 과거시제이므로 종속절의 현재시제 like를 과거시제 liked로 바꾼다.

17 전달동사가 과거시제이므로 종속절의 현재시제 is를 과거시제 was로 바꾸고, 전달하는 사람의 입장에 맞게 인칭대명사 My를 his로 바꾸고 부사 today를 that day로 바꾼다.

18 주절이 과거시제이고, Jason의 여동생이 그의 컴퓨터를 고장 낸 것은 그가 알게 된 시점보다 더 이전에 발생한 일이므로 과거완료 시제 had broken his computer를 쓴다.

19 의문사가 없는 의문문의 간접 화법은 if나 whether로 주절과 종속절을 연결하고, 전달동사 say to는 ask로 바꾼다. 전달하는 사람의 입장에 맞게 인칭대명사 you를 I로 바꾸고, 전달동사가 과거시제이므로 종속절의 현재시제 Are를 과거시제 was로 바꾼다.

20 의문사가 없는 의문문의 간접 화법은 if나 whether로 주절과 종속절을 연결한다.

21 ④ one is → is one

22 (A) 전달동사가 과거시제이므로 종속절의 현재시제 aren't를 과거시제 wasn't로 바꾸고, 전달하는 사람의 입장에 맞게 부사 today를 that day로, 인칭대명사 you를 he로 바꾼다.
(B) 전달동사가 과거시제이므로 종속절의 현재시제 am을 과거시제 was로 바꾼다. 전달하는 사람의 입장에 맞게 I를 he로 바꾼다.

23 전달동사 say는 그대로 쓰고, 전달동사가 과거시제라서 종속절에 과거형 would가 쓰였으므로 현재형 will을 쓴다. Mr. Lee의 입장에 맞게 인칭대명사 he를 I로 바꾼다.

24 전달동사 say to는 ask로 바꾸고, 전달동사가 과거시제이므로 종속절의 have를 과거시제 had로 바꾼다. 전달하는 사람의 입장에 맞게 인칭대명사 you를 she로 바꾼다.

25 ⓑ is which book → which book was
ⓔ I → he

MEMO

MEMO

MEMO

기출로 적중

해커스
중학영문법

2학년

핵심만 담았다!

문법 암기리스트

+

단어 암기장

MEMO

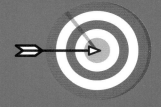

CHAPTER 1 문장의 형식

POINT 2 3형식과 4형식

4형식 문장은 동사에 따라 전치사 to/for/of 중 하나를 사용하여 3형식으로 바꿀 수 있다.

to를 쓰는 동사	give, send, bring, pass, show, teach, tell, write, read, lend, sell, pay 등	The clerk showed me a nice shirt. → The clerk showed a nice shirt to me. 그 점원은 나에게 멋진 셔츠를 보여줬다.
for를 쓰는 동사	buy, cook, find, make, get, build 등	Dad cooked us a delicious meal. → Dad cooked a delicious meal for us. 아빠는 우리에게 맛있는 식사를 요리해주셨다.
of를 쓰는 동사	ask 등	Can I ask you a favor? → Can I ask a favor of you? 내가 너에게 부탁 하나를 해도 되니?

POINT 3-1 ~ 3-4 동사

1. 명사/형용사를 목적격 보어로 쓰는 동사

동사	call	make	keep	find

2. to부정사를 목적격 보어로 쓰는 동사

동사	want	ask	tell	expect	allow	advise	order	get (준사역동사)

3. 원형부정사를 목적격 보어로 쓰는 동사

사역동사	make	have	let

4. 원형부정사/to부정사를 목적격 보어로 쓰는 동사

준사역동사	help

5. 원형부정사/V-ing형을 목적격 보어로 쓰는 동사

지각동사	see	watch	hear	listen to	smell	feel

CHAPTER 3 시제

POINT 2-2 과거시제: 동사의 과거형과 과거분사형

1. A-A-A형: 원형-과거형-과거분사형이 모두 같다.

원형	과거형	과거분사형	원형	과거형	과거분사형
cost 비용이 들다	cost	cost	hurt 다치게 하다	hurt	hurt
let ~하게 하다	let	let	read[ri:d] 읽다	read[red]	read[red]
shut 닫다	shut	shut	spread 펼치다	spread	spread

2. A-B-A형: 원형-과거분사형이 같다.

원형	과거형	과거분사형	원형	과거형	과거분사형
become ~이 되다	became	become 되다	come 오다	came	come
overcome 극복하다	overcame	overcome 극복하다	run 달리다	ran	run

3. A-B-B형: 과거형-과거분사형이 같다.

원형	과거형	과거분사형	원형	과거형	과거분사형
bring 가져오다	brought	brought	build 짓다, 만들다	built	built
feed 먹이를 주다	fed	fed	feel 느끼다	felt	felt
find 찾다	found	found	get 얻다	got	got(ten)
have 가지다	had	had	hear 듣다	heard	heard
keep 유지하다	kept	kept	lay 놓다, 눕히다	laid	laid
lead 이끌다	led	led	leave 떠나다	left	left
lose 잃다, 지다	lost	lost	make 만들다	made	made
meet 만나다	met	met	send 보내다	sent	sent
sleep 자다	slept	slept	spend 쓰다	spent	spent
think 생각하다	thought	thought	understand 이해하다	understood	understood

CHAPTER 5 수동태

POINT 7 수동태 관용 표현

be made of	~으로 만들어지다 (재료 성질이 변하지 않음)	be known to	~에게 알려져 있다
be made from	~으로 만들어지다 (재료 성질이 변함)	be known for	~으로 유명하다
be filled with	~으로 가득 차 있다	be known as	~으로 알려져 있다
be covered with	~으로 덮여 있다	be interested in	~에 흥미가 있다
be satisfied with	~에 만족하다	be surprised at	~에 놀라다
be pleased with	~에 기뻐하다	be disappointed at[by]	~에 실망하다

4. A-B-C형: 원형-과거형-과거분사형이 모두 다르다.

원형	과거형	과거분사형	원형	과거형	과거분사형
be ~이다, ~있다	was/were	been	begin 시작하다	began	begun
break 깨다	broke	broken	choose 선택하다	chose	chosen
do 하다	did	done	drive 운전하다	drove	driven
eat 먹다	ate	eaten	fall 떨어지다, 넘어지다	fell	fallen
fly 날다	flew	flown	forget 잊다	forgot	forgotten
give 주다	gave	given	go 가다	went	gone
grow 자라다	grew	grown	know 알다	knew	known
mistake 실수하다	mistook	mistaken	ride 타다	rode	ridden
ring 울리다	rang	rung	rise 오르다	rose	risen
see 보다	saw	seen	sing 노래하다	sang	sung
steal 훔치다	stole	stolen	swim 수영하다	swam	swum
take 가지고 가다	took	taken	throw 던지다	threw	thrown
wear 입고 있다	wore	worn	write 쓰다	wrote	written

CHAPTER 6 부정사

POINT 2-2 명사적 용법: to부정사를 목적어로 쓰는 동사

want	hope	wish	decide	plan	need	agree
would like	would love	expect	promise	learn	choose	refuse

POINT 2-3 명사적 용법: to부정사를 목적격 보어로 쓰는 동사

want	ask	tell	expect	allow	advise	order

CHAPTER 7 동명사

POINT 3-1 동명사를 목적어로 쓰는 동사

enjoy	finish	avoid	keep	mind	give up	imagine
stop	quit	practice	deny	suggest	put off	postpone

POINT 3-2, 3-3 동명사와 to부정사를 모두 목적어로 쓰는 동사 I, II

1. 동명사와 to부정사 둘 중 무엇을 써도 의미가 달라지지 않는 동사

like	love	hate	prefer	begin	start	continue

2. 동명사와 to부정사 둘 중 무엇을 쓰는지에 따라 의미가 달라지는 동사

forget	+ 동명사	(과거에) ~한 것을 잊다	He **forgot sending** the letter. 그는 그 편지를 보낸 것을 잊었다.
	+ to부정사	(미래에) ~할 것을 잊다	He **forgot to send** the letter. 그는 그 편지를 보낼 것을 잊었다.
remember	+ 동명사	(과거에) ~한 것을 기억하다	Do you **remember calling** him? 너는 그에게 전화한 것을 기억하니?
	+ to부정사	(미래에) ~할 것을 기억하다	Do you **remember to call** him? 너는 그에게 전화할 것을 기억하니?

POINT 4-1, 4-2 동명사 관용 표현 I, II

1. 전치사의 목적어로 동명사를 쓰는 관용 표현

be good at + V-ing ~하는 것을 잘하다	be bad at + V-ing ~하는 것을 잘 못하다
succeed in + V-ing ~하는 데 성공하다	be interested in + V-ing ~하는 것에 흥미가 있다
think of + V-ing ~할 것을 생각하다	be tired of + V-ing ~하는 것에 싫증이 나다
be afraid of + V-ing ~하는 것을 두려워하다	feel like + V-ing ~하고 싶다
thank ... for + V-ing ~에 대해 …에게 감사하다	be sorry for[about] + V-ing ~에 대해 미안해하다
be used to + V-ing ~하는 데 익숙하다	get used to + V-ing ~하는 데 익숙해지다
look forward to + V-ing ~하는 것을 기대하다	keep[prevent] ... from + V-ing …가 ~하지 못하게 하다
on + V-ing ~하자마자	by + V-ing ~함으로써

2. 동명사를 쓰는 관용 표현

go + V-ing ~하러 가다	be busy + V-ing ~하느라 바쁘다
It's no use + V-ing ~해도 소용없다	be worth + V-ing ~할 가치가 있다
spend + 돈/시간 + V-ing ~하는 데 돈/시간을 쓰다	have trouble + V-ing ~하는 데 어려움을 겪다
cannot help + V-ing ~하지 않을 수 없다 (= cannot but + 동사원형)	How[What] about + V-ing ~? ~하는 게 어때? (= What do you say to + V-ing ~?)

regret	+ to부정사	~하게 되어 유감이다	**I regret to tell you the news.** 나는 너에게 그 소식을 말하게 되어 유감이다.
	+ 동명사	~한 것을 후회하다	**I regret telling you my secret.** 나는 너에게 나의 비밀을 말했던 것을 후회한다.
try	+ to부정사	~하려고 노력하다	**Sally tried to write a fantasy novel.** Sally는 판타지 소설을 쓰려고 노력했다.
	+ 동명사	(시험 삼아) ~해보다	**Sally tried writing a fantasy novel.** Sally는 판타지 소설을 써봤다.

CHAPTER 8 분사

감정을 나타내는 분사

현재분사(~한 감정을 일으키는)		과거분사(~한 감정을 느끼는)	
surprising	놀라게 하는	surprised	놀란
amazing	놀라게 하는	amazed	놀란
worrying	걱정하게 하는	worried	걱정하는
interesting	흥미롭게 하는	interested	흥미로워하는
boring	지루하게 하는	bored	지루해하는
exciting	신이 나게 하는	excited	신이 난
pleasing	기쁘게 하는	pleased	기뻐하는
depressing	우울하게 하는	depressed	우울해하는
tiring	피곤하게 하는	tired	피곤해하는
moving	감동하게 하는	moved	감동한
touching	감동하게 하는	touched	감동한
shocking	충격을 주는	shocked	충격을 받은
confusing	혼란스럽게 하는	confused	혼란스러워하는
satisfying	만족스럽게 하는	satisfied	만족스러워하는
disappointing	실망스럽게 하는	disappointed	실망스러워하는
embarrassing	당황스럽게 하는	embarrassed	당황해하는
fascinating	황홀하게 하는	fascinated	황홀해하는

CHAPTER 10 대명사

POINT 2 재귀대명사

재귀대명사를 쓰는 관용 표현

by oneself 혼자서, 홀로
in itself 그 자체가, 본질적으로
talk to oneself 혼잣말을 하다
help oneself to ~을 마음껏 먹다

for oneself 혼자 힘으로, 스스로
enjoy oneself 즐거운 시간을 보내다
think to oneself 혼자 생각하다
make oneself at home (집에서처럼) 편히 쉬다

CHAPTER 12 부사

POINT 5 타동사 + 부사

turn on ~을 켜다	turn off ~을 끄다	put on ~을 입다/쓰다
take off ~을 벗다	try on ~을 입어보다/신어보다	pick up ~을 줍다/들어 올리다
wake up ~를 깨우다	give up ~을 포기하다/그만두다	write down ~을 적다
throw away ~을 버리다	put off ~을 미루다	hand[turn] in ~을 제출하다
find out ~을 알아내다	look up ~을 찾아보다	give back ~을 돌려주다

CHAPTER 13 비교구문

POINT 1-2 불규칙변화

원급		비교급	최상급	원급		비교급	최상급
good	좋은	better	best	many	(수가) 많은	more	most
well	건강한, 잘			much	(양이) 많은		
bad	나쁜			little	(양이) 적은	less	least
badly	나쁘게	worse	worst	late	(시간이) 늦은	later	latest
ill	아픈, 병든				(순서가) 늦은	latter	last
old	나이 든, 오래된	older	oldest	far	(거리가) 먼	farther	farthest
	연상의	elder	eldest		(정도가) 더욱	further	furthest

CHAPTER 14 전치사

| POINT 6-1, 6-2 | 전치사 관용 표현 |

1. 형용사 + 전치사

be good at ~을 잘하다
be afraid of ~을 무서워하다
be full of ~으로 가득 차 있다
be good for ~에 좋다
be famous for ~으로 유명하다
be sorry for[about] ~에 대해 미안해하다
be similar to ~과 비슷하다

be bad at ~을 못하다
be proud of ~을 자랑스러워하다
be late for ~에 늦다
be bad for ~에 나쁘다
be ready for ~에 준비가 되다
be curious about ~에 대해 호기심이 있다
be different from ~과 다르다

2. 동사 + 전치사

look at ~을 보다
wait for ~을 기다리다
laugh at ~을 보고/듣고 웃다, 비웃다
belong to ~에 속하다
run[bump] into ~와 우연히 충돌하다

look for ~을 찾다
thank … for ~에 대해 …에게 감사해하다
listen to ~을 듣다
spend 시간/돈 on ~에 돈/시간을 쓰다
take care of ~을 돌보다, ~을 잘 돌보다

CHAPTER 16 관계사

| POINT 1 | 관계대명사의 역할과 종류 |

선행사	격	주격	목적격	소유격
사람, 사물, 동물		that	that	–
사물, 동물		which	which	whose
사람		who	who(m)	whose

| POINT 7 | 관계부사 |

선행사		관계부사	「전치사 + 관계대명사」
장소	the place, the city, the house 등	where	in/on/at/to + which
시간	the time, the year, the day 등	when	in/on/at + which
이유	the reason	why	for + which
방법	the way	how	in + which

해커스북 중·고등
www.HackersBook.com

| 기출로 잡은 해커스 중학영단어 2800제

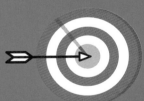

단어 외우기
학생들 단어왕기

- 단어 기억하기
- 단어 테스트

• 잘 외워지지 않는 단어는 박스에 체크하여 복습하세요.

🎧 2학년_단어암기장_CH1.mp3

☐ 1	laugh	동 웃다	☐ 31	wash the dishes		설거지를 하다
☐ 2	beautifully	부 아름답게	☐ 32	allow	동	허락하다
☐ 3	castle	명 성	☐ 33	expect	동	기대하다
☐ 4	hill	명 언덕	☐ 34	apologize	동	사과하다
☐ 5	lawyer	명 변호사	☐ 35	order	동	명령하다
☐ 6	convenient	형 편리한	☐ 36	advise	동	조언하다
☐ 7	calm	형 침착한	☐ 37	tidy	형	깔끔한
☐ 8	melt	동 녹다	☐ 38	positively	부	긍정적으로
☐ 9	dentist	명 치과의사	☐ 39	understand	동	이해하다
☐ 10	museum	명 박물관	☐ 40	promise	명	약속
☐ 11	rich	형 부유한	☐ 41	lesson	명	교훈
☐ 12	happen	동 일어나다	☐ 42	explain	동	설명하다
☐ 13	shine	동 빛나다	☐ 43	librarian	명	(도서관) 사서
☐ 14	voice	명 목소리	☐ 44	worldwide	부	전 세계적으로
☐ 15	neighbor	명 이웃	☐ 45	bark	동	짖다
☐ 16	terrible	형 끔찍한	☐ 46	shake	동	흔들리다
☐ 17	science	명 과학	☐ 47	burn	동	(불에) 타다
☐ 18	question	명 질문	☐ 48	whisper	동	귓속말하다
☐ 19	opinion	명 의견	☐ 49	landscape	명	풍경
☐ 20	finish	동 끝내다	☐ 50	fantastic	형	환상적인
☐ 21	delicious	형 맛있는	☐ 51	famous	형	유명한
☐ 22	meal	명 식사	☐ 52	laundry	명	빨래
☐ 23	journalist	명 기자	☐ 53	silent	형	조용한
☐ 24	president	명 대통령	☐ 54	confident	형	자신 있는
☐ 25	vegetable	명 채소	☐ 55	chemistry	명	화학
☐ 26	healthy	형 건강한	☐ 56	novel	명	소설
☐ 27	captain	명 주장	☐ 57	count	동	세다
☐ 28	history	명 역사	☐ 58	carefully	부	신중히
☐ 29	garden	명 정원	☐ 59	garbage	명	쓰레기
☐ 30	celebrity	명 유명 인사	☐ 60	forgive	동	용서하다

CHAPTER 2 다양한 문장의 종류

단어 테스트 p.33

• 잘 외워지지 않는 단어는 박스에 체크하여 복습하세요.　　🔊 25회 단어암기강의_CH2.mp3

☐ 1	useful	형 유용한		☐ 31	diligent	형 성실한
☐ 2	boring	형 지루한		☐ 32	turn red	빨개지다
☐ 3	trip	명 여행		☐ 33	quite	부 꽤
☐ 4	excellent	형 훌륭한		☐ 34	clever	형 영리한
☐ 5	speech	명 연설		☐ 35	advice	명 조언
☐ 6	comfortable	형 편한		☐ 36	joke	명 농담
☐ 7	wonderful	형 아주 멋진		☐ 37	forget	동 잊다
☐ 8	helpful	형 도움이 되는		☐ 38	beef	명 소고기
☐ 9	difficult	형 어려운		☐ 39	pillow	명 베개
☐ 10	exercise	동 운동하다		☐ 40	biology	명 생물학
☐ 11	quit	동 그만두다		☐ 41	land	동 착륙하다
☐ 12	machine	명 기계		☐ 42	recipe	명 조리법
☐ 13	press	동 누르다		☐ 43	different	형 다른
☐ 14	toilet	명 화장실		☐ 44	mirror	명 거울
☐ 15	information	명 정보		☐ 45	shocked	형 충격을 받은
☐ 16	airport	명 공항		☐ 46	problem	명 문제
☐ 17	culture	명 문화		☐ 47	marry	동 결혼하다
☐ 18	traditional	형 전통의		☐ 48	thief	명 도둑
☐ 19	prefer	동 선호하다		☐ 49	stripe	명 줄무늬
☐ 20	false	형 가짜의		☐ 50	celebrate	동 기념하다
☐ 21	classical	형 클래식의		☐ 51	moment	명 순간
☐ 22	visit	동 방문하다		☐ 52	answer	명 답
☐ 23	wonder	동 궁금하다		☐ 53	well-known	형 잘 알려진
☐ 24	gift	명 선물		☐ 54	plant	동 심다
☐ 25	arrive	동 도착하다		☐ 55	return	동 반납하다
☐ 26	disappear	동 사라지다		☐ 56	truth	명 사실
☐ 27	remember	동 기억하다		☐ 57	change	동 바꾸다
☐ 28	imagine	동 상상하다, 상상해보다		☐ 58	recommend	동 추천하다
☐ 29	storm	명 폭풍		☐ 59	exhibition	명 전시회
☐ 30	vacation	명 휴가		☐ 60	ancient	형 고대의

CHAPTER 3 시제

단어 테스트 p.34

• 잘 외워지지 않는 단어는 박스에 체크하여 복습하세요.

◎ 2강의_단어장1강_CH3.mp3

□ 1	weekend	명 주말	□ 31	temperature	명 기온
□ 2	boil	동 끓다	□ 32	research	명 연구
□ 3	action	명 행동	□ 33	marathon	명 마라톤
□ 4	belong to	~에 속하다	□ 34	pilot	명 조종사
□ 5	gravity	명 중력	□ 35	release	동 풀어주다, 공개하다
□ 6	company	명 회사	□ 36	fall down	동 넘어지다
□ 7	end	동 끝나다	□ 37	mistake	명 실수
□ 8	break out	동 발생하다	□ 38	cause	동 초래하다
□ 9	hold	동 개최하다	□ 39	rumor	명 소문
□ 10	sci-fi	명 공상 과학 소설	□ 40	Antarctic	명 남극 (지역)
□ 11	field trip	현장 학습	□ 41	experiment	명 실험
□ 12	medicine	명 약	□ 42	documentary	명 다큐멘터리
□ 13	fix	동 고치다	□ 43	volunteer	동 자원 봉사하다
□ 14	festival	명 축제	□ 44	sunset	명 일몰
□ 15	invite	동 초대하다	□ 45	riddle	명 수수께끼
□ 16	shut	동 닫다	□ 46	participate in	~에 참가하다
□ 17	spread	동 퍼뜨리다	□ 47	government	명 정부
□ 18	overcome	동 극복하다	□ 48	nervous	형 초조한
□ 19	feed	동 먹이를 주다	□ 49	citizen	명 시민
□ 20	steal	동 훔치다	□ 50	save	동 모으다 (돈을)
□ 21	improve	동 개선하다	□ 51	explore	동 탐험하다, 탐구하다
□ 22	invent	동 발명하다	□ 52	lately	부 최근에
□ 23	delay	동 늦추다	□ 53	publish	동 출판하다
□ 24	typhoon	명 태풍	□ 54	cover	동 덮다
□ 25	location	명 장소	□ 55	surface	명 표면
□ 26	doorbell	명 초인종	□ 56	graduate	동 졸업하다
□ 27	soldier	명 군인	□ 57	depart	동 출발하다
□ 28	argue	동 말다툼하다	□ 58	perform	동 연주하다
□ 29	appear	동 나타나다	□ 59	interesting	형 흥미로운
□ 30	recently	부 최근에	□ 60	fear	명 두려움

CHAPTER 4 조동사

단어 테스트 p.35

• 꼭 외워지지 않는 단어는 박스에 체크하여 복습하세요.

🔊 2권료_단어암기장_CH4.mp3

☐ 1 **cancel**	동 취소하다	☐ 31 **actively** 부 적극적으로
☐ 2 **reservation**	명 예약	☐ 32 **rude** 형 무례한
☐ 3 **recycle**	동 재활용하다	☐ 33 **fall asleep** 잠들다
☐ 4 **language**	명 언어	☐ 34 **crowded** 형 붐비는
☐ 5 **fluently**	부 유창하게	☐ 35 **lottery** 명 복권
☐ 6 **space**	명 우주	☐ 36 **peel** 동 껍질을 벗기다
☐ 7 **survive**	동 살아남다	☐ 37 **breath** 명 숨
☐ 8 **solve**	동 해결하다	☐ 38 **vegetarian** 명 채식주의자
☐ 9 **without**	전 ~없이	☐ 39 **gently** 부 부드럽게
☐ 10 **whole**	형 전체의	☐ 40 **temple** 명 사원, 절
☐ 11 **regularly**	부 규칙적으로	☐ 41 **exhausted** 형 탈진한
☐ 12 **agree**	동 동의하다	☐ 42 **sour** 형 (맛이) 신
☐ 13 **passport**	명 여권	☐ 43 **headache** 명 두통
☐ 14 **hallway**	명 복도	☐ 44 **sign** 명 신호
☐ 15 **skip**	동 거르다	☐ 45 **careful** 형 조심하는
☐ 16 **correct**	형 옳은	☐ 46 **take off** 동 이륙하다
☐ 17 **allergic**	형 알레르기가 있는	☐ 47 **eyesight** 명 시력
☐ 18 **ceremony**	명 의식	☐ 48 **floor** 명 바닥
☐ 19 **reserve**	동 예약하다	☐ 49 **yellow dust** 황사
☐ 20 **lie**	동 거짓말하다	☐ 50 **decision** 명 결정
☐ 21 **loudly**	부 큰 소리로	☐ 51 **gorgeous** 형 아름다운
☐ 22 **cactus**	명 선인장	☐ 52 **beverage** 명 음료
☐ 23 **avoid**	동 피하다	☐ 53 **fasten** 동 매다
☐ 24 **environment**	명 환경	☐ 54 **send** 동 보내다
☐ 25 **harmful**	형 해로운	☐ 55 **noisy** 형 시끄러운
☐ 26 **respect**	동 존중하다	☐ 56 **safe** 형 안전한
☐ 27 **trash**	명 쓰레기	☐ 57 **popular** 형 인기 있는
☐ 28 **responsibility**	명 책임	☐ 58 **sharp** 형 날카로운
☐ 29 **fee**	명 요금	☐ 59 **claw** 명 발톱
☐ 30 **discussion**	명 토론	☐ 60 **prize** 명 상

CHAPTER 5 수능탑

단어 테스트 p.36

• 잘 외워지지 않는 단어는 박스에 체크하여 복습하세요.

음원 단어암기장_CH5.mp3

☐ 1 organic	형 유기농의		☐ 31 satisfied	형 만족하는
☐ 2 repair	동 수리하다		☐ 32 disappointed	형 실망한
☐ 3 raise	동 기르다		☐ 33 cabinet	명 수납장
☐ 4 discover	동 발견하다		☐ 34 physics	명 물리학
☐ 5 wooden	형 나무로 된		☐ 35 foreign	형 외국의
☐ 6 sentence	명 문장		☐ 36 mud	명 진흙
☐ 7 tourist	명 관광객		☐ 37 flight	명 항공편
☐ 8 produce	동 생산하다		☐ 38 tradition	명 전통
☐ 9 teenager	명 10대		☐ 39 slice	동 (얇게) 썰다
☐ 10 poem	명 시		☐ 40 damage	동 훼손하다
☐ 11 shrimp	명 새우		☐ 41 flu	명 독감
☐ 12 reason	명 이유		☐ 42 sneeze	동 재채기하다
☐ 13 pick	동 뽑다, 고르다		☐ 43 groceries	명 식료품
☐ 14 class president	반장		☐ 44 lend	동 빌려주다
☐ 15 rob	동 도둑질하다		☐ 45 traveler	명 여행자
☐ 16 decorate	동 꾸미다		☐ 46 purchase	동 구매하다
☐ 17 practice	동 연습하다		☐ 47 customer	명 고객
☐ 18 bite	동 물다		☐ 48 greet	동 환영하다
☐ 19 bracelet	명 팔찌		☐ 49 provide	동 제공하다
☐ 20 telephone	명 전화기		☐ 50 deliver	동 배달하다
☐ 21 extra	형 여분의		☐ 51 restroom	명 화장실
☐ 22 predict	동 예측하다		☐ 52 cartoon	명 만화
☐ 23 hunt	동 사냥하다		☐ 53 create	동 만들다
☐ 24 newspaper	명 신문		☐ 54 chop	동 다지다
☐ 25 mayor	명 시장		☐ 55 election	명 선거
☐ 26 reporter	명 기자		☐ 56 treat	동 다루다
☐ 27 award	명 상		☐ 57 unique	형 독특한
☐ 28 favor	명 호의		☐ 58 talent	명 재능
☐ 29 elect	동 선출하다		☐ 59 audience	명 청중
☐ 30 leader	명 대표		☐ 60 tomb	명 무덤

☐ 1 **waste** 동 낭비하다
☐ 2 **secret** 명 비밀
☐ 3 **enough** 형 충분한
☐ 4 **important** 형 중요한
☐ 5 **achieve** 동 달성하다
☐ 6 **manage** 동 운영하다, 관리하다
☐ 7 **confusing** 형 혼란스러운
☐ 8 **necessary** 형 필수적인
☐ 9 **climb** 동 오르다
☐ 10 **impossible** 형 불가능한
☐ 11 **artist** 명 화가, 예술가
☐ 12 **protect** 동 보호하다
☐ 13 **refuse** 동 거절하다
☐ 14 **giraffe** 명 기린
☐ 15 **rush hour** 명 혼잡 시간대
☐ 16 **escape** 동 달아나다
☐ 17 **volume** 명 음량
☐ 18 **come up with** ~을 생각해내다
☐ 19 **suitcase** 명 여행 가방
☐ 20 **show** 동 보여주다
☐ 21 **rest** 동 쉬다
☐ 22 **season** 명 계절
☐ 23 **weekday** 명 평일
☐ 24 **tourist site** 관광지
☐ 25 **topic** 명 주제
☐ 26 **activity** 명 활동
☐ 27 **excited** 형 신이 난
☐ 28 **honest** 형 정직한
☐ 29 **foolish** 형 어리석은
☐ 30 **trust** 동 믿다

☐ 31 **bank account** 명 은행 계좌
☐ 32 **scream** 동 소리 지르다
☐ 33 **careless** 형 부주의한
☐ 34 **selfish** 형 이기적인
☐ 35 **grammar** 명 문법
☐ 36 **rule** 명 규칙
☐ 37 **ceiling** 명 천장
☐ 38 **concentrate** 동 집중하다
☐ 39 **curry** 명 카레
☐ 40 **ill** 형 아픈
☐ 41 **throw a party** 파티를 열다
☐ 42 **sleepy** 형 졸린
☐ 43 **competition** 명 경기
☐ 44 **knock** 동 문을 두드리다
☐ 45 **earthquake** 명 지진
☐ 46 **photograph** 명 사진
☐ 47 **shout** 동 소리치다
☐ 48 **astronaut** 명 우주비행사
☐ 49 **empty** 형 빈
☐ 50 **mushroom** 명 버섯
☐ 51 **shooting star** 명 별똥별
☐ 52 **communicate** 동 의사소통하다
☐ 53 **trunk** 명 (코끼리의) 코
☐ 54 **generous** 형 관대한
☐ 55 **alien** 명 외계인
☐ 56 **miracle** 명 기적
☐ 57 **receive** 동 받다
☐ 58 **attack** 동 공격하다
☐ 59 **poisonous** 형 독이 있는
☐ 60 **jealous** 형 질투하는

• 잘 외워지지 않는 단어는 박스에 체크하여 복습하세요.

🎧 2혜료 단어암기장_CH6.mp3

CHAPTER 6 누적시사

CHAPTER 7 동의어

단어 테스트 p.38

• 잘 외워지지 않는 단어는 박스에 체크하여 복습하세요.

🔊 2권 단어암기장_CH7.mp3

□	1	regret	동 후회하다
□	2	dig	동 파다
□	3	collect	동 모으다
□	4	habit	명 습관
□	5	favorite	형 가장 좋아하는
□	6	goal	명 목표
□	7	hide	동 숨기다
□	8	deny	동 부인하다
□	9	put off	미루다
□	10	finally	부 마침내
□	11	country	명 나라
□	12	scenery	명 풍경
□	13	develop	동 개발하다
□	14	suggest	동 제안하다
□	15	postpone	동 미루다
□	16	turn off	~을 끄다
□	17	continue	동 계속하다
□	18	each other	서로
□	19	wait in line	줄 서서 기다리다
□	20	accident	명 사고
□	21	calm	동 진정시키다
□	22	bicycle	명 자전거
□	23	present	명 선물
□	24	look forward to	~을 기대하다
□	25	take care of	~을 돌보다
□	26	farm	명 농장
□	27	focus	동 집중하다
□	28	prevent	동 ~가 못 하게 하다
□	29	succeed	동 성공하다
□	30	telescope	명 망원경
□	31	get used to	~에 익숙해지다
□	32	mystery	명 수수께끼
□	33	perfect	형 완벽한
□	34	courage	명 용기
□	35	costume	명 의상
□	36	nap	명 낮잠
□	37	scary	형 무서운
□	38	relax	동 휴식을 취하다
□	39	electricity	명 전기
□	40	fair	부 공정하게
□	41	technology	명 기술
□	42	dangerous	형 위험한
□	43	behavior	명 행동
□	44	search	동 검색하다
□	45	exist	동 존재하다
□	46	lose	동 잃어버리다
□	47	nail	명 손톱
□	48	record	동 기록하다
□	49	remind	동 상기시키다
□	50	reduce	동 줄이다
□	51	edit	동 편집하다
□	52	magazine	명 잡지
□	53	article	명 기사
□	54	complaint	명 불평
□	55	success	명 성공
□	56	inconvenient	형 불편한
□	57	aquarium	명 수족관
□	58	thrilling	형 짜릿한, 아주 신나는
□	59	put out	(불을) 끄다
□	60	require	동 필요로 하다

• 잘 안외워지지 않는 단어는 박스에 체크하여 복습하세요.

2천사_단어기강_CH8.mp3

□ 1 build	통 짓다	□ 31 report	명 보고서
□ 2 human	명 인간의	□ 32 sweat	통 땀을 흘리다
□ 3 brain	명 뇌	□ 33 ankle	명 발목
□ 4 get out of	~에서 나가다	□ 34 observe	통 관찰하다
□ 5 artwork	명 예술작품	□ 35 parrot	명 앵무새
□ 6 frozen	형 언	□ 36 especially	부 특히
□ 7 peaceful	형 평화로운	□ 37 effect	명 효과
□ 8 purse	명 지갑	□ 38 musical	명 뮤지컬
□ 9 rise	통 뜨다 (해가)	□ 39 cage	명 새장, 우리
□ 10 midnight	명 자정	□ 40 take out	통 꺼내다
□ 11 fill	통 채우다	□ 41 plate	명 접시
□ 12 depressing	형 우울하게 하는	□ 42 talented	형 재능이 있는
□ 13 painting	명 그림	□ 43 price	명 가격
□ 14 amazing	형 놀라운	□ 44 experience	명 경험
□ 15 grade	명 성적	□ 45 sculpture	명 조각
□ 16 fascinating	형 흥미로운, 대단히	□ 46 strange	형 이상한
□ 17 principal	명 교장	□ 47 out of order	고장 난
□ 18 journey	명 여정	□ 48 offer	통 제안하다
□ 19 embarrassing	형 당황스러운	□ 49 rare	형 희귀한
□ 20 performance	명 공연	□ 50 coin	명 동전
□ 21 direction	명 방향	□ 51 package	명 소포
□ 22 architect	명 건축가	□ 52 wild	형 야생
□ 23 forward	부 앞으로	□ 53 crime	명 범죄
□ 24 yell	통 소리치다	□ 54 decrease	통 감소하다
□ 25 dive into	~로 뛰어들다	□ 55 wisely	부 현명하게
□ 26 scared	형 무서워하는	□ 56 thirsty	형 목마른
□ 27 hospital	명 병원	□ 57 worth	형 ~할 가치가 있는
□ 28 face	통 ~을 향하다	□ 58 complete	통 완료하다
□ 29 take a bath	목욕하다	□ 59 injure	통 다치게 하다
□ 30 slip	통 미끄러지다	□ 60 realize	통 깨닫다

CHAPTER 9 명사와 관사

단어 테스트 p.40

• 잘 외워지지 않는 단어는 박스에 체크하여 복습하세요.　🎧 2분 단어암기장_CH9.mp3

☐ 1 consist of	~으로 이루어지다	
☐ 2 oxygen	몡 산소	
☐ 3 jar	몡 병	
☐ 4 dictionary	몡 사전	
☐ 5 question	몡 질문	
☐ 6 climb	통 오르다	
☐ 7 neighborhood	몡 동네	
☐ 8 fox	몡 여우	
☐ 9 salmon	몡 연어	
☐ 10 memory	몡 기억	
☐ 11 roof	몡 지붕	
☐ 12 cliff	몡 절벽	
☐ 13 on sale	할인 중인	
☐ 14 public	몡 공공의	
☐ 15 autumn	몡 가을	
☐ 16 run away	통 도망치다	
☐ 17 university	몡 대학	
☐ 18 address	몡 주소	
☐ 19 pot	몡 냄비	
☐ 20 weigh	통 무게가 나가다	
☐ 21 furniture	몡 가구	
☐ 22 hang	통 걸리다	
☐ 23 fireplace	몡 벽난로	
☐ 24 donate	통 기부하다	
☐ 25 drawer	몡 서랍	
☐ 26 fact	몡 사실	
☐ 27 climate	몡 기후	
☐ 28 announcement	몡 발표	
☐ 29 tail	몡 꼬리	
☐ 30 distance	몡 거리	

☐ 31 flag	몡 깃발	
☐ 32 uniform	몡 교복	
☐ 33 title	몡 제목	
☐ 34 owl	몡 부엉이	
☐ 35 active	혱 활동적인	
☐ 36 eat out	통 외식하다	
☐ 37 creature	몡 생명체	
☐ 38 hole	몡 구멍	
☐ 39 planet	몡 행성	
☐ 40 person	몡 사람	
☐ 41 had better	~하는 것이 낫다	
☐ 42 be known for	~으로 유명하다	
☐ 43 subject	몡 과목	
☐ 44 universe	몡 우주	
☐ 45 pond	몡 연못	
☐ 46 church	몡 교회	
☐ 47 amusement park	몡 놀이공원	
☐ 48 luck	몡 행운	
☐ 49 trail	몡 오솔길	
☐ 50 shape	몡 모양	
☐ 51 proud	혱 자랑스러운	
☐ 52 knowledge	몡 지식	
☐ 53 refrigerator	몡 냉장고	
☐ 54 order	통 주문하다	
☐ 55 unusual	혱 특이한	
☐ 56 tourist	몡 관광객	
☐ 57 prepare	통 준비하다	
☐ 58 field	몡 들판	
☐ 59 clue	몡 단서	
☐ 60 dust	몡 먼지	

CHAPTER 10 대명사

단어 테스트 p.41

• 잘 외워지지 않는 단어는 박스에 체크하여 복습하세요.

🎧 정답 단어암기장_CH10.mp3

☐ 1	stand	동 참다		☐ 31	appearance	명 외관
☐ 2	semester	명 학기		☐ 32	flour	명 밀가루
☐ 3	skill	명 기술		☐ 33	through	전 ~을 통해
☐ 4	population	명 인구		☐ 34	example	명 사례
☐ 5	laptop	명 노트북		☐ 35	snack	명 간식
☐ 6	shiny	형 반짝거리는		☐ 36	for free	무료로
☐ 7	introduce	동 소개하다		☐ 37	ingredient	명 재료
☐ 8	bookshelf	명 책꽂이		☐ 38	personality	명 성격
☐ 9	clothes	명 옷		☐ 39	turn in	동 ~을 제출하다
☐ 10	impressive	형 인상적인		☐ 40	smoothly	부 순조롭게
☐ 11	business	명 사업		☐ 41	final	형 최종의
☐ 12	homeroom teacher	명 담임선생님		☐ 42	match	명 경기
☐ 13	building	명 건물		☐ 43	pull	동 끌어당기다
☐ 14	author	명 작가		☐ 44	spill	동 쏟다
☐ 15	expensive	형 비싼		☐ 45	crop	명 작물
☐ 16	idea	명 생각		☐ 46	athlete	명 선수
☐ 17	password	명 비밀번호		☐ 47	attention	명 관심
☐ 18	destroy	동 파괴하다		☐ 48	genre	명 장르
☐ 19	scientific	형 과학적인		☐ 49	book	동 예약하다
☐ 20	riverside	명 강변		☐ 50	express	동 표현하다
☐ 21	along	전 ~을 따라		☐ 51	theater	명 극장
☐ 22	certain	형 확실한		☐ 52	basket	명 바구니
☐ 23	gold	명 금		☐ 53	totally	부 완전히
☐ 24	mark	동 표시하다		☐ 54	bright	형 밝은 •
☐ 25	fault	명 잘못		☐ 55	blame	동 ~을 탓하다
☐ 26	obey	동 지키다, 따르다		☐ 56	official	형 공식의
☐ 27	law	명 법		☐ 57	uncomfortable	형 불편한
☐ 28	plan	동 계획하다		☐ 58	balloon	명 풍선
☐ 29	sell	동 팔다		☐ 59	earth	명 지구
☐ 30	judge	동 판단하다		☐ 60	number	명 번호

CHAPTER 11 영영사

단어 테스트 p.42

• 잘 외워지지 않는 단어는 박스에 체크하여 복습하세요.　🎧 2교시 단어암기장_CH11.mp3

☐ 1 asleep	형 잠든	☐ 31 firefighter	명 소방관
☐ 2 alive	형 살아있는	☐ 32 month	명 개월, 달
☐ 3 alike	형 비슷한	☐ 33 guidebook	명 안내서
☐ 4 glad	형 기쁜	☐ 34 require	동 요구하다
☐ 5 pleased	형 기쁜	☐ 35 patience	명 인내
☐ 6 stone	명 돌	☐ 36 peace	명 평화
☐ 7 diamond	명 다이아몬드	☐ 37 a number of	많은
☐ 8 octopus	명 문어	☐ 38 fight	동 싸우다
☐ 9 familiar	형 친숙한	☐ 39 mentor	명 멘토
☐ 10 abroad	부 외국으로	☐ 40 desert	명 사막
☐ 11 sticky	형 끈적한	☐ 41 vaccine	명 백신
☐ 12 tax	명 세금	☐ 42 spaceship	명 우주선
☐ 13 blind	형 눈이 먼	☐ 43 successfully	부 성공적으로
☐ 14 poor	형 가난한	☐ 44 chase	동 쫓다
☐ 15 charity	명 자선단체	☐ 45 decay	동 썩다
☐ 16 positive	형 긍정적인	☐ 46 credit card	명 신용카드
☐ 17 homeless	형 노숙자의	☐ 47 towel	명 수건
☐ 18 pocket	명 주머니	☐ 48 subtitle	명 자막
☐ 19 daughter	명 딸	☐ 49 foreigner	명 외국인
☐ 20 guest	명 손님	☐ 50 stomachache	명 복통
☐ 21 ancient	형 고대의	☐ 51 interested	형 흥미가 있는
☐ 22 heavy	형 무거운	☐ 52 creative	형 창의적인
☐ 23 bowl	명 그릇	☐ 53 pollute	동 오염시키다
☐ 24 deaf	형 귀가 먼	☐ 54 notice	동 알아차리다
☐ 25 communicate	동 의사소통하다	☐ 55 jellyfish	명 해파리
☐ 26 disabled	형 장애를 가진	☐ 56 bone	명 뼈
☐ 27 support	명 지원	☐ 57 immediately	부 즉시
☐ 28 date	명 날짜	☐ 58 hen	명 암탉
☐ 29 various	형 다양한	☐ 59 heat	동 가열하다
☐ 30 plenty of	많은	☐ 60 gather	동 모이다

• 잘 외워지지 않는 단어는 박스에 체크하여 복습하세요.

🎧 2학년_단어암기장_CH12.mp3

□	1	section	명	구역	□	31	write down	동	~을 적다
□	2	extremely	부	매우	□	32	inside	부	안으로
□	3	decision	명	결정	□	33	document	명	문서
□	4	championship	명	선수권 대회	□	34	textbook	명	교과서
□	5	completely	부	완전히	□	35	salty	형	짠
□	6	dull	형	지루한	□	36	statue	명	조각상
□	7	basic	형	기본적인	□	37	diligent	형	부지런한
□	8	energetic	형	활기찬	□	38	crime	명	범죄
□	9	clap	동	손뼉을 치다	□	39	increase	동	증가하다
□	10	costly	형	값비싼	□	40	city	명	도시
□	11	serious	형	심각한	□	41	hastily	부	성급하게
□	12	simple	형	간단한	□	42	citizen	명	시민
□	13	responsible	형	책임감 있는	□	43	vitamin	명	비타민
□	14	quiet	형	조용한	□	44	prevent	동	예방하다
□	15	horrible	형	끔찍한	□	45	space	명	우주
□	16	sincere	형	진실한	□	46	keep in touch		연락하다
□	17	observe	동	관찰하다	□	47	journalist	명	기자
□	18	remember	동	기억하다	□	48	recognize	동	알아보다
□	19	gym	명	체육관	□	49	polite	형	공손한
□	20	travel	동	여행하다	□	50	effective	형	효과적인
□	21	modern	형	현대의	□	51	check	동	검사하다
□	22	lightning	명	번개	□	52	spill	동	쏟다
□	23	upset	형	속상한	□	53	apply	동	신청하다
□	24	package	명	소포	□	54	ladder	명	사다리
□	25	vote	동	투표하다	□	55	reach	동	~에 닿다
□	26	raw	형	날것의	□	56	explore	동	탐험하다
□	27	riddle	명	수수께끼	□	57	enormously	부	엄청나게
□	28	peanut	명	땅콩	□	58	quickly	부	빠르게
□	29	find out	동	~을 알아내다	□	59	jog	동	조깅하다
□	30	give back	동	~을 돌려주다	□	60	nowadays	부	요즘에는

CHAPTER 13 비교급

단어 테스트 p.44

• 잘 외워지지 않는 단어는 박스에 체크하여 복습하세요.

🎧 2번씩 단어암기장_CH13.mp3

□	1	lazy	형	게으른
□	2	thin	형	얇은
□	3	young	형	젊은
□	4	cheap	형	싼
□	5	wide	형	넓은
□	6	useless	형	쓸모없는
□	7	pillow	명	베개
□	8	dry	형	마른
□	9	feather	명	깃털
□	10	strawberry	명	딸기
□	11	polite	형	예의 바른
□	12	temperature	명	기온
□	13	complete	동	완성하다
□	14	visitor	명	방문객
□	15	return	동	돌아오다
□	16	height	명	키
□	17	Jupiter	명	목성
□	18	thick	형	두꺼운
□	19	earthworm	명	지렁이
□	20	normally	부	보통
□	21	family	명	가족
□	22	tight	형	꽉 끼는
□	23	airplane	명	비행기
□	24	ocean	명	바다
□	25	become	동	~해지다
□	26	customer	명	손님
□	27	weather	명	날씨
□	28	gloomy	형	우울한
□	29	actor	명	배우
□	30	invite	동	초대하다
□	31	volleyball	명	배구
□	32	game	명	경기
□	33	artificial	형	인공적인
□	34	intelligence	명	지능
□	35	blow	동	(바람이) 불다
□	36	kite	명	연
□	37	yard	명	마당
□	38	flea	명	벼룩
□	39	closet	명	옷장
□	40	town	명	마을
□	41	life	명	삶
□	42	colorful	형	형형색색한
□	43	spring	명	봄
□	44	gallery	명	미술관
□	45	live	동	살다
□	46	common	형	흔한
□	47	orchestra	명	오케스트라
□	48	solar system	명	태양계
□	49	mysterious	형	불가사의한
□	50	raindrop	명	빗방울
□	51	confused	형	혼란스러운
□	52	dolphin	명	돌고래
□	53	invention	명	발명품
□	54	eco-friendly	형	환경친화적인
□	55	means	명	수단
□	56	transportation	명	교통
□	57	pollution	명	오염
□	58	reply	동	응답하다
□	59	luxurious	형	호화스러운
□	60	scene	명	장면

• 잘 외워지지 않는 단어는 박스에 체크하여 복습하세요.

🎧 2학년_단어암기장_CH14.mp3

☐	1	exhibition	명 전시회	☐	31	beard	명 수염
☐	2	ticket	명 티켓, 표	☐	32	cash	명 현금
☐	3	cave	명 동굴	☐	33	spinach	명 시금치
☐	4	awake	형 깨어 있는	☐	34	stick	동 붙이다
☐	5	cross	동 건너다	☐	35	enter	동 들어가다
☐	6	bake	동 굽다	☐	36	angel	명 천사
☐	7	discount	명 할인	☐	37	curious	형 호기심 있는
☐	8	for a while	잠시 동안	☐	38	site	명 장소
☐	9	evening	명 저녁	☐	39	similar	형 비슷한
☐	10	heat up	데우다	☐	40	run into	~를 우연히 만나다
☐	11	electronic	형 전자의	☐	41	silly	형 유치한
☐	12	owner	명 주인	☐	42	detective	명 탐정
☐	13	grass	명 잔디	☐	43	evidence	명 증거
☐	14	map	명 지도	☐	44	silence	명 조용함
☐	15	magnet	명 자석	☐	45	complain	동 불평하다
☐	16	share	동 나누다	☐	46	bookstore	명 서점
☐	17	lizard	명 도마뱀	☐	47	come up	동 다가오다
☐	18	danger	명 위험	☐	48	pharmacy	명 약국
☐	19	criminal	명 범죄자	☐	49	separate	동 구분하다
☐	20	prison	명 감옥	☐	50	independence	명 독립
☐	21	cloud	명 구름	☐	51	sail	동 나아가다, 항해하다
☐	22	stove	명 스토브, 가스레인지	☐	52	swing	명 그네
☐	23	walnut	명 호두	☐	53	path	명 길
☐	24	instant	형 인스턴트의, 즉각적인	☐	54	wizard	명 마법사
☐	25	police station	명 경찰서	☐	55	traffic	명 교통
☐	26	campfire	명 모닥불	☐	56	forest	명 숲
☐	27	tunnel	명 터널	☐	57	attract	동 끌어 모으다
☐	28	street	명 길, 거리	☐	58	remove	동 없애다
☐	29	magician	명 마술사	☐	59	bury	동 (땅속에) 묻다
☐	30	dawn	명 새벽	☐	60	seafood	명 해산물

CHAPTER 15 단어퀴즈

단어 테스트 p.46

• 잘 외워지지 않는 단어는 박스에 체크하여 복습하세요.

🎧 2교시_단어암기장_CH15.mp3

☐ 1 surf	통 서핑하다	
☐ 2 catch a cold	감기에 걸리다	
☐ 3 watch out	통 조심하다	
☐ 4 expand	통 팽창하다	
☐ 5 sculptor	명 조각가	
☐ 6 muddy	형 진흙의	
☐ 7 brush	명 붓	
☐ 8 sore throat	명 인후통	
☐ 9 true	형 사실인	
☐ 10 genius	명 천재	
☐ 11 health	명 건강	
☐ 12 director	명 감독	
☐ 13 luggage	명 짐	
☐ 14 join	통 가입하다	
☐ 15 seat	명 좌석	
☐ 16 as soon as	~하자마자	
☐ 17 metal	명 금속	
☐ 18 surgery	명 수술	
☐ 19 kindergarten	명 유치원	
☐ 20 pour	통 붓다	
☐ 21 angry	형 화난	
☐ 22 twice	부 두 번	
☐ 23 loud	형 큰 (소리가)	
☐ 24 glacier	명 빙하	
☐ 25 global warming	명 지구 온난화	
☐ 26 latest	형 최신의	
☐ 27 scold	통 혼내다	
☐ 28 charge	통 충전하다	
☐ 29 later	부 나중에	
☐ 30 habitat	명 서식지	

☐ 31 refund	명 환불	
☐ 32 receipt	명 영수증	
☐ 33 autograph	명 사인	
☐ 34 mix	통 섞다	
☐ 35 despite	전 ~에도 불구하고	
☐ 36 twin	명 쌍둥이	
☐ 37 install	통 설치하다	
☐ 38 wise	형 현명한	
☐ 39 impatient	형 못 참는	
☐ 40 cough	명 기침	
☐ 41 review	통 복습하다	
☐ 42 lift	통 들다	
☐ 43 directly	부 직접	
☐ 44 guess	통 ~라고 짐작하다, 추측하다	
☐ 45 crow	명 까마귀	
☐ 46 branch	명 나뭇가지	
☐ 47 bring	통 가져오다	
☐ 48 symbol	명 상징	
☐ 49 view	명 경치	
☐ 50 wrong	형 잘못된	
☐ 51 trouble	명 곤란, 문제	
☐ 52 coast	명 해안	
☐ 53 mess	명 엉망진창	
☐ 54 farming	명 농사	
☐ 55 jewelry	명 보석	
☐ 56 lock	통 잠그다	
☐ 57 national	형 국가의	
☐ 58 furious	형 격분한	
☐ 59 manner	명 예의	
☐ 60 east	명 동쪽	

CHAPTER 16 관계사

단어 테스트 p.47

• 잘 외워지지 않는 단어는 박스에 체크하여 복습하세요.

🎧 2학년_단어암기장_CH16.mp3

☐	1	postcard	명 엽서	☐	31	same	형 같은

☐ 1 postcard 명 엽서

☐ 2 handle 명 손잡이

☐ 3 destroy 동 무너뜨리다

☐ 4 deliver 동 배달하다

☐ 5 trophy 명 트로피

☐ 6 retire 동 은퇴하다

☐ 7 poet 명 시인

☐ 8 trust 동 믿다

☐ 9 scientist 명 과학자

☐ 10 plastic 명 플라스틱

☐ 11 printer 명 프린터

☐ 12 discover 동 발견하다

☐ 13 subway 명 지하철

☐ 14 hair 명 털

☐ 15 teen 명 십 대

☐ 16 score 명 점수

☐ 17 battery 명 배터리

☐ 18 admire 동 존경하다

☐ 19 politician 명 정치가

☐ 20 purchase 동 사다

☐ 21 be full of ~으로 가득 차다

☐ 22 park 동 주차하다

☐ 23 road 명 길

☐ 24 move 동 감동하게 하다

☐ 25 depend on ~에 의지하다

☐ 26 patient 명 환자

☐ 27 wave 동 (손·팔을) 흔들다

☐ 28 market 명 시장

☐ 29 piece 명 조각

☐ 30 request 동 신청하다

☐ 31 same 형 같은

☐ 32 vase 명 꽃병

☐ 33 hand in 동 제출하다

☐ 34 joke 명 농담

☐ 35 celebrity 명 유명 인사

☐ 36 reason 명 이유

☐ 37 explain 동 설명하다

☐ 38 spend 동 (시간을) 보내다

☐ 39 turn into ~으로 바뀌다

☐ 40 region 명 지역

☐ 41 film 동 촬영하다

☐ 42 carrot 명 당근

☐ 43 say 동 말하다

☐ 44 ignore 동 무시하다

☐ 45 gentle 형 순한

☐ 46 passenger 명 승객

☐ 47 skillful 형 숙련된

☐ 48 incredible 형 놀랄 만한

☐ 49 drop 동 떨어뜨리다

☐ 50 gather 동 모으다

☐ 51 honey 명 꿀

☐ 52 advice 명 조언

☐ 53 fever 명 열

☐ 54 potato 명 감자

☐ 55 bloom 동 (꽃이) 피다

☐ 56 prince 명 왕자

☐ 57 police 명 경찰

☐ 58 composer 명 작곡가

☐ 59 author 명 작가

☐ 60 shop 동 쇼핑하다

CHAPTER 17 가장친

단어 테스트 p.48

• 잘 외워지지 않는 단어는 박스에 체크하여 복습하세요.   🎧 교재 단어암기장_CH17.mp3

☐ 1 **often**	부 자주	
☐ 2 **free**	형 한가한	
☐ 3 **drive**	동 운전하다	
☐ 4 **lottery**	명 복권	
☐ 5 **conversation**	명 대화	
☐ 6 **shy**	형 수줍음이 많은	
☐ 7 **stranger**	명 낯선 사람	
☐ 8 **lonely**	형 외로운	
☐ 9 **chilly**	형 추운	
☐ 10 **sold out**	매진된	
☐ 11 **disappointed**	형 실망한	
☐ 12 **river**	명 강	
☐ 13 **miss**	동 놓치다	
☐ 14 **sunrise**	명 일출	
☐ 15 **slippery**	형 미끄러운	
☐ 16 **clean**	동 청소하다	
☐ 17 **millionaire**	명 백만장자	
☐ 18 **rainbow**	명 무지개	
☐ 19 **depressed**	형 우울한	
☐ 20 **camping**	명 캠핑, 야영	
☐ 21 **water**	동 (식물 등에) 물을 주다	
☐ 22 **decide**	동 결정하다	
☐ 23 **lend**	동 빌려주다	
☐ 24 **in fact**	사실은	
☐ 25 **boring**	형 지루한	
☐ 26 **yesterday**	부 어제	
☐ 27 **rain forest**	명 열대 우림	
☐ 28 **appear**	동 ~처럼 보이다	
☐ 29 **test**	명 시험	
☐ 30 **foot**	명 발	
☐ 31 **someday**	부 언젠가	
☐ 32 **play**	명 연극	
☐ 33 **show**	동 보여주다	
☐ 34 **garden**	명 정원	
☐ 35 **costume**	명 의상	
☐ 36 **agree**	동 동의하다	
☐ 37 **rumor**	명 소문	
☐ 38 **unfortunately**	부 불행하게도	
☐ 39 **read**	동 읽다	
☐ 40 **favorite**	형 가장 좋아하는	
☐ 41 **own**	형 자기 자신의, 소유하다	
☐ 42 **race**	명 경주	
☐ 43 **leave**	동 떠나다	
☐ 44 **soon**	부 곧	
☐ 45 **spider**	명 거미	
☐ 46 **insect**	명 곤충	
☐ 47 **ghost**	명 유령	
☐ 48 **on time**	정각에	
☐ 49 **spicy**	형 매운	
☐ 50 **practice**	동 연습하다	
☐ 51 **stage**	명 무대	
☐ 52 **perform**	동 공연하다	
☐ 53 **Chinese**	명 중국어	
☐ 54 **learn**	동 배우다	
☐ 55 **take a shower**	샤워하다	
☐ 56 **from now on**	이제부터	
☐ 57 **behave**	동 행동하다	
☐ 58 **adult**	명 성인, 어른	
☐ 59 **emergency**	명 비상 상황	
☐ 60 **reservation**	명 예약	

• 잘 외워지지 않는 단어는 박스에 체크하여 복습하세요.

🎧 2학년_단어암기장_CH18.mp3

☐ 1 **realize**	동 깨닫다	☐ 31 **teach**	동 가르치다
☐ 2 **apologize**	동 사과하다	☐ 32 **together**	부 함께
☐ 3 **noise**	명 소음	☐ 33 **taste**	동 맛이 ~하다
☐ 4 **upstairs**	명 위층	☐ 34 **a little**	약간
☐ 5 **speaker**	명 발표자	☐ 35 **speak**	동 말하다, 이야기하다
☐ 6 **tour**	명 관광	☐ 36 **mall**	명 쇼핑몰
☐ 7 **guide**	명 가이드, 안내인	☐ 37 **picture**	명 사진
☐ 8 **traditional**	형 전통적인	☐ 38 **among**	전 ~ 사이에
☐ 9 **haste**	명 서두름	☐ 39 **cabin**	명 오두막
☐ 10 **knowledge**	명 지식	☐ 40 **ambulance**	명 구급차
☐ 11 **light**	명 빛	☐ 41 **fence**	명 울타리
☐ 12 **travel**	동 이동하다	☐ 42 **dirty**	형 더러운
☐ 13 **capital**	명 수도	☐ 43 **wonder**	동 궁금하다
☐ 14 **industrial**	형 산업의	☐ 44 **proud**	형 자랑스러운
☐ 15 **revolution**	명 혁명	☐ 45 **instead**	부 대신에
☐ 16 **expand**	동 팽창하다	☐ 46 **anywhere**	부 어디에서(도)
☐ 17 **tonight**	부 오늘 밤에	☐ 47 **jar**	명 병
☐ 18 **previous**	형 이전의	☐ 48 **translate**	동 통역하다
☐ 19 **satisfied**	형 만족한	☐ 49 **thankful**	형 고마워하는
☐ 20 **graduate**	동 졸업하다	☐ 50 **repair**	동 수리하다
☐ 21 **dish**	명 요리	☐ 51 **do one's best**	최선을 다하다
☐ 22 **ask**	동 묻다	☐ 52 **album**	명 (음악) 앨범
☐ 23 **chef**	명 요리사	☐ 53 **cook**	동 요리하다
☐ 24 **underwater**	부 물속에서	☐ 54 **tell**	동 말하다
☐ 25 **lawn**	명 잔디밭	☐ 55 **bored**	형 지루해하는
☐ 26 **keep one's promise**	약속을 지키다	☐ 56 **following**	형 다음의
☐ 27 **breathe**	동 숨을 쉬다	☐ 57 **project**	명 프로젝트, 과제
☐ 28 **volunteer**	동 자원 봉사하다	☐ 58 **club**	명 동아리
☐ 29 **invent**	동 발명하다	☐ 59 **math**	명 수학
☐ 30 **sure**	형 확신하는	☐ 60 **go out**	동 나가다

• 영어는 우리말로 쓰고, 우리말은 영어로 쓰시오.

1 calm		31 과학	
2 journalist		32 목소리	
3 expect		33 건강한	
4 hill		34 유명한	
5 castle		35 빛나다	
6 delicious		36 조언하다	
7 garbage		37 변호사	
8 wash the dishes		38 채소	
9 shake		39 (불에) 타다	
10 confident		40 대통령	
11 beautifully		41 화학	
12 landscape		42 긍정적으로	
13 lesson		43 박물관	
14 happen		44 용서하다	
15 promise		45 역사	
16 order		46 녹다	
17 silent		47 유명 인사	
18 worldwide		48 이웃	
19 tidy		49 설명하다	
20 terrible		50 식사	
21 rich		51 이해하다	
22 convenient		52 세다	
23 novel		53 귓속말하다	
24 finish		54 의견	
25 fantastic		55 (도서관) 사서	
26 bark		56 허락하다	
27 laugh		57 정원	
28 captain		58 치과의사	
29 apologize		59 빨래	
30 carefully		60 질문	

*정답은 HackersBook.com에서 확인할 수 있습니다.

• 영어는 우리말로 쓰고, 우리말은 영어로 쓰시오.

1	helpful	31	궁금하다
2	quite	32	잊다
3	clever	33	결혼하다
4	imagine	34	거울
5	false	35	정보
6	biology	36	선호하다
7	trip	37	다른
8	turn red	38	조리법
9	land	39	방문하다
10	storm	40	도둑
11	toilet	41	고대의
12	celebrate	42	공항
13	press	43	지루한
14	return	44	농담
15	difficult	45	답
16	arrive	46	문제
17	diligent	47	클래식의
18	wonderful	48	충격을 받은
19	vacation	49	연설
20	exhibition	50	베개
21	well-known	51	소고기
22	gift	52	기억하다
23	excellent	53	문화
24	truth	54	사라지다
25	useful	55	전통의
26	recommend	56	편한
27	plant	57	순간
28	quit	58	바꾸다
29	exercise	59	기계
30	advice	60	줄무늬

*정답은 HackersBook.com에서 확인할 수 있습니다.

단어 테스트 | CHAPTER 3 시제

• 영어는 우리말로 쓰고, 우리말은 영어로 쓰시오.

1	invite	31	발발하다
2	location	32	마라톤
3	belong to	33	끓다
4	explore	34	약
5	end	35	개선하다
6	cause	36	태풍
7	lately	37	실험
8	appear	38	흥미로운
9	depart	39	먹이를 주다
10	participate in	40	정부
11	volunteer	41	현장 학습
12	argue	42	실수
13	citizen	43	주말
14	research	44	초인종
15	shut	45	남극 (지역)
16	delay	46	공상 과학 소설
17	hold	47	중력
18	recently	48	소문
19	perform	49	기온
20	fall down	50	축제
21	save	51	두려움
22	riddle	52	극복하다
23	release	53	표면
24	publish	54	조종사
25	cover	55	훔치다
26	invent	56	일몰
27	documentary	57	졸업하다
28	fix	58	펼치다
29	company	59	초조한
30	action	60	군인

*정답은 HackersBook.com에서 확인할 수 있습니다.

• 영어는 우리말로 쓰고, 우리말은 영어로 쓰시오.

1 space	31 해로운
2 fee	32 언어
3 actively	33 동의하다
4 prize	34 ~ 없이
5 reserve	35 인기 있는
6 exhausted	36 거짓말하다
7 gorgeous	37 선인장
8 regularly	38 발톱
9 decision	39 복권
10 noisy	40 취소하다
11 fall asleep	41 유창하게
12 safe	42 환경
13 avoid	43 숨
14 correct	44 알레르기가 있는
15 temple	45 신호
16 discussion	46 껍질을 벗기다
17 fasten	47 황사
18 responsibility	48 복도
19 careful	49 날카로운
20 rude	50 살아남다
21 floor	51 채식주의자
22 beverage	52 재활용하다
23 gently	53 붐비는
24 whole	54 시력
25 skip	55 보내다
26 ceremony	56 여권
27 take off	57 해결하다
28 loudly	58 (맛이) 신
29 trash	59 존중하다
30 reservation	60 두통

*정답은 HackersBook.com에서 확인할 수 있습니다.

• 영어는 우리말로 쓰고, 우리말은 영어로 쓰시오.

1 pick		31 선출하다	
2 bite		32 외국의	
3 extra		33 사냥하다	
4 discover		34 호의	
5 treat		35 만족하는	
6 leader		36 전통	
7 raise		37 시	
8 election		38 배달하다	
9 damage		39 전화기	
10 customer		40 팔찌	
11 decorate		41 식료품	
12 award		42 (얇게) 썰다	
13 reporter		43 관광객	
14 lend		44 무덤	
15 greet		45 이유	
16 provide		46 새우	
17 mayor		47 항공편	
18 disappointed		48 생산하다	
19 create		49 나무로 된	
20 class president		50 물리학	
21 purchase		51 문장	
22 organic		52 진흙	
23 practice		53 신문	
24 chop		54 독특한	
25 repair		55 수납장	
26 rob		56 10대	
27 predict		57 독감	
28 talent		58 청중	
29 traveler		59 재채기하다	
30 restroom		60 만화	

*정답은 HackersBook.com에서 확인할 수 있습니다.

• 영어는 우리말로 쓰고, 우리말은 영어로 쓰시오.

1	confusing	31	천장
2	refuse	32	필수적인
3	miracle	33	계절
4	throw a party	34	부주의한
5	poisonous	35	주제
6	protect	36	빈
7	trunk	37	외계인
8	show	38	중요한
9	communicate	39	경기
10	foolish	40	혼잡 시간대
11	concentrate	41	졸린
12	tourist site	42	버섯
13	achieve	43	정직한
14	excited	44	충분한
15	astronaut	45	음량
16	trust	46	지진
17	shout	47	활동
18	escape	48	문을 두드리다
19	rest	49	문법
20	manage	50	여행 가방
21	come up with	51	비밀
22	climb	52	낭비하다
23	scream	53	이기적인
24	ill	54	공격하다
25	photograph	55	카레
26	receive	56	기린
27	bank account	57	화가, 예술가
28	weekday	58	규칙
29	generous	59	불가능한
30	jealous	60	별똥별

*정답은 HackersBook.com에서 확인할 수 있습니다.

단어 테스트 | CHAPTER 7 동사1

• 영어는 우리말을 쓰고, 우리말은 영어로 쓰시오.

1 put off		31 파다	
2 mystery		32 완벽한	
3 inconvenient		33 자라기	
4 focus		34 편안하다	
5 collect		35 잡기	
6 present		36 개최하다	
7 reduce		37 벗김	
8 country		38 후원하다	
9 look forward to		39 마치다	
10 require		40 야망찬	
11 relax		41 진정시키다	
12 magazine		42 사실	
13 exist		43 상승하다	
14 success		44 안달강	
15 behavior		45 슬픔	
16 suggest		46 동의	
17 get used to		47 짜릿함, 아주 신나는	
18 lose		48 연기시키다	
19 courage		49 믿음	
20 prevent		50 ~을 돌보다	
21 favorite		51 인상	
22 scenery		52 풍경	
23 fair		53 사고	
24 put out		54 줄이다	
25 wait in line		55 암시문	
26 article		56 계속하다	
27 goal		57 ~을 끄다	
28 deny		58 수줍음	
29 postpone		59 기울	
30 search		60 기록하다	

*정답은 HackersBook.com에서 확인할 수 있습니다.

• 영어는 우리말로 쓰고, 우리말은 영어로 쓰시오.

1	rise	31	앞으로
2	performance	32	교장
3	sculpture	33	~할 가치가 있는
4	build	34	~에서 나오다
5	depressing	35	여정
6	talented	36	앵무새
7	complete	37	뮤지컬
8	injure	38	언
9	dive into	39	미끄러지다
10	embarrassing	40	가격
11	yell	41	범죄
12	face	42	성적
13	report	43	채우다
14	wisely	44	야생
15	coin	45	경험
16	out of order	46	예술작품
17	fascinating	47	발목
18	observe	48	소포
19	rare	49	효과
20	plate	50	뇌
21	scared	51	땀을 흘리다
22	take a bath	52	특히
23	painting	53	병원
24	offer	54	새장, 우리
25	direction	55	지갑
26	realize	56	인간의
27	decrease	57	목마른
28	peaceful	58	건축가
29	take out	59	자정
30	amazing	60	이상한

*정답은 HackersBook.com에서 확인할 수 있습니다.

• 영어는 우리말로 쓰고, 우리말은 영어로 쓰시오.

1	public	31	서랍
2	on sale	32	기억
3	proud	33	냄비
4	clue	34	행성
5	universe	35	오솔길
6	knowledge	36	제목
7	active	37	동네
8	donate	38	벽난로
9	prepare	39	무게가 나가다
10	climb	40	꼬리
11	field	41	외식하다
12	jar	42	교회
13	amusement park	43	먼지
14	had better	44	연어
15	cliff	45	구멍
16	oxygen	46	가구
17	distance	47	생명체
18	consist of	48	질문
19	autumn	49	사람
20	uniform	50	사전
21	order	51	과목
22	fact	52	냉장고
23	unusual	53	주소
24	run away	54	여우
25	announcement	55	행운
26	be known for	56	연못
27	tourist	57	지붕
28	hang	58	기후
29	university	59	부엉이
30	shape	60	깃발

*정답은 HackersBook.com에서 확인할 수 있습니다.

단어 테스트 | CHAPTER 10 대명사

• 영어는 우리말로 쓰고, 우리말은 영어로 쓰시오.

1 destroy	31 법
2 smoothly	32 지구
3 final	33 사례
4 population	34 담임선생님
5 athlete	35 건물
6 official	36 번호
7 pull	37 소개하다
8 stand	38 간식
9 author	39 경기
10 ingredient	40 바구니
11 uncomfortable	41 비밀번호
12 book	42 풍선
13 scientific	43 극장
14 fault	44 판단하다
15 obey	45 노트북
16 impressive	46 ~을 탓하다
17 spill	47 옷
18 totally	48 ~을 통해
19 bright	49 작물
20 idea	50 무료로
21 turn in	51 비싼
22 sell	52 반짝거리는
23 skill	53 장르
24 appearance	54 금
25 certain	55 강변
26 along	56 표시하다
27 attention	57 학기
28 personality	58 책꽂이
29 plan	59 사업
30 express	60 밀가루

*정답은 HackersBook.com에서 확인할 수 있습니다.

단어 테스트 | CHAPTER 11 형용사

• 영어는 우리말을 쓰고, 우리말은 영어를 쓰시오.

1 pleased	31 균형한
2 a number of	32 붙이다
3 heat	33 인공의
4 glad	34 메모
5 abroad	35 자선단체
6 patience	36 세금
7 notice	37 안내서
8 asleep	38 문화
9 disabled	39 개념, 말
10 guest	40 녹음하다
11 communicate	41 씹다
12 chase	42 불꽃
13 daughter	43 우주선
14 pollute	44 가난한
15 bone	45 고래
16 deaf	46 운동화인
17 alike	47 지점
18 various	48 충분한
19 plenty of	49 싸우다
20 gather	50 곰이
21 stone	51 수리
22 creative	52 다이아몬드
23 interested	53 혈통
24 hen	54 배지
25 pocket	55 신용카드
26 subtitle	56 사원
27 immediately	57 응급상황으로
28 bowl	58 해파리
29 familiar	59 곡이 난
30 require	60 마감날

*정답은 HackersBook.com에서 확인하실 수 있습니다.

단어 테스트 | CHAPTER 12 부사

• 영어는 우리말로 쓰고, 우리말은 영어로 쓰시오.

1	costly	31	짠
2	journalist	32	기억하다
3	extremely	33	성급하게
4	apply	34	투표하다
5	recognize	35	활기찬
6	decision	36	도시
7	horrible	37	안으로
8	diligent	38	기본적인
9	sincere	39	공손한
10	write down	40	빠르게
11	completely	41	체육관
12	statue	42	날것의
13	upset	43	연락하다
14	find out	44	조깅하다
15	explore	45	번개
16	riddle	46	여행하다
17	document	47	선수권 대회
18	responsible	48	증가하다
19	enormously	49	사다리
20	spill	50	시민
21	dull	51	간단한
22	quiet	52	비타민
23	space	53	구역
24	reach	54	땅콩
25	effective	55	손뼉을 치다
26	nowadays	56	검사하다
27	give back	57	소포
28	serious	58	현대의
29	observe	59	예방하다
30	crime	60	교과서

*정답은 HackersBook.com에서 확인할 수 있습니다.

• 영어는 우리말로 쓰고, 우리말은 영어로 쓰시오.

1	thin	31	싼
2	normally	32	마당
3	temperature	33	연
4	volleyball	34	오염
5	luxurious	35	키
6	raindrop	36	목성
7	wide	37	알록달록한
8	live	38	깃털
9	transportation	39	비행기
10	confused	40	봄
11	become	41	벼룩
12	polite	42	젊은
13	game	43	가족
14	invention	44	미술관
15	customer	45	옷장
16	useless	46	초대하다
17	reply	47	인공적인
18	lazy	48	지능
19	means	49	지렁이
20	blow	50	마른
21	thick	51	삶
22	visitor	52	날씨
23	return	53	오케스트라
24	gloomy	54	완료하다
25	scene	55	딸기
26	mysterious	56	꽉 끼는
27	ocean	57	환경친화적인
28	solar system	58	돌고래
29	actor	59	베개
30	common	60	마을

*정답은 HackersBook.com에서 확인할 수 있습니다.

• 영어는 우리말로 쓰고, 우리말은 영어로 쓰시오.

1	run into	31	모닥불
2	enter	32	교통
3	detective	33	주인
4	independence	34	시금치
5	silly	35	인스턴트의, 즉각적인
6	share	36	호기심 있는
7	remove	37	마술사
8	silence	38	구름
9	for a while	39	그네
10	attract	40	굽다
11	discount	41	해산물
12	police station	42	잔디
13	site	43	서점
14	separate	44	저녁
15	electronic	45	위험
16	bury	46	불평하다
17	cross	47	감옥
18	evidence	48	동굴
19	exhibition	49	티켓, 표
20	street	50	새벽
21	wizard	51	지도
22	stick	52	스토브, 가스레인지
23	tunnel	53	호두
24	path	54	자석
25	criminal	55	천사
26	come up	56	도마뱀
27	forest	57	수염
28	heat up	58	현금
29	sail	59	약국
30	similar	60	깨어 있는

*정답은 HackersBook.com에서 확인할 수 있습니다.

• 영어는 우리말로 쓰고, 우리말은 영어로 쓰시오.

1	sculptor	31	서식지
2	lift	32	기침
3	genius	33	보석
4	despite	34	팽창하다
5	watch out	35	설치하다
6	angry	36	붓
7	manner	37	인후통
8	coast	38	까마귀
9	directly	39	섞다
10	luggage	40	수술
11	global warming	41	동쪽의
12	latest	42	금속
13	mess	43	잘못된
14	furious	44	빙하
15	bring	45	나중에
16	refund	46	~인 것 같다, 추측하다
17	symbol	47	감기에 걸리다
18	charge	48	서핑하다
19	director	49	사인
20	true	50	진흙의
21	scold	51	복습하다
22	national	52	쌍둥이
23	seat	53	~하자마자
24	join	54	건강
25	lock	55	곤란, 문제
26	pour	56	두 번
27	impatient	57	현명한
28	farming	58	영수증
29	view	59	유치원
30	loud	60	나뭇가지

*정답은 HackersBook.com에서 확인할 수 있습니다.

단어 테스트 | CHAPTER 16 관계사

• 영어는 우리말로 쓰고, 우리말은 영어로 쓰시오.

1 destroy	31 주사하다
2 market	32 정답
3 say	33 플라스틱
4 region	34 현자
5 handle	35 이유
6 skillful	36 프린터
7 admire	37 (눈·빗물 등) 흘리다
8 hand in	38 트로피
9 politician	39 승객
10 road	40 뿔
11 incredible	41 피다 (꽃이)
12 discover	42 정수
13 author	43 배터리
14 advice	44 고객가
15 turn into	45 환자
16 celebrity	46 조각
17 move	47 열쇠
18 purchase	48 빌려주다 (시간등)
19 teen	49 지하철
20 gentle	50 배달하다
21 ignore	51 털
22 shop	52 포즈
23 depend on	53 시인
24 trust	54 칭찬하다
25 drop	55 좌절
26 gather	56 영혼
27 be full of	57 감시
28 request	58 훌륭하다
29 composer	59 동의
30 retire	60 은근

단어 테스트 | CHAPTER 17 가정법

• 영어는 우리말로 쓰고, 우리말은 영어로 쓰시오.

1	emergency	31	낯선 사람
2	play	32	매진된
3	decide	33	발
4	on time	34	불행하게도
5	miss	35	정원
6	depressed	36	한가한
7	soon	37	(식물 등에) 물을 주다
8	test	38	무지개
9	often	39	연습하다
10	conversation	40	무대
11	show	41	언젠가
12	reservation	42	수줍음이 많은
13	rumor	43	어제
14	boring	44	떠나다
15	favorite	45	곤충
16	appear	46	사실은
17	rain forest	47	매운
18	millionaire	48	배우다
19	chilly	49	귀신
20	agree	50	복권
21	behave	51	청소하다
22	costume	52	외로운
23	own	53	경주
24	take a shower	54	거미
25	disappointed	55	미끄러운
26	lend	56	일출
27	perform	57	운전하다
28	from now on	58	캠핑, 야영
29	Chinese	59	강
30	adult	60	읽다

*정답은 HackersBook.com에서 확인할 수 있습니다.

• 영어는 우리말로 쓰고, 우리말은 영어로 쓰시오.

1 bored		31 맛이 ~하다	
2 haste		32 대신에	
3 travel		33 잔디밭	
4 apologize		34 고마워하는	
5 do one's best		35 깨닫다	
6 ambulance		36 프로젝트, 과제	
7 translate		37 동아리	
8 keep one's promise		38 혁명	
9 chef		39 (음악) 앨범	
10 volunteer		40 가르치다	
11 traditional		41 사진	
12 wonder		42 가이드, 안내인	
13 previous		43 발명하다	
14 anywhere		44 발표자	
15 tell		45 울타리	
16 satisfied		46 함께	
17 jar		47 물속에서	
18 among		48 빛	
19 ask		49 약간	
20 sure		50 위층	
21 proud		51 요리하다	
22 knowledge		52 오두막	
23 following		53 수도	
24 expand		54 졸업하다	
25 noise		55 오늘 밤에	
26 dish		56 관광	
27 go out		57 쇼핑몰	
28 industrial		58 더러운	
29 repair		59 숨을 쉬다	
30 speak		60 수학	

*정답은 HackersBook.com에서 확인할 수 있습니다.